D0882703

DIODORUS OF SICILY
I

LCL 279

DIODORUS OF SICILY

IN TWELVE VOLUMES

I

BOOKS I AND II, 1–34

WITH AN ENGLISH TRANSLATION BY

C. H. OLDFATHER

HARVARD UNIVERSITY PRESS
CAMBRIDGE, MASSACHUSETTS
LONDON, ENGLAND

First published 1933
Reprinted 1946, 1960, 1968, 1989

ISBN 0-674-99307-1

Printed in Great Britain by St. Edmundsbury Press Ltd,
Bury St. Edmunds, Suffolk, on wood-free paper.
Bound by Hunter & Foulis Ltd, Edinburgh, Scotland.

CONTENTS

CONTENTS

INTRODUCTION

GENERAL INTRODUCTION

WITH but one exception antiquity affords no further information on the life and work of Diodorus of Sicily than is to be found in his own *Library of History*. The exception is St. Jerome, who, in his *Chronology* under the Year of Abraham 1968 (= 49 B.C.), writes: " Diodorus of Sicily, a writer of Greek history, became illustrious." [1]

Diodorus himself says (1. 4. 4) that the city of his birth was Agyrium in Sicily, one of the oldest settlements of the interior, which was visited even by Heracles (4. 24), whose cult was maintained by the inhabitants on a scale rivalling that of the Olympians, and this statement is rendered plausible by the importance accorded the city in his History, an importance quite out of proportion in a World History of only forty Books.[2] It is a striking coincidence that one of the only two Greek inscriptions from Agyrium (*IG.* XIV, 588) marked the final resting-place of a " Diodorus the son of Apollonius."

The earliest date at which Diodorus is known to

---

[1] *Diodorus Siculus Graecae scriptor historiae clarus habetur* (p. 155, i, ed. Helm). This date must mark the first appearance of a portion of his History.

[2] At that he is more reserved in this respect than Ephorus, who, according to Strabo (13. 3. 6), was so insistent on mentioning the city of his origin, Cyme, that he once added, " At the same time the Cymaeans were at peace."

have been gathering material for his history is the
180th Olympiad (60/59–57/6 B.C.), in the course of
which he visited Egypt (1. 44. 1).   Diodorus records
that while there he saw with his own eyes a mob of
Egyptians demand, and apparently secure, the death
of a man connected with a Roman embassy, because
he had accidentally killed a cat, and this despite
the fear which the Egyptians felt for the Romans,
and despite the fact that " Ptolemy their king had
not as yet been given the appellation of ' friend ' "
by the Romans (1. 83. 8).   Ptolemy XI, " the Piper,"
had ascended the throne of the last nominally
independent Hellenistic kingdom in 80 B.C., and
after waiting twenty years, a period in which the
Roman Senate would neither avow nor repudiate
him, finally secured recognition by the Senate
through the efforts of Caesar and Pompey in 59 B.C.[1]
This embassy is not mentioned in the Roman sources,
but the huge sum required of Ptolemy by Caesar
and Pompey in exchange for this recognition must
certainly have required some such a diplomatic
mission, and it may be assumed that it was dispatched
from Rome fairly early after January 1st, when
Caesar entered upon his consulship, or at least soon
after February 1st, when he first had the fasces.
The date of this recognition of Ptolemy by Rome
clearly shows that Diodorus was in Egypt in the
year 59 B.C., the length of his visit remaining still
uncertain.

---

[1] Suetonius, *Julius*, 54. 3 : *Societates ac regna pretio dedit*
(sc. *Caesar*), *ut qui uni Ptolemaeo prope sex milia talentorum
suo Pompeique nomine abstulerit*.   Ptolemy was driven from
his throne by the people in 57 and restored by Gabinius in
55; cp. the comments of Butler-Cary, *ad loc.*

INTRODUCTION

Diodorus had already commenced his work as early as 56 B.C. This is evident from the passage (1. 44. 1–4) [1] in which he lists the number of years during which Egypt was under the control of foreigners. The last aliens to rule over Egypt, he says, are the Macedonians and their dynasty who have held the land for two hundred and seventy-six years. Now since the conquest of Egypt by Alexander is put by Diodorus (17. 49) in the year 331 B.C., he must have been at work upon the composition of his *Library of History* at least as early as 56 B.C.

The latest contemporary event mentioned by Diodorus is a reference to the city of Tauromenium in Sicily, when he records (16. 7. 1) that " Caesar removed the citizens from their native state and the city received a Roman colony." This may have taken place in 36 B.C., or soon thereafter, since Appian, *Civil Wars*, 5. 109 ff. tells how the city in 36 closed its gates to Octavian, who was caught on the same day by Sextus Pompey and in the ensuing naval battle lost practically all his ships, barely escaping with his life. This disaster he could have avoided had the city received him and his forces, and the anger which he must have felt toward the city supplies the motive for the drastic punishment meted out to it. [2] The founding of this colony

---

[1] The significance of this evidence has, so far as I know, been overlooked by previous writers, even by O. Cuntz, *De Augusto Plinii geographicorum auctore* (Bonn, 1888), pp. 32 ff., who has listed most fully the references in Diodorus to contemporary events.

[2] This is the date first suggested by O. Cuntz, *op. cit.*, p. 35, accepted as " probable " by Beloch, *Die Bevölkerung der griechisch-romischen Welt*, p. 337, and by Schwartz, *R-E²*, 5. 663, and fully approved by Kornemann, *R-E²*, 4. 526.

has been placed also in 21 B.C., the year in which, according to Cassius Dio (54. 7. 1), Augustus reorganized Sicily;[1] but it seems most improbable that such an act of angry revenge should have been delayed for fifteen years on the occasion of a mere administrative reorganization which surely could have called for nothing like this.

That Tauromenium was made a Roman colony in 36 B.C. or a little later, and that, therefore, the latest date at which Diodorus is known to have been composing or revising his history is that year or a little later, would appear to be supported by two further considerations. Diodorus informs us (1. 4. 1) that he had spent thirty years in the composition of his history, and it may justly be assumed that this period includes the travels which he made and the dangers which he met in visiting the most important sites about which he intended to write. The beginning of this period must surely be set some years before 59 B.C., when he was in Egypt, since it is only reasonable to suppose that he had been turning over his great undertaking in his mind and been reading and excerpting some authorities upon Egypt before he set out upon his travels. Furthermore, in view of the great admiration of the Roman Empire expressed by Diodorus it is difficult to believe that

---

Cassius Dio (49. 12. 5) states that, after the defeat of Sextus Pompey and the humbling of Lepidus in 36 B.C., Octavian did actually punish certain unspecified cities of Sicily, and among these must have been Tauromenium.

[1] This is the view of Mommsen, *C.I.L.*, X, p. 718; *Römische Forschung*, 2. p. 549, n. 1, of C. Wachsmuth, *Über das Geschichtswerk des Sikelioten Diodoros* (Leipzig, 1892), I, p. 3, and of M. Büdinger, *Die Universalhistorie im Alterthume*, 114, n. 4.

he would have said that the Macedonians were the
last aliens to rule over Egypt, had he been working
on his History after the incorporation of Egypt in
the Roman Empire in 30 B.C. And this accords
with the statement of Suidas,[1] that the *floruit* of
Diodorus fell in the period of Augustus Caesar and
before.[2]

The task which Diodorus set himself was to write
one of " the general histories " (αἱ κοιναὶ ἱστορίαι),[3]
or " the general events " (αἱ κοιναὶ πράξεις) [4] (1. 4. 6;
5. 1. 4); in other words, to compose a Universal,
or World, History from the Creation to his day.
The adjective " general " or " common " is used
so much by him that it may be possible to find
in its connotation the clue to his motive in taking
upon himself so great a task. In the decade
between 70 and 60 B.C. he had seen the entire
Mediterranean shore brought under the control of
Rome by Pompey—Egypt was still independent
only in name, for its kings held their throne at the
will of the Roman Senate—the sea swept clean of
pirates, Roman supremacy extended " to the bounds

---

[1] γέγονε (sc. Διόδωρος) δὲ ἐπὶ τῶν χρόνων Αὐγούστου Καίσαρος
καὶ ἐπάνω.

[2] Although parts of his History must have appeared by
49 B.C., it is reasonable to suppose that Diodorus published it
as a whole, with consequent revision, at one time, between
36 and 30 B.C. at the latest; cp. below, p. xvi, n. 1.

[3] Dionysius of Halicarnassus (1. 6) uses the same words in
speaking of the writings of Timaeus.

[4] Cp. 1. 3. 2, when he contrasts " isolated wars waged by a
single nation or a single state " with " the general events "
(αἱ κοιναὶ πράξεις). The same sharp distinction appears also
in 1. 4. 6, and he uses the same words to describe the *Universal
History* of Ephorus (4. 1. 3).

of the inhabited world " (1. 4. 3). If Diodorus had
not witnessed the celebration of this incorporation
of the Eastern world in the Roman state, he had
certainly heard from others of the great triumph of
Pompey in 61 b.c., in the course of which banners
announced that he had subdued fourteen nations,
brought back 20,000 talents to the treasury, and
almost doubled the annual revenue of the state.
Under the dominion of Rome the Stoic idea of a
cosmopolis was on the way to becoming an actuality.
All mankind was coming to form a " common "
civilization, a " common " society, and Diodorus
could speak of a " common life " in the sense that
the whole Mediterranean world was now interested
in the same things and what benefited one nation
was of common value to all. If the term " Western
civilization " may properly include two cultures so
different, for instance, as those of the United States
and Spain, it is no exaggeration to say that by
60 b.c. Syrian, Greek, Iberian and Roman had
become one. The limitations of the old city state,
whereby a man was a stranger in any city but the
one of his origin, were gone for ever. Surely, then,
the history of each one of these nations was a matter
of interest to all, since the past of every people was
making its distinctive contribution to this most
catholic of all civilizations, and he who would gather
the records of all these peoples and present them in
convenient form would have " composed a treatise
of the utmost value to those who are studiously
inclined " (1. 3. 6). Some such considerations as
these must have moved Diodorus to lay hand to
such a work, and even if he was not the man fully
to control the material before him, still we cannot

deny him at all events the apology of Propertius
(2. 10. 6):

in magnis et voluisse sat est.

In preparation for his History Diodorus states
(1. 4. 1) that with much hardship and many dangers
he visited all the most important regions of Europe
and Asia. There is no evidence in his work that he
travelled in any other land than Egypt, where he
may have ascended the Nile as far as Memphis, in
connection with which city he mentions a shrine of
Isis which " is pointed out to this day in the temple-
area of Hephaestus " (1. 22. 2); all the other details
of his account of that marvellous land could have
been gathered from his literary sources. The only
other place where he claims to have stayed was
Rome, which furnished him in abundance the
materials necessary for his study (1. 4. 2). Certainly
he never went to Mesopotamia, since he places
Nineveh on the Euphrates, and it is kinder to suppose
that he never visited Athens than to think that the
glory of the Acropolis, if he had once seen it, was
not considered important enough to deserve mention.

Not only does Diodorus claim to have travelled
widely in preparation for his History, but to have
gained through his contact with the Romans in Sicily
" considerable familiarity " (πολλὴ ἐμπειρία, 1. 4. 4) with
their language. In the general disparagement of
Diodorus, his knowledge of Latin has not been overlooked, and he has been accused even of finding a
nominative *Fidenates* from an ablative *Fidenate*.[1]

---

[1] So Christ-Schmid, *Griechische Litteraturgeschichte* [6] (1920),
2. p. 403, n. 9, but without basis, as had been shown by G.
Sigwart, *Römische Fasten und Annalen bei Diodor* (Greisswald,
1906), pp. 5 f.

INTRODUCTION

Other criticisms on this score, such as that he did not know the meaning of *bellare cum aliquo*,[1] must be held in abeyance, so long as the question whether Diodorus in his account of Roman affairs used a Latin or Greek source (or sources) is still *sub judice*. And since criticism is beginning to adopt a more reasonable attitude toward Diodorus,[2] the better course is to trust his word that he could use the Latin language; he knew it at least well enough for his purposes.

Diodorus commenced with the mythical period and brought his History down to 59 B.C., the year of Julius Caesar's first consulship. Of the forty Books only the first five and Books XI–XX are preserved, although fragments of the other twenty-five are found in different authors, notably in Eusebius and Byzantine excerptors. According to his own plan (1. 4. 6–7), Books I–VI embraced the period before the Trojan War, the first three treating of the history of the non-Greeks, the other three, of that of the Greeks. The next eleven, Books VII–XVII, were designed to form a Universal History from the Trojan War to the death of Alexander the Great, and the last twenty-three carried the account down to the Archonship of Herodes in 60/59 B.C., *i.e.* to include the year 61/60 B.C.[3] As for the years covered by his History, he makes no effort to estimate those which had elapsed before the Trojan War,

---

[1] Cp. Büdinger, *op. cit.*, p. 122, n. 1.

[2] O. Leuze, *Die römische Jahrzählung* (Tübingen, 1909), gives the most recent detailed defence of Diodorus; cp. p. 78, n. 107, for the exaggerated detractions by Reuss, Wachsmuth, and Schwartz.

[3] Cp. Leuze, *op. cit.*, p. 72.

since for that earlier period there existed no chronological table " that was trustworthy," [1] but for the subsequent period he records that he followed the *Chronology* of Apollodorus of Athens [2] in setting 80 years between the Trojan War (1184 B.C.) and the Return of the Heracleidae (1104 B.C.), thence 328 years to the First Olympiad (776/5 B.C.), and from the First Olympiad to the beginning of the Celtic War (60/59 B.C.), a date which Apollodorus did not reach, Diodorus counted 730 years. There can be no question about the correctness of these numbers of years, 80, 328, 730, because in the next sentence he makes the sum of them 1138; and yet 730 years after the First Olympiad is 46/5 B.C., just fifteen years later than the date at which he says his History closes. It is impossible to think that his work came down to so late a date, since his last book opened with the year 70 B.C., the latest fragment mentioning the conspiracy of Catiline in 63, and he states specifically that his History closed before the year 60/59 B.C.[3]

The contents of the several Books are briefly :

Book I : The myths, kings and customs of Egypt.
Book II : History of Assyria, description of India, Scythia, Arabia, and the islands of the Ocean.

---

[1] In 40. 8 Diodorus says that he had no chronological table for this period, and on the basis of that passage from an excerptor, Schwartz, *R-E²*., 5. 665, argues that he could not have used the *Chronology* of Castor; but Beloch, *Römische Geschichte*, p. 122, properly calls the attention of Schwartz to this passage and its πιστευόμενον.

[2] His *Chronology* spanned the years 1184/3 to at least 120/19 B.C.

[3] For a possible explanation of this discrepancy, cp. below, p. xix.

INTRODUCTION

Book III: Ethiopia, the Amazons of Africa, the inhabitants of Atlantis and the origins of the first gods.

Book IV: The principal Greek gods, the Argonauts, Theseus, the Seven against Thebes.

Book V: The islands and peoples of the West, Rhodes and Crete.

Books VI–X: Fragments, from the Trojan War to 480 B.C.

Commencing with Book XI the *Library of History* covers:

Book XI: Years 480–451 B.C.
Book XII: Years 450–416 B.C.
Book XIII: Years 415–405 B.C.
Book XIV: Years 404–387 B.C.
Book XV: Years 386–361 B.C.
Book XVI: Years 360–336 B.C.
Book XVII: Years 335–324 B.C.
Book XVIII: Years 323–318 B.C.
Book XIX: Years 317–311 B.C.
Book XX: Years 310–302 B.C.
Books XXI–XL: Fragments, years 301–60 B.C.

To compose a history of the entire world down to his day was " an immense labour," as Diodorus says (1. 3. 6), looking back upon it,[1] because the material

---

[1] The Preface was certainly (cp. 1. 4. 6) revised after the whole work had been completed. Diodorus laments (40. 8) that parts of his work had reached the public before his final revision and publication as a whole, probably in 49 B.C. (see above, p. vii, n. 1). Just how seriously his words are to be taken remains a question. Might they not be a reserved suggestion to the reading public that, in order to get his final account, they should purchase the latest revision ?

for it lay scattered about in so many different authors,
and because the authors themselves varied so widely.
Perhaps this was his way of telling his readers that
what they should expect of his history is no more
than a compilation of what former writers had set
down. And the choice of so unusual a title, *Library
of History*,[1] is further evidence that Diodorus made
no pretence of doing anything more than giving a
convenient summary of events which were to be
found in greater detail in many works. The alloca-
tion of this and that bit of information among the
various writers whom Diodorus names has occupied
the attention of many scholars.[2] The earlier view
was that Diodorus took a single author and copied
him for many chapters and even Books of his history.
From that extreme position criticism soon was forced
to recede, and it is generally held now that while
Diodorus probably leaned very strongly upon a single
author for one or another section of his work, he
used at the same time other writers as well. It is
the feeling of the present translator that there is
much more of the individuality of Diodorus in his
Library of History than has been generally supposed,
and that he picked and chose more widely and more
wisely than has been allowed him by most critics.[3]

---

[1] Pliny, *Nat. Hist.*, Preface, 25, praised this straightforward
title (*Apud Graecos desiit nugari Diodorus et Βιβλιοθήκης
historiam suam inscripsit*).

[2] A convenient summary and rebuttal of some of the
earlier literature is given by L. O. Bröcker, *Moderne Quellen-
forscher und antike Geschichtschreiber* (Innsbruch, 1882),
pp. 83 ff.

[3] I fully subscribe to the following words of Jacoby, *F. Gr.
Hist.* 2, B D, p. 356 : " . . . direkte benutzung Theopompos
bei Diodor ist so wenig wahrscheinlich, wie eine Diodor-

INTRODUCTION

A brief discussion of the sources used by Diodorus is given in the Introductions to the several volumes.

One mistake of method made it almost impossible for Diodorus to write either a readable story or an accurate history. So soon as he entered the period which allowed precise dating he became an annalist, or, in other words, he endeavoured to present under one year the events which took place in Greece, Sicily, Africa and Italy, to write a synchronistic universal history. For a closely related series of incidents which covered several years this meant that he either had to break the story as many times as there were years, or crowd the events of several years into one. Moreover, he tried to synchronize the Roman consular year, which in his day commenced January 1st—and he uses this date even for the earlier period—with the Athenian archon year, which commenced about the middle of July. It should be observed to his credit that Diodorus recognized (20. 43. 7) the shortcomings of this annalistic arrangement, but he still felt that the recital of events in the order in which they were taking place gave a more truthful presentation of history.

It may be noted, in connection with this annalistic arrangement, that, although Diodorus says in his Preface to the First Book that he has brought his history down to 60/59 B.C., yet in three other places

analyse, die satz für satz Theopompos, eigene züsatze des Ephoros und solche aus Xenophon scheidet, reichlich unsicher ist,'' and to the conclusion of Holm, *Geschichte Siciliens*, 2, p. 369, '' dass Diodor nicht bloss mit der Scheere gearbeitet hat, sondern auch mit der Feder und mit dem Kopf.''

(3. 38. 2; 5. 21. 2; 5. 22. 1) he remarks that he will speak of Britain more in detail when he gives an account of the deeds of Gaius Caesar, and that, as observed above, in the *Chronology* which he gives of his entire work, 1138 years from the Trojan War brings his history down to 46/45 B.C. It has been suggested by Schwartz [1] that Diodorus found these figures in some Chronology which he had in his hands at the time. Such an assumption would indeed convict him not only of carelessness, but of plain stupidity. It seems more reasonable to suppose that, as Diodorus was engaged upon the writing of his earlier Books, he fully intended to bring his history down to include the year 46/45 B.C., which would make an excellent stopping-point. In March of 45 B.C. Caesar met and defeated at Munda the last army of republicans which still held the field against him. The first period of civil war was at an end. However, as Diodorus grew old and perhaps a little tired, he gave up his original plan. He stopped his account at 60/59 B.C., which year, marking the agreement reached by Caesar, Pompey and Crassus, was a definite turning-point in the history of the Roman Republic. The "1138 years" may be explained in two ways. Since some of his Books, and presumably the earlier ones, came into the hands of the public before his final revision and the publication of his History as a whole, Diodorus may himself have overlooked the need of correcting that number in the final revision. Or the earlier figures may in some way have slipped from an earlier MS. into one of the final revision.

[1] *R-E²*., 5. 665.

INTRODUCTION

From scattered observations, which bear every mark of being from Diodorus himself and not from his sources, and from the emphasis upon certain phenomena or particular features of history, it is possible to get some idea of his views and interests. Again and again, and not alone in the Preface to the First Book, the Stoic doctrine of the *utilitas* of history is stressed, and nowhere does he demand that history be entertaining. Of the customs of Egypt he will mention, he tells us, only those which are especially strange and those which can be of most advantage to his readers (1. 69. 2), of its laws only those that can be of help to lovers of reading (1. 77. 1). It is obviously to this end that, as he states (11. 46. 1), he makes it his practice to increase the fame of good men by extolling them and to censure evil characters; the latter he does, for instance, at the death of Pausanias (*loc. cit.*), and the defeat of Leuctra offers an occasion to observe what heavy punishments await the proud and unjust, while Gelon (11. 38. 6) and Epaminondas (15. 88. 1) receive the praise which is due to noble men. More often than any extant ancient historian Diodorus stresses the view that history should instruct in the good life. With great detail (16. 61 ff.) he describes the fate which met the various leaders of the Phocians, who had dared to lay impious hands upon the treasure of Delphi, how the allied cities lost their freedom, and even how one woman who had tricked herself out with the chain of Helen ended her days as a prostitute, while another, who had put on the chain of Eriphyle, was burned to death in her home by her own son. Philip, on the other hand, because he came to the defence of the oracle, increased in power from that day forth and finally made his country the mightiest state in Europe. The great earthquakes and inundations in the Peloponnesus of 373 B.C. were certainly due to the anger of the gods, more particularly to that of Poseidon. Admitting that the natural philosophers gave another reason, yet he thinks that they were wrong, and goes on to show what it was that angered Poseidon (15. 48). He emphasizes the qualities of the spirit, such as meekness, gentleness, kindliness, very much in the manner of Herodotus; but he thinks very little of democracy (1. 74. 7; 13. 95. 1), the natural counterpart of such a conviction being a great admiration for the strong man in history.

While characteristics such as these exclude Diodorus from a place among the abler historians of the ancient world, there is every reason to believe that he used the best sources and that he reproduced them faithfully. His First Book, which deals almost exclusively with Egypt, is the fullest literary account of the history and customs of that country after Herodotus. Books II–V cover a wide range, and because of their inclusion of much mythological material are of less value. In the period from 480 to 301 B.C., which he treats in annalistic fashion and in which his main source was the *Universal History* of Ephorus, his importance varies according as he is the sole continuous source, or again as he is paralleled by superior writers. To the fifty years from 480 to 430 B.C. Thucydides devotes only a little more than thirty chapters; Diodorus covers it more fully (11. 37–12. 38) and his is the only consecutive literary account for the chronology of the period. On the other hand, he is of less importance for the years

INTRODUCTION

430–362 B.C., since the history of this period is covered in the contemporary accounts of Thucydides and Xenophon. For the years 362–302 B.C. Diodorus is again the only consecutive literary account, and although the *Epitome* by Justin of the *History of Philip* by Pompeius Trogus is preserved for the earlier period, and the *Anabasis* of Arrian and *The History of Alexander the Great* by Q. Curtius Rufus, more than half of which is extant, for the years 336–323, Diodorus offers the only chronological survey of the period of Philip, and supplements the writers mentioned and contemporary sources in many matters. For the period of the Successors to Alexander, 323–302 B.C. (Books XVIII–XX), he is the chief literary authority and his history of this period assumes, therefore, an importance which it does not possess for the other years. These three Books are based mainly upon the work of Hieronymus of Cardia, an historian of outstanding ability who brought to his account both the experience gained in the service, first of Eumenes, and then of Antigonus, and an exceptional sense of the importance of the history of the period. As for Sicily, it has well been said that no history of that island could be written were it not for Diodorus, and as for Roman history, the *Fasti* of Diodorus are recognized in the most recent research to be by far the oldest and most trustworthy.

One merit even those critics who have dealt most severely with Diodorus accord him. Long speeches, happily used but unhappily introduced by Thucydides, Diodorus avoids, as he promises that he will do in the Preface to Book XX. With the exception of four instances he eliminates entirely that rhetorical device, which must have wearied even a contemporary audience. He gave great care to little details of writing, and when he errs in fact the fault is not so much his as that of his source. A kindly judgment upon such errors may be found in the words of Cicero when he acknowledges that the story was generally recognized to be incorrect that Eupolis, the poet of Old Comedy, was thrown into the sea by Alcibiades, and adds: "But surely that is no reason for sneering at Duris of Samos, who was a careful scholar, because he erred in the company of many others."[1]

Editions and Translations

The following are the more important editions:

Poggio Bracciolini: Latin translation of Books I–V; published at Bologna, 1472, and many times thereafter at Paris, Venice and Lyons.

Vincentius Opsopoeus: the first Greek edition, containing Books XVI–XX only; Basel, 1539.

H. Stephanus: Greek edition of Books I–V, XI–XX, and some fragments of Books XXI–XL; Geneva, 1559.

L. Rhodoman: the edition of Stephanus with a Latin translation, indices and chronological tables; Hanau, 1604.

Petrus Wesseling: the Greek text, and the Latin version of Rhodoman, with the critical work of former scholars; 2 vols., Amsterdam, 1746. This is the only annotated edition of Diodorus and a monument of zeal and scholarship.

[1] *Ad Att.* 6. 1. 18: "*Num idcirco Duris Samius, homo in historia diligens, quod cum multis erravit, inridetur?*"

INTRODUCTION

Bipontine Edition, 11 vols., Zweibrücken and Strassburg, 1793–1807. This is the edition of Wesseling, to which were added essays by C. G. Heyne and I. N. Eyring.

H. Eichstädt: the Greek text of Books I–V, X–XIV; 2 vols., Halle, 1800–1802.

L. Dindorf: four editions of the Greek text: 4 vols., Leipzig (Weidmann), 1826; 5 vols., with critical apparatus, Leipzig (Hartmann), 1828–31; 2 vols. in a Didot edition, the Latin by C. Müller, Paris, 1842–4; 5 vols., Leipzig (Teubner), 1866–8.

I. Bekker: the Greek text; 4 vols., Leipzig (Teubner), 1853–4.

The present text is based upon that of Vogel-Fischer, Leipzig (Teubner), 1888 ff., and the most important variants of the editions of Bekker and Dindorf (1866–8) have been noted; the reading which follows the colon is, unless otherwise stated, that of the *textus receptus*.

Translations of Diodorus have not kept pace with the intrinsic interest of his History. Worthy of mention is that into English in two volumes by G. Booth, London, 1700; another edition, in a series entitled " Corpus Historicum," is of London, 1814. The English is quaint, *archon* being sometimes rendered " lord high-chancellor," " high-chancellor," " chief magistrate; " the chapter divisions are quite arbitrary, and the early date, before the commentary of Wesseling, makes it of little value. The translation into German by J. F. Wurm, Stuttgart, 1827–40, is a serious work, and that of A. Wahrmund of Books I–X, Stuttgart, 1866–9, with many notes, has also been of considerable aid in the preparation of this translation. It is hoped that infelicities of the present translation will be viewed by scholars with some indulgence, in consideration of the fact that it is the first in English for more than two hundred years.

One feature of the style of Diodorus calls for remark. A large part of his earlier Books is in indirect discourse, which is introduced with " they say " or " it is said " or " history records," and the like, or with the name of the writer he is following. Yet at times he inserts into this reported speech sentences of direct discourse which are presumably original with himself. In general, an attempt has been made to distinguish this reported speech from the remarks of Diodorus himself; but I have not done so if it involved any great interruption of the flow of his narrative.

MANUSCRIPTS

A. Codex Coislinianus, of the 15th century.
B. Codex Mutinensis, of the 15th century.
C. Codex Vaticanus, of the 12th century.
D. Codex Vindobonensis 79, of the 11th century.
E. Codex Parisinus, of the 16th century.
F. G. Codices Claromontani, of the 16th century.
M. Codex Venetus, of the 15th century.
N. Codex Vindobonensis, of the 16th century.

The designations of the MSS. are those of the Preface to the first volume of the edition of Vogel-Fischer, to which the reader is referred for further details on each MS. and its worth. In the critical notes " Vulgate " designates the reading of all MSS. except D, and " II " designates the reading of all MSS. of the " second class," *i.e.* of all but A B D.

INTRODUCTION

INTRODUCTION TO BOOKS I–II, 34

After the Preface to his whole work Diodorus describes the origin of animal life, and then, " since Egypt is the country where mythology places the origin of the gods " (1. 9. 6), and since " animal life appeared first of all " (1. 10. 2) in that country, he devotes the entire First Book to the gods, kings, laws and customs of that land. His interest in religion causes him to pay more attention to that subject than to political institutions and military affairs, in marked contrast to his later Books. As for his literary sources, he is generally held to have drawn primarily upon Hecataeus of Abdera, who visited Egypt early in the 3rd century B.C., for his account of the customs of the Egyptians, upon Agatharchides of Cnidus, an historian and geographer of the 2nd century B.C., for his geographical data, and especially for the description of the Nile (cc. 32–41. 3), and upon Herodotus. He also mentions what is told by the priests of Egypt and natives of Ethiopia, and it is entirely possible that many a detail was picked up by personal observation and inquiry. By the time of his visit Greek had been the official language of the land for nearly three hundred years and was widely used in the better circles, and hence he was not in such danger of being imposed upon by guides and priests as was Herodotus.

In the opening chapters of the Second Book Diodorus moves to Asia and Assyrian affairs. Most of his material was drawn from Ctesias of Cnidus, who spent seventeen years as physician at the court of the Persian king, Artaxerxes Mnemon, returning to Greece some time after 390 B.C. Ctesias wrote a

INTRODUCTION

Persica in twenty-three Books, the first six of which dealt with Assyrian and Median history. Whether Diodorus used Ctesias directly or through a medium is still a question.[1] He also used Cleitarchus and " certain of those who at a later time crossed into Asia with Alexander " (2. 7. 3). Incidentally, he quotes from a particular Athenaeus, otherwise unknown, and " certain other historians " (2. 20. 3) to the effect that Semiramis was nothing more than a beautiful courtesan. While there is some shadowy outline of the long history of Egypt in Book I, what Diodorus (or rather Ctesias, Cleitarchus and others) has to offer on Babylonian history is scarcely deserving of the name. It is astonishing to observe that a writer with the opportunities which Ctesias enjoyed should have been content to do little more than pass on the folk tales which constitute the " history " of the Assyrian Empire.

Into the daily widening field of the history of Egypt and Babylonia, which is the theme of this volume of Diodorus, and in which many dates change from year to year and many are still the subject of controversy among competent Orientalists, a classicist enters with extreme reluctance. It has seemed the better policy to draw upon the latest general survey of this period, *The Cambridge Ancient History*, for the chronology, recognizing at the same time that even the contributors to this single enterprise are not always in agreement.

[1] Cp. P. Schnabel, *Berossos und die babylonisch-hellenistische Literatur* (Leipzig, 1923), p. 34.

THE LIBRARY OF HISTORY

OF

DIODORUS OF SICILY

BOOK I

Τάδε ἔνεστιν ἐν τῇ πρώτῃ τῶν
Διοδώρου βίβλων

Προοίμιον τῆς ὅλης πραγματείας.

Περὶ τῶν παρ' Αἰγυπτίοις λεγομένων περὶ τῆς τοῦ κόσμου γενέσεως.

Περὶ τῶν θεῶν ὅσοι πόλεις ἔκτισαν κατ' Αἴγυπτον.

Περὶ τῶν πρώτων γενομένων ἀνθρώπων καὶ τοῦ παλαιοτάτου βίου.

Περὶ τῆς τῶν ἀθανάτων τιμῆς καὶ τῆς τῶν ναῶν κατασκευῆς.

Περὶ τῆς τοποθεσίας τῆς κατ' Αἴγυπτον χώρας καὶ τῶν περὶ τὸν Νεῖλον ποταμὸν παραδοξολογουμένων, τῆς τε τούτου πληρώσεως τὰς αἰτίας [1] καὶ τῶν ἱστορικῶν καὶ φιλοσόφων ἀποφάσεις.

Περὶ τῶν πρώτων γενομένων κατ' Αἴγυπτον βασιλέων καὶ τῶν κατὰ μέρος αὐτῶν πράξεων.

Περὶ κατασκευῆς τῶν πυραμίδων τῶν ἀναγραφομένων ἐν τοῖς ἑπτὰ θαυμαζομένοις ἔργοις.

Περὶ τῶν νόμων καὶ τῶν δικαστηρίων.

Περὶ τῶν ἀφιερωμένων ζῴων παρ' Αἰγυπτίοις.

Περὶ τῶν νομίμων τῶν περὶ τοὺς τετελευτηκότας παρ' Αἰγυπτίοις γενομένων.

Περὶ τῶν Ἑλλήνων ὅσοι τῶν ἐπὶ παιδείᾳ θαυμαζομένων παραβαλόντες εἰς Αἴγυπτον καὶ πολλὰ τῶν χρησίμων μαθόντες μετήνεγκαν εἰς τὴν Ἑλλάδα.

---

[1] Some verb is needed here, such as περιέχει, which is found in chap. 42, from which most of this outline is drawn.

CONTENTS OF THE FIRST BOOK
OF DIODORUS

[1] There are no chapters which are especially devoted to this topic.

ΔΙΟΔΩΡΟΥ

ΤΟΥ ΣΙΚΕΛΙΩΤΟΥ
ΒΙΒΛΙΟΘΗΚΗΣ ΙΣΤΟΡΙΚΗΣ

ΒΙΒΛΟΣ ΠΡΩΤΗ

1. Τοῖς τὰς κοινὰς ἱστορίας πραγματευσαμένοις
μεγάλας χάριτας ἀπονέμειν δίκαιον πάντας ἀνθρώπους, ὅτι τοῖς ἰδίοις πόνοις ὠφελῆσαι τὸν
κοινὸν βίον ἐφιλοτιμήθησαν· ἀκίνδυνον γὰρ διδασκαλίαν τοῦ συμφέροντος εἰσηγησάμενοι καλλίστην ἐμπειρίαν διὰ τῆς πραγματείας ταύτης
2 περιποιοῦσι τοῖς ἀναγινώσκουσιν. ἡ μὲν γὰρ ἐκ
τῆς πείρας ἑκάστου μάθησις μετὰ πολλῶν πόνων
καὶ κινδύνων ποιεῖ τῶν χρησίμων ἕκαστα δια-
γινώσκειν, καὶ διὰ τοῦτο τῶν ἡρώων ὁ πολυπειρό-
τατος μετὰ μεγάλων ἀτυχημάτων

πολλῶν ἀνθρώπων ἴδεν ἄστεα καὶ νόον ἔγνω·

ἡ δὲ διὰ τῆς ἱστορίας περιγινομένη σύνεσις τῶν
ἀλλοτρίων ἀποτευγμάτων τε καὶ κατορθωμάτων
3 ἀπείρατον κακῶν ἔχει τὴν διδασκαλίαν. ἔπειτα
πάντας ἀνθρώπους, μετέχοντας μὲν τῆς πρὸς

---

[1] Here Diodorus markedly connects "universal" (κοιναὶ)
history with human society "as a whole" (κοινός). Cp. the
Introduction, pp. xi f.

[2] Odysseus. The quotation is from the *Odyssey* 1. 3.

THE LIBRARY OF HISTORY

OF

DIODORUS OF SICILY

BOOK I

1. IT is fitting that all men should ever accord
great gratitude to those writers who have composed
universal[1] histories, since they have aspired to help
by their individual labours human society as a whole;
for by offering a schooling, which entails no danger,
in what is advantageous they provide their readers,
through such a presentation of events, with a most
excellent kind of experience. For although the
learning which is acquired by experience in each
separate case, with all the attendant toils and
dangers, does indeed enable a man to discern in
each instance where utility lies—and this is the
reason why the most widely experienced of our
heroes[2] suffered great misfortunes before he

> Of many men the cities saw and learned
> Their thoughts;—

yet the understanding of the failures and successes
of other men, which is acquired by the study of
history, affords a schooling that is free from actual
experience of ills. Furthermore, it has been the
aspiration of these writers to marshal all men, who,

5

ἀλλήλους συγγενείας, τόποις δὲ καὶ χρόνοις
διεστηκότας, ἐφιλοτιμήθησαν ὑπὸ μίαν καὶ τὴν
αὐτὴν σύνταξιν ἀγαγεῖν, ὥσπερ τινὲς ὑπουργοὶ
τῆς θείας προνοίας γενηθέντες. ἐκείνη τε γὰρ
τὴν τῶν ὁρωμένων ἄστρων διακόσμησιν καὶ τὰς
τῶν ἀνθρώπων φύσεις εἰς κοινὴν ἀναλογίαν συν-
θεῖσα κυκλεῖ συνεχῶς ἅπαντα τὸν αἰῶνα, τὸ
ἐπιβάλλον ἑκάστοις ἐκ τῆς πεπρωμένης μερί-
ζουσα, οἵ τε τὰς κοινὰς τῆς οἰκουμένης πράξεις
καθάπερ μιᾶς πόλεως ἀναγράψαντες ἕνα λόγον
καὶ κοινὸν χρηματιστήριον τῶν συντετελεσμένων
4 ἀπέδειξαν τὰς ἑαυτῶν πραγματείας. καλὸν γὰρ
τὸ δύνασθαι τοῖς τῶν ἄλλων ἀγνοήμασι πρὸς
διόρθωσιν χρῆσθαι παραδείγμασι, καὶ πρὸς τὰ
συγκυροῦντα ποικίλως κατὰ τὸν βίον ἔχειν μὴ
ζήτησιν τῶν πραττομένων, ἀλλὰ μίμησιν τῶν
ἐπιτετευγμένων. καὶ γὰρ τοὺς πρεσβυτάτους
ταῖς ἡλικίαις ἅπαντες τῶν νεωτέρων προκρίνουσιν
ἐν ταῖς συμβουλίαις διὰ τὴν ἐκ τοῦ χρόνου περι-
γεγενημένην αὐτοῖς ἐμπειρίαν· ἧς τοσοῦτον ὑπερέχειν συμβέβηκε τὴν ἐκ τῆς ἱστορίας μάθησιν
ὅσον καὶ τῷ πλήθει τῶν πραγμάτων προτεροῦσαν
αὐτὴν ἐπεγνώκαμεν. διὸ καὶ πρὸς ἁπάσας τὰς
τοῦ βίου περιστάσεις χρησιμωτάτην ἄν τις εἶναι
5 νομίσειε τὴν ταύτης ἀνάληψιν. τοῖς μὲν γὰρ
νεωτέροις τὴν τῶν γεγηρακότων περιποιεῖ σύνεσιν, τοῖς δὲ πρεσβυτέροις πολλαπλασιάζει τὴν
ὑπάρχουσαν ἐμπειρίαν, καὶ τοὺς μὲν ἰδιώτας

---

[1] The reference is to the Stoic doctrine of the universal
kinship of mankind.

although united one to another by their kinship,[1] are yet separated by space and time, into one and the same orderly body. And such historians have therein shown themselves to be, as it were, ministers of Divine Providence. For just as Providence, having brought the orderly arrangement of the visible stars and the natures of men together into one common relationship, continually directs their courses through all eternity, apportioning to each that which falls to it by the direction of fate, so likewise the historians, in recording the common affairs of the inhabited world as though they were those of a single state, have made of their treatises a single reckoning of past events and a common clearing-house of knowledge concerning them. For it is an excellent thing to be able to use the ignorant mistakes of others as warning examples for the correction of error, and, when we confront the varied vicissitudes of life, instead of having to investigate what is being done now, to be able to imitate the successes which have been achieved in the past. Certainly all men prefer in their counsels the oldest men to those who are younger, because of the experience which has accrued to the former through the lapse of time; but it is a fact that such experience is in so far surpassed by the understanding which is gained from history, as history excels, we know, in the multitude of facts at its disposal. For this reason one may hold that the acquisition of a knowledge of history is of the greatest utility for every conceivable circumstance of life. For it endows the young with the wisdom of the aged, while for the old it multiplies the experience which they already possess; citizens in private station it qualifies for leadership, and the

ἀξίους ἡγεμονίας κατασκευάζει, τοὺς δ᾽ ἡγεμόνας
τῷ διὰ τῆς δόξης ἀθανατισμῷ προτρέπεται τοῖς
καλλίστοις τῶν ἔργων ἐπιχειρεῖν, χωρὶς δὲ τούτων τοὺς μὲν στρατιώτας τοῖς μετὰ τὴν τελευτὴν
ἐπαίνοις ἑτοιμοτέρους κατασκευάζει πρὸς τοὺς
ὑπὲρ τῆς πατρίδος κινδύνους, τοὺς δὲ πονηροὺς
τῶν ἀνθρώπων ταῖς αἰωνίοις βλασφημίαις ἀπο-
τρέπει τῆς ἐπὶ τὴν κακίαν ὁρμῆς.

2. Καθόλου δὲ διὰ τὴν ἐκ ταύτης ἐπ᾽ ἀγαθῷ
μνήμην οἱ μὲν κτίσται πόλεων γενέσθαι προε-
κλήθησαν, οἱ δὲ νόμους εἰσηγήσασθαι περιέχοντας
τῷ κοινῷ βίῳ τὴν ἀσφάλειαν, πολλοὶ δ᾽ ἐπιστή-
μας καὶ τέχνας ἐξευρεῖν ἐφιλοτιμήθησαν πρὸς
εὐεργεσίαν τοῦ γένους τῶν ἀνθρώπων. ἐξ ἁπάντων δὲ συμπληρουμένης τῆς εὐδαιμονίας, ἀπο-
δοτέον τῶν ἐπαίνων τὸ πρωτεῖον τῇ τούτων
2 μάλιστ᾽ αἰτίᾳ, ἱστορίᾳ. ἡγητέον γὰρ εἶναι ταύτην φύλακα μὲν τῆς τῶν ἀξιολόγων ἀρετῆς,
μάρτυρα δὲ τῆς τῶν φαύλων κακίας, εὐεργέτιν
δὲ τοῦ κοινοῦ γένους τῶν ἀνθρώπων. εἰ γὰρ
ἡ τῶν ἐν ᾅδου μυθολογία τὴν ὑπόθεσιν πεπλασ-
μένην ἔχουσα πολλὰ συμβάλλεται τοῖς ἀνθρώποις πρὸς εὐσέβειαν καὶ δικαιοσύνην, πόσῳ
μᾶλλον¹ ὑποληπτέον τὴν προφῆτιν τῆς ἀληθείας
ἱστορίαν, τῆς ὅλης φιλοσοφίας οἱονεὶ μητρόπολιν
οὖσαν, ἐπισκευάσαι δύνασθαι τὰ ἤθη μᾶλλον
3 πρὸς καλοκἀγαθίαν; πάντες γὰρ ἄνθρωποι διὰ

---

¹ μᾶλλον Bekker, Vogel: omitted C F, Dindorf.

¹ The Greek "metropolis," the "home country" or "mother-
city" of all the colonies which it had sent forth, was venerated
by them as the source of their race and of their institutions.
For the striking figure cp. the passage in Athenæus 104 B,

leaders it incites, through the immortality of the glory which it confers, to undertake the noblest deeds; soldiers, again, it makes more ready to face dangers in defence of their country because of the public encomiums which they will receive after death, and wicked men it turns aside from their impulse towards evil through the everlasting opprobrium to which it will condemn them.

2. In general, then, it is because of that commemoration of goodly deeds which history accords men that some of them have been induced to become the founders of cities, that others have been led to introduce laws which encompass man's social life with security, and that many have aspired to discover new sciences and arts in order to benefit the race of men. And since complete happiness can be attained only through the combination of all these activities, the foremost meed of praise must be awarded to that which more than any other thing is the cause of them, that is, to history. For we must look upon it as constituting the guardian of the high achievements of illustrious men, the witness which testifies to the evil deeds of the wicked, and the benefactor of the entire human race. For if it be true that the myths which are related about Hades, in spite of the fact that their subject-matter is fictitious, contribute greatly to fostering piety and justice among men, how much more must we assume that history, the prophetess of truth, she who is, as it were, the mother-city [1] of philosophy as a whole, is still more potent to equip men's characters for noble living! For all men, by reason of the frailty of our nature,

where Chrysippus calls the *Gastrology* of Archestratus a "metropolis" of the philosophy of Epicurus.

τὴν τῆς φύσεως ἀσθένειαν βιοῦσι μὲν ἀκαριαῖόν
τι μέρος τοῦ παντὸς αἰῶνος, τετελευτήκασι δὲ
πάντα τὸν ὕστερον χρόνον, καὶ τοῖς μὲν ἐν τῷ
ζῆν μηδὲν ἀξιόλογον πράξασιν ἅμα ταῖς τῶν
σωμάτων τελευταῖς συναποθνήσκει καὶ τὰ ἄλλα
πάντα τὰ κατὰ τὸν βίον, τοῖς δὲ δι' ἀρετὴν
περιποιησαμένοις δόξαν αἱ πράξεις ἅπαντα τὸν
αἰῶνα μνημονεύονται, διαβοώμεναι τῷ θειοτάτῳ
τῆς ἱστορίας στόματι.

4 Καλὸν δ', οἶμαι, τοῖς εὖ φρονοῦσι θνητῶν
πόνων ἀντικαταλλάξασθαι τὴν ἀθάνατον εὐφη-
μίαν. Ἡρακλῆς μὲν γὰρ ὁμολογεῖται πάντα
τὸν γενόμενον αὐτῷ κατ' ἀνθρώπους χρόνον
ὑπομεῖναι μεγάλους καὶ συνεχεῖς πόνους καὶ κινδύνους ἑκουσίως, ἵνα τὸ γένος τῶν ἀνθρώπων
εὐεργετήσας τύχῃ τῆς ἀθανασίας· τῶν δὲ ἄλλων
ἀγαθῶν ἀνδρῶν οἱ μὲν ἡρωικῶν, οἱ δὲ ἰσοθέων
τιμῶν ἔτυχον, πάντες δὲ μεγάλων ἐπαίνων
ἠξιώθησαν, τὰς ἀρετὰς αὐτῶν τῆς ἱστορίας
5 ἀπαθανατιζούσης. τὰ μὲν γὰρ ἄλλα μνημεῖα
διαμένει χρόνον ὀλίγον, ὑπὸ πολλῶν ἀναιρούμενα
περιστάσεων, ἡ δὲ τῆς ἱστορίας δύναμις ἐπὶ
πᾶσαν τὴν οἰκουμένην διήκουσα τὸν πάντα
τἆλλα λυμαινόμενον χρόνον ἔχει φύλακα τῆς
αἰωνίου παραδόσεως τοῖς ἐπιγινομένοις.

Συμβάλλεται δ' αὕτη καὶ πρὸς λόγου δύναμιν,
οὗ κάλλιον ἕτερον οὐκ ἄν τις ῥᾳδίως εὕροι.
6 τούτῳ γὰρ οἱ μὲν Ἕλληνες τῶν βαρβάρων, οἱ
δὲ πεπαιδευμένοι τῶν ἀπαιδεύτων προέχουσι,
πρὸς δὲ τούτοις διὰ μόνου τούτου δυνατόν ἐστιν

live but an infinitesimal portion of eternity and are
dead throughout all subsequent time; and while in
the case of those who in their lifetime have done
nothing worthy of note, everything which has per-
tained to them in life also perishes when their bodies
die, yet in the case of those who by their virtue have
achieved fame, their deeds are remembered for
evermore, since they are heralded abroad by history's
voice most divine.

Now it is an excellent thing, methinks, as all men
of understanding must agree, to receive in exchange
for mortal labours an immortal fame. In the case
of Heracles, for instance, it is generally agreed that
during the whole time which he spent among men he
submitted to great and continuous labours and perils
willingly, in order that he might confer benefits
upon the race of men and thereby gain immortality;
and likewise in the case of other great and good men,
some have attained to heroic honours and others to
honours equal to the divine, and all have been thought
to be worthy of great praise, since history immor-
talizes their achievements. For whereas all other
memorials abide but a brief time, being continually
destroyed by many vicissitudes, yet the power of
history, which extends over the whole inhabited
world, possesses in time, which brings ruin upon all
things else, a custodian which ensures its perpetual
transmission to posterity.

History also contributes to the power of speech,
and a nobler thing than that may not easily be
found. For it is this that makes the Greeks superior
to the barbarians, and the educated to the unedu-
cated, and, furthermore, it is by means of speech
alone that one man is able to gain ascendancy over

ἕνα τῶν πολλῶν περιγενέσθαι· καθόλου δὲ
φαίνεται πᾶν τὸ προτεθὲν τοιοῦτον ὁποῖον ἂν
ᾖ τοῦ λέγοντος δύναμις παραστήσῃ, καὶ τοὺς
ἀγαθοὺς ἄνδρας ἀξίους λόγου προσαγορεύομεν,
ὡς τοῦτο τὸ πρωτεῖον τῆς ἀρετῆς περιπεποιη-
7 μένους. εἰς πλείω δὲ μέρη τούτου διῃρημένου,
συμβαίνει τὴν μὲν ποιητικὴν τέρπειν μᾶλλον
ἤπερ ὠφελεῖν, τὴν δὲ νομοθεσίαν κολάζειν, οὐ
διδάσκειν, παραπλησίως δὲ καὶ τἆλλα μέρη τὰ
μὲν μηδὲν συμβάλλεσθαι πρὸς εὐδαιμονίαν, τὰ
δὲ μεμιγμένην ἔχειν τῷ συμφέροντι τὴν βλάβην,
ἔνια δὲ κατεψεῦσθαι τῆς ἀληθείας, μόνην δὲ τὴν
ἱστορίαν, συμφωνούντων ἐν αὐτῇ τῶν λόγων
τοῖς ἔργοις, ἅπαντα τἆλλα χρήσιμα τῇ γραφῇ
8 περιειληφέναι· ὁρᾶσθαι γὰρ αὐτὴν προτρεπο-
μένην ἐπὶ δικαιοσύνην, κατηγοροῦσαν τῶν φαύλων, ἐγκωμιάζουσαν τοὺς ἀγαθούς, τὸ σύνολον
ἐμπειρίαν μεγίστην περιποιοῦσαν τοῖς ἐντυγχά-
νουσι.

3. Διὸ καὶ θεωροῦντες ἡμεῖς δικαίας ἀποδοχῆς
τυγχάνοντας τοὺς ταύτην πραγματευσαμένους
προήχθημεν ἐπὶ τὸν ὅμοιον τῆς ὑποθέσεως ζῆλον.
ἐπιστήσαντες δὲ τὸν νοῦν τοῖς πρὸ ἡμῶν συγγραφεῦσιν ἀπεδεξάμεθα μὲν ὡς ἔνι μάλιστα τὴν
προαίρεσιν αὐτῶν, οὐ μὴν ἐξειργάσθαι πρὸς τὸ
συμφέρον κατὰ[1] τὸ δυνατὸν τὰς πραγματείας
2 αὐτῶν ὑπελάβομεν. κειμένης γὰρ τοῖς ἀνα-
γινώσκουσι τῆς ὠφελείας ἐν τῷ πλείστας καὶ
ποικιλωτάτας περιστάσεις λαμβάνειν, οἱ πλεῖστοι
μὲν ἑνὸς[2] ἔθνους ἢ μιᾶς πόλεως αὐτοτελεῖς
πολέμους ἀνέγραψαν, ὀλίγοι δ᾽ ἀπὸ τῶν ἀρχαίων

---

[1] κατὰ Stephanus : καὶ. [2] ἑνὸς added by Porson.

the many; and, in general, the impression made by every measure that is proposed corresponds to the power of the speaker who presents it, and we describe great and good men as " worthy of speech," [1] as though therein they had won the highest prize of excellence. And when speech is resolved into its several kinds, we find that, whereas poetry is more pleasing than profitable, and codes of law punish but do not instruct, and similarly, all the other kinds either contribute nothing to happiness or else contain a harmful element mingled with the beneficial, while some of them actually pervert the truth, history alone, since in it word and fact are in perfect agreement, embraces in its narration all the other qualities as well that are useful; for it is ever to be seen urging men to justice, denouncing those who are evil, lauding the good, laying up, in a word, for its readers a mighty store of experience.

3. Consequently we, observing that writers of history are accorded a merited approbation, were led to feel a like enthusiasm for the subject. But when we turned our attention to the historians before our time, although we approved their purpose without reservation, yet we were far from feeling that their treatises had been composed so as to contribute to human welfare as much as might have been the case. For although the profit which history affords its readers lies in its embracing a vast number and variety of circumstances, yet most writers have recorded no more than isolated wars waged by a single nation or a single state, and but few have undertaken, beginning with the earliest times and coming down

---

[1] *i.e.* worthy to be the subject of speech. ἀξιόλογος is a favourite word of Diodorus in the usual meaning of " distinguished," " notable."

χρόνων ἀρξάμενοι τὰς κοινὰς πράξεις ἐπεχείρη-
σαν ἀναγράφειν μέχρι τῶν καθ᾿ αὑτοὺς καιρῶν,
καὶ τούτων οἱ μὲν τοὺς οἰκείους χρόνους ἑκάστοις οὐ παρέζευξαν, οἱ δὲ τὰς τῶν βαρβάρων
πράξεις ὑπερέβησαν, ἔτι δ᾿ οἱ μὲν τὰς παλαιὰς
μυθολογίας διὰ τὴν δυσχέρειαν τῆς πραγματείας
ἀπεδοκίμασαν, οἱ δὲ τὴν ὑπόστασιν τῆς ἐπιβολῆς
οὐ συνετέλεσαν, μεσολαβηθέντες τὸν βίον ὑπὸ
3 τῆς πεπρωμένης. τῶν δὲ τὴν ἐπιβολὴν ταύτης
τῆς πραγματείας πεποιημένων οὐδεὶς προεβίβασε
τὴν ἱστορίαν κατωτέρω τῶν Μακεδονικῶν καιρῶν·
οἱ μὲν γὰρ εἰς τὰς Φιλίππου πράξεις, οἱ δ᾿ εἰς
τὰς Ἀλεξάνδρου, τινὲς δ᾿ εἰς τοὺς διαδόχους ἢ
τοὺς ἐπιγόνους κατέστρεψαν τὰς συντάξεις·
πολλῶν δὲ καὶ μεγάλων τῶν μετὰ ταῦτα
πράξεων ἀπολελειμμένων μέχρι τοῦ καθ᾿ ἡμᾶς
βίου τῶν ἱστοριογράφων οὐδεὶς ἐπεβάλετο αὐτὰς
μιᾶς συντάξεως περιγραφῇ πραγματεύσασθαι διὰ
4 τὸ μέγεθος τῆς ὑποθέσεως. διὸ καὶ διερριμμένων[1] τῶν τε χρόνων καὶ τῶν πράξεων ἐν
πλείοσι πραγματείαις καὶ διαφόροις συγγραφεῦσι δυσπερίληπτος ἡ τούτων ἀνάληψις γίνεται καὶ δυσμνημόνευτος.
5 Ἐξετάσαντες οὖν τὰς ἑκάστου τούτων δια-
θέσεις ἐκρίναμεν ὑπόθεσιν ἱστορικὴν πραγματεύσασθαι τὴν πλεῖστα μὲν ὠφελῆσαι δυναμένην,

---

[1] διερριμμένων Hertlein and Bezzel: ἐρριμμένων.

---

[1] Of the writers who may be said to have composed universal
histories, Diodorus may have had in mind Herodotus, who had
no chronological system, Anaximenes of Lampsacus, who
confined his *Hellenica*, as the title shows, to the Greeks, and
Ephorus of Cyme, who omitted the mythological period and

to their own day, to record the events connected with all peoples; and of the latter, some have not attached to the several events their own proper dates, and others have passed over the deeds of barbarian peoples; and some, again, have rejected the ancient legends because of the difficulties involved in their treatment, while others have failed to complete the plan to which they had set their hand, their lives having been cut short by fate.[1] And of those who have undertaken this account of all peoples not one has continued his history beyond the Macedonian period. For while some have closed their accounts with the deeds of Philip, others with those of Alexander, and some with the Diadochi or the Epigoni,[2] yet, despite the number and importance of the events subsequent to these and extending even to our own lifetime which have been left neglected, no historian has essayed to treat of them within the compass of a single narrative, because of the magnitude of the undertaking. For this reason, since both the dates of the events and the events themselves lie scattered about in numerous treatises and in divers authors, the knowledge of them becomes difficult for the mind to encompass and for the memory to retain.

Consequently, after we had examined the composition of each of these authors' works, we resolved to write a history after a plan which might yield to

whose death brought his history to a close with the year 340 B.C., although he had witnessed the stirring events of the subsequent twenty years.

[2] The Diadochi, or Successors, were those rulers who shortly after 323 B.C. formed separate kingdoms out of the territory conquered by Alexander. The Epigoni were the next and succeeding generations.

ἐλάχιστα δὲ τοὺς ἀναγινώσκοντας ἐνοχλήσου-
6 σαν. εἰ γάρ τις τὰς εἰς μνήμην παραδεδομένας
τοῦ σύμπαντος κόσμου πράξεις, ὥσπερ τινὸς
μιᾶς πόλεως, ἀρξάμενος ἀπὸ τῶν ἀρχαιοτάτων
χρόνων ἀναγράψαι κατὰ τὸ δυνατὸν μέχρι τῶν
καθ᾽ αὑτὸν καιρῶν, πόνον μὲν ἂν πολὺν ὑπομεῖναι δῆλον ὅτι, πραγματείαν δὲ πασῶν εὐχρη-
στοτάτην συντάξαιτο τοῖς φιλαναγνωστοῦσιν.
7 ἐξέσται γὰρ ἐκ ταύτης ἕκαστον πρὸς τὴν ἰδίαν
ὑπόστασιν ἑτοίμως λαμβάνειν τὸ χρήσιμον,
8 ὥσπερ ἐκ μεγάλης ἀρυόμενον πηγῆς. τοῖς μὲν
γὰρ ἐπιβαλλομένοις διεξιέναι τὰς τῶν τοσούτων
συγγραφέων ἱστορίας πρῶτον μὲν οὐ ῥάδιον
εὐπορῆσαι τῶν εἰς τὴν χρείαν πιπτουσῶν βίβλων, ἔπειτα διὰ τὴν ἀνωμαλίαν καὶ τὸ πλῆθος
τῶν συνταγμάτων δυσκατάληπτος γίνεται τελέως
καὶ δυσέφικτος ἡ τῶν πεπραγμένων ἀνάληψις·
ἡ δ᾽ ἐν μιᾶς [1] συντάξεως περιγραφῇ πραγματεία
τὸ τῶν πράξεων εἰρόμενον ἔχουσα τὴν μὲν
ἀνάγνωσιν ἑτοίμην παρέχεται, τὴν δ᾽ ἀνάληψιν
ἔχει παντελῶς εὐπαρακολούθητον. καθόλου δὲ
τῶν ἄλλων τοσοῦτον ὑπερέχειν ταύτην ἡγητέον
ὅσῳ χρησιμώτερόν ἐστι τὸ πᾶν τοῦ μέρους καὶ τὸ
συνεχὲς τοῦ διερρηγμένου, πρὸς δὲ τούτοις τὸ
διηκριβωμένον τοῖς χρόνοις τοῦ μηδὲ γινωσκο-
μένου τίσιν ἐπράχθη καιροῖς.
4. Διόπερ ἡμεῖς ὁρῶντες ταύτην τὴν ὑπόθεσιν
χρησιμωτάτην μὲν οὖσαν, πολλοῦ δὲ πόνου καὶ
χρόνου προσδεομένην, τριάκοντα μὲν ἔτη περὶ
αὐτὴν ἐπραγματεύθημεν, μετὰ δὲ πολλῆς κακο-

_____
[1] μιᾶς Schäfer : μιᾷ.

its readers the greatest benefit and at the same
time incommode them the least. For if a man
should begin with the most ancient times and record
to the best of his ability the affairs of the entire
world down to his own day, so far as they have been
handed down to memory, as though they were the
affairs of some single city, he would obviously have
to undertake an immense labour, yet he would have
composed a treatise of the utmost value to those
who are studiously inclined. For from such a
treatise every man will be able readily to take what
is of use for his special purpose, drawing as it were
from a great fountain. The reason for this is that,
in the first place, it is not easy for those who propose
to go through the writings of so many historians to
procure the books which come to be needed, and, in
the second place, that, because the works vary so
widely and are so numerous, the recovery of past
events becomes extremely difficult of comprehension
and of attainment; whereas, on the other hand,
the treatise which keeps within the limits of a single
narrative and contains a connected account of events
facilitates the reading and contains such recovery of
the past in a form that is perfectly easy to follow.
In general, a history of this nature must be held to
surpass all others to the same degree as the whole
is more useful than the part and continuity than dis-
continuity, and, again, as an event whose date has
been accurately determined is more useful than one
of which it is not known in what period it happened.

4. And so we, appreciating that an undertaking
of this nature, while most useful, would yet require
much labour and time, have been engaged upon it
for thirty years, and with much hardship and many

παθείας καὶ κινδύνων ἐπήλθομεν πολλὴν τῆς τε
Ἀσίας καὶ τῆς Εὐρώπης, ἵνα τῶν ἀναγκαιοτάτων
καὶ πλείστων μερῶν αὐτόπται γενηθῶμεν·
πολλὰ γὰρ παρὰ τὰς ἀγνοίας τῶν τόπων διήμαρτον οὐχ οἱ τυχόντες τῶν συγγραφέων, ἀλλά
2 τινες καὶ τῶν τῇ δόξῃ πεπρωτευκότων. ἀφορμῇ
δὲ πρὸς τὴν ἐπιβολὴν ταύτην ἐχρησάμεθα
μάλιστα μὲν τῇ πρὸς τὴν πραγματείαν ἐπιθυμίᾳ,
δι' ἣν πᾶσιν ἀνθρώποις τὸ δοκοῦν ἄπορον εἶναι
τυγχάνει συντελείας, ἔπειτα καὶ τῇ ἐν Ῥώμῃ
χορηγίᾳ[1] τῶν πρὸς τὴν ὑποκειμένην ὑπόθεσιν
3 ἀνηκόντων. ἡ γὰρ ταύτης τῆς πόλεως ὑπεροχή,
διατείνουσα τῇ δυνάμει πρὸς τὰ πέρατα τῆς
οἰκουμένης, ἑτοιμοτάτας καὶ πλείστας ἡμῖν
ἀφορμὰς παρέσχετο παρεπιδημήσασιν ἐν αὐτῇ
4 πλείω χρόνον. ἡμεῖς γὰρ ἐξ Ἀγυρίου τῆς
Σικελίας ὄντες, καὶ διὰ τὴν ἐπιμιξίαν τοῖς ἐν
τῇ νήσῳ πολλὴν ἐμπειρίαν τῆς Ῥωμαίων διαλέκτου περιπεποιημένοι, πάσας τὰς τῆς ἡγεμονίας ταύτης πράξεις ἀκριβῶς ἀνελάβομεν ἐκ
τῶν παρ' ἐκείνοις ὑπομνημάτων ἐκ πολλῶν
5 χρόνων τετηρημένων. πεποιήμεθα δὲ τὴν ἀρχὴν
τῆς ἱστορίας ἀπὸ τῶν μυθολογουμένων παρ'
Ἕλλησί τε καὶ βαρβάροις, ἐξετάσαντες τὰ παρ'
ἑκάστοις ἱστορούμενα κατὰ τοὺς ἀρχαίους χρόνους, ἐφ' ὅσον ἡμῖν δύναμις.
6 Ἐπεὶ δ' ἡ μὲν ὑπόθεσις ἔχει τέλος, αἱ βίβλοι
δὲ μέχρι τοῦ νῦν ἀνέκδοτοι τυγχάνουσιν οὖσαι,

[1] τῇ . . . χορηγίᾳ Hertlein : διὰ τὴν . . . χορηγίαν.

---

[1] On the travels undertaken by Diodorus in preparation for
the writing of his history, see the Introduction, p. xiii.

dangers we have visited a large portion of both
Asia and Europe that we might see with our own
eyes all the most important regions [1] and as many
others as possible; for many errors have been committed through ignorance of the sites, not only by
the common run of historians, but even by some of
the highest reputation. As for the resources which
have availed us in this undertaking, they have been,
first and foremost, that enthusiasm for the work
which enables every man to bring to completion the
task which seems impossible, and, in the second place,
the abundant supply which Rome affords of the
materials pertaining to the proposed study. For
the supremacy of this city, a supremacy so powerful
that it extends to the bounds of the inhabited
world, has provided us in the course of our long
residence there with copious resources in the most
accessible form. For since the city of our origin
was Agyrium in Sicily, and by reason of our contact
with the Romans in that island we had gained a
wide acquaintance with their language,[2] we have
acquired an accurate knowledge of all the events
connected with this empire from the records which
have been carefully preserved among them over a
long period of time. Now we have begun our
history with the legends of both Greeks and barbarians, after having first investigated to the best
of our ability the accounts which each people records
of its earliest times.

Since my undertaking is now completed, although
the volumes are as yet unpublished, I wish to pre-

[2] The prevailing language in Sicily in this period was Greek.
On the acquaintance of Diodorus with Latin see the Introduction, pp. xiii f.

βούλομαι βραχέα προδιορίσαι περὶ ὅλης τῆς πραγματείας. τῶν γὰρ βίβλων ἡμῖν ἐξ μὲν αἱ πρῶται περιέχουσι τὰς πρὸ τῶν Τρωικῶν πράξεις καὶ μυθολογίας, καὶ τούτων αἱ μὲν προηγούμεναι τρεῖς τὰς βαρβαρικάς, αἱ δ' ἑξῆς σχεδὸν τὰς τῶν Ἑλλήνων ἀρχαιολογίας· ἐν δὲ ταῖς μετὰ ταύτας ἕνδεκα τὰς ἀπὸ τῶν Τρωικῶν κοινὰς πράξεις ἀναγεγράφαμεν ἕως τῆς Ἀλεξάνδρου 7 τελευτῆς· ἐν δὲ ταῖς ἑξῆς εἴκοσι καὶ τρισὶ βίβλοις τὰς λοιπὰς ἁπάσας κατετάξαμεν μέχρι τῆς ἀρχῆς τοῦ συστάντος πολέμου Ῥωμαίοις πρὸς Κελτούς, καθ' ὃν ἡγούμενος Γάιος Ἰούλιος Καῖσαρ ὁ διὰ τὰς πράξεις προσαγορευθεὶς θεὸς κατεπολέμησε μὲν τὰ πλεῖστα καὶ μαχιμώτατα τῶν Κελτῶν ἔθνη, προεβίβασε δὲ τὴν ἡγεμονίαν τῆς Ῥώμης μέχρι τῶν Βρεττανικῶν νήσων· τούτου δ' αἱ πρῶται πράξεις ἐπετελέσθησαν Ὀλυμπιάδος τῆς ἑκατοστῆς καὶ ὀγδοηκοστῆς κατὰ τὸ πρῶτον ἔτος ἐπ' ἄρχοντος Ἀθήνησιν Ἡρώδου.

5. Τῶν δὲ χρόνων τούτων περιειλημμένων ἐν ταύτῃ τῇ πραγματείᾳ τοὺς μὲν πρὸ τῶν Τρωικῶν οὐ διοριζόμεθα βεβαίως διὰ τὸ μηδὲν παράπηγμα παρειληφέναι περὶ τούτων πιστευόμενον, ἀπὸ δὲ τῶν Τρωικῶν ἀκολούθως Ἀπολλοδώρῳ τῷ Ἀθηναίῳ τίθεμεν ὀγδοήκοντ' ἔτη πρὸς τὴν κάθοδον τῶν Ἡρακλειδῶν, ἀπὸ δὲ ταύτης ἐπὶ τὴν πρώτην Ὀλυμπιάδα δυσὶ λείποντα τῶν τριακοσίων καὶ τριάκοντα, συλλογιζόμενοι τοὺς χρόνους ἀπὸ τῶν ἐν Λακεδαίμονι βασιλευσάντων, ἀπὸ δὲ τῆς

---

[1] For the subjects of the several Books see the Introduction, pp. xvi f.

sent a brief preliminary outline of the work as a whole. Our first six Books embrace the events and legends previous to the Trojan War, the first three setting forth the antiquities of the barbarians, and the next three almost exclusively those of the Greeks;[1] in the following eleven we have written a universal history of events from the Trojan War to the death of Alexander; and in the succeeding twenty-three Books we have given an orderly account of all subsequent events down to the beginning of the war between the Romans and the Celts, in the course of which the commander, Gaius Julius Caesar, who has been deified because of his deeds, subdued the most numerous and most warlike tribes of the Celts, and advanced the Roman Empire as far as the British Isles. The first events of this war occurred in the first year of the One Hundred and Eightieth 60–59 Olympiad, when Herodes was archon in Athens.[2] B.C.

5. As for the periods included in this work, we do not attempt to fix with any strictness the limits of those before the Trojan War, because no trustworthy chronological table covering them has come into our hands: but from the Trojan War 1184 we follow Apollodorus of Athens[3] in setting the B.C. interval from then to the Return of the Heracleidae 1104 as eighty years, from then to the First Olympiad B.C. three hundred and twenty-eight years, reckoning 776–5 the dates by the reigns of the kings of Lacedaemon, B.C.

[2] On these periods and dates, as given more fully in the following paragraph, see the Introduction, p. xv.

[3] A philosopher and historian of the second century B.C. whose *Chronology* covered the years 1184–119 B.C. The *Chronology* of Castor of Rhodes, of the first century B.C., which came down to 60 B.C., and was probably also used by Diodorus after the date where Apollodorus stopped, included the period before the Trojan War.

πρώτης Ὀλυμπιάδος εἰς τὴν ἀρχὴν τοῦ Κελτικοῦ
πολέμου, ἣν τελευτὴν πεποιήμεθα τῆς ἱστορίας,
ἑπτακόσια καὶ τριάκοντα· ὥστε τὴν ὅλην πραγματείαν ἡμῶν τετταράκοντα βίβλων οὖσαν περιέ-
χειν ἔτη δυσὶ λείποντα τῶν χιλίων ἑκατὸν
τετταράκοντα χωρὶς τῶν χρόνων τῶν περιεχόν-
των τὰς πρὸ τῶν Τρωικῶν πράξεις.

2 Ταῦτα μὲν οὖν ἀκριβῶς προδιωρισάμεθα, βουλόμενοι τοὺς μὲν ἀναγινώσκοντας εἰς ἔννοιαν
ἀγαγεῖν τῆς ὅλης προθέσεως, τοὺς δὲ διασκευάζειν
εἰωθότας τὰς βίβλους ἀποτρέψαι τοῦ λυμαίνεσθαι
τὰς ἀλλοτρίας πραγματείας. ἡμῖν δὲ παρ' ὅλην
τὴν ἱστορίαν τὰ μὲν γραφέντα καλῶς μὴ μετεχέτω
φθόνου, τὰ δὲ ἀγνοηθέντα τυγχανέτω διορθώσεως
ὑπὸ τῶν δυνατωτέρων.

3 Διεληλυθότες δὲ ὑπὲρ ὧν προηρούμεθα, τὴν
ἐπαγγελίαν τῆς γραφῆς βεβαιοῦν ἐγχειρήσομεν.

6. Περὶ μὲν οὖν θεῶν τίνας ἐννοίας ἔσχον οἱ
πρῶτοι καταδείξαντες τιμᾶν τὸ θεῖον, καὶ τῶν
μυθολογουμένων περὶ ἑκάστου[1] τῶν ἀθανάτων,
τὰ μὲν πολλὰ συντάξασθαι παρήσομεν[2] κατ'
ἰδίαν διὰ τὸ τὴν ὑπόθεσιν ταύτην πολλοῦ λόγου
προσδεῖσθαι, ὅσα δ' ἂν ταῖς προκειμέναις ἱστορίαις
οἰκεῖα[3] δόξωμεν ὑπάρχειν, παραθήσομεν ἐν
κεφαλαίοις, ἵνα μηδὲν τῶν ἀκοῆς ἀξίων ἐπιζη-
2 τῆται. περὶ δὲ τοῦ γένους τῶν ἁπάντων ἀνθρώ-

---

[1] So Dindorf : περὶ τῶν μυθολογουμένων ἑκάστου.
[2] παρήσομεν Madvig : πειρασόμεθα.
[3] οἰκεῖα Vogel : ἐοικότα.

---

[1] In Book 40. 8 Diodorus remarks that some of his Books
had been circulated before the publication of the work as a

and from the First Olympiad to the beginning of the Celtic War, which we have made the end of our history, seven hundred and thirty years; so that our whole treatise of forty Books embraces eleven hundred and thirty-eight years, exclusive of the periods which embrace the events before the Trojan War.

We have given at the outset this precise outline, since we desire to inform our readers about the project as a whole, and at the same time to deter those who are accustomed to make their books by compilation,[1] from mutilating works of which they are not the authors. And throughout our entire history it is to be hoped that what we have done well may not be the object of envy, and that the matters wherein our knowledge is defective may receive correction at the hands of more able historians.

Now that we have set forth the plan and purpose of our undertaking we shall attempt to make good our promise of such a treatise.

6. Concerning the various conceptions of the gods formed by those who were the first to introduce the worship of the deity, and concerning the myths which are told about each of the immortals, although we shall refrain from setting forth the most part in detail, since such a procedure would require a long account, yet whatever on these subjects we may feel to be pertinent to the several parts of our proposed history we shall present in a summary fashion, that nothing which is worth hearing may be found missing. Concerning, however, every race

whole. Whether they had been materially altered, as was often done by the diaskeuasts, is not known.

πων καὶ τῶν πραχθέντων ἐν τοῖς γνωριζομένοις
μέρεσι τῆς οἰκουμένης, ὡς ἂν ἐνδέχηται περὶ τῶν
οὕτω παλαιῶν, ἀκριβῶς ἀναγράψομεν ἀπὸ τῶν
3 ἀρχαιοτάτων χρόνων ἀρξάμενοι. περὶ τῆς πρώτης τοίνυν γενέσεως τῶν ἀνθρώπων διτταὶ γεγό-
νασιν ἀποφάσεις παρὰ τοῖς νομιμωτάτοις τῶν τε
φυσιολόγων καὶ τῶν ἱστορικῶν· οἱ μὲν γὰρ
αὐτῶν ἀγέννητον καὶ ἄφθαρτον ὑποστησάμενοι
τὸν κόσμον, ἀπεφήναντο καὶ τὸ γένος τῶν ἀνθρώπων ἐξ αἰῶνος ὑπάρχειν, μηδέποτε τῆς αὐτῶν
τεκνώσεως ἀρχὴν ἐσχηκυίας. οἱ δὲ γεννητὸν καὶ
φθαρτὸν εἶναι νομίσαντες ἔφησαν ὁμοίως ἐκείνῳ[1]
τοὺς ἀνθρώπους τυχεῖν τῆς πρώτης γενέσεως
ὡρισμένοις χρόνοις.

7. Κατὰ γὰρ τὴν ἐξ ἀρχῆς τῶν ὅλων σύστασιν
μίαν ἔχειν ἰδέαν οὐρανόν τε καὶ γῆν, μεμιγμένης
αὐτῶν τῆς φύσεως· μετὰ δὲ ταῦτα διαστάντων
τῶν σωμάτων ἀπ᾽ ἀλλήλων, τὸν μὲν κόσμον
περιλαβεῖν ἅπασαν τὴν ὁρωμένην ἐν αὐτῷ
σύνταξιν, τὸν δ᾽ ἀέρα κινήσεως τυχεῖν συνεχοῦς,
καὶ τὸ μὲν πυρῶδες αὐτοῦ πρὸς τοὺς μετεωροτά-
τους τόπους συνδραμεῖν, ἀνωφεροῦς οὔσης τῆς
τοιαύτης φύσεως διὰ τὴν κουφότητα· ἀφ᾽ ἧς
αἰτίας τὸν μὲν ἥλιον καὶ τὸ λοιπὸν πλῆθος τῶν
ἄστρων ἐναπολ ηφθῆναι τῇ πάσῃ δίνῃ· τὸ δὲ
ἰλυῶδες καὶ θολερὸν μετὰ τῆς τῶν ὑγρῶν συγκρίσεως ἐπὶ ταὐτὸ καταστῆναι διὰ τὸ βάρος·

[1] ἐκείνῳ Rhodoman : ἐκείνοις.

---

[1] That the universe, as well as the earth and the human
race, was eternal was the view of Aristotle and the early

of men, and all events that have taken place in the
known parts of the inhabited world, we shall give
an accurate account, so far as that is possible in the
case of things that happened so long ago, beginning
with the earliest times. Now as regards the first
origin of mankind two opinions have arisen among
the best authorities both on nature and on history.
One group, which takes the position that the universe
did not come into being and will not decay, has
declared that the race of men also has existed from
eternity, there having never been a time when
men were first begotten; the other group, however,
which holds that the universe came into being and
will decay, has declared that, like it, men had their
first origin at a definite time.[1]

7. When in the beginning, as their account runs, the
universe was being formed, both heaven and earth were
indistinguishable in appearance, since their elements
were intermingled: then, when their bodies separated
from one another, the universe took on in all its parts
the ordered form in which it is now seen; the air
set up a continual motion, and the fiery element in
it gathered into the highest regions, since anything
of such a nature moves upward by reason of its
lightness (and it is for this reason that the sun and
the multitude of other stars became involved in the
universal whirl); while all that was mud-like and
thick and contained an admixture of moisture sank
because of its weight into one place; and as this

Peripatetics, and was defended by Theophrastus against Zeno,
the founder of the Stoic school. The arguments used by
Theophrastus are found in Philo Judaeus, *De Aeternitate
Mundi*, especially chaps. 23–27; cp. E. Zeller, *Aristotle and the
Earlier Peripatetics* (Eng. transl.), 2. pp. 380 f.

DIODORUS OF SICILY

2 εἰλούμενον δ᾽ ἐν ἑαυτῷ συνεχῶς καὶ συστρεφό-
μενον¹ ἐκ μὲν τῶν ὑγρῶν τὴν θάλατταν, ἐκ δὲ
τῶν στερεμνιωτέρων ποιῆσαι τὴν γῆν πηλώδη
3 καὶ παντελῶς ἁπαλήν. ταύτην δὲ τὸ μὲν πρῶτον
τοῦ περὶ τὸν ἥλιον πυρὸς καταλάμψαντος πῆξιν
λαβεῖν, ἔπειτα διὰ τὴν θερμασίαν ἀναζυμουμένης
τῆς ἐπιφανείας συνοιδῆσαί τινα τῶν ὑγρῶν κατὰ
πολλοὺς τόπους, καὶ γενέσθαι περὶ αὐτὰ σηπεδόνας
ὑμέσι λεπτοῖς περιεχομένας· ὅπερ ἐν τοῖς ἕλεσι καὶ
τοῖς λιμνάζουσι τῶν τόπων ἔτι καὶ νῦν ὁρᾶσθαι
γινόμενον, ἐπειδὰν τῆς χώρας κατεψυγμένης ἄφνω
διάπυρος ὁ ἀὴρ γένηται, μὴ λαβὼν τὴν μεταβολὴν
4 ἐκ τοῦ κατ᾽ ὀλίγον. ζωογονουμένων δὲ τῶν ὑγρῶν
διὰ τῆς θερμασίας τὸν εἰρημένον τρόπον τὰς μὲν
νύκτας λαμβάνειν αὐτίκα τὴν τροφὴν ἐκ τῆς πι-
πτούσης ἀπὸ τοῦ περιέχοντος ὁμίχλης, τὰς δ᾽
ἡμέρας ὑπὸ τοῦ καύματος στερεοῦσθαι· τὸ δ᾽
ἔσχατον τῶν κυοφορουμένων τὴν τελείαν αὔξησιν
λαβόντων, καὶ τῶν ὑμένων διακαυθέντων τε καὶ
περιρραγέντων, ἀναφυῆναι παντοδαποὺς τύπους
5 ζῴων. τούτων δὲ τὰ μὲν πλείστης θερμασίας
κεκοινωνηκότα πρὸς τοὺς μετεώρους τόπους ἀπελ-
θεῖν γενόμενα πτηνά, τὰ δὲ γεώδους ἀντεχόμενα
συγκρίσεως ἐν τῇ τῶν ἑρπετῶν καὶ τῶν ἄλλων
τῶν ἐπιγείων τάξει καταριθμηθῆναι, τὰ δὲ
φύσεως ὑγρᾶς μάλιστα μετειληφότα πρὸς τὸν
ὁμογενῆ τόπον συνδραμεῖν, ὀνομασθέντα πλωτά.
6 τὴν δὲ γῆν ἀεὶ μᾶλλον στερεουμένην ὑπό τε τοῦ
περὶ τὸν ἥλιον πυρὸς καὶ τῶν πνευμάτων τὸ
τελευταῖον μηκέτι δύνασθαι μηδὲν τῶν μειζόνων

¹ So Vogel: καὶ συστρεφόμενον συνεχῶς Vulgate, Bekker,
Dindorf.

26

continually turned about upon itself and became
compressed, out of the wet it formed the sea, and
out of what was firmer, the land, which was like
potter's clay and entirely soft. But as the sun's
fire shone upon the land, it first of all became firm,
and then, since its surface was in a ferment because
of the warmth, portions of the wet swelled up in
masses in many places, and in these pustules covered
with delicate membranes made their appearance.
Such a phenomenon can be seen even yet in swamps
and marshy places whenever, the ground having
become cold, the air suddenly and without any
gradual change becomes intensely warm. And
while the wet was being impregnated with life by
reason of the warmth in the manner described, by
night the living things forthwith received their
nourishment from the mist that fell from the envelop-
ing air, and by day were made solid by the intense
heat ; and finally, when the embryos had attained
their full development and the membranes had been
thoroughly heated and broken open, there was produced every form of animal life.[1] Of these, such as
had partaken of the most warmth set off to the
higher regions, having become winged, and such as
retained an earthy consistency came to be numbered
in the class of creeping things and of the other
land animals, while those whose composition partook
the most of the wet element gathered into the region
congenial to them, receiving the name of water
animals. And since the earth constantly grew more
solid through the action of the sun's fire and of the
winds, it was finally no longer able to generate any

---

[1] Cp. chap. 10. 2.

27

ζωογονεῖν, ἀλλ' ἐκ τῆς πρὸς ἄλληλα μίξεως
ἔκαστα γεννᾶσθαι τῶν ἐμψύχων.

7 Ἔοικε δὲ περὶ τῆς τῶν ὅλων φύσεως οὐδ'
Εὐριπίδης διαφωνεῖν τοῖς προειρημένοις, μαθητὴς
ὢν Ἀναξαγόρου τοῦ φυσικοῦ· ἐν γὰρ τῇ Μελα-
νίππῃ τίθησιν οὕτως,

> ὡς οὐρανός τε γαῖά τ' ἦν μορφὴ μία·
> ἐπεὶ δ' ἐχωρίσθησαν ἀλλήλων δίχα,
> τίκτουσι πάντα κἀνέδωκαν εἰς φάος,
> δένδρη, πετηνά, θῆρας, οὕς θ' ἅλμη τρέφει,
> γένος τε θνητῶν.

8. Καὶ περὶ μὲν τῆς πρώτης τῶν ὅλων γενέσεως τοιαῦτα παρειλήφαμεν, τοὺς δ' ἐξ ἀρχῆς
γεννηθέντας τῶν ἀνθρώπων φασὶν ἐν ἀτάκτῳ καὶ
θηριώδει βίῳ καθεστῶτας σποράδην ἐπὶ τὰς
νομὰς ἐξιέναι, καὶ προσφέρεσθαι τῆς τε βοτάνης
τὴν προσηνεστάτην καὶ τοὺς αὐτομάτους ἀπὸ
2 τῶν δένδρων καρπούς. καὶ πολεμουμένους μὲν
ὑπὸ τῶν θηρίων ἀλλήλοις βοηθεῖν ὑπὸ τοῦ συμφέροντος διδασκομένους, ἀθροιζομένους δὲ διὰ τὸν
φόβον ἐπιγινώσκειν ἐκ τοῦ κατὰ μικρὸν τοὺς
3 ἀλλήλων τύπους. τῆς φωνῆς δ' ἀσήμου καὶ
συγκεχυμένης οὔσης ἐκ τοῦ κατ' ὀλίγον διαρθροῦν
τὰς λέξεις, καὶ πρὸς ἀλλήλους τιθέντας σύμβολα
περὶ ἑκάστου τῶν ὑποκειμένων γνώριμον σφίσιν
αὐτοῖς ποιῆσαι τὴν περὶ ἁπάντων ἑρμηνείαν.
4 τοιούτων δὲ συστημάτων γινομένων καθ' ἅπασαν
τὴν οἰκουμένην, οὐχ ὁμόφωνον πάντας ἔχειν τὴν

---

[1] Frg. 488, Nauck.
[2] G. Busolt, "Diodor's Verhältniss z. Stoicismus," *Jahrb. cl. Phil.* 139 (1889), 297 ff., ascribes to Posidonius most of the Preface of Diodorus, but finds in this and the preceding

of the larger animals, but each kind of living creatures was now begotten by breeding with one another.

And apparently Euripides also, who was a pupil of Anaxagoras the natural philosopher, is not opposed to this account of the nature of the universe, for in his *Melanippe* [1] he writes as follows:

'Tis thus that heav'n and earth were once one form;
But since the two were sundered each from each,
They now beget and bring to light all things,
The trees and birds, the beasts, the spawn of sea,
And race of mortals.

8. Concerning the first generation of the universe this is the account which we have received.[2] But the first men to be born, they say, led an undisciplined and bestial life, setting out one by one to secure their sustenance and taking for their food both the tenderest herbs and the fruits of wild trees. Then, since they were attacked by the wild beasts, they came to each other's aid, being instructed by expediency, and when gathered together in this way by reason of their fear, they gradually came to recognize their mutual characteristics. And though the sounds which they made were at first unintelligible and indistinct, yet gradually they came to give articulation to their speech, and by agreeing with one another upon symbols for each thing which presented itself to them, made known among themselves the significance which was to be attached to each term. But since groups of this kind arose over every part of the inhabited world, not all men had the

chapter Epicurean influence. The fact is that Diodorus' philosophy, if he may be said to have had any, was highly eclectic.

διάλεκτον, ἑκάστων ὡς ἔτυχε συνταξάντων τὰς
λέξεις· διὸ καὶ παντοίους τε ὑπάρξαι χαρακτῆρας
διαλέκτων καὶ τὰ πρῶτα γενόμενα συστήματα
τῶν ἁπάντων ἐθνῶν ἀρχέγονα γενέσθαι.

5 Τοὺς οὖν πρώτους τῶν ἀνθρώπων μηδενὸς τῶν
πρὸς βίον χρησίμων εὑρημένου ἐπιπόνως διάγειν,
γυμνοὺς μὲν ἐσθῆτος ὄντας, οἰκήσεως δὲ καὶ πυρὸς
ἀήθεις, τροφῆς δ' ἡμέρου παντελῶς ἀνεννοήτους.

6 καὶ γὰρ τὴν συγκομιδὴν τῆς ἀγρίας τροφῆς ἀγνο-
οῦντας μηδεμίαν τῶν καρπῶν εἰς τὰς ἐνδείας
ποιεῖσθαι παράθεσιν· διὸ καὶ πολλοὺς αὐτῶν
ἀπόλλυσθαι κατὰ τοὺς χειμῶνας διά τε τὸ ψῦχος

7 καὶ τὴν σπάνιν τῆς τροφῆς. ἐκ δὲ τοῦ[1] κατ'
ὀλίγον ὑπὸ τῆς πείρας διδασκομένους εἴς τε τὰ
σπήλαια καταφεύγειν ἐν τῷ χειμῶνι καὶ τῶν
καρπῶν τοὺς φυλάττεσθαι δυναμένους ἀποτί-

8 θεσθαι. γνωσθέντος δὲ τοῦ πυρὸς καὶ τῶν ἄλλων
τῶν χρησίμων κατὰ μικρὸν καὶ τὰς τέχνας εὑρεθῆναι καὶ τἆλλα τὰ δυνάμενα τὸν κοινὸν βίον

9 ὠφελῆσαι. καθόλου γὰρ πάντων τὴν χρείαν
αὐτὴν διδάσκαλον γενέσθαι τοῖς ἀνθρώποις,
ὑφηγουμένην οἰκείως τὴν ἑκάστου μάθησιν
εὐφυεῖ ζῴῳ καὶ συνεργοὺς ἔχοντι πρὸς ἅπαντα
χεῖρας καὶ λόγον καὶ ψυχῆς ἀγχίνοιαν.

10 Καὶ περὶ μὲν τῆς πρώτης γενέσεως τῶν ἀνθρώπων καὶ τοῦ παλαιοτάτου βίου τοῖς ῥηθεῖσιν
ἀρκεσθησόμεθα, στοχαζόμενοι τῆς συμμετρίας.
9. Περὶ δὲ τῶν πράξεων τῶν παραδεδομένων
μὲν εἰς μνήμην, γενομένων δὲ ἐν τοῖς γνωριζομένοις
τόποις τῆς οἰκουμένης, διεξιέναι πειρασόμεθα.

---

[1] τοῦ Schäfer : τούτου.

same language, inasmuch as every group organized the elements of its speech by mere chance. This is the explanation of the present existence of every conceivable kind of language, and, furthermore, out of these first groups to be formed came all the original nations of the world.

Now the first men, since none of the things useful for life had yet been discovered, led a wretched existence, having no clothing to cover them, knowing not the use of dwelling and fire, and also being totally ignorant of cultivated food. For since they also even neglected the harvesting of the wild food, they laid by no store of its fruits against their needs; consequently large numbers of them perished in the winters because of the cold and the lack of food. Little by little, however, experience taught them both to take to the caves in winter and to store such fruits as could be preserved. And when they had become acquainted with fire and other useful things, the arts also and whatever else is capable of furthering man's social life were gradually discovered. Indeed, speaking generally, in all things it was necessity itself that became man's teacher, supplying in appropriate fashion instruction in every matter to a creature which was well endowed by nature and had, as its assistants for every purpose, hands and speech and sagacity of mind.

And as regards the first origin of men and their earliest manner of life we shall be satisfied with what has been said, since we would keep due proportion in our account. 9. But as regards all the events which have been handed down to memory and took place in the known regions of the inhabited world, we shall now undertake to give a full account of them.

2 Τοὺς μὲν οὖν πρώτους ὑπάρξαντας βασιλεῖς
οὔτ' αὐτοὶ λέγειν ἔχομεν οὔτε τῶν ἱστορικῶν τοῖς
ἐπαγγελλομένοις εἰδέναι συγκατατιθέμεθα· ἀδύνατον γὰρ τὴν εὕρεσιν τῶν γραμμάτων οὕτως
εἶναι παλαιὰν ὥστε τοῖς πρώτοις βασιλεῦσιν
ἡλικιώτιδα γενέσθαι· εἰ δέ τις καὶ τοῦτο συγ-
χωρήσαι, τό γε τῶν ἱστοριογράφων γένος παντελῶς φαίνεται νεωστὶ τῷ κοινῷ βίῳ συνεστα-
3 μένον. περὶ δὲ τῆς τοῦ γένους ἀρχαιότητος οὐ
μόνον ἀμφισβητοῦσιν Ἕλληνες, ἀλλὰ καὶ πολλοὶ
τῶν βαρβάρων, ἑαυτοὺς αὐτόχθονας λέγοντες καὶ
πρώτους τῶν ἁπάντων ἀνθρώπων εὑρετὰς γενέσθαι τῶν ἐν τῷ βίῳ χρησίμων, καὶ τὰς γενομένας
παρ' αὑτοῖς πράξεις ἐκ πλείστων χρόνων ἀναγρα-
4 φῆς ἠξιῶσθαι. ἡμεῖς δὲ περὶ μὲν τῆς ἑκάστων
παλαιότητος τἀκριβὲς καὶ τίνων προτερεῖ τὰ ἔθνη
τῶν ἄλλων τοῖς χρόνοις καὶ πόσοις ἔτεσιν οὐκ ἂν
διορισαίμεθα, τὰ δὲ λεγόμενα παρ' ἑκάστοις περὶ
τῆς ἀρχαιότητος καὶ τῶν παλαιῶν πράξεων ἐν
κεφαλαίοις ἀναγράψομεν, στοχαζόμενοι τῆς συμ-
5 μετρίας. περὶ πρώτων δὲ τῶν βαρβάρων διέξιμεν, οὐκ ἀρχαιοτέρους αὐτοὺς ἡγούμενοι τῶν
Ἑλλήνων, καθάπερ Ἔφορος εἴρηκεν, ἀλλὰ προ-
διελθεῖν βουλόμενοι τὰ πλεῖστα τῶν περὶ αὐτούς,
ὅπως ἀρξάμενοι τῶν παρὰ τοῖς Ἕλλησιν ἱστορουμένων μηδεμίαν ἐν ταῖς ἀρχαιολογίαις ἑτερογενῆ
6 πρᾶξιν παρεμβάλωμεν. ἐπεὶ δὲ κατὰ τὴν
Αἴγυπτον θεῶν τε γενέσεις ὑπάρξαι μυθολο-
γοῦνται, αἵ τε τῶν ἄστρων ἀρχαιόταται παρα-

Now as to who were the first kings we are in no position to speak on our own authority, nor do we give assent to those historians who profess to know; for it is impossible that the discovery of writing was of so early a date as to have been contemporary with the first kings. But if a man should concede even this last point, it still seems evident that writers of history are as a class a quite recent appearance in the life of mankind. Again, with respect to the antiquity of the human race, not only do Greeks put forth their claims but many of the barbarians as well, all holding that it is they who are auto-chthonous and the first of all men to discover the things which are of use in life, and that it was the events in their own history which were the earliest to have been held worthy of record. So far as we are concerned, however, we shall not make the attempt to determine with precision the antiquity of each nation or what is the race whose nations are prior in point of time to the rest and by how many years, but we shall record summarily, keeping due proportion in our account, what each nation has to say concerning its antiquity and the early events in its history. The first peoples which we shall discuss will be the barbarians, not that we consider them to be earlier than the Greeks, as Ephorus has said, but because we wish to set forth most of the facts about them at the outset, in order that we may not, by beginning with the various accounts given by the Greeks, have to interpolate in the different narrations of their early history any event connected with another people. And since Egypt is the country where mythology places the origin of the gods, where the earliest observations of the stars are said to have

τηρήσεις εὑρῆσθαι λέγονται, πρὸς δὲ τούτοις
πράξεις ἀξιόλογοι καὶ πολλαὶ μεγάλων ἀνδρῶν
ἱστοροῦνται, ποιησόμεθα τῆς ἱστορίας τὴν ἀρχὴν
διὰ τῶν κατ' Αἴγυπτον πραχθέντων.

10. Φασὶ τοίνυν Αἰγύπτιοι κατὰ τὴν ἐξ
ἀρχῆς τῶν ὅλων γένεσιν πρώτους ἀνθρώπους
γενέσθαι κατὰ τὴν Αἴγυπτον διά τε τὴν
εὐκρασίαν τῆς χώρας καὶ διὰ τὴν φύσιν τοῦ
Νείλου. τοῦτον γὰρ πολύγονον ὄντα καὶ τὰς
τροφὰς αὐτοφυεῖς παρεχόμενον ῥᾳδίως ἐκτρέφειν
τὰ ζῳογονηθέντα· τήν τε γὰρ τοῦ καλάμου ῥίζαν
καὶ τὸν λωτόν, ἔτι δὲ τὸν Αἰγύπτιον κύαμον καὶ
τὸ καλούμενον κορσαῖον καὶ πολλὰ τοιαῦθ' ἕτερα
τροφὴν ἑτοίμην παρέχεσθαι τῷ γένει τῶν ἀνθρώ-
2 πων. τῆς δ' ἐξ ἀρχῆς παρ' αὐτοῖς ζῳογονίας
τεκμήριον πειρῶνται φέρειν τὸ καὶ νῦν ἔτι τὴν
ἐν Θηβαΐδι χώραν κατά τινας καιροὺς τοσούτους
καὶ τηλικούτους μῦς γεννᾶν ὥστε τοὺς ἰδόντας τὸ
γινόμενον ἐκπλήττεσθαι· ἐνίους γὰρ αὐτῶν ἕως
μὲν τοῦ στήθους καὶ τῶν ἐμπροσθίων ποδῶν
διατετυπῶσθαι καὶ κίνησιν λαμβάνειν, τὸ δὲ
λοιπὸν τοῦ σώματος ἔχειν ἀδιατύπωτον, μενούσης
3 ἔτι κατὰ φύσιν τῆς βώλου. ἐκ τούτου δ' εἶναι
φανερὸν ὅτι κατὰ τὴν ἐξ ἀρχῆς τοῦ κόσμου σύστασιν τῆς γῆς εὐκράτου καθεστώσης μάλιστ' ἂν
ἔσχε τὴν γένεσιν τῶν ἀνθρώπων ἡ κατ' Αἴγυπτον
χώρα· καὶ γὰρ νῦν, οὐδαμοῦ τῆς ἄλλης γῆς
φυούσης οὐδὲν τῶν τοιούτων, ἐν μόνῃ ταύτῃ

---

[1] These plants are more fully described in chap. 34. For
the "root of the reed" cp. chap. 80, where the preparation

been made, and where, furthermore, many noteworthy deeds of great men are recorded, we shall
begin our history with the events connected with
Egypt.

10. Now the Egyptians have an account like this:
When in the beginning the universe came into being,
men first came into existence in Egypt, both because
of the favourable climate of the land and because of
the nature of the Nile. For this stream, since it
produces much life and provides a spontaneous supply
of food, easily supports whatever living things have
been engendered; for both the root of the reed
and the lotus, as well as the Egyptian bean and
corsaeum, as it is called, and many other similar
plants, supply the race of men with nourishment
all ready for use.[1] As proof that animal life appeared
first of all in their land they would offer the fact
that even at the present day the soil of the Thebaid
at certain times generates mice in such numbers
and of such size as to astonish all who have witnessed
the phenomenon; for some of them are fully formed
as far as the breast and front feet and are able to
move, while the rest of the body is unformed, the
clod of earth still retaining its natural character.
And from this fact it is manifest that, when the
world was first taking shape, the land of Egypt could
better than any other have been the place where
mankind came into being because of the well-
tempered nature of its soil; for even at the present
time, while the soil of no other country generates
any such things, in it alone certain living creatures

---

of such food is described. The *corsaeum* was the tuber of the
Nile water-lily.

θεωρεῖσθαί τινα τῶν ἐμψύχων παραδόξως ζῳογο-
νούμενα.

4 Καθόλου δὲ λέγουσιν, εἴτε κατὰ τὸν ἐπὶ
Δευκαλίωνος γενόμενον κατακλυσμὸν ἐφθάρη τὰ
πλεῖστα τῶν ζῴων, εἰκὸς μάλιστα διασεσῶσθαι
τοὺς κατὰ τὴν Αἴγυπτον ὑπὸ τὴν μεσημβρίαν
κατοικοῦντας, ὡς ἂν τῆς χώρας αὐτῶν οὔσης
ἀνόμβρου κατὰ τὸ πλεῖστον, εἴτε, καθάπερ τινές
φασι, παντελοῦς γενομένης τῶν ἐμψύχων φθορᾶς
ἡ γῆ πάλιν ἐξ ἀρχῆς καινὰς ἤνεγκε τῶν ζῴων
φύσεις, ὅμως καὶ κατὰ τοῦτον τὸν λόγον πρέπειν
τὴν ἀρχηγὸν τῶν ἐμψύχων γένεσιν προσάπτειν
5 ταύτῃ τῇ χώρᾳ. τῆς γὰρ παρὰ τοῖς ἄλλοις ἐπομ-
βρίας τῷ παρ᾽ ἑαυτοῖς [1] γινομένῳ καύματι
μιγείσης εἰκὸς εὐκρατότατον γενέσθαι τὸν ἀέρα
6 πρὸς τὴν ἐξ ἀρχῆς τῶν πάντων ζῳογονίαν. καὶ
γὰρ ἐν τοῖς καθ᾽ ἡμᾶς ἔτι χρόνοις κατὰ τὴν
ἐπίκλυστον Αἴγυπτον ἐν τοῖς ὀψίμοις τῶν
ὑδάτων φανερῶς ὁρᾶσθαι γεννωμένας φύσεις
7 ἐμψύχων· ὅταν γὰρ τοῦ ποταμοῦ τὴν ἀναχώ-
ρησιν ποιουμένου τὴν πρώτην τῆς ἰλύος ὁ ἥλιος
διαξηράνῃ, φασὶ συνίστασθαι ζῷα, τινὰ μὲν
εἰς τέλος ἀπηρτισμένα, τινὰ δὲ ἡμιτελῆ καὶ πρὸς
αὐτῇ συμφυῆ τῇ γῇ.

11. Τοὺς δ᾽ οὖν κατ᾽ Αἴγυπτον ἀνθρώπους τὸ
παλαιὸν γενομένους, ἀναβλέψαντας εἰς τὸν
κόσμον καὶ τὴν τῶν ὅλων φύσιν καταπλαγέντας
τε [2] καὶ θαυμάσαντας, ὑπολαβεῖν εἶναι δύο θεοὺς
ἀιδίους τε καὶ πρώτους, τόν τε ἥλιον καὶ τὴν
σελήνην, ὧν τὸν μὲν Ὄσιριν, τὴν δὲ Ἶσιν ὀνο-

---

[1] ἑαυτοῖς Vogel: ἑαυτῆς D, αὐτοῖς F, Bekker, Dindorf.

may be seen coming into being in a marvellous fashion.

In general, they say that if in the flood which occurred in the time of Deucalion most living things were destroyed, it is probable that the inhabitants of southern Egypt survived rather than any others, since their country is rainless for the most part; or if, as some maintain, the destruction of living things was complete and the earth then brought forth again new forms of animals, nevertheless, even on such a supposition the first genesis of living things fittingly attaches to this country. For when the moisture from the abundant rains, which fell among other peoples, was mingled with the intense heat which prevails in Egypt itself, it is reasonable to suppose that the air became very well tempered for the first generation of all living things. Indeed, even in our day during the inundations of Egypt the generation of forms of animal life can clearly be seen taking place in the pools which remain the longest; for, whenever the river has begun to recede and the sun has thoroughly dried the surface of the slime, living animals, they say, take shape, some of them fully formed, but some only half so and still actually united with the very earth.

11. Now the men of Egypt, they say, when ages ago they came into existence, as they looked up at the firmament and were struck with both awe and wonder at the nature of the universe, conceived that two gods were both eternal and first, namely, the sun and the moon, whom they called respectively Osiris and Isis, these appellations having in each

---

[2] τε Vogel: omitted by Vulgate, Bekker, Dindorf.

μάσαι, ἀπό τινος ἐτύμου τεθείσης ἑκατέρας τῆς
2 προσηγορίας ταύτης. μεθερμηνευομένων γὰρ
τούτων εἰς τὸν Ἑλληνικὸν τῆς διαλέκτου τρόπον
εἶναι τὸν μὲν Ὄσιριν πολυόφθαλμον, εἰκότως·
πανταχῇ γὰρ ἐπιβάλλοντα τὰς ἀκτῖνας ὥσπερ
ὀφθαλμοῖς πολλοῖς βλέπειν ἅπασαν γῆν καὶ
θάλατταν. καὶ τὸν ποιητὴν δὲ λέγειν σύμφωνα
τούτοις

ἠέλιός θ', ὃς πάντ' ἐφορᾷ καὶ πάντ' ἐπακούει.

3 τῶν δὲ παρ' Ἕλλησι παλαιῶν μυθολόγων τινὲς
τὸν Ὄσιριν Διόνυσον προσονομάζουσι καὶ
Σείριον παρωνύμως· ὧν Εὔμολπος μὲν ἐν τοῖς
Βακχικοῖς ἔπεσί φησιν

ἀστροφαῆ Διόνυσον ἐν ἀκτίνεσσι πυρωπόν,

Ὀρφεὺς δὲ

τούνεκά μιν καλέουσι Φάνητά τε καὶ Διόνυσον.

4 φασὶ δέ τινες καὶ τὸ ἔναμμα αὐτῷ τὸ τῆς νεβρίδος
ἀπὸ τῆς τῶν ἄστρων ποικιλίας περιῆφθαι. τὴν
δὲ Ἶσιν μεθερμηνευομένην εἶναι παλαιάν, τεθει-
μένης τῆς προσηγορίας ἀπὸ τῆς ἀιδίου καὶ
παλαιᾶς γενέσεως. κέρατα δ' αὐτῇ ἐπιτιθέασιν
ἀπό τε τῆς ὄψεως ἣν ἔχουσα φαίνεται καθ' ὃν
ἂν χρόνον ὑπάρχῃ μηνοειδής, καὶ ἀπὸ τῆς καθιε-
ρωμένης αὐτῇ βοὸς παρ' Αἰγυπτίοις.
5 Τούτους δὲ τοὺς θεοὺς ὑφίστανται τὸν σύμ-
παντα κόσμον διοικεῖν τρέφοντάς τε καὶ αὔξοντας

---

[1] " The poet " for the Greeks was Homer; the line occurs
frequently, e.g. *Odyssey* 12. 323.

38

case been based upon a certain meaning in them.
For when the names are translated into Greek Osiris
means " many-eyed," and properly so; for in shed-
ding his rays in every direction he surveys with
many eyes, as it were, all land and sea. And the
words of the poet [1] are also in agreement with this
conception when he says:

The sun, who sees all things and hears all things.

And of the ancient Greek writers of mythology some
give to Osiris the name Dionysus or, with a slight
change in form, Sirius. One of them, Eumolpus,
in his *Bacchic Hymn* speaks of

Our Dionysus, shining like a star,
With fiery eye in ev'ry ray;

while Orpheus [2] says:

And this is why men call him Shining One
And Dionysus.

Some say that Osiris is also represented with the
cloak of fawn-skin about his shoulders [3] as imitating
the sky spangled with the stars. As for Isis, when
translated the word means " ancient," the name
having been given her because her birth was from
everlasting and ancient. And they put horns on her
head both because of the appearance which she has
to the eye when the moon is crescent-shaped, and
because among the Egyptians a cow is held sacred
to her.

These two gods, they hold, regulate the entire
universe, giving both nourishment and increase to

[2] Frg. 237, Kern.
[3] That is, as Dionysus was commonly represented.

πάντα τριμερέσιν ὥραις ἀοράτῳ κινήσει τὴν
περίοδον ἀπαρτιζούσαις, τῇ τε ἐαρινῇ καὶ θερινῇ
καὶ χειμερινῇ· ταύτας δ' ἐναντιωτάτην ἀλλήλαις
τὴν φύσιν ἐχούσας ἀπαρτίζειν τὸν ἐνιαυτὸν
ἀρίστῃ συμφωνίᾳ· φύσιν δὲ συμβάλλεσθαι
πλείστην εἰς τὴν τῶν ἁπάντων ζῳογονίαν τῶν
θεῶν τούτων τὸν μὲν πυρώδους καὶ πνεύματος,
τὴν δὲ ὑγροῦ καὶ ξηροῦ, κοινῇ δ' ἀμφοτέρους
ἀέρος· καὶ διὰ τούτων πάντα γεννᾶσθαι καὶ
6 τρέφεσθαι. διὸ καὶ τὸ μὲν ἅπαν σῶμα τῆς τῶν
ὅλων φύσεως ἐξ ἡλίου καὶ σελήνης ἀπαρτίζεσθαι,
τὰ δὲ τούτων μέρη πέντε τὰ προειρημένα, τό τε
πνεῦμα καὶ τὸ πῦρ καὶ τὸ ξηρόν, ἔτι δὲ τὸ ὑγρὸν
καὶ τὸ τελευταῖον τὸ ἀερῶδες, ὥσπερ ἐπ' ἀνθρώπου κεφαλὴν καὶ χεῖρας καὶ πόδας καὶ τἆλλα
μέρη καταριθμοῦμεν, τὸν αὐτὸν τρόπον τὸ σῶμα
τοῦ κόσμου συγκεῖσθαι πᾶν ἐκ τῶν προειρημένων.

12. Τούτων δ' ἕκαστον θεὸν νομίσαι καὶ
προσηγορίαν ἰδίαν ἑκάστῳ θεῖναι κατὰ τὸ οἰκεῖον
τοὺς πρώτους διαλέκτῳ χρησαμένους διηρθρωμένῃ
2 τῶν κατ' Αἴγυπτον ἀνθρώπων. τὸ μὲν οὖν πνεῦμα
Δία προσαγορεῦσαι μεθερμηνευομένης τῆς λέξεως,
ὃν αἴτιον ὄντα τοῦ ψυχικοῦ τοῖς ζῴοις ἐνόμισαν
ὑπάρχειν πάντων οἱονεί τινα πατέρα. συμφωνεῖν δὲ τούτοις φασὶ καὶ τὸν ἐπιφανέστατον
τῶν παρ' Ἕλλησι ποιητῶν ἐπὶ τοῦ θεοῦ τούτου
λέγοντα

πατὴρ ἀνδρῶν τε θεῶν τε.

3 τὸ δὲ πῦρ μεθερμηνευόμενον Ἥφαιστον ὀνομάσαι,
νομίσαντας μέγαν εἶναι θεὸν καὶ πολλὰ συμ-

all things by means of a system of three seasons which complete the full cycle through an unobservable movement, these being spring and summer and winter; and these seasons, though in nature most opposed to one another, complete the cycle of the year in the fullest harmony. Moreover, practically all the physical matter which is essential to the generation of all things is furnished by these gods, the sun contributing the fiery element and the spirit, the moon the wet and the dry, and both together the air; and it is through these elements that all things are engendered and nourished. And so it is out of the sun and moon that the whole physical body of the universe is made complete; and as for the five parts just named of these bodies—the spirit, the fire, the dry, as well as the wet, and, lastly, the air-like—just as in the case of a man we enumerate head and hands and feet and the other parts, so in the same way the body of the universe is composed in its entirety of these parts.

12. Each of these parts they regard as a god and to each of them the first men in Egypt to use articulate speech gave a distinct name appropriate to its nature. Now the spirit they called, as we translate their expression, Zeus, and since he was the source of the spirit of life in animals they considered him to be in a sense the father of all things. And they say that the most renowned of the Greek poets [1] also agrees with this when he speaks of this god as

The father of men and of gods.

The fire they called Hephaestus, as it is translated, holding him to be a great god and one who con-

---

[1] Homer; the phrase occurs in many passages.

βάλλεσθαι πᾶσιν εἰς γένεσίν τε καὶ τελείαν
4 αὔξησιν. τὴν δὲ γῆν ὥσπερ ἀγγεῖόν τι τῶν
φυομένων ὑπολαμβάνοντας μητέρα προσαγορεῦ-
σαι· καὶ τοὺς Ἕλληνας δὲ ταύτην παραπλησίως
Δήμητραν καλεῖν, βραχὺ μετατεθείσης διὰ τὸν
χρόνον τῆς λέξεως· τὸ γὰρ παλαιὸν ὀνομάζεσθαι
γῆν μητέρα, καθάπερ καὶ τὸν Ὀρφέα προσμαρτυ-
ρεῖν λέγοντα

Γῆ μήτηρ πάντων, Δημήτηρ πλουτοδότειρα.

5 τὸ δ' ὑγρὸν ὀνομάσαι λέγουσι τοὺς παλαιοὺς
Ὠκεάνην,[1] ὃ μεθερμηνευόμενον μὲν εἶναι τροφὴν
μητέρα, παρ' ἐνίοις δὲ τῶν Ἑλλήνων Ὠκεανὸν
ὑπάρχειν ὑπειλῆφθαι, περὶ οὗ καὶ τὸν ποιητὴν
λέγειν

Ὠκεανόν τε θεῶν γένεσιν καὶ μητέρα Τηθύν.

6 οἱ γὰρ Αἰγύπτιοι νομίζουσιν Ὠκεανὸν εἶναι τὸν
παρ' αὐτοῖς ποταμὸν Νεῖλον, πρὸς ᾧ καὶ τὰς
τῶν θεῶν γενέσεις ὑπάρξαι· τῆς γὰρ πάσης
οἰκουμένης κατὰ μόνην τὴν Αἴγυπτον εἶναι
πόλεις πολλὰς ὑπὸ τῶν ἀρχαίων θεῶν ἐκτισμέ-
νας, οἷον Διός, Ἡλίου, Ἑρμοῦ, Ἀπόλλωνος,
Πανός, Εἰλειθυίας, ἄλλων πλειόνων.

7 Τὸν δ' ἀέρα προσαγορεῦσαί φασιν Ἀθηνᾶν
μεθερμηνευομένης τῆς λέξεως, καὶ Διὸς θυγατέρα
νομίσαι ταύτην, καὶ παρθένον ὑποστήσασθαι
διά τε τὸ ἄφθορον εἶναι φύσει τὸν ἀέρα καὶ τὸν
ἀκρότατον ἐπέχειν τόπον τοῦ σύμπαντος κόσμου·
διόπερ ἐκ τῆς κορυφῆς τοῦ Διὸς μυθολογηθῆναι

---

[1] Ὠκεάνην Wesseling : ὠκέλμην F, ὠκεανόν CD.

---

[1] Frg. 302, Kern.

tributes much both to the birth and full development
of all things. The earth, again, they looked upon as
a kind of vessel which holds all growing things and so
gave it the name "mother"; and in like manner the
Greeks also call it Demeter, the word having been
slightly changed in the course of time; for in olden
times they called her Gê Meter (Earth Mother), to
which Orpheus [1] bears witness when he speaks of

Earth the Mother of all, Demeter giver of wealth.

And the wet, according to them, was called by the
men of old Oceanê, which, when translated, means
Fostering-mother, though some of the Greeks have
taken it to be Oceanus, in connection with whom
the poet [2] also speaks of

Oceanus source of gods and mother Tethys.

For the Egyptians consider Oceanus to be their
river Nile, on which also their gods were born; since,
they say, Egypt is the only country in the whole
inhabited world where there are many cities which
were founded by the first gods, such as Zeus, Helius,
Hermes, Apollo, Pan, Eileithyia, and many more.[3]

The air, they say, they called Athena, as the name
is translated, and they considered her to be the
daughter of Zeus and conceived of her as a virgin,
because of the fact that the air is by its nature
uncorrupted and occupies the highest part of the
entire universe; for the latter reason also the myth
arose that she was born from the head of Zeus.

[2] Tethys was the wife of Oceanus. The line is from the
Iliad 14. 302.

[3] By the time Diodorus visited Egypt many an old
Egyptian city bore a Greek name, such as Diospolis (cp.
chap. 45), Heliopolis, Hermupolis, Apollinopolis, Panopolis,
and the like.

8 ταύτην γενέσθαι. ὠνομάσθαι δὲ αὐτὴν Τριτο-
γένειαν ἀπὸ τοῦ τρὶς μεταβάλλειν αὐτῆς τὴν
φύσιν κατ' ἐνιαυτόν, ἔαρος καὶ θέρους καὶ χειμῶνος. λέγεσθαι δ' αὐτὴν καὶ Γλαυκῶπιν, οὐχ
ὥσπερ ἔνιοι τῶν Ἑλλήνων ὑπέλαβον, ἀπὸ τοῦ
τοὺς ὀφθαλμοὺς ἔχειν γλαυκούς· τοῦτο μὲν γὰρ
εὔηθες ὑπάρχειν· ἀλλ' ἀπὸ τοῦ τὸν ἀέρα τὴν
πρόσοψιν ἔχειν ἔγγλαυκον.

9 Φασὶ δὲ τοὺς πέντε θεοὺς τοὺς προειρημένους
πᾶσαν τὴν οἰκουμένην ἐπιπορεύεσθαι, φανταζο-
μένους τοῖς ἀνθρώποις ἐν ἱερῶν ζῴων μορφαῖς,
ἔστι δ' ὅτε εἰς ἀνθρώπων ἰδέας ἤ τινων ἄλλων
μεταβάλλοντας· καὶ τοῦτο μὴ μυθῶδες ὑπάρχειν,
ἀλλὰ δυνατόν, εἴπερ οὗτοι πρὸς ἀλήθειάν εἰσιν
οἱ πάντα γεννῶντες. καὶ τὸν ποιητὴν δὲ εἰς
10 Αἴγυπτον παραβαλόντα καὶ μετασχόντα παρὰ
τῶν ἱερέων τῶν τοιούτων λόγων θεῖναί που κατὰ
τὴν ποίησιν τὸ προειρημένον ὡς γινόμενον,

καί τε θεοὶ ξείνοισιν ἐοικότες ἀλλοδαποῖσι
παντοῖοι τελέθοντες ἐπιστρωφῶσι πόληας,
ἀνθρώπων ὕβριν τε καὶ εὐνομίην ἐσορῶντες.

Περὶ μὲν οὖν τῶν ἐν οὐρανῷ θεῶν καὶ γένεσιν
ἀίδιον ἐσχηκότων τοσαῦτα λέγουσιν Αἰγύπτιοι.

13. Ἄλλους δ' ἐκ τούτων ἐπιγείους γενέσθαι
φασίν, ὑπάρξαντας μὲν θνητούς, διὰ δὲ σύνεσιν
καὶ κοινὴν ἀνθρώπων εὐεργεσίαν τετευχότας τῆς
ἀθανασίας, ὧν ἐνίους καὶ βασιλεῖς γεγονέναι κατὰ
2 τὴν Αἴγυπτον. μεθερμηνευομένων δ' αὐτῶν τινὰς
μὲν ὁμωνύμους ὑπάρχειν τοῖς οὐρανίοις, τινὰς
δ' ἰδίαν ἐσχηκέναι προσηγορίαν, Ἥλιόν τε καὶ

Another name given her was Tritogeneia (Thrice-born), because her nature changes three times in the course of the year, in the spring, summer, and winter. They add that she is also called Glaucopis (Blue-eyed),[1] not because she has blue eyes, as some Greeks have held—a silly explanation, indeed—but because the air has a bluish cast.

These five deities, they say, visit all the inhabited world, revealing themselves to men in the form of sacred animals, and at times even appearing in the guise of men or in other shapes; nor is this a fabulous thing, but possible, if these are in very truth the gods who give life to all things. And also the poet, who visited Egypt and became acquainted with such accounts as these from the lips of the priests, in some place in his writings [2] sets forth as actual fact what has been said:

> The gods, in strangers' form from alien lands,
> Frequent the cities of men in ev'ry guise,
> Observing their insolence and lawful ways.

Now so far as the celestial gods are concerned whose genesis is from eternity, this is the account given by the Egyptians.

13. And besides these there are other gods, they say, who were terrestrial, having once been mortals, but who, by reason of their sagacity and the good services which they rendered to all men, attained immortality, some of them having even been kings in Egypt. Their names, when translated, are in some cases the same as those of the celestial gods, while others have a distinct appellation, such as

---

[1] This common epithet of Athena in Homer is more generally taken to mean " gleaming-eyed."
[2] *Odyssey* 17. 485–7.

Κρόνον καὶ 'Ρέαν, ἔτι δὲ Δία τὸν ὑπό τινων
"Αμμωνα προσαγορευόμενον, πρὸς δὲ τούτοις
"Ηραν καὶ "Ηφαιστον, ἔτι δ' 'Εστίαν καὶ τελευταῖον 'Ερμῆν. καὶ πρῶτον μὲν "Ηλιον βασιλεῦσαι τῶν κατ' Αἴγυπτον, ὁμώνυμον ὄντα τῷ κατ'
3 οὐρανὸν ἄστρῳ. ἔνιοι δὲ τῶν ἱερέων φασὶ
πρῶτον "Ηφαιστον βασιλεῦσαι, πυρὸς εὑρετὴν
γενόμενον καὶ διὰ τὴν εὐχρηστίαν ταύτην
τυχόντα τῆς ἡγεμονίας· γενομένου γὰρ ἐν τοῖς
ὄρεσι κεραυνοβόλου δένδρου καὶ τῆς πλησίον
ὕλης καομένης προσελθόντα τὸν "Ηφαιστον κατὰ
τὴν χειμέριον ὥραν ἡσθῆναι διαφερόντως ἐπὶ τῇ
θερμασίᾳ, λήγοντος δὲ τοῦ πυρὸς ἀεὶ τῆς ὕλης
ἐπιβάλλειν, καὶ τούτῳ τῷ τρόπῳ διατηροῦντα
τὸ πῦρ προκαλεῖσθαι[1] τοὺς ἄλλους ἀνθρώπους
4 πρὸς τὴν ἐξ αὐτοῦ γινομένην εὐχρηστίαν. μετὰ
δὲ ταῦτα τὸν Κρόνον ἄρξαι, καὶ γήμαντα τὴν
ἀδελφὴν 'Ρέαν γεννῆσαι κατὰ μέν τινας τῶν
μυθολόγων "Οσιριν καὶ 'Ισιν, κατὰ δὲ τοὺς
πλείστους Δία τε καὶ "Ηραν, οὓς δι' ἀρετὴν
βασιλεῦσαι τοῦ σύμπαντος κόσμου. ἐκ δὲ
τούτων γενέσθαι πέντε θεούς, καθ' ἑκάστην τῶν
ἐπαγομένων παρ' Αἰγυπτίοις πένθ' ἡμερῶν ἑνὸς
γεννηθέντος· ὀνόματα δὲ ὑπάρξαι τοῖς τεκνω-
θεῖσιν "Οσιριν καὶ 'Ισιν, ἔτι δὲ Τυφῶνα καὶ
5 'Απόλλωνα καὶ 'Αφροδίτην· καὶ τὸν μὲν "Οσιριν
μεθερμηνευόμενον εἶναι Διόνυσον, τὴν δὲ 'Ισιν
ἔγγιστά πως Δήμητραν. ταύτην δὲ γήμαντα τὸν
"Οσιριν καὶ τὴν βασιλείαν διαδεξάμενον πολλὰ
πρᾶξαι πρὸς εὐεργεσίαν τοῦ κοινοῦ βίου.

14. Πρῶτον μὲν γὰρ παῦσαι τῆς ἀλληλοφαγίας

[1] προκαλεῖσθαι Dindorf : προσκαλεῖσθαι.

Helius, Cronus, and Rhea, and also the Zeus who is called Ammon by some, and besides these Hera and Hephaestus, also Hestia, and, finally, Hermes. Helius was the first king of the Egyptians, his name being the same as that of the heavenly star.[1] Some of the priests, however, say that Hephaestus was their first king, since he was the discoverer of fire and received the rule because of this service to mankind; for once, when a tree on the mountains had been struck by lightning and the forest near by was ablaze, Hephaestus went up to it, for it was winter-time, and greatly enjoyed the heat; as the fire died down he kept adding fuel to it, and while keeping the fire going in this way he invited the rest of mankind to enjoy the advantage which came from it. Then Cronus became the ruler, and upon marrying his sister Rhea he begat Osiris and Isis, according to some writers of mythology, but, according to the majority, Zeus and Hera, whose high achievements gave them dominion over the entire universe. From these last were sprung five gods, one born on each of the five days which the Egyptians intercalate;[2] the names of these children were Osiris and Isis, and also Typhon, Apollo, and Aphrodite; and Osiris when translated is Dionysus, and Isis is more similar to Demeter than to any other goddess; and after Osiris married Isis and succeeded to the kingship he did many things of service to the social life of man.

14. Osiris was the first, they record, to make man-

---

[1] That is, the sun.
[2] The Egyptians used a calendar of twelve months of thirty days each, with five days intercalated at the end of the year. Cp. chap. 50.

τὸ τῶν ἀνθρώπων γένος, εὑρούσης μὲν Ἴσιδος
τόν τε τοῦ πυροῦ καὶ τῆς κριθῆς καρπόν, φυό-
μενον μὲν ὡς ἔτυχε κατὰ τὴν χώραν μετὰ τῆς
ἄλλης βοτάνης, ἀγνοούμενον δὲ ὑπὸ τῶν ἀνθρώπων, τοῦ δὲ Ὀσίριδος ἐπινοησαμένου καὶ τὴν
τούτων κατεργασίαν τῶν καρπῶν, ἡδέως μετα-
θέσθαι πάντας τὴν τροφὴν διά τε τὴν ἡδονὴν τῆς
φύσεως τῶν εὑρεθέντων καὶ διὰ τὸ φαίνεσθαι
συμφέρον ὑπάρχειν ἀπέχεσθαι τῆς κατ᾽ ἀλλήλων
2 ὠμότητος. μαρτύριον δὲ φέρουσι τῆς εὑρέσεως
τῶν εἰρημένων καρπῶν τὸ τηρούμενον παρ᾽
αὐτοῖς ἐξ ἀρχαίων νόμιμον· ἔτι γὰρ καὶ νῦν
κατὰ τὸν θερισμὸν τοὺς πρώτους ἀμηθέντας
στάχυς θέντας τοὺς ἀνθρώπους κόπτεσθαι πλησίον τοῦ δράγματος καὶ τὴν Ἴσιν ἀνακαλεῖσθαι,
καὶ τοῦτο πράττειν τιμὴν ἀπονέμοντας τῇ θεῷ
τῶν εὑρημένων κατὰ τὸν ἐξ ἀρχῆς τῆς εὑρέσεως
3 καιρόν. παρ᾽ ἐνίαις δὲ τῶν πόλεων καὶ τοῖς
Ἰσείοις ἐν τῇ πομπῇ μετὰ τῶν ἄλλων φέρεσθαι
καὶ πυθμένας πυρῶν καὶ κριθῶν, ἀπομνημόνευμα
τῶν ἐξ ἀρχῆς τῇ θεῷ φιλοτέχνως εὑρεθέντων.
θεῖναι δέ φασι καὶ νόμους τὴν Ἴσιν, καθ᾽ οὓς
ἀλλήλοις διδόναι τοὺς ἀνθρώπους τὸ δίκαιον καὶ
τῆς ἀθέσμου βίας καὶ ὕβρεως παύσασθαι διὰ
4 τὸν ἀπὸ τῆς τιμωρίας φόβον· διὸ καὶ τοὺς
παλαιοὺς Ἕλληνας τὴν Δήμητραν θεσμοφόρον
ὀνομάζειν, ὡς τῶν νόμων πρῶτον ὑπὸ ταύτης
τεθειμένων.

15. Κτίσαι δὲ φασι τοὺς περὶ τὸν Ὄσιριν
πόλιν ἐν τῇ Θηβαΐδι τῇ κατ᾽ Αἴγυπτον ἑκατόμπυλον, ἣν ἐκείνους μὲν ἐπώνυμον ποιῆσαι τῆς
μητρός, τοὺς δὲ μεταγενεστέρους αὐτὴν ὀνομάζειν

kind give up cannibalism; for after Isis had dis covered the fruit of both wheat and barley which grew wild over the land along with the other plants but was still unknown to man, and Osiris had also devised the cultivation of these fruits, all men were glad to change their food, both because of the pleasing nature of the newly-discovered grains and because it seemed to their advantage to refrain from their butchery of one another. As proof of the discovery of these fruits they offer the following ancient custom which they still observe: Even yet at harvest time the people make a dedication of the first heads of the grain to be cut, and standing beside the sheaf beat themselves and call upon Isis, by this act rendering honour to the goddess for the fruits which she discovered, at the season when she first did this. Moreover in some cities, during the Festival of Isis as well, stalks of wheat and barley are carried among the other objects in the procession, as a memorial of what the goddess so ingeniously discovered at the beginning. Isis also established laws, they say, in accordance with which the people regularly dispense justice to one another and are led to refrain through fear of punishment from illegal violence and insolence; and it is for this reason also that the early Greeks gave Demeter the name Thesmophorus,[1] acknowledging in this way that she had first established their laws.

15. Osiris, they say, founded in the Egyptian Thebaid a city with a hundred gates, which the men of his day named after his mother, though later generations called it Diospolis,[2] and some named it

---

[1] Law-giver.   [2] City of Zeus.

2 Διὸς πόλιν, ἐνίους δὲ Θήβας. ἀμφισβητεῖται δ'
ἡ κτίσις τῆς πόλεως ταύτης οὐ μόνον παρὰ τοῖς
συγγραφεῦσιν, ἀλλὰ καὶ παρ' αὐτοῖς τοῖς κατ'
Αἴγυπτον ἱερεῦσι· πολλοὶ γὰρ ἱστοροῦσιν οὐχ
ὑπὸ τῶν περὶ τὸν Ὄσιριν κτισθῆναι τὰς Θήβας,
ἀλλὰ πολλοῖς ὕστερον ἔτεσιν ὑπό τινος βασιλέως,
περὶ οὗ τὰ κατὰ μέρος ἐν τοῖς οἰκείοις χρόνοις
3 ἀναγράψομεν. ἱδρύσασθαι δὲ καὶ ἱερὸν τῶν
γονέων Διός τε καὶ Ἥρας ἀξιόλογον τῷ τε
μεγέθει καὶ τῇ λοιπῇ πολυτελείᾳ, καὶ ναοὺς
χρυσοῦς δύο Διός, τὸν μὲν μείζονα τοῦ οὐρανίου,
τὸν δὲ ἐλάττονα τοῦ βεβασιλευκότος καὶ πατρὸς
4 αὐτῶν, ὅν τινες Ἄμμωνα καλοῦσι. κατασκευάσαι δὲ καὶ τῶν ἄλλων θεῶν τῶν προειρημένων ναοὺς χρυσοῦς, ὧν ἑκάστῳ τιμὰς ἀπονεῖμαι
καὶ καταστῆσαι τοὺς ἐπιμελομένους ἱερεῖς. προ-
τιμᾶσθαι δὲ παρὰ τῷ Ὀσίριδι καὶ τῇ Ἴσιδι τοὺς
τὰς τέχνας ἀνευρίσκοντας ἢ μεθοδεύοντάς τι τῶν
5 χρησίμων· διόπερ ἐν τῇ Θηβαΐδι χαλκουργείων
εὑρεθέντων καὶ χρυσείων ὅπλα τε κατασκευάσασθαι, δι' ὧν τὰ θηρία κτείνοντας καὶ τὴν γῆν
ἐργαζομένους φιλοτίμως ἐξημερῶσαι τὴν χώραν,
ἀγάλματά τε καὶ χρυσοῦς ναοὺς κατασκευάσασθαι
τῶν θεῶν διαπρεπεῖς.

6 Γενέσθαι δὲ καὶ φιλογέωργον τὸν Ὄσιριν, καὶ
τραφῆναι μὲν τῆς εὐδαίμονος Ἀραβίας ἐν Νύσῃ
πλησίον Αἰγύπτου, Διὸς ὄντα παῖδα, καὶ τὴν
προσηγορίαν ἔχειν παρὰ τοῖς Ἕλλησιν ἀπό τε
τοῦ πατρὸς καὶ τοῦ τόπου Διόνυσον ὀνομασ-
7 θέντα.[1] μεμνῆσθαι δὲ τῆς Νύσης καὶ τὸν

---

[1] ὀνομασθέντα Vogel: μετονομασθέντα F, Bekker, Dindorf.

Thebes. There is no agreement, however, as to when this city was founded, not only among the historians, but even among the priests of Egypt themselves; for many writers say that Thebes was not founded by Osiris, but many years later by a certain king of whom we shall give a detailed account in connection with his period.[1] Osiris, they add, also built a temple to his parents, Zeus and Hera, which was famous both for its size and its costliness in general, and two golden chapels to Zeus, the larger one to him as god of heaven, the smaller one to him as former king and father of the Egyptians, in which rôle he is called by some Ammon. He also made golden chapels for the rest of the gods mentioned above, allotting honours to each of them and appointing priests to have charge over these. Special esteem at the court of Osiris and Isis was also accorded to those who should invent any of the arts or devise any useful process; consequently, since copper and gold mines had been discovered in the Thebaid, they fashioned implements with which they killed the wild beasts and worked the soil, and thus in eager rivalry brought the country under cultivation, and they made images of the gods and magnificent golden chapels for their worship.

Osiris, they say, was also interested in agriculture and was reared in Nysa, a city of Arabia Felix near Egypt, being a son of Zeus; and the name which he bears among the Greeks is derived both from his father and from the birthplace, since he is called Dionysus.[2] Mention is also made of Nysa by the

[1] The founder was a certain Busiris, according to chap. 45.
[2] A far-fetched etymology: *Dio-* (from *Dios*, the genitive form of the nominative *Zeus*) and *Nysus* (*Nysa*).

ποιητὴν ἐν τοῖς ὕμνοις, ὅτι περὶ τὴν Αἴγυπτον
γέγονεν, ἐν οἷς λέγει

ἔστι δέ τις Νύση, ὕπατον ὄρος ἀνθέον ὕλῃ,
τηλοῦ Φοινίκης, σχεδὸν Αἰγύπτοιο ῥοάων.

8 εὑρετὴν δ' αὐτὸν γενέσθαι φασὶ τῆς ἀμπέλου
περὶ τὴν Νῦσαν, καὶ τὴν κατεργασίαν τοῦ ταύτης
καρποῦ προσεπινοήσαντα πρῶτον οἴνῳ χρήσασθαι, καὶ διδάξαι τοὺς ἄλλους ἀνθρώπους τήν
τε φυτείαν τῆς ἀμπέλου καὶ τὴν χρῆσιν τοῦ
οἴνου καὶ τὴν συγκομιδὴν αὐτοῦ καὶ τήρησιν.
9 τιμᾶσθαι δ' ὑπ' αὐτοῦ μάλιστα πάντων τὸν
Ἑρμῆν, διαφόρῳ φύσει κεχορηγημένον πρὸς
ἐπίνοιαν τῶν δυναμένων ὠφελῆσαι τὸν κοινὸν
βίον.
16. Ὑπὸ γὰρ τούτου πρῶτον μὲν τήν τε
κοινὴν διάλεκτον διαρθρωθῆναι καὶ πολλὰ τῶν
ἀνωνύμων τυχεῖν προσηγορίας, τήν τε εὕρεσιν
τῶν γραμμάτων γενέσθαι καὶ τὰ περὶ τὰς τῶν
θεῶν τιμὰς καὶ θυσίας διαταχθῆναι· περί τε
τῆς τῶν ἄστρων τάξεως καὶ περὶ τῆς τῶν φθόγγων
ἁρμονίας καὶ φύσεως τοῦτον πρῶτον γενέσθαι
παρατηρητήν, καὶ παλαίστρας εὑρετὴν ὑπάρξαι,
καὶ τῆς εὐρυθμίας καὶ τῆς περὶ τὸ σῶμα πρε-
πούσης πλάσεως ἐπιμεληθῆναι. λύραν τε νευ-
ρίνην ποιῆσαι τρίχορδον, μιμησάμενον τὰς κατ'
ἐνιαυτὸν ὥρας· τρεῖς γὰρ αὐτὸν ὑποστήσασθαι
φθόγγους, ὀξὺν καὶ βαρὺν καὶ μέσον, ὀξὺν μὲν
ἀπὸ τοῦ θέρους, βαρὺν δὲ ἀπὸ τοῦ χειμῶνος,
2 μέσον δὲ ἀπὸ τοῦ ἔαρος. καὶ τοὺς Ἕλληνας
διδάξαι τοῦτον τὰ περὶ τὴν ἑρμηνείαν, ὑπὲρ ὧν

poet in his Hymns,[1] to the effect that it was in the vicinity of Egypt, when he says:

> There is a certain Nysa, mountain high,
> With forests thick, in Phoenicê afar,
> Close to Aegyptus' streams.

And the discovery of the vine, they say, was made by him near Nysa, and that, having further devised the proper treatment of its fruit, he was the first to drink wine and taught mankind at large the culture of the vine and the use of wine, as well as the way to harvest the grape and to store the wine. The one most highly honoured by him was Hermes, who was endowed with unusual ingenuity for devising things capable of improving the social life of man.

16. It was by Hermes, for instance, according to them, that the common language of mankind was first further articulated, and that many objects which were still nameless received an appellation, that the alphabet was invented, and that ordinances regarding the honours and offerings due to the gods were duly established; he was the first also to observe the orderly arrangement of the stars and the harmony of the musical sounds and their nature, to establish a wrestling school, and to give thought to the rhythmical movement of the human body and its proper development. He also made a lyre and gave it three strings, imitating the seasons of the year; for he adopted three tones, a high, a low, and a medium; the high from the summer, the low from the winter, and the medium from the spring. The Greeks also were taught by him how to expound (*hermeneia*) their thoughts, and it was for this reason

---

[1] *Homeric Hymns* 1. 8–9.

Ἑρμῆν αὐτὸν ὠνομάσθαι. καθόλου δὲ τοὺς
περὶ τὸν Ὄσιριν τοῦτον ἔχοντας ἱερογραμματέα
ἅπαντ' αὐτῷ προσανακοινοῦσθαι καὶ μάλιστα
χρῆσθαι τῇ τούτου συμβουλίᾳ. καὶ τῆς ἐλαίας
δὲ τὸ φυτὸν αὐτὸν εὑρεῖν, ἀλλ' οὐκ Ἀθηνᾶν,
ὥσπερ Ἕλληνές φασι.

17. Τὸν δὲ Ὄσιριν λέγουσιν, ὥσπερ εὐεργετικὸν
ὄντα καὶ φιλόδοξον, στρατόπεδον μέγα συστήσασθαι, διανοούμενον ἐπελθεῖν ἅπασαν τὴν οἰκουμένην καὶ διδάξαι τὸ γένος τῶν ἀνθρώπων τήν τε
τῆς ἀμπέλου φυτείαν καὶ τὸν σπόρον τοῦ τε
2 πυρίνου καὶ κριθίνου καρποῦ· ὑπολαμβάνειν
γὰρ αὐτὸν ὅτι παύσας τῆς ἀγριότητος τοὺς ἀνθρώπους καὶ διαίτης ἡμέρου μεταλαβεῖν ποιήσας
τιμῶν ἀθανάτων τεύξεται διὰ τὸ μέγεθος τῆς
εὐεργεσίας. ὅπερ δὴ καὶ γενέσθαι· οὐ μόνον γὰρ
τοὺς κατ' ἐκείνους τοὺς χρόνους τυχόντας τῆς
δωρεᾶς ταύτης, ἀλλὰ καὶ πάντας τοὺς μετὰ
ταῦτα ἐπιγενομένους διὰ τὴν ἐν ταῖς εὑρεθείσαις
τροφαῖς χάριτα τοὺς εἰσηγησαμένους ὡς ἐπιφανεστάτους θεοὺς τετιμηκέναι.

3 Τὸν δ' οὖν Ὄσιρίν φασι τὰ κατὰ τὴν Αἴγυπτον
καταστήσαντα καὶ τὴν τῶν ὅλων ἡγεμονίαν
Ἴσιδι τῇ γυναικὶ παραδόντα, ταύτῃ μὲν παρα-
καταστῆσαι σύμβουλον τὸν Ἑρμῆν διὰ τὸ
φρονήσει τοῦτον διαφέρειν τῶν ἄλλων φίλων,
καὶ στρατηγὸν μὲν ἀπολιπεῖν ἁπάσης τῆς ὑφ'
αὑτὸν χώρας Ἡρακλέα γένει τε προσήκοντα καὶ
θαυμαζόμενον ἐπ' ἀνδρείᾳ τε καὶ σώματος ῥώμῃ,
ἐπιμελητὰς δὲ τάξαι τῶν μὲν πρὸς Φοινίκην
κεκλιμένων μερῶν καὶ τῶν ἐπὶ θαλάττῃ τόπων
Βούσιριν, τῶν δὲ κατὰ τὴν Αἰθιοπίαν καὶ Λιβύην

that he was given the name Hermes. In a word, Osiris, taking him for his priestly scribe, communicated with him on every matter and used his counsel above that of all others. The olive tree also, they claim, was his discovery, not Athena's, as Greeks say.

17. Of Osiris they say that, being of a beneficent turn of mind, and eager for glory, he gathered together a great army, with the intention of visiting all the inhabited earth and teaching the race of men how to cultivate the vine and sow wheat and barley; for he supposed that if he made men give up their savagery and adopt a gentle manner of life he would receive immortal honours because of the magnitude of his benefactions. And this did in fact take place, since not only the men of his time who received this gift, but all succeeding generations as well, because of the delight which they take in the foods which were discovered, have honoured those who introduced them as gods most illustrious.

Now after Osiris had established the affairs of Egypt and turned the supreme power over to Isis his wife, they say that he placed Hermes at her side as counsellor because his prudence raised him above the king's other friends, and as general of all the land under his sway he left Heracles, who was both his kinsman and renowned for his valour and physical strength, while as governors he appointed Busiris over those parts of Egypt which lie towards Phoenicia and border upon the sea and Antaeus over those adjoining Ethiopia and Libya; then he

'Ανταῖον, αὐτὸν δ' ἐκ τῆς Αἰγύπτου μετὰ τῆς δυνάμεως ἀναζεῦξαι πρὸς τὴν στρατείαν, ἔχοντα μεθ' αὑτοῦ καὶ τὸν ἀδελφόν, ὃν οἱ Ἕλληνες 4 Ἀπόλλωνα καλοῦσιν. εὑρετὴν δὲ καὶ τοῦτόν φασι γενέσθαι τοῦ φυτοῦ τῆς δάφνης, ἣν καὶ περιτιθέασι τούτῳ τῷ θεῷ μάλιστα πάντες ἄνθρωποι. τοῦ δὲ κιττοῦ τὴν εὕρεσιν ἀνατιθέασιν Ὀσίριδι, καὶ καθιεροῦσιν αὐτὸν τούτῳ τῷ θεῷ, 5 καθάπερ καὶ οἱ Ἕλληνες Διονύσῳ. καὶ κατὰ τὴν Αἰγυπτίων μὲν[1] διάλεκτον ὀνομάζεσθαί φασι τὸν κιττὸν φυτὸν Ὀσίριδος, προκεκρίσθαι δὲ τῆς ἀμπέλου τοῦτον πρὸς τὴν ἀφιέρωσιν διὰ τὸ τὴν μὲν φυλλορροεῖν, τὸν δὲ πάντα τὸν χρόνον ἀειθαλῆ διαμένειν· ὅπερ τοὺς παλαιοὺς καὶ ἐφ' ἑτέρων φυτῶν ἀεὶ θαλλόντων πεποιηκέναι, τῇ μὲν Ἀφροδίτῃ τὴν μυρσίνην, τῷ δ' Ἀπόλλωνι τὴν δάφνην προσάψαντας.[2]

18. Τῷ δ' οὖν Ὀσίριδι συνεστρατεῦσθαι δύο λέγουσιν υἱοὺς Ἄνουβίν τε καὶ Μακεδόνα, διαφέροντας ἀνδρείᾳ. ἀμφοτέρους δὲ χρήσασθαι τοῖς ἐπισημοτάτοις ὅπλοις ἀπό τινων ζῴων οὐκ ἀνοικείων τῇ περὶ αὐτοὺς εὐτολμίᾳ· τὸν μὲν γὰρ Ἄνουβιν περιθέσθαι κυνῆν, τὸν δὲ Μακεδόνα λύκου προτομήν· ἀφ' ἧς αἰτίας καὶ τὰ ζῷα ταῦτα 2 τιμηθῆναι παρὰ τοῖς Αἰγυπτίοις. παραλαβεῖν δ' ἐπὶ τὴν στρατείαν καὶ τὸν Πᾶνα, διαφερόντως ὑπὸ τῶν Αἰγυπτίων τιμώμενον· τούτῳ γὰρ τοὺς ἐγχωρίους οὐ μόνον ἀγάλματα πεποιηκέναι κατὰ πᾶν ἱερόν, ἀλλὰ καὶ πόλιν ἐπώνυμον κατὰ τὴν Θηβαΐδα, καλουμένην μὲν ὑπὸ τῶν ἐγχωρίων Χεμμώ, μεθερμηνευομένην δὲ Πανὸς πόλιν. συν-

---

[1] μὲν Bekker, Vogel: omitted C F, Dindorf.

himself left Egypt with his army to make his campaign, taking in his company also his brother, whom the Greeks call Apollo. And it was Apollo, they say, who discovered the laurel, a garland of which all men place about the head of this god above all others. The discovery of ivy is also attributed to Osiris by the Egyptians and made sacred to this god, just as the Greeks also do in the case of Dionysus. And in the Egyptian language, they say, the ivy is called the " plant of Osiris " and for purposes of dedication is preferred to the vine, since the latter sheds its leaves while the former ever remains green; the same rule, moreover, the ancients have followed in the case of other plants also which are perennially green, ascribing, for instance, the myrtle to Aphrodite and the laurel to Apollo.

18. Now Osiris was accompanied on his campaign, as the Egyptian account goes, by his two sons Anubis and Macedon, who were distinguished for their valour. Both of them carried the most notable accoutrements of war, taken from certain animals whose character was not unlike the boldness of the men, Anubis wearing a dog's skin and Macedon the fore-parts of a wolf; and it is for this reason that these animals are held in honour among the Egyptians. He also took Pan along on his campaign, who is held in special honour by the Egyptians; for the inhabitants of the land have not only set up statues of him at every temple but have also named a city after him in the Thebaid, called by the natives Chemmo, which when translated means City of Pan.[1]

[1] The god Min, being ithyphallic, was usually identified by the Greeks with Pan; cp. Herodotus, 2. 46.

[2] τῇ δ' Ἀθηνᾷ τὴν ἐλαίαν added F, Bekker, Dindorf.

ἕπεσθαι δὲ καὶ τῆς γεωργίας ἐμπειρίαν ἔχοντας,
τῆς μὲν περὶ τὴν ἄμπελον φυτείας Μάρωνα, τοῦ
δὲ κατὰ τὸν σῖτον σπόρου καὶ τῆς ὅλης συγκο-
3 μιδῆς Τριπτόλεμον. πάντων δ' εὐτρεπῶν γενομένων τὸν Ὄσιριν, εὐξάμενον τοῖς θεοῖς θρέψειν
τὴν κόμην μέχρι ἂν εἰς Αἴγυπτον ἀνακάμψῃ, τὴν
πορείαν ποιεῖσθαι δι' Αἰθιοπίας· δι' ἣν αἰτίαν
μέχρι τῶν νεωτέρων χρόνων ἐνισχῦσαι τὸ περὶ
τῆς κόμης νόμιμον παρ' Αἰγυπτίοις, καὶ τοὺς
ποιουμένους τὰς ἀποδημίας μέχρι τῆς εἰς οἶκον
ἀνακομιδῆς κομοτροφεῖν.
4 Ὄντι δ' αὐτῷ περὶ τὴν Αἰθιοπίαν ἀχθῆναι
λέγουσι πρὸς αὐτὸν τὸ τῶν Σατύρων γένος, οὕς
φασιν ἐπὶ τῆς ὀσφύος ἔχειν κόμας. εἶναι γὰρ
τὸν Ὄσιριν φιλογέλωτά τε καὶ χαίροντα μουσικῇ
καὶ χοροῖς· διὸ καὶ περιάγεσθαι πλῆθος μου-
σουργῶν, ἐν οἷς παρθένους ἐννέα δυναμένας ᾄδειν
καὶ κατὰ τὰ ἄλλα πεπαιδευμένας, τὰς παρὰ
τοῖς Ἕλλησιν ὀνομαζομένας Μούσας· τούτων δ'
ἡγεῖσθαι τὸν Ἀπόλλωνα λέγουσιν, ἀφ' οὗ καὶ
5 Μουσηγέτην αὐτὸν ὠνομάσθαι. τούς τε Σατύρους
πρὸς ὄρχησιν καὶ μελῳδίαν καὶ πᾶσαν ἄνεσιν
καὶ παιδιὰν ὄντας εὐθέτους παραληφθῆναι πρὸς
τὴν στρατείαν· οὐ γὰρ πολεμικὸν εἶναι τὸν Ὄσιριν
οὐδὲ παρατάξεις συνίστασθαι καὶ κινδύνους, ἅτε
παντὸς ἔθνους ὡς θεὸν ἀποδεχομένου διὰ τὰς
6 εὐεργεσίας. κατὰ δὲ τὴν Αἰθιοπίαν διδάξαντα
τοὺς ἀνθρώπους τὰ περὶ τὴν γεωργίαν καὶ πόλεις
ἀξιολόγους κτίσαντα καταλιπεῖν τοὺς ἐπιμελησομένους τῆς χώρας καὶ φόρους πραξομένους.
19. Τούτων δ' ὄντων περὶ ταῦτα, τὸν Νεῖλόν
φασι κατὰ τὴν τοῦ σειρίου ἄστρου ἐπιτολήν,

In his company were also men who were experienced in agriculture, such as Maron in the cultivation of the vine, and Triptolemus in the sowing of grain and in every step in the harvesting of it. And when all his preparations had been completed Osiris made a vow to the gods that he would let his hair grow until his return to Egypt and then made his way through Ethiopia; and this is the reason why this custom with regard to their hair was observed among the Egyptians until recent times, and why those who journeyed abroad let their hair grow until their return home.

While he was in Ethiopia, their account continues, the Satyr people were brought to him, who, they say, have hair upon their loins. For Osiris was laughter-loving and fond of music and the dance; consequently he took with him a multitude of musicians, among whom were nine maidens who could sing and were trained in the other arts, these maidens being those who among the Greeks are called the Muses; and their leader (*hegetes*), as the account goes, was Apollo, who was for that reason also given the name Musegetes. As for the Satyrs, they were taken along on the campaign because they were proficient in dancing and singing and every kind of relaxation and pastime; for Osiris was not warlike, nor did he have to organize pitched battles or engagements, since every people received him as a god because of his benefactions. In Ethiopia he instructed the inhabitants in agriculture and founded some notable cities, and then left behind him men to govern the country and collect the tribute.

19. While Osiris and his army were thus employed, the Nile, they say, at the time of the rising of Sirius,

ἐν ᾧ καιρῷ μάλιστα εἴωθε πληροῦσθαι, ῥαγέντα
κατακλύσαι πολλὴν τῆς Αἰγύπτου, καὶ μάλιστα
τοῦτο τὸ μέρος ἐπελθεῖν οὗ Προμηθεὺς εἶχε τὴν
ἐπιμέλειαν· διαφθαρέντων δὲ σχεδὸν ἁπάντων
τῶν κατὰ ταύτην τὴν χώραν τὸν Προμηθέα διὰ
τὴν λύπην κινδυνεύειν ἐκλιπεῖν τὸν βίον ἑκουσίως.
2 διὰ δὲ τὴν ὀξύτητα καὶ τὴν βίαν τοῦ κατ-
ενεχθέντος ῥεύματος τὸν μὲν ποταμὸν Ἀετὸν
ὀνομασθῆναι, τὸν δ' Ἡρακλέα, μεγαλεπίβολον
ὄντα καὶ τὴν ἀνδρείαν ἐζηλωκότα, τό τε γενόμενον ἔκρηγμα ταχέως ἐμφράξαι καὶ τὸν ποταμὸν
3 ἐπὶ τὴν προϋπάρξασαν ῥύσιν ἀποστρέψαι. διὸ
καὶ τῶν παρ' Ἕλλησι ποιητῶν τινας εἰς μῦθον
ἀγαγεῖν τὸ πραχθέν, ὡς Ἡρακλέους τὸν ἀετὸν
ἀνῃρηκότος τὸν τὸ τοῦ Προμηθέως ἧπαρ ἐσθίοντα.
4 τὸν δὲ ποταμὸν ἀρχαιότατον μὲν ὄνομα σχεῖν
Ὠκεάνην, ὅς ἐστιν ἑλληνιστὶ Ὠκεανός· ἔπειτα
διὰ τὸ γενόμενον ἔκρηγμά φασιν Ἀετὸν ὀνομασθῆναι, ὕστερον δ' Αἴγυπτον ἀπὸ τοῦ βασιλεύσαντος τῆς χώρας προσαγορευθῆναι· μαρτυρεῖν
δὲ καὶ τὸν ποιητὴν λέγοντα

στῆσα δ' ἐν Αἰγύπτῳ ποταμῷ νέας ἀμφιε-
λίσσας.

κατὰ γὰρ τὴν καλουμένην Θῶνιν ἐμβάλλοντος
εἰς θάλατταν τοῦ ποταμοῦ, τοῦτον τὸν τόπον
ἐμπόριον εἶναι τὸ παλαιὸν τῆς Αἰγύπτου· τελευ-
ταίας δὲ τυχεῖν αὐτὸν ἧς νῦν ἔχει προσηγορίας
ἀπὸ τοῦ βασιλεύσαντος Νειλέως.

5 Τὸν δ' οὖν Ὄσιριν παραγενόμενον ἐπὶ τοὺς
τῆς Αἰθιοπίας ὅρους τὸν ποταμὸν ἐξ ἀμφοτέρων
τῶν μερῶν χώμασιν ἀναλαβεῖν, ὥστε κατὰ τὴν

which is the season when the river is usually at flood, breaking out of its banks inundated a large section of Egypt and covered especially that part where Prometheus was governor; and since practically everything in this district was destroyed, Prometheus was so grieved that he was on the point of quitting life wilfully. Because its water sweeps down so swiftly and with such violence the river was given the name Aëtus;[1] but Heracles, being ever intent upon great enterprises and eager for the reputation of a manly spirit, speedily stopped the flood at its breach and turned the river back into its former course. Consequently certain of the Greek poets worked the incident into a myth, to the effect that Heracles had killed the eagle which was devouring the liver of Prometheus. The river in the earliest period bore the name Oceanê, which in Greek is Oceanus; then because of this flood, they say, it was called Aëtus, and still later it was known as Aegyptus after a former king of the land. And the poet also adds his testimony to this when he writes:[2]

On the river Aegyptus my curvéd ships I stayed.

For it is at Thonis, as it is called, which in early times was the trading-port of Egypt, that the river empties into the sea. Its last name and that which the river now bears it received from the former king Nileus.

Now when Osiris arrived at the borders of Ethiopia, he curbed the river by dikes on both banks, so that

---

[1] Eagle.
[2] *Odyssey* 14. 258.

πλήρωσιν αὐτοῦ τὴν χώραν μὴ λιμνάζειν παρὰ
τὸ συμφέρον, ἀλλὰ διά τινων κατεσκευασμένων
θυρῶν εἰσαφίεσθαι τὸ ῥεῦμα πράως καθ' ὅσον
6 ἂν ᾖ χρεία. ἔπειτα ποιήσασθαι τὴν πορείαν
δι' Ἀραβίας παρὰ τὴν Ἐρυθρὰν θάλατταν ἕως
7 Ἰνδῶν καὶ τοῦ πέρατος τῆς οἰκουμένης. κτίσαι
δὲ καὶ πόλεις οὐκ ὀλίγας ἐν Ἰνδοῖς, ἐν αἷς καὶ
Νῦσαν ὀνομάσαι, βουλόμενον μνημεῖον ἀπολιπεῖν
ἐκείνης καθ' ἣν ἐτράφη κατ' Αἴγυπτον. φυτεῦσαι
δὲ καὶ κιττὸν ἐν τῇ παρ' Ἰνδοῖς Νύσῃ, καὶ διαμένειν τοῦτο τὸ φυτὸν ἐν ἐκείνῳ μόνῳ τῷ τόπῳ
τῶν τε κατὰ τὴν Ἰνδικὴν καὶ τὴν ὅμορον χώραν.
8 πολλὰ δὲ καὶ ἄλλα σημεῖα τῆς ἑαυτοῦ παρουσίας
ἀπολελοιπέναι κατ' ἐκείνην τὴν χώραν, δι' ὧν
προαχθέντας τοὺς μεταγενεστέρους τῶν Ἰνδῶν
ἀμφισβητῆσαι τοῦ θεοῦ, λέγοντας Ἰνδὸν εἶναι
τὸ γένος.

20. Γενέσθαι δὲ καὶ περὶ τὴν τῶν ἐλεφάντων
θήραν, καὶ στήλας πανταχοῦ καταλιπεῖν[1] τῆς
ἰδίας στρατείας. ἐπελθεῖν δὲ καὶ τἆλλα τὰ
κατὰ τὴν Ἀσίαν ἔθνη, καὶ περαιωθῆναι κατὰ
2 τὸν Ἑλλήσποντον εἰς τὴν Εὐρώπην. καὶ κατὰ
μὲν τὴν Θρᾴκην Λυκοῦργον τὸν βασιλέα τῶν
βαρβάρων ἐναντιούμενον τοῖς ὑπ' αὐτοῦ πρατ-
τομένοις ἀποκτεῖναι, Μάρωνα δὲ γηραιὸν ἤδη
καθεστῶτα καταλιπεῖν ἐπιμελητὴν τῶν ἐν ταύτῃ
τῇ χώρᾳ φυτευομένων, καὶ κτίστην αὐτὸν ποιῆσαι
τῆς ἐπωνύμου πόλεως, ἣν ὀνομάσαι Μαρώνειαν.
3 καὶ Μακεδόνα μὲν τὸν υἱὸν ἀπολιπεῖν βασιλέα
τῆς ἀπ' ἐκείνου προσαγορευθείσης Μακεδονίας,
Τριπτολέμῳ δ' ἐπιτρέψαι τὰς κατὰ τὴν Ἀττικὴν
γεωργίας. τέλος δὲ τὸν Ὄσιριν πᾶσαν τὴν

at flood-time it might not form stagnant pools over
the land to its detriment, but that the flood-water
might be let upon the countryside, in a gentle flow
as it might be needed, through gates which he had
built. After this he continued his march through
Arabia along the shore of the Red Sea[1] as far as
India and the limits of the inhabited world. He also
founded not a few cities in India, one of which he
named Nysa, wishing to leave there a memorial of
that city in Egypt where he had been reared. He
also planted ivy in the Indian Nysa, and throughout
India and those countries which border upon it the
plant to this day is still to be found only in this
region. And many other signs of his stay he left
in that country, which have led the Indians of a later
time to lay claim to the god and say that he was by
birth a native of India.

20. Osiris also took an interest in hunting elephants,
and everywhere left behind him inscribed pillars telling of his campaign. And he visited all the other
nations of Asia as well and crossed into Europe at
the Hellespont. In Thrace he slew Lycurgus, the
king of the barbarians, who opposed his undertakings, and Maron, who was now old, he left there to
supervise the culture of the plants which he introduced into that land and caused him to found a city
to bear his name, which he called Maroneia. Macedon his son, moreover, he left as king of Macedonia,
which was named after him, while to Triptolemus he
assigned the care of agriculture in Attica. Finally,
Osiris in this way visited all the inhabited world and

[1] Not the present Red Sea, but the Persian Gulf and the
Indian Ocean.

---

[1] καταλιπεῖν πανταχοῦ Vulgate, Bekker, Dindorf.

οἰκουμένην ἐπελθόντα τὸν κοινὸν βίον τοῖς ἡμε-
4 ρωτάτοις καρποῖς εὐεργετῆσαι. εἰ δέ τις χώρα
τὸ φυτὸν τῆς ἀμπέλου μὴ προσδέχοιτο, διδάξαι
τὸ ἐκ τῆς κριθῆς κατασκευαζόμενον πόμα, λειπόμενον οὐ πολὺ τῆς περὶ τὸν οἶνον εὐωδίας τε καὶ
5 δυνάμεως. ἐπανελθόντα δ᾽ εἰς τὴν Αἴγυπτον
συναποκομίσαι δῶρά τε πανταχόθεν τὰ κράτιστα
καὶ διὰ τὸ μέγεθος τῶν εὐεργεσιῶν συμπεφωνη-
μένην λαβεῖν παρὰ πᾶσι τὴν ἀθανασίαν καὶ τὴν
6 ἴσην τοῖς οὐρανίοις τιμήν. μετὰ δὲ ταῦτ᾽ ἐξ
ἀνθρώπων εἰς θεοὺς μεταστάντα τυχεῖν ὑπὸ
Ἴσιδος καὶ Ἑρμοῦ θυσιῶν καὶ τῶν ἄλλων τῶν
ἐπιφανεστάτων τιμῶν. τούτους δὲ καὶ τελετὰς
καταδεῖξαι καὶ πολλὰ μυστικῶς εἰσηγήσασθαι,
μεγαλύνοντας τοῦ θεοῦ τὴν δύναμιν.

21. Τῶν δ᾽ ἱερέων περὶ τῆς Ὀσίριδος τελευτῆς
ἐξ ἀρχαίων ἐν ἀπορρήτοις παρειληφότων, τῷ
χρόνῳ ποτὲ συνέβη διά τινων εἰς τοὺς πολλοὺς
2 ἐξενεχθῆναι τὸ σιωπώμενον. φασὶ γὰρ νομίμως
βασιλεύοντα τῆς Αἰγύπτου τὸν Ὄσιριν ὑπὸ
Τυφῶνος ἀναιρεθῆναι τἀδελφοῦ, βιαίου καὶ
ἀσεβοῦς ὄντος· ὃν διελόντα τὸ σῶμα τοῦ φονευ-
θέντος εἰς ἓξ καὶ εἴκοσι μέρη δοῦναι τῶν συνεπιθεμένων ἑκάστῳ μερίδα, βουλόμενον πάντας μετασχεῖν τοῦ μύσους, καὶ διὰ τούτου[1] νομίζοντα
συναγωνιστὰς ἕξειν καὶ φύλακας τῆς βασιλείας
3 βεβαίους. τὴν δὲ Ἶσιν ἀδελφὴν οὖσαν Ὀσίριδος καὶ γυναῖκα μετελθεῖν τὸν φόνον, συναγωνι-
ζομένου τοῦ παιδὸς αὐτῆς Ὥρου, ἀνελοῦσαν δὲ
τὸν Τυφῶνα καὶ τοὺς συμπράξαντας βασιλεῦσαι
4 τῆς Αἰγύπτου. γενέσθαι δὲ τὴν μάχην παρὰ

---

[1] τούτου Vogel: τοῦτο Vulgate, Bekker, Dindorf.

advanced community life by the introduction of the fruits which are most easily cultivated. And if any country did not admit of the growing of the vine he introduced the drink prepared from barley,[1] which is little inferior to wine in aroma and in strength. On his return to Egypt he brought with him the very greatest presents from every quarter and by reason of the magnitude of his benefactions received the gift of immortality with the approval of all men and honour equal to that offered to the gods of heaven. After this he passed from the midst of men into the company of the gods and received from Isis and Hermes sacrifices and every other highest honour. These also instituted rites for him and introduced many things of a mystic nature, magnifying in this way the power of the god.

21. Although the priests of Osiris had from the earliest times received the account of his death as a matter not to be divulged, in the course of years it came about that through some of their number this hidden knowledge was published to the many. This is the story as they give it: When Osiris was ruling over Egypt as its lawful king, he was murdered by his brother Typhon, a violent and impious man; Typhon then divided the body of the slain man into twenty-six pieces and gave one portion to each of the band of murderers, since he wanted all of them to share in the pollution and felt that in this way he would have in them steadfast supporters and defenders of his rule. But Isis, the sister and wife of Osiris, avenged his murder with the aid of her son Horus, and after slaying Typhon and his accomplices became queen over Egypt. The struggle

---

[1] The Egyptian beer, called below *zythos* (chap. 34).

τὸν ποταμὸν πλησίον τῆς νῦν Ἀνταίου κώμης
καλουμένης, ἣν κεῖσθαι μὲν λέγουσιν ἐν τῷ κατὰ
τὴν Ἀραβίαν μέρει, τὴν προσηγορίαν δ' ἔχειν
ἀπὸ τοῦ κολασθέντος ὑφ' Ἡρακλέους Ἀνταίου,
5 τοῦ κατὰ τὴν Ὀσίριδος ἡλικίαν γενομένου. τὴν
δ' οὖν Ἶσιν πάντα τὰ μέρη τοῦ σώματος πλὴν
τῶν αἰδοίων ἀνευρεῖν· βουλομένην δὲ τὴν τἀνδρὸς ταφὴν ἄδηλον ποιῆσαι καὶ τιμωμένην παρὰ
πᾶσι τοῖς τὴν Αἴγυπτον κατοικοῦσι, συντελέσαι
τὸ δόξαν τοιῷδέ τινι τρόπῳ. ἑκάστῳ τῶν μερῶν
περιπλάσαι λέγουσιν αὐτὴν τύπον ἀνθρωποειδῆ,
παραπλήσιον Ὀσίριδι τὸ μέγεθος, ἐξ ἀρωμάτων
6 καὶ κηροῦ· εἰσκαλεσαμένην δὲ κατὰ γένη τῶν
ἱερέων ἐξορκίσαι πάντας μηδενὶ δηλώσειν τὴν
δοθησομένην αὐτοῖς πίστιν, κατ' ἰδίαν δ' ἑκάστοις
εἰπεῖν ὅτι μόνοις ἐκείνοις παρατίθεται τὴν τοῦ
σώματος ταφήν, καὶ τῶν εὐεργεσιῶν ὑπομνήσα-
σαν παρακαλέσαι θάψαντας ἐν τοῖς ἰδίοις τόποις
τὸ σῶμα τιμᾶν ὡς θεὸν τὸν Ὄσιριν, καθιερῶσαι
δὲ καὶ τῶν γινομένων παρ' αὐτοῖς ζῴων ἐν ὁποῖον
ἂν βουληθῶσι, καὶ τοῦτ' ἐν μὲν τῷ ζῆν τιμᾶν,
καθάπερ καὶ πρότερον τὸν Ὄσιριν, μετὰ δὲ τὴν
τελευτὴν τῆς ὁμοίας ἐκείνῳ κηδείας ἀξιοῦν.
7 βουλομένην δὲ τὴν Ἶσιν καὶ τῷ λυσιτελεῖ
προτρέψασθαι τοὺς ἱερεῖς ἐπὶ τὰς προειρημένας τιμάς, τὸ τρίτον μέρος τῆς χώρας αὐτοῖς
δοῦναι πρὸς τὰς τῶν θεῶν θεραπείας τε καὶ
8 λειτουργίας. τοὺς δ' ἱερεῖς λέγεται, μνημονεύοντας τῶν Ὀσίριδος εὐεργεσιῶν καὶ τῇ παρα-

---

¹ Antaeus was a giant of Libya, the son of Poseidon
and Earth, who was slain by Heracles (cp. Book 4. 17. 4).
According to one version of the story he received strength

between them took place on the banks of the Nile near the village now known as Antaeus, which, they say, lies on the Arabian side of the river and derives its name from that Antaeus,[1] a contemporary of Osiris, who was punished by Heracles. Now Isis recovered all the pieces of the body except the privates, and wishing that the burial-place of her husband should remain secret and yet be honoured by all the inhabitants of Egypt, she fulfilled her purpose in somewhat the following manner. Over each piece of the body, as the account goes, she fashioned out of spices and wax a human figure about the size of Osiris; then summoning the priests group by group, she required of all of them an oath that they would reveal to no one the trust which she was going to confide to them, and taking each group of them apart privately she said that she was consigning to them alone the burial of the body, and after reminding them of the benefactions of Osiris she exhorted them to bury his body in their own district and pay honours to him as to a god, and to consecrate to him also some one that they might choose of the animals native to their district, pay it while living the honours which they had formerly rendered to Osiris, and upon its death accord it the same kind of funeral as they had given to him. And since Isis wished to induce the priests to render these honours by the incentive of their own profit also, she gave them the third part of the country to defray the cost of the worship and service of the gods. And the priests, it is said, being mindful of the benefactions of Osiris and eager to please the queen

whenever he touched his mother Earth and Heracles overcame him only by holding him in the air.

67

καλούσῃ βουλομένους χαρίζεσθαι, πρὸς δὲ τούτοις τῷ λυσιτελεῖ προκληθέντας, πάντα πρᾶξαι
9 κατὰ τὴν Ἴσιδος ὑποθήκην. διὸ καὶ μέχρι τοῦ
νῦν ἑκάστους τῶν ἱερέων ὑπολαμβάνειν παρ'
ἑαυτοῖς τεθάφθαι τὸν Ὄσιριν, καὶ τά τε ἐξ ἀρχῆς
καθιερωθέντα ζῷα τιμᾶν, καὶ τελευτησάντων
αὐτῶν ἐν ταῖς ταφαῖς ἀνανεοῦσθαι τὸ τοῦ Ὀσίριδος
10 πένθος. τοὺς δὲ ταύρους τοὺς ἱερούς, τόν τε
ὀνομαζόμενον Ἆπιν καὶ τὸν Μνεῦιν, Ὀσίριδι
καθιερωθῆναι, καὶ τούτους σέβεσθαι καθάπερ
θεοὺς κοινῇ καταδειχθῆναι πᾶσιν Αἰγυπτίοις·
11 ταῦτα γὰρ τὰ ζῷα τοῖς εὑροῦσι τὸν τοῦ σίτου
καρπὸν συνεργῆσαι μάλιστα πρός τε τὸν
σπόρον καὶ τὰς κοινὰς ἁπάντων ἐκ τῆς γεωργίας
ὠφελείας.

22. Τὴν δὲ Ἰσίν φασι μετὰ τὴν Ὀσίριδος
τελευτὴν ὀμόσαι μηδενὸς ἀνδρὸς ἔτι συνουσίαν
προσδέξεσθαι,[1] διατελέσαι δὲ τὸν λοιπὸν τοῦ
βίου χρόνον βασιλεύουσαν νομιμώτατα καὶ ταῖς
εἰς τοὺς ἀρχομένους εὐεργεσίαις ἅπαντας ὑπερ-
2 βαλλομένην. ὁμοίως δὲ καὶ ταύτην μεταστᾶσαν
ἐξ ἀνθρώπων τυχεῖν ἀθανάτων τιμῶν καὶ ταφῆναι
κατὰ τὴν Μέμφιν, ὅπου δείκνυται μέχρι τοῦ νῦν
ὁ σηκός, ὑπάρχων ἐν τῷ τεμένει τοῦ Ἡφαίστου.
3 ἔνιοι δέ φασιν οὐκ ἐν Μέμφει κεῖσθαι τὰ σώματα
τούτων τῶν θεῶν, ἀλλ' ἐπὶ τῶν ὅρων τῆς Αἰθιοπίας
καὶ τῆς Αἰγύπτου κατὰ τὴν ἐν τῷ Νείλῳ νῆσον,
κειμένην μὲν πρὸς ταῖς καλουμέναις Φίλαις,

---

[1] προσδέξεσθαι Hertlein : προσδέξασθαι.

[1] Cp. chaps. 84 f.
[2] Though the island of Philae, once " the pearl of Egypt,"
was a sacred place of early Egypt, the beautiful temples which
68

who was petitioning them, and incited as well by their own profit, did everything just as Isis had suggested. It is for this reason that even to this day each group of priests supposes that Osiris lies buried in their district, pays honours to the animals which were originally consecrated to him, and, when these die, renews in the funeral rites for them the mourning for Osiris. The consecration to Osiris, however, of the sacred bulls, which are given the names Apis and Mnevis,[1] and the worship of them as gods were introduced generally among all the Egyptians, since these animals had, more than any others, rendered aid to those who discovered the fruit of the grain, in connection with both the sowing of the seed and with every agricultural labour from which mankind profits.

22. Isis, they say, after the death of Osiris took a vow never to marry another man, and passed the remainder of her life reigning over the land with complete respect for the law and surpassing all sovereigns in benefactions to her subjects. And like her husband she also, when she passed from among men, received immortal honours and was buried near Memphis, where her shrine is pointed out to this day in the temple-area of Hephaestus. According to some writers, however, the bodies of these two gods rest, not in Memphis, but on the border between Egypt and Ethiopia, on the island in the Nile which lies near the city which is called Philae,[2] but is

have made it so famous were constructions of the Ptolemies of the last two centuries B.C. and of the Roman emperors of the first three Christian centuries. Since the height of the Aswan dam has been increased the temples are completely submerged except during July–October.

ἔχουσαν δὲ προσηγορίαν ἀπὸ τοῦ συμβεβηκότος
4 ἱεροῦ πεδίου. σημεῖα δὲ τούτου δεικνύουσιν ἐν
τῇ νήσῳ ταύτῃ διαμένοντα τόν τε τάφον τὸν
κατεσκευασμένον Ὀσίριδι, κοινῇ τιμώμενον ὑπὸ
τῶν κατ᾽ Αἴγυπτον ἱερέων, καὶ τὰς περὶ τούτον
5 κειμένας ἑξήκοντα καὶ τριακοσίας χοάς· ταύτας
γὰρ καθ᾽ ἑκάστην ἡμέραν γάλακτος πληροῦν
τοὺς πρὸς τούτοις ταχθέντας ἱερεῖς, καὶ θρηνεῖν
6 ἀνακαλουμένους τὰ τῶν θεῶν ὀνόματα. διὰ ταύτην δὲ τὴν αἰτίαν καὶ τὴν νῆσον ταύτην ἄβατον
εἶναι τοῖς παριοῦσι.¹ καὶ πάντας τοὺς τὴν
Θηβαΐδα κατοικοῦντας, ἥπερ ἐστὶν ἀρχαιοτάτη
τῆς Αἰγύπτου, μέγιστον ὅρκον κρίνειν, ὅταν τις
τὸν Ὄσιριν τὸν ἐν Φίλαις κείμενον ὀμόσῃ.

Τὰ μὲν οὖν ἀνευρεθέντα τοῦ Ὀσίριδος μέρη
ταφῆς ἀξιωθῆναί φασι τὸν εἰρημένον τρόπον, τὸ
δὲ αἰδοῖον ὑπὸ μὲν Τυφῶνος εἰς τὸν ποταμὸν
ῥιφῆναι λέγουσι² διὰ τὸ μηδένα τῶν συνεργη-
σάντων αὐτὸ λαβεῖν βουληθῆναι, ὑπὸ δὲ τῆς Ἴσιδος
οὐδὲν ἧττον τῶν ἄλλων ἀξιωθῆναι τιμῶν ἰσοθέων·
ἔν τε γὰρ τοῖς ἱεροῖς εἴδωλον αὐτοῦ κατασκευάσα-
σαν τιμᾶν καταδεῖξαι καὶ κατὰ τὰς τελετὰς καὶ
τὰς θυσίας τὰς τῷ θεῷ τούτῳ γινομένας ἐντιμότα-
τον ποιῆσαι καὶ πλείστου σεβασμοῦ τυγχάνειν.
7 διὸ καὶ τοὺς Ἕλληνας, ἐξ Αἰγύπτου παρειληφότας
τὰ περὶ τοὺς ὀργιασμοὺς καὶ τὰς Διονυσιακὰς
ἑορτάς, τιμᾶν τοῦτο τὸ μόριον ἔν τε τοῖς μυστηρίοις
καὶ ταῖς τοῦ θεοῦ τούτου τελεταῖς τε καὶ θυσίαις,
ὀνομάζοντας αὐτὸ φαλλόν.

¹ τοῖς παριοῦσι Vogel, following nearly all the MSS. : πλὴν
τοῖς ἱερεῦσι E, Bekker, Dindorf.
² λέγουσι deleted by Bekker, Dindorf.

referred to because of this burial as the Holy Field.
In proof of this they point to remains which still
survive on this island, both to the tomb constructed
for Osiris, which is honoured in common by all the
priests of Egypt, and to the three hundred and sixty
libation bowls which are placed around it; for the
priests appointed over these bowls fill them each day
with milk, singing all the while a dirge in which they
call upon the names of these gods. It is for this
reason that travellers are not allowed to set foot on
this island. And all the inhabitants of the Thebaid,
which is the oldest portion of Egypt, hold it to be the
strongest oath when a man swears " by Osiris who
lieth in Philae."

Now the parts of the body of Osiris which were
found were honoured with burial, they say, in the
manner described above, but the privates, according
to them, were thrown by Typhon into the Nile
because no one of his accomplices was willing to take
them. Yet Isis thought them as worthy of divine
honours as the other parts, for, fashioning a likeness
of them, she set it up in the temples, commanded
that it be honoured, and made it the object of the
highest regard and reverence in the rites and sacrifices accorded to the god. Consequently the Greeks
too, inasmuch as they received from Egypt the cele-
brations of the orgies and the festivals connected
with Dionysus, honour this member in both the
mysteries and the initiatory rites and sacrifices of
this god, giving it the name " phallus." [1]

[1] P. Foucart (*Le Culte de Dionysos en Attique*) maintained
the Egyptian origin of the rites of Dionysus, but his view was
strongly opposed by L. R. Farnell (*The Cults of the Greek
City States*, 5. pp. 174 ff.).

23. Εἶναι δὲ ἔτη φασὶν ἀπὸ Ὀσίριδος καὶ Ἴσιδος ἕως τῆς Ἀλεξάνδρου βασιλείας τοῦ κτίσαντος ἐν Αἰγύπτῳ τὴν ἐπώνυμον αὐτοῦ πόλιν πλείω τῶν μυρίων, ὡς δ᾽ ἔνιοι γράφουσι, βραχὺ
2 λείποντα τῶν δισμυρίων καὶ τρισχιλίων. τοὺς δὲ λέγοντας ἐν Θήβαις τῆς Βοιωτίας γεγονέναι τὸν θεὸν ἐκ Σεμέλης καὶ Διός φασι σχεδιάζειν. Ὀρφέα γὰρ εἰς Αἴγυπτον παραβαλόντα καὶ μετασχόντα τῆς τελετῆς καὶ τῶν Διονυσιακῶν μυστηρίων μεταλαβεῖν,[1] τοῖς δὲ[2] Καδμείοις φίλον ὄντα καὶ τιμώμενον ὑπ᾽ αὐτῶν μεταθεῖναι τοῦ θεοῦ τὴν γένεσιν ἐκείνοις χαριζόμενον· τοὺς δ᾽ ὄχλους τὰ μὲν διὰ τὴν ἄγνοιαν, τὰ δὲ διὰ τὸ βούλεσθαι τὸν θεὸν Ἕλληνα νομίζεσθαι, προσδέξασθαι προσηνῶς τὰς τελετὰς καὶ τὰ μυσ-
3 τήρια. ἀφορμὰς δ᾽ ἔχειν τὸν Ὀρφέα πρὸς τὴν μετάθεσιν τῆς τοῦ θεοῦ γενέσεώς τε καὶ τελετῆς τοιαύτας.

4 Κάδμον ἐκ Θηβῶν ὄντα τῶν Αἰγυπτίων γεννῆσαι σὺν ἄλλοις τέκνοις καὶ Σεμέλην, ταύτην δὲ ὑφ᾽ ὅτου δήποτε[3] φθαρεῖσαν ἔγκυον γενέσθαι, καὶ τεκεῖν ἑπτὰ μηνῶν διελθόντων βρέφος τὴν ὄψιν οἱόνπερ οἱ κατ᾽ Αἴγυπτον τὸν Ὄσιριν γεγονέναι νομίζουσι· ζωογονεῖσθαι δ᾽ οὐκ εἰωθέναι τὸ τοιοῦτο, εἴτε τῶν θεῶν μὴ βουλομένων εἴτε
5 τῆς φύσεως μὴ συγχωρούσης. Κάδμον δ᾽ αἰσθόμενον τὸ γεγονός, καὶ χρησμὸν ἔχοντα διατηρεῖν τὰ τῶν πατέρων νόμιμα, χρυσῶσαί τε τὸ βρέφος καὶ τὰς καθηκούσας αὐτῷ ποιήσασθαι θυσίας,

---

[1] μεταλαβεῖν Vogel : μεταλαβόντα A E, Bekker, Dindorf.
[2] δὲ Vogel : τε D, Bekker, Dindorf.
[3] So Stephanus : ὑπὸ τοῦ δήποτε.

23. The number of years from Osiris and Isis, they say, to the reign of Alexander, who founded the city which bears his name in Egypt, is over ten thousand, but, according to other writers, a little less than twenty-three thousand. And those who say that the god[1] was born of Semelê and Zeus in Boeotian Thebes are, according to the priests, simply inventing the tale. For they say that Orpheus, upon visiting Egypt and participating in the initiation and mysteries of Dionysus, adopted them and as a favour to the descendants of Cadmus, since he was kindly disposed to them and received honours at their hands, transferred the birth of the god to Thebes; and the common people, partly out of ignorance and partly out of their desire to have the god thought to be a Greek, eagerly accepted his initiatory rites and mysteries. What led Orpheus to transfer the birth and rites of the god, they say, was something like this.

Cadmus, who was a citizen of Egyptian Thebes, begat several children, of whom one was Semelê; she was violated by an unknown person, became pregnant, and after seven months gave birth to a child whose appearance was such as the Egyptians hold had been that of Osiris. Now such a child is not usually brought into the world alive, either because it is contrary to the will of the gods or because the law of nature does not admit of it. But when Cadmus found out what had taken place, having at the same time a reply from an oracle commanding him to observe the laws of his fathers, he both gilded the infant and paid it the appropriate sacrifices, on the ground that there had been a sort of

331 B.C.

[1] Dionysus.

73

ὡς ἐπιφανείας τινὸς κατ' ἀνθρώπους Ὀσίριδος
6 γεγενημένης. ἀνάψαι δὲ καὶ τὴν γένεσιν εἰς
Δία, σεμνύνοντα τὸν Ὄσιριν καὶ τῆς φθαρείσης
τὴν διαβολὴν ἀφαιρούμενον· διὸ καὶ παρὰ τοῖς
Ἕλλησιν ἐκδοθῆναι λόγον ὡς ἡ Κάδμου Σεμέλη
τέτοκεν ἐκ Διὸς Ὄσιριν. ἐν δὲ τοῖς ὕστερον
χρόνοις Ὀρφέα, μεγάλην ἔχοντα δόξαν παρὰ τοῖς
Ἕλλησιν ἐπὶ μελῳδίᾳ καὶ τελεταῖς καὶ θεολογίαις,
ἐπιξενωθῆναι τοῖς Καδμείοις καὶ διαφερόντως
7 ἐν ταῖς Θήβαις τιμηθῆναι. μετεσχηκότα δὲ
τῶν παρ' Αἰγυπτίοις θεολογουμένων μετενεγκεῖν
τὴν Ὀσίριδος τοῦ παλαιοῦ γένεσιν ἐπὶ τοὺς
νεωτέρους χρόνους, χαριζόμενον δὲ τοῖς Καδμείοις
ἐνστήσασθαι καινὴν τελετήν, καθ' ἣν παραδοῦναι
τοῖς μυουμένοις ἐκ Σεμέλης καὶ Διὸς γεγεννῆσθαι
τὸν Διόνυσον. τοὺς δ' ἀνθρώπους τὰ μὲν διὰ τὴν
ἄγνοιαν ἐξαπατωμένους, τὰ δὲ διὰ τὴν Ὀρφέως
ἀξιοπιστίαν καὶ δόξαν ἐν τοῖς τοιούτοις προσ-
έχοντας, τὸ δὲ μέγιστον ἡδέως προσδεχομένους
τὸν θεὸν Ἕλληνα νομιζόμενον, καθάπερ προείρη-
8 ται, χρήσασθαι ταῖς τελεταῖς. ἔπειτα παρα-
λαβόντων τῶν μυθογράφων καὶ ποιητῶν τὸ
γένος, ἐμπεπλῆσθαι τὰ θέατρα, καὶ τοῖς ἐπιγινομένοις ἰσχυρὰν πίστιν καὶ ἀμετάθετον γενέσθαι.

Καθόλου δέ φασι τοὺς Ἕλληνας ἐξιδιάζεσθαι
τοὺς ἐπιφανεστάτους ἥρωάς τε καὶ θεούς, ἔτι
δ' ἀποικίας τὰς παρ' ἑαυτῶν.

24. Καὶ γὰρ Ἡρακλέα τὸ γένος Αἰγύπτιον

---

[1] i.e., an appearance in the flesh of a deity. Cp. Book 2.
47. 6 f., where it is related that Apollo visited the Hyper-
boreans every nineteen years at the time of the vernal
equinox.

epiphany [1] of Osiris among men. The fatherhood of the child he attributed to Zeus, in this way magnifying Osiris and averting slander from his violated daughter; and this is the reason why the tale was given out among the Greeks to the effect that Semelê, the daughter of Cadmus, was the mother of Osiris by Zeus. Now at a later time Orpheus, who was held in high regard among the Greeks for his singing, initiatory rites, and instructions on things divine, was entertained as a guest by the descendants of Cadmus and accorded unusual honours in Thebes. And since he had become conversant with the teachings of the Egyptians about the gods, he transferred the birth of the ancient Osiris to more recent times, and, out of regard for the descendants of Cadmus, instituted a new initiation, in the ritual of which the initiates were given the account that Dionysus had been born of Semelê and Zeus. And the people observed these initiatory rites, partly because they were deceived through their ignorance, partly because they were attracted to them by the trustworthiness of Orpheus and his reputation in such matters, and most of all because they were glad to receive the god as a Greek, which, as has been said, is what he was considered to be. Later, after the writers of myths and poets had taken over this account of his ancestry, the theatres became filled with it and among following generations faith in the story grew stubborn and immutable.

In general, they say, the Greeks appropriate to themselves the most renowned of both Egyptian heroes and gods, and so also the colonies sent out by them.

24. Heracles, for instance, was by birth an

ὄντα, δι᾽ ἀνδρείαν ἐπελθεῖν πολλὴν τῆς οἰκουμένης, καὶ τὴν ἐπὶ τῆς Λιβύης θέσθαι στήλην·
2 ὑπὲρ οὗ πειρῶνται τὰς ἀποδείξεις παρὰ τῶν
Ἑλλήνων λαμβάνειν. ὁμολογουμένου γὰρ ὄντος
παρὰ πᾶσιν ὅτι τοῖς Ὀλυμπίοις θεοῖς Ἡρακλῆς
συνηγωνίσατο τὸν πρὸς τοὺς γίγαντας πόλεμον,
φασὶ τῇ γῇ μηδαμῶς ἁρμόττειν γεγεννηκέναι τοὺς
γίγαντας κατὰ τὴν ἡλικίαν ἣν οἱ Ἕλληνές φασιν
Ἡρακλέα γεγενῆσθαι, γενεᾷ πρότερον τῶν
Τρωικῶν, ἀλλὰ μᾶλλον, ὡς αὐτοὶ λέγουσι, κατὰ
τὴν ἐξ ἀρχῆς γένεσιν τῶν ἀνθρώπων· ἀπ᾽ ἐκείνης
μὲν γὰρ παρ᾽ Αἰγυπτίοις ἔτη καταριθμεῖσθαι
πλείω τῶν μυρίων, ἀπὸ δὲ τῶν Τρωικῶν ἐλάττω
3 τῶν χιλίων καὶ διακοσίων. ὁμοίως δὲ τό τε
ῥόπαλον καὶ τὴν λεοντῆν τῷ παλαιῷ πρέπειν
Ἡρακλεῖ διὰ τὸ κατ᾽ ἐκείνους τοὺς χρόνους μήπω
τῶν ὅπλων εὑρημένων τοὺς ἀνθρώπους τοῖς μὲν
ξύλοις ἀμύνεσθαι τοὺς ἀντιταττομένους, ταῖς δὲ
δοραῖς τῶν θηρίων σκεπαστηρίοις ὅπλοις χρῆσθαι.
καὶ Διὸς μὲν υἱὸν αὐτὸν ἀναγορεύουσι, μητρὸς δὲ
4 ἧς ἐστιν οὔ φασι γινώσκειν. τὸν δ᾽ ἐξ Ἀλκμήνης
γενόμενον ὕστερον πλείοσιν ἔτεσιν ἢ μυρίοις,
Ἀλκαῖον ἐκ γενετῆς καλούμενον, ὕστερον Ἡρακλέα
μετονομασθῆναι, οὐχ ὅτι δι᾽ Ἥραν ἔσχε κλέος, ὥς
φησιν ὁ Μᾶτρις, ἀλλ᾽ ὅτι τὴν αὐτὴν ἐζηλωκὼς
προαίρεσιν Ἡρακλεῖ τῷ παλαιῷ τὴν ἐκείνου
δόξαν ἅμα καὶ προσηγορίαν ἐκληρονόμησε.

---

[1] The Pillars of Heracles are described in Book 4. 18. 4–7.
[2] Heracles, according to Greek mythology, was a contemporary of Laomedon, the father of Priam king of Troy,
and with the help of Poseidon built for him the walls of
Troy.

Egyptian, who by virtue of his manly vigour visited a large part of the inhabited world and set up his pillar in Libya;[1] and their proofs of this assertion they endeavour to draw from the Greeks themselves. For inasmuch as it is generally accepted that Heracles fought on the side of the Olympian gods in their war against the Giants, they say that it in no way accords with the age of the earth for the Giants to have been born in the period when, as the Greeks say, Heracles lived, which was a generation before the Trojan War,[2] but rather at the time, as their own account gives it, when mankind first appeared on the earth; for from the latter time to the present the Egyptians reckon more than ten thousand years, but from the Trojan War less than twelve hundred. Likewise, both the club and the lion's skin are appropriate to their ancient Heracles, because in those days arms had not yet been invented, and men defended themselves against their enemies with clubs of wood and used the hides of animals for defensive armour. They also designate him as the son of Zeus, but about the identity of his mother they say that they know nothing. The son of Alcmenê, who was born more than ten thousand years later and was called Alcaeus[3] at birth, in later life became known instead as Heracles, not because he gained glory (*kleos*) by the aid of Hera, as Matris says, but because, having avowed the same principles as the ancient Heracles, he inherited that one's fame and name as well.[4]

[3] Alcaeus was the name of the grandfather of Heracles. The career of Heracles is recounted in Book 4. 9 ff.

[4] The date of Matris, who was the author of an encomium upon Heracles, is unknown.

77

5 Συμφωνεῖν δὲ τοῖς ὑφ᾽ ἑαυτῶν λεγομένοις καὶ τὴν παρὰ τοῖς Ἕλλησιν ἐκ πολλῶν χρόνων παραδεδομένην φήμην, ὅτι καθαρὰν τὴν γῆν τῶν θηρίων ἐποίησεν Ἡρακλῆς· ὅπερ μηδαμῶς ἁρμόττειν τῷ γεγονότι σχεδὸν κατὰ τοὺς Τρωικοὺς χρόνους, ὅτε τὰ πλεῖστα μέρη τῆς οἰκουμένης ἐξημέρωτο γεωργίαις καὶ πόλεσι καὶ πλήθει τῶν 6 κατοικούντων τὴν χώραν πανταχοῦ. μᾶλλον οὖν πρέπειν τῷ γεγονότι κατὰ τοὺς ἀρχαίους χρόνους τὴν ἡμέρωσιν τῆς χώρας, κατισχυομένων ἔτι τῶν ἀνθρώπων ὑπὸ τοῦ πλήθους τῶν θηρίων, καὶ μάλιστα κατὰ τὴν Αἴγυπτον ἧς [1] τὴν ὑπερκειμένην χώραν μέχρι τοῦ νῦν ἔρημον εἶναι [2] 7 καὶ θηριώδη. εἰκὸς γὰρ ταύτης ὡς πατρίδος προνοηθέντα τὸν Ἡρακλέα, καὶ καθαρὰν τὴν γῆν τῶν θηρίων ποιήσαντα, παραδοῦναι τοῖς γεωργοῖς τὴν χώραν, καὶ διὰ τὴν εὐεργεσίαν τυχεῖν ἰσοθέου 8 τιμῆς. φασὶ δὲ καὶ τὸν Περσέα γεγονέναι κατ᾽ Αἴγυπτον, καὶ τῆς Ἴσιδος τὴν γένεσιν ὑπὸ τῶν Ἑλλήνων εἰς Ἄργος μεταφέρεσθαι, μυθολογούντων τὴν Ἰὼ τὴν εἰς βοὸς τύπον μεταμορφωθεῖσαν.

25. Καθόλου δὲ πολλή τίς ἐστι διαφωνία περὶ τούτων τῶν θεῶν. τὴν αὐτὴν γὰρ οἱ μὲν Ἶσιν, οἱ δὲ Δήμητραν, οἱ δὲ Θεσμοφόρον, οἱ δὲ Σελήνην, οἱ δὲ Ἥραν, οἱ δὲ πάσαις ταῖς προσηγορίαις 2 ὀνομάζουσι. τὸν δὲ Ὄσιριν οἱ μὲν Σάραπιν, οἱ δὲ Διόνυσον, οἱ δὲ Πλούτωνα, οἱ δὲ Ἄμμωνα, τινὲς δὲ Δία, πολλοὶ δὲ Πᾶνα τὸν αὐτὸν νενομίκασι· λέγουσι δέ τινες Σάραπιν εἶναι τὸν παρὰ τοῖς Ἕλλησι Πλούτωνα ὀνομαζόμενον.

---

[1] For ἧς Vogel reads καὶ and retains οὖσαν below.
[2] εἶναι Dindorf : οὖσαν.

The account of the Egyptians agrees also with the tradition which has been handed down among the Greeks since very early times, to the effect that Heracles cleared the earth of wild beasts, a story which is in no way suitable for a man who lived in approximately the period of the Trojan War, when most parts of the inhabited world had already been reclaimed from their wild state by agriculture and cities and the multitude of men settled everywhere over the land. Accordingly this reclamation of the land suits better a man who lived in early times, when men were still held in subjection by the vast numbers of wild beasts, a state of affairs which was especially true in the case of Egypt, the upper part of which is to this day desert and infested with wild beasts. Indeed it is reasonable to suppose that the first concern of Heracles was for this country as his birthplace, and that, after he had cleared the land of wild beasts, he presented it to the peasants, and for this benefaction was accorded divine honours. And they say that Perseus also was born in Egypt, and that the origin of Isis is transferred by the Greeks to Argos in the myth which tells of that Io who was changed into a heifer.

25. In general, there is great disagreement over these gods. For the same goddess is called by some Isis, by others Demeter, by others Thesmophorus, by others Selenê, by others Hera, while still others apply to her all these names. Osiris has been given the name Sarapis by some, Dionysus by others, Pluto by others, Ammon by others, Zeus by some, and many have considered Pan to be the same god; and some say that Sarapis is the god whom the Greeks call Pluto.

Φασὶ δ' Αἰγύπτιοι τὴν Ἶσιν φαρμάκων τε πολλῶν πρὸς ὑγίειαν εὑρέτιν γεγονέναι καὶ τῆς ἰατρικῆς ἐπιστήμης μεγάλην ἔχειν ἐμπειρίαν·
3 διὸ καὶ τυχοῦσαν τῆς ἀθανασίας ἐπὶ ταῖς θεραπείαις τῶν ἀνθρώπων μάλιστα χαίρειν, καὶ κατὰ τοὺς ὕπνους τοῖς ἀξιοῦσι διδόναι βοηθήματα, φανερῶς ἐπιδεικνυμένην τήν τε ἰδίαν ἐπιφάνειαν καὶ τὸ πρὸς τοὺς δεομένους τῶν ἀνθρώπων
4 εὐεργετικόν. ἀποδείξεις δὲ τούτων φασὶ φέρειν ἑαυτοὺς οὐ μυθολογίας ὁμοίως τοῖς Ἕλλησιν, ἀλλὰ πράξεις ἐναργεῖς· πᾶσαν γὰρ σχεδὸν τὴν οἰκουμένην μαρτυρεῖν ἑαυτοῖς, εἰς τὰς ταύτης τιμὰς φιλοτιμουμένην διὰ τὴν ἐν ταῖς θεραπείαις
5 ἐπιφάνειαν. κατὰ γὰρ τοὺς ὕπνους ἐφισταμένην διδόναι τοῖς κάμνουσι βοηθήματα πρὸς τὰς νόσους, καὶ τοὺς ὑπακούσαντας αὐτῇ παραδόξως ὑγιάζεσθαι· καὶ πολλοὺς μὲν ὑπὸ τῶν ἰατρῶν διὰ τὴν δυσκολίαν τοῦ νοσήματος ἀπελπισθέντας ὑπὸ ταύτης σώζεσθαι, συχνοὺς δὲ παντελῶς πηρωθέντας τὰς ὁράσεις ἤ τινα τῶν ἄλλων μερῶν τοῦ σώματος, ὅταν πρὸς ταύτην τὴν θεὸν καταφύγωσιν, εἰς τὴν προϋπάρξασαν ἀποκαθί-
6 στασθαι τάξιν. εὑρεῖν δ' αὐτὴν καὶ τὸ τῆς ἀθανασίας φάρμακον, δι' οὗ τὸν υἱὸν Ὧρον, ὑπὸ τῶν Τιτάνων ἐπιβουλευθέντα καὶ νεκρὸν εὑρεθέντα καθ' ὕδατος, μὴ μόνον ἀναστῆσαι, δοῦσαν

---

[1] A reference to the common practice of incubation, briefly described below. The patients spent the nights in the temple-precincts and were ministered to in their sleep by the god. An interesting picture of such an incubation is in

As for Isis, the Egyptians say that she was the discoverer of many health-giving drugs and was greatly versed in the science of healing; consequently, now that she has attained immortality, she finds her greatest delight in the healing of mankind and gives aid in their sleep [1] to those who call upon her, plainly manifesting both her very presence and her beneficence towards men who ask her help. In proof of this, as they say, they advance not legends, as the Greeks do, but manifest facts; for practically the entire inhabited world [2] is their witness, in that it eagerly contributes to the honours of Isis because she manifests herself in healings. For standing above the sick in their sleep she gives them aid for their diseases and works remarkable cures upon such as submit themselves to her; and many who have been despaired of by their physicians because of the difficult nature of their malady are restored to health by her, while numbers who have altogether lost the use of their eyes or of some other part of their body, whenever they turn for help to this goddess, are restored to their previous condition. Furthermore, she discovered also the drug which gives immortality, by means of which she not only raised from the dead her son Horus, who had been the object of plots on the part of the Titans and had been found dead under the water, giving him his

Aristophanes, *Plutus*, 659 ff., where a description is given of how the god of wealth, who because of his blindness distributes his gifts with little discrimination, is taken to the temple of Asclepius to be healed.

[2] Under the influence of the Ptolemies, soon after 300 B.C., the cult of Isis began to spread over the Mediterranean, and by the time of Diodorus was in practically every city of any importance.

τὴν ψυχήν, ἀλλὰ καὶ τῆς ἀθανασίας ποιῆσαι
7 μεταλαβεῖν. δοκεῖ δ' ὕστατος τῶν θεῶν οὗτος
βασιλεῦσαι μετὰ τὴν τοῦ πατρὸς Ὀσίριδος ἐξ
ἀνθρώπων μετάστασιν. τὸν δὲ Ὧρον μεθερμη-
νευόμενόν φασιν Ἀπόλλωνα ὑπάρχειν, καὶ τήν
τε ἰατρικὴν καὶ τὴν μαντικὴν ὑπὸ τῆς μητρὸς
Ἴσιδος διδαχθέντα διὰ τῶν χρησμῶν καὶ τῶν
θεραπειῶν εὐεργετεῖν τὸ τῶν ἀνθρώπων γένος.
26. Οἱ δ' ἱερεῖς τῶν Αἰγυπτίων τὸν χρόνον
ἀπὸ τῆς Ἡλίου βασιλείας συλλογιζόμενοι μέχρι
τῆς Ἀλεξάνδρου διαβάσεως εἰς τὴν Ἀσίαν φασὶν
ὑπάρχειν ἐτῶν μάλιστά πως δισμυρίων καὶ
2 τρισχιλίων. μυθολογοῦσι δὲ καὶ τῶν θεῶν τοὺς
μὲν ἀρχαιοτάτους βασιλεῦσαι πλείω τῶν χιλίων
καὶ διακοσίων ἐτῶν, τοὺς δὲ μεταγενεστέρους οὐκ
3 ἐλάττω τῶν τριακοσίων. ἀπίστου δ' ὄντος τοῦ
πλήθους τῶν ἐτῶν, ἐπιχειροῦσί τινες λέγειν ὅτι
τὸ παλαιόν, οὔπω τῆς περὶ τὸν ἥλιον κινήσεως
ἐπεγνωσμένης, συνέβαινε κατὰ τὴν τῆς σελήνης
4 περίοδον ἄγεσθαι τὸν ἐνιαυτόν. διόπερ τῶν ἐτῶν
τριακονθημέρων ὄντων οὐκ ἀδύνατον εἶναι βεβιω-
κέναι τινὰς ἔτη χίλια καὶ διακόσια· καὶ γὰρ νῦν
δωδεκαμήνων[1] ὄντων τῶν ἐνιαυτῶν οὐκ ὀλίγους
5 ὑπὲρ ἑκατὸν ἔτη ζῆν. παραπλήσια δὲ λέγουσι
καὶ περὶ τῶν τριακόσια ἔτη δοκούντων ἄρξαι·
κατ' ἐκείνους γὰρ τοὺς χρόνους τὸν ἐνιαυτὸν
ἀπαρτίζεσθαι τέτταρσι μησὶ τοῖς γινομένοις κατὰ
τὰς ἑκάστων τῶν χρόνων ὥρας, οἷον ἔαρος,
θέρους, χειμῶνος· ἀφ' ἧς αἰτίας καὶ παρ' ἐνίοις
τῶν Ἑλλήνων τοὺς ἐνιαυτοὺς ὥρους καλεῖσθαι

---

[1] δωδεκαμήνων Dindorf : δυοκαίδεκα μηνῶν.

soul again, but also made him immortal. And it appears that Horus was the last of the gods to be king after his father Osiris departed from among men. Moreover, they say that the name Horus, when translated, is Apollo, and that, having been instructed by his mother Isis in both medicine and divination, he is now a benefactor of the race of men through his oracular responses and his healings.

26. The priests of the Egyptians, reckoning the time from the reign of Helius to the crossing of Alexander into Asia, say that it was in round numbers twenty-three thousand years. And, as their legends say, the most ancient of the gods ruled more than twelve hundred years and the later ones not less than three hundred. But since this great number of years surpasses belief, some men would maintain that in early times, before the movement of the sun had as yet been recognized, it was customary to reckon the year by the lunar cycle. Consequently, since the year consisted of thirty days, it was not impossible that some men lived twelve hundred years; for in our own time, when our year consists of twelve months, not a few men live over one hundred years. A similar explanation they also give regarding those who are supposed to have reigned for three hundred years; for at their time, namely, the year was composed of the four months which comprise the seasons of each year, that is, spring, summer, and winter; and it is for this reason that among some of the Greeks the years are called

334 B.O.

καὶ τὰς κατ' ἔτος ἀναγραφὰς ὡρογραφίας προσαγορεύεσθαι.

6 Οἱ δ' οὖν Αἰγύπτιοι μυθολογοῦσι κατὰ τὴν
Ἴσιδος ἡλικίαν γεγονέναι τινὰς πολυσωμάτους
τοὺς ὑπὸ μὲν τῶν Ἑλλήνων ὀνομαζομένους γίγαντας, ὑφ' ἑαυτῶν δὲ . . .[1] διακοσμουμένους
τερατωδῶς ἐπὶ τῶν ἱερῶν καὶ τυπτομένους ὑπὸ
7 τῶν περὶ τὸν Ὄσιριν. ἔνιοι μὲν οὖν αὐτοὺς
γηγενεῖς φασιν ὑπάρξαι, προσφάτου τῆς τῶν
ζῴων γενέσεως ἐκ τῆς γῆς ὑπαρχούσης, ἔνιοι
δὲ λέγουσι σώματος ῥώμῃ διενεγκόντας καὶ
πολλὰς πράξεις ἐπιτελεσαμένους ἀπὸ τοῦ συμβε-
8 βηκότος μυθολογηθῆναι πολυσωμάτους. συμφωνεῖται δὲ παρὰ τοῖς πλείστοις ὅτι τοῖς περὶ τὸν
Δία καὶ τὸν Ὄσιριν θεοῖς πόλεμον ἐνστησάμενοι
πάντες ἀνῃρέθησαν.

27. Νομοθετῆσαι δέ φασι τοὺς Αἰγυπτίους
παρὰ τὸ κοινὸν ἔθος τῶν ἀνθρώπων γαμεῖν
ἀδελφὰς διὰ τὸ γεγονὸς ἐν τούτοις τῆς Ἴσιδος
ἐπίτευγμα· ταύτην γὰρ συνοικήσασαν Ὀσίριδι
τῷ ἀδελφῷ, καὶ ἀποθανόντος ὀμόσασαν οὐδενὸς
ἔτι συνουσίαν ἀνδρὸς προσδέξεσθαι,[2] μετελθεῖν
τόν τε φόνον τἀνδρὸς καὶ διατελέσαι βασιλεύουσαν νομιμώτατα, καὶ τὸ σύνολον πλείστων καὶ
μεγίστων ἀγαθῶν αἰτίαν γενέσθαι πᾶσιν ἀνθρώ-
2 ποις. διὰ δὴ ταύτας τὰς αἰτίας καταδειχθῆναι
μείζονος ἐξουσίας καὶ τιμῆς τυγχάνειν τὴν

---

[1] Vogel suggests that a noun has dropped out here.
[2] προσδέξεσθαι Dindorf: προσδέξασθαι.

---

[1] " Records of the seasons.'' This designation for yearly
records was used, for instance, by the inhabitants of the
island of Naxos.

" seasons " (*horoi*) and that their yearly records are given the name " horographs."[1]

Furthermore, the Egyptians relate in their myths that in the time of Isis there were certain creatures of many bodies, who are called by the Greeks Giants,[2] but by themselves . . ., these being the men who are represented on their temples in monstrous form and as being cudgelled by Osiris. Now some say that they were born of the earth at the time when the genesis of living things from the earth was still recent,[3] while some hold that they were only men of unusual physical strength who achieved many deeds and for this reason were described in the myths as of many bodies. But it is generally agreed that when they stirred up war against Zeus and Osiris they were all destroyed.

27. The Egyptians also made a law, they say, contrary to the general custom of mankind, permitting men to marry their sisters, this being due to the success attained by Isis in this respect; for she had married her brother Osiris, and upon his death, having taken a vow never to marry another man, she both avenged the murder of her husband and reigned all her days over the land with complete respect for the laws, and, in a word, became the cause of more and greater blessings to all men than any other. It is for these reasons, in fact, that it was ordained that the queen should have greater

[2] But the Giants of Greek mythology were represented with "huge," not "many," bodies.

[3] Cp. *Genesis* 6. 4 : " 'There were giants in the earth in those days ; and also after that, when the sons of God came in unto the daughters of men, and they bare children to them, the same became mighty men, which were of old, men of renown."

βασίλισσαν τοῦ βασιλέως, καὶ παρὰ τοῖς ἰδιώταις
κυριεύειν τὴν γυναῖκα τἀνδρός, ἐν τῇ τῆς προικὸς
συγγραφῇ προσομολογούντων τῶν γαμούντων
ἅπαντα πειθαρχήσειν τῇ γαμουμένῃ.[1]

3 Οὐκ ἀγνοῶ δὲ διότι τινὲς τῶν συγγραφέων
ἀποφαίνονται τοὺς τάφους τῶν θεῶν τούτων
ὑπάρχειν ἐν Νύσῃ τῆς Ἀραβίας, ἀφ' ἧς καὶ
Νυσαῖον τὸν Διόνυσον ὠνομάσθαι. εἶναι δὲ καὶ
στήλην ἑκατέρου τῶν θεῶν ἐπιγεγραμμένην τοῖς
4 ἱεροῖς γράμμασιν. ἐπὶ μὲν οὖν τῆς Ἴσιδος ἐπιγεγράφθαι " Ἐγὼ Ἶσίς εἰμι ἡ βασίλισσα πάσης
χώρας, ἡ παιδευθεῖσα ὑπὸ Ἑρμοῦ, καὶ ὅσα ἐγὼ
ἐνομοθέτησα, οὐδεὶς αὐτὰ δύναται λῦσαι. ἐγώ

---

[1] Here A B D E N add: ταφῆναι δὲ λέγουσι τὴν Ἶσιν ἐν
Μέμφει, καθ' ἣν μέχρι τοῦ νῦν δείκνυσθαι τὸν σηκόν, ἐν τῷ
τεμένει τοῦ Ἡφαίστου. ἔνιοι δέ φασι τὰ σώματα τῶν θεῶν
τούτων [κεῖσθαι κατὰ τὴν ἐν Φίλαις τοῦ Νείλου νῆσον, ὥσπερ
προείρηταί μοι added by A E N which stop at this point, B D
continuing] ἐπὶ τῶν ὅρων κεῖσθαι τῆς Αἰθιοπίας καὶ τῆς Αἰγύπτου
κατὰ τὴν ἐν τῷ Νείλῳ νῆσον, τὴν κειμένην μὲν ἐπὶ ταῖς Φίλαις,
ἔχουσαν δὲ τὸ προσαγορευόμενον ἀπὸ τοῦ συμβεβηκότος ἱερὸν
πεδίον· σημεῖον δὲ τούτου δεικνύουσιν ἐν τῇ νήσῳ ταύτῃ διαμένοντα τόν τε τάφον κατεσκευασμένον Ὀσίριδι, κοινῇ τιμώμενον
ὑπὸ τῶν κατ' Αἴγυπτον ἱερέων· καί φασι περὶ τούτου κειμένας
χοὰς ἑξήκοντα καὶ τριακοσίας· ταύτας γὰρ καθ' ἑκάστην ἡμέραν
γάλακτος πληροῦν τοὺς πρὸς τούτοις ταχθέντας ἱερεῖς καὶ θρηνεῖν
ἀνακαλουμένους τὰ τῶν θεῶν ὀνόματα. διὰ ταύτην δὲ τὴν αἰτίαν
καὶ τὴν νῆσον ἄβατον εἶναι πλὴν τοῖς ἱερεῦσι. καὶ πάντας τοὺς
τὴν Θηβαΐδα κατοικοῦντας, ἥπερ ἐστὶν ἀρχαιοτάτη τῆς Αἰγύπτου,
μέγιστον ὅρκον κρίνειν, ὅταν τις Ὄσιριν τὸν ἐν Φίλαις κείμενον
ὀμόσῃ.

power and honour than the king and that among private persons the wife should enjoy authority over her husband,[1] the husbands agreeing in the marriage contract that they will be obedient in all things to their wives.[2]

Now I am not unaware that some historians give the following account of Isis and Osiris: The tombs of these gods lie in Nysa in Arabia, and for this reason Dionysus is also called Nysaeus. And in that place there stands also a stele of each of the gods bearing an inscription in hieroglyphs. On the stele of Isis it runs: " I am Isis, the queen of every land, she who was instructed of Hermes, and whatsoever laws I have established, these can no man make

---

[1] Cp. Sophocles, *Oedipus at Colonus*, 337 ff.:

> Their thoughts and actions all
> Are framed and modelled on Egyptian ways.
> For there the men sit at the loom indoors
> While the wives slave abroad for daily bread.
>
> (Tr. by Storr, in *L.C.L.*)

[2] Here some MSS. add the following sentences (cp. critical note), which are taken almost bodily from chap. 22. 2-6: " And they say that Isis is buried in Memphis, where her tomb is pointed out to this day in the temple-area of Hephaestus. According to some writers, however, the bodies of these gods [rest in Philae on the island in the Nile, as I have already stated] rest on the border between Ethiopia and Egypt, on the island in the Nile which lies near Philae, but is referred to because of this burial as the Holy Field. In proof of this they point to the tomb which was constructed for Osiris on this island and is honoured in common by all the priests of Egypt; and they mention three hundred and sixty libation bowls which are placed around it; for the priests appointed over these bowls fill them each day with milk, singing all the while a dirge in which they call upon the names of these gods. It is for this reason that only the priests are allowed to set foot on this island. And all the inhabitants of the Thebaid, which is the oldest portion of Egypt, hold it to be the strongest oath when a man swears ' by Osiris who lieth in Philae.' "

εἰμὶ ἡ τοῦ νεωτάτου Κρόνου θεοῦ θυγάτηρ πρεσ-
βυτάτη· ἐγώ εἰμι γυνὴ καὶ ἀδελφὴ Ὀσίριδος
βασιλέως· ἐγώ εἰμι ἡ πρώτη καρπὸν ἀνθρώποις
εὑροῦσα· ἐγώ εἰμι μήτηρ Ὥρου τοῦ βασιλέως·
ἐγώ εἰμι ἡ ἐν τῷ ἄστρῳ τῷ ἐν τῷ κυνὶ ἐπιτέλ-
λουσα· ἐμοὶ Βούβαστος ἡ πόλις ᾠκοδομήθη.
5 χαῖρε χαῖρε Αἴγυπτε ἡ θρέψασά με." ἐπὶ δὲ
τῆς Ὀσίριδος ἐπιγεγράφθαι λέγεται " Πατὴρ μέν
ἐστί μοι Κρόνος νεώτατος θεῶν ἁπάντων, εἰμὶ δὲ
Ὄσιρις ὁ βασιλεύς, ὁ στρατεύσας ἐπὶ πᾶσαν
χώραν ἕως εἰς τοὺς ἀοικήτους τόπους τῶν Ἰνδῶν
καὶ τοὺς πρὸς ἄρκτον κεκλιμένους, μέχρι Ἴστρου
ποταμοῦ πηγῶν, καὶ πάλιν ἐπὶ τἄλλα μέρη ἕως
ὠκεανοῦ. εἰμὶ δὲ υἱὸς Κρόνου πρεσβύτατος, καὶ
βλαστὸς ἐκ καλοῦ τε καὶ εὐγενοῦς ᾠοῦ[1] σπέρμα
συγγενὲς ἐγεννήθην ἡμέρας. καὶ οὐκ ἔστι τόπος
τῆς οἰκουμένης εἰς ὃν ἐγὼ οὐκ ἀφῖγμαι, διαδοὺς
6 πᾶσιν ὧν ἐγὼ εὑρετὴς[2] ἐγενόμην." τοσαῦτα
τῶν γεγραμμένων ἐν ταῖς στήλαις φασὶ δύνασθαι
ἀναγνῶναι, τὰ δ' ἄλλα ὄντα πλείω κατεφθάρθαι
διὰ τὸν χρόνον. τὰ μὲν οὖν περὶ τῆς ταφῆς τῶν
θεῶν τούτων διαφωνεῖται παρὰ τοῖς πλείστοις διὰ
τὸ τοὺς ἱερεῖς ἐν ἀπορρήτοις παρειληφότας τὴν

---

[1] ᾠοῦ Wesseling : ᾤου C, ᾧ οὐ G, σῴου other MSS.
[2] εὑρετὴς Wesseling : εὐεργέτης.

---

[1] According to Pseudo-Eratosthenes (*Catasterismus*, 33) the
star on the head of Canis Maior was called Isis as well as Sirius.
[2] The Danube.
[3] This may be drawn from the Orphic legends which conceived of the undeveloped universe as a mystic egg, from
which came Phanes, the first principle of life. Cp. the parody
of the Orphic cosmogony in Aristophanes, *The Birds*, 693 ff.:

void. I am the eldest daughter of the youngest god
Cronus; I am the wife and sister of the king Osiris;
I am she who first discovered fruits for mankind; I
am the mother of Horus the king; I am she who
riseth in the star that is in the Constellation of
the Dog;[1] by me was the city of Bubastus built.
Farewell, farewell, O Egypt that nurtured me."
And on the stele of Osiris the inscription is said to
run: " My father is Cronus, the youngest of all the
gods, and I am Osiris the king, who campaigned
over every country as far as the uninhabited regions
of India and the lands to the north, even to the
sources of the river Ister,[2] and again to the remaining parts of the world as far as Oceanus. I am the
eldest son of Cronus, and being sprung from a fair
and noble egg[3] I was begotten a seed of kindred birth
to Day. There is no region of the inhabited world
to which I have not come, dispensing to all men the
things of which I was the discoverer." So much of
the inscriptions on the stelae can be read, they say,
but the rest of the writing, which was of greater
extent, has been destroyed by time. However this
may be, varying accounts of the burial of these gods
are found in most writers by reason of the fact that
the priests, having received the exact facts about

> There was Chaos at first, and Darkness, and Night,
>   and Tartarus vasty and dismal;
> But the Earth was not there, nor the Sky, nor the Air,
>   till at length in the bosom abysmal
> Of Darkness an egg, from the whirlwind conceived,
>   was laid by the sable-plumed Night.
> And out of that egg, as the seasons revolved,
>   sprang Love, the entrancing, the bright,
> Love brilliant and bold with his pinions of gold,
>   like a whirlwind, refulgent and sparkling!
>   (Tr. by Rogers, in *L.C.L.*)

περὶ τούτων ἀκρίβειαν μὴ βούλεσθαι τἀληθὲς
ἐκφέρειν εἰς τοὺς πολλούς, ὡς ἂν καὶ κινδύνων
ἐπικειμένων τοῖς τἀπόρρητα περὶ τῶν θεῶν τούτων
μηνύσασιν εἰς τοὺς ὄχλους.

28. Οἱ δ' οὖν Αἰγύπτιοί φασι καὶ μετὰ ταῦτα
ἀποικίας πλείστας ἐξ Αἰγύπτου κατὰ πᾶσαν
διασπαρῆναι τὴν οἰκουμένην. εἰς Βαβυλῶνα μὲν
γὰρ ἀγαγεῖν ἀποίκους Βῆλον τὸν νομιζόμενον
Ποσειδῶνος εἶναι καὶ Λιβύης· ὃν παρὰ τὸν Εὐφράτην ποταμὸν καθιδρυθέντα τούς τε ἱερεῖς καταστή-
σασθαι παραπλησίως τοῖς κατ' Αἴγυπτον ἀτελεῖς
καὶ πάσης λειτουργίας ἀπολελυμένους, οὓς
Βαβυλώνιοι καλοῦσι Χαλδαίους, τάς τε παρατηρήσεις τῶν ἄστρων τούτους ποιεῖσθαι, μιμου-
μένους τοὺς παρ' Αἰγυπτίοις ἱερεῖς καὶ φυσικούς,
2 ἔτι δὲ ἀστρολόγους. λέγουσι δὲ καὶ τοὺς περὶ
τὸν Δαναὸν ὁρμηθέντας ὁμοίως ἐκεῖθεν συνοικίσαι
τὴν ἀρχαιοτάτην σχεδὸν τῶν παρ' Ἕλλησι
πόλεων Ἄργος, τό τε τῶν Κόλχων ἔθνος ἐν τῷ
Πόντῳ καὶ τὸ τῶν Ἰουδαίων ἀνὰ μέσον Ἀραβίας
καὶ Συρίας οἰκίσαι τινὰς ὁρμηθέντας παρ' ἑαυτῶν·
3 διὸ καὶ παρὰ τοῖς γένεσι τούτοις ἐκ παλαιοῦ
παραδεδόσθαι τὸ περιτέμνειν τοὺς γεννωμένους
παῖδας, ἐξ Αἰγύπτου μετενηνεγμένου τοῦ νομίμου.
4 καὶ τοὺς Ἀθηναίους δέ φασιν ἀποίκους εἶναι
Σαϊτῶν τῶν ἐξ Αἰγύπτου, καὶ πειρῶνται τῆς
οἰκειότητος ταύτης φέρειν ἀποδείξεις· παρὰ
μόνοις γὰρ τῶν Ἑλλήνων τὴν πόλιν ἄστυ
καλεῖσθαι, μετενηνεγμένης τῆς προσηγορίας ἀπὸ
τοῦ παρ' αὐτοῖς Ἄστεος. ἔτι δὲ[1] τὴν πολιτείαν
τὴν αὐτὴν ἐσχηκέναι τάξιν καὶ διαίρεσιν τῇ παρ'

[1] δὲ Dindorf : τέ.

these matters as a secret not to be divulged, are unwilling to give out the truth to the public, on the ground that perils overhang any men who disclose to the common crowd the secret knowledge about these gods.

28. Now the Egyptians say that also after these events a great number of colonies were spread from Egypt over all the inhabited world. To Babylon, for instance, colonists were led by Belus, who was held to be the son of Poseidon and Libya; and after establishing himself on the Euphrates river he appointed priests, called Chaldaeans by the Babylonians, who were exempt from taxation and free from every kind of service to the state, as are the priests of Egypt;[1] and they also make observations of the stars, following the example of the Egyptian priests, physicists, and astrologers. They say also that those who set forth with Danaus, likewise from Egypt, settled what is practically the oldest city of Greece, Argos, and that the nation of the Colchi in Pontus and that of the Jews, which lies between Arabia and Syria, were founded as colonies by certain emigrants from their country; and this is the reason why it is a long-established institution among these two peoples to circumcise their male children, the custom having been brought over from Egypt. Even the Athenians, they say, are colonists from Saïs in Egypt, and they undertake to offer proofs of such a relationship; for the Athenians are the only Greeks who call their city " Asty," a name brought over from the city Asty in Egypt. Furthermore, their body politic had the same classification and division

---

[1] On the exemption of the priests of Egypt from taxation, cp. chap. 73; on the Chaldaeans, cp. Book 2. 29 f.

5 Αἰγυπτίοις, εἰς τρία μέρη διανεμηθείσῃ· καὶ
πρώτην μὲν ὑπάρξαι μερίδα τοὺς εὐπατρίδας
καλουμένους, οἵτινες[1] ὑπῆρχον ἐν παιδείᾳ μάλιστα διατετριφότες καὶ τῆς μεγίστης ἠξιωμένοι
τιμῆς παραπλησίως τοῖς κατ᾽ Αἴγυπτον ἱερεῦσι·
δευτέραν δὲ τάξιν γενέσθαι τὴν τῶν γεωμόρων
τῶν ὀφειλόντων ὅπλα κεκτῆσθαι καὶ πολεμεῖν
ὑπὲρ τῆς πόλεως ὁμοίως τοῖς κατ᾽ Αἴγυπτον
ὀνομαζομένοις γεωργοῖς καὶ τοὺς μαχίμους παρ-
εχομένοις· τελευταίαν δὲ μερίδα καταριθμηθῆναι
τὴν τῶν δημιουργῶν τῶν τὰς βαναύσους τέχνας
μεταχειριζομένων καὶ λειτουργίας τελούντων τὰς
ἀναγκαιοτάτας, τὸ παραπλήσιον ποιούσης τῆς
τάξεως ταύτης παρ᾽ Αἰγυπτίοις.

6 Γεγονέναι δὲ καὶ τῶν ἡγεμόνων τινὰς Αἰγυπτίους παρὰ τοῖς Ἀθηναίοις· τὸν γὰρ Πέτην τὸν
πατέρα Μενεσθέως τοῦ στρατεύσαντος εἰς Τροίαν
φανερῶς Αἰγύπτιον ὑπάρξαντα τυχεῖν ὕστερον
Ἀθήνησι πολιτείας τε καὶ βασιλείας. . . .

7 διφυοῦς δ᾽ αὐτοῦ γεγονότος, τοὺς μὲν Ἀθηναίους
μὴ δύνασθαι κατὰ τὴν ἰδίαν ὑπόστασιν ἀποδοῦναι
περὶ τῆς φύσεως ταύτης τὰς ἀληθεῖς αἰτίας, ἐν
μέσῳ κειμένου πᾶσιν ὅτι δυοῖν πολιτειῶν μετα-
σχών, Ἑλληνικῆς καὶ βαρβάρου, διφυὴς ἐνομίσθη,
τὸ μὲν ἔχων μέρος θηρίου, τὸ δὲ ἀνθρώπου.

29. Ὁμοίως δὲ τούτῳ καὶ τὸν Ἐρεχθέα λέγουσι
τὸ γένος Αἰγύπτιον ὄντα βασιλεῦσαι τῶν Ἀθηνῶν,

---

[1] οἵτινες Vogel : οἵτινες ἱεροποιοί.

---

[1] i.e. "of noble sires."
[2] i.e. "holders of a share of land."

of the people as is found in Egypt, where the citizens have been divided into three orders: the first Athenian class consisted of the "eupatrids,"[1] as they were called, being those who were such as had received the best education and were held worthy of the highest honour, as is the case with the priests of Egypt; the second was that of the "geomoroi,"[2] who were expected to possess arms and to serve in defence of the state, like those in Egypt who are known as husbandmen and supply the warriors; and the last class was reckoned to be that of the "demiurgoi,"[3] who practise the mechanical arts and render only the most menial services to the state, this class among the Egyptians having a similar function.

Moreover, certain of the rulers of Athens were originally Egyptians, they say. Petes,[4] for instance, the father of that Menestheus who took part in the expedition against Troy, having clearly been an Egyptian, later obtained citizenship at Athens and the kingship.[5] . . . He was of double form, and yet the Athenians are unable from their own point of view to give the true explanation of this nature of his, although it is patent to all that it was because of his double citizenship, Greek and barbarian, that he was held to be of double form, that is, part animal and part man.

29. In the same way, they continue, Erechtheus also, who was by birth an Egyptian, became king of

---

[3] *i.e.* "workers for the people."
[4] Called Peteus in *Iliad* 2. 552.
[5] There is a break at this point in the text, since what follows can refer only to Cecrops, the traditional first king of Athens, whose body in the lower part was that of a serpent.

τοιαύτας τινὰς φέροντες ἀποδείξεις· γενομένων
γὰρ ὁμολογουμένως αὐχμῶν μεγάλων κατὰ πᾶσαν
σχεδὸν τὴν οἰκουμένην πλὴν Αἰγύπτου διὰ τὴν
ἰδιότητα τῆς χώρας, καὶ φθορᾶς ἐπιγενομένης
τῶν τε καρπῶν καὶ πλήθους ἀνθρώπων, ἐξ
Αἰγύπτου τὸν Ἐρεχθέα κομίσαι διὰ τὴν συγγέ-
νειαν σίτου πλῆθος εἰς τὰς Ἀθήνας· ἀνθ' ὧν
τοὺς εὖ παθόντας βασιλέα καταστῆσαι τὸν
2 εὐεργέτην. τοῦτον δὲ παραλαβόντα τὴν ἡγεμονίαν καταδεῖξαι τὰς τελετὰς τῆς Δήμητρος ἐν
Ἐλευσῖνι καὶ τὰ μυστήρια ποιῆσαι, μετενεγκόντα
τὸ περὶ τούτων νόμιμον ἐξ Αἰγύπτου. καὶ τῆς[1]
θεοῦ δὲ παρουσίαν εἰς τὴν Ἀττικὴν γεγονυῖαν
κατὰ τούτους τοὺς χρόνους παραδεδόσθαι κατὰ
λόγον, ὡς ἂν τῶν ἐπωνύμων ταύτης καρπῶν τότε
κομισθέντων εἰς τὰς Ἀθήνας, καὶ διὰ τοῦτο δόξαι
πάλιν ἐξ ἀρχῆς τὴν εὕρεσιν γεγονέναι τοῦ σπέρ-
3 ματος, δωρησαμένης τῆς Δήμητρος. ὁμολογεῖν
δὲ καὶ τοὺς Ἀθηναίους ὅτι βασιλεύοντος Ἐρεχ-
θέως καὶ τῶν καρπῶν διὰ τὴν ἀνομβρίαν προ-
ηφανισμένων ἡ τῆς Δήμητρος ἐγένετο παρουσία
πρὸς αὐτοὺς καὶ ἡ δωρεὰ τοῦ σίτου. πρὸς δὲ
τούτοις αἱ τελεταὶ καὶ τὰ μυστήρια ταύτης τῆς
4 θεοῦ τότε κατεδείχθησαν ἐν Ἐλευσῖνι. τά τε
περὶ τὰς θυσίας καὶ τὰς ἀρχαιότητας ὡσαύτως
ἔχειν Ἀθηναίους καὶ τοὺς Αἰγυπτίους· τοὺς μὲν
γὰρ Εὐμολπίδας ἀπὸ τῶν κατ' Αἴγυπτον ἱερέων
μετενηνέχθαι, τοὺς δὲ Κήρυκας ἀπὸ τῶν παστο-
φόρων. τήν τε Ἶσιν μόνους τῶν Ἑλλήνων

---

[1] καὶ τῆς B N, Bekker, Vogel: καὶ τὴν τῆς Hertlein, Dindorf.

[1] The Eumolpidae ("Descendants of Eumolpus") and the

Athens, and in proof of this they offer the following considerations. Once when there was a great drought, as is generally agreed, which extended over practically all the inhabited earth except Egypt because of the peculiar character of that country, and there followed a destruction both of crops and of men in great numbers, Erechtheus, through his racial connection with Egypt, brought from there to Athens a great supply of grain, and in return those who had enjoyed this aid made their benefactor king. After he had secured the throne he instituted the initiatory rites of Demeter in Eleusis and established the mysteries, transferring their ritual from Egypt. And the tradition that an advent of the goddess into Attica also took place at that time is reasonable, since it was then that the fruits which are named after her were brought to Athens, and this is why it was thought that the discovery of the seed had been made again, as though Demeter had bestowed the gift. And the Athenians on their part agree that it was in the reign of Erechtheus, when a lack of rain had wiped out the crops, that Demeter came to them with the gift of grain. Furthermore, the initiatory rites and mysteries of this goddess were instituted in Eleusis at that time. And their sacrifices as well as their ancient ceremonies are observed by the Athenians in the same way as by the Egyptians; for the Eumolpidae were derived from the priests of Egypt and the Ceryces from the *pastophoroi*.[1] They are also the only Greeks

Ceryces ("Heralds") were two noble Athenian families, in charge of the more important religious ceremonies of Attica; the *pastophoroi* were those Egyptian priests who carried in processions small shrines of the gods.

ὀμνύειν, καὶ ταῖς ἰδέαις καὶ τοῖς ἤθεσιν ὁμοιοτά-
5 τους εἶναι τοῖς Αἰγυπτίοις. πολλὰ δὲ καὶ ἄλλα
τούτοις παραπλήσια λέγοντες φιλοτιμότερον ἤπερ
ἀληθινώτερον, ὥς γ᾽ ἐμοὶ φαίνεται, τῆς ἀποικίας
ταύτης ἀμφισβητοῦσι διὰ τὴν δόξαν τῆς πόλεως.

Καθόλου δὲ πλείστας ἀποικίας Αἰγύπτιοί
φασιν ἐκπέμψαι τοὺς ἑαυτῶν προγόνους ἐπὶ
πολλὰ μέρη τῆς οἰκουμένης διά τε τὴν ὑπεροχὴν
τῶν βασιλευσάντων παρ᾽ αὐτοῖς καὶ διὰ τὴν ὑπερ-
6 βολὴν τῆς πολυανθρωπίας· ὑπὲρ ὧν μήτε ἀπο-
δείξεως φερομένης μηδεμιᾶς ἀκριβοῦς μήτε συγγραφέως ἀξιοπίστου μαρτυροῦντος, οὐκ ἐκρίναμεν
ὑπάρχειν τὰ λεγόμενα γραφῆς ἄξια.

Καὶ περὶ μὲν τῶν θεολογουμένων παρ᾽ Αἰγυπτίοις τοσαῦθ᾽ ἡμῖν εἰρήσθω, στοχαζομένοις τῆς
συμμετρίας· περὶ δὲ τῆς χώρας καὶ τοῦ Νείλου
καὶ τῶν ἄλλων τῶν ἀκοῆς ἀξίων ἐν κεφαλαίοις
ἕκαστα διεξιέναι πειρασόμεθα.

30. Ἡ γὰρ Αἴγυπτος κεῖται μὲν μάλιστά πως
κατὰ μεσημβρίαν, ὀχυρότητι δὲ φυσικῇ καὶ
κάλλει χώρας οὐκ ὀλίγῳ δοκεῖ προέχειν τῶν εἰς
2 βασιλείαν ἀφωρισμένων τόπων. ἀπὸ μὲν γὰρ
τῆς δύσεως ὠχύρωκεν αὐτὴν ἡ ἔρημος καὶ θηριώ-
δης τῆς Λιβύης, ἐπὶ πολὺ μὲν παρεκτείνουσα,
διὰ δὲ τὴν ἀνυδρίαν καὶ τὴν σπάνιν τῆς ἁπάσης
τροφῆς ἔχουσα τὴν διέξοδον οὐ μόνον ἐπίπονον,
ἀλλὰ καὶ παντελῶς ἐπικίνδυνον· ἐκ δὲ τῶν πρὸς
νότον μερῶν οἵ τε καταράκται τοῦ Νείλου καὶ
3 τῶν ὀρῶν τὰ συνορίζοντα τούτοις· ἀπὸ γὰρ τῆς

---

[1] T. Birt (*Das antike Buchwesen*, pp. 151 ff.) feels that by
this phrase, which is often used by Diodorus, he referred to his

who swear by Isis, and they closely resemble the
Egyptians in both their appearance and manners.
By many other statements like these, spoken more
out of a love for glory than with regard for the
truth, as I see the matter, they claim Athens as a
colony of theirs because of the fame of that city.

In general, the Egyptians say that their ancestors
sent forth numerous colonies to many parts of the
inhabited world, by reason of the pre-eminence of
their former kings and their excessive population;
but since they offer no precise proof whatsoever for
these statements, and since no historian worthy of
credence testifies in their support, we have not
thought that their accounts merited recording.

So far as the ideas of the Egyptians about the
gods are concerned, let what we have said suffice,
since we are aiming at due proportion in our account,[1]
but with regard to the land, the Nile, and everything else worth hearing about we shall endeavour,
in each case, to give the several facts in summary.

30. The land of Egypt stretches in a general way
from north to south, and in natural strength and
beauty of landscape is reputed to excel in no small
degree all other regions that have been formed into
kingdoms. For on the west it is fortified by the
desert of Libya, which is full of wild beasts and
extends along its border for a long distance, and by
reason of its lack of rain and want of every kind of
food makes the passage through it not only toilsome
but even highly dangerous; while on the south the
same protection is afforded by the cataracts of the
Nile and the mountains flanking them, since from

effort to keep the several Books of his history of approximately the same size.

97

Τρωγοδυτικῆς [1] καὶ τῶν ἐσχάτων τῆς Αἰθιοπίας
μερῶν ἐντὸς σταδίων πεντακισχιλίων καὶ πεντακοσίων οὔτε πλεῦσαι διὰ τοῦ ποταμοῦ ῥᾴδιον
οὔτε πεζῇ πορευθῆναι μὴ τυχόντα βασιλικῆς ἢ
4 παντελῶς μεγάλης τινὸς χορηγίας. τῶν δὲ πρὸς
τὴν ἀνατολὴν νευόντων μερῶν τὰ μὲν ὁ ποταμὸς
ὠχύρωκε, τὰ δ' ἔρημος περιέχει καὶ πεδία τελμα-
τώδη τὰ προσαγορευόμενα Βάραθρα. ἔστι γὰρ
ἀνὰ μέσον τῆς Κοίλης Συρίας καὶ τῆς Αἰγύπτου
λίμνη τῷ μὲν πλάτει στενὴ παντελῶς, τῷ δὲ
βάθει θαυμάσιος, τὸ δὲ μῆκος ἐπὶ διακοσίους
παρήκουσα σταδίους, ἣ προσαγορεύεται μὲν
Σερβωνίς, τοῖς δ' ἀπείροις τῶν προσπελαζόντων
5 ἀνελπίστους ἐπιφέρει κινδύνους. στενοῦ γὰρ
τοῦ ῥεύματος ὄντος καὶ ταινίᾳ παραπλησίου,
θινῶν τε μεγάλων πάντῃ περικεχυμένων, ἐπειδὰν νότοι συνεχεῖς πνεύσωσιν, ἐπισείεται πλῆ-
6 θος ἄμμου. αὕτη δὲ τὸ μὲν ὕδωρ κατὰ τὴν
ἐπιφάνειαν ἄσημον ποιεῖ, τὸν δὲ τῆς λίμνης
τύπον συμφυῆ τῇ χέρσῳ καὶ κατὰ πᾶν ἀδιάγνωσ-
τον. διὸ καὶ πολλοὶ τῶν ἀγνοούντων τὴν ἰδιότητα τοῦ τόπου μετὰ στρατευμάτων ὅλων
ἠφανίσθησαν τῆς ὑποκειμένης ὁδοῦ διαμαρτόντες.
7 ἡ μὲν γὰρ ἄμμος ἐκ τοῦ κατ' ὀλίγον πατουμένη
τὴν ἔνδοσιν λαμβάνει, καὶ τοὺς ἐπιβάλλοντας

---

[1] For this form, without the λ, see Vogel I. lxxii and
Kallenberg, *Textkritik und Sprachgebrauch Diodors*, I. 1.

---

[1] The "Cave-dwellers" are located by Diodorus along the
Red Sea as far north as the Greek port of Berenicê, and are
described at length in Book 3. 32 f.

[2] The word comes from a root meaning "to devour," which
suits the nature of the region, as Diodorus observes below.

the country of the Trogodytes [1] and the farthest
parts of Ethiopia, over a distance of five thousand
five hundred stades, it is not easy to sail by the
river or to journey by land, unless a man is fitted
out like a king or at least on a very great scale.
And as for the parts of the country facing the east,
some are fortified by the river and some are embraced
by a desert and a swampy flat called the Barathra. [2]
For between Coele-Syria and Egypt there lies a
lake, quite narrow, but marvellously deep and some
two hundred stades in length, which is called Ser-
bonis [3] and offers unexpected perils to those who
approach it in ignorance of its nature. For since
the body of the water is narrow, like a ribbon, and
surrounded on all sides by great dunes, when there
are constant south winds great quantities of sand
are strewn over it. This sand hides the surface of
the water and makes the outline of the lake continuous with the solid land and entirely indistinguishable from it. For this reason many who were
unacquainted with the peculiar nature of the place
have disappeared together with whole armies, [4] when
they wandered from the beaten road. For as the
sand is walked upon it gives way but gradually,
deceiving with a kind of malevolent cunning those

The famous Barathron, or " Pit," at Athens was a cleft west
of the Hill of the Nymphs into which condemned criminals
were flung.

[3] Cp. Milton, *Paradise Lost*, 2. 592 ff.:

> A gulf profound as that Serbonian bog
> Betwixt Damiata and Mount Casius old,
> Where armies whole have sunk.

[4] An instance of the loss of part of an army is given in Book
16. 46.

ὥσπερ προνοίᾳ τινὶ πονηρᾷ παρακρούεται, μέχρι
ἂν ὅτου λαβόντες ὑπόνοιαν τοῦ συμβησομένου
βοηθήσωσιν ἑαυτοῖς, οὐκ οὔσης ἔτι φυγῆς οὐδὲ
8 σωτηρίας. ὁ γὰρ ὑπὸ τοῦ τέλματος καταπινό-
μενος οὔτε νήχεσθαι δύναται, παραιρουμένης τῆς
ἰλύος τὴν τοῦ σώματος κίνησιν, οὔτ' ἐκβῆναι
κατισχύει, μηδὲν ἔχων στερέμνιον εἰς ἐπίβασιν·
μεμιγμένης γὰρ τῆς ἄμμου τοῖς ὑγροῖς, καὶ διὰ
τοῦτο τῆς ἑκατέρων φύσεως ἠλλοιωμένης, συμβαίνει τὸν τόπον μήτε πορευτὸν εἶναι μήτε πλω-
9 τόν. διόπερ οἱ τοῖς μέρεσι τούτοις ἐπιβάλλοντες
φερόμενοι πρὸς τὸν βυθὸν οὐδεμίαν ἀντίληψιν
βοηθείας ἔχουσι, συγκατολισθανούσης τῆς ἄμμου
τῆς παρὰ τὰ χείλη. τὰ μὲν οὖν προειρημένα
πεδία τοιαύτην ἔχοντα τὴν φύσιν οἰκείας ἔτυχε
προσηγορίας, ὀνομασθέντα Βάραθρα.

31. Ἡμεῖς δ' ἐπεὶ τὰ περὶ τῶν ἀπὸ τῆς
χέρσου τριῶν μερῶν τῶν ὀχυρούντων τὴν Αἴγυπτον διήλθομεν, προσθήσομεν τοῖς εἰρημένοις τὸ
2 λειπόμενον. ἡ τετάρτη τοίνυν πλευρὰ πᾶσα
σχεδὸν ἀλιμένῳ θαλάττῃ προσκλυζομένη προβέ-
βληται τὸ Αἰγύπτιον πέλαγος,[1] ὃ τὸν μὲν παρά-
πλουν ἔχει μακρότατον, τὴν δ' ἀπόβασιν τὴν ἐπὶ
τὴν χώραν δυσπροσόρμιστον· ἀπὸ γὰρ Παραιτο-
νίου τῆς Λιβύης ἕως Ἰόπης τῆς ἐν τῇ Κοίλῃ
Συρίᾳ, ὄντος τοῦ παράπλου σταδίων σχεδὸν
πεντακισχιλίων, οὐκ ἔστιν εὑρεῖν ἀσφαλῆ λιμένα
3 πλὴν τοῦ Φάρου. χωρὶς δὲ τούτων ταινία παρ'
ὅλην σχεδὸν τὴν Αἴγυπτον παρήκει τοῖς ἀπείροις

---

[1] That part of the Mediterranean lying off Egypt.

who advance upon it, until, suspecting some impending mishap, they begin to help one another only when it is no longer possible to turn back or escape. For anyone who has been sucked in by the mire cannot swim, since the slime prevents all movement of the body, nor is he able to wade out, since he has no solid footing; for by reason of the mixing of the sand with the water and the consequent change in the nature of both it comes about that the place cannot be crossed either on foot or by boat. Consequently those who enter upon these regions are borne towards the depths and have nothing to grasp to give them help, since the sand along the edge slips in with them. These flats have received a name appropriate to their nature as we have described it, being called Barathra.

31. Now that we have set forth the facts about the three regions which fortify Egypt by land we shall add to them the one yet remaining. The fourth side, which is washed over its whole extent by waters which are practically harbourless, has for a defence before it the Egyptian Sea.[1] The voyage along the coast of this sea is exceedingly long, and any landing is especially difficult; for from Paraetonium[2] in Libya as far as Iopê[3] in Coele-Syria, a voyage along the coast of some five thousand stades, there is not to be found a safe harbour except Pharos.[4] And, apart from these considerations, a sandbank extends along practically the whole length of Egypt, not discernible to any

[2] The first important city on the coast west of Alexandria.
[3] Joppa.
[4] The island which lies before Alexandria and gave its name to the harbour.

DIODORUS OF SICILY

4 τῶν προσπλεόντων ἀθεώρητος· διόπερ οἱ τὸν ἐκ
πελάγους κίνδυνον ἐκπεφευγέναι νομίζοντες, καὶ
διὰ τὴν ἄγνοιαν ἄσμενοι πρὸς τὴν γῆν κατα-
πλέοντες, ἐξαίφνης ἐποκελλόντων τῶν σκαφῶν
5 ἀνελπίστως ναυαγοῦσιν· ἔνιοι δὲ διὰ τὴν ταπει-
νότητα τῆς χώρας οὐ δυνάμενοι προϊδέσθαι τὴν
γῆν λανθάνουσιν ἑαυτοὺς ἐκπίπτοντες οἱ μὲν εἰς
ἑλώδεις καὶ λιμνάζοντας τόπους, οἱ δ᾽ εἰς χώραν
ἔρημον.

6   Ἡ μὲν οὖν Αἴγυπτος πανταχόθεν φυσικῶς
ὠχύρωται τὸν εἰρημένον τρόπον, τῷ δὲ σχήματι
παραμήκης οὖσα δισχιλίων μὲν σταδίων ἔχει τὴν
παραθαλάττιον πλευράν, εἰς μεσόγειον δ᾽ ἀνήκει
σχεδὸν ἐπὶ σταδίους ἑξακισχιλίους.   πολυανθρωπίᾳ δὲ τὸ μὲν παλαιὸν πολὺ προέσχε πάντων
τῶν γνωριζομένων τόπων κατὰ τὴν οἰκουμένην,
καὶ καθ᾽ ἡμᾶς δὲ οὐδενὸς τῶν ἄλλων δοκεῖ
7 λείπεσθαι· ἐπὶ μὲν γὰρ τῶν ἀρχαίων χρόνων
ἔσχε κώμας ἀξιολόγους καὶ πόλεις πλείους τῶν
μυρίων καὶ ὀκτακισχιλίων, ὡς ἐν ταῖς ἱεραῖς
ἀναγραφαῖς ὁρᾶν ἔστι κατακεχωρισμένον, ἐπὶ δὲ
Πτολεμαίου τοῦ Λάγου πλείους τῶν τρισμυρίων
ἠριθμήθησαν, ὧν τὸ πλῆθος διαμεμένηκεν ἕως
8 τῶν καθ᾽ ἡμᾶς χρόνων.   τοῦ δὲ σύμπαντος λαοῦ
τὸ μὲν παλαιὸν φασι γεγονέναι περὶ ἑπτακοσίας

---

[1] Ptolemy Lagus, general of Alexander the Great, was the
founder of the line of the Ptolemies.   He obtained the governorship of Egypt shortly after the death of Alexander in 323 B.C.,
assumed the title of king in 305, and reigned until 283.

who approach without previous experience of these waters. Consequently those who think that they have escaped the peril of the sea, and in their ignorance turn with gladness towards the shore, suffer unexpected shipwreck when their vessels suddenly run aground; and now and then mariners who cannot see land in time because the country lies so low are cast ashore before they realize it, some of them on marshy and swampy places and others on a desert region.

The land of Egypt, then, is fortified on all sides by nature in the manner described, and is oblong in shape, having a coast-line of two thousand stades and extending inland about six thousand stades. In density of population it far surpassed of old all known regions of the inhabited world, and even in our own day is thought to be second to none other; for in ancient times it had over eighteen thousand important villages and cities, as can be seen entered in their sacred records, while under Ptolemy son of Lagus[1] these were reckoned at over thirty thousand,[2] this great number continuing down to our own time. The total population, they say, was of old about seven million and the number

---

[2] Herodotus (2. 177) gives the number of " inhabited cities " in the time of Amasis (sixth century B.C.) as twenty thousand. The " over thirty thousand " of Diodorus may be approximately correct, when the " villages " are included, although he may be using the figures given by Theocritus (17. 82 ff.), who was born about 305 B.C. and performed a feat of metrical juggling of the number 33,333 : " The cities builded therein are three hundreds and three thousands and three tens of thousands, and threes twain and nines three, and in them the lord and master of all is proud Ptolemy " (tr. Edmonds, in *L.C.L.*).

μυριάδας, καὶ καθ᾽ ἡμᾶς δὲ οὐκ ἐλάττους εἶναι
9 τούτων.[1] διὸ καὶ τοὺς ἀρχαίους βασιλεῖς ἱστοροῦσι κατὰ τὴν Αἴγυπτον ἔργα μεγάλα καὶ
θαυμαστὰ διὰ τῆς πολυχειρίας κατασκευάσαντας
ἀθάνατα τῆς ἑαυτῶν δόξης ἀπολιπεῖν ὑπομνήματα. ἀλλὰ περὶ μὲν τούτων τὰ κατὰ μέρος
μικρὸν ὕστερον ἀναγράψομεν, περὶ δὲ τῆς τοῦ
ποταμοῦ φύσεως καὶ τῶν κατὰ τὴν χώραν
ἰδιωμάτων νῦν διέξιμεν.

32. Ὁ γὰρ Νεῖλος φέρεται μὲν ἀπὸ μεσημβρίας
ἐπὶ τὴν ἄρκτον, τὰς πηγὰς ἔχων ἐκ τόπων
ἀοράτων, οἳ κεῖνται τῆς ἐσχάτης Αἰθιοπίας κατὰ
τὴν ἔρημον, ἀπροσίτου τῆς χώρας οὔσης διὰ τὴν
2 τοῦ καύματος ὑπερβολήν. μέγιστος δ᾽ ὢν τῶν
ἁπάντων ποταμῶν καὶ πλείστην γῆν διεξιὼν
καμπὰς ποιεῖται μεγάλας, ποτὲ μὲν ἐπὶ τὴν
ἀνατολὴν καὶ τὴν Ἀραβίαν ἐπιστρέφων, ποτὲ δ᾽
ἐπὶ τὴν δύσιν καὶ τὴν Λιβύην ἐκκλίνων· φέρεται
γὰρ ἀπὸ τῶν Αἰθιοπικῶν ὁρῶν μέχρι τῆς εἰς
θάλατταν ἐκβολῆς στάδια μάλιστά πως μύρια
3 καὶ δισχίλια σὺν αἷς ποιεῖται καμπαῖς.[2] κατὰ
δὲ τοὺς ὑποκάτω τόπους συστέλλεται τοῖς ὄγκοις
ἀεὶ μᾶλλον, ἀποσπωμένου τοῦ ῥεύματος ἐπ᾽
4 ἀμφοτέρας τὰς ἠπείρους. τῶν δ᾽ ἀποσχιζο-
μένων μερῶν τὸ μὲν εἰς τὴν Λιβύην ἐκκλῖνον ὑφ᾽

[1] All MSS. except M read τριακοσίων, which has been
deleted by every editor since Dindorf. But U. Wilcken
(Griechische Ostraka aus Ägypten und Nubien, 1., pp. 489 f.)
follows Ed. Meyer in feeling that τριακοσίων is a corruption
and makes a strong case for τούτων, which I have
adopted.

[2] περιείληφε δὲ καὶ νήσους ἐν αὐτῷ κατὰ μὲν τὴν Αἰθιοπίαν
ἄλλας τε πλείους καὶ μίαν εὐμεγέθη, τὴν ὀνομαζομένην Μερόην, ἣ

has remained no less down to our day.[1] It is for this reason that, according to our historical accounts, the ancient kings of Egypt built great and marvellous works with the aid of so many hands and left in them immortal monuments to their glory. But these matters we shall set forth in detail a little later; now we shall tell of the nature of the river and the distinctive features of the country.

32. The Nile flows from south to north, having its sources in regions which have never been seen, since they lie in the desert at the extremity of Ethiopia in a country that cannot be approached because of the excessive heat. Being as it is the largest of all rivers as well as the one which traverses the greatest territory, it forms great windings, now turning towards the east and Arabia, now bending back towards the west and Libya; for its course from the mountains of Ethiopia to where it empties into the sea is a distance, inclusive of its windings, of some twelve thousand stades. In its lower stretches it is more and more reduced in volume, as the flow is drawn off to the two continents.[2] Of the streams which thus break off from it, those which turn off into Libya are swallowed up by the

---

[1] U. Wilcken (cp. critical note) feels that this sum for the population of Egypt about the middle of the first century B.C. is approximately correct. Josephus (*Jewish War*, 2. 385), writing a little more than a century later, gives the population as 7,500,000, exclusive of Alexandria. In Book 17. 52. 6 Diodorus says that the " free inhabitants " of that city numbered over 300,000.

[2] The earlier Greek writers made the Nile the dividing line between the continents of Asia and Africa.

εἴκοσι δυοῖν σταδίων ἐστὶ τὸ πλάτος added by C F from chap. 33. 1.

ἄμμου καταπίνεται τὸ βάθος ἐχούσης ἄπιστον,
τὸ δ' εἰς τὴν Ἀραβίαν ἐναντίως εἰσχεόμενον εἰς
τέλματα παμμεγέθη καὶ λίμνας ἐκτρέπεται μεγά-
5 λας καὶ περιοικουμένας γένεσι πολλοῖς. εἰς δὲ
τὴν Αἴγυπτον ἐμβάλλει τῇ μὲν δέκα σταδίων,
τῇ δ' ἔλαττον τούτων, οὐκ ἐπ' εὐθείας φερόμενος,
ἀλλὰ καμπὰς παντοίας ποιούμενος· ποτὲ μὲν
γὰρ ἑλίττεται πρὸς τὴν ἔω, ποτὲ δὲ πρὸς τὴν
ἑσπέραν, ἔστι δ' ὅτε πρὸς τὴν μεσημβρίαν, εἰς
6 τοὐπίσω λαμβάνων τὴν παλίρροιαν. ὄρη γὰρ
ἐξ ἑκατέρου μέρους τοῦ ποταμοῦ παρήκει, πολλὴν
μὲν τῆς παραποταμίας ἐπέχοντα, διειλημμένα
δὲ φάραγξι κατακρήμνοις¹ στενοπόροις, οἷς
ἐμπῖπτον τὸ ῥεῦμα παλισσυτεῖ διὰ τῆς πεδιάδος,
καὶ πρὸς τὴν μεσημβρίαν ἐφ' ἱκανὸν τόπον
ἐνεχθὲν πάλιν ἐπὶ τὴν κατὰ φύσιν φορὰν
ἀποκαθίσταται.
7 Τηλικαύτην δ' ἔχων ὑπεροχὴν ἐν πᾶσιν ὁ
ποταμὸς οὗτος μόνος τῶν ἄλλων ἄνευ βίας καὶ
κυματώδους ὁρμῆς τὴν ῥύσιν ποιεῖται, πλὴν ἐν
8 τοῖς καλουμένοις καταράκταις. τόπος γάρ τίς
ἐστι μήκει μὲν ὡς δέκα σταδίων, κατάντης δὲ καὶ
κρημνοῖς συγκλειόμενος εἰς στενὴν ἐντομήν, ἅπας
δὲ τραχὺς καὶ φαραγγώδης, ἔτι δὲ πέτρους ἔχων
πυκνοὺς καὶ μεγάλους ἐοικότας σκοπέλοις· τοῦ
δὲ ῥεύματος περὶ τούτους σχιζομένου βιαιότερον
καὶ πολλάκις διὰ τὰς ἐγκοπὰς ἀνακλωμένου πρὸς
ἐναντίαν τὴν καταφορὰν συνίστανται δῖναι θαυ-
9 μασταί· πᾶς δ' ὁ μεσάζων τόπος ὑπὸ τῆς παλιρ-

---

¹ κατακρήμνοις Capps : καὶ κρημνοῖς.

sand, which lies there to an incredible depth, while
those which pour in the opposite direction into
Arabia are diverted into immense fens and large
marshes[1] on whose shores dwell many peoples. But
where it enters Egypt it has a width of ten stades,
sometimes less, and flows, not in a straight course,
but in windings of every sort; for it twists now
towards the east, now towards the west, and at
times even towards the south, turning entirely back
upon itself. For sharp hills extend along both sides
of the river, which occupy much of the land border-
ing upon it and are cut through by precipitous
ravines, in which are narrow defiles; and when it
comes to these hills the stream rushes rapidly backward through the level country,[2] and after being
borne southward over an area of considerable extent
resumes once more its natural course.

Distinguished as it is in these respects above all
other streams, the Nile is also the only river which
makes its way without violence or onrushing waves,
except at the cataracts, as they are called. This is
a place which is only about ten stades in length, but
has a steep descent and is shut in by precipices so
as to form a narrow cleft, rugged in its entire length
and ravine-like, full, moreover, of huge boulders
which stand out of the water like peaks. And since
the river is split about these boulders with great
force and is often turned back so that it rushes in
the opposite direction because of the obstacles,
remarkable whirlpools are formed; the middle space,
moreover, for its entire length is filled with foam

---

[1] Herodotus (2. 32) speaks of "large marshes" on the
upper course of the Nile.

[2] *i.e.* the valley which lies between the hills.

ροίας ἀφροῦ τε πληροῦται καὶ τοῖς προσιοῦσι
μεγάλην παρέχεται κατάπληξιν· καὶ γὰρ ἡ
καταφορὰ τοῦ ποταμοῦ οὕτως ἐστὶν ὀξεῖα καὶ
10 βίαιος ὥστε δοκεῖν μηδὲν βέλους διαφέρειν. κατὰ
δὲ τὴν πλήρωσιν τοῦ Νείλου, τῶν σκοπέλων
κατακλυζομένων καὶ παντὸς τοῦ τραχύνοντος
τόπου τῷ πλήθει τοῦ ῥεύματος καλυπτομένου,
καταπλέουσι μέν τινες κατὰ τοῦ καταράκτου
λαμβάνοντες ἐναντίους τοὺς ἀνέμους, ἀναπλεῦ-
σαι δὲ οὐδεὶς δύναται, νικώσης τῆς τοῦ ποταμοῦ
11 βίας πᾶσαν ἐπίνοιαν ἀνθρωπίνην. καταράκται
μὲν οὖν εἰσι τοιοῦτοι πλείους, μέγιστος δ' ὁ πρὸς
τοῖς μεθορίοις τῆς Αἰθιοπίας τε καὶ τῆς Αἰγύπτου.

33. Περιείληφε δ' ὁ ποταμὸς καὶ νήσους ἐν
αὑτῷ, κατὰ μὲν τὴν Αἰθιοπίαν ἄλλας τε πλείους
καὶ μίαν εὐμεγέθη, τὴν ὀνομαζομένην Μερόην, ἐν
ᾗ καὶ πόλις ἐστὶν ἀξιόλογος ὁμώνυμος τῇ νήσῳ,
κτίσαντος αὐτὴν Καμβύσου καὶ θεμένου τὴν
προσηγορίαν ἀπὸ τῆς μητρὸς αὐτοῦ Μερόης.
2 ταύτην δὲ τῷ μὲν σχήματί φασιν ὑπάρχειν
θυρεῷ παραπλησίαν, τῷ δὲ μεγέθει πολὺ προέχειν
τῶν ἄλλων νήσων τῶν ἐν τούτοις τοῖς τόποις· τὸ
μὲν γὰρ μῆκος αὐτῆς εἶναι λέγουσι σταδίων
τρισχιλίων, τὸ δὲ πλάτος χιλίων. ἔχειν δ'
αὐτὴν καὶ πόλεις οὐκ ὀλίγας, ὧν ἐπιφανεστάτην
3 ὑπάρχειν τὴν Μερόην. παρήκειν δὲ τῆς νήσου
τὸν περικλυζόμενον πάντα τόπον ἀπὸ μὲν τῆς
Λιβύης θῖνας ἔχοντας ἄμμου μέγεθος ἀέριον, ἀπὸ
δὲ τῆς Ἀραβίας κρημνοὺς κατερρωγότας. ὑπάρχειν δ' ἐν αὐτῇ καὶ μέταλλα χρυσοῦ τε καὶ
ἀργύρου καὶ σιδήρου καὶ χαλκοῦ· πρὸς δὲ τούτοις ἔχειν πλῆθος ἐβένου, λίθων τε πολυτελῶν

made by the backward rush of the water, and strikes those who approach it with great terror. And, in fact, the descent of the river is so swift and violent that it appears to the eye like the very rush of an arrow. During the flood-time of the Nile, when the peaked rocks are covered and the entire rapids are hidden by the large volume of the water, some men descend the cataract when they find the winds against them,[1] but no man can make his way up it, since the force of the river overcomes every human device. Now there are still other cataracts of this nature, but the largest is the one on the border between Ethiopia and Egypt.

33. The Nile also embraces islands within its waters, of which there are many in Ethiopia and one of considerable extent called Meroë, on which there also lies a famous city bearing the same name as the island, which was founded by Cambyses and named by him after his mother Meroë. This island, they say, has the shape of a long shield and in size far surpasses the other islands in these parts; for they state that it is three thousand stades long and a thousand wide. It also contains not a few cities, the most famous of which is Meroë. Extending the entire length of the island where it is washed by the river there are, on the side towards Libya, dunes containing an infinite amount of sand, and, on the side towards Arabia, rugged cliffs. There are also to be found in it mines of gold, silver, iron, and copper, and it contains in addition much ebony and

[1] i.e. and so are able to check their speed by using the sails.

4 γένη παντοδαπά. καθόλου δὲ τοσαύτας νήσους ποιεῖν τὸν ποταμὸν ὥστε τοὺς ἀκούοντας μὴ ῥαδίως πιστεῦσαι· χωρὶς γὰρ τῶν περικλυζομένων τόπων ἐν τῷ καλουμένῳ Δέλτα τὰς ἄλλας εἶναι νήσους πλείους τῶν ἑπτακοσίων, ὧν τὰς μὲν ὑπὸ Αἰθιόπων ἐπαντλουμένας γεωργεῖσθαι κέγχρῳ, τὰς δὲ πλήρεις ὑπάρχειν ὄφεων καὶ κυνοκεφάλων καὶ ἄλλων θηρίων παντοδαπῶν, καὶ διὰ τοῦτο ἀπροσίτους εἶναι τοῖς ἀνθρώποις.

5 Ὁ δ' οὖν Νεῖλος κατὰ τὴν Αἴγυπτον εἰς πλείω μέρη σχιζόμενος ποιεῖ τὸ καλούμενον ἀπὸ
6 τοῦ σχήματος Δέλτα. τούτου δὲ τὰς μὲν πλευρὰς καταγράφει τὰ τελευταῖα τῶν ῥευμάτων, τὴν δὲ βάσιν ἀναπληροῖ τὸ δεχόμενον
7 πέλαγος τὰς ἐκβολὰς τοῦ ποταμοῦ. ἐξίησι δ' εἰς τὴν θάλατταν ἑπτὰ στόμασιν, ὧν τὸ μὲν πρὸς ἔω κεκλιμένον καὶ πρῶτον καλεῖται Πηλουσιακόν, τὸ δὲ δεύτερον Τανιτικόν, εἶτα Μενδήσιον καὶ Φατνιτικὸν καὶ Σεβεννυτικόν, ἔτι δὲ Βολβίτινον, καὶ τελευταῖον Κανωβικόν, ὅ τινες
8 Ἡρακλεωτικὸν ὀνομάζουσιν. ἔστι δὲ καὶ ἕτερα στόματα χειροποίητα, περὶ ὧν οὐδὲν κατεπείγει γράφειν. ἐφ' ἑκάστῳ δὲ πόλις τετείχισται διαιρουμένη τῷ ποταμῷ καὶ καθ' ἑκάτερον μέρος τῆς ἐκβολῆς ζεύγμασι καὶ φυλακαῖς εὐκαίροις διειλημμένη. ἀπὸ δὲ τοῦ Πηλουσιακοῦ στόματος διῶρύξ ἐστι χειροποίητος εἰς τὸν Ἀράβιον
9 κόλπον καὶ τὴν Ἐρυθρὰν θάλατταν. ταύτην δ' ἐπεβάλετο πρῶτος κατασκευάζειν Νεκῶς ὁ Ψαμμητίχου, μετὰ δὲ τοῦτον Δαρεῖος ὁ Πέρσης, καὶ προκόψας τοῖς ἔργοις ἕως τινὸς τὸ τελευταῖον

every kind of precious stone. Speaking generally, the river forms so many islands that the report of them can scarcely be credited; for, apart from the regions surrounded by water in what is called the Delta, there are more than seven hundred other islands, of which some are irrigated by the Ethiopians and planted with millet, though others are so overrun by snakes and dog-faced baboons [1] and other animals of every kind that human beings cannot set foot upon them.

Now where the Nile in its course through Egypt divides into several streams it forms the region which is called from its shape the Delta. The two sides of the Delta are described by the outermost branches, while its base is formed by the sea which receives the discharge from the several outlets of the river. It empties into the sea in seven mouths, of which the first, beginning at the east, is called the Pelusiac, the second the Tanitic, then the Mendesian, Phatnitic, and Sebennytic, then the Bolbitine, and finally the Canopic, which is called by some the Heracleotic. There are also other mouths, built by the hand of man, about which there is no special need to write. At each mouth is a walled city, which is divided into two parts by the river and provided on each side of the mouth with pontoon bridges and guard-houses at suitable points. From the Pelusiac mouth there is an artificial canal to the Arabian Gulf and the Red Sea. The first to undertake the construction of this was Necho the son of Psammetichus, and after him Darius the Persian made progress with the work for

[1] These are described in Book 3. 35.

10 εἴασεν αὐτὴν ἀσυντέλεστον· ἐδιδάχθη γὰρ ὑπό
τινων ὅτι διορύξας τὸν ἰσθμὸν αἴτιος ἔσται τοῦ
κατακλυσθῆναι τὴν Αἴγυπτον· μετεωροτέραν γὰρ
ἀπεδείκνυον ὑπάρχειν τῆς Αἰγύπτου τὴν Ἐρυ-
11 θρὰν θάλατταν. ὕστερον δὲ ὁ δεύτερος Πτολεμαῖος συνετέλεσεν αὐτήν, καὶ κατὰ τὸν ἐπικαιρότατον τόπον ἐμηχανήσατό τι φιλότεχνον
διάφραγμα. τοῦτο δ' ἐξήνοιγεν, ὁπότε βούλοιτο
διαπλεῦσαι, καὶ ταχέως πάλιν συνέκλειεν, εὐ-
12 στόχως ἐκλαμβανομένης τῆς χρείας. ὁ δὲ διὰ
τῆς διώρυχος ταύτης ῥέων ποταμὸς ὀνομάζεται
μὲν ἀπὸ τοῦ κατασκευάσαντος Πτολεμαῖος, ἐπὶ
δὲ τῆς ἐκβολῆς πόλιν ἔχει τὴν προσαγορευομένην
Ἀρσινόην.

34. Τὸ δ' οὖν Δέλτα τῇ Σικελίᾳ τῷ σχήματι
παραπλήσιον ὑπάρχον τῶν μὲν πλευρῶν ἑκατέραν
ἔχει σταδίων ἑπτακοσίων καὶ πεντήκοντα, τὴν δὲ
βάσιν θαλάττῃ προσκλυζομένην σταδίων χιλίων
2 καὶ τριακοσίων. ἡ δὲ νῆσος αὕτη πολλαῖς
διώρυξι χειροποιήτοις διείληπται καὶ χώραν
περιέχει καλλίστην τῆς Αἰγύπτου. ποταμόχω-
στος γὰρ οὖσα καὶ κατάρρυτος πολλοὺς καὶ
παντοδαποὺς ἐκφέρει καρπούς, τοῦ μὲν ποταμοῦ
διὰ τὴν κατ' ἔτος ἀνάβασιν νεαρὰν ἰλὺν ἀεὶ
καταχέοντος, τῶν δ' ἀνθρώπων ῥᾳδίως ἅπασαν
ἀρδευόντων διά τινος μηχανῆς, ἣν ἐπενόησε μὲν

---

[1] Necho reigned from 609 to 593 B.C., Darius from 521 to
485 B.C.

[2] This canal, not to be confused with the Suez Canal, left

a time but finally left it unfinished;[1] for he was informed by certain persons that if he dug through the neck of land he would be responsible for the submergence of Egypt, for they pointed out to him that the Red Sea was higher than Egypt.[2] At a later time the second Ptolemy completed it and in the most suitable spot constructed an ingenious kind of a lock. This he opened, whenever he wished to pass through, and quickly closed again, a contrivance which usage proved to be highly successful. The river which flows through this canal is named Ptolemy, after the builder of it, and has at its mouth the city called Arsinoë.

285-246 B.C.

34. The Delta is much like Sicily in shape, and its sides are each seven hundred and fifty stades long and its base, where it is washed by the sea, thirteen hundred stades. This island is intersected by many artificial canals and includes the fairest land in Egypt. For since it is alluvial soil and well watered, it produces many crops of every kind, inasmuch as the river by its annual rise regularly deposits on it fresh slime, and the inhabitants easily irrigate its whole area by means of a contrivance

the Nile a little above Bubastis, followed the Wadi Tûmilât to the Bitter Lakes, and then turned south, along the course of the present canal, to the Red Sea. Its construction has been placed as far back as the 19th and even the 12th Dynasty. At any rate, it was again put in operation by Darius, as is clear from the inscription on the best-preserved of the five stelae discovered: "I am a Persian. From Persia I captured Egypt. I commanded this canal to be built from the Nile, which flows in Egypt, to the Sea which comes from Persia. So was this canal built, as I had commanded, and ships passed from Egypt through this canal to Persia, as was my purpose" (translation in R. W. Rogers, *History of Ancient Persia*, p. 120). Remains show that it was about 150 feet wide and 16 to 17 feet deep.

Ἀρχιμήδης ὁ Συρακόσιος, ὀνομάζεται δὲ ἀπὸ τοῦ σχήματος κοχλίας.

3 Πραεῖαν δὲ τοῦ Νείλου τὴν ῥύσιν ποιουμένου, καὶ γῆν πολλὴν καὶ παντοδαπὴν καταφέροντος, ἔτι δὲ κατὰ τοὺς κοίλους τόπους λιμνάζοντος,

4 ἕλη γίνεται πάμφορα. ῥίζαι γὰρ ἐν αὐτοῖς φύονται παντοδαπαὶ τῇ γεύσει καὶ καρπῶν καὶ καυλῶν ἰδιάζουσαι φύσεις, πολλὰ συμβαλλόμεναι τοῖς ἀπόροις τῶν ἀνθρώπων καὶ τοῖς

5 ἀσθενέσι πρὸς αὐτάρκειαν. οὐ γὰρ μόνον τροφὰς παρέχονται ποικίλας καὶ πᾶσι τοῖς δεομένοις ἑτοίμας καὶ δαψιλεῖς, ἀλλὰ καὶ τῶν ἄλλων τῶν εἰς τὸ ζῆν ἀναγκαίων οὐκ ὀλίγα φέρουσι βοηθή-

6 ματα· λωτός τε γὰρ φύεται πολύς, ἐξ οὗ κατασκευάζουσιν ἄρτους οἱ κατ' Αἴγυπτον δυναμένους ἐκπληροῦν τὴν φυσικὴν τοῦ σώματος ἔνδειαν, τό τε κιβώριον δαψιλέστατον ὑπάρχον φέρει τὸν

7 καλούμενον Αἰγύπτιον κύαμον. ἔστι δὲ καὶ δένδρων γένη πλείονα, καὶ τούτων αἱ μὲν ὀνομαζόμεναι περσαῖαι καρπὸν διάφορον ἔχουσι τῇ γλυκύτητι, μετενεχθέντος ἐξ Αἰθιοπίας ὑπὸ Περσῶν τοῦ φυτοῦ καθ' ὃν καιρὸν Καμβύσης

8 ἐκράτησεν ἐκείνων τῶν τόπων· τῶν δὲ συκαμίνων αἱ μὲν τὸν τῶν μόρων καρπὸν φέρουσιν, αἱ δὲ τὸν τοῖς σύκοις ἐμφερῆ, καὶ παρ' ὅλον σχεδὸν τὸν ἐνιαυτὸν αὐτοῦ φυομένου συμβαίνει τοὺς ἀπόρους

9 καταφυγὴν ἑτοίμην ἔχειν τῆς ἐνδείας. τὰ δὲ βάτα καλούμενα[1] συνάγεται μὲν κατὰ τὴν ἀποχώρησιν

---

[1] μυξάρια after καλούμενα deleted by Dindorf.

---

[1] According to the description of Vitruvius (10. 6) this was a screw with spiral channels, "like those of a snail shell," which

which was invented by Archimedes of Syracuse and is called, after its shape, a screw.[1]

Since the Nile has a gentle current, carries down a great quantity of all kinds of earth, and, furthermore, gathers in stagnant pools in low places, marshes are formed which abound in every kind of plant. For tubers of every flavour grow in them and fruits and vegetables which grow on stalks, of a nature peculiar to the country, supplying an abundance sufficient to render the poor and the sick among the inhabitants self-sustaining. For not only do they afford a varied diet, ready at hand and abundant for all who need it, but they also furnish not a few of the other things which contribute to the necessities of life; the lotus, for instance, grows in great profusion, and from it the Egyptians make a bread which is able to satisfy the physical needs of the body, and the *ciborium*, which is found in great abundance, bears what is called the " Egyptian " bean.[2] There are also many kinds of trees, of which that called *persea*,[3] which was introduced from Ethiopia by the Persians when Cambyses conquered those regions, has an unusually sweet fruit, while of the fig-mulberry [4] trees one kind bears the black mulberry and another a fruit resembling the fig; and since the latter produces throughout almost the whole year, the result is that the poor have a ready source to turn to in their need. The fruit called the blackberry is picked at the time the river is

turned within a wooden shaft. It was worked by man-power and did not raise the water so high as did the water-wheel.

[2] The *Nelumbium speciosum*; cp. Theophrastus, *Enquiry into Plants*, 4. 8. 7 (tr. by Hort in *L.C.L.*).

[3] The *Mimusops Schimperi*; cp. Theophrastus, *ibid.* 4. 2. 5.

[4] The *Ficus Sycamorus*; cp. Theophrastus, *ibid.* 6. 6. 4.

τοῦ ποταμοῦ, διὰ δὲ τὴν γλυκύτητα τῆς φύσεως
αὐτῶν ἐν τραγήματος μέρει καταναλίσκεται.
10 κατασκευάζουσι δὲ καὶ ἐκ τῶν κριθῶν Αἰγύπτιοι
πόμα λειπόμενον οὐ πολὺ τῆς περὶ τὸν οἶνον
11 εὐωδίας, ὃ καλοῦσι ζῦθος. χρῶνται δὲ καὶ πρὸς
τὴν τῶν λύχνων καῦσιν ἐπιχέοντες ἀντ' ἐλαίου
τὸ ἀποθλιβόμενον ἔκ τινος φυτοῦ, προσαγορευόμενον δὲ κίκι. πολλὰ δὲ καὶ ἄλλα τὰ δυνάμενα
τὰς ἀναγκαίας χρείας παρέχεσθαι τοῖς ἀνθρώποις
δαψιλῆ φύεται κατὰ τὴν Αἴγυπτον, ὑπὲρ ὧν
μακρὸν ἂν εἴη γράφειν.
35. Θηρία δ' ὁ Νεῖλος τρέφει πολλὰ μὲν καὶ
ἄλλα ταῖς ἰδέαις ἐξηλλαγμένα, δύο δὲ διάφορα,
τόν τε κροκόδειλον καὶ τὸν καλούμενον ἵππον.
2 τούτων δ' ὁ μὲν κροκόδειλος ἐξ ἐλαχίστου γίνεται
μέγιστος, ὡς ἂν ᾠὰ μὲν τοῦ ζῴου τούτου τίκτοντος
τοῖς χηνείοις παραπλήσια, τοῦ δὲ γεννηθέντος
3 αὐξομένου μέχρι πηχῶν ἑκκαίδεκα. καὶ μακρό-
βιον μέν ἐστιν ὡς κατ' ἄνθρωπον, γλῶτταν δὲ
οὐκ ἔχει. τὸ δὲ σῶμα θαυμαστῶς ὑπὸ τῆς
φύσεως ὠχύρωται· τὸ μὲν γὰρ δέρμα αὐτοῦ πᾶν
φολιδωτόν ἐστι καὶ τῇ σκληρότητι διάφορον,
ὀδόντες δ' ἐξ ἀμφοτέρων τῶν μερῶν ὑπάρχουσι
πολλοί, δύο δὲ οἱ χαυλιόδοντες πολὺ τῷ μεγέθει
4 τῶν ἄλλων διαλλάττοντες. σαρκοφαγεῖ δ' οὐ
μόνον ἀνθρώπους, ἀλλὰ καὶ τῶν ἄλλων τῶν ἐπὶ
τῆς γῆς ζῴων τὰ προσπελάζοντα τῷ ποταμῷ.
καὶ τὰ μὲν δήγματα ποιεῖ ἁδρὰ καὶ χαλεπά,
τοῖς δ' ὄνυξι δεινῶς σπαράττει, καὶ τὸ διαιρεθὲν
τῆς σαρκὸς παντελῶς ἀπεργάζεται δυσίατον.
5 ἐθηρεύετο δὲ ταῦτα τὰ ζῷα τὸ μὲν παλαιὸν ὑπὸ
τῶν Αἰγυπτίων ἀγκίστροις ἔχουσιν ἐπιδεδελεασ-

receding and by reason of its natural sweetness is eaten as a dessert. The Egyptians also make a drink out of barley which they call *zythos*, the bouquet of which is not much inferior to that of wine. Into their lamps they pour for lighting purposes, not the oil of the olive, but a kind which is extracted from a plant and called *kiki*.[1] Many other plants, capable of supplying men with the necessities of life, grow in Egypt in great abundance, but it would be a long task to tell about them.

35. As for animals, the Nile breeds many of peculiar form, and two which surpass the others, the crocodile and what is called the " horse." [2] Of these animals the crocodile grows to be the largest from the smallest beginning, since this animal lays eggs about the size of those of a goose, but after the young is hatched it grows to be as long as sixteen cubits. It is as long-lived as man, and has no tongue. The body of the animal is wondrously protected by nature; for its skin is covered all over with scales and is remarkably hard, and there are many teeth in both jaws, two being tusks, much larger than the rest. It devours the flesh not only of men but also of any land animal which approaches the river. The bites which it makes are huge and severe and it lacerates terribly with its claws, and whatever part of the flesh it tears it renders altogether difficult to heal. In early times the Egyptians used to catch these beasts with hooks baited with

[1] Castor-oil.
[2] Called by the Greeks also *hippopotamos*, " horse of the river," and " horse of the Nile."

μένας ὑείας σάρκας, ὕστερον δὲ ποτὲ μὲν δικτύοις
παχέσιν ὡσπερεί τινες ἰχθῦς, ποτὲ δ᾽ ἐμβολίοις
σιδηροῖς ἐκ τῶν ἀκάτων τυπτόμενα συνεχῶς εἰς
6 τὴν κεφαλήν. πλῆθος δ᾽ αὐτῶν ἀμύθητόν ἐστι
κατά τε τὸν ποταμὸν καὶ τὰς παρακειμένας
λίμνας, ὡς ἂν πολυγόνων τε ὄντων καὶ σπανίως
ὑπὸ τῶν ἀνθρώπων ἀναιρουμένων· τῶν μὲν
γὰρ ἐγχωρίων τοῖς πλείστοις νόμιμόν ἐστιν ὡς
θεὸν σέβεσθαι τὸν κροκόδειλον, τοῖς δ᾽ ἀλλο-
φύλοις ἀλυσιτελής ἐστιν ἡ θήρα παντελῶς, οὐκ
7 οὔσης ἐδωδίμου τῆς σαρκός. ἀλλ᾽ ὅμως τοῦ
πλήθους τούτου φυομένου κατὰ τῶν ἀνθρώπων
ἡ φύσις κατεσκεύασε μέγα βοήθημα· ὁ γὰρ
καλούμενος ἰχνεύμων, παραπλήσιος ὢν μικρῷ
κυνί, περιέρχεται τὰ τῶν κροκοδείλων ᾠὰ συν-
τρίβων, τίκτοντος τοῦ ζῴου παρὰ τὸν ποταμόν,
καὶ τὸ θαυμασιώτατον, οὔτε κατεσθίων οὔτε
ὠφελούμενος οὐδὲν διατελεῖ φυσικήν τινα χρείαν
καὶ κατηναγκασμένην ἐνεργῶν εἰς ἀνθρώπων
εὐεργεσίαν.
8 Ὁ δὲ καλούμενος ἵππος τῷ μεγέθει μέν ἐστιν
οὐκ ἐλάττων πηχῶν πέντε, τετράπους δ᾽ ὢν καὶ
δίχηλος παραπλησίως τοῖς βουσὶ τοὺς χαυλιό-
δοντας ἔχει μείζους τῶν ἀγρίων ὑῶν, τρεῖς ἐξ
ἀμφοτέρων τῶν μερῶν, ὦτα δὲ καὶ κέρκον καὶ
φωνὴν ἵππῳ παρεμφερῆ, τὸ δ᾽ ὅλον κύτος τοῦ
σώματος οὐκ ἀνόμοιον ἐλέφαντι, καὶ δέρμα
9 πάντων σχεδὸν τῶν θηρίων ἰσχυρότατον. ποτά-
μιον δὲ[1] ὑπάρχον καὶ χερσαῖον τὰς μὲν ἡμέρας
ἐν τοῖς ὕδασι ποιεῖ γυμναζόμενον κατὰ βάθους,
τὰς δὲ νύκτας ἐπὶ τῆς χώρας κατανέμεται τόν τε
σῖτον καὶ τὸν χόρτον, ὥστε εἰ πολύτεκνον ἦν

the flesh of pigs, but since then they have hunted them sometimes with heavy nets, as they catch some kinds of fish, and sometimes from their boats with iron spears which they strike repeatedly into the head. The multitude of them in the river and the adjacent marshes is beyond telling, since they are prolific and are seldom slain by the inhabitants; for it is the custom of most of the natives of Egypt to worship the crocodile as a god, while for foreigners there is no profit whatsoever in the hunting of them since their flesh is not edible. But against this multitude's increasing and menacing the inhabitants nature has devised a great help; for the animal called the *ichneumon*, which is about the size of a small dog, goes about breaking the eggs of the crocodiles, since the animal lays them on the banks of the river, and—what is most astonishing of all—without eating them or profiting in any way it continually performs a service which, in a sense, has been prescribed by nature and forced upon the animal for the benefit of men.

The animal called the " horse " is not less than five cubits high, and is four-footed and cloven-hoofed like the ox; it has tusks larger than those of the wild boar, three on each side, and ears and tail and a cry somewhat like those of the horse; but the trunk of its body, as a whole, is not unlike that of the elephant, and its skin is the toughest of almost any beast's. Being a river and land animal, it spends the day in the streams exercising in the deep water, while at night it forages about the countryside on the grain and hay, so that, if this animal were

---

[1] δὲ Dindorf : γάρ.

τοῦτο τὸ ζῷον καὶ κατ' ἐνιαυτὸν ἔτικτεν, ἐλυ-
μαίνετ' ἂν ὁλοσχερῶς τὰς γεωργίας τὰς κατ'
10 Αἴγυπτον. ἁλίσκεται δὲ καὶ τοῦτο πολυχειρίᾳ
τῶν τυπτόντων τοῖς σιδηροῖς ἐμβολίοις· ὅπου
γὰρ ἂν φανῇ, συνάγουσιν ἐπ' αὐτὸ πλοῖα, καὶ
περιστάντες κατατραυματίζουσιν ὥσπερ τισὶ
κοπεῦσιν ἐπὶ σιδηροῖς ἀγκίστροις, εἶθ' ἑνὶ τῶν
ἐμπαγέντων ἐνάπτοντες ἀρχὰς στυππίνας ἀφιᾶσι,
μέχρι ἂν ὅτου παραλυθῇ γενόμενον ἔξαιμον.
11 τὴν μὲν οὖν σάρκα σκληρὰν ἔχει καὶ δύσπεπτον,
τῶν δ' ἔντοσθεν οὐδὲν ἐδώδιμον, οὔτε σπλάγχνον
οὔτ' ἐγκοίλιον.

36. Χωρὶς δὲ τῶν εἰρημένων θηρίων ὁ Νεῖλος
ἔχει παντοῖα γένη ἰχθύων καὶ κατὰ τὸ πλῆθος
ἄπιστα· τοῖς γὰρ ἐγχωρίοις οὐ μόνον ἐκ τῶν
προσφάτως ἁλισκομένων παρέχεται δαψιλῆ τὴν
ἀπόλαυσιν, ἀλλὰ καὶ πλῆθος εἰς ταριχείαν
2 ἀνίησιν ἀνέκλειπτον. καθόλου δὲ ταῖς εἰς ἀνθρώπους εὐεργεσίαις ὑπερβάλλει πάντας τοὺς
κατὰ τὴν οἰκουμένην ποταμούς. τῆς γὰρ πληρώσεως τὴν ἀρχὴν ἀπὸ θερινῶν τροπῶν ποιούμενος
αὔξεται μὲν μέχρι τῆς ἰσημερίας τῆς μετοπωρινῆς,
ἐπάγων δ' ἀεὶ νέαν ἰλὺν βρέχει τὴν γῆν ὁμοίως
τήν τε ἀργὴν καὶ σπόριμον καὶ φυτεύσιμον
τοσοῦτον χρόνον ὅσον ἂν οἱ γεωργοῦντες τὴν
3 χώραν ἐθελήσωσι. τοῦ γὰρ ὕδατος πραέως
φερομένου ῥᾳδίως ἀποτρέπουσιν αὐτὸν μικροῖς
χώμασι, καὶ πάλιν ἐπάγουσιν εὐχερῶς ταῦτα
4 διαιροῦντες, ὅταν δόξῃ συμφέρειν. καθόλου δὲ
τοσαύτην τοῖς μὲν ἔργοις εὐκοπίαν παρέχεται,
τοῖς δ' ἀνθρώποις λυσιτέλειαν, ὥστε τοὺς μὲν
πλείστους τῶν γεωργῶν τοῖς ἀναξηραινομένοις

prolific and reproduced each year, it would entirely destroy the farms of Egypt. But even it is caught by the united work of many men who strike it with iron spears; for whenever it appears they converge their boats upon it, and gathering about it wound it repeatedly with a kind of chisel fitted with iron barbs,[1] and then, fastening the end of a rope of tow to one of them which has become imbedded in the animal, they let it go until it dies from loss of blood. Its meat is tough and hard to digest and none of its inward parts is edible, neither the viscera[2] nor the intestines.

36. Beside the beasts above mentioned the Nile contains every variety of fish and in numbers beyond belief; for it supplies the natives not only with abundant subsistence from the fish freshly caught, but it also yields an unfailing multitude for salting. Speaking generally, we may say that the Nile surpasses all the rivers of the inhabited world in its benefactions to mankind. For, beginning to rise at the summer solstice, it increases in volume until the autumnal equinox, and, since it is bringing down fresh mud all the time, it soaks both the fallow land and the seed land as well as the orchard land for so long a time as the farmers may wish. For since the water comes with a gentle flow, they easily divert the river from their fields by small dams of earth, and then, by cutting these, as easily let the river in again upon the land whenever they think this to be advantageous. And in general the Nile contributes so greatly to the lightening of labour as well as to the profit of the inhabitants, that the majority of the farmers, as they

---

[1] *i.e.* a harpoon.   [2] *i.e.* the heart, liver, lungs, kidneys.

τῆς γῆς τόποις ἐφισταμένους καὶ τὸ σπέρμα
βάλλοντας ἐπάγειν τὰ βοσκήματα, καὶ τούτοις
συμπατήσαντας μετὰ τέτταρας ἢ πέντε μῆνας
ἀπαντᾶν ἐπὶ τὸν θερισμόν, ἐνίους δὲ κούφοις
ἀρότροις ἐπαγαγόντας βραχέως τὴν ἐπιφάνειαν
τῆς βεβρεγμένης χώρας σωροὺς ἀναιρεῖσθαι τῶν
καρπῶν χωρὶς δαπάνης πολλῆς καὶ κακοπαθείας.
5 ὅλως γὰρ πᾶσα γεωργία παρὰ μὲν τοῖς ἄλλοις
ἔθνεσι μετὰ μεγάλων ἀναλωμάτων καὶ ταλαι-
πωριῶν διοικεῖται, παρὰ δ' Αἰγυπτίοις μόνοις
ἐλαχίστοις δαπανήμασι καὶ πόνοις συγκομίζεται.
ἥ τε ἀμπελόφυτος ὁμοίως ἀρδευομένη δαψίλειαν
6 οἴνου τοῖς ἐγχωρίοις παρασκευάζει. οἱ δὲ χερ-
σεύειν ἐάσαντες τὴν χώραν τὴν ἐπικεκλυσμένην
καὶ τοῖς ποιμνίοις ἀνέντες μηλόβοτον διὰ τὸ
πλῆθος τῆς νομῆς δὶς τεκόντα καὶ δὶς ἀποκαρέντα
τὰ πρόβατα καρποῦνται.
7 Τὸ δὲ γινόμενον περὶ τὴν ἀνάβασιν τοῦ Νείλου
τοῖς μὲν ἰδοῦσι θαυμαστὸν φαίνεται, τοῖς δ'
ἀκούσασι παντελῶς ἄπιστον. τῶν γὰρ ἄλλων
ποταμῶν ἁπάντων περὶ τὰς θερινὰς τροπὰς
ἐλαττουμένων καὶ κατὰ τὸν ἑξῆς χρόνον τοῦ
θέρους ἀεὶ μᾶλλον ταπεινουμένων, οὗτος μόνος
τότε τὴν[1] ἀρχὴν λαβὼν τῆς πληρώσεως ἐπὶ
τοσοῦτον αὔξεται καθ' ἡμέραν ὥστε τὸ τελευταῖον
8 πᾶσαν σχεδὸν ἐπικλύζειν τὴν Αἴγυπτον. ὡσαύτως
δὲ πάλιν εἰς τοὐναντίον μεταβαλὼν[2] τὸν ἴσον

---

[1] τὴν omitted by F, Bekker, Dindorf.
[2] μεταβάλλων A B, Bekker, Dindorf.

begin work upon the areas of the land which are becoming dry, merely scatter their seed, turn their herds and flocks in on the fields, and after they have used these for trampling the seed in return after four or five months to harvest it;[1] while some, applying light ploughs to the land, turn over no more than the surface of the soil after its wetting and then gather great heaps of grain without much expense or exertion. For, generally speaking, every kind of field labour among other peoples entails great expense and toil, but among the Egyptians alone is the harvest gathered in with very slight outlay of money and labour. Also the land planted with the vine, being irrigated as are the other fields, yields an abundant supply of wine to the natives. And those who allow the land, after it has been inundated, to lie uncultivated and give it over to the flocks to graze upon, are rewarded with flocks which, because of the rich pasturage, lamb twice and are twice shorn every year.[2]

The rise of the Nile is a phenomenon which appears wonderful enough to those who have witnessed it, but to those who have only heard of it, quite incredible. For while all other rivers begin to fall at the summer solstice and grow steadily lower and lower during the course of the following summer, this one alone begins to rise at that time and increases so greatly in volume day by day that it finally overflows practically all Egypt. And in like manner it afterwards follows precisely the opposite

---

[1] A monument of the Old Kingdom represents sheep treading in the seed (the reproduction appears in J. H. Breasted, *A History of Egypt*, p. 92).

[2] Cp. the *Odyssey* 4. 86.

χρόνον καθ᾽ ἡμέραν ἐκ τοῦ κατ᾽ ὀλίγον ταπεινοῦ-
ται, μέχρι ἂν εἰς τὴν προϋπάρξασαν ἀφίκηται
τάξιν. καὶ τῆς μὲν χώρας οὔσης πεδιάδος, τῶν
δὲ πόλεων καὶ τῶν κωμῶν, ἔτι δὲ τῶν ἀγροικιῶν
κειμένων ἐπὶ χειροποιήτων χωμάτων, ἡ πρόσοψις
9 ὁμοία γίνεται ταῖς Κυκλάσι νήσοις. τῶν δὲ χερ-
σαίων θηρίων τὰ πολλὰ μὲν ὑπὸ τοῦ ποταμοῦ
περιληφθέντα διαφθείρεται βαπτιζόμενα, τινὰ δ᾽
εἰς τοὺς μετεωροτέρους ἐκφεύγοντα τόπους διασώ-
ζεται, τὰ δὲ βοσκήματα κατὰ τὸν τῆς ἀναβάσεως
χρόνον ἐν ταῖς κώμαις καὶ ταῖς ἀγροικίαις δια-
τρέφεται, προπαρασκευαζομένης αὐτοῖς τῆς τρο-
10 φῆς. οἱ δ᾽ ὄχλοι πάντα τὸν τῆς πληρώσεως
χρόνον ἀπολελυμένοι τῶν ἔργων εἰς ἄνεσιν τρέ-
πονται, συνεχῶς ἑστιώμενοι καὶ πάντων τῶν
πρὸς ἡδονὴν ἀνηκόντων ἀνεμποδίστως ἀπολαύ-
11 οντες. διὰ δὲ τὴν ἀγωνίαν τὴν ἐκ τῆς ἀναβάσεως
τοῦ ποταμοῦ γινομένην κατεσκεύασται Νειλο-
σκοπεῖον ὑπὸ τῶν βασιλέων ἐν τῇ Μέμφει· ἐν
τούτῳ δὲ τὴν ἀνάβασιν ἀκριβῶς ἐκμετροῦντες οἱ
τὴν τούτου διοίκησιν ἔχοντες ἐξαποστέλλουσιν
εἰς τὰς πόλεις ἐπιστολάς, διασαφοῦντες πόσους
πήχεις ἢ δακτύλους ἀναβέβηκεν ὁ ποταμὸς καὶ
πότε τὴν ἀρχὴν πεποίηται τῆς ἐλαττώσεως.
12 διὰ δὲ τοῦ τοιούτου τρόπου τῆς μὲν ἀγωνίας
ἀπολύεται πᾶς ὁ λαός, πυθόμενος τὴν τῆς αὐξήσεως εἰς τοὐναντίον μεταβολήν, τὸ δὲ πλῆθος
τῶν ἐσομένων καρπῶν εὐθὺς ἅπαντες προεπεγνώ-
κασιν, ἐκ πολλῶν χρόνων τῆς παρατηρήσεως
ταύτης παρὰ τοῖς Αἰγυπτίοις ἀκριβῶς ἀναγε-
γραμμένης.

course and for an equal length of time gradually
falls each day, until it has returned to its former
level. And since the land is a level plain, while the
cities and villages, as well as the farm-houses, lie
on artificial mounds, the scene comes to resemble
the Cyclades Islands.[1] The wild land animals for
the larger part are cut off by the river and perish in
its waters, but a few escape by fleeing to higher
ground; the herds and flocks, however, are maintained at the time of the flood in the villages and
farm-houses, where fodder is stored up for them in
advance. The masses of the people, being relieved
of their labours during the entire time of the inundation, turn to recreation, feasting all the while
and enjoying without hindrance every device of
pleasure. And because of the anxiety occasioned
by the rise of the river the kings have constructed
a Nilometer[2] at Memphis, where those who are
charged with the administration of it accurately
measure the rise and despatch messages to the
cities, and inform them exactly how many cubits or
fingers the river has risen and when it has commenced
to fall. In this manner the entire nation, when it
has learned that the river has ceased rising and
begun to fall, is relieved of its anxiety, while at the
same time all immediately know in advance how
large the next harvest will be, since the Egyptians
have kept an accurate record of their observations
of this kind over a long period of terms.

[1] These are small islands, some of which " cluster " (as the
name signifies) about the island of Delos.
[2] The Nilometer (Diodorus calls it in fact a " Niloscope ")
is described by Strabo (17. 1. 48) as a well on the bank of the
Nile with lines on the wall to indicate the stage of the river.

37. Μεγάλης δ' οὔσης ἀπορίας περὶ τῆς τοῦ
ποταμοῦ πληρώσεως, ἐπικεχειρήκασι πολλοὶ τῶν
τε φιλοσόφων καὶ τῶν ἱστορικῶν ἀποδιδόναι [1] τὰς
ταύτης αἰτίας, περὶ ὧν ἐν κεφαλαίοις ἐροῦμεν, ἵνα
μήτε μακρὰς ποιώμεθα τὰς παρεκβάσεις μήτε
ἄγραφον τὸ παρὰ πᾶσιν ἐπιζητούμενον ἀπολεί-
2 πωμεν. ὅλως γὰρ ὑπὲρ τῆς ἀναβάσεως τοῦ
Νείλου καὶ τῶν πηγῶν, ἔτι δὲ τῆς εἰς θάλατταν
ἐκβολῆς καὶ τῶν ἄλλων ὧν ἔχει διαφορῶν παρὰ
τοὺς ἄλλους ποταμούς, μέγιστος ὢν τῶν κατὰ
τὴν οἰκουμένην, τινὲς μὲν τῶν συγγραφέων
ἁπλῶς οὐκ ἐτόλμησαν οὐδὲν εἰπεῖν, καίπερ
εἰωθότες μηκύνειν ἐνίοτε περὶ χειμάρρου τοῦ
τυχόντος, τινὲς δ' ἐπιβαλόμενοι λέγειν περὶ τῶν
ἐπιζητουμένων πολὺ τῆς ἀληθείας διήμαρτον.
3 οἱ μὲν γὰρ περὶ τὸν Ἑλλάνικον καὶ Κάδμον, ἔτι
δ' Ἑκαταῖον, καὶ πάντες οἱ τοιοῦτοι, παλαιοὶ
παντάπασιν ὄντες, εἰς τὰς μυθώδεις ἀποφά-
4 σεις ἀπέκλιναν· Ἡρόδοτος δὲ ὁ πολυπράγ-
μων, εἰ καί τις ἄλλος, γεγονὼς καὶ πολλῆς
ἱστορίας ἔμπειρος ἐπικεχείρηκε μὲν περὶ τούτων
ἀποδιδόναι λόγον, ἠκολουθηκὼς δὲ ἀντιλεγο-
μέναις ὑπονοίαις εὑρίσκεται· Ξενοφῶν δὲ καὶ
Θουκυδίδης, ἐπαινούμενοι κατὰ τὴν ἀλήθειαν τῶν
ἱστοριῶν, ἀπέσχοντο τελέως κατὰ τὴν γραφὴν
τῶν τόπων τῶν κατ' Αἴγυπτον· οἱ δὲ περὶ τὸν
Ἔφορον καὶ Θεόπομπον μάλιστα πάντων εἰς
ταῦτ' ἐπιταθέντες ἥκιστα τῆς ἀληθείας ἐπέτυχον.

---

[1] ἀποδοῦναι A B E, Dindorf.

---

[1] These early chroniclers belonged to the group whom
Thucydides (1. 21) called *logographoi* ("writers of prose")
to distinguish them from the writers of epic. The two chief

37. Since there is great difficulty in explaining the swelling of the river, many philosophers and historians have undertaken to set forth the causes of it; regarding this we shall speak summarily, in order that we may neither make our digression too long nor fail to record that which all men are curious to know. For on the general subject of the rise of the Nile and its sources, as well as on the manner in which it reaches the sea and the other points in which this, the largest river of the inhabited world, differs from all others, some historians have actually not ventured to say a single word, although wont now and then to expatiate at length on some winter torrent or other, while others have undertaken to speak on these points of inquiry, but have strayed far from the truth. Hellanicus and Cadmus, for instance, as well as Hecataeus and all the writers like them, belonging as they do one and all to the early school,[1] turned to the answers offered by the myths; Herodotus, who was a curious inquirer if ever a man was, and widely acquainted with history, undertook, it is true, to give an explanation of the matter, but is now found to have followed contradictory guesses; Xenophon and Thucydides, who are praised for the accuracy of their histories, completely refrained in their writings from any mention of the regions about Egypt; and Ephorus and Theopompus, who of all writers paid most attention to these matters, hit upon the truth the least. The

characteristics of the group were interest in mythology and lack of criticism. Hellanicus of Mitylene died soon after 406 B.C.; the historical character of Cadmus of Miletus (*fl.* sixth century B.C.) is questioned by Schmid-Stählin (*Geschichte der griechischen Literatur*, I. pp. 691 f.); Hecataeus of Miletus visited Egypt before 526 B.C. and died soon after 494 B.C.

καὶ διεσφάλησαν οὗτοι πάντες οὐ διὰ τὴν ἀμέ-
5 λειαν, ἀλλὰ διὰ τὴν τῆς χώρας ἰδιότητα. ἀπὸ
γὰρ τῶν ἀρχαίων χρόνων ἄχρι Πτολεμαίου τοῦ
Φιλαδέλφου προσαγορευθέντος οὐχ ὅπως τινὲς
τῶν Ἑλλήνων ὑπερέβαλον εἰς Αἰθιοπίαν, ἀλλ'
οὐδὲ μέχρι τῶν ὅρων τῆς Αἰγύπτου προσανέβη-
σαν· οὕτως ἄξενα πάντα ἦν τὰ περὶ τοὺς τόπους
τούτους καὶ παντελῶς ἐπικίνδυνα· τοῦ δὲ προειρημένου βασιλέως μεθ' Ἑλληνικῆς δυνάμεως εἰς
Αἰθιοπίαν πρῶτου στρατεύσαντος ἐπεγνώσθη τὰ
κατὰ τὴν χώραν ταύτην ἀκριβέστερον ἀπὸ τούτων τῶν χρόνων.

6   Τῆς μὲν οὖν τῶν προτέρων συγγραφέων ἀγνοίας
τοιαύτας τὰς αἰτίας συνέβη γενέσθαι· τὰς δὲ
πηγὰς τοῦ Νείλου, καὶ τὸν τόπον ἐξ οὗ λαμβάνει
τὴν ἀρχὴν τοῦ ῥεύματος, ἑορακέναι μὲν μέχρι
τῶνδε τῶν ἱστοριῶν γραφομένων οὐδεὶς εἴρηκεν
οὐδ' ἀκοὴν ἀπεφήνατο παρὰ τῶν ἑορακέναι
7 διαβεβαιουμένων. διὸ καὶ τοῦ πράγματος εἰς
ὑπόνοιαν καὶ καταστοχασμὸν πιθανὸν κατανν-
τῶντος, οἱ μὲν κατ' Αἴγυπτον ἱερεῖς ἀπὸ τοῦ
περιρρέοντος τὴν οἰκουμένην ὠκεανοῦ φασιν αὐτὸν
τὴν σύστασιν λαμβάνειν, ὑγιὲς μὲν οὐδὲν
λέγοντες, ἀπορίᾳ δὲ τὴν ἀπορίαν λύοντες καὶ
λόγον φέροντες εἰς πίστιν αὐτὸν[1] πολλῆς πί-

---

[1] αὐτὸν Stephanus : αὐτῶν.

---

[1] The second of the line, who reigned from 285 to 246 B.C.
Following the custom of the Egyptian kings (cp. chap. 27)
he married his sister Arsinoë, and upon her death (or possibly
even before; cp. J. Beloch, *Griechische Geschichte*, IV. 2. p.

error on the part of all these writers was due, not to their negligence, but to the peculiar character of the country. For from earliest times until Ptolemy who was called Philadelphus,[1] not only did no Greeks ever cross over into Ethiopia, but none ascended even as far as the boundaries of Egypt—to such an extent were all these regions inhospitable to foreigners and altogether dangerous; but after this king had made an expedition into Ethiopia with an army of Greeks, being the first to do so, the facts about that country from that time forth have been more accurately learned.

Such, then, were the reasons for the ignorance of the earlier historians; and as for the sources of the Nile and the region where the stream arises, not a man, down to the time of the writing of this history, has ever affirmed that he has seen them, or reported from hearsay an account received from any who have maintained that they have seen them. The question, therefore, resolves itself into a matter of guesswork and plausible conjecture; and when, for instance, the priests of Egypt assert that the Nile has its origin in the ocean which surrounds the inhabited world, there is nothing sound in what they say, and they are merely solving one perplexity by substituting another, and advancing as proof an explanation which itself stands much in need of proof.

586. n. 1 and 1. pp. 370 f.) established a cult of himself as ruler and of his sister-wife and consort as *theoi adelphoi* ("Brother-Sister Gods"). The epithet *philadelphos* ("sister-loving") was never borne by Ptolemy II during his lifetime; to his contemporaries he was known as "Ptolemy the son of Ptolemy" (cp. E. R. Bevan, *A History of Egypt under the Ptolemaic Dynasty*, p. 56, and Ferguson in *Cambridge Ancient History*, 7, p. 17.

8 στεως προσδεόμενον· τῶν δὲ Τρωγοδυτῶν οἱ μετ-
αναστάντες ἐκ τῶν ἄνω τόπων διὰ καῦμα, προσ-
αγορευόμενοι δὲ Βόλγιοι,[1] λέγουσιν ἐμφάσεις
τινὰς εἶναι περὶ τοὺς τόπους ἐκείνους, ἐξ ὧν ἄν τις
συλλογίσαιτο διότι πολλῶν πηγῶν εἰς ἕνα τόπον
ἀθροιζομένων συνίσταται τὸ ῥεῦμα τοῦ Νείλου·
διὸ καὶ πολυγονώτατον αὐτὸν ὑπάρχειν πάντων
9 τῶν γνωριζομένων ποταμῶν. οἱ δὲ περιοικοῦντες
τὴν νῆσον τὴν ὀνομαζομένην Μερόην, οἷς καὶ
μάλιστ᾽ ἄν τις συγκατάθοιτο, τῆς μὲν κατὰ τὸ
πιθανὸν εὑρησιλογίας πολὺ κεχωρισμένοις, τῶν
δὲ τόπων τῶν ζητουμένων ἔγγιστα κειμένοις, τοσοῦτον ἀπέχουσι τοῦ λέγειν τι περὶ τούτων
ἀκριβῶς ὥστε καὶ τὸν ποταμὸν ᾿Αστάπουν προσ-
ηγορεύκασιν, ὅπερ ἐστὶ μεθερμηνευόμενον εἰς τὴν
Ἑλλήνων διάλεκτον ἐκ τοῦ σκότους ὕδωρ.

10 Οὗτοι μὲν οὖν τῷ Νείλῳ τῆς ἐν τοῖς τόποις
ἀθεωρησίας καὶ τῆς ἰδίας ἀγνοίας οἰκείαν ἔταξαν
προσηγορίαν· ἡμῖν δ᾽ ἀληθέστατος εἶναι δοκεῖ
λόγος ὁ πλεῖστον ἀπέχων τοῦ προσποιήματος.
11 οὐκ ἀγνοῶ δὲ ὅτι τὴν πρὸς τὴν ἔω τοῦ ποταμοῦ
τούτου καὶ τὴν πρὸς ἑσπέραν Λιβύην ἀφορίζων
Ἡρόδοτος ἀνατίθησι Λίβυσι τοῖς ὀνομαζομένοις
Νασαμῶσι τὴν ἀκριβῆ θεωρίαν τοῦ ῥείθρου, καί
φησιν ἔκ τινος λίμνης λαμβάνοντα τὴν ἀρχὴν
τὸν Νεῖλον φέρεσθαι διὰ χώρας Αἰθιοπικῆς
ἀμυθήτου· οὐ μὴν αὐτόθεν οὔτε τοῖς εἰποῦσι
Λίβυσιν, εἴπερ καὶ πρὸς ἀλήθειαν εἰρήκασιν,
οὔτε τῷ συγγραφεῖ προσεκτέον ἀναπόδεικτα
λέγοντι.

[1] Βόλγιοι C D F, Vogel : μόλγιοι A B E, Bekker, Dindorf.

On the other hand, those Trogodytes,[1] known as the Bolgii, who migrated from the interior because of the heat, say that there are certain phenomena connected with those regions, from which a man might reason that the body of the Nile is gathered from many sources which converge upon a single place, and that this is the reason for its being the most fertile of all known rivers. But the inhabitants of the country about the island called Meroë, with whom a man would be most likely to agree, since they are far removed from the art of finding reasons in accordance with what is plausible and dwell nearest the regions under discussion, are so far from saying anything accurate about these problems that they even call the river Astapus, which means, when translated into Greek, "Water from Darkness."

This people, then, have given the Nile a name which accords with the want of any first-hand information about those regions and with their own ignorance of them; but in our opinion the explanation nearest the truth is the one which is farthest from pure assumption. I am not unaware that Herodotus,[2] when distinguishing between the Libya which lies to the east and that which lies to the west of this river, attributes to the Libyans known as the Nasamones the exact observation of the stream, and says that the Nile rises in a certain lake and then flows through the land of Ethiopia for a distance beyond telling; and yet assuredly no hasty assent should be given to the statements either of Libyans, even though they may have spoken truthfully, or of the historian when what he says does not admit of proof.

[1] Cp. p. 98, n. 1.   [2] Book 2. 32.

38. Ἐπειδὴ δὲ περὶ τῶν πηγῶν καὶ τῆς ῥύσεως αὐτοῦ διεληλύθαμεν, πειρασόμεθα τὰς
2 αἰτίας ἀποδιδόναι τῆς πληρώσεως. Θαλῆς μὲν οὖν, εἷς τῶν ἑπτὰ σοφῶν ὀνομαζόμενος, φησὶ τοὺς ἐτησίας ἀντιπνέοντας ταῖς ἐκβολαῖς τοῦ ποταμοῦ κωλύειν εἰς θάλατταν προχεῖσθαι τὸ ῥεῦμα, καὶ διὰ τοῦτ' αὐτὸν πληρούμενον ἐπικλύζειν ταπεινὴν οὖσαν καὶ πεδιάδα τὴν Αἴγυπ-
3 τον. τοῦ δὲ λόγου τούτου, καίπερ εἶναι δοκοῦντος πιθανοῦ, ῥᾴδιον ἐξελέγξαι τὸ ψεῦδος. εἰ γὰρ ἦν ἀληθὲς τὸ προειρημένον, οἱ ποταμοὶ πάντες ἂν οἱ τοῖς ἐτησίαις ἐναντίας τὰς ἐκβολὰς ἔχοντες ἐποιοῦντο τὴν ὁμοίαν ἀνάβασιν· οὐ μηδαμοῦ τῆς οἰκουμένης συμβαίνοντος ζητητέον ἑτέραν αἰτίαν
4 ἀληθινὴν τῆς πληρώσεως. Ἀναξαγόρας δ' ὁ φυσικὸς ἀπεφήνατο τῆς ἀναβάσεως αἰτίαν εἶναι τὴν τηκομένην χιόνα κατὰ τὴν Αἰθιοπίαν, ᾧ καὶ ὁ ποιητὴς Εὐριπίδης μαθητὴς ὢν ἠκολούθηκε· λέγει γοῦν

Νείλου λιπὼν κάλλιστον ἐκ γαίας ὕδωρ,
ὃς ἐκ μελαμβρότοιο πληροῦται ῥοὰς
Αἰθιοπίδος γῆς, ἡνίκ' ἂν τακῇ χιών.

5 καὶ ταύτην δὲ τὴν ἀπόφασιν οὐ πολλῆς ἀντιρρήσεως δεῖσθαι συμβέβηκε, φανεροῦ πᾶσιν ὄντος ὅτι διὰ τὴν ὑπερβολὴν τῶν καυμάτων ἀδύνατον
6 χιόνα πίπτειν περὶ τὴν Αἰθιοπίαν· καθόλου γὰρ περὶ τοὺς τόπους τούτους οὔτε πάγος οὔτε ψῦχος οὔθ' ὅλως χειμῶνος ἔμφασις γίνεται, καὶ μάλιστα περὶ τὴν ἀνάβασιν τοῦ Νείλου. εἰ δέ τις καὶ

---

[1] Thales doubtless meant by "etesian" the north-west winds which blow in summer from the Mediterranean, but

38. Now that we have discussed the sources and course of the Nile we shall endeavour to set forth the causes of its swelling. Thales, who is called one of the seven wise men, says that when the etesian winds [1] blow against the mouths of the river they hinder the flow of the water into the sea, and that this is the reason why it rises and overflows Egypt, which is low and a level plain. But this explanation, plausible as it appears, may easily be shown to be false. For if what he said were true, all the rivers whose mouths face the etesian winds would rise in a similar way; but since this is the case nowhere in the inhabited world the true cause of the swelling must be sought elsewhere. Anaxagoras the physical philosopher has declared that the cause of the rising is the melting snow in Ethiopia, and the poet Euripides, a pupil of his, is in agreement with him. At least he writes: [2]

He quit Nile's waters, fairest that gush from earth,
The Nile which, drawn from Ethiop land, the black
Man's home, flows with full flood when melts the snow.

But the fact is that this statement also requires but a brief refutation, since it is clear to everyone that the excessive heat makes it impossible that any snow should fall in Ethiopia; for, speaking generally, in those regions there is no frost or cold or any sign whatsoever of winter, and this is especially true at the time of the rising of the Nile. And even

the term is not a precise one, as Diodorus shows in the following chapter.
[2] Frg. 228, Nauck[2].

συγχωρῆσαι χιόνος εἶναι πλῆθος ἐν τοῖς ὑπὲρ
Αἰθιοπίαν τόποις, ὅμως ἐλέγχεται τὸ ψεῦδος τῆς
7 ἀποφάσεως· πᾶς γὰρ ποταμὸς ἀπὸ χιόνος ῥέων
ὁμολογουμένως αὔρας ἀναδίδωσι ψυχρὰς καὶ τὸν
ἀέρα παχύνει· περὶ δὲ τὸν Νεῖλον μόνον τῶν
ποταμῶν οὔτε νέφους ὑποστάσεις ὑπάρχουσιν
οὔτ' αὖραι ψυχραὶ γίνονται οὔθ' ὁ ἀὴρ παχύ-
νεται.

8 Ἡρόδοτος δέ φησι τὸν Νεῖλον εἶναι μὲν φύσει
τηλικοῦτον ἡλίκος γίνεται κατὰ τὴν πλήρωσιν,
ἐν δὲ τῷ χειμῶνι τὸν ἥλιον κατὰ τὴν Λιβύην
φερόμενον ἐπισπᾶσθαι πρὸς ἑαυτὸν πολλὴν
ὑγρασίαν ἐκ τοῦ Νείλου, καὶ διὰ τοῦτο περὶ τοὺς
καιροὺς τούτους παρὰ φύσιν ἐλάττονα γίνεσθαι
9 τὸν ποταμόν· τοῦ δὲ θέρους ἐπιστάντος ἀποχω-
ροῦντα τῇ φορᾷ τὸν ἥλιον πρὸς τὰς ἄρκτους
ἀναξηραίνειν καὶ ταπεινοῦν τούς τε περὶ τὴν
Ἑλλάδα ποταμοὺς καὶ τοὺς κατὰ τὴν ἄλλην
10 χώραν τὴν ὁμοίως ἐκείνῃ κειμένην. οὐκέτ' οὖν
εἶναι παράδοξον τὸ γινόμενον περὶ τὸν Νεῖλον·
οὐ γὰρ ἐν τοῖς καύμασιν αὔξεσθαι, κατὰ τὸν
χειμῶνα δὲ ταπεινοῦσθαι διὰ τὴν προειρημένην
11 αἰτίαν. ῥητέον οὖν καὶ πρὸς τοῦτον ὅτι καθῆκον
ἦν, ὥσπερ ἀπὸ τοῦ Νείλου τὴν ὑγρασίαν ὁ ἥλιος
ἐφ' ἑαυτὸν ἐπισπᾶται κατὰ τοὺς τοῦ χειμῶνος
καιρούς, οὕτω καὶ ἀπὸ τῶν ἄλλων τῶν κατὰ
τὴν Λιβύην ὄντων ποταμῶν ἀναλαμβάνειν τι
τῶν ὑγρῶν καὶ ταπεινοῦν τὰ φερόμενα ῥεύματα.
12 ἐπεὶ δ' οὐδαμοῦ τῆς Λιβύης οὐδὲν τοιοῦτον
γινόμενον θεωρεῖται, περιφανῶς ὁ συγγραφεὺς
σχεδιάζων εὑρίσκεται· καὶ γὰρ οἱ περὶ τὴν
Ἑλλάδα ποταμοὶ τὴν αὔξησιν ἐν τῷ χειμῶνι

if a man should admit the existence of great quantities of snow in the regions beyond Ethiopia, the falsity of the statement is still shown by this fact: every river which flows out of snow gives out cool breezes, as is generally agreed, and thickens the air about it; but the Nile is the only river about which no clouds form, and where no cool breezes rise and the air is not thickened.

Herodotus [1] says that the size of the Nile at its swelling is its natural one, but that as the sun travels over Libya in the winter it draws up to itself from the Nile a great amount of moisture, and this is the reason why at that season the river becomes smaller than its natural size; but at the beginning of summer, when the sun turns back in its course towards the north, it dries out and thus reduces the level of both the rivers of Greece and those of every other land whose geographical position is like that of Greece. [2] Consequently there is no occasion for surprise, he says, in the phenomenon of the Nile; for, as a matter of fact, it does not increase in volume in the hot season and then fall in the winter, for the reason just given. Now the answer to be made to this explanation also is that it would follow that, if the sun drew moisture to itself from the Nile in the winter, it would also take some moisture from all the other rivers of Libya and reduce the flow of their waters. But since nowhere in Libya is anything like this to be seen taking place, it is clear that the historian is caught inventing an explanation; for the fact is that the rivers of Greece increase in winter, not

---

[1] Book 2. 25.
[2] *i.e.* in the north latitude.

λαμβάνουσιν οὐ διὰ τὸ μακρότερον ἀφίστασθαι
τὸν ἥλιον, ἀλλὰ διὰ τὸ πλῆθος τῶν γινομένων
ὄμβρων.

39. Δημόκριτος δ' ὁ Ἀβδηρίτης φησὶν οὐ τὸν
περὶ τὴν μεσημβρίαν τόπον χιονίζεσθαι, καθάπερ
εἴρηκεν Εὐριπίδης καὶ Ἀναξαγόρας, ἀλλὰ τὸν
περὶ τὰς ἄρκτους, καὶ τοῦτο ἐμφανὲς εἶναι πᾶσι.
2 τὸ δὲ πλῆθος τῆς σωρευομένης χιόνος ἐν τοῖς
βορείοις μέρεσι περὶ μὲν τὰς τροπὰς μένειν
πεπηγός, ἐν δὲ τῷ θέρει διαλυομένων ὑπὸ τῆς
θερμασίας τῶν πάγων πολλὴν τηκεδόνα γίνεσθαι, καὶ διὰ τοῦτο πολλὰ γεννᾶσθαι καὶ παχέα
νέφη περὶ τοὺς μετεωροτέρους τῶν τόπων, δαψι-
λοῦς τῆς ἀναθυμιάσεως πρὸς τὸ ὕψος αἰρομένης.
3 ταῦτα δ' ὑπὸ τῶν ἐτησίων ἐλαύνεσθαι, μέχρι ἂν
ὅτου προσπέσῃ τοῖς μεγίστοις ὄρεσι τῶν κατὰ
τὴν οἰκουμένην, ἅ φησιν εἶναι περὶ τὴν Αἰθιοπίαν·
ἔπειτα πρὸς τούτοις οὖσιν ὑψηλοῖς βιαίως
θραυόμενα παμμεγέθεις ὄμβρους γεννᾶν, ἐξ ὧν
πληροῦσθαι τὸν ποταμὸν μάλιστα κατὰ τὴν τῶν
4 ἐτησίων ὥραν. ῥᾴδιον δὲ καὶ τοῦτον ἐξελέγξαι
τοὺς χρόνους τῆς αὐξήσεως ἀκριβῶς ἐξετάζοντα·
ὁ γὰρ Νεῖλος ἄρχεται μὲν πληροῦσθαι κατὰ τὰς
θερινὰς τροπάς, οὔπω τῶν ἐτησίων πνεόντων,
λήγει δ' ὕστερον ἰσημερίας φθινοπωρινῆς, πάλαι
5 προπεπαυμένων τῶν εἰρημένων ἀνέμων. ὅταν
οὖν ἡ τῆς πείρας ἀκρίβεια κατισχύῃ τὴν τῶν
λόγων πιθανότητα, τὴν μὲν ἐπίνοιαν τἀνδρὸς
ἀποδεκτέον, τὴν δὲ πίστιν τοῖς ὑπ' αὐτοῦ λεγο-
6 μένοις οὐ δοτέον. παρίημι γὰρ καὶ διότι τοὺς
ἐτησίας ἰδεῖν ἔστιν οὐδέν τι μᾶλλον ἀπὸ τῆς

because the sun is farther away, but by reason of the enormous rainfall.

39. Democritus of Abdera [1] says that it is not the regions of the south that are covered with snow, as Euripides and Anaxagoras have asserted, but only those of the north, and that this is evident to everyone. The great quantities of heaped-up snow in the northern regions still remain frozen until about the time of the winter solstice, but when in summer its solid masses are broken up by the heat, a great melting sets up, and this brings about the formation of many thick clouds in the higher altitudes, since the vapour rises upwards in large quantities. These clouds are then driven by the etesian winds until they strike the highest mountains in the whole earth, which, he says, are those of Ethiopia; then by their violent impact upon these peaks, lofty as they are, they cause torrential rains which swell the river, to the greatest extent at the season of the etesian winds. But it is easy for anyone to refute this explanation also, if he will but note with precision the time when the increase of the river takes place; for the Nile begins to swell at the summer solstice, when the etesian winds are not yet blowing, and commences to fall after the autumnal equinox, when the same winds have long since ceased. Whenever, therefore, the precise knowledge derived from experience prevails over the plausibility of mere argumentation, while we should recognize the man's ingenuity, yet no credence should be given to his statements. Indeed, I pass over the further fact that the etesian winds can be seen to blow just

---

[1] Democritus was a contemporary of Socrates and the first Greek who attempted to embrace in his writings all the knowledge of his time.

ἄρκτου πνέοντας ἤπερ τῆς ἑσπέρας· οὐ βορέαι
γὰρ οὐδ' ἀπαρκτίαι μόνοι, ἀλλὰ καὶ οἱ πνέοντες
ἀπὸ θερινῆς δύσεως ἀργέσται κοινωνοῦσι τῆς τῶν
ἐτησίων προσηγορίας. τό τε λέγειν ὡς μέγιστα
συμβαίνει τῶν ὀρῶν ὑπάρχειν τὰ περὶ τὴν
Αἰθιοπίαν οὐ μόνον ἀναπόδεικτόν ἐστιν, ἀλλ'
οὐδὲ τὴν πίστιν ἔχει διὰ τῆς ἐναργείας[1] συγχω-
ρουμένην.

7   Ἔφορος δὲ καινοτάτην αἰτίαν εἰσφέρων πιθα-
νολογεῖν μὲν πειρᾶται, τῆς δ' ἀληθείας οὐδαμῶς
ἐπιτυγχάνων θεωρεῖται. φησὶ γὰρ τὴν Αἴγυπτον
ἅπασαν οὖσαν ποταμόχωστον καὶ χαύνην, ἔτι
δὲ κισηρώδη τὴν φύσιν, ῥαγάδας τε μεγάλας καὶ
διηνεκεῖς ἔχειν, διὰ δὲ τούτων εἰς ἑαυτὴν ἀναλαμβάνειν ὑγροῦ πλῆθος, καὶ κατὰ μὲν τὴν
χειμερινὴν ὥραν συνέχειν ἐν ἑαυτῇ τοῦτο, κατὰ
δὲ τὴν θερινὴν ὥσπερ ἱδρῶτάς τινας ἐξ αὐτῆς πανταχόθεν ἀνιέναι, καὶ διὰ τούτων πληροῦν τὸν
8 ποταμόν. ὁ δὲ συγγραφεὺς οὗτος οὐ μόνον ἡμῖν
φαίνεται μὴ τεθεαμένος τὴν φύσιν τῶν κατὰ
τὴν Αἴγυπτον τόπων, ἀλλὰ μηδὲ παρὰ τῶν
εἰδότων τὰ κατὰ τὴν χώραν ταύτην ἐπιμελῶς
9 πεπυσμένος. πρῶτον μὲν γάρ, εἴπερ ἐξ αὐτῆς
τῆς Αἰγύπτου ὁ Νεῖλος τὴν αὔξησιν ἐλάμβανεν,
οὐκ ἂν ἐν τοῖς ἀνωτέρω μέρεσιν ἐπληροῦτο, διά
τε πετρώδους καὶ στερεᾶς χώρας φερόμενος· νῦν
δὲ πλείω τῶν ἑξακισχιλίων σταδίων διὰ τῆς
Αἰθιοπίας ῥέων τὴν πλήρωσιν ἔχει πρὶν ἢ

---

[1] ἐναργείας Wesseling : ἐνεργείας.

---

[1] Two names given to north winds.
[2] *i.e.* the north-west.

as much from the west as from the north; since
Borean and Aparctian[1] winds are not the only winds
which are called etesian, but also the Argestean,
which blow from the direction of the sun's summer
setting.[2] Also the statement that by general agreement the highest mountains are those of Ethiopia
is not only advanced without any proof, but it does
not possess, either, the credibility which is accorded
to facts established by observation.[3]

Ephorus, who presents the most recent explanation, endeavours to adduce a plausible argument,
but, as may be seen, by no means arrives at the
truth. For he says that all Egypt, being alluvial
soil and spongy,[4] and in nature like pumice-stone, is
full of large and continuous cracks, through which
it takes up a great amount of water; this it retains
within itself during the winter season, but in the
summer season it pours this out from itself everywhere like sweat, as it were, and by means of this
exudation it causes the flood of the river. But this
historian, as it appears to us, has not only never
personally observed the nature of the country in
Egypt, but has not even inquired with any care
about it of those who are acquainted with the character of this land. For in the first place, if the
Nile derived its increase from Egypt itself, it would
then not experience a flood in its upper stretches,
where it flows through a stony and solid country;
yet, as a matter of fact, it floods while flowing over
a course of more than six thousand stades through

[3] *i.e.* there is no evidence from witnesses that they appear
to be exceedingly high.

[4] The words mean literally "poured out by a river" and
"gaping."

10 ψαῦσαι τῆς Αἰγύπτου. ἔπειτ᾽ εἰ μὲν τὸ ῥεῦμα
τοῦ Νείλου ταπεινότερον ἦν τῶν κατὰ τὴν ποταμόχωστον γῆν ἀραιωμάτων, ἐπιπολαίους ἂν
εἶναι τὰς ῥαγάδας συνέβαινε, καθ᾽ ἃς ἀδύνατον
ἦν διαμένειν τοσοῦτο πλῆθος ὕδατος· εἰ δ᾽
ὑψηλότερον τόπον ἐπεῖχεν ὁ ποταμὸς τῶν
ἀραιωμάτων, ἀδύνατον ἦν ἐκ τῶν ταπεινοτέρων
κοιλωμάτων εἰς τὴν ὑψηλοτέραν ἐπιφάνειαν τὴν
τῶν ὑγρῶν σύρρυσιν γίνεσθαι.

11 Καθόλου δὲ τίς ἂν δυνατὸν ἡγήσαιτο τοὺς ἐκ
τῶν κατὰ τὴν γῆν ἀραιωμάτων ἱδρῶτας τοσαύτην αὔξησιν τοῦ ποταμοῦ ποιεῖν ὥστε ὑπ᾽
αὐτοῦ σχεδὸν πᾶσαν τὴν Αἴγυπτον ἐπικλύζε-
σθαι; ἀφίημι γὰρ καὶ τὸ ψεῦδος τῆς τε ποτα-
μοχώστου γῆς καὶ τῶν ἐν τοῖς ἀραιώμασι
τηρουμένων ὑδάτων, ἐμφανῶν ὄντων τῶν ἐν

12 τούτοις ἐλέγχων. ὁ μὲν γὰρ Μαίανδρος ποταμὸς
κατὰ τὴν Ἀσίαν πολλὴν χώραν πεποίηκε
ποταμόχωστον, ἐν ᾗ τῶν συμβαινόντων περὶ
τὴν ἀναπλήρωσιν τοῦ Νείλου τὸ σύνολον οὐδὲν

13 θεωρεῖται γινόμενον. ὁμοίως δὲ τούτῳ περὶ μὲν
τὴν Ἀκαρνανίαν ὁ καλούμειος Ἀχελῷος ποταμός, περὶ δὲ τὴν Βοιωτίαν ὁ Κηφισὸς φερόμενος
ἐκ τῶν Φωκέων προσκέχωκεν οὐκ ὀλίγην χώραν,
ἐφ᾽ ὧν ἀμφοτέρων ἐλέγχεται φανερῶς τὸ ψεῦδος
τοῦ συγγραφέως. ἀλλὰ γὰρ οὐκ ἄν τις παρ᾽
Ἐφόρῳ ζητήσειεν ἐκ παντὸς τρόπου τἀκριβές,
ὁρῶν αὐτὸν ἐν πολλοῖς ὠλιγωρηκότα τῆς ἀληθείας.

40. Τῶν δ᾽ ἐν Μέμφει τινὲς φιλοσόφων ἐπεχεί-
ρησαν αἰτίαν φέρειν τῆς πληρώσεως ἀνεξέλεγκτον
μᾶλλον ἢ πιθανήν, ᾗ πολλοὶ συγκατατέθεινται.

Ethiopia before ever it touches Egypt. Secondly, if the stream of the Nile were, on the one hand, lower than the rifts in the alluvial soil, the cracks would then be on the surface and so great an amount of water could not possibly remain in them; and if, on the other hand, the river occupied a higher level than the rifts, there could not possibly be a flow of water from the lower hollows to the higher surface.

In general, can any man think it possible that the exudations from rifts in the ground should produce so great an increase in the waters of the river that practically all Egypt is inundated by it! For I pass over the false statements of Ephorus about the ground being alluvial and the water being stored up in the rifts, since the refutation of them is manifest. For instance, the Meander river in Asia has laid down a great amount of alluvial land, yet not a single one of the phenomena attending the flooding of the Nile is to be seen in its case. And like the Meander the river in Acarnania known as the Acheloüs, and the Cephisus in Boeotia, which flows out of Phocis, have built up not a little land, and in the case of both there is clear proof that the historian's statements are erroneous. However, under no circumstances would any man look for strict accuracy in Ephorus, when he sees that in many matters he has paid little regard to the truth.

40. Certain of the wise men in Memphis have undertaken to advance an explanation of the flooding, which is incapable of disproof rather than credible, and yet it is accepted by many. They

2 διαιρούμενοι γὰρ τὴν γῆν εἰς τρία μέρη φασὶν
ὑπάρχειν ἓν μὲν τὸ κατὰ τὴν ἡμετέραν οἰκουμένην, ἕτερον δὲ τὸ τούτοις τοῖς τόποις ἀντιπε-
πονθὸς ταῖς ὥραις, τὸ δὲ τρίτον μεταξὺ μὲν
κεῖσθαι τούτων, ὑπάρχειν δὲ διὰ καῦμα ἀοίκητον.
3 εἰ μὲν οὖν ὁ Νεῖλος ἀνέβαινε κατὰ τὸν τοῦ
χειμῶνος καιρόν, δῆλον ἂν [1] ὑπῆρχεν ὡς ἐκ τῆς
καθ᾽ ἡμᾶς ζώνης λαμβάνει τὴν ἐπίρρυσιν διὰ
τὸ περὶ τούτους τοὺς καιροὺς μάλιστα γίνεσθαι
παρ᾽ ἡμῖν τὰς ἐπομβρίας· ἐπεὶ δὲ τοὐναντίον
περὶ τὸ θέρος πληροῦται, πιθανὸν εἶναι κατὰ
τοὺς ἀντικειμένους τόπους γεννᾶσθαι τοὺς χειμῶνας, καὶ τὸ πλεονάζον τῶν κατ᾽ ἐκείνους τοὺς
τόπους ὑδάτων εἰς τὴν καθ᾽ ἡμᾶς οἰκουμένην
4 φέρεσθαι. διὸ καὶ πρὸς τὰς πηγὰς τοῦ Νείλου
μηδένα δύνασθαι παρελθεῖν, ὡς ἂν ἐκ τῆς
ἐναντίας ζώνης διὰ τῆς ἀοικήτου φερομένου τοῦ
ποταμοῦ. μαρτυρεῖν δὲ τούτοις καὶ τὴν ὑπερβολὴν
τῆς γλυκύτητος τοῦ κατὰ τὸν Νεῖλον ὕδατος·
διὰ γὰρ τῆς κατακεκαυμένης αὐτὸν ῥέοντα
καθέψεσθαι, καὶ διὰ τοῦτο γλυκύτατον εἶναι
πάντων τῶν ποταμῶν, ἅτε φύσει τοῦ πυρώδους
πᾶν τὸ ὑγρὸν ἀπογλυκαίνοντος.
5 Οὗτος δ᾽ ὁ λόγος ἔχει μέν τινα [2] πρόχειρον
ἀντίρρησιν, ὅτι παντελῶς ἀδύνατον εἶναι δοκεῖ
ποταμὸν ἐκ τῆς ἀντικειμένης οἰκουμένης εἰς τὴν
ἡμετέραν ἀναφέρεσθαι, καὶ μάλιστ᾽ εἴ τις ὑπό-

---

[1] ἂν added by Hertlein.
[2] τινὰ D, Vogel : τινὰ φανερὰν καὶ other MSS., Bekker,
Dindorf.

divide the earth into three parts, and say that one part is that which forms our inhabited world, that the second is exactly opposed to these regions in its seasons, and that the third lies between these two but is uninhabited by reason of the heat.[1] Now if the Nile rose in the winter, it would be clear that it was receiving its additional waters from our zone because of the heavy rains which fall with us in that season especially; but since, on the contrary, its flood occurs in the summer, it is probable that in the regions opposite to us the winter storms are being produced and that the surplus waters of those distant regions flow into our inhabited world. And it is for this reason that no man can journey to the sources of the Nile, because the river flows from the opposite zone through the uninhabited one. A further witness to this is the excessive sweetness of the water of the Nile; for in the course of the river through the torrid zone it is tempered by the heat, and that is the reason for its being the sweetest of all rivers, inasmuch as by the law of nature that which is fiery always sweetens [2] what is wet.

But this explanation admits of an obvious rebuttal, for plainly it is quite impossible for a river to flow uphill into our inhabited world from the inhabited world opposite to ours, especially if one holds to

---

[1] *i.e.*, they postulated a south temperate zone, corresponding to the north temperate, and separated from it by the torrid zone. The Nile, according to them, rose in the south temperate zone. They were not in fact so far astray in the matter, the White Nile rising just a little south of the equator, although the waters of the annual inundation come from the Blue Nile, which has its sources in the table-land of Abyssinia.

[2] *i.e.*, water is freshened ("sweetened") by being heated.

θοιτο σφαιροειδῆ τὴν γῆν ὑπάρχειν. καὶ γὰρ
ἐάν τις τοῖς λόγοις κατατολμήσας βιάζηται τὴν
ἐνάργειαν, ἥ γε φύσις τῶν πραγμάτων οὐδαμῶς
συγχωρήσει. καθόλου μὲν γὰρ ἀνεξέλεγκτον
ἀπόφασιν εἰσηγούμενοι, καὶ τὴν ἀοίκητον χώραν
μεταξὺ τιθέμενοι, ταύτῃ διαφεύξεσθαι τοὺς
6 ἀκριβεῖς ἐλέγχους νομίζουσι· δίκαιον δὲ τοὺς
περί τινων διαβεβαιουμένους ἢ τὴν ἐνάργειαν
παρέχεσθαι μαρτυροῦσαν ἢ τὰς ἀποδείξεις
λαμβάνειν ἐξ ἀρχῆς συγκεχωρημένας. πῶς δὲ
μόνος ὁ Νεῖλος ἐξ ἐκείνης τῆς οἰκουμένης φέρεται
πρὸς τοὺς καθ' ἡμᾶς τόπους; εἰκὸς γὰρ εἶναι
καὶ ἑτέρους ποταμούς, καθάπερ καὶ παρ' ἡμῖν.
7 ἥ τε τῆς περὶ τὸ ὕδωρ γλυκύτητος αἰτία παντελῶς
ἄλογος. εἰ γὰρ καθεψόμενος ὑπὸ τῶν καυμάτων
ὁ ποταμὸς ἐγλυκαίνετο, πολύγονος οὐκ ἂν ἦν
οὐδὲ ποικίλας ἰχθύων καὶ θηρίων ἰδέας εἶχε· πᾶν
γὰρ ὕδωρ ὑπὸ τῆς πυρώδους φύσεως ἀλλοιωθὲν
8 ἀλλοτριώτατόν ἐστι ζωογονίας. διόπερ τῇ
παρεισαγομένῃ καθεψήσει τῆς φύσεως τοῦ
Νείλου παντάπασιν ἐναντιουμένης ψευδεῖς τὰς
εἰρημένας αἰτίας τῆς πληρώσεως ἡγητέον.

41. Οἰνοπίδης δὲ ὁ Χίος φησι κατὰ μὲν τὴν
θερινὴν ὥραν τὰ ὕδατα κατὰ τὴν γῆν εἶναι
ψυχρά, τοῦ δὲ χειμῶνος τοὐναντίον θερμά, καὶ
τοῦτο εὔδηλον ἐπὶ τῶν βαθέων φρεάτων γίνεσθαι·
κατὰ μὲν γὰρ τὴν ἀκμὴν τοῦ χειμῶνος ἥκιστα
τὸ ὕδωρ ἐν αὐτοῖς ὑπάρχειν ψυχρόν, κατὰ δὲ
τὰ μέγιστα καύματα ψυχρότατον ἐξ αὐτῶν

---

[1] Practically nothing more is known of Oenopides than
that he was an astronomer and mathematician of the fifth
century B.C.

the theory that the earth is shaped like a sphere. And indeed, if any man makes bold to do violence, by means of mere words, to facts established by observation, Nature at least will in no wise yield to him. For, in general, such men think that, by introducing a proposition incapable of being disproved and placing the uninhabited region between the two inhabited ones, they will in this way avoid all precise refutations of their argument; but the proper course for such as take a firm position on any matter is either to adduce the observed facts as evidence or to find their proofs in statements which have been agreed upon at the outset. But how can the Nile be the only river which flows from that inhabited world to our parts? For it is reasonable to suppose that other rivers as well are to be found there, just as there are many among us. Moreover, the cause which they advance for the sweetness of the water is altogether absurd. For if the river were sweetened by being tempered by the heat, it would not be so productive as it is of life, nor contain so many kinds of fishes and animals; for all water upon being changed by the fiery element is quite incapable of generating life. Therefore, since by the " tempering " process which they introduce they entirely change the real nature of the Nile, the causes which they advance for its flooding must be considered false.

41. Oenopides of Chios [1] says that in the summer the waters under the earth are cold, but in the winter, on the contrary, warm; and that this may be clearly observed in deep wells, for in midwinter their water is least cold, while in the hottest weather

2 ὑγρὸν ἀναφέρεσθαι. διὸ καὶ τὸν Νεῖλον εὐλόγως
κατὰ μὲν τὸν χειμῶνα μικρὸν εἶναι καὶ συστέλλεσθαι, διὰ τὸ τὴν μὲν κατὰ γῆν θερμασίαν τὸ
πολὺ τῆς ὑγρᾶς οὐσίας ἀναλίσκειν, ὄμβρους δὲ
κατὰ τὴν Αἴγυπτον μὴ γίνεσθαι· κατὰ δὲ τὸ
θέρος μηκέτι τῆς κατὰ γῆν ἀπαναλώσεως γινομένης ἐν τοῖς κατὰ βάθος τόποις πληροῦσθαι
τὴν κατὰ φύσιν αὐτοῦ ῥύσιν ἀνεμποδίστως.

3 ῥητέον δὲ καὶ πρὸς τοῦτον ὅτι πολλοὶ ποταμοὶ
τῶν κατὰ τὴν Λιβύην ὁμοίως μὲν κείμενοι τοῖς
στόμασι, παραπλησίους δὲ τὰς ῥύσεις ποιούμενοι, τὴν ἀνάβασιν οὐκ ἔχουσιν ἀνάλογον τῷ
Νείλῳ· τοὐναντίον γὰρ ἐν μὲν τῷ χειμῶνι
πληρούμενοι, κατὰ δὲ τὸ θέρος λήγοντες ἐλέγχουσι
τὸ ψεῦδος τοῦ πειρωμένου τοῖς πιθανοῖς κατα-
μάχεσθαι τὴν ἀλήθειαν.

4 Ἔγγιστα δὲ τῇ ἀληθείᾳ προσελήλυθεν Ἀγα-
θαρχίδης ὁ Κνίδιος. φησὶ γὰρ κατ' ἐνιαυτὸν ἐν
τοῖς κατὰ τὴν Αἰθιοπίαν ὄρεσι γίνεσθαι συνεχεῖς
ὄμβρους ἀπὸ θερινῶν τροπῶν μέχρι τῆς μετο-
5 πωρινῆς ἰσημερίας· εὐλόγως οὖν τὸν Νεῖλον ἐν
μὲν τῷ χειμῶνι συστέλλεσθαι, τὴν κατὰ φύσιν
ἔχοντα ῥύσιν ἀπὸ μόνων τῶν πηγῶν, κατὰ δὲ
τὸ θέρος διὰ τοὺς ἐκχεομένους ὄμβρους λαμβά-
6 νειν τὴν αὔξησιν. εἰ δὲ τὰς αἰτίας μηδεὶς ἀποδοῦναι δύναται μέχρι τοῦ νῦν τῆς τῶν ὑδάτων
γενέσεως, οὐ προσήκειν[1] ἀθετεῖσθαι τὴν ἰδίαν
ἀπόφασιν· πολλὰ γὰρ τὴν φύσιν ἐναντίως φέρειν,
ὧν τὰς αἰτίας οὐκ ἐφικτὸν ἀνθρώποις ἀκριβῶς

---

[1] προσήκειν Rhodomann: προσήκει.

the coldest water is drawn up from them. Consequently it is reasonable that the Nile should be small and should diminish in the winter, since the heat in the earth consumes the larger part of the moisture and there are no rains in Egypt; while in the summer, since there is no longer any consumption of the moisture down in the depths of the earth, the natural flow of the river is increased without hindrance. But the answer to be given to this explanation also is that there are many rivers in Libya, whose mouths are situated like those of the Nile and whose courses are much the same, and yet they do not rise in the same manner as the Nile; on the contrary, flooding as they do in the winter and receding in the summer, they refute the false statement of any man who tries to overcome the truth with specious arguments.

The nearest approach to the truth has been made by Agatharchides of Cnidus.[1] His explanation is as follows: Every year continuous rains fall in the mountains of Ethiopia from the summer solstice to the autumnal equinox; and so it is entirely reasonable that the Nile should diminish in the winter when it derives its natural supply of water solely from its sources, but should increase its volume in the summer on account of the rains which pour into it. And just because no one up to this time has been able to set forth the causes of the origin of the flood waters, it is not proper, he urges, that his personal explanation be rejected; for nature presents many contradictory phenomena, the exact causes of which are beyond the power of mankind

[1] Agatharchides was a historian and geographer of the second century B.C.

7 ἐξευρεῖν. μαρτυρεῖν δὲ τοῖς ὑφ' ἑαυτοῦ λεγομένοις καὶ τὸ γινόμενον περί τινας τόπους τῆς
Ἀσίας· πρὸς μὲν γὰρ τοῖς ὅροις τῆς Σκυθίας
τοῖς πρὸς τὸ Καυκάσιον ὄρος συνάπτουσι, παρε-
ληλυθότος ἤδη τοῦ χειμῶνος, καθ' ἕκαστον ἔτος
νιφετοὺς ἐξαισίους γίνεσθαι συνεχῶς ἐπὶ πολλὰς
ἡμέρας, ἐν δὲ τοῖς πρὸς βορρᾶν ἐστραμμένοις
μέρεσι τῆς Ἰνδικῆς ὡρισμένοις καιροῖς καὶ
χάλαζαν ἄπιστον τὸ μέγεθος καὶ τὸ πλῆθος
καταράττειν, καὶ περὶ μὲν τὸν Ὑδάσπην ποταμὸν ἀρχομένου θέρους συνεχεῖς ὄμβρους γίνεσθαι,
κατὰ δὲ τὴν Αἰθιοπίαν μεθ' ἡμέρας τινὰς ταὐτὸ
συμβαίνειν, καὶ ταύτην τὴν περίστασιν κυκλου-
μένην ἀεὶ τοὺς συνεχεῖς τόπους χειμάζειν.
8 οὐδὲν οὖν εἶναι παράδοξον εἰ καὶ κατὰ τὴν
Αἰθιοπίαν τὴν κειμένην ὑπὲρ Αἰγύπτου συνεχεῖς
ἐν τοῖς ὄρεσιν ὄμβροι καταράττοντες ἐν τῷ θέρει
πληροῦσι τὸν ποταμόν, ἄλλως τε καὶ τῆς ἐναργείας [1] αὐτῆς μαρτυρουμένης ὑπὸ τῶν περὶ τοὺς
9 τόπους οἰκούντων βαρβάρων. εἰ δὲ τοῖς παρ'
ἡμῖν γινομένοις ἐναντίαν ἔχει τὰ λεγόμενα φύσιν,
οὐ διὰ τοῦτ' ἀπιστητέον· καὶ γὰρ τὸν νότον παρ'
ἡμῖν μὲν εἶναι χειμέριον, περὶ δὲ τὴν Αἰθιοπίαν
αἴθριον ὑπάρχειν, καὶ τὰς βορείους πνοὰς περὶ
μὲν τὴν Εὐρώπην εὐτόνους εἶναι, κατ' ἐκείνην δὲ
τὴν χώραν βληχρὰς καὶ ἀτόνους.[2]
10   Καὶ περὶ μὲν τῆς πληρώσεως τοῦ Νείλου, δυνάμενοι ποικιλώτερον ἀντειπεῖν πρὸς ἅπαντας,
ἀρκεσθησόμεθα τοῖς εἰρημένοις, ἵνα μὴ τὴν ἐξ
ἀρχῆς ἡμῖν προκειμένην συντομίαν ὑπερβαίνω-
μεν. ἐπεὶ δὲ τὴν βίβλον ταύτην διὰ τὸ μέγεθος

___
[1] ἐναργείας Wesseling : ἐνεργείας.

to discover. As to his own statement, he adds, testimony to its truth is furnished by what takes place in certain regions of Asia. For on the borders of Scythia which abut upon the Caucasus mountains, annually, after the winter is over, exceptionally heavy snowstorms occur over many consecutive days; in the northern parts of India at certain seasons hailstones come beating down which in size and quantity surpass belief; about the Hydaspes river continuous rains fall at the opening of summer; and in Ethiopia, likewise, the same thing occurs some days later, this climatical condition, in its regular recurrence, always causing storms in the neighbouring regions. And so, he argues, it is nothing surprising if in Ethiopia as well, which lies above Egypt, continuous rains in the mountains, beating down during the summer, swell the river, especially since the plain fact itself is witnessed to by the barbarians who inhabit those regions. And if what has been said is of a nature opposite to what occurs among us, it should not be disbelieved on that score; for the south wind, for example, with us is accompanied by stormy weather, but in Ethiopia by clear skies, and in Europe the north winds are violent, but in that land they are gentle and light.

With regard, then, to the flooding of the Nile, though we are able to answer with more varied arguments all who have offered explanations of it, we shall rest content with what has been said, in order that we may not overstep the principle of brevity which we resolved upon at the beginning. And since we have divided this Book into two parts

---

[2] καὶ παντελῶς ἀσθενεῖς added by D.

εἰς δύο μέρη διῃρήκαμεν, στοχαζόμενοι τῆς συμμετρίας, τὴν πρώτην μερίδα τῶν ἱστορουμένων αὐτοῦ περιγράψομεν, τὰ δὲ συνεχῆ τῶν κατὰ τὴν Αἴγυπτον ἱστορουμένων ἐν τῇ δευτέρᾳ κατατάξομεν, ἀρχὴν ποιησάμενοι τὴν ἀπαγγελίαν τῶν γενομένων βασιλέων τῆς Αἰγύπτου καὶ τοῦ παλαιοτάτου βίου παρ' Αἰγυπτίοις.

because of its length, inasmuch as we are aiming at due proportion in our account,[1] at this point we shall close the first portion of our history, and in the second we shall set forth the facts in the history of Egypt which come next in order, beginning with the account of the former kings of Egypt and of the earliest manner of life among the Egyptians.

[1] Cp. p. 96, n. 1.

ΜΕΡΙΣ ΔΕΥΤΕΡΑ ΤΗΣ ΠΡΩΤΗΣ ΒΙΒΛΟΥ[1]

42. Τῆς πρώτης τῶν Διοδώρου βίβλων διὰ τὸ μέγεθος εἰς δύο βίβλους διῃρημένης ἡ πρώτη μὲν περιέχει προοίμιον περὶ ὅλης τῆς πραγματείας καὶ τὰ λεγόμενα παρ' Αἰγυπτίοις περὶ τῆς τοῦ κόσμου γενέσεως καὶ τῆς τῶν ὅλων ἐξ ἀρχῆς συστάσεως, πρὸς δὲ τούτοις περὶ τῶν θεῶν, ὅσοι πόλεις ἔκτισαν κατ' Αἴγυπτον ἐπωνύμους ἑαυτῶν ποιήσαντες, περί τε τῶν πρώτων γενομένων ἀνθρώπων καὶ τοῦ παλαιοτάτου βίου, τῆς τε τῶν ἀθανάτων τιμῆς καὶ τῆς τῶν ναῶν κατασκευῆς, ἑξῆς δὲ περὶ τῆς τοποθεσίας τῆς κατ' Αἴγυπτον χώρας καὶ τῶν περὶ τὸν Νεῖλον ποταμὸν παρα-δοξολογουμένων, τῆς τε τούτου πληρώσεως τὰς αἰτίας καὶ τῶν ἱστορικῶν καὶ φιλοσόφων ἀποφά-σεις, ἔτι δὲ τὰς πρὸς ἕκαστον τῶν συγγραφέων

2 ἀντιρρήσεις· ἐν ταύτῃ δὲ τῇ βίβλῳ τὰ συνεχῆ τοῖς προειρημένοις διέξιμεν. ἀρχόμεθα δὲ ἀπὸ τῶν γενομένων πρώτων κατ' Αἴγυπτον βασιλέων, καὶ τὰς κατὰ μέρος αὐτῶν πράξεις ἐκθησόμεθα μέχρι Ἀμάσιδος τοῦ βασιλέως, προεκθέμενοι κεφαλαιωδῶς τὴν ἀρχαιοτάτην ἀγωγὴν τῶν κατ' Αἴγυπτον.

43. Βίῳ γὰρ τὸ παλαιὸν Αἰγυπτίους φασὶ χρῆσθαι τὸ μὲν ἀρχαιότατον πόαν ἐσθίοντας καὶ

---

[1] This title is found in A.

152

PART TWO OF THE FIRST BOOK

42. THE First Book of Diodorus being divided because of its length into two volumes, the first contains the preface to the whole treatise and the accounts given by the Egyptians of the genesis of the world and the first forming of the universe; then he tells of the gods who founded cities in Egypt and named them after themselves, of the first men and the earliest manner of life, of the honour paid to the immortals and the building of their temples to them, then of the topography of Egypt and the marvels related about the river Nile, and also of the causes of its flooding and the opinions thereupon of the historians and the philosophers as well as the refutation of each writer.[1] In this volume we shall discuss the topics which come next in order after the foregoing. We shall begin with the first kings of Egypt and set forth their individual deeds down to King Amasis, after we have first described in summary fashion the most ancient manner of life in Egypt.

569–526 B.C.

43. As for their means of living in primitive times, the Egyptians, they say, in the earliest period got

---

[1] This sentence as it stands is almost certainly not from the hand of Diodorus. But the following words do not connect well with the end of chapter 41. In Book 17, which is also broken into two Parts, the narrative continues without any such interruption as occurs here.

τῶν ἐν τοῖς ἕλεσι γινομένων τοὺς καυλοὺς καὶ
τὰς ῥίζας, πεῖραν διὰ τῆς γεύσεως ἑκάστου λαμ-
βάνοντας, πρώτην δὲ καὶ μάλιστα προσενέγκασθαι
τὴν ὀνομαζομένην ἄγρωστιν διὰ τὸ καὶ τῇ γλυκύτητι διάφορον εἶναι καὶ τὴν τροφὴν ἀρκοῦσαν
2 παρέχεσθαι τοῖς σώμασι τῶν ἀνθρώπων· καὶ γὰρ
τοῖς κτήνεσι ταύτην θεωρεῖσθαι προσηνῆ καὶ ταχὺ
τοὺς ὄγκους αὐτῶν προσανατρέφειν. διὸ καὶ
τῆς εὐχρηστίας τῆς περὶ τὴν βοτάνην ταύτην
μνημονεύοντας τοὺς ἀνθρώπους μέχρι τοῦ νῦν,
ὅταν πρὸς θεοὺς βαδίζωσι, τῇ χειρὶ ταύτης λαμ-
βάνοντας προσεύχεσθαι· οἴονται γὰρ τὸν ἄνθρωπον ἕλειον καὶ λιμνῶδες εἶναι ζῷον, ἀπό τε τῆς
λειότητος τεκμαιρόμενοι καὶ τῆς φυσικῆς ποιό-
τητος, ἔτι δὲ τοῦ προσδεῖσθαι τροφῆς τῆς ὑγρᾶς
3 μᾶλλον ἢ τῆς ξηρᾶς. δευτέραν δὲ λέγουσιν ἔχειν
διαγωγὴν τοὺς Αἰγυπτίους τὴν τῶν ἰχθύων
βρῶσιν, πολλὴν δαψίλειαν παρεχομένου τοῦ
ποταμοῦ, καὶ μάλισθ᾿ ὅτε μετὰ τὴν ἀνάβασιν
4 ταπεινούμενος ἀναξηραίνοιτο. ὁμοίως δὲ καὶ τῶν
βοσκημάτων ἔνια σαρκοφαγεῖν, καὶ ταῖς δοραῖς
τῶν κατεσθιομένων ἐσθῆσι χρῆσθαι, καὶ τὰς
οἰκήσεις ἐκ τῶν καλάμων κατασκευάζεσθαι.
ἴχνη δὲ τούτων διαμένειν παρὰ τοῖς νομεῦσι
τοῖς κατ᾿ Αἴγυπτον, οὓς ἅπαντάς φασι μέχρι
τοῦ νῦν μηδεμίαν ἄλλην οἴκησιν ἢ τὴν ἐκ τῶν
καλάμων ἔχειν, δοκιμάζοντας ἀρκεῖσθαι ταύτῃ.
5 πολλοὺς δὲ χρόνους τούτῳ τῷ βίῳ διεξαγαγόντας[1] τὸ τελευταῖον ἐπὶ τοὺς ἐδωδίμους μετα-
βῆναι καρπούς, ὧν εἶναι καὶ τὸν ἐκ τοῦ λωτοῦ
γινόμενον ἄρτον. καὶ τούτων τὴν εὕρεσιν οἱ μὲν

---

[1] διεξαγαγόντας Dindorf : διεξάγοντας.

their food from herbs and the stalks and roots of the
plants which grew in the marshes, making trial of
each one of them by tasting it, and the first one eaten
by them and the most favoured was that called
Agrostis,[1] because it excelled the others in sweetness
and supplied sufficient nutriment for the human
body; for they observed that this plant was attractive to the cattle and quickly increased their bulk.
Because of this fact the natives, in remembrance of
the usefulness of this plant, to this day, when
approaching the gods, hold some of it in their hands
as they pray to them; for they believe that man is a
creature of swamp and marsh, basing this conclusion
on the smoothness of his skin and his physical constitution, as well as on the fact that he requires a wet
rather than a dry diet. A second way by which the
Egyptians subsisted was, they say, by the eating of
fish, of which the river provided a great abundance,
especially at the time when it receded after its flood
and dried up.[2] They also ate the flesh of some of the
pasturing animals, using for clothing the skins of the
beasts that were eaten, and their dwellings they built
out of reeds. And traces of these customs still remain
among the herdsmen of Egypt, all of whom, they say,
have no other dwelling up to this time than one of
reeds, considering that with this they are well enough
provided for. After subsisting in this manner over
a long period of time they finally turned to the edible
fruits of the earth, among which may be included the
bread made from the lotus. The discovery of these

[1] Dog's-tooth grass.
[2] This must refer to the drying-up of the pools left by the
flood.

εἰς τὴν Ἶσιν ἀναφέρουσιν, οἱ δ᾽ εἴς τινα τῶν
παλαιῶν βασιλέων τὸν ὀνομαζόμενον Μηνᾶν.
6 οἱ δ᾽ ἱερεῖς εὑρετὴν τῶν μὲν¹ παιδειῶν καὶ τῶν
τεχνῶν μυθολογοῦσι τὸν Ἑρμῆν γεγονέναι, τῶν
δ᾽ εἰς τὸν βίον ἀναγκαίων τοῖς βασιλεῖς· διὸ καὶ
τὸ παλαιὸν παραδίδοσθαι τὰς βασιλείας μὴ τοῖς
ἐκγόνοις τῶν ἀρξάντων, ἀλλὰ τοῖς πλεῖστα καὶ
μέγιστα τὸ πλῆθος εὐεργετοῦσιν, εἴτε προκαλου-
μένων τῶν ἀνθρώπων τοὺς ἐφ᾽ ἑαυτῶν βασιλεῖς
ἐπὶ τὴν κοινὴν εὐεργεσίαν, εἴτε καὶ κατ᾽ ἀλήθειαν
ἐν ταῖς ἱεραῖς ἀναγραφαῖς οὕτω παρειληφότων.

44. Μυθολογοῦσι δ᾽ αὐτῶν τινες τὸ μὲν πρῶτον
ἄρξαι τῆς Αἰγύπτου θεοὺς καὶ ἥρωας ἔτη βραχὺ
λείποντα τῶν μυρίων καὶ ὀκτακισχιλίων, καὶ
θεῶν ἔσχατον βασιλεῦσαι τὸν Ἴσιδος Ὧρον· ὑπ᾽
ἀνθρώπων δὲ τὴν χώραν βεβασιλεῦσθαί φασιν
ἔτη² βραχὺ λείποντα τῶν πεντακισχιλίων μέχρι
τῆς ἑκατοστῆς καὶ ὀγδοηκοστῆς Ὀλυμπιάδος,
καθ᾽ ἣν ἡμεῖς μὲν παρεβάλομεν εἰς Αἴγυπτον,
ἐβασίλευε δὲ Πτολεμαῖος ὁ νέος Διόνυσος χρημα-
2 τίζων. τούτων δὲ τὰ μὲν πλεῖστα κατασχεῖν
τὴν ἀρχὴν ἐγχωρίους βασιλεῖς, ὀλίγα δὲ Αἰθίοπας
καὶ Πέρσας καὶ Μακεδόνας. Αἰθίοπας μὲν οὖν
ἄρξαι τέτταρας, οὐ κατὰ τὸ ἑξῆς, ἀλλ᾽ ἐκ διαστήματος, ἔτη τὰ πάντα βραχὺ λείποντα τῶν ἓξ καὶ
3 τριάκοντα· Πέρσας δ᾽ ἡγήσασθαι Καμβύσου τοῦ
βασιλέως τοῖς ὅπλοις καταστρεψαμένου τὸ ἔθνος
πέντε πρὸς τοῖς ἑκατὸν καὶ τριάκοντα ἔτεσι σὺν

---

¹ τῶν μὲν Dindorf : μὲν τῶν.
² ἀπὸ Μοίριδος before ἔτη deleted by Dindorf.

---

¹ Cp. chap. 14.

is attributed by some to Isis,[1] but by others to one of their early kings called Menas. The priests, however, have the story that the discoverer of the branches of learning and of the arts was Hermes, but that it was their kings who discovered such things as are necessary for existence; and that this was the reason why the kingship in early times was bestowed, not upon the sons of their former rulers, but upon such as conferred the greatest and most numerous benefits upon the peoples, whether it be that the inhabitants in this way sought to provoke their kings to useful service for the benefit of all, or that they have in very truth received an account to this effect in their sacred writings.

44. Some of them give the story that at first gods and heroes ruled Egypt for a little less than eighteen thousand years, the last of the gods to rule being Horus, the son of Isis; and mortals have been kings over their country, they say, for a little less than five thousand years down to the One Hundred and Eightieth Olympiad, the time when we visited Egypt and the king was Ptolemy, who took the name of The New Dionysus.[2] For most of this period the rule was held by native kings, and for a small part of it by Ethiopians, Persians, and Macedonians.[3] Now four Ethiopians held the throne, not consecutively but with intervals between, for a little less than thirty-six years in all; and the Persians, after their king Cambyses had subdued the nation by arms, ruled for one hundred and thirty-five years, including the

60-56 B.C.

[2] Ptolemy XI (80–51 B.C.), better known as Auletes (" The Piper ") and as the father of the famous Cleopatra.
[3] The Ethiopian Period (Twenty-fifth Dynasty), *ca.* 715–663 B.C.; the Persian, 525–332 B.C.; on the Macedonian, 332–30 B.C., see the Introduction, pp. ix ff.

ταῖς τῶν Αἰγυπτίων ἀποστάσεσιν, ἃς ἐποιήσαντο
φέρειν οὐ δυνάμενοι τὴν τραχύτητα τῆς ἐπιστα-
σίας καὶ τὴν εἰς τοὺς ἐγχωρίους θεοὺς ἀσέβειαν.
4 ἐσχάτους δὲ Μακεδόνας ἄρξαι καὶ τοὺς ἀπὸ
Μακεδόνων ἐξ ἔτη πρὸς τοῖς διακοσίοις καὶ
ἑβδομήκοντα. τοὺς δὲ λοιποὺς χρόνους ἅπαντας
διατελέσαι βασιλεύοντας τῆς χώρας ἐγχωρίους,
ἄνδρας μὲν ἑβδομήκοντα πρὸς τοῖς τετρακοσίοις,
γυναῖκας δὲ πέντε· περὶ ὧν ἁπάντων οἱ μὲν
ἱερεῖς εἶχον ἀναγραφὰς ἐν ταῖς ἱεραῖς βίβλοις
ἐκ παλαιῶν χρόνων ἀεὶ τοῖς διαδόχοις παραδεδομένας, ὁπηλίκος ἕκαστος τῶν βασιλευσάντων ἐγένετο τῷ μεγέθει καὶ ὁποῖός τις τῇ
φύσει καὶ τὰ κατὰ τοὺς ἰδίους χρόνους ἑκάστῳ
5 πραχθέντα· ἡμῖν δὲ περὶ ἑκάστου τὰ κατὰ μέρος
μακρὸν ἂν εἴη καὶ περίεργον γράφειν, ὡς ἂν τῶν
πλείστων ἀχρήστων περιειλημμένων. διόπερ τῶν
ἀξίων ἱστορίας τὰ κυριώτατα συντόμως διεξιέναι
πειρασόμεθα.

45. Μετὰ τοὺς θεοὺς τοίνυν πρῶτόν φασι
βασιλεῦσαι τῆς Αἰγύπτου Μηνᾶν, καὶ καταδεῖξαι
τοῖς λαοῖς θεούς τε σέβεσθαι καὶ θυσίας ἐπι-
τελεῖν, πρὸς δὲ τούτοις παρατίθεσθαι τραπέζας
καὶ κλίνας καὶ στρωμνῇ πολυτελεῖ χρῆσθαι, καὶ
τὸ σύνολον τρυφὴν καὶ πολυτελῆ βίον εἰσηγή-
2 σασθαι. διὸ καὶ πολλαῖς ὕστερον γενεαῖς βασιλεύοντα Τνέφαχθον τὸν Βοκχόριδος τοῦ σοφοῦ
πατέρα λέγουσιν εἰς τὴν Ἀραβίαν στρατεύσαντα,
τῶν ἐπιτηδείων αὐτὸν διά τε τὴν ἐρημίαν καὶ
τὰς δυσχωρίας ἐκλιπόντων, ἀναγκασθῆναι μίαν
ἡμέραν ἐνδεᾶ γενόμενον χρήσασθαι διαίτῃ παντελῶς εὐτελεῖ παρά τισι τῶν τυχόντων ἰδιωτῶν,

periods of revolt on the part of the Egyptians which they raised because they were unable to endure the harshness of their dominion and their lack of respect for the native gods. Last of all the Macedonians and their dynasty held rule for two hundred and seventy-six years. For the rest of the time all the kings of the land were natives, four hundred and seventy of them being men and five women. About all of them the priests had records which were regularly handed down in their sacred books to each successive priest from early times, giving the stature of each of the former kings, a description of his character, and what he had done during his reign; as for us, however, it would be a long task to write of each of them severally, and superfluous also, seeing that most of the material included is of no profit. Consequently we shall undertake to recount briefly only the most important of the facts which deserve a place in history.

45. After the gods the first king of Egypt, according to the priests, was Menas, who taught the people to worship gods and offer sacrifices, and also to supply themselves with tables and couches and to use costly bedding, and, in a word, introduced luxury and an extravagant manner of life. For this reason when, many generations later, Tnephachthus,[1] the father of Bocchoris the wise, was king and, while on a campaign in Arabia, ran short of supplies because the country was desert and rough, we are told that he was obliged to go without food for one day and then to live on quite simple fare at the home of some ordinary folk in private station, and that he, enjoying

---

[1] Not identified. Wiedemann conjected that he might be Tef-sucht, of the 23rd Dynasty.

ἡσθέντα δὲ καθ' ὑπερβολὴν καταγνῶναι τῆς
τρυφῆς καὶ τῷ καταδείξαντι τὴν πολυτέλειαν
ἐξ ἀρχῆς βασιλεῖ καταρᾶσθαι· οὕτω δ' ἐγκάρδιον
αὐτῷ τὴν μεταβολὴν γενέσθαι τὴν περὶ τὴν
βρῶσιν καὶ πόσιν καὶ κοίτην ὥστε τὴν κατάραν
ἀναγράψαι τοῖς ἱεροῖς γράμμασιν εἰς τὸν τοῦ
Διὸς ναὸν ἐν Θήβαις· ὃ δὴ δοκεῖ μάλιστα αἴτιον
γενέσθαι τοῦ μὴ διαμεῖναι τὴν δόξαν τοῦ Μηνᾶ
3 καὶ τὰς τιμὰς εἰς τοὺς ὕστερον χρόνους. ἑξῆς δ'
ἄρξαι λέγεται τοῦ προειρημένου βασιλέως τοὺς
ἀπογόνους δύο πρὸς τοῖς πεντήκοντα τοὺς ἅπαντας
ἔτη πλείω τῶν χιλίων καὶ τετταράκοντα· ἐφ' ὧν
μηδὲν ἄξιον ἀναγραφῆς γενέσθαι.

4 Μετὰ δὲ ταῦτα κατασταθέντος βασιλέως
Βουσίριδος καὶ τῶν τούτου πάλιν ἐκγόνων ὀκτώ,
τὸν τελευταῖον ὁμώνυμον ὄντα τῷ πρώτῳ φασὶ
κτίσαι τὴν ὑπὸ μὲν τῶν [1] Αἰγυπτίων καλουμένην
Διὸς πόλιν τὴν μεγάλην, ὑπὸ δὲ τῶν Ἑλλήνων
Θήβας. τὸν μὲν οὖν περίβολον αὐτὸν ὑποστήσασθαι σταδίων ἑκατὸν καὶ τετταράκοντα, οἰκο-
δομήμασι δὲ μεγάλοις καὶ ναοῖς ἐκπρεπέσι καὶ
τοῖς ἄλλοις ἀναθήμασι κοσμῆσαι θαυμαστῶς·
5 ὁμοίως δὲ καὶ τὰς τῶν ἰδιωτῶν οἰκίας, ἃς μὲν
τετρωρόφους, ἃς δὲ πεντωρόφους κατασκευάσαι,
καὶ καθόλου τὴν πόλιν εὐδαιμονεστάτην οὐ μόνον
τῶν κατ' Αἴγυπτον, ἀλλὰ καὶ τῶν ἄλλων πασῶν
6 ποιῆσαι. διὰ δὲ τὴν ὑπερβολὴν τῆς περὶ αὐτὴν
εὐπορίας τε καὶ δυνάμεως εἰς πάντα τόπον τῆς

the experience exceedingly, denounced luxury and pronounced a curse on the king who had first taught the people their extravagant way of living; and so deeply did he take to heart the change which had taken place in the people's habits of eating, drinking, and sleeping, that he inscribed his curse in hiero-glyphs on the temple of Zeus in Thebes; and this, in fact, appears to be the chief reason why the fame of Menas and his honours did not persist into later ages. And it is said that the descendants of this king, fifty-two in number all told, ruled in unbroken succession more than a thousand and forty years, but that in their reigns nothing occurred that was worthy of record.

Subsequently, when Busiris became king and his descendants in turn, eight in number, the last of the line, who bore the same name as the first, founded, they say, the city which the Egyptians call Diospolis [1] the Great, though the Greeks call it Thebes. Now the circuit of it he made one hundred and forty stades, and he adorned it in marvellous fashion with great buildings and remarkable temples and dedica-tory monuments of every other kind; in the same way he caused the houses of private citizens to be constructed in some cases four stories high, in other five, and in general made it the most prosperous city, not only of Egypt, but of the whole world. And since, by reason of the city's pre-eminent wealth and power, its fame has been spread abroad to every

[1] "City of Zeus," the Diospolis Magna of the Romans. The Egyptian name by which it was most commonly known was *Nu* (or *No*), "the city."

---

[1] τῶν omitted by Vulgate, Bekker, Dindorf.

φήμης διαδεδομένης ἐπιμεμνῆσθαι καὶ τὸν ποιητὴν
αὐτῆς φασιν ἐν οἷς λέγει

οὐδ᾽ ὅσα Θήβας
Αἰγυπτίας, ὅθι πλεῖστα δόμοις ἔνι κτήματα
κεῖται,
αἴθ᾽ ἑκατόμπυλοί εἰσι, διηκόσιοι δ᾽ ἀν᾽ ἑκάστην
ἀνέρες ἐξοιχνεῦσι σὺν ἵπποισιν καὶ ὄχεσφιν.

7 ἔνιοι δέ φασιν οὐ πύλας ἑκατὸν ἐσχηκέναι τὴν
πόλιν, ἀλλὰ πολλὰ καὶ μεγάλα προπύλαια τῶν
ἱερῶν, ἀφ᾽ ὧν ἑκατόμπυλον ὠνομάσθαι, καθαπερεὶ
πολύπυλον. δισμύρια δ᾽ ἅρματα πρὸς ἀλήθειαν
ἐξ αὐτῆς εἰς τοὺς πολέμους ἐκπορεύεσθαι· τοὺς
γὰρ ἱππῶνας ἑκατὸν γεγονέναι κατὰ τὴν παρα-
ποταμίαν τὴν ἀπὸ Μέμφεως ἄχρι Θηβῶν τῶν
κατὰ τὴν Λιβύην, ἑκάστου δεχομένου ἀνὰ διακοσίους ἵππους, ὧν ἔτι νῦν τὰ θεμέλια δείκνυσθαι.

46. Οὐ μόνον δὲ τοῦτον τὸν βασιλέα παρειλήφαμεν, ἀλλὰ καὶ τῶν ὕστερον ἀρξάντων
πολλοὺς εἰς τὴν αὔξησιν τῆς πόλεως πεφιλοτι-
μῆσθαι. ἀναθήμασί τε γὰρ πολλοῖς καὶ μεγάλοις
ἀργυροῖς καὶ χρυσοῖς, ἔτι δ᾽ ἐλεφαντίνοις, καὶ
κολοττικῶν ἀνδριάντων πλήθει, πρὸς δὲ τούτοις
κατασκευαῖς μονολίθων ὀβελίσκων μηδεμίαν τῶν
2 ὑπὸ τὸν ἥλιον οὕτω κεκοσμῆσθαι. τεττάρων γὰρ
ἱερῶν κατασκευασθέντων τό τε κάλλος καὶ τὸ
μέγεθος θαυμαστὸν [1] εἶναι τὸ παλαιότατον,
τρισκαίδεκα μὲν σταδίων τὴν περίμετρον, πέντε
δὲ καὶ τετταράκοντα πηχῶν τὸ ὕψος, εἴκοσι

---

[1] θαυμαστὸν D, Vogel : θαυμαστῶν ἐν C, Bekker, Dindorf.

---

[1] *Iliad* 9. 381–4, where Achilles replies to Odysseus, reject-
ing the proffer of gifts from Agamemnon.

region, even the poet, we are told, has mentioned it
when he says:[1]

> Nay, not for all the wealth
> Of Thebes in Egypt, where in ev'ry hall
> There lieth treasure vast; a hundred are
> Her gates, and warriors by each issue forth
> Two hundred, each of them with car and steeds.

Some, however, tell us that it was not one hundred
" gates " (*pulai*) which the city had, but rather many
great propylaea in front of its temples, and that it
was from these that the title " hundred-gated " was
given it, that is, " having many gateways." Yet
twenty thousand chariots did in truth, we are told,
pass out from it to war; for there were once scattered
along the river from Memphis to the Thebes which is
over against Libya one hundred post-stations,[2] each
one having accommodation for two hundred horses,
whose foundations are pointed out even to this day.

46. Not only this king, we have been informed, but
also many of the later rulers devoted their attention
to the development of the city. For no city under
the sun has ever been so adorned by votive offerings,
made of silver and gold and ivory, in such number
and of such size, by such a multitude of colossal
statues, and, finally, by obelisks made of single
blocks of stone. Of four temples erected there the
oldest [3] is a source of wonder for both its beauty and
size, having a circuit of thirteen stades, a height of

---

[2] Stables where relays of horses were kept. Eichstädt
would reject the whole of § 7 as spurious, and the words τῶν
κατὰ τὴν Λιβύην appear to be unnecessary.

[3] This is undoubtedly the Great Temple of Ammon at
Karnak, the most imposing of all the monuments of Egypt.

δὲ καὶ τεττάρων ποδῶν τὸ πλάτος τῶν τοίχων.
3 ἀκόλουθον δὲ τῇ μεγαλοπρεπείᾳ ταύτῃ καὶ τὸν
ἐν αὐτῷ κόσμον τῶν ἀναθημάτων γενέσθαι,
τῇ τε δαπάνῃ θαυμαστὸν καὶ τῇ χειρουργίᾳ
4 περιττῶς εἰργασμένον. τὰς μὲν οὖν οἰκοδομὰς
διαμεμενηκέναι μέχρι τῶν νεωτέρων χρόνων, τὸν
δ' ἄργυρον καὶ χρυσὸν καὶ τὴν δι' ἐλέφαντος
καὶ λιθείας πολυτέλειαν ὑπὸ Περσῶν σεσυλῆσθαι καθ' οὓς καιροὺς ἐνέπρησε τὰ κατ' Αἴγυπτον
ἱερὰ Καμβύσης· ὅτε δή φασι τοὺς Πέρσας
μετενεγκόντας τὴν εὐπορίαν ταύτην εἰς τὴν Ἀσίαν
καὶ τεχνίτας ἐξ Αἰγύπτου παραλαβόντας κατασκευάσαι τὰ περιβόητα βασίλεια τά τε ἐν
Περσεπόλει καὶ τὰ ἐν Σούσοις καὶ τὰ ἐν Μηδίᾳ.
5 τοσοῦτο δὲ πλῆθος χρημάτων ἀποφαίνουσι
γεγονέναι τότε κατ' Αἴγυπτον ὥστε τῶν κατὰ
τὴν σύλησιν ἀπολειμμάτων κατακαυθέντων τὰ
συναχθέντα κατὰ μικρὸν εὑρεθῆναι χρυσίου μὲν
πλείω τῶν τριακοσίων ταλάντων, ἀργυρίου δ' οὐκ
ἐλάττω τῶν δισχιλίων καὶ τριακοσίων ταλάντων.
6 εἶναι δέ φασι καὶ τάφους ἐνταῦθα τῶν ἀρχαίων
βασιλέων θαυμαστοὺς καὶ τῶν μεταγενεστέρων
τοῖς εἰς τὰ παραπλήσια φιλοτιμουμένοις ὑπερβολὴν οὐκ ἀπολείποντας.
7 Οἱ μὲν οὖν ἱερεῖς ἐκ τῶν ἀναγραφῶν ἔφασαν
εὑρίσκειν ἑπτὰ πρὸς τοῖς τετταράκοντα τάφους
βασιλικούς· εἰς δὲ Πτολεμαῖον τὸν Λάγου δια-
μεῖναί φασιν ἑπτακαίδεκα μόνον, ὧν τὰ πολλὰ
κατέφθαρτο καθ' οὓς χρόνους παρεβάλομεν
ἡμεῖς εἰς ἐκείνους τοὺς τόπους, ἐπὶ τῆς ἑκατοστῆς
8 καὶ ὀγδοηκοστῆς Ὀλυμπιάδος. οὐ μόνον δ' οἱ

forty-five cubits, and walls twenty-four feet thick.
In keeping with this magnificence was also the embellishment of the votive offerings within the circuit
wall, marvellous for the money spent upon it and
exquisitely wrought as to workmanship. Now the
buildings of the temple survived down to rather recent
times, but the silver and gold and costly works of ivory
and rare stone were carried off by the Persians when
Cambyses burned the temples of Egypt;[1] and it was
at this time, they say, that the Persians, by transferring all this wealth to Asia and taking artisans
along from Egypt, constructed their famous palaces
in Persepolis and Susa and throughout Media. So
great was the wealth of Egypt at that period, they
declare, that from the remnants left in the course of
the sack and after the burning the treasure which
was collected little by little was found to be worth
more than three hundred talents of gold and no less
than two thousand three hundred talents of silver.
There are also in this city, they say, remarkable
tombs of the early kings and of their successors,
which leave to those who aspire to similar magnificence no opportunity to outdo them.

Now the priests said that in their records they find
forty-seven tombs of kings; but down to the time of
Ptolemy son of Lagus, they say, only fifteen remained, 323–283
most of which had been destroyed at the time we B.C.
visited those regions, in the One Hundred and 60–56
Eightieth Olympiad. Not only do the priests of B.C.

---

[1] Cambyses was in Egypt from 525 to 522 B.C. The account
of his excesses against the Egyptian religion and customs,
given in great detail by Herodotus (3. 16 ff.), is almost certainly much exaggerated (see Gray in *The Cambridge Ancient
History*, 4. pp. 22–3, but cp. Hall, *ibid*. 3. pp. 311–12); at any
rate they fall toward the end of his stay in the country.

κατ' Αἴγυπτον ἱερεῖς ἐκ τῶν ἀναγραφῶν ἱστοροῦ·
σιν, ἀλλὰ καὶ πολλοὶ τῶν Ἑλλήνων τῶν παραβαλόντων μὲν εἰς τὰς Θήβας ἐπὶ Πτολεμαίου
τοῦ Λάγου, συνταξαμένων δὲ τὰς Αἰγυπτιακὰς
ἱστορίας, ὧν ἐστι καὶ Ἑκαταῖος, συμφωνοῦσι
τοῖς ὑφ' ἡμῶν εἰρημένοις.

47. Ἀπὸ γὰρ τῶν πρώτων τάφων, ἐν οἷς
παραδέδοται τὰς παλλακίδας τοῦ Διὸς τεθάφθαι,
δέκα σταδίων φησὶν ὑπάρξαι βασιλέως μνῆμα
τοῦ προσαγορευθέντος Ὀσυμανδύου. τούτου δὲ
κατὰ μὲν τὴν εἴσοδον ὑπάρχειν πυλῶνα λίθου
ποικίλου, τὸ μὲν μῆκος δίπλεθρον, τὸ δ' ὕψος
2 τετταράκοντα καὶ πέντε πηχῶν· διελθόντι δ'
αὐτὸν εἶναι λίθινον περίστυλον τετράγωνον,
ἑκάστης πλευρᾶς οὔσης τεττάρων πλέθρων·
ὑπηρεῖσθαι δ' ἀντὶ τῶν κιόνων ζῴδια πηχῶν
ἑκκαίδεκα μονόλιθα, τὸν τύπον εἰς τὸν ἀρχαῖον
τρόπον εἰργασμένα· τὴν ὀροφήν τε πᾶσαν ἐπὶ
πλάτος δυοῖν ὀργυιῶν ὑπάρχειν μονόλιθον,
ἀστέρας ἐν κυανῷ καταπεποικιλμένην· ἑξῆς δὲ
τοῦ περιστύλου τούτου πάλιν ἑτέραν εἴσοδον
καὶ πυλῶνα τὰ μὲν ἄλλα παραπλήσιον τῷ
προειρημένῳ, γλυφαῖς δὲ παντοίαις περιττότερον
3 εἰργασμένον· παρὰ δὲ τὴν εἴσοδον ἀνδριάντας
εἶναι τρεῖς ἐξ ἑνὸς τοὺς πάντας λίθου μέλανος[1]
τοῦ Συηνίτου, καὶ τούτων ἕνα μὲν καθήμενον

---

[1] μέλανος Hertlein : Μέμνονος.

---

[1] Hecataeus of Abdera was an historian of the early third
century B.C., author of an *Aigyptiaka*, from which the following
description (47. 1–49. 5) of the tomb of Osymandyas (Müller,

Egypt give these facts from their records, but many also of the Greeks who visited Thebes in the time of Ptolemy son of Lagus and composed histories of Egypt, one of whom was Hecataeus,[1] agree with what we have said.

47. Ten stades from the first tombs, he says, in which, according to tradition, are buried the concubines of Zeus, stands a monument of the king known as Osymandyas.[2] At its entrance there is a pylon, constructed of variegated stone, two plethra in breadth and forty-five cubits high; passing through this one enters a rectangular peristyle, built of stone, four plethra long on each side; it is supported, in place of pillars, by monolithic figures sixteen cubits high, wrought in the ancient manner as to shape;[3] and the entire ceiling, which is two fathoms wide, consists of a single stone, which is highly decorated with stars on a blue field. Beyond this peristyle there is yet another entrance and pylon, in every respect like the one mentioned before, save that it is more richly wrought with every manner of relief; beside the entrance are three statues, each of a single block of black stone from Syene, of which one, that

Fragmenta historicorum Graecorum, 2. 389-91) is drawn. What Diodorus gives here is no more than a paraphrase, not a quotation, of Hecataeus (cp. the Introduction, p. xvii).

[2] This is the great sanctuary erected by Ramses II for his mortuary service and known to every visitor at Thebes as the Ramesseum. In chap. 49, where Diodorus is not following Hecataeus, he calls it specifically a "tomb." H. R. Hall (*Ancient History of the Near East*[6], p. 317) derives the name Osymandyas from User-ma-Ra (or "Uashmuariya" as the Semites wrote it), one of the royal names of Ramses.

[3] These were square pillars with engaged statues of Osiris, but they were not monoliths (cp. H. R. Hall, *l.c.*, with illustration).

ὑπάρχειν μέγιστον πάντων τῶν κατ' Αἴγυπτον,
οὗ τὸν πόδα μετρούμενον ὑπερβάλλειν τοὺς ἑπτὰ
πήχεις, ἑτέρους δὲ δύο πρὸς τοῖς γόνασι, τὸν
μὲν ἐκ δεξιῶν, τὸν δὲ ἐξ εὐωνύμων, θυγατρὸς
καὶ μητρός, τῷ μεγέθει λειπομένους τοῦ προειρη-
4 μένου. τὸ δ' ἔργον τοῦτο μὴ μόνον εἶναι κατὰ
τὸ μέγεθος ἀποδοχῆς ἄξιον, ἀλλὰ καὶ τῇ τέχνῃ
θαυμαστὸν καὶ τῇ τοῦ λίθου φύσει διαφέρον, ὡς
ἂν ἐν τηλικούτῳ μεγέθει μήτε διαφυάδος μήτε
κηλῖδος μηδεμιᾶς θεωρουμένης. ἐπιγεγράφθαι δ'
ἐπ' αὐτοῦ "Βασιλεὺς βασιλέων Ὀσυμανδύας
εἰμί. εἰ δέ τις εἰδέναι βούλεται πηλίκος εἰμὶ
καὶ ποῦ κεῖμαι, νικάτω τι τῶν ἐμῶν ἔργων."
5 εἶναι δὲ καὶ ἄλλην εἰκόνα τῆς μητρὸς αὐτοῦ καθ'
αὑτὴν πηχῶν εἴκοσι μονόλιθον, ἔχουσαν δὲ τρεῖς
βασιλείας ἐπὶ τῆς κεφαλῆς, ἃς διασημαίνειν
ὅτι καὶ θυγάτηρ καὶ γυνὴ καὶ μήτηρ βασιλέως
ὑπῆρξε.
6 Μετὰ δὲ τὸν πυλῶνα περίστυλον εἶναι τοῦ
προτέρου ἀξιολογώτερον, ἐν ᾧ γλυφὰς ὑπάρχειν
παντοίας δηλούσας τὸν πόλεμον τὸν γενόμενον
αὐτῷ πρὸς τοὺς ἐν τοῖς Βάκτροις ἀποστάντας·
ἐφ' οὓς ἐστρατεῦσθαι πεζῶν μὲν τετταράκοντα
μυριάσιν, ἱππεῦσι δὲ δισμυρίοις, εἰς τέτταρα
μέρη διῃρημένης τῆς πάσης στρατιᾶς, ὧν ἁπάντων υἱοὺς τοῦ βασιλέως ἐσχηκέναι τὴν ἡγεμονίαν.
48. Καὶ κατὰ μὲν τὸν πρῶτον τῶν τοίχων
τὸν βασιλέα κατεσκευάσθαι πολιορκοῦντα τεῖχος
ὑπὸ ποταμοῦ περίρρυτον καὶ προκινδυνεύοντα

---

[1] The estimated weight of this colossus of Ramses II is
one thousand tons.

is seated, is the largest of any in Egypt,[1] the foot measuring over seven cubits, while the other two at the knees of this, the one on the right and the other on the left, daughter and mother respectively, are smaller than the one first mentioned. And it is not merely for its size that this work merits approbation, but it is also marvellous by reason of its artistic quality and excellent because of the nature of the stone, since in a block of so great a size there is not a single crack or blemish to be seen. The inscription upon it runs: " King of Kings am I, Osymandyas. If anyone would know how great I am and where I lie, let him surpass one of my works." There is also another statue of his mother standing alone, a monolith twenty cubits high, and it has three diadems on its head, signifying that she was both daughter and wife and mother of a king.

Beyond the pylon, he says, there is a peristyle more remarkable than the former one; in it there are all manner of reliefs depicting the war which the king waged against those Bactrians who had revolted; against these he had made a campaign with four hundred thousand foot-soldiers and twenty thousand cavalry, the whole army having been divided into four divisions, all of which were under the command of sons of the king.[2]

48. On the first wall the king, he says, is represented in the act of besieging a walled city which is surrounded by a river, and of leading the attack against

[2] This is the campaign of Ramses II against the Hittites in 1288 B.C. and the great battle around the city of Kadesh on the upper Orontes. The battle has been fully described by J. H. Breasted, *The Battle of Kadesh* (Decennial Publications of the University of Chicago, 1904), who estimates the size of the army at little more than 20,000.

DIODORUS OF SICILY

πρός τινας ἀντιτεταγμένους μετὰ λέοντος, συν-
αγωνιζομένου τοῦ θηρίου καταπληκτικῶς· ὑπὲρ
οὗ τῶν ἐξηγουμένων οἱ μὲν ἔφασαν πρὸς ἀλήθειαν
χειροήθη λέοντα τρεφόμενον ὑπὸ τοῦ βασιλέως
συγκινδυνεύειν αὐτῷ κατὰ τὰς μάχας καὶ τροπὴν
ποιεῖν τῶν ἐναντίων διὰ τὴν ἀλκήν, τινὲς δ᾽
ἱστόρουν ὅτι καθ᾽ ὑπερβολὴν ἀνδρεῖος ὢν καὶ
φορτικῶς¹ ἑαυτὸν ἐγκωμιάζειν βουλόμενος, διὰ
τῆς τοῦ λέοντος εἰκόνος τὴν διάθεσιν ἑαυτοῦ τῆς
2 ψυχῆς ἐσήμαινεν. ἐν δὲ τῷ δευτέρῳ τοίχῳ τοὺς
αἰχμαλώτους ὑπὸ τοῦ βασιλέως ἀγομένους εἰργά-
σθαι τά τε αἰδοῖα καὶ τὰς χεῖρας οὐκ ἔχοντας,
δι᾽ ὧν δοκεῖν δηλοῦσθαι διότι ταῖς ψυχαῖς
ἄνανδροι καὶ κατὰ τὰς ἐν τοῖς δεινοῖς ἐνεργείας
3 ἄχειρες ἦσαν. τὸν δὲ τρίτον ἔχειν γλυφὰς
παντοίας καὶ διαπρεπεῖς γραφάς, δι᾽ ὧν δηλοῦσθαι
βουθυσίας τοῦ βασιλέως καὶ θρίαμβον ἀπὸ τοῦ
4 πολέμου καταγόμενον. κατὰ δὲ μέσον τὸν περίστυλον ὑπαίθριον βωμὸν ᾠκοδομῆσθαι τοῦ καλ-
λίστου λίθου τῇ τε χειρουργίᾳ διάφορον καὶ τῷ
5 μεγέθει θαυμαστόν. κατὰ δὲ τὸν τελευταῖον
τοίχον ὑπάρχειν ἀνδριάντας καθημένους δύο μονολίθους ἑπτὰ καὶ εἴκοσι πηχῶν, παρ᾽ οὓς εἰσόδους
τρεῖς ἐκ τοῦ περιστύλου κατεσκευάσθαι, καθ᾽
ἃς οἶκον ὑπάρχειν ὑπόστυλον, ᾠδείου τρόπον
κατεσκευασμένον, ἑκάστην πλευρὰν ἔχοντα δί-
6 πλεθρον. ἐν τούτῳ δ᾽ εἶναι πλῆθος ἀνδριάντων

¹ φορτικῶς Vogel : φορτικὸς Vulgate, Bekker, Dindorf.

¹ This sentence is apparently not from Hecataeus.
Breasted (l.c., pp. 44–5) holds that this lion is purely
decorative, though the reliefs of the battle show a tame lion
accompanying Ramses on the campaign.

opposing troops; he is accompanied by a lion, which is
aiding him with terrifying effect. Of those who have
explained the scene some have said that in very truth
a tame lion which the king kept accompanied him in
the perils of battle and put the enemy to rout by his
fierce onset; but others have maintained that the
king, who was exceedingly brave and desirous of prais-
ing himself in a vulgar way, was trying to portray
his own bold spirit in the figure of the lion.[1] On the
second wall, he adds, are wrought the captives as they
are being led away by the king; they are without their
privates and their hands, which apparently signifies
that they were effeminate in spirit and had no hands
when it came to the dread business of warfare.[2]
The third wall carries every manner of relief and
excellent paintings, which portray the king perform-
ing a sacrifice of oxen and celebrating a triumph after
the war. In the centre of the peristyle there had
been constructed of the most beautiful stone an altar,
open to the sky, both excellent in its workmanship
and marvellous because of its size. By the last wall
are two monolithic seated statues, twenty-seven
cubits high, beside which are set three entrances
from the peristyle; and by way of these entrances one
comes into a hall whose roof was supported by
pillars, constructed in the style of an Odeum,[3] and
measuring two plethra on each side. In this hall
there are many wooden statues representing parties

[2] The reliefs of the battle show Ramses in his chariot and
the severed hands of the slain, not of the captives, being cast
before him (Breasted, *l.c.*, p. 45).

[3] *i.e.* a Music Hall, distinguished, in general, by the ancients
from a theatre by its roof and supporting pillars. This is
the great hypostyle hall behind the second court (cp. the
Plan in *Baedeker's Egypt*, opp. p. 301).

ξυλίνων, διασημαῖνον τοὺς ἀμφισβητήσεις [1]
ἔχοντας καὶ προσβλέποντας τοῖς τὰς δίκας
κρίνουσι· τούτους δ' ἐφ' ἑνὸς τῶν τοίχων ἐγγε-
γλύφθαι τριάκοντα τὸν ἀριθμόν ἄχειρας,[2] καὶ
κατὰ τὸ μέσον τὸν ἀρχιδικαστήν, ἔχοντα τὴν
Ἀλήθειαν ἐξηρτημένην ἐκ τοῦ τραχήλου καὶ
τοὺς ὀφθαλμοὺς ἐπιμύοντα,[3] καὶ βιβλίων αὐτῷ
παρακείμενον πλῆθος· ταύτας δὲ τὰς εἰκόνας
ἐνδείκνυσθαι διὰ τοῦ σχήματος ὅτι τοὺς μὲν
δικαστὰς οὐδὲν δεῖ λαμβάνειν, τὸν ἀρχιδικαστὴν
δὲ πρὸς μόνην βλέπειν τὴν ἀλήθειαν.

49. Ἑξῆς δ' ὑπάρχειν περίπατον οἴκων παντοδαπῶν πλήρη, καθ' οὓς παντοῖα γένη βρωτῶν
κατεσκευάσθαι τῶν πρὸς ἀπόλαυσιν ἡδίστων.
2 καθ' ὃν δὴ γλυφαῖς ἐντυχεῖν [4] εἶναι καὶ χρώμασιν
ἐπηνθισμένον τὸν βασιλέα, φέροντα τῷ θεῷ
χρυσὸν καὶ ἄργυρον, ὃν ἐξ ἁπάσης ἐλάμβανε
τῆς Αἰγύπτου κατ' ἐνιαυτὸν ἐκ τῶν ἀργυρείων
καὶ χρυσείων μετάλλων· ὑπογεγράφθαι δὲ καὶ
τὸ πλῆθος, ὃ συγκεφαλαιούμενον εἰς ἀργυρίου
λόγον εἶναι μνῶν τρισχιλίας καὶ διακοσίας
3 μυριάδας. ἑξῆς δ' ὑπάρχειν τὴν ἱερὰν βιβλιο-
θήκην, ἐφ' ἧς ἐπιγεγράφθαι Ψυχῆς ἰατρεῖον,
συνεχεῖς δὲ ταύτῃ τῶν κατ' Αἴγυπτον θεῶν
ἁπάντων εἰκόνας, τοῦ βασιλέως ὁμοίως δωρο-
φοροῦντος ἃ προσῆκον ἦν ἑκάστοις, καθάπερ
ἐνδεικνυμένου πρός τε τὸν Ὄσιριν καὶ τοὺς

---

[1] τὰς before ἀμφισβητήσεις omitted by D, Vogel: retained
by Bekker, Dindorf.
[2] ἄχειρας added by Hertlein, cp. Plutarch, Mor. 355 A.
[3] ἐπιμύοντα Hertlein : ἐπιμύνουσαν.
[4] The text is defective. Reiske conjectures γλυφὰς ἐν
τοίχῳ ἰδεῖν εἶναι.

172

in litigation, whose eyes are fixed upon the judges who decide their cases; and these, in turn, are shown in relief on one of the walls, to the number of thirty and without any hands,[1] and in their midst the chief justice, with a figure of Truth hanging from his neck and holding his eyes closed, and at his side a great number of books. And these figures show by their attitude that the judges shall receive no gift and that the chief justice shall have his eyes upon the truth alone.[2]

49. Next to these courts, he says, is an ambulatory crowded with buildings of every kind, in which there are representations of the foods that are sweetest to the taste, of every variety. Here are to be found reliefs in which the king, adorned in colours, is represented as offering to the god the gold and silver which he received each year from the silver and gold mines of all Egypt; and an inscription below gives also the total amount, which, summed up according to its value in silver, is thirty-two million minas. Next comes the sacred library, which bears the inscription "Healing-place of the Soul," and contiguous to this building are statues of all the gods of Egypt, to each of whom the king in like manner makes the offering appropriate to him, as though he were submitting proof before Osiris and his assessors

---

[1] A word to this effect, which is found in a description of "figures in Thebes" by Plutarch (*On Isis and Osiris*, 10), must almost certainly have stood in the text, to give a basis for the thought in the next sentence that the judges should not receive gifts; cp. Plutarch, *l.c.*, ὡς ἄδωρον ἅμα τὴν δικαιοσύνην καὶ ἀνέντευκτον οὖσαν ("showing that justice should take no gifts and should be inaccessible to influence").

[2] On this Supreme Court see chap. 75.

κάτω παρέδρους ὅτι τὸν βίον ἐξετέλεσεν εὐσεβῶν
καὶ δικαιοπραγῶν πρός τε ἀνθρώπους καὶ θεούς.
4 ὁμότοιχον δὲ τῇ βιβλιοθήκῃ κατεσκευάσθαι περιττῶς οἶκον εἰκοσίκλινον, ἔχοντα τοῦ τε Διὸς
καὶ τῆς Ἥρας, ἔτι δὲ τοῦ βασιλέως, εἰκόνας,
ἐν ᾧ δοκεῖν καὶ τὸ σῶμα τοῦ βασιλέως ἐντε-
5 θάφθαι. κύκλῳ δὲ τούτου πλῆθος οἰκημάτων
κατεσκευάσθαι γραφὴν ἐχόντων ἐκπρεπῆ πάντων
τῶν καθιερωμένων ἐν Αἰγύπτῳ ζῴων· ἀνάβασίν
τε δι' αὐτῶν εἶναι πρὸς ὅλον[1] τὸν τάφον· ἦν
διελθοῦσιν ὑπάρχειν ἐπὶ τοῦ μνήματος κύκλον
χρυσοῦν τριακοσίων καὶ ἑξήκοντα καὶ πέντε
πηχῶν τὴν περίμετρον, τὸ δὲ πάχος[2] πηχυαῖον·
ἐπιγεγράφθαι δὲ καὶ διῃρῆσθαι καθ' ἕκαστον
πῆχυν τὰς ἡμέρας τοῦ ἐνιαυτοῦ, παραγεγραμ-
μένων τῶν κατὰ φύσιν γινομένων τοῖς ἄστροις
ἀνατολῶν τε καὶ δύσεων καὶ τῶν διὰ ταύτας
ἐπιτελουμένων ἐπισημασιῶν κατὰ τοὺς Αἰγυπτίους ἀστρολόγους. τοῦτον δὲ τὸν κύκλον ὑπὸ
Καμβύσου καὶ Περσῶν ἔφασαν σεσυλῆσθαι καθ'
οὓς χρόνους ἐκράτησεν Αἰγύπτου.

6   Τὸν μὲν οὖν Ὀσυμανδύου τοῦ βασιλέως τάφον
τοιοῦτον γενέσθαι φασίν, ὃς οὐ μόνον δοκεῖ τῇ
κατὰ τὴν δαπάνην χορηγίᾳ πολὺ τῶν ἄλλων
διενεγκεῖν, ἀλλὰ καὶ τῇ τῶν τεχνιτῶν ἐπινοίᾳ.

50. Οἱ δὲ Θηβαῖοί φασιν ἑαυτοὺς ἀρχαιοτάτους
εἶναι πάντων ἀνθρώπων, καὶ παρ' ἑαυτοῖς πρώτοις

---

[1] ὅλον has been suspected. Hertlein conjectured ἄκρον,
" to the top of the tomb."
[2] πάχος all editors. Capps conjectures πλάτος.

in the underworld that to the end of his days he had lived a life of piety and justice towards both men and gods. Next to the library and separated from it by a party wall is an exquisitely constructed hall, which contains a table with couches for twenty and statues of Zeus and Hera as well as of the king; here, it would seem, the body of the king is also buried. In a circle about this building are many chambers which contain excellent paintings of all the animals which are held sacred in Egypt. There is an ascent leading through these chambers to the tomb as a whole. At the top of this ascent there is a circular border of gold crowning the monument, three hundred and sixty-five cubits in circumference and one cubit thick;[1] upon this the days of the year are inscribed, one in each cubit of length, and by each day the risings and settings of the stars as nature ordains them and the signs indicating the effects which the Egyptian astrologers hold that they produce.[2] This border, they said, had been plundered by Cambyses and the Persians when he conquered Egypt.

Such, they say, was the tomb of Osymandyas the king, which is considered far to have excelled all others, not only in the amount of money lavished upon it, but also in the ingenuity shown by the artificers.

50. The Thebans say that they are the earliest of all men and the first people among whom philosophy[3]

---

[1] In place of " one cubit thick " one should certainly expect " one cubit wide." In that case the space for the portrayal of each day would be one cubit square.

[2] Here ends the account drawn, except for occasional remarks of Diodorus, from Hecataeus.

[3] *i.e.* in the wider sense of study of knowledge.

φιλοσοφίαν τε εὑρῆσθαι καὶ τὴν ἐπ' ἀκριβὲς
ἀστρολογίαν, ἅμα καὶ τῆς χώρας αὐτοῖς συνερ-
γούσης πρὸς τὸ τηλαυγέστερον ὁρᾶν τὰς ἐπιτολάς
2 τε καὶ δύσεις τῶν ἄστρων. ἰδίως δὲ καὶ τὰ
περὶ τοὺς μῆνας αὐτοῖς καὶ τοὺς ἐνιαυτοὺς
διατετάχθαι.[1] τὰς γὰρ ἡμέρας οὐκ ἄγουσι κατὰ
σελήνην, ἀλλὰ κατὰ τὸν ἥλιον, τριακονθημέρους
μὲν τιθέμενοι τοὺς μῆνας, πέντε δ' ἡμέρας καὶ
τέταρτον τοῖς δώδεκα μησὶν ἐπάγουσι, καὶ τούτῳ
τῷ τρόπῳ τὸν ἐνιαύσιον κύκλον ἀναπληροῦσιν.
ἐμβολίμους δὲ μῆνας οὐκ ἄγουσιν οὐδ' ἡμέρας
ὑφαιροῦσι, καθάπερ οἱ πλεῖστοι τῶν Ἑλλήνων.
περὶ δὲ τῶν ἐκλείψεων ἡλίου τε καὶ σελήνης
ἀκριβῶς ἐπεσκέφθαι δοκοῦσι, καὶ προρρήσεις
περὶ τούτων ποιοῦνται, πάντα τὰ κατὰ μέρος
γινόμενα προλέγοντες ἀδιαπτώτως.

3 Τῶν δὲ τούτου τοῦ βασιλέως ἀπογόνων ὄγδοος
ὁ[2] προσαγορευθεὶς Οὐχορεὺς ἔκτισε πόλιν Μέμφιν, ἐπιφανεστάτην τῶν κατ' Αἴγυπτον. ἐξελέξατο μὲν γὰρ τόπον ἐπικαιρότατον ἁπάσης
τῆς χώρας, ὅπου σχιζόμενος ὁ Νεῖλος εἰς πλείονα
μέρη ποιεῖ τὸ καλούμενον ἀπὸ τοῦ σχήματος
Δέλτα· διὸ καὶ συνέβη τὴν πόλιν εὐκαίρως
κειμένην ἐπὶ τῶν κλείθρων εἶναι κυριεύουσαν
4 τῶν εἰς τὴν ἄνω χώραν ἀναπλεόντων. τὸ μὲν
οὖν περίβολον τῆς πόλεως ἐποίησε σταδίων
ἑκατὸν καὶ πεντήκοντα, τὴν δ' ὀχυρότητα καὶ

---

[1] Camusatus conjectured διατέτακται, which is adopted by
Bekker, Dindorf.

[2] ἀπὸ τοῦ πατρὸς after ὁ omitted by C F.

---

[1] The Egyptians undoubtedly knew the proper length of
the year, but their year was one of 365 days and there is no

and the exact science of the stars were discovered, since their country enables them to observe more distinctly than others the risings and settings of the stars. Peculiar to them also is their ordering of the months and years. For they do not reckon the days by the moon, but by the sun, making their month of thirty days, and they add five and a quarter days [1] to the twelve months and in this way fill out the cycle of the year. But they do not intercalate months or subtract days, as most of the Greeks do. They appear to have made careful observations of the eclipses both of the sun and of the moon, and predict them, foretelling without error all the events which actually occur.

Of the descendants of this king, the eighth, known as Uchoreus, founded Memphis, the most renowned city of Egypt. For he chose the most favourable spot in all the land, where the Nile divides into several branches to form the " Delta," as it is called from its shape; and the result was that the city, excellently situated as it was at the gates of the Delta, continually controlled the commerce passing into upper Egypt. Now he gave the city a circumference of one hundred and fifty stades, and made it

record of their ever officially intercalating a day every four years, as, indeed, Diodorus tells us in the next sentence (cp. *The Cambridge Ancient History*, 1. p. 168). The distinct contribution of the Egyptians to the calendar was the rejection of the lunar month and the recognition that the length of the divisions of the year should be conventional. It was this conventional month which Julius Caesar introduced into the lunar month calendar of the Romans, practically all ancient writers saying in one way or another that the idea for his calendar came from Egypt (cp. J. H. Breasted, *A History of Egypt*, pp. 32-3).

τὴν εὐχρηστίαν θαυμαστήν, τοιῷδέ τινι τρόπῳ
5 κατασκευάσας. ῥέοντος γὰρ τοῦ Νείλου περὶ
τὴν πόλιν καὶ κατὰ τὰς ἀναβάσεις ἐπικλύζοντος,
ἀπὸ μὲν τοῦ νότου προεβάλετο χῶμα παμμέγεθες, πρὸς μὲν τὴν πλήρωσιν τοῦ ποταμοῦ
προβλήματος, πρὸς δὲ τοὺς ἀπὸ τῆς γῆς πολεμίους ἀκροπόλεως ἔχον τάξιν· ἐκ δὲ τῶν ἄλλων
μερῶν πανταχόθεν ὤρυξε λίμνην μεγάλην καὶ
βαθεῖαν, ἣ τὸ σφοδρὸν τοῦ ποταμοῦ δεχομένη
καὶ πάντα τὸν περὶ τὴν πόλιν τόπον πληροῦσα,
πλὴν ᾗ τὸ χῶμα κατεσκεύαστο, θαυμαστὴν
6 ἐποίει τὴν ὀχυρότητα. οὕτω δὲ καλῶς ὁ κτίσας
αὐτὴν ἐστοχάσατο τῆς τῶν τόπων εὐκαιρίας ὥστε
τοὺς ἑξῆς βασιλεῖς σχεδὸν ἅπαντας καταλιπόντας
τὰς Θήβας τά τε βασίλεια καὶ τὴν οἴκησιν ἐν
ταύτῃ ποιεῖσθαι. διόπερ ἀπὸ τούτων τῶν χρόνων ἤρξατο ταπεινοῦσθαι μὲν τὰ περὶ τὰς Θήβας,
αὔξεσθαι δὲ τὰ περὶ τὴν Μέμφιν, ἕως Ἀλεξάνδρου τοῦ βασιλέως· τούτου γὰρ ἐπὶ θαλάττῃ
τὴν ἐπώνυμον αὐτῷ πόλιν οἰκίσαντος οἱ κατὰ
τὸ ἑξῆς βασιλεύσαντες τῆς Αἰγύπτου πάντες
7 ἐφιλοτιμήθησαν εἰς τὴν ταύτης αὔξησιν. οἱ μὲν
γὰρ βασιλείοις μεγαλοπρεπέσιν, οἱ δὲ νεωρίοις
καὶ λιμέσιν, οἱ δ᾽ ἑτέροις ἀναθήμασι καὶ κατασκευάσμασιν ἀξιολόγοις ἐπὶ τοσοῦτον ἐκόσμησαν
αὐτὴν ὥστε παρὰ τοῖς πλείστοις πρώτην ἢ
δευτέραν ἀριθμεῖσθαι τῶν κατὰ τὴν οἰκουμένην
πόλεων. ἀλλὰ περὶ μὲν ταύτης τὰ κατὰ μέρος
ἐν τοῖς ἰδίοις χρόνοις ἀναγράψομεν.

51. Ὁ δὲ τὴν Μέμφιν κτίσας μετὰ τὴν τοῦ
χώματος καὶ τῆς λίμνης κατασκευὴν ᾠκοδόμησε
βασίλεια τῶν μὲν παρὰ τοῖς ἄλλοις οὐ λειπό-

remarkably strong and adapted to its purpose by works of the following nature. Since the Nile flowed around the city and covered it at the time of inundation, he threw out a huge mound of earth on the south to serve as a barrier against the swelling of the river and also as a citadel against the attacks of enemies by land; and all around the other sides he dug a large and deep lake, which, by taking up the force of the river and occupying all the space about the city except where the mound had been thrown up, gave it remarkable strength. And so happily did the founder of the city reckon upon the suitableness of the site that practically all subsequent kings left Thebes and established both their palaces and official residences here. Consequently from this time Thebes began to wane and Memphis to increase,[1] until the time of Alexander the king; for after he had founded the city on the sea which bears his name, all the kings of Egypt after him concentrated their interest on the development of it. Some adorned it with magnificent palaces, some with docks and harbours, and others with further notable dedications and buildings, to such an extent that it is generally reckoned the first or second city of the inhabited world. But a detailed description of this city we shall set forth in the appropriate period.[2]

51. The founder of Memphis, after constructing the mound and the lake, erected a palace, which, while not inferior to those of other nations, yet was

[1] In common with all the Greek writers, Diodorus knew nothing about the chronological development of Egyptian history. The great period of Thebes was to come with the Eighteenth Dynasty, after 1600 B.C., many centuries subsequent to the founding of Memphis.

[2] Alexandria is more fully described in Book 17. 52.

μενα, τῆς δὲ τῶν προβασιλευσάντων μεγα-
2 λοψυχίας καὶ φιλοκαλίας οὐκ ἄξια. οἱ γὰρ
ἐγχώριοι τὸν μὲν ἐν τῷ ζῆν χρόνον εὐτελῆ
παντελῶς εἶναι νομίζουσι, τὸν δὲ μετὰ τὴν
τελευτὴν δι' ἀρετὴν μνημονευθησόμενον περὶ
πλείστου ποιοῦνται, καὶ τὰς μὲν τῶν ζώντων
οἰκήσεις καταλύσεις ὀνομάζουσιν, ὡς ὀλίγον
χρόνον ἐν ταύταις οἰκούντων ἡμῶν, τοὺς δὲ τῶν
τετελευτηκότων τάφους ἀιδίους οἴκους προσαγο-
ρεύουσιν, ὡς ἐν ἅδου διατελούντων τὸν ἄπειρον
αἰῶνα· διόπερ τῶν μὲν κατὰ τὰς οἰκίας κατα-
σκευῶν ἧττον φροντίζουσι, περὶ δὲ τὰς ταφὰς
ὑπερβολὴν οὐκ ἀπολείπουσι φιλοτιμίας.

3 Τὴν δὲ προειρημένην πόλιν ὀνομασθῆναί τινές
φασιν ἀπὸ τῆς θυγατρὸς τοῦ κτίσαντος αὐτὴν
βασιλέως. ταύτης δὲ μυθολογοῦσιν ἐρασθῆναι
τὸν ποταμὸν Νεῖλον ὁμοιωθέντα ταύρῳ, καὶ
γεννῆσαι τὸν ἐπ' ἀρετῇ θαυμασθέντα παρὰ τοῖς
ἐγχωρίοις Αἴγυπτον, ἀφ' οὗ καὶ τὴν σύμπασαν
4 χώραν τυχεῖν τῆς προσηγορίας. διαδεξάμενον
γὰρ τοῦτον τὴν ἡγεμονίαν γενέσθαι βασιλέα
φιλάνθρωπον καὶ δίκαιον καὶ καθόλου σπου-
δαῖον ἐν πᾶσι· διὸ καὶ μεγάλης ἀποδοχῆς ἀξιού-
μενον ὑπὸ πάντων διὰ τὴν εὔνοιαν τυχεῖν τῆς
προειρημένης τιμῆς.

5 Μετὰ δὲ τὸν προειρημένον βασιλέα δώδεκα
γενεαῖς ὕστερον διαδεξάμενος τὴν κατ' Αἴγυπτον
ἡγεμονίαν Μοῖρις ἐν μὲν τῇ Μέμφει κατεσκεύασε
τὰ βόρεια προπύλαια, τῇ μεγαλοπρεπείᾳ πολὺ
τῶν ἄλλων ὑπερέχοντα, ἐπάνω δὲ τῆς πόλεως
ἀπὸ δέκα σχοίνων λίμνην ὤρυξε τῇ μὲν εὐχρη-
στίᾳ θαυμαστήν, τῷ δὲ μεγέθει τῶν ἔργων

no match for the grandeur of design and love of the beautiful shown by the kings who preceded him. For the inhabitants of Egypt consider the period of this life to be of no account whatever, but place the greatest value on the time after death when they will be remembered for their virtue, and while they give the name of " lodgings " to the dwellings of the living, thus intimating that we dwell in them but a brief time, they call the tombs of the dead " eternal homes," since the dead spend endless eternity in Hades; consequently they give less thought to the furnishings of their houses, but on the manner of their burials they do not forgo any excess of zeal.

The aforementioned city was named, according to some, after the daughter of the king who founded it. They tell the story that she was loved by the river Nile, who had assumed the form of a bull, and gave birth to Egyptus, a man famous among the natives for his virtue, from whom the entire land received its name. For upon succeeding to the throne he showed himself to be a kindly king, just, and, in a word, upright in all matters; and so, since he was held by all to merit great approbation because of his goodwill, he received the honour mentioned.

Twelve generations after the king just named, Moeris succeeded to the throne of Egypt and built in Memphis itself the north propylaea, which far surpasses the others in magnificence, while ten schoeni[1] above the city he excavated a lake which was remarkable for its utility and an undertaking of

---

[1] Herodotus (2. 6) says that the *schoenus* was an Egyptian measure, equal to sixty stades or approximately seven miles, but according to Strabo (17. 1. 24) it varied from thirty to one hundred and twenty stades. At any rate the Fayûm is about sixty miles from the site of ancient Memphis.

6 ἄπιστον· τὴν μὲν γὰρ περίμετρον αὐτῆς φασιν
ὑπάρχειν σταδίων τρισχιλίων καὶ ἑξακοσίων, τὸ
δὲ βάθος ἐν τοῖς πλείστοις μέρεσιν ὀργυιῶν
πεντήκοντα· ὥστε τίς οὐκ ἂν ἀναλογιζόμενος τὸ
μέγεθος τοῦ κατασκευάσματος εἰκότως ζητήσαι
πόσαι μυριάδες ἀνδρῶν ἐν πόσοις ἔτεσι τοῦτο
7 συνετέλεσαν; τὴν δὲ χρείαν τὴν ἐκ ταύτης καὶ
κοινωφελίαν τοῖς τὴν Αἴγυπτον οἰκοῦσιν, ἔτι δὲ
τὴν τοῦ βασιλέως ἐπίνοιαν, οὐκ ἄν τις ἐπαινέσειε
τῆς ἀληθείας ἀξίως.

52. Ἐπειδὴ γὰρ ὁ μὲν Νεῖλος οὐχ ὡρισμένας
ἐποιεῖτο τὰς ἀναβάσεις, ἡ δὲ χώρα τὴν εὐκαρ-
πίαν παρεσκεύαζεν ἀπὸ τῆς ἐκείνου συμμετρίας,
εἰς ὑποδοχὴν τοῦ πλεονάζοντος ὕδατος ὤρυξε τὴν
λίμνην, ὅπως μήτε διὰ τὸ πλῆθος τῆς ῥύσεως
ἐπικλύζων ἀκαίρως τὴν χώραν ἕλη καὶ λίμνας
κατασκευάζῃ, μήτ' ἐλάττω τοῦ συμφέροντος τὴν
πλήρωσιν ποιούμενος τῇ λειψυδρίᾳ τοὺς καρποὺς
2 λυμαίνηται. καὶ διώρυχα μὲν ἐκ τοῦ ποταμοῦ
κατεσκεύασεν εἰς τὴν λίμνην ὀγδοήκοντα μὲν
σταδίων τὸ μῆκος, τρίπλεθρον δὲ τὸ πλάτος·
διὰ δὲ ταύτης ποτὲ μὲν δεχόμενος τὸν ποταμόν,
ποτὲ δ' ἀποστρέφων, παρείχετο τοῖς γεωργοῖς
τὴν τῶν ὑδάτων εὐκαιρίαν, ἀνοιγομένου τοῦ
στόματος καὶ πάλιν κλειομένου φιλοτέχνως καὶ
πολυδαπάνως· οὐκ ἐλάττω γὰρ τῶν πεντήκοντα
ταλάντων δαπανᾶν ἦν ἀνάγκη τὸν ἀνοῖξαι βουλόμενον ἢ κλεῖσαι τὸ προειρημένον κατασκεύασμα.
3 διαμεμένηκε δ' ἡ λίμνη τὴν εὐχρηστίαν παρεχο-
μένη τοῖς κατ' Αἴγυπτον ἕως τῶν καθ' ἡμᾶς
χρόνων, καὶ τὴν προσηγορίαν ἀπὸ τοῦ κατα-

incredible magnitude.[1] For its circumference, they say, is three thousand six hundred stades and its depth in most parts fifty fathoms; what man, accordingly, in trying to estimate the magnitude of the work, would not reasonably inquire how many myriads of men labouring for how many years were required for its completion? And as for the utility of this lake and its contribution to the welfare of all the inhabitants of Egypt, as well as for the ingenuity of the king, no man may praise them highly enough to do justice to the truth.

52. For since the Nile did not rise to a fixed height each year and yet the fruitfulness of the country depended on the constancy of the flood-level, he excavated the lake to receive the excess water, in order that the river might not, by an excessive volume of flow, immoderately flood the land and form marshes and pools, nor, by failing to rise to the proper height, ruin the harvests by the lack of water. He also dug a canal, eighty stades long and three plethra wide,[2] from the river to the lake, and by this canal, sometimes turning the river into the lake and sometimes shutting it off again, he furnished the farmers with an opportune supply of water, opening and closing the entrance by a skilful device and yet at considerable expense; for it cost no less than fifty talents if a man wanted to open or close this work. The lake has continued to serve well the needs of the Egyptians down to our time, and bears

[1] The reference is to the great depression known as the Fayûm, into which the Nile flowed during the period of inundation. The control of this flow, as described below, was first undertaken by the Pharaohs of the Twelfth Dynasty, especially by Amenemhet III.

[2] *i.e.* about nine miles long and three hundred feet wide.

σκευάσαντος ἔχει, καλουμένη μέχρι τοῦ νῦν
4 Μοίριδος λίμνη. ὁ δ' οὖν βασιλεὺς ὀρύττων
ταύτην κατέλιπεν ἐν μέσῃ τόπον, ἐν ᾧ τάφον
ᾠκοδόμησε καὶ δύο πυραμίδας, τὴν μὲν ἑαυτοῦ,
τὴν δὲ τῆς γυναικός, σταδιαίας τὸ ὕψος, ἐφ'
ὧν ἐπέστησεν εἰκόνας λιθίνας καθημένας ἐπὶ
θρόνου, νομίζων διὰ τούτων τῶν ἔργων ἀθάνατον ἑαυτοῦ καταλείψειν τὴν ἐπ' ἀγαθῷ μνήμην.
5 τὴν δ' ἐκ τῆς λίμνης ἀπὸ τῶν ἰχθύων γινομένην
πρόσοδον ἔδωκε τῇ γυναικὶ πρὸς μύρα καὶ τὸν
ἄλλον καλλωπισμόν, φερούσης τῆς θήρας ἀργυ-
6 ρίου τάλαντον ἑκάστης ἡμέρας· εἴκοσι γὰρ καὶ
δύο γένη τῶν κατ' αὐτὴν φασιν ἰχθύων εἶναι,
καὶ τοσοῦτον αὐτῶν ἁλίσκεσθαι πλῆθος ὥστε
τοὺς προσκαρτεροῦντας ταῖς ταριχείαις ὄντας
παμπληθεῖς δυσχερῶς περιγίνεσθαι τῶν ἔργων.

Περὶ μὲν οὖν Μοίριδος τοσαῦθ' ἱστοροῦσιν
Αἰγύπτιοι.

53. Σεσόωσιν δέ φασιν ὕστερον ἑπτὰ γενεαῖς
βασιλέα γενόμενον ἐπιφανεστάτας καὶ μεγίστας
τῶν πρὸ αὐτοῦ πράξεις ἐπιτελέσασθαι. ἐπεὶ δὲ
περὶ τούτου τοῦ βασιλέως οὐ μόνον οἱ συγγρα-
φεῖς οἱ παρὰ τοῖς Ἕλλησι διαπεφωνήκασι πρὸς

---

[1] This practice is better known in the case of the Persian
rulers. Villages in Syria had been given the Queen Mother
" for her girdle" (cp. the English " pin-money "; Xenophon,
Anabasis, 1. 4. 9), and when Themistocles was received by
the Persian king after his exile from Athens three cities of
Asia Minor were given him—Magnesia for bread, Lampsacus
for wine, and Myus for meat (Thucydides, 1. 138. 5).
Herodotus (2. 149) gives the same figure for the income from

the name of its builder, being called to this day the
Lake of Moeris. Now the king in excavating it left
a spot in the centre, where he built a tomb and two
pyramids, a stade in height, one for himself and the
other for his wife, on the tops of which he placed stone
statues seated upon thrones, thinking that by these
monuments he would leave behind him an imperish-
able commemoration of his good deeds. The income
accruing from the fish taken from the lake he gave to
his wife for her unguents and general embellishment,
the value of the catch amounting to a talent of silver
daily;[1] for there are twenty-two different kinds of
fish in the lake, they say, and they are caught in such
abundance that the people engaged in salting them,
though exceedingly many, can scarcely keep up with
their task.

Now this is the account which the Egyptians give
of Moeris.

53. Sesoösis,[2] they say, who became king seven
generations later, performed more renowned and
greater deeds than did any of his predecessors.
And since, with regard to this king, not only are the
Greek writers at variance with one another but also

the catch, but only for the six months when the water "flows
from the lake." A daily catch of the value of more than a
thousand dollars and a cost of fifty times that sum for
opening the locks seem highly improbable.

[2] Practically all Greek and Latin writers called him
Sesostris, and about him stories gathered as about no other
ruler in ancient history with the exception of Alexander the
Great. "In Greek times Sesostris had long since become
but a legendary figure which cannot be identified with any
particular king" (J. H. Breasted, *A History of Egypt*, p. 189).
But certain facts narrated in connection with him were
certainly drawn from memories of the reign of Ramses II of
the Nineteenth Dynasty.

ἀλλήλους, ἀλλὰ καὶ τῶν κατ᾿ Αἴγυπτον οἵ τε
ἱερεῖς καὶ οἱ διὰ τῆς ᾠδῆς αὐτὸν ἐγκωμιάζοντες
οὐχ ὁμολογούμενα λέγουσιν, ἡμεῖς πειρασόμεθα
τὰ πιθανώτατα καὶ τοῖς ὑπάρχουσιν ἔτι κατὰ
τὴν χώραν σημείοις τὰ μάλιστα συμφωνοῦντα
2 διελθεῖν. γεννηθέντος γὰρ τοῦ Σεσοώσιος ἐποίησεν ὁ πατὴρ αὐτοῦ μεγαλοπρεπές τι καὶ βασιλι-
κόν·[1] τοὺς γὰρ κατὰ τὴν αὐτὴν ἡμέραν γεννηθέντας παῖδας ἐξ ὅλης τῆς Αἰγύπτου συναγαγὼν
καὶ τροφοὺς καὶ τοὺς ἐπιμελησομένους ἐπιστήσας
τὴν αὐτὴν ἀγωγὴν καὶ παιδείαν ὥρισε τοῖς πᾶσιν,
ὑπολαμβάνων τοὺς μάλιστα συντραφέντας καὶ
τῆς αὐτῆς παρρησίας κεκοινωνηκότας εὐνουστά-
τους καὶ συναγωνιστὰς ἐν τοῖς πολέμοις ἀρίστους
3 ἔσεσθαι. πάντα δὲ δαψιλῶς χορηγήσας διε-
πόνησε τοὺς παῖδας ἐν γυμνασίοις συνεχέσι καὶ
πόνοις· οὐδενὶ γὰρ αὐτῶν ἐξῆν προσενέγκασθαι
τροφήν, εἰ μὴ πρότερον δράμοι σταδίους ἑκατὸν
4 καὶ ὀγδοήκοντα. διὸ καὶ πάντες ἀνδρωθέντες
ὑπῆρξαν ἀθληταὶ μὲν τοῖς σώμασιν εὔρωστοι,
ἡγεμονικοὶ δὲ καὶ καρτερικοὶ ταῖς ψυχαῖς διὰ τὴν
τῶν ἀρίστων ἐπιτηδευμάτων ἀγωγήν.

5   Τὸ μὲν οὖν πρῶτον ὁ Σεσόωσις ἀποσταλεὶς
ὑπὸ τοῦ πατρὸς μετὰ δυνάμεως εἰς τὴν Ἀραβίαν,
συστρατευομένων καὶ τῶν συντρόφων, περί τε
τὰς θήρας διεπονήθη καὶ ταῖς ἀνυδρίαις καὶ
σπανοσιτίαις ἐγκαρτερήσας κατεστρέψατο τὸ
ἔθνος ἅπαν τὸ τῶν Ἀράβων,[2] ἀδούλωτον τὸν
6 πρὸ τοῦ χρόνον γεγονός· ἔπειτα εἰς τοὺς πρὸς
τὴν ἑσπέραν τόπους ἀποσταλεὶς τὴν πλείστην

---

[1] Bekker and Dindorf follow II in omitting ἐποίησεν and
adding ἔπραξε after βασιλικόν.

among the Egyptians the priests and the poets who
sing his praises give conflicting stories, we for our part
shall endeavour to give the most probable account
and that which most nearly agrees with the monuments still standing in the land.   Now at the birth of
Sesoösis his father did a thing worthy of a great man
and a king: Gathering together from over all Egypt
the male children which had been born on the same
day and assigning to them nurses and guardians, he
prescribed the same training and education for them
all, on the theory that those who had been reared in
the closest companionship and had enjoyed the same
frank relationship would be most loyal and as fellow-
combatants in the wars most brave.   He amply
provided for their every need and then trained the
youths by unremitting exercises and hardships; for
no one of them was allowed to have anything to eat
unless he had first run one hundred and eighty stades.[1]
Consequently upon attaining to manhood they were
all veritable athletes of robustness of body, and in
spirit qualified for leadership and endurance because
of the training which they had received in the most
excellent pursuits.

First of all Sesoösis, his companions also accompanying him, was sent by his father with an army
into Arabia, where he was subjected to the laborious
training of hunting wild animals and, after hardening
himself to the privations of thirst and hunger, conquered the entire nation of the Arabs, which had
never been enslaved before his day; and then, on
being sent to the regions to the west, he subdued the

---

[1] About twenty miles.

[2] Ἀράβων Wesseling : βαρβάρων.

τῆς Λιβύης ὑπήκοον ἐποιήσατο, παντελῶς νέος
7 ὢν τὴν ἡλικίαν. τοῦ δὲ πατρὸς τελευτήσαντος
διαδεξάμενος τὴν βασιλείαν καὶ ταῖς προκατ-
εργασθείσαις πράξεσι μετεωρισθείς, ἐπεβάλετο
8 τὴν οἰκουμένην κατακτήσασθαι. ἔνιοι δὲ λέγουσιν αὐτὸν ὑπὸ τῆς ἰδίας θυγατρὸς Ἀθύρτιος
παρακληθῆναι πρὸς τὴν τῶν ὅλων δυναστείαν,
ἣν οἱ μὲν συνέσει πολὺ τῶν ἄλλων διαφέρουσάν
φασι διδάξαι τὸν πατέρα ῥᾳδίως ἐσομένην[1] τὴν
στρατείαν, οἱ δὲ μαντικῇ χρωμένην καὶ τὸ μέλλον
ἔσεσθαι προγινώσκουσαν ἔκ τε τῆς θυτικῆς καὶ
τῆς ἐγκοιμήσεως τῆς ἐν τοῖς ἱεροῖς, ἔτι δ' ἐκ[2] τῶν
9 κατὰ τὸν οὐρανὸν γινομένων σημείων. γεγρά-
φασι δέ τινες καὶ διότι κατὰ τὴν γένεσιν τοῦ
Σεσοώσιος ὁ πατὴρ αὐτοῦ καθ' ὕπνον δόξαι τὸν
Ἥφαιστον αὐτῷ λέγειν ὅτι πάσης τῆς οἰκου-
10 μένης ὁ γεννηθεὶς παῖς κρατήσει· διὰ ταύτην
οὖν τὴν αἰτίαν τὸν μὲν πατέρα τοὺς ἡλικιώτας
τοῦ προειρημένου ἀθροῖσαι καὶ βασιλικῆς ἀγω-
γῆς ἀξιῶσαι, προκατασκευαζόμενον εἰς τὴν τῶν
ὅλων ἐπίθεσιν, αὐτὸν δ' ἀνδρωθέντα καὶ τῇ τοῦ
θεοῦ προρρήσει πιστεύσαντα κατενεχθῆναι πρὸς
τὴν εἰρημένην στρατείαν.

54. Πρὸς δὲ ταύτην τὴν ἐπιβολὴν πρῶτον μὲν
τὴν πρὸς αὐτὸν εὔνοιαν κατεσκεύασε πᾶσι τοῖς
κατ' Αἴγυπτον, ἡγούμενος δεῖν τοὺς μὲν συστρα-
τεύοντας ἑτοίμως ὑπὲρ τῶν ἡγουμένων ἀποθνήσκειν, τοὺς δ' ἀπολειπομένους ἐπὶ τῶν
πατρίδων μηδὲν νεωτερίζειν, εἰ μέλλει τὴν προαί-

----

[1] ἂν before ἐσομένην deleted by Dindorf.
[2] δ' ἐκ Capps : δέ.

larger part of Libya, though in years still no more than a youth. And when he ascended the throne upon the death of his father, being filled with confidence by reason of his earlier exploits he undertook to conquer the inhabited earth. There are those who say that he was urged to acquire empire over the whole world by his own daughter Athyrtis, who, according to some, was far more intelligent than any of her day and showed her father that the campaign would be an easy one, while according to others she had the gift of prophecy and knew beforehand, by means both of sacrifices and the practice of sleeping in temples,[1] as well as from the signs which appear in the heavens, what would take place in the future. Some have also written that, at the birth of Sesoösis, his father had thought that Hephaestus had appeared to him in a dream and told him that the son who had been born would rule over the whole civilized world; and that for this reason, therefore, his father collected the children of the same age as his son and granted them a royal training, thus preparing them beforehand for an attack upon the whole world, and that his son, upon attaining manhood, trusting in the prediction of the god was led to undertake this campaign.

54. In preparation for this undertaking he first of all confirmed the goodwill of all the Egyptians towards himself, feeling it to be necessary, if he were to bring his plan to a successful end, that his soldiers on the campaign should be ready to die for their leaders, and that those left behind in their native

[1] The ancient practice of incubation, during which the god of the temple would grant a revelation through a dream; cp. p. 80, n. 1.

2 ρεσιν ἐπὶ τέλος ἄξειν. διὸ καὶ πάντας ἐκ τῶν
ἐνδεχομένων εὐηργέτει, τοὺς μὲν χρημάτων δωρεαῖς ἐκθεραπεύων, τοὺς δὲ χώρας δόσει, τινὰς δὲ
τιμωρίας ἀπολύσει, πάντας δὲ ταῖς ὁμιλίαις καὶ
τῇ τῶν τρόπων ἐπιεικείᾳ προσήγετο· τῶν τε γὰρ
βασιλικῶν ἐγκλημάτων ἅπαντας ἀθῴους ἀφῆκε
καὶ τοὺς πρὸς ἀργύριον συγκεκλειμένους ἀπέλυσε
τοῦ χρέους, ὄντος πολλοῦ πλήθους ἐν ταῖς
3 φυλακαῖς. τὴν δὲ χώραν ἅπασαν εἰς ἓξ καὶ
τριάκοντα μέρη διελών, ἃ καλοῦσιν Αἰγύπτιοι
νομούς, ἐπέστησεν ἅπασι νομάρχας τοὺς ἐπιμελησομένους τῶν τε προσόδων τῶν βασιλικῶν καὶ
διοικήσοντας ἅπαντα τὰ κατὰ τὰς ἰδίας μερίδας.
4 ἐπελέξατο δὲ καὶ [1] τῶν ἀνδρῶν τοὺς ταῖς ῥώμαις
διαφέροντας καὶ συνεστήσατο στρατόπεδον ἄξιον
τοῦ μεγέθους τῆς ἐπιβολῆς· κατέγραψε γὰρ
πεζῶν μὲν ἑξήκοντα μυριάδας, ἱππεῖς δὲ δισμυ-
ρίους καὶ τετρακισχιλίους, ζεύγη δὲ πολεμιστήρια
5 δισμύρια καὶ ἑπτακισχίλια. ἐπὶ δὲ τὰς κατὰ
μέρος ἡγεμονίας τῶν στρατιωτῶν ἔταξε τοὺς
συντρόφους, ἠνθηληκότας μὲν ἤδη τοῖς πολέμοις,
ἀρετὴν δ᾽ ἐζηλωκότας ἐκ παίδων, εὔνοιαν δὲ
ἀδελφικὴν ἔχοντας πρός τε τὸν βασιλέα καὶ
πρὸς ἀλλήλους, ὄντας τὸν ἀριθμὸν πλείους τῶν
6 χιλίων καὶ ἑπτακοσίων. πᾶσι δὲ τοῖς προειρημένοις κατεκληρούχησε τὴν ἀρίστην τῆς χώρας,
ὅπως ἔχοντες ἱκανὰς προσόδους καὶ μηδενὸς
ἐνδεεῖς ὄντες ἀσκῶσι τὰ περὶ τοὺς πολέμους.

55. Κατασκευάσας δὲ τὴν δύναμιν ἐστράτευσεν
ἐπὶ πρώτους Αἰθίοπας τοὺς πρὸς τῇ μεσημβρίᾳ
κατοικοῦντας, καὶ καταπολεμήσας ἠνάγκασε τὸ
ἔθνος φόρους τελεῖν ἔβενον καὶ χρυσὸν καὶ τῶν

lands should not rise in revolt. He therefore showed
kindnesses to everyone by all means at his disposal,
winning over some by presents of money, others by
gifts of land, and others by remission of penalties,
and the entire people he attached to himself by his
friendly intercourse and kindly ways; for he set free
unharmed everyone who was held for some crime
against the king and cancelled the obligations of
those who were in prison for debt, there being a great
multitude in the gaols. And dividing the entire
land into thirty-six parts which the Egyptians call
nomes, he set over each a nomarch, who should
superintend the collection of the royal revenues
and administer all the affairs of his division. He
then chose out the strongest of the men and formed
an army worthy of the greatness of his undertaking;
for he enlisted six hundred thousand foot-soldiers,
twenty-four thousand cavalry, and twenty-seven
thousand war chariots. In command of the several
divisions of his troops he set his companions, who were
by this time inured to warfare, had striven after a
reputation for valour from their youth, and cherished
with a brotherly love both their king and one another,
the number of them being over seventeen hundred.
And upon all these commanders he bestowed allot-
ments of the best land in Egypt, in order that, enjoying sufficient income and lacking nothing, they might
sedulously practise the art of war.

55. After he had made ready his army he marched
first of all against the Ethiopians who dwell south of
Egypt, and after conquering them he forced that
people to pay a tribute in ebony, gold and the

---

[1] τούτων after καὶ deleted by Dindorf.

2 ἐλεφάντων τοὺς ὀδόντας. ἔπειτ᾽ εἰς μὲν τὴν
Ἐρυθρὰν θάλατταν ἀπέστειλε στόλον νεῶν
τετρακοσίων, πρῶτος τῶν ἐγχωρίων μακρὰ σκάφη
ναυπηγησάμενος, καὶ τάς τε νήσους τὰς ἐν τοῖς
τόποις κατεκτήσατο καὶ τῆς ἠπείρου τὰ παρὰ
θάλατταν μέρη κατεστρέψατο μέχρι τῆς Ἰνδικῆς·
αὐτὸς δὲ μετὰ τῆς δυνάμεως πεζῇ τὴν πορείαν
ποιησάμενος κατεστρέψατο πᾶσαν τὴν Ἀσίαν.
3 οὐ μόνον γὰρ τὴν ὕστερον ὑπ᾽ Ἀλεξάνδρου τοῦ
Μακεδόνος κατακτηθεῖσαν χώραν ἐπῆλθεν, ἀλλὰ
καί τινα τῶν ἐθνῶν ὧν ἐκεῖνος οὐ παρέβαλεν εἰς
4 τὴν χώραν. καὶ γὰρ τὸν Γάγγην ποταμὸν διέβη
καὶ τὴν Ἰνδικὴν ἐπῆλθε πᾶσαν ἕως ὠκεανοῦ καὶ
τὰ τῶν Σκυθῶν ἔθνη μέχρι Τανάιδος ποταμοῦ
τοῦ διορίζοντος τὴν Εὐρώπην ἀπὸ τῆς Ἀσίας·
ὅτε δή φασι τῶν Αἰγυπτίων τινὰς καταλειφθέντας
περὶ τὴν Μαιῶτιν λίμνην συστήσασθαι τὸ τῶν
5 Κόλχων ἔθνος. ὅτι δὲ τοῦτο τὸ γένος Αἰγυπτια-
κόν ἐστι σημεῖον εἶναι τὸ περιτέμνεσθαι τοὺς
ἀνθρώπους παραπλησίως τοῖς κατ᾽ Αἴγυπτον,
διαμένοντος τοῦ νομίμου παρὰ τοῖς ἀποίκοις,
καθάπερ καὶ παρὰ τοῖς Ἰουδαίοις.
6 Ὁμοίως δὲ καὶ τὴν λοιπὴν Ἀσίαν ἅπασαν
ὑπήκοον ἐποιήσατο καὶ τῶν Κυκλάδων νήσων
τὰς πλείους. διαβὰς δ᾽ εἰς τὴν Εὐρώπην καὶ
διεξιὼν ἅπασαν τὴν Θρᾴκην ἐκινδύνευσεν ἀπο-
βαλεῖν τὴν δύναμιν διὰ σπάνιν τροφῆς καὶ
7 τόπων δυσχωρίας. διόπερ ὅρια τῆς στρατείας
ποιησάμενος ἐν τῇ Θρᾴκῃ, στήλας κατεσκεύασεν
ἐν πολλοῖς τόποις τῶν ὑπ᾽ αὐτοῦ κατακτηθέντων·
αὗται δὲ τὴν ἐπιγραφὴν εἶχον Αἰγυπτίοις γράμ-

tusks of elephants. Then he sent out a fleet of
four hundred ships into the Red Sea,[1] being the
first Egyptian to build warships, and not only took
possession of the islands in those waters, but also
subdued the coast of the mainland as far as India,
while he himself made his way by land with his army
and subdued all Asia. Not only did he, in fact, visit
the territory which was afterwards won by Alexander
of Macedon, but also certain peoples into whose
country Alexander did not cross. For he even
passed over the river Ganges and visited all of India
as far as the ocean, as well as the tribes of the
Scythians as far as the river Tanaïs, which divides
Europe from Asia; and it was at this time, they say,
that some of the Egyptians, having been left behind
near the Lake Maeotis, founded the nation of the
Colchi.[2] And the proof which they offer of the
Egyptian origin of this nation is the fact that the
Colchi practise circumcision even as the Egyptians
do, the custom continuing among the colonists sent
out from Egypt as it also did in the case of the Jews.

In the same way he brought all the rest of Asia into
subjection as well as most of the Cyclades islands.
And after he had crossed into Europe and was on his
way through the whole length of Thrace he nearly
lost his army through lack of food and the difficult
nature of the land. Consequently he fixed the limits
of his expedition in Thrace, and set up stelae in many
parts of the regions which he had acquired; and
these carried the following inscription in the Egyptian

[1] Not the present Red Sea, but the Persian Gulf and the
Indian Ocean.
[2] The Tanaïs river and the Lake Maeotis are the Don and
the Sea of Azof respectively, but the country of the Colchi
is generally placed in the Caucasus.

μασι τοῖς ἱεροῖς λεγομένοις, " Τήνδε τὴν χώραν
ὅπλοις κατεστρέψατο τοῖς ἑαυτοῦ βασιλεὺς
βασιλέων καὶ δεσπότης δεσποτῶν Σεσόωσις."
8 τὴν δὲ στήλην κατεσκεύασεν ἔχουσαν αἰδοῖον ἐν
μὲν τοῖς μαχίμοις ἔθνεσιν ἀνδρός, ἐν δὲ τοῖς
ἀγεννέσι καὶ δειλοῖς γυναικός, ἀπὸ τοῦ κυριωτέρου
μέρους τὴν διάθεσιν τῆς ἑκάστων ψυχῆς φανερω-
9 τάτην τοῖς ἐπιγινομένοις ἔσεσθαι νομίζων. ἐν
ἐνίοις δὲ τόποις καὶ τὴν ἑαυτοῦ κατεσκεύασεν
εἰκόνα λιθίνην, τόξα καὶ λόγχην ἔχουσαν, τῷ
μεγέθει τέτταρσι παλαισταῖς μείζονα τῶν τεττάρων πηχῶν, ἡλίκος ὢν καὶ αὐτὸς ἐτύγχανεν.
10 ἐπιεικῶς δὲ προσενεχθεὶς ἅπασι τοῖς ὑποτεταγ-
μένοις καὶ συντελέσας τὴν στρατείαν ἐν ἔτεσιν
ἐννέα, τοῖς μὲν ἔθνεσι κατὰ δύναμιν προσέταξε
δωροφορεῖν κατ' ἐνιαυτὸν εἰς Αἴγυπτον, αὐτὸς
δ' ἀθροίσας αἰχμαλώτων τε καὶ τῶν ἄλλων
λαφύρων πλῆθος ἀνυπέρβλητον ἐπανῆλθεν εἰς
τὴν πατρίδα, μεγίστας πράξεις τῶν πρὸ αὐτοῦ
11 κατειργασμένος. καὶ τὰ μὲν ἱερὰ πάντα τὰ κατ'
Αἴγυπτον ἀναθήμασιν ἀξιολόγοις καὶ σκύλοις
ἐκόσμησε, τῶν δὲ στρατιωτῶν τοὺς ἀνδραγαθή-
12 σαντας δωρεαῖς κατὰ τὴν ἀξίαν ἐτίμησε. καθόλου
δὲ ἀπὸ ταύτης τῆς στρατείας οὐ μόνον ἡ συναν-
δραγαθήσασα δύναμις μεγάλην εὐπορίαν κτησα-
μένη τὴν ἐπάνοδον ἐποιήσατο λαμπράν, ἀλλὰ καὶ
τὴν Αἴγυπτον ἅπασαν συνέβη παντοίας ὠφελείας
ἐμπλησθῆναι.

---

[1] H. R. Hall (*The Ancient History of the Near East* [6], pp.
161–2) gives a translation of a stele set up at Semneh by
Senusret III of the Twelfth Dynasty, who is often identified
with the Sesoösis of Diodorus, and observes that its language,

writing which is called "sacred": "This land the
King of Kings and Lord of Lords, Sesoösis, subdued
with his own arms." And he fashioned the stele with
a representation, in case the enemy people were warlike, of the privy parts of a man, but in case they were
abject and cowardly, of those of a woman, holding
that the quality of the spirit of each people would be
set forth most clearly to succeeding generations by
the dominant member of the body.[1] And in some
places he also erected a stone statue of himself, armed
with bow and arrows and a spear, in height four cubits
and four palms, which was indeed his own stature.[2]
He dealt gently with all conquered peoples and, after
concluding his campaign in nine years, commanded
the nations to bring presents each year to Egypt
according to their ability, while he himself, assembling
a multitude of captives which has never been surpassed and a mass of other booty, returned to his
country, having accomplished the greatest deeds of
any king of Egypt to his day. All the temples of
Egypt, moreover, he adorned with notable votive
offerings and spoils, and honoured with gifts according to his merits every soldier who had distinguished
himself for bravery. And in general, as a result of
this campaign not only did the army, which had
bravely shared in the deeds of the king and had
gathered great wealth, make a brilliant homeward
journey, but it also came to pass that all Egypt was
filled to overflowing with benefits of every kind.

unique in this period for its scorn of the conquered negroes,
is strikingly reminiscent of the stelae described in this passage
and by Herodotus 2. 102.

[2] About seven feet; cp. the bed of Og, king of Bashan
(*Deut.* 3. 11), which was nine cubits long and four wide; "is
it not in Rabbath of the children of Ammon?"

56. Ὁ δὲ Σεσόωσις ἀποστήσας τὰ πλήθη ἀπὸ
τῶν πολεμικῶν ἔργων τοῖς μὲν συνανδραγαθήσασι
συνεχώρησε τὴν ῥαστώνην καὶ τὴν ἀπόλαυσιν
τῶν κατακτηθέντων ἀγαθῶν, αὐτὸς δὲ φιλόδοξος
ὢν καὶ τῆς εἰς τὸν αἰῶνα μνήμης ὀρεγόμενος
κατεσκεύασεν ἔργα μεγάλα καὶ θαυμαστὰ ταῖς
ἐπινοίαις καὶ ταῖς χορηγίαις, ἑαυτῷ μὲν ἀθάνατον
περιποιοῦντα δόξαν, τοῖς δ' Αἰγυπτίοις τὴν εἰς
ἅπαντα τὸν χρόνον ἀσφάλειαν μετὰ ῥαστώνης.
2 πρῶτον μὲν γὰρ ἀπὸ θεῶν ἀρξάμενος ᾠκοδόμησεν
ἐν πάσαις ταῖς κατ' Αἴγυπτον πόλεσιν ἱερὸν
θεοῦ τοῦ μάλιστα παρ' ἑκάστοις τιμωμένου.
πρὸς δὲ τὰς ἐργασίας τῶν μὲν Αἰγυπτίων οὐδένα
παρέλαβε, δι' αὐτῶν δὲ τῶν αἰχμαλώτων ἅπαντα
κατεσκεύασε· διόπερ ἐπὶ πᾶσι τοῖς ἱεροῖς ἐπέ-
γραψεν ὡς οὐδεὶς ἐγχώριος εἰς αὐτὰ μεμόχθηκε.
3 λέγεται δὲ τῶν αἰχμαλώτων τοὺς ἐκ τῆς Βαβυλωνίας ἁλόντας ἀποστῆναι τοῦ βασιλέως, μὴ
δυναμένους φέρειν τὰς ἐν τοῖς ἔργοις ταλαιπωρίας·
οὓς καταλαβομένους παρὰ τὸν ποταμὸν χωρίον
καρτερὸν διαπολεμεῖν τοῖς Αἰγυπτίοις καὶ τὴν
σύνεγγυς χώραν καταφθείρειν, τέλος δὲ δοθείσης
ἀδείας αὐτοῖς κατοικῆσαι τὸν τόπον, ὃν καὶ ἀπὸ
4 τῆς πατρίδος Βαβυλῶνα προσαγορεῦσαι. δι'
αἰτίας δὲ παραπλησίους φασὶν ὠνομάσθαι καὶ
τὴν Τροίαν τὴν ἔτι[1] νῦν οὖσαν παρὰ τὸν Νεῖλον·
τὸν μὲν γὰρ Μενέλαον ἐξ Ἰλίου πλέοντα μετὰ

---

[1] καὶ after ἔτι omitted by D and Vogel, retained by Bekker
and Dindorf.

---

[1] " Few of the great temples of Egypt have not some
chamber, hall, colonnade or pylon which bears his (Ramses II)

56. Sesoösis now relieved his peoples of the labours of war and granted to the comrades who had bravely shared in his deeds a care-free life in the enjoyment of the good things which they had won, while he himself, being ambitious for glory and intent upon everlasting fame, constructed works which were great and marvellous in their conception as well as in the lavishness with which their cost was provided, winning in this way immortal glory for himself and for the Egyptians security combined with ease for all time. For beginning with the gods first, he built in each city of Egypt a temple to the god who was held in special reverence by its inhabitants.[1] On these labours he used no Egyptians, but constructed them all by the hands of his captives alone; and for this reason he placed an inscription on every temple to the effect that no native had toiled upon it. And it is said that the captives brought from Babylonia revolted from the king, being unable to endure the hardships entailed by his works; and they, seizing a strong position on the banks of the river, maintained a warfare against the Egyptians and ravaged the neighbouring territory, but finally, on being granted an amnesty, they established a colony on the spot, which they also named Babylon after their native land. For a similar reason, they say, the city of Troy likewise, which even to this day exists on the bank of the Nile, received its name:[2] for Menelaus, on his voyage from Ilium with a great

name, in perpetuating which the king stopped at no desecration or destruction of the ancient monuments of the country " (J. H. Breasted, *History of Egypt*, p. 443).

[2] Strabo (17. 1. 34) mentions a village of this name near the pyramids.

πολλῶν αἰχμαλώτων παραβαλεῖν εἰς Αἴγυπτον,
τοὺς δὲ Τρῶας ἀποστάντας αὐτοῦ καταλαβέσθαι
τινὰ τόπον καὶ διαπολεμῆσαι μέχρι ὅτου συγ-
χωρηθείσης αὐτοῖς τῆς ἀσφαλείας ἔκτισαν πόλιν,
5 ἣν ὁμώνυμον αὐτοὺς ποιῆσαι τῇ πατρίδι. οὐκ
ἀγνοῶ δ' ὅτι περὶ τῶν εἰρημένων πόλεων Κτησίας
ὁ Κνίδιος διαφόρως ἱστόρησε, φήσας τῶν μετὰ
Σεμιράμιδος παραβαλόντων εἰς Αἴγυπτόν τινας
ἐκτικέναι ταύτας, ἀπὸ τῶν ἰδίων πατρίδων
6 θεμένους τὴν προσηγορίαν. περὶ δὲ τούτων τὸ
μὲν ἀληθὲς ἐκθέσθαι μετὰ ἀκριβείας οὐ ῥάδιον,
τὸ δ' ἀναγραφῆς ἀξιῶσαι τὰ διαφωνούμενα παρὰ
τοῖς συγγραφεῦσιν ἀναγκαῖον, ὅπως ἀκέραιος ἡ
περὶ τῆς ἀληθείας κρίσις ἀπολείπηται τοῖς ἀναγινώσκουσιν.

57. Ὁ δ' οὖν Σεσόωσις χώματα πολλὰ καὶ
μεγάλα κατασκευάσας τὰς πόλεις εἰς ταῦτα
μετῴκισεν, ὅσαι μὴ φυσικῶς τὸ ἔδαφος ἐτύγχανον
ἐπηρμένον ἔχουσαι, ὅπως κατὰ τὰς πληρώσεις
τοῦ ποταμοῦ καταφυγὰς ἔχωσιν ἀκινδύνους οἵ τε
2 ἄνθρωποι καὶ τὰ κτήνη. κατὰ πᾶσαν δὲ τὴν
χώραν τὴν ἀπὸ Μέμφεως ἐπὶ θάλατταν ὤρυξε
πυκνὰς ἐκ τοῦ ποταμοῦ διώρυχας, ἵνα τὰς μὲν
συγκομιδὰς τῶν καρπῶν ποιῶνται συντόμως καὶ
ῥαδίως, ταῖς δὲ πρὸς ἀλλήλους τῶν λαῶν ἐπι-
μιξίαις καὶ πᾶσι τοῖς τόποις ὑπάρχῃ ῥᾳστώνη
καὶ πάντων τῶν πρὸς ἀπόλαυσιν πολλὴ δαψίλεια·
τὸ δὲ μέγιστον, πρὸς τὰς τῶν πολεμίων ἐφόδους
ὀχυρὰν καὶ δυσέμβολον ἐποίησε τὴν χώραν·
3 τὸν γὰρ πρὸ τοῦ χρόνου ἡ κρατίστη τῆς Αἰγύ-

number of captives, crossed over into Egypt; and
the Trojans, revolting from him, seized a certain
place and maintained a warfare until he granted
them safety and freedom, whereupon they founded
a city, to which they gave the name of their native
land. I am not unaware that regarding the cities
named above Ctesias of Cnidus has given a different
account, saying that some of those who had come
into Egypt with Semiramis founded them, calling
them after their native lands.[1] But on such matters
as these it is not easy to set forth the precise truth,
and yet the disagreements among historians must
be considered worthy of record, in order that the
reader may be able to decide upon the truth without
prejudice.

57. Now Sesoösis threw up many great mounds
of earth and moved to them such cities as happened
to be situated on ground that was not naturally
elevated, in order that at the time of the flooding
of the river both the inhabitants and their herds
might have a safe place of retreat. And over the
entire land from Memphis to the sea he dug frequent
canals leading from the river, his purpose being that
the people might carry out the harvesting of their
crops quickly and easily, and that, through the constant intercourse of the peasants with one another,
every district might enjoy both an easy livelihood
and a great abundance of all things which minister
to man's enjoyment. The greatest result of this
work, however, was that he made the country secure
and difficult of access against attacks by enemies;
for practically all the best part of Egypt, which

---

[1] This campaign of Semiramis is described in Book 2. 14;
on Ctesias cp. the Introduction, pp. xxvi f.

DIODORUS OF SICILY

πτου πᾶσα σχεδὸν ἱππάσιμος οὖσα καὶ ταῖς
συνωρίσιν εὔβατος ἀπ' ἐκείνου τοῦ χρόνου διὰ τὸ
πλῆθος τῶν ἐκ τοῦ ποταμοῦ διωρύχων δυσεφοδω-
4 τάτη γέγονεν. ἐτείχισε δὲ καὶ τὴν πρὸς ἀνα-
τολὰς νεύουσαν πλευρὰν τῆς Αἰγύπτου πρὸς τὰς
ἀπὸ τῆς Συρίας καὶ τῆς Ἀραβίας ἐμβολὰς ἀπὸ
Πηλουσίου μέχρι Ἡλιουπόλεως διὰ τῆς ἐρήμου,
τὸ μῆκος ἐπὶ σταδίους χιλίους καὶ πεντακοσίους.
5 ἐναυπηγήσατο δὲ καὶ πλοῖον κέδρινον τὸ μὲν
μῆκος πηχῶν διακοσίων καὶ ὀγδοήκοντα, τὴν δ'
ἐπιφάνειαν ἔχον τὴν μὲν ἔξωθεν ἐπίχρυσον, τὴν
δ' ἔνδοθεν κατηργυρωμένην· καὶ τοῦτο μὲν
ἀνέθηκε τῷ θεῷ τῷ μάλιστα ἐν Θήβαις τιμω-
μένῳ, δύο τε[1] λιθίνους ὀβελίσκους ἐκ τοῦ σκληροῦ
λίθου πηχῶν τὸ ὕψος εἴκοσι πρὸς τοῖς ἑκατόν,
ἐφ' ὧν ἐπέγραψε τό τε μέγεθος τῆς δυνάμεως καὶ
τὸ πλῆθος τῶν προσόδων καὶ τὸν ἀριθμὸν τῶν
καταπολεμηθέντων ἐθνῶν· ἐν Μέμφει δ' ἐν τῷ
τοῦ Ἡφαίστου ἱερῷ μονολίθους εἰκόνας ἑαυτοῦ
τε καὶ τῆς γυναικὸς τὸ ὕψος τριάκοντα πηχῶν,
τῶν δ' υἱῶν εἴκοσι πηχῶν, διὰ σύμπτωμα τοιόνδε.
6 ἐκ τῆς μεγάλης στρατείας ἀνακάμψαντος εἰς
Αἴγυπτον τοῦ Σεσοώσιος καὶ διατρίβοντος περὶ
τὸ Πηλούσιον, ἑστιῶν αὐτὸν ὁ ἀδελφὸς μετὰ
τῆς γυναικὸς καὶ τῶν τέκνων ἐπιβουλὴν συνε-
στήσατο· ἀναπαυσαμένων γὰρ αὐτῶν ἀπὸ τῆς
μέθης, ἔχων καλάμου ξηροῦ πλῆθος ἐκ χρόνου
παρεσκευασμένον, καὶ τοῦτο νυκτὸς τῇ σκηνῇ

[1] τε Wesseling : δέ.

before this time had been easy of passage for horses and carts, has from that time on been very difficult for an enemy to invade by reason of the great number of canals leading from the river. He also fortified with a wall the side of Egypt which faces east, as a defence against inroads from Syria and Arabia; the wall extended through the desert from Pelusium to Heliopolis, and its length was some fifteen hundred stades. Moreover, he also built a ship of cedar wood, which was two hundred and eighty cubits long and plated on the exterior with gold and on the interior with silver. This ship he presented as a votive offering to the god who is held in special reverence in Thebes, as well as two obelisks of hard stone one hundred and twenty cubits high, upon which he inscribed the magnitude of his army, the multitude of his revenues, and the number of the peoples he had subdued; also in Memphis in the temples of Hephaestus he dedicated monolithic statues of himself and of his wife, thirty cubits high,[1] and of his sons, twenty cubits high, the occasion of their erection being as follows. When Sesoösis had returned to Egypt after his great campaign and was tarrying at Pelusium, his brother, who was entertaining Sesoösis and his wife and children, plotted against them; for when they had fallen asleep after the drinking he piled great quantities of dry rushes, which he had kept in readiness for some time, around the tent in the night and

---

[1] The account through here of Sesoösis closely follows that given by Herodotus 2. 102 ff. Near Memphis are two colossi of Ramses II, the larger of which was about forty-two feet high, approximately the thirty cubits of Diodorus and of Herodotus 2. 110 (*Baedeker's Egypt*, p. 141).

7 περιθείς, ἐνέπρησεν. ἄφνω δὲ τοῦ πυρὸς ἐκλάμ-
ψαντος οἱ μὲν ἐπὶ τῆς θεραπείας τοῦ βασιλέως
τεταγμένοι παρεβοήθουν ἀγεννῶς ὡς ἂν οἰνωμένοι,
ὁ δὲ Σεσόωσις ἀμφοτέρας τὰς χεῖρας ἀνατείνας
καὶ ὑπὲρ τῆς σωτηρίας τῶν τε παίδων καὶ τῆς
γυναικὸς τοῖς θεοῖς εὐξάμενος διεξέπεσε διὰ τῆς
8 φλογός. σωθεὶς δὲ παραδόξως τοὺς ἄλλους
θεοὺς ἐτίμησεν ἀναθήμασι, καθότι προείρηται,
πάντων δὲ μάλιστα τὸν Ἥφαιστον, ὡς ὑπὸ
τούτου τετευχὼς τῆς σωτηρίας.

58. Πολλῶν δὲ καὶ μεγάλων περὶ τὸν Σεσόωσιν ὑπαρξάντων δοκεῖ μεγαλοπρεπέστατον αὐτῷ
γεγονέναι τὸ συντελούμενον ἐν ταῖς ἐξόδοις περὶ
2 τοὺς ἡγεμόνας. τῶν γὰρ καταπεπολεμημένων
ἐθνῶν οἵ τε τὰς συγκεχωρημένας βασιλείας
ἔχοντες καὶ τῶν ἄλλων οἱ τὰς μεγίστας ἡγεμονίας παρειληφότες ἀπήντων εἰς Αἴγυπτον ἐν
τακτοῖς χρόνοις φέροντες δῶρα· οὓς ὁ βασιλεὺς
ἐκδεχόμενος ἐν μὲν τοῖς ἄλλοις ἐτίμα καὶ διαφερόντως προῆγεν, ὁπότε δὲ πρὸς ἱερὸν ἢ πόλιν
προσιέναι μέλλοι, τοὺς ἵππους ἀπὸ τοῦ τεθρίππου
λύων ὑπεζεύγνυεν ἀντὶ τούτων κατὰ τέτταρας
τούς τε βασιλεῖς καὶ τοὺς ἄλλους ἡγεμόνας,
ἐνδεικνύμενος, ὡς ᾤετο, πᾶσιν ὅτι τοὺς τῶν
ἄλλων κρατίστους καὶ δι' ἀρετὴν ἐπιφανεστάτους
καταπολεμήσας εἰς ἅμιλλαν ἀρετῆς οὐκ ἔχει
3 τὸν δυνάμενον συγκριθῆναι. δοκεῖ δ' οὗτος ὁ
βασιλεὺς πάντας τοὺς πώποτε γενομένους ἐν
ἐξουσίαις ὑπερβεβηκέναι ταῖς τε πολεμικαῖς
πράξεσι καὶ τῷ μεγέθει καὶ τῷ πλήθει τῶν τε
ἀναθημάτων καὶ τῶν ἔργων τῶν κατεσκευασμένων κατ' Αἴγυπτον. ἔτη δὲ τρία πρὸς τοῖς τριά-

set them afire. When the fire suddenly blazed up, those who had been assigned to wait upon the king came to his aid in a churlish fashion, as would men heavy with wine, but Sesoösis, raising both hands to the heavens with a prayer to the gods for the preservation of his children and wife, dashed out safe through the flames. For this unexpected escape he honoured the rest of the gods with votive offerings, as stated above, and Hephaestus most of all, on the ground that it was by his intervention that he had been saved.

58. Although many great deeds have been credited to Sesoösis, his magnificence seems best to have been shown in the treatment which he accorded to the foreign potentates when he went forth from his palace. The kings whom he had allowed to continue their rule over the peoples which he had subdued and all others who had received from him the most important positions of command would present themselves in Egypt at specified times, bringing him gifts, and the king would welcome them and in all other matters show them honour and special preferment; but whenever he intended to visit a temple or city he would remove the horses from his four-horse chariot and in their place yoke the kings and other potentates, taking them four at a time, in this way showing to all men, as he thought, that, having conquered the mightiest of other kings and those most renowned for their excellence, he now had no one who could compete with him for the prize of excellence. This king is thought to have surpassed all former rulers in power and military exploits, and also in the magnitude and number of the votive offerings and public works which he built in Egypt. And after a reign of thirty-three years

κοντα βασιλεύσας ἐκ προαιρέσεως ἐξέλιπε τὸν
βίον, ὑπολιπόντων αὐτὸν τῶν ὀμμάτων· καὶ
τοῦτο πράξας οὐ μόνον παρὰ τοῖς ἱερεῦσιν, ἀλλὰ
καὶ παρὰ τοῖς ἄλλοις Αἰγυπτίοις ἐθαυμάσθη,
δόξας τῇ μεγαλοψυχίᾳ τῶν πεπραγμένων
ἀκόλουθον πεποιῆσθαι τὴν τοῦ βίου κατα-
στροφήν.

4   Ἐπὶ τοσοῦτο δ᾽ ἴσχυσε καὶ διέτεινε τοῖς
χρόνοις ἡ δόξα τούτου τοῦ βασιλέως ὥστε τῆς
Αἰγύπτου πολλαῖς γενεαῖς ὕστερον πεσούσης ὑπὸ
τὴν ἐξουσίαν τῶν Περσῶν, καὶ Δαρείου τοῦ
Ξέρξου πατρὸς σπουδάσαντος ἐν Μέμφει τὴν
ἰδίαν εἰκόνα στῆσαι πρὸ τῆς¹ Σεσοώσιος, ὁ μὲν
ἀρχιερεὺς ἀντεῖπε λόγου προτεθέντος ἐν ἐκκλη-
σίᾳ τῶν ἱερέων, ἀποφηνάμενος ὡς οὔπω Δαρεῖος
ὑπερβέβηκε τὰς Σεσοώσιος πράξεις, ὁ δὲ βασιλεὺς οὐχ ὅπως ἠγανάκτησεν, ἀλλὰ καὶ τοὐναντίον
ἡσθεὶς ἐπὶ τῇ παρρησίᾳ σπουδάσειν ἔφησεν
ὅπως κατὰ μηδὲν ἐκείνου λειφθείη βιώσας τὸν
ἴσον χρόνον, καὶ παρεκάλει συγκρίνειν τὰς
ἡλικιώτιδας πράξεις· τοῦτον γὰρ δικαιότατον
ἔλεγχον εἶναι τῆς ἀρετῆς.

5   Περὶ μὲν οὖν Σεσοώσιος ἀρκεσθησόμεθα τοῖς
λόγοις τοῖς ῥηθεῖσιν.

59. Ὁ δ᾽ υἱὸς αὐτοῦ διαδεξάμενος τὴν βασιλείαν καὶ τὴν τοῦ πατρὸς προσηγορίαν ἑαυτῷ
περιθέμενος πρᾶξιν μὲν πολεμικὴν ἢ μνήμης
ἀξίαν οὐδ᾽ ἡντινοῦν συνετελέσατο, συμπτώματι
2 δὲ περιέπεσεν ἰδιάζοντι. ἐστερήθη μὲν γὰρ τῆς
ὁράσεως εἴτε διὰ τὴν πρὸς τὸν πατέρα τῆς
φύσεως κοινωνίαν εἴθ᾽, ὥς τινες μυθολογοῦσι, διὰ
τὴν εἰς τὸν ποταμὸν ἀσέβειαν, ἐν ᾧ χειμαζόμενός

he deliberately took his own life, his eyesight having failed him; and this act won for him the admiration not only of the priests of Egypt but of the other inhabitants as well, for it was thought that he had caused the end of his life to comport with the loftiness of spirit shown in his achievements.

So great became the fame of this king and so enduring through the ages that when, many generations later, Egypt fell under the power of the Persians and Darius, the father of Xerxes, was bent upon placing a statue of himself in Memphis before that of Sesoösis, the chief priest opposed it in a speech which he made in an assembly of the priests, to the effect that Darius had not yet surpassed the deeds of Sesoösis; and the king was far from being angered, but, on the contrary, being pleased at his frankness of speech, said that he would strive not to be found behind that ruler in any point when he had attained his years, and asked them to base their judgment upon the deeds of each at the same age, for that was the fairest test of their excellence.

As regards Sesoösis, then, we shall rest content with what has been said.

59. But his son, succeeding to the throne and assuming his father's appellation, did not accomplish a single thing in war or otherwise worthy of mention, though he did have a singular experience.[1] He lost his sight, either because he shared in his father's bodily constitution or, as some fictitiously relate, because of his impiety towards the river, since once when caught in a storm upon it he had

[1] The following folk story, with some variations, is given in Herodotus 2, 111.

---

[1] πρὸ τῆς Dindorf: πρὸ τῆς τοῦ.

ποτε τὸ φερόμενον ῥεῦμα κατηκόντισε· διὰ δὲ
τὴν ἀτυχίαν ἀναγκασθεὶς καταφυγεῖν ἐπὶ τὴν
τῶν θεῶν βοήθειαν, ἐπὶ χρόνους ἱκανοὺς πλείσταις
θυσίαις καὶ τιμαῖς τὸ θεῖον ἐξιλασκόμενος οὐδε-
3 μιᾶς ἐτύγχανε πολυωρίας· τῷ δεκάτῳ δ' ἔτει
μαντείας αὐτῷ γενομένης τιμῆσαί τε τὸν θεὸν
τὸν ἐν Ἡλιουπόλει καὶ γυναικὸς οὔρῳ νίζεσθαι
τὸ πρόσωπον ἥτις ἑτέρου πεῖραν ἀνδρὸς οὐκ
εἴληφε, τῶν μὲν γυναικῶν ἀπὸ τῆς ἰδίας ἀρξάμενος καὶ πολλὰς ἐξετάσας οὐδεμίαν εὗρεν ἀδιά-
φθορον πλὴν κηπουροῦ τινος, ἣν ὑγιὴς γενόμενος
ἔγημε· τὰς δ' ἄλλας ζώσας ἐν κώμῃ τινὶ κατέκαυσεν, ἣν Αἰγύπτιοι διὰ τὸ σύμπτωμα τοῦτο
4 προσηγόρευσαν ἱερὰν βῶλον· τῷ δ' ἐν Ἡλιουπόλει θεῷ τὰς χάριτας ἀπονέμων τῆς εὐεργεσίας κατὰ τὸν χρησμὸν ὀβελίσκους ἀνέθηκε δύο
μονολίθους, τὸ μὲν πλάτος ὀκτώ, τὸ δὲ μῆκος
πηχῶν ἑκατόν.

60. Μετὰ δὲ τοῦτον τὸν βασιλέα συχνοὶ τῶν
διαδεξαμένων τὴν ἀρχήν τινες οὐδὲν ἔπραξαν
ἀναγραφῆς ἄξιον. πολλαῖς δ' ὕστερον γενεαῖς
Ἄμασις γενόμενος βασιλεὺς ἦρχε τῶν ὄχλων
βιαιότερον· πολλοὺς μὲν γὰρ παρὰ τὸ δίκαιον
ἐτιμωρεῖτο, συχνοὺς δὲ τῶν οὐσιῶν ἐστέρισκε,
πᾶσι δ' ὑπεροπτικῶς καὶ κατὰ πᾶν ὑπερηφάνως
2 προσεφέρετο. μέχρι μὲν οὖν τινος οἱ πάσχοντες
ἐκαρτέρουν, οὐ δυνάμενοι κατ' οὐδένα τρόπον
ἀμύνασθαι τοὺς πλέον ἰσχύοντας· ἐπεὶ δ'
Ἀκτισάνης ὁ τῶν Αἰθιόπων βασιλεὺς ἐστράτευσεν ἐπ' αὐτόν, τότε τοῦ μίσους καιρὸν λα-

---

[1] One of these obelisks still stands, of red granite of Syene
and 66 feet high. The largest obelisk in the world, that

hurled a spear into the rushing current. Forced by this ill fortune to turn to the gods for aid, he strove over a long period to propitiate the deity by numerous sacrifices and honours, but received no consideration. But in the tenth year an oracular command was given to him to do honour to the god in Heliopolis and bathe his face in the urine of a woman who had never known any other man than her husband. Thereupon he began with his own wife and then made trial of many, but found not one that was chaste save a certain gardener's wife, whom he married as soon as he was recovered. All the other women he burned alive in a certain village to which the Egyptians because of this incident gave the name Holy Field; and to the god in Heliopolis, out of gratitude for his benefaction, he dedicated, in accordance with the injunction of the oracle, two monolithic obelisks,[1] eight cubits wide and one hundred high.

60. After this king a long line of successors on the throne accomplished no deed worth recording. But Amasis, who became king many generations later, ruled the masses of the people with great harshness; many he punished unjustly, great numbers he deprived of their possessions, and towards all his conduct was without exception contemptuous and arrogant. Now for a time his victims bore up under this, being unable in any way to protect themselves against those of greater power; but when Actisanes,[2] the king of the Ethiopians, led an army against Amasis, their hatred seized the opportunity

569-526 B.C.

---

before the Lateran, is 100 feet high; the 150 feet of Diodorus seems a little too big.

[2] A. Wiedemann (*Ägyptische Geschichte*, p. 582, n. 1) thinks that Actisanes is no more than a double of the Ethiopian Sabaco of chap. 65.

207

3 βόντος[1] ἀπέστησαν οἱ πλεῖστοι. διόπερ ῥᾳδίως
αὐτοῦ χειρωθέντος ἡ μὲν Αἴγυπτος ἔπεσεν ὑπὸ
τὴν τῶν Αἰθιόπων βασιλείαν, ὁ δ᾽ Ἀκτισάνης
ἀνθρωπίνως ἐνέγκας τὴν εὐτυχίαν ἐπιεικῶς
4 προσεφέρετο τοῖς ὑποτεταγμένοις· ὅτε δὴ καὶ
συνετέλεσεν ἴδιόν τι περὶ τοὺς λῃστάς, οὔτε
θανατώσας τοὺς ἐνόχους οὔτε ὁλοσχερῶς ἀφεὶς
5 ἀτιμωρήτους· συναγαγὼν γὰρ ἐξ ἁπάσης τῆς
χώρας τοὺς ἐν ἐγκλήμασιν ὄντας κακουργίας,
καὶ τὴν διάγνωσιν αὐτῶν δικαιοτάτην ποιησάμενος, ἤθροισεν ἅπαντας τοὺς καταδεδικασμένους,
ἀποτεμὼν δ᾽ αὐτῶν τοὺς μυκτῆρας κατῴκισεν ἐν
τοῖς ἐσχάτοις τῆς ἐρήμου,[2] κτίσας πόλιν τὴν ἀπὸ
τοῦ συμπτώματος τῶν οἰκητόρων Ῥινοκόλουρα
προσαγορευθεῖσαν.
6 Αὕτη δὲ κειμένη πρὸς τοῖς μεθορίοις τῆς
Αἰγύπτου καὶ Συρίας οὐ μακρὰν τοῦ παρήκοντος
αἰγιαλοῦ πάντων σχεδὸν τῶν πρὸς ἀνθρωπίνην
7 δίαιταν ἀνηκόντων ἐστέρηται· περιέχει μὲν γὰρ
αὐτὴν χώρα πλήρης ἁλμυρίδος, ἐντὸς δὲ τοῦ
τείχους ὀλίγον ἐστὶν ὕδωρ ἐν φρέασι, καὶ τοῦτο
διεφθαρμένον καὶ παντελῶς τῇ γεύσει πικρόν.
8 κατῴκισε δ᾽ αὐτοὺς εἰς ταύτην τὴν χώραν, ὅπως
μήτε τοὺς ἐξ ἀρχῆς ἐπιτηδευθέντας βίους διατη-
ροῦντες λυμαίνωνται τοὺς μηδὲν ἀδικοῦντας, μήτε
κατὰ τὰς πρὸς τοὺς ἄλλους ἐπιμιξίας ἀγνοού-
9 μενοι λανθάνωσιν. ἀλλ᾽ ὅμως ἐκριφέντες εἰς
χώραν ἔρημον καὶ πάντων σχεδὸν τῶν χρησίμων
ἄπορον ἐπενόησαν βίον οἰκεῖον τῆς περὶ αὐτοὺς
ἐνδείας, ἀναγκαζούσης τῆς φύσεως πρὸς τὴν

---

[1] λαβόντος Dindorf: λαβόντες.
[2] ἐρήμου D, Bekker, Vogel: ἐρήμου χώρας Vulgate, Dindorf.

and most of the Egyptians revolted. As a consequence, since he was easily overcome, Egypt fell
under the rule of the Ethiopians. But Actisanes
carried his good fortune as a man should and conducted himself in a kindly manner towards his
subjects. For instance, he had his own manner of
dealing with thieves, neither putting to death such
as were liable to that punishment, nor letting them
go with no punishment at all; for after he had
gathered together out of the whole land those who
were charged with some crime and had held a
thoroughly fair examination of their cases, he took
all who had been judged guilty, and, cutting off
their noses, settled them in a colony on the edge
of the desert, founding the city which was called
Rhinocolura [1] after the lot of its inhabitants.

This city, which lies on the border between Egypt
and Syria not far from the sea-coast, is wanting in
practically everything which is necessary for man's
existence; for it is surrounded by land which is full
of brine, while within the walls there is but a small
supply of water from wells, and this is impure and
very bitter to the taste. But he settled them in
this country in order that, in case they continued to
practise their original manner of life, they might
not prey upon innocent people, and also that they
might not pass unrecognized as they mingled with
the rest of mankind. And yet, despite the fact
that they had been cast out into a desert country
which lacked practically every useful thing, they
contrived a way of living appropriate to the dearth
about them, since nature forced them to devise

---

[1] *i.e.* Nose-clipped.

10 ἀπορίαν πάντα μηχανᾶσθαι. καλάμην γὰρ κεί-
ροντες ἐκ τῆς ὁμόρου χώρας, καὶ ταύτην σχί-
ζοντες, λίνα παραμήκη κατεσκεύαζον, ταῦτα δὲ
παρὰ τὸν αἰγιαλὸν ἐπὶ πολλοὺς σταδίους
ἱστάντες τὰς θήρας τῶν ὀρτύγων ἐποιοῦντο·
φέρονται γὰρ οὗτοι κατ' ἀγέλας μείζονας ἐκ τοῦ
πελάγους· οὓς θηρεύοντες ἤθροιζον πλῆθος ἱκανὸν
εἰς διατροφὴν ἑαυτοῖς.

61. Τοῦ δὲ βασιλέως τούτου τελευτήσαντος
ἀνεκτήσαντο τὴν ἀρχὴν Αἰγύπτιοι, καὶ κατέστησαν ἐγχώριον βασιλέα Μένδην, ὅν τινες Μάρρον
2 προσονομάζουσιν. οὗτος δὲ πολεμικὴν μὲν πρᾶξιν οὐδ' ἡντινοῦν ἐπετελέσατο, τάφον δ' αὑτῷ
κατεσκεύασε τὸν ὀνομαζόμενον λαβύρινθον, οὐχ
οὕτω κατὰ τὸ μέγεθος τῶν ἔργων θαυμαστὸν ὡς
πρὸς τὴν φιλοτεχνίαν δυσμίμητον· ὁ γὰρ εἰσελ-
θὼν εἰς αὐτὸν οὐ δύναται ῥᾳδίως τὴν ἔξοδον
εὑρεῖν, ἐὰν μὴ τύχῃ τινὸς ὁδηγοῦ παντελῶς
3 ἐμπείρου. φασὶ δέ τινες καὶ τὸν Δαίδαλον εἰς
Αἴγυπτον παραβαλόντα καὶ θαυμάσαντα τὴν ἐν
τοῖς ἔργοις τέχνην κατασκευάσαι τῷ βασιλεύοντι
τῆς Κρήτης Μίνῳ λαβύρινθον ὅμοιον τῷ κατ'
Αἴγυπτον, ἐν ᾧ γενέσθαι μυθολογοῦσι τὸν
4 λεγόμενον Μινώταυρον. ἀλλ' ὁ μὲν κατὰ τὴν
Κρήτην ἠφανίσθη τελέως, εἴτε δυνάστου τινὸς
κατασκάψαντος εἴτε τοῦ χρόνου τοὔργον λυμη-
ναμένου· ὁ δὲ κατ' Αἴγυπτον ἀκέραιον τὴν
ὅλην κατασκευὴν τετήρηκε μέχρι τοῦ καθ' ἡμᾶς
βίου.

62. Μετὰ δὲ τὴν τοῦ βασιλέως τούτου τελευτὴν
ἐπὶ γενεὰς πέντε γενομένης ἀναρχίας τῶν ἀδόξων

every possible means to combat their destitution. For instance, by cutting down reeds in the neighbourhood and splitting them, they made long nets, which they set up along the beach for a distance of many stades and hunted quails; for these are driven in large coveys from the open sea, and in hunting them they caught a sufficient number to provide themselves with food.

61. After the death of this king the Egyptians regained the control of their government and placed on the throne a native king, Mendes, whom some call Marrus. So far as war is concerned this ruler did not accomplish anything at all, but he did build himself a tomb known as the Labyrinth,[1] which was not so remarkable for its size as it was impossible to imitate in respect to its ingenious design; for a man who enters it cannot easily find his way out, unless he gets a guide who is thoroughly acquainted with the structure. And some say that Daedalus, visiting Egypt and admiring the skill shown in the building, also constructed for Minos, the king of Crete, a labyrinth like the one in Egypt, in which was kept, as the myth relates, the beast called Minotaur. However, the labyrinth in Crete has entirely disappeared, whether it be that some ruler razed it to the ground or that time effaced the work, but the one in Egypt has stood intact in its entire structure down to our lifetime.

62. After the death of this king there were no rulers for five generations, and then a man of obscure

---

[1] This building is described in chap. 66. The classical authors did not agree on the name of its builder and the Mendes or Marrus of Diodorus is otherwise entirely unknown (cp. A. Wiedemann, *Ägyptische Geschichte*, p. 259).

τις ἡρέθη βασιλεύς, ὃν Αἰγύπτιοι μὲν ὀνομάζουσι
Κέτηνα, παρὰ δὲ τοῖς Ἕλλησιν εἶναι δοκεῖ
Πρωτεὺς ὁ κατὰ τὸν Ἰλιακὸν γεγονὼς πόλεμον.

2 τούτου δὲ παραδεδομένου τῶν τε πνευμάτων ἔχειν
ἐμπειρίαν καὶ τὴν μορφὴν μεταβάλλειν ὁτὲ μὲν
εἰς ζῴων τύπους, ὁτὲ δὲ εἰς δένδρον ἢ πῦρ ἤ τι
τῶν ἄλλων, ὁμολογούμενα τούτοις συμβαίνει καὶ
3 τοὺς ἱερεῖς λέγειν περὶ αὐτοῦ. ἐκ μὲν γὰρ τῆς
μετὰ τῶν ἀστρολόγων συμβιώσεως, ἣν ἐποιεῖτο
συνεχῶς, ἐμπειρίαν ἐσχηκέναι τὸν βασιλέα τῶν
τοιούτων, ἐκ δὲ τοῦ νομίμου τοῦ παραδεδομένου
τοῖς βασιλεῦσι τὸ περὶ τὰς μεταβολὰς τῆς ἰδέας
4 μυθολογηθῆναι παρὰ τοῖς Ἕλλησιν. ἐν ἔθει
γὰρ εἶναι τοῖς κατ' Αἴγυπτον δυνάσταις περιτί-
θεσθαι περὶ τὴν κεφαλὴν λεόντων καὶ ταύρων
καὶ δρακόντων προτομάς, σημεῖα τῆς ἀρχῆς· καὶ
ποτὲ μὲν δένδρα, ποτὲ δὲ πῦρ, ἔστι δ' ὅτε καὶ
θυμιαμάτων εὐωδῶν ἔχειν ἐπὶ τῆς κεφαλῆς οὐκ
ὀλίγα, καὶ διὰ τούτων ἅμα μὲν ἑαυτοὺς εἰς
εὐπρέπειαν κοσμεῖν, ἅμα δὲ τοὺς ἄλλους εἰς
κατάπληξιν ἄγειν καὶ δεισιδαίμονα διάθεσιν.

5 Μετὰ δὲ τὴν Πρωτέως τελευτὴν διαδεξάμενος
τὴν βασιλείαν ὁ υἱὸς Ῥέμφις διετέλεσε πάντα
τὸν τοῦ ζῆν χρόνον ἐπιμελόμενος τῶν προσόδων
καὶ σωρεύων πανταχόθεν τὸν πλοῦτον, διὰ δὲ
μικροψυχίαν καὶ φιλαργυρίαν ἤθους οὔτε εἰς
ἀναθήματα θεῶν οὔτ' εἰς εὐεργεσίαν ἀνθρώπων

---

[1] Diodorus in his account of Proteus follows Herodotus
(2. 112 ff.), who, it has been suggested, may have confused
an Egyptian title, Proutî, with the familiar " Proteus " (cp.
How and Wells, *A Commentary on Herodotus*, 1. p. 223). Cetes,
apparently, cannot be identified with any Egyptian ruler.

origin was chosen king, whom the Egyptians call
Cetes, but who among the Greeks is thought to be
that Proteus [1] who lived at the time of the war about
Ilium. Some tradition records that this Proteus was
experienced in the knowledge of the winds and that
he would change his body, sometimes into the form
of different animals, sometimes into a tree or fire or
something else, and it so happens that the account
which the priests give of Cetes is in agreement with
that tradition. For, according to the priests, from
the close association which the king constantly maintained with the astrologers, he had gained experience
in such matters, and from a custom which has been
passed down among the kings of Egypt has arisen the
myths current among the Greeks about the way
Proteus changed his shape. For it was a practice
among the rulers of Egypt to wear upon their heads
the forepart of a lion, or bull, or snake as symbols of
their rule; at times also trees or fire, and in some
cases they even carried on their heads large bunches
of fragrant herbs for incense, these last serving to
enhance their comeliness and at the same time to fill
all other men with fear and religious awe.[2]

On the death of Proteus his son Remphis [3] succeeded to the throne. This ruler spent his whole
life looking after the revenues and amassing riches
from every source, and because of his niggardly and
miserly character spent nothing either on votive
offerings to the gods or on benefactions to the inhabi-

---

[2] On some of these insignia cp. J. H. Breasted, *History of
Egypt*, p. 38; the snake was the symbol of the Northern
Kingdom, the sacred uraeus.
[3] Ramses III, the Rhampsinitus in connection with whom
Herodotus (2. 121) recounts the famous tale of the thieves.

6 οὐδὲν ἀνήλωσε. διὸ καὶ γενόμενος οὐ βασιλεὺς
ἀλλ᾽ οἰκονόμος ἀγαθὸς ἀντὶ τῆς ἐπ᾽ ἀρετῇ δόξης
ἀπέλιπε πλεῖστα χρήματα τῶν πρὸ αὐτοῦ βασι-
λευσάντων· ἀργύρου[1] γὰρ καὶ χρυσοῦ[2] παραδέδοται συναγαγεῖν αὐτὸν εἰς τετταράκοντα
μυριάδας ταλάντων.

63. Τούτου δὲ τελευτήσαντος ἐπὶ γενεὰς ἑπτὰ
διεδέξαντο τὴν ἀρχὴν βασιλεῖς ἀργοὶ παντελῶς
καὶ πρὸς ἄνεσιν καὶ τρυφὴν ἅπαντα πράττοντες.
διόπερ ἐν ταῖς ἱεραῖς ἀναγραφαῖς οὐδὲν αὐτῶν
ἔργον πολυτελὲς οὐδὲ πρᾶξις ἱστορίας ἀξία
παραδέδοται πλὴν ἑνὸς Νειλέως, ἀφ᾽ οὗ συμβαίνει
τὸν ποταμὸν ὀνομασθῆναι[3] Νεῖλον, τὸ πρὸ τοῦ
καλούμενον Αἴγυπτον· οὗτος δὲ πλείστας εὐκαί-
ρους διώρυχας κατασκευάσας καὶ πολλὰ περὶ τὴν
εὐχρηστίαν τοῦ Νείλου φιλοτιμηθεὶς αἴτιος
κατέστη τῷ ποταμῷ ταύτης τῆς προσηγορίας.

2 Ὄγδοος δὲ βασιλεὺς γενόμενος Χέμμις ὁ Μεμ-
φίτης ἦρξε μὲν ἔτη πεντήκοντα, κατεσκεύασε δὲ
τὴν μεγίστην τῶν τριῶν πυραμίδων τῶν ἐν τοῖς
ἑπτὰ τοῖς ἐπιφανεστάτοις ἔργοις ἀριθμουμένων.
3 αὗται δὲ κείμεναι κατὰ τὴν Λιβύην τῆς Μέμφεως
ἀπέχουσι σταδίους ἑκατὸν καὶ εἴκοσι, τοῦ δὲ
Νείλου πέντε πρὸς τοῖς τετταράκοντα, τῷ δὲ
μεγέθει τῶν ἔργων καὶ τῇ κατὰ τὴν χειρουργίαν
τέχνῃ[4] θαυμαστήν τινα κατάπληξιν παρέχονται
4 τοῖς θεωμένοις. ἡ μὲν γὰρ μεγίστη τετράπλευρος

[1] ἀργυρίου D, Bekker, Dindorf.
[2] χρυσίου Bekker, Dindorf.
[3] ὀνομασθῆναι A B D, Bekker, Vogel: ὠνομάσθαι Vulgate, Dindorf.
[4] So Reiske: τέχνην χειρουργία.

214

tants. Consequently, since he had been not so much
a king as only an efficient steward, in the place of a
fame based upon virtue he left a treasure larger than
that of any king before him; for according to tradition he amassed some four hundred thousand talents
of silver and gold.

63. After Remphis died, kings succeeded to the
throne for seven generations who were confirmed
sluggards and devoted only to indulgence and
luxury. Consequently, in the priestly records, no
costly building of theirs nor any deed worthy of
historical record is handed down in connection with
them, except in the case of one ruler, Nileus, from
whom the river came to be named the Nile, though
formerly called Aegyptus. This ruler constructed
a very great number of canals at opportune places
and in many ways showed himself eager to increase
the usefulness of the Nile, and therefore became the
cause of the present appellation of the river.

The eighth king, Chemmis [1] of Memphis, ruled
fifty years and constructed the largest of the three
pyramids, which are numbered among the seven
wonders of the world. These pyramids, which are
situated on the side of Egypt which is towards Libya,
are one hundred and twenty stades from Memphis
and forty-five from the Nile, and by the immensity
of their structures and the skill shown in their execution they fill the beholder with wonder and astonish-
ment. For the largest is in the form of a square and

---

[1] Chemmis is the Cheops of Herodotus (2. 124), the Khufu
of the monuments. Diodorus makes the same mistake as
Herodotus in putting the pyramid-builders of the Fourth
Dynasty (c. 3000 B.C.) after Ramses III of the Twentieth
Dynasty (c. 1200 B.C.).

οὖσα τῷ σχήματι τὴν ἐπὶ τῆς βάσεως πλευρὰν
ἑκάστην ἔχει πλέθρων ἑπτά, τὸ δ' ὕψος πλέον
τῶν ἓξ πλέθρων· συναγωγὴν δ' ἐκ τοῦ κατ'
ὀλίγον λαμβάνουσα μέχρι τῆς κορυφῆς ἑκάστην
5 πλευρὰν ποιεῖ πηχῶν ἕξ. πᾶσα δὲ στερεοῦ
λίθου κατεσκεύασται, τὴν μὲν ἐργασίαν ἔχοντος
δυσχερῆ, τὴν δὲ διαμονὴν αἰώνιον· οὐκ ἐλαττόνων
γὰρ ἢ χιλίων ἐτῶν, ὥς φασι, διεληλυθότων εἰς
τὸν καθ' ἡμᾶς βίον, ὡς δὲ ἔνιοι γράφουσι, πλειόνων ἢ τρισχιλίων καὶ τετρακοσίων, διαμένουσι
μέχρι τοῦ νῦν οἱ λίθοι τὴν ἐξ ἀρχῆς σύνθεσιν καὶ
τὴν ὅλην κατασκευὴν ἄσηπτον διαφυλάττοντες.
6 λέγεται δὲ τὸν μὲν λίθον ἐκ τῆς Ἀραβίας ἀπὸ
πολλοῦ διαστήματος κομισθῆναι, τὴν δὲ κατασκευὴν διὰ χωμάτων γενέσθαι, μήπω τῶν μηχανῶν
7 εὑρημένων κατ' ἐκείνους τοὺς χρόνους· καὶ τὸ
θαυμασιώτατον, τηλικούτων ἔργων κατεσκευασμένων καὶ τοῦ περιέχοντος τόπου παντὸς ἀμμώ-
δους ὄντος οὐδὲν ἴχνος οὔτε τοῦ χώματος οὔτε
τῆς τῶν λίθων ξεστουργίας ἀπολείπεσθαι,[1] ὥστε
δοκεῖν μὴ κατ' ὀλίγον ὑπ' ἀνθρώπων ἐργασίας,
ἀλλὰ συλλήβδην ὥσπερ ὑπὸ θεοῦ τινος τὸ κατασκεύασμα τεθῆναι πᾶν εἰς τὴν περιέχουσαν ἄμμον.
8 ἐπιχειροῦσι δέ τινες τῶν Αἰγυπτίων τερατολογεῖν
ὑπὲρ τούτων, λέγοντες ὡς ἐξ ἁλῶν καὶ νίτρου τῶν
χωμάτων γεγονότων ἐπαφεθεὶς ὁ ποταμὸς ἔτηξεν
αὐτὰ καὶ παντελῶς ἠφάνισεν ἄνευ τῆς χειροποιή-
9 του πραγματείας. οὐ μὴν καὶ τἀληθὲς οὕτως

---

[1] ἀπολείπεται II, Bekker, Dindorf.

has a base length on each side of seven plethra and a height of over six plethra; it also gradually tapers to the top, where each side is six cubits long.[1] The entire construction is of hard stone, which is difficult to work but lasts for ever; for though no fewer than a thousand years have elapsed, as they say, to our lifetime, or, as some writers have it, more than three thousand four hundred, the stones remain to this day still preserving their original position and the entire structure undecayed. It is said that the stone was conveyed over a great distance from Arabia [2] and that the construction was effected by means of mounds, since cranes had not yet been invented at that time; and the most remarkable thing in the account is that, though the constructions were on such a great scale and the country round about them consists of nothing but sand, not a trace remains either of any mound or of the dressing of the stones, so that they do not have the appearance of being the slow handiwork of men but look like a sudden creation, as though they had been made by some god and set down bodily in the surrounding sand. Certain Egyptians would make a marvel out of these things, saying that, inasmuch as the mounds were built of salt and saltpetre, when the river was let in it melted them down and completely effaced them without the intervention of man's hand. However, there is not a

---

[1] Including the facing, which has now almost entirely disappeared, the Great Pyramid was originally about 768 feet broad on the base and 482 feet high.

[2] The term "Arabia" also designated the region lying between the Nile and the Red Sea, as in Herodotus (2. 8) and Strabo (17. 1. 34). Apparently all the material for the Great Pyramid came from the immediate neighbourhood (cp. *Baedeker's Egypt*, pp. 124–5).

DIODORUS OF SICILY

ἔχει, διὰ δὲ τῆς πολυχειρίας τῆς τὰ χώματα
βαλούσης πάλιν τὸ πᾶν ἔργον εἰς τὴν προϋπάρχουσαν ἀποκατεστάθη τάξιν· τριάκοντα μὲν
γὰρ καὶ ἐξ μυριάδες ἀνδρῶν, ὥς φασι, ταῖς τῶν
ἔργων λειτουργίαις προσήδρευσαν, τὸ δὲ πᾶν
κατασκεύασμα τέλος ἔσχε μόγις ἐτῶν εἴκοσι
διελθόντων.

64. Τελευτήσαντος δὲ τοῦ βασιλέως τούτου
διεδέξατο τὴν ἀρχὴν ὁ ἀδελφὸς Κεφρὴν καὶ ἦρξεν
ἔτη ἐξ πρὸς τοῖς πεντήκοντα· ἔνιοι δέ φασιν οὐκ
ἀδελφόν, ἀλλ' υἱὸν παραλαβεῖν τὴν ἀρχήν,
2 ὀνομαζόμενον Χαβρύην. συμφωνεῖται δὲ παρὰ
πᾶσιν ὅτι ζηλώσας ὁ διαδεξάμενος τὴν τοῦ προβασιλεύσαντος προαίρεσιν κατεσκεύασε τὴν
δευτέραν πυραμίδα, τῇ μὲν κατὰ τὴν χειρουργίαν
τέχνῃ[1] παραπλησίαν τῇ προειρημένῃ, τῷ δὲ
μεγέθει πολὺ λειπομένην, ὡς ἂν τῆς ἐν τῇ βάσει
3 πλευρᾶς ἑκάστης οὔσης σταδιαίας. ἐπιγέγραπται
δ' ἐπὶ τῆς μείζονος τὸ πλῆθος τῶν ἀναλωθέντων
χρημάτων, ὡς εἰς λάχανα καὶ συρμαίαν τοῖς
ἐργάταις μηνύεται[2] διὰ τῆς γραφῆς τάλαντα
δεδαπανῆσθαι πλείω τῶν χιλίων καὶ ἑξακοσίων.
4 ἡ δ' ἐλάττων ἀνεπίγραφος μέν ἐστιν, ἀνάβασιν
δ' ἔχει διὰ μιᾶς τῶν πλευρῶν ἐγκεκολαμμένην.
τῶν δὲ βασιλέων τῶν κατασκευασάντων αὐτὰς
ἑαυτοῖς τάφους συνέβη μηδέτερον αὐτῶν ταῖς
5 πυραμίσιν ἐνταφῆναι· τὰ γὰρ πλήθη διά τε ταλαι-
πωρίαν τὴν ἐν τοῖς ἔργοις καὶ διὰ τὸ τούτους τοὺς
βασιλεῖς ὠμὰ καὶ βίαια πολλὰ πρᾶξαι δι'
ὀργῆς εἶχε τοὺς αἰτίους, καὶ τὰ σώματα ἠπείλει

---

[1] So Reiske : τέχνην χειρουργίᾳ.
[2] μηνύεται Vogel : καὶ μηνύεται C, Bekker, Dindorf.

word of truth in this, but the entire material for the mounds, raised as they were by the labour of many hands, was returned by the same means to the place from which it came; for three hundred and sixty thousand men, as they say, were employed on the undertaking, and the whole structure was scarcely completed in twenty years.[1]

64. Upon the death of this king his brother Cephren [2] succeeded to the throne and ruled fifty-six years; but some say that it was not the brother of Chemmis, but his son, named Chabryes, who took the throne. All writers, however, agree that it was the next ruler who, emulating the example of his predecessor, built the second pyramid, which was the equal of the one just mentioned in the skill displayed in its execution but far behind it in size, since its base length on each side is only a stade.[3] And an inscription on the larger pyramid gives the sum of money expended on it, since the writing sets forth that on vegetables and purgatives for the workmen there were paid out over sixteen hundred talents. The smaller bears no inscription but has steps cut into one side. And though the two kings built the pyramids to serve as their tombs, in the event neither of them was buried in them; for the multitudes, because of the hardships which they had endured in the building of them and the many cruel and violent acts of these kings, were filled with anger against those who had caused their sufferings and openly threatened to tear

[1] The classic description of the building of the pyramids is in Herodotus 2. 124–5.

[2] The Chephren of Herodotus (2. 127), Khafre of the monuments.

[3] *i.e.* six plethra, while the former was seven.

διασπάσειν καὶ μεθ' ὕβρεως ἐκρίψειν ἐκ τῶν
6 τάφων· διὸ καὶ τελευτῶν ἑκάτερος ἐνετείλατο
τοῖς προσήκουσιν ἐν ἀσήμῳ τόπῳ καὶ λάθρᾳ
θάψαι τὸ σῶμα.

Μετὰ δὲ τούτους ἐγένετο βασιλεὺς Μυκερῖνος,
ὅν τινες Μεγχερῖνον ὀνομάζουσιν, υἱὸς ὢν τοῦ
7 ποιήσαντος τὴν προτέραν πυραμίδα. οὗτος δ'
ἐπιβαλόμενος τρίτην κατασκευάζειν, πρότερον
ἐτελεύτησε πρὶν ἢ τὸ πᾶν ἔργον λαβεῖν συντέλειαν. τῆς μὲν γὰρ βάσεως ἑκάστην πλευρὰν
ὑπεστήσατο πλέθρων τριῶν, τοὺς δὲ τοίχους ἐπὶ
μὲν πεντεκαίδεκα δόμους κατεσκεύασεν ἐκ μέλανος
λίθου τῷ Θηβαϊκῷ παραπλησίου, τὸ δὲ λοιπὸν
ἀνεπλήρωσεν ἐκ λίθων ὁμοίων ταῖς ἄλλαις πυρα-
8 μίσιν. τῷ δὲ μεγέθει λειπόμενον τοῦτο τὸ ἔργον
τῶν προειρημένων τῇ κατὰ τὴν χειρουργίαν τέχνῃ
πολὺ διαλλάττει καὶ τῇ τοῦ λίθου πολυτελείᾳ·
ἐπιγέγραπται δὲ κατὰ τὴν βόρειον αὐτῆς πλευρὰν
9 ὁ κατασκευάσας αὐτὴν Μυκερῖνος. τοῦτον δέ
φασι μισήσαντα τὴν τῶν προβασιλευσάντων
ὠμότητα ζηλῶσαι βίον ἐπιεικῆ καὶ πρὸς τοὺς
ἀρχομένους εὐεργετικόν, καὶ ποιεῖν αὐτὸν συνεχῶς
ἄλλα τε πλείω δι' ὧν ἦν μάλιστα ἐκκαλέσασθαι
τὴν τοῦ πλήθους πρὸς αὐτὸν εὔνοιαν, καὶ κατὰ
τοὺς χρηματισμοὺς ἀναλίσκειν χρημάτων πλῆθος,
διδόντα δωρεὰς τῶν ἐπιεικῶν τοῖς δοκοῦσιν ἐν
ταῖς κρίσεσι μὴ κατὰ τρόπον ἀπαλλάττειν.
10 Εἰσὶ δὲ καὶ ἄλλαι τρεῖς πυραμίδες, ὧν ἑκάστη
μὲν πλευρὰ πλεθριαία ὑπάρχει, τὸ δ' ὅλον ἔργον

---

[1] The remains, such as " massive blocks of granite, placed
in position after the interment of the mummy to protect the

their bodies asunder and cast them in despite out of the tombs. Consequently each ruler when dying enjoined upon his kinsmen to bury his body secretly in an unmarked place.[1]

After these rulers Mycerinus,[2] to whom some give the name Mencherinus, a son of the builder of the first pyramid, became king. He undertook the construction of a third pyramid, but died before the entire structure had been completed. The base length of each side he made three plethra, and for fifteen courses he built the walls of black stone[3] like that found about Thebes, but the rest of it he filled out with stone like that found in the other pyramids. In size this structure falls behind those mentioned above, but far surpasses them in the skill displayed in its execution and the great cost of the stone; and on the north side of the pyramid is an inscription stating that its builder was Mycerinus. This ruler, they say, out of indignation at the cruelty of his predecessors aspired to live an honourable life and one devoted to the welfare of his subjects; and he continually did many other things which might best help to evoke the goodwill of the people towards himself, and more especially, when he gave audiences, he spent a great amount of money, giving presents to such honest men as he thought had not fared in the courts of law as they deserved.

There are also three more pyramids, each of which is one plethrum long on each side and in general

grave from robbers," and other considerations all show that this cannot have been the case (cp. *Baedeker's Egypt*, pp. 123, 126).

[2] The Menkaure of the monuments.

[3] The lower courses of the third pyramid are of red granite, the " Ethiopian stone " of Herodotus 2. 134.

παραπλήσιον τῇ κατασκευῇ ταῖς ἄλλαις πλὴν τοῦ
μεγέθους· ταύτας δέ φασι τοὺς προειρημένους
τρεῖς βασιλεῖς ταῖς ἰδίαις κατασκευάσαι γυναιξίν.

11 Ὁμολογεῖται δὲ ταῦτα τὰ ἔργα πολὺ προέχειν
τῶν κατ' Αἴγυπτον οὐ μόνον τῷ βάρει τῶν κατασκευασμάτων καὶ ταῖς δαπάναις, ἀλλὰ καὶ τῇ
12 φιλοτεχνίᾳ τῶν ἐργασαμένων. καί φασι δεῖν
θαυμάζειν μᾶλλον τοὺς ἀρχιτέκτονας τῶν ἔργων
ἢ τοὺς βασιλεῖς τοὺς παρασχομένους τὰς εἰς
ταῦτα χορηγίας· τοὺς μὲν γὰρ ταῖς ἰδίαις ψυχαῖς
καὶ ταῖς φιλοτιμίαις, τοὺς δὲ τῷ κληρονομηθέντι
πλούτῳ καὶ ταῖς ἀλλοτρίαις κακουχίαις ἐπὶ τέλος
13 ἀγαγεῖν τὴν προαίρεσιν. περὶ δὲ τῶν πυραμίδων
οὐδὲν ὅλως οὔτε παρὰ τοῖς ἐγχωρίοις οὔτε παρὰ
τοῖς συγγραφεῦσι συμφωνεῖται· οἱ μὲν γὰρ τοὺς
προειρημένους βασιλεῖς κατασκευάσαι φασὶν
αὐτάς, οἱ δὲ ἑτέρους τινάς· οἷον τὴν μὲν[1] μεγίστην ποιῆσαι λέγουσιν Ἀρμαῖον, τὴν δὲ δευτέραν
14 Ἄμωσιν, τὴν δὲ τρίτην Ἰναρῶν. ταύτην δ'
ἔνιοι λέγουσι Ῥοδώπιδος τάφον εἶναι τῆς ἑταίρας,
ἧς φασι τῶν νομαρχῶν τινας ἐραστὰς γενομένους
διὰ φιλοστοργίαν ἐπιτελέσαι κοινῇ τὸ κατασκεύασμα.

65. Μετὰ δὲ τοὺς προειρημένους βασιλεῖς

---

[1] μὲν omitted by Vulgate, Bekker, Dindorf.

[1] As regards Rhodopis the theory of H. R. Hall (*Journal of
Hellenic Studies*, 24 (1904), pp. 208–13) is attractive : The
Sphinx, the cheeks of which were tinted red, was called by the
Greeks " Rhodopis " (" rosy-cheeked "), and erroneously sup-
posed to be female. Later they took it to be a portrait of
the greatest Rhodopis they knew, the rosy-cheeked Doricha
(although Athenaeus, 13. 596 b, denies that her name was
Doricha), the famous courtesan of the Milesian colony of

construction is like the others save in size; and these pyramids, they say, were built by the three kings named above for their wives.

It is generally agreed that these monuments far surpass all other constructions in Egypt, not only in their massiveness and cost but also in the skill displayed by their builders. And they say that the architects of the monuments are more deserving of admiration than the kings who furnished the means for their execution; for in bringing their plans to completion the former called upon their individual souls and their zeal for honour, but the latter only used the wealth which they had inherited and the grievous toil of other men. But with regard to the pyramids there is no complete agreement among either the inhabitants of the country or the historians; for according to some the kings mentioned above were their builders, according to others they were different kings; for instance, it is said that Armaeus built the largest, Amosis the second, and Inaros the third. And this last pyramid, some say, is the tomb of the courtesan Rhodopis,[1] for some of the nomarchs[2] became her lovers, as the account goes, and out of their passion for her carried the building through to completion as a joint undertaking.

65. After the kings mentioned above Bocchoris[3]

Naucratis in the Delta (cp. Herodotus 2. 134 ff.). The infatuation for her of Sappho's brother Charaxus invoked Sappho's rebuke; cp. Edmonds, *Lyra Graeca*, I. p. 205 (*L.C.L.*).

[2] The governors of the provinces (nomes) of Egypt.

[3] On Bocchoris cp. chaps. 79 and 94. His Egyptian name was Bokenranef (*c.* 726—*c.* 712 B.C.), the second of the two kings of the Twenty-fourth Dynasty (cp. *The Cambridge Ancient History*, 3. 276 f.).

διεδέξατο τὴν ἀρχὴν Βόκχορις, τῷ μὲν σώματι
παντελῶς εὐκαταφρόνητος, ἀγχινοίᾳ δὲ πολὺ
2 διαφέρων τῶν προβασιλευσάντων. πολλοῖς δ᾽
ὕστερον χρόνοις ἐβασίλευσε τῆς Αἰγύπτου Σα-
βάκων, τὸ μὲν γένος ὢν Αἰθίοψ, εὐσεβείᾳ δὲ καὶ
χρηστότητι πολὺ διαφέρων τῶν πρὸ αὐτοῦ.
3 τῆς μὲν οὖν ἐπιεικείας αὐτοῦ λάβοι τις ἂν τεκμήριον τὸ τῶν νομίμων προστίμων ἆραι τὸ μέγιστον,
4 λέγω δὲ τὴν τοῦ ζῆν στέρησιν· ἀντὶ γὰρ τοῦ
θανάτου[1] τοὺς καταδικασθέντας ἠνάγκαζε λει-
τουργεῖν ταῖς πόλεσι δεδεμένους, καὶ διὰ τούτων
πολλὰ μὲν χώματα κατεσκεύαζεν, οὐκ ὀλίγας δὲ
διώρυχας ὤρυττεν εὐκαίρους· ὑπελάμβανε γὰρ
τοῖς μὲν κολαζομένοις τὸ τῆς τιμωρίας ἀπότομον
ἠλαττωκέναι, ταῖς δὲ πόλεσιν ἀντὶ προστίμων
ἀνωφελῶν μεγάλην εὐχρηστίαν περιπεποιηκέναι.[2]
5 τὴν δὲ τῆς εὐσεβείας ὑπερβολὴν συλλογίσαιτ᾽
ἄν τις ἐκ τῆς κατὰ τὸν ὄνειρον φαντασίας καὶ
6 τῆς κατὰ τὴν ἀρχὴν ἀποθέσεως. ἔδοξε μὲν γὰρ
κατὰ τὸν ὕπνον λέγειν αὐτῷ τὸν ἐν Θήβαις θεὸν
ὅτι βασιλεύειν οὐ δυνήσεται τῆς Αἰγύπτου
μακαρίως οὐδὲ πολὺν χρόνον, ἐὰν μὴ τοὺς ἱερεῖς
ἅπαντας διατεμὼν διὰ μέσων αὐτῶν διέλθῃ μετὰ
7 τῆς θεραπείας. πολλάκις δὲ τούτου γινομένου
μεταπεμψάμενος πανταχόθεν τοὺς ἱερεῖς ἔφη
λυπεῖν τὸν θεὸν ἐν τῇ χώρᾳ μένων· οὐ γὰρ ἂν

---

[1] θανατοῦν Dindorf.
[2] πεποιηκέναι Vulgate, Bekker, Dindorf.

---

[1] Shabaka (c. 712—c. 700 B.C.), the first king of the Twenty-fifth Dynasty.

succeeded to the throne, a man who was altogether contemptible in personal appearance but in sagacity far surpassed all former kings. Much later Egypt was ruled by Sabaco,[1] who was by birth an Ethiopian and yet in piety and uprightness far surpassed his predecessors. A proof of his goodness may be found in his abolition of the severest one of the customary penalties (I refer to the taking of life); for instead of executing the condemned he put them in chains at forced labour for the cities, and by their services constructed many dykes and dug out not a few well-placed canals; for he held that in this way he had reduced for those who were being chastised the severity of their punishment, while for the cities he had procured, in exchange for useless penalties, something of great utility. And the excessiveness of his piety may be inferred from a vision which he had in a dream and his consequent abdication of the throne. For he thought that the god of Thebes told him while he slept that he would not be able to reign over Egypt in happiness or for any great length of time, unless he should cut the bodies of all the priests in twain and accompanied by his retinue pass through the very midst of them.[2] And when this dream came again and again, he summoned the priests from all over the land and told them that by his presence in the country he was offending the god;

[2] This story is reminiscent of the belief that one may be preserved from harm by passing between the parts of a sacrificed animal; cp. *Genesis*, 15. 10, 17; *Jeremiah*, 34. 18–19, and the account in Herodotus (7. 39) of the son of Pythius, whose body was cut in two and one half set on the right side of the road and the other on the left, that the Persian army might pass between them on its way to the conquest of Greece.

αὐτῷ τοιαῦτα προστάττειν κατὰ τὸν ὕπνον.
8 ἀπελθὼν οὖν βούλεσθαι καθαρὸς παντὸς μύσους
ἀποδοῦναι τὸ ζῆν τῇ πεπρωμένῃ μᾶλλον ἢ λυπῶν
τὸν κύριον καὶ μιάνας ἀσεβεῖ φόνῳ τὸν ἴδιον
βίον ἄρχειν τῆς Αἰγύπτου· καὶ πέρας τοῖς ἐγχωρίοις ἀποδοὺς τὴν βασιλείαν ἐπανῆλθεν εἰς τὴν
Αἰθιοπίαν.

66. Ἀναρχίας δὲ γενομένης κατὰ τὴν Αἴγυπτον
ἐπ᾽ ἔτη δύο, καὶ τῶν ὄχλων εἰς ταραχὰς καὶ
φόνους ἐμφυλίους τρεπομένων, ἐποιήσαντο συνωμοσίαν οἱ μέγιστοι τῶν ἡγεμόνων δώδεκα· συνε-
δρεύσαντες δὲ ἐν Μέμφει καὶ συνθήκας γραψά-
μενοι περὶ τῆς πρὸς ἀλλήλους ὁμονοίας καὶ
2 πίστεως ἀνέδειξαν ἑαυτοὺς βασιλεῖς. ἐπ᾽ ἔτη
δὲ πεντεκαίδεκα κατὰ τοὺς ὅρκους καὶ τὰς
ὁμολογίας ἄρξαντες καὶ τὴν πρὸς ἀλλήλους
ὁμόνοιαν διατηρήσαντες, ἐπεβάλοντο κατασκευάσαι κοινὸν ἑαυτῶν τάφον, ἵνα καθάπερ ἐν τῷ ζῆν
εὐνοοῦντες ἀλλήλοις τῶν ἴσων ἐτύγχανον τιμῶν,
οὕτω καὶ μετὰ τὴν τελευτὴν ἐν ἑνὶ τόπῳ τῶν
σωμάτων κειμένων τὸ κατασκευασθὲν μνῆμα κοινῇ
3 περιέχῃ τὴν τῶν ἐνταφέντων δόξαν. εἰς ταύτην
δὲ τὴν ἐπιβολὴν φιλοκαλοῦντες ἔσπευσαν ὑπερ-
βαλέσθαι τῷ μεγέθει τῶν ἔργων ἅπαντας τοὺς πρὸ
αὑτῶν. ἐκλεξάμενοι γὰρ τόπον παρὰ τὸν εἴσπλουν
τὸν εἰς τὴν Μοίριδος [1] λίμνην ἐν τῇ Λιβύῃ κατεσκεύαζον τὸν τάφον ἐκ τῶν καλλίστων λίθων, καὶ
τῷ μὲν σχήματι τετράγωνον ὑπεστήσαντο, τῷ
δὲ μεγέθει σταδιαίαν ἑκάστην πλευράν, ταῖς δὲ
γλυφαῖς καὶ ταῖς ἄλλαις χειρουργίαις ὑπερβολὴν

---

[1] Μοίριδος Wesseling : μύριδος.

for were that not the case such a command would not be given to him in his sleep. And so he would rather, he continued, departing pure of all defilement from the land, deliver his life to destiny than offend the Lord, stain his own life by an impious slaughter, and reign over Egypt. And in the end he returned the kingdom to the Egyptians and retired again to Ethiopia.

66. There being no head of the government in Egypt for two years, and the masses betaking themselves to tumults and the killing of one another, the twelve most important leaders formed a solemn league among themselves, and after they had met together for counsel in Memphis and had drawn up agreements setting forth their mutual goodwill and loyalty they proclaimed themselves kings. After they had reigned in accordance with their oaths and promises and had maintained their mutual concord for a period of fifteen years, they set about to construct a common tomb for themselves, their thought being that, just as in their lifetime they had cherished a cordial regard for one another and enjoyed equal honours, so also after their death their bodies would all rest in one place and the memorial which they had erected would hold in one embrace the glory of those buried within. Being full of zeal for this undertaking they eagerly strove to surpass all preceding rulers in the magnitude of their structure. For selecting a site at the entrance to Lake Moeris in Libya [1] they constructed their tomb of the finest stone, and they made it in form a square but in magnitude a stade in length on each side; and in the carvings and, indeed, in all the workmanship they left nothing wherein

---

[1] *i.e.* on the west side of the Nile.

4 οὐκ ἀπέλιπον τοῖς ἐπιγινομένοις. εἰσελθόντι μὲν
γὰρ τὸν περίβολον οἶκος ἦν περίστυλος, ἑκάστης
πλευρᾶς ἐκ τετταράκοντα κιόνων ἀναπληρου-
μένης, καὶ τούτου μονόλιθος ἦν ὀροφή, φάτναις
διαγεγλυμμένη καὶ γραφαῖς διαφόροις πεποικιλ-
5 μένη. εἶχε δὲ τῆς πατρίδος τῆς ἑκάστου τῶν
βασιλέων ὑπομνήματα καὶ τῶν ἱερῶν καὶ θυσιῶν
τῶν ἐν αὐτῇ ταῖς καλλίσταις γραφαῖς φιλοτέχνως
6 δεδημιουργημένα. καθόλου δὲ τοιαύτην τῇ πολυτελείᾳ καὶ τηλικαύτην τῷ μεγέθει τὴν ὑπόστασιν
τοῦ τάφου λέγεται ποιήσασθαι τοὺς βασιλεῖς,
ὥστ' εἰ μὴ πρὸ τοῦ συντελέσαι τὴν ἐπιβολὴν
κατελύθησαν, μηδεμίαν ἂν ὑπερβολὴν ἑτέροις
πρὸς κατασκευὴν ἔργων ἀπολιπεῖν.

7 Ἀρξάντων δὲ τούτων τῆς Αἰγύπτου πεντεκαίδεκα ἔτη συνέβη τὴν βασιλείαν εἰς ἕνα περιστῆναι
8 διὰ τοιαύτας αἰτίας. Ψαμμήτιχος ὁ Σαΐτης, εἷς
ὢν τῶν δώδεκα βασιλέων καὶ τῶν παρὰ θάλατταν
μερῶν κυριεύων, παρείχετο φορτία πᾶσι τοῖς
ἐμπόροις, μάλιστα δὲ τοῖς τε Φοίνιξι καὶ τοῖς
9 Ἕλλησι. διὰ δὲ[1] τοιούτου τρόπου τά τε ἐκ
τῆς ἰδίας χώρας λυσιτελῶς διατιθέμενος καὶ τῶν
παρὰ τοῖς ἄλλοις ἔθνεσι φυομένων μεταλαμβάνων,
οὐ μόνον εὐπορίαν εἶχε μεγάλην ἀλλὰ καὶ φιλίαν
10 πρὸς ἔθνη καὶ δυνάστας. διὰ δὲ ταῦτά φασι
φθονήσαντας αὐτῷ τοὺς ἄλλους βασιλεῖς πόλεμον ἐξενεγκεῖν. ἔνιοι δὲ τῶν ἀρχαίων συγγραφέων μυθολογοῦσι χρησμὸν γενέσθαι τοῖς ἡγε-

[1] τοῦ after δὲ deleted by Dindorf.

---

[1] This is the Labyrinth which was mentioned before in chap.
61. It was the seat of the central government, and was not
built by the " twelve kings," but by Amenemhet III of the

228

succeeding rulers could excel them.[1] For as a man passed through the enclosing wall he found himself in a court surrounded by columns, forty on each side, and the roof of the court consisted of a single stone, which was worked into coffers [2] and adorned with excellent paintings. This court also contained memorials of the native district of each king and of the temples and sacrificial rites therein, artistically portrayed in most beautiful paintings. And in general, the kings are said to have made the plan of their tomb on such an expensive and enormous scale that, had they not died before the execution of their purpose, they would have left no possibility for others to surpass them, so far as the construction of monuments is concerned.

After these kings had reigned over Egypt for fifteen years it came to pass that the sovereignty devolved upon one man for the following reasons. Psammetichus of Sais, who was one of the twelve kings and in charge of the regions lying along the sea, furnished wares for all merchants and especially for the Phoenicians and the Greeks; and since in this manner he disposed of the products of his own district at a profit and exchanged them for those of other peoples, he was not only possessed of great wealth but also enjoyed friendly relations with peoples and rulers. And this was the reason, they say, why the other kings became envious and opened war against him. Some of the early historians,[3] however, tell this fanciful story: The generals had

663–609
B.C.

Twelfth Dynasty (cp. *The Cambridge Ancient History*, 1. p. 309; J. H. Breasted, p. 194).

[2] *i.e.* ornamental panels were deeply recessed in the stone.

[3] The account is given by Herodotus 2. 151 f.

μόσιν, ὃς ἂν αὐτῶν ἐκ χαλκῆς φιάλης πρῶτος
ἐν Μέμφει σπείσῃ τῷ θεῷ, κρατήσειν αὐτὸν
πάσης τῆς Αἰγύπτου· τὸν δὲ Ψαμμήτιχον, ἐξενέγ-
καντος ἐκ τοῦ ἱεροῦ τῶν ἱερέων τινὸς φιάλας
ἔνδεκα[1] χρυσᾶς, περιελόμενον τὴν περικεφαλαίαν
11 σπεῖσαι. ὑπιδομένους[2] οὖν τοὺς συνάρχοντας τὸ
πραχθὲν ἀποκτεῖναι μὲν αὐτὸν μὴ βουληθῆναι,
φυγαδεῦσαι δὲ καὶ προστάξαι διατρίβειν ἐν τοῖς
12 ἕλεσι τοῖς παρὰ θάλατταν. εἴτε δὴ διὰ ταύτην
τὴν αἰτίαν εἴτε διὰ τὸν φθόνον, καθότι προείρηται,
γενομένης τῆς διαφορᾶς, ὁ μὲν[3] Ψαμμήτιχος ἔκ
τε τῆς Καρίας καὶ τῆς Ἰωνίας μισθοφόρους
μεταπεμψάμενος ἐνίκησε παρατάξει περὶ πόλιν
τὴν ὀνομαζομένην Μώμεμφιν, τῶν δ' ἀντιταξαμένων βασιλέων οἱ μὲν κατὰ τὴν μάχην ἀνῃρέθησαν, οἱ δ' εἰς Λιβύην ἐκδιωχθέντες οὐκέτι
περὶ τῆς ἀρχῆς ἴσχυσαν ἀμφισβητῆσαι.

67. Τῆς δ' ὅλης βασιλείας κυριεύσας ὁ Ψαμμήτιχος τῷ μὲν ἐν Μέμφει θεῷ τὸ πρὸς ἕω
προπύλαιον κατεσκεύασε καὶ τῷ ναῷ τὸν περίβολον, κολοττοὺς ὑποστήσας ἀντὶ τῶν κιόνων
δωδεκαπήχεις· τοῖς δὲ μισθοφόροις χωρὶς τῶν
ὡμολογημένων συντάξεων δωρεάς τε ἀξιολόγους
ἀπένειμε καὶ τὰ καλούμενα στρατόπεδα τόπον
οἰκεῖν ἔδωκε καὶ χώραν πολλὴν κατεκληρούχησε
μικρὸν ἐπάνω τοῦ Πηλουσιακοῦ στόματος· οὓς
ἐντεῦθεν Ἄμασις ὕστερον πολλοῖς ἔτεσι βασι-

[1] Reading ἔνδεκα (ιαʹ) with Herodotus 2. 151 for the
δώδεκα (ιβʹ) of the MSS.; cp. E. Evers, *Ein Beitrag zur
Untersuchung der Quellenbenutzung bei Diodor*, p. 26.

[2] ὑπιδομένους Dindorf: ὑπειδομένους.

[3] μὲν Vogel: μὲν γὰρ Vulgate, Bekker: μὲν οὖν Dindorf.

received an oracle to the effect that the first one of
their number to pour a libation from a bronze bowl
to the god in Memphis should rule over all Egypt,
and when one of the priests brought out of the temple
eleven [1] golden bowls, Psammetichus took off his
helmet and poured the libation from it. Now his
colleagues, although suspecting his act, were not yet
ready to put him to death, but drove him instead
from public life, with orders that he should spend his
days in the marshes along the sea. Whether they
fell out for this reason or because of the envy which,
as mentioned above, they felt towards him, at any
rate Psammetichus, calling mercenaries from Caria
and Ionia, overcame the others in a pitched battle
near the city called Momemphis, and of the kings
who opposed him some were slain in the battle and
some were driven out into Libya and were no longer
able to dispute with him for the throne.

67. After Psammetichus had established his
authority over the entire kingdom he built for the
god in Memphis the east propylon and the enclosure
about the temple, supporting it with colossi [2] twelve
cubits high in place of pillars; and among the
mercenaries he distributed notable gifts over and
above their promised pay, gave them the region
called The Camps to dwell in, and apportioned to
them much land in the region lying a little up the
river from the Pelusiac mouth; they being subsequently removed thence by Amasis, who reigned

[1] All former editors retain the reading "twelve" of the
MSS.; but the parallel account in Herodotus gives the number
as "eleven," thus furnishing the occasion for the use of his
helmet by Psammetichus.

[2] Here are meant square pillars with an attached statue
in front; cp. p. 167, n. 3.

2 λεύσας ἀνέστησε καὶ κατῴκισεν εἰς Μέμφιν. διὰ
δὲ τῶν μισθοφόρων κατωρθωκὼς τὴν βασιλείαν
ὁ Ψαμμήτιχος τούτοις τὸ λοιπὸν μάλιστ' ἐνεπί-
στευε τὰ κατὰ τὴν ἀρχὴν καὶ διετέλεσε ξενο-
3 τροφῶν μεγάλας δυνάμεις. στρατεύσαντος δ'
εἰς τὴν Συρίαν αὐτοῦ καὶ κατὰ τὰς παρατάξεις
τοὺς μὲν μισθοφόρους προτιμῶντος καὶ τάττοντος
εἰς τὰ δεξιὰ μέρη, τοὺς δ' ἐγχωρίους ἀτιμότερον
ἄγοντος καὶ τὸν εὐώνυμον τόπον ἀπονέμοντος
τῆς φάλαγγος, οἱ μὲν Αἰγύπτιοι διὰ τὴν ὕβριν
παροξυνθέντες καὶ γενόμενοι τὸ πλῆθος πλείους
τῶν εἴκοσι μυριάδων ἀπέστησαν καὶ προῆγον
ἐπ' Αἰθιοπίας, κεκρικότες ἰδίαν χώραν ἑαυτοῖς
4 κατακτᾶσθαι· ὁ δὲ βασιλεὺς τὸ μὲν πρῶτον
ἔπεμψέ τινας τῶν ἡγεμόνων τοὺς ἀπολογησο-
μένους ὑπὲρ τῆς ἀτιμίας, ὡς δ' οὐ προσεῖχον
αὐτοῖς, αὐτὸς μετὰ τῶν φίλων ἐδίωξε πλοίοις.
5 προαγόντων δ' αὐτῶν παρὰ τὸν Νεῖλον καὶ τοὺς
ὅρους ὑπερβαλλόντων τῆς Αἰγύπτου, ἐδεῖτο μετα-
νοῆσαι καὶ τῶν τε ἱερῶν καὶ τῶν πατρίδων, ἔτι
6 δὲ καὶ γυναικῶν καὶ τέκνων ὑπεμίμνησκεν. οἱ
δ' ἅμα πάντες ἀναβοήσαντες καὶ τοῖς κοντοῖς
τὰς ἀσπίδας πατάξαντες ἔφασαν, ἕως ἂν κυριεύ-
ωσι τῶν ὅπλων, ῥᾳδίως εὑρήσειν πατρίδας·
ἀναστειλάμενοι δὲ τοὺς χιτῶνας καὶ τὰ γεννητικὰ μέρη[1] τοῦ σώματος δείξαντες οὔτε γυναικῶν
οὔτε τέκνων ἀπορήσειν ἔφασαν ταῦτ' ἔχοντες.
7 τοιαύτη δὲ μεγαλοψυχίᾳ χρησάμενοι καὶ κατα-

---

[1] μόρια G, Bekker, Dindorf.

---

[1] A similar account is in Herodotus (2. 154), who locates
(2. 30) the Camps more precisely at Daphnae, the modern

many years later, and settled by him in Memphis.[1]
And since Psammetichus had established his rule
with the aid of the mercenaries, he henceforth
entrusted these before others with the administration of his empire and regularly maintained large
mercenary forces. Once in connection with a campaign in Syria, when he was giving the mercenaries
a more honourable place in his order of battle by
putting them on the right wing and showing the
native troops less honour by assigning them the
position on the left wing of the phalanx, the Egyptians,
angered by this slight and being over two hundred
thousand strong, revolted and set out for Ethiopia,
having determined to win for themselves a country
of their own. The king at first sent some of his
generals to make excuse for the dishonour done to
them, but since no heed was paid to these he set out
in person after them by boat, accompanied by his
friends. And when they still continued their march
along the Nile and were about to cross the boundary
of Egypt, he besought them to change their purpose
and reminded them of their temples, their homeland,
and of their wives and children. But they, all crying
aloud and striking their spears against their shields,
declared that so long as they had weapons in their
hands they would easily find homelands; and lifting
their garments and pointing to their genitals they
said that so long as they had those they would never
be in want either of wives or of children. After such
a display of high courage and of utter disdain for

Tell Defenneh on the Pelusiac arm of the Nile, now a canal.
The mercenaries were thus strategically placed at the Syrian
entrance into Egypt.

φρονήσαντες τῶν παρὰ τοῖς ἄλλοις μεγίστων
εἶναι δοκούντων, κατελάβοντο μὲν τῆς Αἰθιοπίας
τὴν κρατίστην, κατακληρουχήσαντες δὲ πολλὴν
χώραν ἐν ταύτῃ κατῴκησαν.

8   Ὁ δὲ Ψαμμήτιχος ἐπὶ μὲν τούτοις οὐ μετρίως
ἐλυπήθη, τὰ δὲ κατὰ τὴν Αἴγυπτον διατάξας καὶ
τῶν προσόδων ἐπιμελόμενος πρός τε Ἀθηναίους
καί τινας τῶν ἄλλων Ἑλλήνων συμμαχίαν ἐποιή-
9   σατο. εὐηργέτει δὲ καὶ τῶν ξένων τοὺς ἐθελοντὴν [1] εἰς τὴν Αἴγυπτον ἀποδημοῦντας, καὶ
φιλέλλην ὢν διαφερόντως τοὺς υἱοὺς τὴν Ἑλληνικὴν ἐδίδαξε παιδείαν· καθόλου δὲ πρῶτος τῶν
κατ᾽ Αἴγυπτον βασιλέων ἀνέῳξε τοῖς ἄλλοις
ἔθνεσι τὰ κατὰ τὴν ἄλλην [2] χώραν ἐμπόρια
καὶ πολλὴν ἀσφάλειαν τοῖς καταπλέουσι ξένοις
10   παρείχετο. οἱ μὲν γὰρ πρὸ τούτου δυναστεύ-
σαντες ἄβατον ἐποίουν τοῖς ξένοις τὴν Αἴγυπτον,
τοὺς μὲν φονεύοντες, τοὺς δὲ καταδουλούμενοι τῶν
11   καταπλεόντων. καὶ γὰρ ἡ περὶ τὸν Βούσιριν
ἀσέβεια διὰ τὴν τῶν ἐγχωρίων ἀξενίαν διεβοήθη
παρὰ τοῖς Ἕλλησιν, οὐκ οὖσα μὲν πρὸς ἀλήθειαν, διὰ δὲ τὴν ὑπερβολὴν τῆς ἀνομίας εἰς
μύθου πλάσμα καταχωρισθεῖσα.

68. Μετὰ δὲ Ψαμμήτιχον ὕστερον τέτταρσι
γενεαῖς Ἀπρίης ἐβασίλευσεν ἔτη δυσὶ πλείω
τῶν εἴκοσι. στρατεύσας δὲ δυνάμεσιν ἀδραῖς
πεζαῖς τε καὶ ναυτικαῖς ἐπὶ Κύπρον καὶ Φοινίκην,

---

[1] ἐθελοντὴν Kälker : ἐθελοντί.
[2] Reiske would delete ἄλλην, as is done by Bekker and
Dindorf, or read ὅλην.

---

[1] This story of the Deserters is given by Herodotus (2. 30),
but in less detail.

what among other men is regarded as of the greatest consequence, they seized the best part of Ethiopia, and after apportioning much land among themselves they made their home there.[1]

Although Psammetichus was greatly grieved over these things, he put in order the affairs of Egypt, looked after the royal revenues, and then formed alliances with both Athens and certain other Greek states. He also regularly treated with kindness any foreigners who sojourned in Egypt of their own free will, and was so great an admirer of the Hellenes that he gave his sons a Greek education; and, speaking generally, he was the first Egyptian king to open to other nations the trading-places throughout the rest[2] of Egypt and to offer a large measure of security to strangers from across the seas. For his predecessors in power had consistently closed Egypt to strangers, either killing or enslaving any who touched its shores. Indeed, it was because of the objection to strangers on the part of the people that the impiety of Busiris became a byword among the Greeks, although this impiety was not actually such as it was described, but was made into a fictitious myth because of the exceptional disrespect of the Egyptians for ordinary customs.

68. Four generations after Psammetichus, Apries was king for twenty-two years. He made a campaign with strong land and sea forces against Cyprus

588–566
B.C.

---

[2] This reading of the MSS., which has disturbed some editors, may properly be retained. It is understood from the beginning of the chapter that Psammetichus could allow foreigners to trade only in the regions of which he was governor. Upon becoming king he extends that privilege over " the rest " of Egypt.

Σιδῶνα μὲν κατὰ κράτος εἷλε, τὰς δ' ἄλλας τὰς
ἐν τῇ Φοινίκῃ πόλεις καταπληξάμενος προσηγά-
γετο· ἐνίκησε δὲ καὶ ναυμαχίᾳ μεγάλῃ Φοίνικάς
τε καὶ Κυπρίους, καὶ λαφύρων ἀθροίσας πλῆθος
2 ἐπανῆλθεν εἰς Αἴγυπτον. μετὰ δὲ ταῦτα δύναμιν
πέμψας ἁδρὰν τῶν ὁμοεθνῶν ἐπὶ Κυρήνην καὶ
Βάρκην, καὶ τὸ πλεῖστον αὐτῆς ἀποβαλών,
ἀλλοτρίους ἔσχε τοὺς διασωθέντας· ὑπολαβόντες
γὰρ αὐτὸν ἐπ' ἀπωλείᾳ συντάξαι τὴν στρατείαν,
ὅπως ἀσφαλέστερον ἄρχῃ τῶν λοιπῶν Αἰγυπτίων,
3 ἀπέστησαν. ἀποσταλεὶς δὲ πρὸς τούτους ὑπὸ
τοῦ βασιλέως Ἄμασις, ἀνὴρ ἐμφανὴς Αἰγύπτιος,
τῶν μὲν ῥηθέντων[1] ὑπ' αὐτοῦ πρὸς ὁμόνοιαν
ἠμέλησε, τοὐναντίον δ' ἐκείνους προτρεψάμενος
εἰς ἀλλοτριότητα συναπέστη καὶ βασιλεὺς αὐτὸς
4 ᾑρέθη. μετ' οὐ πολὺν δὲ χρόνον καὶ τῶν ἄλλων
ἐγχωρίων ἁπάντων συνεπιθεμένων, ὁ βασιλεὺς
διαπορούμενος ἠναγκάσθη καταφυγεῖν ἐπὶ τοὺς
5 μισθοφόρους, ὄντας εἰς τρισμυρίους. γενομένης
οὖν παρατάξεως περὶ τὴν Μάρειαν κώμην, καὶ
τῶν Αἰγυπτίων τῇ μάχῃ κρατησάντων, ὁ μὲν
Ἀπρίης ζωγρηθεὶς ἀνήχθη καὶ στραγγαλισθεὶς[2]
ἐτελεύτησεν, Ἄμασις δὲ διατάξας τὰ κατὰ τὴν
βασιλείαν ὥς ποτ' ἔδοξεν αὐτῷ συμφέρειν, ἦρχε
νομίμως τῶν Αἰγυπτίων καὶ μεγάλης ἐτύγχανεν
6 ἀποδοχῆς. κατεστρέψατο δὲ καὶ τὰς ἐν Κύπρῳ
πόλεις καὶ πολλὰ τῶν ἱερῶν ἐκόσμησεν ἀναθήμασιν ἀξιολόγοις. βασιλεύσας δ' ἔτη πέντε

[1] Bekker and Dindorf, following Wesseling, read ῥηθεισῶν
and retain ἐντολῶν of the MSS. after ὁμόνοιαν; Vogel
following Eichstädt, retains ῥηθέντων of the MSS. and
deletes ἐντολῶν.

and Phoenicia, took Sidon by storm, and so terrified
the other cities of Phoenicia that he secured their
submission; he also defeated the Phoenicians and
Cyprians in a great sea-battle and returned to Egypt
with much booty. After this he sent a strong native
force against Cyrenê and Barcê and, when the larger
part of it was lost, the survivors became estranged
from him; for they felt that he had organized the expedition with a view to its destruction in order that
his rule over the rest of the Egyptians might be more
secure, and so they revolted. The man sent by the
king to treat with them, one Amasis, a prominent
Egyptian, paid no attention to the orders given him to
effect a reconciliation, but, on the contrary, increased
their estrangement, joined their revolt, and was himself chosen king.[1] When a little later all the rest of
the native Egyptians also went over to Amasis, the
king was in such straits that he was forced to flee for
safety to the mercenaries, who numbered some thirty
thousand men. A pitched battle accordingly took
place near the village of Maria and the Egyptians
prevailed in the struggle; Apries fell alive into the
hands of the enemy and was strangled to death, and
Amasis, arranging the affairs of the kingdom in
whatever manner seemed to him best, ruled over the
Egyptians in accordance with the laws and was held
in great favour. He also reduced the cities of Cyprus
and adorned many temples with noteworthy votive
offerings. After a reign of fifty-five years he ended

[1] Amasis (Ahmose II of the Twenty-sixth Dynasty) reigned
569—526-5 B.C., the first three years of his reign coinciding
with the last three years of Apries.

[2] στραγγαλισθείς Dindorf : στραγγαλήθεις.

πρὸς τοῖς πεντήκοντα κατέστρεψε τὸν βίον
καθ' ὃν χρόνον Καμβύσης ὁ τῶν Περσῶν βασιλεὺς ἐστράτευσεν ἐπὶ τὴν Αἴγυπτον, κατὰ τὸ
τρίτον ἔτος τῆς ἑξηκοστῆς καὶ τρίτης Ὀλυμπιάδος,
ἣν ἐνίκα στάδιον Παρμενίδης Καμαριναῖος.

69. Ἐπεὶ δὲ τὰς τῶν ἐν Αἰγύπτῳ βασιλέων
πράξεις ἀπὸ τῶν ἀρχαιοτάτων χρόνων διεληλύθαμεν ἀρκούντως μέχρι τῆς Ἀμάσιδος τελευτῆς,
τὰς λοιπὰς ἀναγράψομεν ἐν τοῖς οἰκείοις χρόνοις·
2 περὶ δὲ τῶν νομίμων τῶν κατ' Αἴγυπτον νῦν
διέξιμεν ἐν κεφαλαίοις τά τε παραδοξότατα καὶ
τὰ μάλιστα ὠφελῆσαι δυνάμενα τοὺς ἀναγινώσκοντας. πολλὰ γὰρ τῶν παλαιῶν ἐθῶν τῶν
γενομένων παρ' Αἰγυπτίοις οὐ μόνον παρὰ τοῖς
ἐγχωρίοις ἀποδοχῆς ἔτυχεν, ἀλλὰ καὶ παρὰ τοῖς
3 Ἕλλησιν οὐ μετρίως ἐθαυμάσθη· διόπερ οἱ
μέγιστοι τῶν ἐν παιδείᾳ δοξασθέντων ἐφιλοτιμήθησαν εἰς Αἴγυπτον παραβαλεῖν, ἵνα μετά-
σχωσι τῶν τε νόμων καὶ τῶν ἐπιτηδευμάτων ὡς
4 ἀξιολόγων ὄντων. καίπερ γὰρ τῆς χώρας τὸ
παλαιὸν δυσεπιβάτου τοῖς ξένοις οὔσης διὰ τὰς
προειρημένας αἰτίας, ὅμως ἔσπευσαν εἰς αὐτὴν
παραβαλεῖν τῶν μὲν ἀρχαιοτάτων Ὀρφεὺς καὶ
ὁ ποιητὴς Ὅμηρος, τῶν δὲ μεταγενεστέρων ἄλλοι
τε πλείους καὶ Πυθαγόρας ὁ Σάμιος, ἔτι δὲ
5 Σόλων ὁ νομοθέτης. λέγουσι τοίνυν Αἰγύπτιοι
παρ' αὑτοῖς τήν τε τῶν γραμμάτων εὕρεσιν
γενέσθαι καὶ τὴν τῶν ἄστρων παρατήρησιν, πρὸς
δὲ τούτοις τά τε κατὰ τὴν γεωμετρίαν θεωρήματα καὶ τῶν τεχνῶν τὰς πλείστας εὑρεθῆναι,
6 νόμους τε τοὺς ἀρίστους τεθῆναι. καὶ τούτων
μεγίστην ἀπόδειξίν φασιν εἶναι τὸ τῆς Αἰγύπτου

his days at the time when Cambyses, the king of the Persians, attacked Egypt, in the third year of the Sixty-third Olympiad, that in which Parmenides of Camarina won the " stadion." [1] 526–5 B.C.

69. Now that we have discussed sufficiently the deeds of the kings of Egypt from the very earliest times down to the death of Amasis, we shall record the other events in their proper chronological setting; but at this point we shall give a summary account of the customs of Egypt, both those which are especially strange and those which can be of most value to our readers. For many of the customs that obtained in ancient days among the Egyptians have not only been accepted by the present inhabitants but have aroused no little admiration among the Greeks; and for that reason those men who have won the greatest repute in intellectual things have been eager to visit Egypt in order to acquaint themselves with its laws and institutions, which they considered to be worthy of note. For despite the fact that for the reasons mentioned above strangers found it difficult in early times to enter the country, it was nevertheless eagerly visited by Orpheus and the poet Homer in the earliest times and in later times by many others, such as Pythagoras of Samos and Solon the lawgiver. [2] Now it is maintained by the Egyptians that it was they who first discovered writing and the observation of the stars, who also discovered the basic principles of geometry and most of the arts, and established the best laws. And the best proof of all this, they say, lies in the fact that Egypt for more than four

---

[1] The famous foot-race at Olympia, 606¾ feet long.
[2] Cp. for Orpheus, chap. 23, for Homer, chap. 12, for Pythagoras and Solon, chap. 98.

πλείω τῶν ἑπτακοσίων καὶ τετρακισχιλίων ἐτῶν
βασιλεῦσαι τοὺς πλείους ἐγγενεῖς καὶ τὴν χώραν
εὐδαιμονεστάτην ὑπάρξαι τῆς ἁπάσης οἰκου-
μένης· ταῦτα γὰρ οὐκ ἄν ποτε γενέσθαι μὴ οὐ
τῶν ἀνθρώπων χρωμένων κρατίστοις ἔθεσι καὶ
νόμοις καὶ τοῖς κατὰ πᾶσαν παιδείαν ἐπιτηδεύ-
7 μασιν. ὅσα μὲν οὖν Ἡρόδοτος καί τινες τῶν τὰς
Αἰγυπτίων πράξεις συνταξαμένων ἐσχεδιάκασιν,
ἑκουσίως προκρίναντες τῆς ἀληθείας τὸ παρα-
δοξολογεῖν καὶ μύθους πλάττειν ψυχαγωγίας
ἕνεκα, παρήσομεν, αὐτὰ δὲ τὰ παρὰ τοῖς ἱερεῦσι
τοῖς κατ' Αἴγυπτον ἐν ταῖς ἀναγραφαῖς γεγραμμένα φιλοτίμως ἐξητακότες ἐκθησόμεθα.

70. Πρῶτον μὲν τοίνυν οἱ βασιλεῖς αὐτῶν βίον
εἶχον οὐχ ὅμοιον τοῖς ἄλλοις τοῖς ἐν μοναρχικαῖς
ἐξουσίαις οὖσι καὶ πάντα πράττουσι κατὰ τὴν
ἑαυτῶν προαίρεσιν ἀνυπευθύνως, ἀλλ' ἦν ἅπαντα
τεταγμένα νόμων ἐπιταγαῖς, οὐ μόνον τὰ περὶ
τοὺς χρηματισμούς, ἀλλὰ καὶ τὰ περὶ τὴν καθ'
2 ἡμέραν διαγωγὴν καὶ δίαιταν. περὶ μὲν γὰρ τὴν
θεραπείαν αὐτῶν οὐδεὶς ἦν οὔτ' ἀργυρώνητος
οὔτ' οἰκογενὴς δοῦλος, ἀλλὰ τῶν ἐπιφανεστάτων
ἱερέων υἱοὶ πάντες, ὑπὲρ εἴκοσι μὲν ἔτη γεγονότες,
πεπαιδευμένοι δὲ κάλλιστα τῶν ὁμοεθνῶν, ἵνα
τοὺς ἐπιμελησομένους τοῦ σώματος καὶ πᾶσαν
ἡμέραν καὶ νύκτα προσεδρεύοντας ὁ βασιλεὺς
ἔχων ἀρίστους μηδὲν ἐπιτηδεύῃ φαῦλον· οὐδεὶς
γὰρ ἐπὶ πλέον κακίας προβαίνει δυνάστης, ἐὰν
μὴ τοὺς ὑπηρετήσοντας ἔχῃ ταῖς ἐπιθυμίαις.
3 διατεταγμέναι δ' ἦσαν αἵ τε τῆς ἡμέρας καὶ τῆς

thousand seven hundred years was ruled over by kings of whom the majority were native Egyptians, and that the land was the most prosperous of the whole inhabited world; for these things could never have been true of any people which did not enjoy most excellent customs and laws and the institutions which promote culture of every kind. Now as for the stories invented by Herodotus and certain writers on Egyptian affairs, who deliberately preferred to the truth the telling of marvellous tales and the invention of myths for the delectation of their readers, these we shall omit, and we shall set forth only what appears in the written records of the priests of Egypt and has passed our careful scrutiny.

70. In the first place, then, the life which the kings of the Egyptians lived was not like that of other men who enjoy autocratic power and do in all matters exactly as they please without being held to account, but all their acts were regulated by prescriptions set forth in laws, not only their administrative acts, but also those that had to do with the way in which they spent their time from day to day, and with the food which they ate. In the matter of their servants, for instance, not one was a slave, such as had been acquired by purchase or born in the home, but all were sons of the most distinguished priests, over twenty years old and the best educated of their fellow-countrymen, in order that the king, by virtue of his having the noblest men to care for his person and to attend him throughout both day and night, might follow no low practices; for no ruler advances far along the road of evil unless he has those about him who will minister to his passions. And the hours of both the day and night were laid out according to a

νυκτὸς ὧραι, καθ' ἃς ἐκ παντὸς τρόπου καθῆκον
ἦν τὸν βασιλέα πράττειν τὸ συντεταγμένον, οὐ
4 τὸ δεδογμένον ἑαυτῷ. ἕωθεν μὲν γὰρ ἐγερθέντα
λαβεῖν αὐτὸν ἔδει πρῶτον τὰς πανταχόθεν ἀπε-
σταλμένας ἐπιστολάς, ἵνα δύνηται πάντα κατὰ
τρόπον χρηματίζειν καὶ πράττειν, εἰδὼς ἀκριβῶς
ἕκαστα τῶν κατὰ τὴν βασιλείαν συντελουμένων·
ἔπειτα λουσάμενον καὶ τοῖς τῆς ἀρχῆς συσσή-
μοις μετ' ἐσθῆτος λαμπρᾶς κοσμήσαντα τὸ σῶμα
θῦσαι τοῖς θεοῖς.

5 Τῷ τε βωμῷ προσαχθέντων τῶν θυμάτων ἔθος
ἦν τὸν ἀρχιερέα στάντα πλησίον τοῦ βασιλέως
εὔχεσθαι μεγάλῃ τῇ φωνῇ, περιεστῶτος τοῦ
πλήθους τῶν Αἰγυπτίων, δοῦναι τήν τε ὑγίειαν
καὶ τἆλλα ἀγαθὰ πάντα τῷ βασιλεῖ διατηροῦντι
6 τὰ πρὸς τοὺς ὑποτεταγμένους δίκαια. ἀνθομολο-
γεῖσθαι δ' ἦν ἀναγκαῖον καὶ τὰς κατὰ μέρος
ἀρετὰς αὐτοῦ, λέγοντα διότι πρός τε τοὺς θεοὺς
εὐσεβῶς καὶ πρὸς τοὺς ἀνθρώπους ἡμερώτατα
διάκειται· ἐγκρατής τε γάρ ἐστι καὶ δίκαιος καὶ
μεγαλόψυχος, ἔτι δ' ἀψευδὴς καὶ μεταδοτικὸς
τῶν ἀγαθῶν καὶ καθόλου πάσης ἐπιθυμίας κρείτ-
των, καὶ τὰς μὲν τιμωρίας ἐλάττους τῆς ἀξίας
ἐπιτιθεὶς τοῖς ἁμαρτήμασι, τὰς δὲ χάριτας
μείζονας τῆς εὐεργεσίας ἀποδιδοὺς τοῖς εὐεργετή-
7 σασι. πολλὰ δὲ καὶ ἄλλα παραπλήσια τούτοις
διελθὼν ὁ κατευχόμενος τὸ τελευταῖον ὑπὲρ τῶν
ἀγνοουμένων ἀρὰν ἐποιεῖτο, τὸν μὲν βασιλέα τῶν
ἐγκλημάτων ἐξαιρούμενος, εἰς δὲ τοὺς ὑπηρε-
τοῦντας καὶ διδάξαντας τὰ φαῦλα καὶ τὴν βλάβην
8 καὶ τὴν τιμωρίαν ἀξιῶν ἀποσκῆψαι. ταῦτα δ'
ἔπραττεν ἅμα μὲν εἰς δεισιδαιμονίαν καὶ θεοφιλῆ

plan, and at the specified hours it was absolutely
required of the king that he should do what the laws
stipulated and not what he thought best. For
instance, in the morning, as soon as he was awake,
he first of all had to receive the letters which had been
sent from all sides, the purpose being that he might
be able to despatch all administrative business and
perform every act properly, being thus accurately
informed about everything that was being done
throughout his kingdom. Then, after he had bathed
and bedecked his body with rich garments and the
insignia of his office, he had to sacrifice to the gods.

When the victims had been brought to the altar
it was the custom for the high priest to stand near
the king, with the common people of Egypt gathered
around, and pray in a loud voice that health and
all the other good things of life be given the king
if he maintains justice towards his subjects. And
an open confession had also to be made of each and
every virtue of the king, the priest saying that
towards the gods he was piously disposed and
towards men most kindly; for he was self-controlled
and just and magnanimous, truthful, and generous
with his possessions, and, in a word, superior to
every desire, and that he punished crimes less
severely than they deserved and rendered to his
benefactors a gratitude exceeding the benefaction.
And after reciting much more in a similar vein he
concluded his prayer with a curse concerning things
done in error, exempting the king from all blame
therefor and asking that both the evil consequences
and the punishment should fall upon those who
served him and had taught him evil things. All
this he would do, partly to lead the king to fear

βίον τὸν βασιλέα προτρεπόμενος, ἅμα δὲ καὶ
κατὰ τρόπον ζῆν ἐθίζων οὐ διὰ πικρᾶς νουθετή-
σεως, ἀλλὰ δι᾽ ἐπαίνων κεχαρισμένων καὶ πρὸς
9 ἀρετὴν μάλιστ᾽ ἀνηκόντων. μετὰ δὲ ταῦτα τοῦ
βασιλέως ἱεροσκοπησαμένου μόσχῳ καὶ καλ-
λιερήσαντος, ὁ μὲν ἱερογραμματεὺς παρανεγί-
νωσκέ τινας συμβουλίας συμφερούσας καὶ
πράξεις ἐκ τῶν ἱερῶν βίβλων τῶν ἐπιφανεστάτων ἀνδρῶν, ὅπως ὁ τῶν ὅλων τὴν ἡγεμονίαν
ἔχων τὰς καλλίστας προαιρέσεις τῇ διανοίᾳ
θεωρήσας οὕτω πρὸς τὴν τεταγμένην τῶν κατὰ
10 μέρος τρέπηται διοίκησιν. οὐ γὰρ μόνον τοῦ
χρηματίζειν ἢ κρίνειν ἦν καιρὸς ὡρισμένος, ἀλλὰ
καὶ τοῦ περιπατῆσαι καὶ λούσασθαι καὶ κοιμη-
θῆναι μετὰ τῆς γυναικὸς καὶ καθόλου τῶν κατὰ
11 τὸν βίον πραττομένων ἁπάντων. τροφαῖς δ᾽
ἔθος ἦν αὐτοῖς ἁπαλαῖς [1] χρῆσθαι, κρέα μὲν
μόσχων καὶ χηνῶν μόνων [2] προσφερομένους,
οἴνου δὲ τακτόν τι μέτρον πίνοντας μὴ δυνάμενον
12 πλησμονὴν ἄκαιρον ἢ μέθην περιποιῆσαι. καθόλου δὲ τὰ περὶ τὴν δίαιταν οὕτως ὑπῆρχε
συμμέτρως διατεταγμένα ὥστε δοκεῖν μὴ νομοθέτην, ἀλλὰ τὸν ἄριστον τῶν ἰατρῶν συντετα-
χέναι τῆς ὑγιείας στοχαζόμενον.

71. Παραδόξου δ᾽ εἶναι δοκοῦντος τοῦ μὴ
πᾶσαν ἔχειν ἐξουσίαν τὸν βασιλέα τῆς καθ᾽
ἡμέραν τροφῆς, πολλῷ θαυμασιώτερον ἦν τὸ
μήτε δικάζειν μήτε χρηματίζειν τὸ τυχὸν αὐτοῖς
ἐξεῖναι, μηδὲ τιμωρήσασθαι μηδένα δι᾽ ὕβριν ἢ
διὰ θυμὸν ἤ τινα ἄλλην αἰτίαν ἄδικον, ἀλλὰ

___
[1] ἁπαλαῖς Vogel (cp. chap. 84. 5): ἁπλαῖς II, Bekker,
Dindorf.

the gods and live a life pleasing to them, and partly
to accustom him to a proper manner of conduct,
not by sharp admonitions, but through praises that
were agreeable and most conducive to virtue. After
this, when the king had performed the divination
from the entrails of a calf and had found the omens
good, the sacred scribe read before the assemblage
from out of the sacred books some of the edifying
counsels and deeds of their most distinguished men,
in order that he who held the supreme leadership
should first contemplate in his mind the most excellent general principles and then turn to the prescribed administration of the several functions. For
there was a set time not only for his holding audiences
or rendering judgments, but even for his taking a
walk, bathing, and sleeping with his wife, and, in a
word, for every act of his life. And it was the
custom for the kings to partake of delicate food,
eating no other meat than veal and duck, and
drinking only a prescribed amount of wine, which
was not enough to make them unreasonably surfeited
or drunken. And, speaking generally, their whole
diet was ordered with such continence that it had
the appearance of having been drawn up, not by a
lawgiver, but by the most skilled of their physicians,
with only their health in view.

71. Strange as it may appear that the king did
not have the entire control of his daily fare, far
more remarkable still was the fact that kings were
not allowed to render any legal decision or transact
any business at random or to punish anyone through
malice or in anger or for any other unjust reason,

---

² μόνων Vogel : μόνον Vulgate, Bekker, Dindorf.

καθάπερ οἱ περὶ ἑκάστων κείμενοι νόμοι προσ-
2 έταττον. ταῦτα δὲ κατὰ τὸ ἔθος πράττοντες
οὐχ ὅπως ἠγανάκτουν ἢ προσέκοπτον ταῖς
ψυχαῖς,[1] ἀλλὰ τοὐναντίον ἡγοῦντο ἑαυτοὺς ζῆν
3 βίον μακαριώτατον· τοὺς μὲν γὰρ ἄλλους ἀνθρώπους ἐνόμιζον ἀλογίστως τοῖς φυσικοῖς πάθεσι
χαριζομένους πολλὰ πράττειν τῶν φερόντων
βλάβας ἢ κινδύνους, καὶ πολλάκις ἐνίους εἰδότας
ὅτι μέλλουσιν ἁμαρτάνειν μηδὲν ἧττον πράττειν
τὰ φαῦλα κατισχυομένους ὑπ' ἔρωτος ἢ μίσους
ἤ τινος ἑτέρου πάθους, ἑαυτοὺς δ' ἐζηλωκότας
βίον τὸν ὑπὸ τῶν φρονιμωτάτων ἀνδρῶν προκεκρι-
4 μένον ἐλαχίστοις περιπίπτειν ἀγνοήμασι. τοιαύτη δὲ χρωμένων τῶν βασιλέων δικαιοσύνῃ
πρὸς τοὺς ὑποτεταγμένους, τὰ πλήθη ταῖς εἰς
τοὺς ἡγουμένους εὐνοίαις πᾶσαν συγγενικὴν
φιλοστοργίαν ὑπερεβάλλετο· οὐ γὰρ μόνον τὸ
σύστημα τῶν ἱερέων, ἀλλὰ καὶ συλλήβδην
ἅπαντες οἱ κατ' Αἴγυπτον οὐχ οὕτω γυναικῶν
καὶ τέκνων καὶ τῶν ἄλλων τῶν ὑπαρχόντων
αὐτοῖς ἀγαθῶν ἐφρόντιζον ὡς τῆς τῶν βασιλέων
5 ἀσφαλείας. τοιγαροῦν πλεῖστον μὲν χρόνον τῶν
μνημονευομένων βασιλέων πολιτικὴν κατάστασιν
ἐτήρησαν, εὐδαιμονέστατον δὲ βίον ἔχοντες διετέλεσαν, ἕως ἔμεινεν ἡ προειρημένη τῶν νόμων
σύνταξις, πρὸς δὲ τούτοις ἐθνῶν τε πλείστων
ἐπεκράτησαν καὶ μεγίστους πλούτους ἔσχον, καὶ
τὰς μὲν χώρας ἔργοις καὶ κατασκευάσμασιν
ἀνυπερβλήτοις, τὰς δὲ πόλεις ἀναθήμασι πολυτελέσι καὶ παντοίοις ἐκόσμησαν.

72. Καὶ τὰ μετὰ τὴν τελευτὴν δὲ γινόμενα

---

[1] ψυχαῖς MSS., Vogel : τυχαῖς Dindorf.

but only in accordance with the established laws relative to each offence. And in following the dictates of custom in these matters, so far were they from being indignant or taking offence in their souls, that, on the contrary, they actually held that they led a most happy life; for they believed that all other men, in thoughtlessly following their natural passions, commit many acts which bring them injuries and perils, and that oftentimes some who realize that they are about to commit a sin nevertheless do base acts when overpowered by love or hatred or some other passion, while they, on the other hand, by virtue of their having cultivated a manner of life which had been chosen before all others by the most prudent of all men, fell into the fewest mistakes. And since the kings followed so righteous a course in dealing with their subjects, the people manifested a goodwill towards their rulers which surpassed even the affection they had for their own kinsmen; for not only the order of the priests but, in short, all the inhabitants of Egypt were less concerned for their wives and children and their other cherished possessions than for the safety of their kings. Consequently, during most of the time covered by the reigns of the kings of whom we have a record, they maintained an orderly civil government and continued to enjoy a most felicitous life, so long as the system of laws described was in force; and, more than that, they conquered more nations and achieved greater wealth than any other people, and adorned their lands with monuments and buildings never to be surpassed, and their cities with costly dedications of every description.

72. Again, the Egyptian ceremonies which fol‗

τῶν βασιλέων παρὰ τοῖς Αἰγυπτίοις οὐ μικρὰν
ἀπόδειξιν εἶχε [1] τῆς τοῦ πλήθους εὐνοίας εἰς τοὺς
ἡγουμένους· εἰς ἀνεπαίσθητον γὰρ χάριν ἡ τιμὴ
τιθεμένη μαρτυρίαν ἀνόθευτον περιεῖχε τῆς ἀλη-
2 θείας. ὁπότε γὰρ ἐκλείποι τις τὸν βίον τῶν
βασιλέων, πάντες οἱ κατὰ τὴν Αἴγυπτον κοινὸν
ἀνῃροῦντο πένθος, καὶ τὰς μὲν ἐσθῆτας κατερρήτ-
τοντο, τὰ δ' ἱερὰ συνέκλειον καὶ τὰς θυσίας
ἐπεῖχον καὶ τὰς ἑορτὰς οὐκ ἦγον ἐφ' ἡμέρας
ἑβδομήκοντα καὶ δύο· καταπεπλασμένοι δὲ τὰς
κεφαλὰς πηλῷ καὶ περιεζωσμένοι σινδόνας ὑποκάτω τῶν μαστῶν ὁμοίως ἄνδρες καὶ γυναῖκες
περιῆσαν ἀθροισθέντες κατὰ διακοσίους ἢ τριακοσίους, καὶ τὸν μὲν θρῆνον ἐν ῥυθμῷ μετ' ᾠδῆς
ποιούμενοι δὶς τῆς ἡμέρας ἐτίμων ἐγκωμίοις,
ἀνακαλούμενοι τὴν ἀρετὴν τοῦ τετελευτηκότος,
τροφὴν δ' οὔτε τὴν ἀπὸ τῶν ἐμψύχων οὔτε τὴν ἀπὸ
τοῦ πυρὸς προσεφέροντο, τοῦ τε οἴνου καὶ πάσης
3 πολυτελείας ἀπείχοντο. οὐδεὶς δ' ἂν οὔτε λουτροῖς
οὔτ' ἀλείμμασιν οὔτε στρωμναῖς προείλετο χρῆσθαι, οὐ μὴν οὐδὲ πρὸς τὰ ἀφροδίσια προσελθεῖν
ἂν ἐτόλμησεν, ἀλλὰ καθάπερ ἀγαπητοῦ τέκνου
τελευτήσαντος ἕκαστος περιώδυνος γινόμενος
4 ἐπένθει τὰς εἰρημένας ἡμέρας. ἐν δὲ τούτῳ τῷ
χρόνῳ τὰ πρὸς ταφὴν λαμπρῶς παρεσκευασ-
μένοι, καὶ τῇ τελευταίᾳ τῶν ἡμερῶν θέντες τὴν
τὸ σῶμα ἔχουσαν λάρνακα πρὸ τῆς εἰς τὸν
τάφον εἰσόδου, προετίθεσαν κατὰ νόμον τῷ
τετελευτηκότι κριτήριον τῶν ἐν τῷ βίῳ πραχθέν-
5 των. δοθείσης δ' ἐξουσίας τῷ βουλομένῳ κατηγορεῖν, οἱ μὲν ἱερεῖς ἐνεκωμίαζον ἕκαστα τῶν
καλῶς αὐτῷ πραχθέντων διεξιόντες, αἱ δὲ πρὸς

lowed upon the death of a king afforded no small
proof of the goodwill of the people towards their
rulers; for the fact that the honour which they
paid was to one who was insensible of it constituted
an authentic testimony to its sincerity. For when
any king died all the inhabitants of Egypt united in
mourning for him, rending their garments, closing
the temples, stopping the sacrifices, and celebrating
no festivals for seventy-two days; and plastering
their heads with mud and wrapping strips of linen
cloth below their breasts, women as well as men
went about in groups of two or three hundred, and
twice each day, reciting the dirge in a rhythmic chant,
they sang the praises of the deceased, recalling his
virtues; nor would they eat the flesh of any living
thing or food prepared from wheat, and they abstained
from wine and luxury of any sort. And no one would
ever have seen fit to make use of baths or unguents
or soft bedding, nay more, would not even have
dared to indulge in sexual pleasures, but every
Egyptian grieved and mourned during those seventy-
two days as if it were his own beloved child that had
died. But during this interval they had made
splendid preparations for the burial, and on the last
day, placing the coffin containing the body before
the entrance to the tomb, they set up, as custom
prescribed, a tribunal to sit in judgment upon the
deeds done by the deceased during his life. And
when permission had been given to anyone who so
wished to lay complaint against him, the priests
praised all his noble deeds one after another, and

---

[1] εἶχε Bekker, Vogel: φέρει A B, Dindorf.

τὴν ἐκφορὰν συνηγμέναι μυριάδες τῶν ὄχλων
ἀκούουσαι συνεπευφήμουν, εἰ τύχοι καλῶς βεβι-
6 ωκώς, εἰ δὲ μή, τοὐναντίον ἐθορύβουν. καὶ
πολλοὶ τῶν βασιλέων διὰ τὴν τοῦ πλήθους
ἐναντίωσιν ἀπεστερήθησαν τῆς ἐμφανοῦς καὶ
νομίμου ταφῆς· διὸ καὶ συνέβαινε τοὺς τὴν
βασιλείαν διαδεχομένους μὴ μόνον διὰ τὰς ἄρτι
ῥηθείσας αἰτίας δικαιοπραγεῖν, ἀλλὰ καὶ διὰ τὸν
φόβον τῆς μετὰ τὴν τελευτὴν ἐσομένης ὕβρεώς
τε τοῦ σώματος καὶ βλασφημίας εἰς ἅπαντα τὸν
αἰῶνα.

Τῶν μὲν οὖν περὶ τοὺς ἀρχαίους βασιλεῖς
νομίμων τὰ μέγιστα ταῦτ' ἔστιν.

73. Τῆς Αἰγύπτου δὲ πάσης εἰς πλείω μέρη
διῃρημένης, ὧν ἕκαστον κατὰ τὴν Ἑλληνικὴν
διάλεκτον ὀνομάζεται νομός, ἐφ' ἑκάστῳ τέτακται
νομάρχης ὁ τὴν ἁπάντων ἔχων ἐπιμέλειάν τε καὶ
2 φροντίδα. τῆς δὲ χώρας ἁπάσης εἰς τρία μέρη
διῃρημένης τὴν μὲν πρώτην ἔχει μερίδα τὸ σύστημα τῶν ἱερέων, μεγίστης ἐντροπῆς τυγχάνον
παρὰ τοῖς ἐγχωρίοις διά τε τὴν εἰς τοὺς θεοὺς
ἐπιμέλειαν καὶ διὰ τὸ πλείστην σύνεσιν τοὺς
3 ἄνδρας τούτους ἐκ παιδείας εἰσφέρεσθαι. ἐκ δὲ
τούτων τῶν προσόδων τάς τε θυσίας ἁπάσας τὰς
κατ' Αἴγυπτον συντελοῦσι καὶ τοὺς ὑπηρέτας
τρέφουσι καὶ ταῖς ἰδίαις χρείαις χορηγοῦσιν·
οὔτε γὰρ τὰς τῶν θεῶν τιμὰς ᾤοντο δεῖν ἀλλάττειν,
ἀλλ' ὑπό τε τῶν αὐτῶν ἀεὶ καὶ παραπλησίως

---

[1] Two instances of this are given in chap. 64.

[2] The Harris Papyrus of the twelfth century B.C. gives the
only definite figures of the vast holdings of the temples.
They owned at that time about two per cent. of the population

the common people who had gathered in myriads
to the funeral, listening to them, shouted their
approval if the king had led a worthy life, but if
he had not, they raised a clamour of protest. And
in fact many kings have been deprived of the public
burial customarily accorded them because of the
opposition of the people;[1] the result was, consequently, that the successive kings practised justice,
not merely for the reasons just mentioned, but also
because of their fear of the despite which would be
shown their body after death and of eternal
obloquy.

Of the customs, then, touching the early kings
these are the most important.

73. And since Egypt as a whole is divided into
several parts which in Greek are called nomes, over
each of these a nomarch is appointed who is charged
with both the oversight and care of all its affairs.
Furthermore, the entire country is divided into
three parts, the first of which is held by the order
of the priests, which is accorded the greatest venera-
tion by the inhabitants both because these men
have charge of the worship of the gods and because
by virtue of their education they bring to bear a
higher intelligence than others. With the income
from these holdings[2] of land they perform all the
sacrifices throughout Egypt, maintain their assistants, and minister to their own needs; for it has
always been held that the honours paid to the gods
should never be changed, but should ever be performed by the same men and in the same manner,

and some fifteen per cent. of the land, not to mention property
of other nature, and their power materially increased in the
succeeding centuries.

συντελεῖσθαι, οὔτε τοὺς πάντων προβουλευομένους
4 ἐνδεεῖς εἶναι τῶν ἀναγκαίων. καθόλου γὰρ περὶ
τῶν μεγίστων οὗτοι προβουλευόμενοι συνδιατρί-
βουσι τῷ βασιλεῖ, τῶν μὲν συνεργοί, τῶν δὲ
εἰσηγηταὶ καὶ διδάσκαλοι γινόμενοι, καὶ διὰ μὲν
τῆς ἀστρολογίας καὶ τῆς ἱεροσκοπίας τὰ μέλλοντα προσημαίνοντες, ἐκ δὲ τῶν ἐν ταῖς ἱεραῖς
βίβλοις ἀναγεγραμμένων πράξεων τὰς ὠφελῆσαι
5 δυναμένας παραναγινώσκοντες. οὐ γάρ, ὥσπερ
παρὰ τοῖς Ἕλλησιν, εἷς ἀνὴρ ἢ μία γυνὴ τὴν
ἱερωσύνην παρείληφεν, ἀλλὰ πολλοὶ περὶ τὰς
τῶν θεῶν θυσίας καὶ τιμὰς διατρίβουσι, καὶ τοῖς
ἐκγόνοις τὴν ὁμοίαν τοῦ βίου προαίρεσιν παραδι-
δόασιν. εἰσὶ δὲ οὗτοι πάντων τε ἀτελεῖς καὶ δευ-
τερεύοντες μετὰ τὸν βασιλέα ταῖς τε δόξαις καὶ
ταῖς ἐξουσίαις.

6 Τὴν δὲ δευτέραν μοῖραν οἱ βασιλεῖς παρειλήφασιν εἰς προσόδους, ἀφ' ὧν εἴς τε τοὺς πολέμους χορηγοῦσι καὶ τὴν περὶ αὑτοὺς λαμπρότητα
διαφυλάττουσι, καὶ τοὺς μὲν ἀνδραγαθήσαντας
δωρεαῖς κατὰ τὴν ἀξίαν τιμῶσι, τοὺς δ' ἰδιώτας
διὰ τὴν ἐκ τούτων εὐπορίαν οὐ βαπτίζουσι ταῖς
εἰσφοραῖς.

7 Τὴν δὲ μερίδα τὴν τελευταίαν ἔχουσιν οἱ
μάχιμοι καλούμενοι καὶ πρὸς τὰς λειτουργίας
τὰς εἰς τὴν στρατείαν ὑπακούοντες, ἵν' οἱ κινδυ-
νεύοντες εὐνούστατοι τῇ χώρᾳ διὰ τὴν κλη-
ρουχίαν ὄντες προθύμως ἐπιδέχωνται τὰ συμβαί-
8 νοντα κατὰ τοὺς πολέμους δεινά. ἄτοπον γὰρ
ἦν τὴν μὲν τῶν ἁπάντων σωτηρίαν τούτοις
ἐπιτρέπειν, ὑπὲρ οὗ δὲ ἀγωνιοῦνται μηδὲν αὐτοῖς
ὑπάρχειν κατὰ τὴν χώραν σπουδῆς ἄξιον· τὸ δὲ

and that those who deliberate on behalf of all should not lack the necessities of life. For, speaking generally, the priests are the first to deliberate upon the most important matters and are always at the king's side, sometimes as his assistants, sometimes to propose measures and give instructions, and they also, by their knowledge of astrology and of divination, forecast future events, and read to the king, out of the record of acts preserved in their sacred books, those which can be of assistance. For it is not the case with the Egyptians as it is with the Greeks, that a single man or a single woman takes over the priesthood, but many are engaged in the sacrifices and honours paid the gods and pass on to their descendants the same rule of life. They also pay no taxes of any kind, and in repute and in power are second after the king.

The second part of the country has been taken over by the kings for their revenues, out of which they pay the cost of their wars, support the splendour of their court, and reward with fitting gifts any who have distinguished themselves; and they do not swamp the private citizens by taxation, since their income from these revenues gives them a great plenty.

The last part is held by the warriors, as they are called, who are subject to call for all military duties, the purpose being that those who hazard their lives may be most loyal to the country because of such allotment of land and thus may eagerly face the perils of war. For it would be absurd to entrust the safety of the entire nation to these men and yet have them possess in the country no property to fight for valuable enough to arouse their ardour.

μέγιστον, εὐπορουμένους αὐτοὺς ῥᾳδίως τεκνο-
ποιήσειν, καὶ διὰ τοῦτο τὴν πολυανθρωπίαν
κατασκευάσειν,[1] ὥστε μὴ προσδεῖσθαι ξενικῆς
9 δυνάμεως τὴν χώραν. ὁμοίως δ' οὗτοι τὴν
τάξιν ταύτην ἐκ προγόνων διαδεχόμενοι ταῖς μὲν
τῶν πατέρων ἀνδραγαθίαις προτρέπονται πρὸς
τὴν ἀνδρείαν, ἐκ παίδων δὲ ζηλωταὶ γινόμενοι
τῶν πολεμικῶν ἔργων ἀνίκητοι ταῖς τόλμαις καὶ
ταῖς ἐμπειρίαις ἀποβαίνουσιν.

74. Ἔστι δ' ἕτερα συντάγματα τῆς πολιτείας
τρία, τό τε τῶν νομέων καὶ τὸ τῶν γεωργῶν, ἔτι
δὲ τὸ τῶν τεχνιτῶν. οἱ μὲν οὖν γεωργοὶ μικροῦ
τινος τὴν καρποφόρον γῆν τὴν παρὰ τοῦ βασιλέως καὶ τῶν ἱερέων καὶ τῶν μαχίμων μισθού-
μενοι διατελοῦσι τὸν πάντα χρόνον περὶ τὴν
ἐργασίαν ὄντες τῆς χώρας· ἐκ νηπίου δὲ συντρεφόμενοι ταῖς γεωργικαῖς ἐπιμελείαις πολὺ προέχουσι τῶν παρὰ τοῖς ἄλλοις ἔθνεσι γεωργῶν
2 ταῖς ἐμπειρίαις· καὶ γὰρ τὴν τῆς γῆς φύσιν
καὶ τὴν τῶν ὑδάτων ἐπίρρυσιν, ἔτι δὲ τοὺς
καιροὺς τοῦ τε σπόρου καὶ τοῦ θερισμοῦ καὶ
τῆς ἄλλης τῶν καρπῶν συγκομιδῆς ἀκριβέστατα
πάντων γινώσκουσι, τὰ μὲν ἐκ τῆς τῶν προγόνων
παρατηρήσεως μαθόντες, τὰ δ' ἐκ τῆς ἰδίας
3 πείρας διδαχθέντες. ὁ δ' αὐτὸς λόγος ἐστὶ καὶ
περὶ τῶν νομέων, οἳ τὴν τῶν θρεμμάτων ἐπιμέλειαν ἐκ πατέρων ὥσπερ κληρονομίας νόμῳ
παραλαμβάνοντες ἐν βίῳ κτηνοτρόφῳ διατελοῦσι
4 πάντα τὸν τοῦ ζῆν χρόνον, καὶ πολλὰ μὲν παρὰ
τῶν προγόνων πρὸς θεραπείαν καὶ διατροφὴν
ἀρίστην τῶν βοσκομένων παρειλήφασιν, οὐκ ὀλίγα

---

[1] κατασκευάσειν Stephanus: κατασκευάζειν.

But the most important consideration is the fact that, if they are well-to-do, they will readily beget children and thus so increase the population that the country will not need to call in any mercenary troops. And since their calling, like that of the priests, is hereditary, the warriors are incited to bravery by the distinguished records of their fathers and, inasmuch as they become zealous students of warfare from their boyhood up, they turn out to be invincible by reason of their daring and skill.[1]

74. There are three other classes of free citizens, namely, the herdsmen, the husbandmen, and the artisans. Now the husbandmen rent on moderate terms the arable land held by the king and the priests and the warriors, and spend their entire time in tilling the soil; and since from very infancy they are brought up in connection with the various tasks of farming, they are far more experienced in such matters than the husbandmen of any other nation; for of all mankind they acquire the most exact knowledge of the nature of the soil, the use of water in irrigation, the times of sowing and reaping, and the harvesting of the crops in general, some details of which they have learned from the observations of their ancestors and others in the school of their own experience. And what has been said applies equally well to the herdsmen, who receive the care of animals from their fathers as if by a law of inheritance, and follow a pastoral life all the days of their existence. They have received, it is true, much from their ancestors relative to the best care and feeding of grazing animals, but to this they add not a little

[1] The fullest account of this warrior caste is in Herodotus 2 164 ff.

δ' αὐτοὶ διὰ τὸν εἰς ταῦτα ζῆλον προσευρί-
σκουσι, καὶ τὸ θαυμασιώτατον, διὰ τὴν ὑπερβολὴν τῆς εἰς ταῦτα σπουδῆς οἵ τε ὀρνιθοτρόφοι
καὶ οἱ χηνοβοσκοὶ χωρὶς τῆς παρὰ τοῖς ἄλλοις
ἀνθρώποις ἐκ φύσεως συντελουμένης γενέσεως
τῶν εἰρημένων ζῴων αὐτοὶ διὰ τῆς ἰδίας φιλοτεχνίας ἀμύθητον πλῆθος ὀρνέων ἀθροίζουσιν·
5 οὐ γὰρ ἐπῳάζουσι διὰ τῶν ὀρνίθων, ἀλλ' αὐτοὶ
παραδόξως χειρουργοῦντες τῇ συνέσει καὶ φιλοτεχνίᾳ τῆς φυσικῆς ἐνεργείας οὐκ ἀπολείπονται.

6 Ἀλλὰ μὴν καὶ τὰς τέχνας ἰδεῖν ἔστι παρὰ
τοῖς Αἰγυπτίοις μάλιστα διαπεπονημένας καὶ
πρὸς τὸ καθῆκον τέλος διηκριβωμένας· παρὰ
μόνοις γὰρ τούτοις οἱ δημιουργοὶ πάντες οὔτ'
ἐργασίας ἄλλης οὔτε πολιτικῆς τάξεως μετα-
λαμβάνειν ἐῶνται πλὴν τῆς ἐκ τῶν νόμων
ὡρισμένης καὶ παρὰ τῶν γονέων παραδεδομένης,
ὥστε μήτε διδασκάλου φθόνον μήτε πολιτικοὺς
περισπασμοὺς μήτ' ἄλλο μηδὲν ἐμποδίζειν
7 αὐτῶν τὴν εἰς ταῦτα σπουδήν. παρὰ μὲν γὰρ
τοῖς ἄλλοις ἰδεῖν ἔστι τοὺς τεχνίτας περὶ πολλὰ
τῇ διανοίᾳ περισπωμένους καὶ διὰ τὴν πλεο-
νεξίαν μὴ μένοντας τὸ παράπαν ἐπὶ τῆς ἰδίας
ἐργασίας· οἱ μὲν γὰρ ἐφάπτονται γεωργίας, οἱ
δ' ἐμπορίας κοινωνοῦσιν, οἱ δὲ δυοῖν ἢ τριῶν
τεχνῶν ἀντέχονται, πλεῖστοι δ' ἐν ταῖς δημοκρα-
τουμέναις πόλεσιν εἰς τὰς ἐκκλησίας συντρέ-
χοντες τὴν μὲν πολιτείαν λυμαίνονται, τὸ δὲ

by reason of their own interest in such matters; and the most astonishing fact is that, by reason of their unusual application to such matters, the men who have charge of poultry and geese, in addition to producing them in the natural way known to all mankind, raise them by their own hands, by virtue of a skill peculiar to them, in numbers beyond telling; for they do not use the birds for hatching the eggs, but, in effecting this themselves artificially by their own wit and skill in an astounding manner, they are not surpassed by the operations of nature.[1]

Furthermore, one may see that the crafts also among the Egyptians are very diligently cultivated and brought to their proper development; for they are the only people where all the craftsmen are forbidden to follow any other occupation or belong to any other class of citizens than those stipulated by the laws and handed down to them from their parents, the result being that neither ill-will towards a teacher nor political distractions nor any other thing interferes with their interest in their work. For whereas among all other peoples it can be observed that the artisans are distracted in mind by many things, and through the desire to advance themselves do not stick exclusively to their own occupation; for some try their hands at agriculture, some dabble in trade, and some cling to two or three crafts, and in states having a democratic form of government vast numbers of them, trooping to the meetings of the Assembly, ruin the work of the government, while they make a profit for themselves at the expense of

---

[1] According to Aristotle (*Historia Animalium*, 6. 2) this artificial hatching was effected by burying the eggs in dung.

λυσιτελὲς περιποιοῦνται παρὰ τῶν μισθοδο-
τούντων· παρὰ δὲ τοῖς Αἰγυπτίοις, εἴ τις τῶν
τεχνιτῶν μετάσχοι τῆς πολιτείας ἢ τέχνας
πλείους ἐργάζοιτο, μεγάλαις περιπίπτει τιμω-
ρίαις.

8 Τὴν μὲν οὖν διαίρεσιν τῆς πολιτείας καὶ τὴν
τῆς ἰδίας τάξεως ἐπιμέλειαν διὰ προγόνων τοιαύτην ἔσχον οἱ τὸ παλαιὸν τὴν Αἴγυπτον κατοι-
κοῦντες.

75. Περὶ δὲ τὰς κρίσεις οὐ τὴν τυχοῦσαν
ἐποιοῦντο σπουδήν, ἡγούμενοι τὰς ἐν τοῖς δικα-
στηρίοις ἀποφάσεις μεγίστην ῥοπὴν τῷ κοινῷ
2 βίῳ φέρειν πρὸς ἀμφότερα. δῆλον γὰρ ἦν ὅτι
τῶν μὲν παρανομούντων κολαζομένων, τῶν δ᾽
ἀδικουμένων βοηθείας τυγχανόντων, ἀρίστη διόρθωσις ἔσται τῶν ἁμαρτημάτων· εἰ δ᾽ ὁ φόβος
ὁ γινόμενος ἐκ τῶν κρίσεων τοῖς παρανομοῦσιν
ἀνατρέποιτο χρήμασιν ἢ χάρισιν, ἐσομένην
3 ἑώρων τοῦ κοινοῦ βίου σύγχυσιν. διόπερ ἐκ
τῶν ἐπιφανεστάτων πόλεων τοὺς ἀρίστους
ἄνδρας ἀποδεικνύντες δικαστὰς κοινοὺς οὐκ
ἀπετύγχανον τῆς προαιρέσεως. ἐξ Ἡλίου γὰρ
πόλεως καὶ Θηβῶν καὶ Μέμφεως δέκα δικαστὰς
ἐξ ἑκάστης προέκρινον· καὶ τοῦτο τὸ συνέδριον
οὐκ ἐδόκει λείπεσθαι τῶν Ἀθήνησιν Ἀρεοπαγι-
τῶν ἢ τῶν παρὰ Λακεδαιμονίοις γερόντων.
4 ἐπεὶ δὲ συνέλθοιεν οἱ τριάκοντα, ἐπέκρινον
ἐξ ἑαυτῶν ἕνα τὸν ἄριστον, καὶ τοῦτον μὲν
ἀρχιδικαστὴν καθίσταντο, εἰς δὲ τὸ τούτου τόπον

---

[1] Speaking as an aristocrat, Diodorus is criticising the
democracies of Greece, Athens in all probability being especially in his mind, where the citizens, according to him, leave

others who pay them their wage,[1] yet among the Egyptians if any artisan should take part in public affairs or pursue several crafts he is severely punished.

Such, then, were the divisions of the citizens, maintained by the early inhabitants of Egypt, and their devotion to their own class which they inherited from their ancestors.

75. In their administration of justice the Egyptians also showed no merely casual interest, holding that the decisions of the courts exercise the greatest influence upon community life, and this in each of their two aspects. For it was evident to them that if the offenders against the law should be punished and the injured parties should be afforded succour there would be an ideal correction of wrongdoing; but if, on the other hand, the fear which wrongdoers have of the judgments of the courts should be brought to naught by bribery or favour, they saw that the break-up of community life would follow. Consequently, by appointing the best men from the most important cities as judges over the whole land they did not fall short of the end which they had in mind. For from Heliopolis and Thebes and Memphis they used to choose ten judges from each, and this court was regarded as in no way inferior to that composed of the Areopagites at Athens or of the Elders[2] at Sparta. And when the thirty assembled they chose the best one of their number and made him chief justice, and in his stead the city sent

their tasks to participate in the affairs of the state, apparently being paid by their employers while thus engaged and receiving an additional compensation from the state.

[2] The bodies were known as the Council of the Areopagus and the Gerousia respectively; the latter is described in Book 17. 104.

ἀπέστελλεν ἡ πόλις ἕτερον δικαστήν. συντάξεις
δὲ τῶν ἀναγκαίων παρὰ τοῦ βασιλέως τοῖς μὲν
δικασταῖς ἱκαναὶ πρὸς διατροφὴν ἐχορηγοῦντο,
5 τῷ δ' ἀρχιδικαστῇ πολλαπλάσιοι. ἐφόρει δ'
οὗτος περὶ τὸν τράχηλον ἐκ χρυσῆς ἁλύσεως
ἠρτημένον ζῴδιον τῶν πολυτελῶν λίθων, ὃ
προσηγόρευον Ἀλήθειαν. τῶν δ' ἀμφισβητήσεων
ἤρχοντο ἐπειδὰν[1] τὴν τῆς Ἀληθείας εἰκόνα ὁ
B ἀρχιδικαστὴς πρόσθοιτο. τῶν δὲ πάντων νόμων
ἐν βιβλίοις ὀκτὼ γεγραμμένων, καὶ τούτων
παρακειμένων τοῖς δικασταῖς, ἔθος ἦν τὸν μὲν
κατήγορον γράψαι καθ' ἓν ὧν ἐνεκάλει καὶ πῶς
γέγονε καὶ τὴν ἀξίαν τοῦ ἀδικήματος ἢ τῆς
βλάβης, τὸν ἀπολογούμενον δὲ λαβόντα τὸ
χρηματισθὲν ὑπὸ τῶν ἀντιδίκων ἀντιγράψαι
πρὸς ἕκαστον ὡς οὐκ ἔπραξεν ἢ πράξας οὐκ
ἠδίκησεν ἢ ἀδικήσας ἐλάττονος ζημίας ἄξιός ἐστι
I τυχεῖν. ἔπειτα νόμιμον ἦν τὸν κατήγορον ἀντιγράψαι καὶ πάλιν τὸν ἀπολογούμενον ἀντιθεῖναι.
ἀμφοτέρων δὲ τῶν ἀντιδίκων τὰ γεγραμμένα δὶς
τοῖς δικασταῖς δόντων, τὸ τηνικαῦτ' ἔδει τοὺς
μὲν τριάκοντα τὰς γνώμας ἐν ἀλλήλοις ἀποφαί-
νεσθαι, τὸν ἀρχιδικαστὴν δὲ τὸ ζῴδιον τῆς
Ἀληθείας προστίθεσθαι τῇ ἑτέρᾳ τῶν ἀμφισβητήσεων.

76. Τούτῳ δὲ τῷ τρόπῳ τὰς κρίσεις πάσας
συντελεῖν τοὺς Αἰγυπτίους, νομίζοντας ἐκ μὲν
τοῦ λέγειν τοὺς συνηγόρους πολλὰ τοῖς δικαίοις
ἐπισκοτήσειν· καὶ γὰρ τὰς τέχνας τῶν ῥητόρων
καὶ τὴν τῆς ὑποκρίσεως γοητείαν καὶ τὰ τῶν

---

[1] ἐπειδὴ Bekker, Dindorf.

another judge. Allowances to provide for their needs were supplied by the king, to the judges sufficient for their maintenance, and many times as much to the chief justice. The latter regularly wore suspended from his neck by a golden chain a small image made of precious stones, which they called Truth; the hearings of the pleas commenced whenever the chief justice put on the image of Truth. The entire body of the laws was written down in eight volumes which lay before the judges, and the custom was that the accuser should present in writing the particulars of his complaint, namely, the charge, how the thing happened, and the amount of injury or damage done, whereupon the defendant would take the document submitted by his opponents in the suit and reply in writing to each charge, to the effect either that he did not commit the deed, or, if he did, that he was not guilty of wrongdoing, or, if he was guilty of wrongdoing, that he should receive a lighter penalty. After that, the law required that the accuser should reply to this in writing and that the defendant should offer a rebuttal. And after both parties had twice presented their statements in writing to the judges, it was the duty of the thirty at once to declare their opinions among themselves and of the chief justice to place the image of Truth upon one or the other of the two pleas which had been presented.

76. This was the manner, as their account goes, in which the Egyptians conducted all court proceedings, since they believed that if the advocates were allowed to speak they would greatly becloud the justice of a case; for they knew that the clever devices of orators, the cunning witchery of their

DIODORUS OF SICILY

κινδυνευόντων δάκρυα πολλοὺς προτρέπεσθαι
παρορᾶν τὸ τῶν νόμων ἀπότομον καὶ τὴν τῆς
2 ἀληθείας ἀκρίβειαν· θεωρεῖσθαι γοῦν τοὺς ἐπαι-
νουμένους ἐν τῷ κρίνειν πολλάκις ἢ δι' ἀπάτην
ἢ διὰ ψυχαγωγίαν ἢ διὰ τὸ πρὸς τὸν ἔλεον
πάθος συνεκφερομένους τῇ δυνάμει τῶν συνηγο-
ρούντων· ἐκ δὲ τοῦ γράφειν τὰ δίκαια τοὺς
ἀντιδίκους ᾤοντο τὰς κρίσεις ἀκριβεῖς ἔσεσθαι,
3 γυμνῶν τῶν πραγμάτων θεωρουμένων. οὕτω
γὰρ[1] μάλιστα μήτε τοὺς εὐφυεῖς τῶν βραδυ-
τέρων πλεονεκτήσειν μήτε τοὺς ἐνηθληκότας τῶν
ἀπείρων μήτε τοὺς ψεύστας καὶ τολμηροὺς τῶν
φιλαλήθων καὶ κατεσταλμένων τοῖς ἤθεσι,
πάντας δ' ἐπ' ἴσης τεύξεσθαι τῶν δικαίων,
ἱκανὸν χρόνον ἐκ τῶν νόμων λαμβανόντων τῶν
μὲν ἀντιδίκων ἐξετάσαι τὰ παρ' ἀλλήλων, τῶν
δὲ δικαστῶν συγκρῖναι τὰ παρ' ἀμφοτέρων.

77. Ἐπεὶ δὲ τῆς νομοθεσίας ἐμνήσθημεν, οὐκ
ἀνοίκειον εἶναι τῆς ὑποκειμένης ἱστορίας νομί-
ζομεν ἐκθέσθαι τῶν νόμων ὅσοι παρὰ τοῖς
Αἰγυπτίοις παλαιότητι διήνεγκαν ἢ παρηλλαγ-
μένην τάξιν ἔσχον ἢ τὸ σύνολον ὠφέλειαν τοῖς
2 φιλαναγνωστοῦσι δύνανται παρασχέσθαι. πρῶτον μὲν οὖν κατὰ τῶν ἐπιόρκων θάνατος ἦν παρ'
αὐτοῖς τὸ πρόστιμον, ὡς δύο τὰ μέγιστα ποιούντων ἀνομήματα, θεούς τε ἀσεβούντων καὶ τὴν

---

[1] ἂν after γὰρ deleted by Dindorf.

delivery, and the tears of the accused would influence
many to overlook the severity of the laws and the
strictness of truth; at any rate they were aware
that men who are highly respected as judges are
often carried away by the eloquence of the advocates, either because they are deceived, or because
they are won over by the speaker's charm, or because
the emotion of pity has been aroused in them;[1]
but by having the parties to a suit present their
pleas in writing, it was their opinion that the judgments would be strict, only the bare facts being
taken into account. For in that case there would
be the least chance that gifted speakers would have
an advantage over the slower, or the well-practised
over the inexperienced, or the audacious liars over
those who were truth-loving and restrained in character, but all would get their just dues on an equal
footing, since by the provision of the laws ample
time is taken, on the one hand by the disputants for
the examination of the arguments of the other side,
and, on the other hand, by the judges for the com-
parison of the allegations of both parties.

77. Since we have spoken of their legislation, we
feel that it will not be foreign to the plan of our
history to present such laws of the Egyptians as
were especially old or took on an extraordinary
form, or, in general, can be of help to lovers of
reading. Now in the first place, their penalty for
perjurers was death, on the ground that such men
are guilty of the two greatest transgressions—being
impious towards the gods and overthrowing the

---

[1] It is interesting to observe that the Egyptians are supposed to be familiar with the weaknesses of the Attic courts.

μεγίστην τῶν παρ' ἀνθρώποις πίστιν ἀνατρε-
3 πόντων. ἔπειτα εἴ τις ἐν ὁδῷ κατὰ τὴν χώραν
ἰδὼν φονευόμενον ἄνθρωπον ἢ τὸ καθόλου βίαιόν
τι πάσχοντα μὴ ῥύσαιτο δυνατὸς ὤν, θανάτῳ
περιπεσεῖν ὤφειλεν· εἰ δὲ πρὸς ἀλήθειαν διὰ τὸ
ἀδύνατον μὴ κατισχύσαι βοηθῆσαι, μηνῦσαί γε
πάντως ὤφειλε τοὺς λῃστὰς καὶ ἐπεξιέναι τὴν
παρανομίαν· τὸν δὲ ταῦτα μὴ πράξαντα κατὰ
τὸν νόμον ἔδει μαστιγοῦσθαι τεταγμένας πληγὰς
καὶ πάσης εἴργεσθαι τροφῆς ἐπὶ τρεῖς ἡμέρας.
4 οἱ δὲ ψευδῶς τινων κατηγορήσαντες ὤφειλον
τοῦτο παθεῖν ὃ τοῖς συκοφαντηθεῖσιν ἐτέτακτο
πρόστιμον, εἴπερ ἔτυχον καταδικασθέντες.
5 προσετέτακτο δὲ καὶ πᾶσι τοῖς Αἰγυπτίοις
ἀπογράφεσθαι πρὸς τοὺς ἄρχοντας ἀπὸ τίνων
ἕκαστος πορίζεται τὸν βίον, καὶ τὸν ἐν τούτοις
ψευσάμενον ἢ πόρον ἄδικον ἐπιτελοῦντα θανάτῳ
περιπίπτειν ἦν ἀναγκαῖον. λέγεται δὲ τοῦτον
τὸν νόμον ὑπὸ Σόλωνος παραβαλόντος εἰς
6 Αἴγυπτον εἰς τὰς Ἀθήνας μετενεχθῆναι. εἰ δέ τις
ἑκουσίως ἀποκτείναι τὸν ἐλεύθερον ἢ τὸν δοῦλον,
ἀποθνήσκειν τοῦτον οἱ νόμοι προσέταττον, ἅμα
μὲν βουλόμενοι μὴ ταῖς διαφοραῖς τῆς τύχης, ἀλλὰ
ταῖς τῶν πράξεων ἐπιβολαῖς εἴργεσθαι πάντας
ἀπὸ τῶν φαύλων, ἅμα δὲ διὰ τῆς τῶν δούλων
φροντίδος ἐθίζοντες τοὺς ἀνθρώπους πολὺ μᾶλλον
εἰς τοὺς ἐλευθέρους μηδὲν ὅλως ἐξαμαρτάνειν.

---

[1] Cp. Euripides, *Medea*, 412–13: θεῶν δ' οὐκέτι πίστις ἄραρε
(" a pledge given in the name of the gods no longer stands
firm ").

[2] Cp. Herodotus, 2. 177: μηδὲ ἀποφαίνοντα δικαίην ζόην
("unless he proved that he had a just way of life").

mightiest pledge known among men.[1] Again, if a
man, walking on a road in Egypt, saw a person
being killed or, in a word, suffering any kind of
violence and did not come to his aid if able to do
so, he had to die; and if he was truly prevented
from aiding the person because of inability, he was
in any case required to lodge information against
the bandits and to bring an action against their
lawless act; and in case he failed to do this as the
law required, it was required that he be scourged
with a fixed number of stripes and be deprived of
every kind of food for three days. Those who brought
false accusations against others had to suffer the
penalty that would have been meted out to the
accused persons had they been adjudged guilty.
All Egyptians were also severally required to submit
to the magistrates a written declaration of the sources
of their livelihood, and any man making a false declaration or gaining an unlawful means of livelihood [2] had
to pay the death penalty. And it is said that Solon,
after his visit to Egypt, brought this law to Athens.[3]
If anyone intentionally killed a free man or a slave
the laws enjoined that he be put to death; for they,
in the first place, wished that it should not be through
the accidental differences in men's condition in life
but through the principles governing their actions
that all men should be restrained from evil deeds,
and, on the other hand, they sought to accustom
mankind, through such consideration for slaves, to
refrain all the more from committing any offence
whatever against freemen.

[3] Herodotus (2. 177) makes the same statement, but
Plutarch (*Solon*, 31), on the authority of Theophrastus,
attributes a similar law, not to Solon, but to Peisistratus.

7   Καὶ κατὰ μὲν τῶν γονέων τῶν ἀποκτεινάντων
τὰ τέκνα θάνατον μὲν οὐχ ὥρισαν, ἡμέρας δὲ
τρεῖς καὶ νύκτας ἴσας συνεχῶς ἦν ἀναγκαῖον
περιειληφότας τὸν νεκρὸν ὑπομένειν φυλακῆς
παρεδρευούσης δημοσίας· οὐ γὰρ δίκαιον ὑπε-
λήφθη τὸ τοῦ βίου στερίσκειν τοὺς τὸν βίον τοῖς
παισὶ δεδωκότας, νουθετήσει δὲ μᾶλλον λύπην
ἐχούσῃ καὶ μεταμέλειαν ἀποτρέπειν τῶν τοιού-
8 των ἐγχειρημάτων· κατὰ δὲ τῶν τέκνων τῶν
γονεῖς φονευσάντων τιμωρίαν ἐξηλλαγμένην ἔθη-
καν· ἔδει γὰρ τοὺς καταδικασθέντας ἐπὶ τούτοις καλάμοις ὀξέσι δακτυλιαῖα μέρη τοῦ σώματος
κατατμηθέντας ἐπ' ἀκάνθαις κατακάεσθαι ζῶντας·
μέγιστον τῶν ἐν ἀνθρώποις ἀδικημάτων κρίνοντες
τὸ βιαίως τὸ ζῆν ἀφαιρεῖσθαι τῶν τὴν ζωὴν
9 αὐτοῖς δεδωκότων. τῶν δὲ γυναικῶν τῶν κατα-
δικασθεισῶν θανάτῳ τὰς ἐγκύους μὴ θανατοῦσθαι
πρὶν ἂν τέκωσι. καὶ τοῦτο τὸ νόμιμον πολλοὶ
καὶ τῶν Ἑλλήνων κατέδειξαν, ἡγούμενοι παντελῶς
ἄδικον εἶναι τὸ μηδὲν ἀδικῆσαν τῷ ἀδικήσαντι
τῆς αὐτῆς μετέχειν τιμωρίας, καὶ παρανομήματος
ἑνὸς γενομένου παρὰ δυοῖν λαμβάνειν τὸ πρόστιμον, πρὸς δὲ τούτοις κατὰ προαίρεσιν πονηρὰν
συντελεσθέντος τοῦ ἀδικήματος τὸ μηδεμίαν πω
σύνεσιν ἔχον ὑπὸ τὴν ὁμοίαν ἄγειν κόλασιν, τὸ
δὲ πάντων μέγιστον, ὅτι ταῖς κυούσαις ἰδίᾳ τῆς
αἰτίας ἐπενηνεγμένης οὐδαμῶς προσήκει τὸ κοινὸν
10 πατρὸς καὶ μητρὸς τέκνον ἀναιρεῖσθαι· ἐπ' ἴσης
γὰρ ἄν τις φαύλους διαλάβοι κριτὰς τούς τε τὸν
ἔνοχον τῷ φόνῳ σῴζοντας καὶ τοὺς τὸ μηδὲν ὅλως
ἀδικῆσαν συναναιροῦντας.

In the case of parents who had slain their children, though the laws did not prescribe death, yet the offenders had to hold the dead body in their arms for three successive days and nights, under the surveillance of a state guard; for it was not considered just to deprive of life those who had given life to their children, but rather by a warning which brought with it pain and repentance to turn them from such deeds. But for children who had killed their parents they reserved an extraordinary punishment; for it was required that those found guilty of this crime should have pieces of flesh about the size of a finger cut out of their bodies with sharp reeds and then be put on a bed of thorns and burned alive; for they held that to take by violence the life of those who had given them life was the greatest crime possible to man. Pregnant women who had been condemned to death were not executed until they had been delivered. The same law has also been enacted by many Greek states, since they held it entirely unjust that the innocent should suffer the same punishment as the guilty, that a penalty should be exacted of two for only one transgression, and, further, that, since the crime had been actuated by an evil intention, a being as yet without intelligence should receive the same correction, and, what is the most important consideration, that in view of the fact that the guilt had been laid at the door of the pregnant mother it was by no means proper that the child, who belongs to the father as well as to the mother, should be despatched; for a man may properly consider judges who spare the life of a murderer to be no worse than other judges who destroy that which is guilty of no crime whatsoever.

11   Τῶν μὲν οὖν φονικῶν νόμων οἱ μάλιστα δο-
κοῦντες ἐπιτετεῦχθαι τοιοῦτοί τινες ἦσαν.

78. Τῶν δ' ἄλλων ὁ μὲν περὶ τῶν πολέμων
κείμενος κατὰ τῶν τὴν τάξιν λιπόντων ἢ τὸ
παραγγελθὲν ὑπὸ τῶν ἡγεμόνων μὴ ποιούντων
ἔταττε πρόστιμον οὐ θάνατον, ἀλλὰ τὴν ἐσχάτην

2 ἀτιμίαν· εἰ δ' ὕστερον ταῖς ἀνδραγαθίαις ὑπερ-
βάλοιντο τὰς ἀτιμίας, εἰς τὴν προϋπάρξασαν
παρρησίαν ἀποκαθίστα, ἅμα μὲν τοῦ νομοθέτου
δεινοτέραν τιμωρίαν ποιοῦντος τὴν ἀτιμίαν ἢ τὸν
θάνατον, ἵνα τὸ μέγιστον τῶν κακῶν ἐθίσῃ
πάντας κρίνειν τὴν αἰσχύνην, ἅμα δὲ τοὺς μὲν
θανατωθέντας ἡγεῖτο μηδὲν ὠφελήσειν τὸν κοινὸν
βίον, τοὺς δὲ ἀτιμωθέντας ἀγαθῶν πολλῶν
αἰτίους ἔσεσθαι διὰ τὴν ἐπιθυμίαν τῆς παρρησίας.

3 καὶ τῶν μὲν τὰ ἀπόρρητα τοῖς πολεμίοις ἀπαγ-
γειλάντων ἐπέταττεν ὁ νόμος ἐκτέμνεσθαι τὴν
γλῶτταν, τῶν δὲ τὸ νόμισμα παρακοπτόντων ἢ
μέτρα καὶ σταθμὰ παραποιούντων ἢ παραγλυ-
φόντων τὰς σφραγῖδας, ἔτι δὲ τῶν γραμματέων
τῶν ψευδεῖς χρηματισμοὺς γραφόντων ἢ ἀφαι-
ρούντων τι τῶν ἐγγεγραμμένων, καὶ τῶν τὰς
ψευδεῖς συγγραφὰς ἐπιφερόντων, ἀμφοτέρας
ἐκέλευσεν ἀποκόπτεσθαι τὰς χεῖρας, ὅπως οἷς
ἕκαστος μέρεσι τοῦ σώματος παρενόμησεν, εἰς
ταῦτα κολαζόμενος αὐτὸς μὲν μέχρι τελευτῆς
ἀνίατον ἔχῃ τὴν συμφοράν, τοὺς δ' ἄλλους διὰ
τῆς ἰδίας τιμωρίας νουθετῶν ἀποτρέπῃ τῶν
ὁμοίων τι πράττειν.

---

[1] The significance of this word, which summed up as well
as any the ideal of Greek freedom and of the Athenian
democracy, cannot be included in a single phrase. It im-

Now of the laws dealing with murder these are those which are thought to have been the most successful.

78. Among their other laws one, which concerned military affairs, made the punishment of deserters or of any who disobeyed the command of their leaders, not death, but the uttermost disgrace; but if later on such men wiped out their disgrace by a display of manly courage, they were restored to their former freedom of speech.[1] Thus the lawgiver at the same time made disgrace a more terrible punishment than death, in order to accustom all the people to consider dishonour the greatest of evils, and he also believed that, while dead men would never be of value to society, men who had been disgraced would do many a good deed through their desire to regain freedom of speech. In the case of those who had disclosed military secrets to the enemy the law prescribed that their tongues should be cut out, while in the case of counterfeiters or falsifiers of measures and weights or imitators of seals, and of official scribes who made false entries or erased items, and of any who adduced false documents, it ordered that both their hands should be cut off, to the end that the offender, being punished in respect of those members of his body that were the instruments of his wrongdoing, should himself keep until death his irreparable misfortune, and at the same time, by serving as a warning example to others, should turn them from the commission of similar offences.

plied that a man was as good as any other, that he could hold up his head among his fellows. " Position of self-respect and equality " is approximately what it means in this sentence and the following.

4 Πικροὶ δὲ καὶ περὶ τῶν γυναικῶν νόμοι παρ'
αὐτοῖς ὑπῆρχον. τοῦ μὲν γὰρ βιασαμένου
γυναῖκα ἐλευθέραν προσέταξαν ἀποκόπτεσθαι
τὰ αἰδοῖα, νομίσαντες τὸν τοιοῦτον μιᾷ πράξει
παρανόμῳ τρία τὰ μέγιστα τῶν κακῶν ἐνηργη-
κέναι, τὴν ὕβριν καὶ τὴν φθορὰν καὶ τὴν τῶν
5 τέκνων σύγχυσιν· εἰ δέ τις πείσας μοιχεύσαι, τὸν
μὲν ἄνδρα ῥάβδοις χιλίας πληγὰς λαμβάνειν
ἐκέλευον, τῆς δὲ γυναικὸς τὴν ῥῖνα κολοβοῦσθαι,
ὑπολαμβάνοντες δεῖν τῆς πρὸς ἀσυγχώρητον
ἀκρασίαν καλλωπιζομένης ἀφαιρεθῆναι τὰ μάλιστα κοσμοῦντα τὴν εὐπρέπειαν.

79. Τοὺς δὲ περὶ τῶν συμβολαίων νόμους
Βοκχόριδος εἶναί φασι. προστάττουσι δὲ τοὺς
μὲν ἀσύγγραφα δανεισαμένους, ἂν μὴ φάσκωσιν
ὀφείλειν, ὀμόσαντας ἀπολύεσθαι τοῦ δανείου,
πρῶτον μὲν ὅπως ἐν μεγάλῳ τιθέμενοι τοὺς ὅρκους
2 δεισιδαιμονῶσι· προδήλου γὰρ ὄντος ὅτι τῷ
πολλάκις ὀμόσαντι συμβήσεται τὴν πίστιν ἀπο-
βαλεῖν, ἵνα τῆς εὐχρηστίας μὴ στερηθῇ, περὶ πλείστου πᾶς τις ἄξει[1] τὸ μὴ καταντᾶν ἐπὶ τὸν ὅρκον·
ἔπειθ' ὑπελάμβανεν ὁ νομοθέτης τὴν ὅλην πίστιν
ἐν τῇ καλοκἀγαθίᾳ ποιήσας προτρέψεσθαι πάντας
σπουδαίους εἶναι τοῖς ἤθεσιν, ἵνα μὴ πίστεως
ἀνάξιοι διαβληθῶσι· πρὸς δὲ τούτοις ἄδικον ἔκρινεν
εἶναι τοὺς χωρὶς ὅρκου πιστευθέντας περὶ τῶν
αὐτῶν συμβολαίων ὀμόσαντας μὴ τυγχάνειν
πίστεως. τοὺς δὲ μετὰ συγγραφῆς δανείσαντας

---

[1] ἄξει Cobet : ἕξει.

---

[1] Cp. chap. 65.

Severe also were their laws touching women. For if a man had violated a free married woman, they stipulated that he be emasculated, considering that such a person by a single unlawful act had been guilty of the three greatest crimes, assault, abduction, and confusion of offspring; but if a man committed adultery with the woman's consent, the laws ordered that the man should receive a thousand blows with the rod, and that the woman should have her nose cut off, on the ground that a woman who tricks herself out with an eye to forbidden licence should be deprived of that which contributes most to a woman's comeliness.

79. Their laws governing contracts they attribute to Bocchoris.[1] These prescribe that men who had borrowed money without signing a bond, if they denied the indebtedness, might take an oath to that effect and be cleared of the obligation. The purpose was, in the first place, that men might stand in awe of the gods by attributing great importance to oaths, for, since it is manifest that the man who has repeatedly taken such an oath will in the end lose the confidence which others had in him, everyone will consider it a matter of the utmost concern not to have recourse to the oath lest he forfeit his credit. In the second place, the lawgiver assumed that by basing confidence entirely upon a man's sense of honour he would incite all men to be virtuous in character, in order that they might not be talked about as being unworthy of confidence; and, furthermore, he held it to be unjust that men who had been trusted with a loan without an oath should not be trusted when they gave their oath regarding the same transaction. And whoever lent money along

ἐκώλυε διὰ τοῦ τόκου τὸ κεφάλαιον πλέον ποιεῖν
ἢ διπλάσιον.

3 Τῶν δὲ ὀφειλόντων τὴν ἔκπραξιν τῶν δανείων
ἐκ τῆς οὐσίας μόνον ἐποιήσατο, τὸ δὲ σῶμα κατ'
οὐδένα τρόπον εἴασεν ὑπάρχειν ἀγώγιμον, ἡγούμενος δεῖν εἶναι τὰς μὲν κτήσεις τῶν ἐργασαμένων
ἢ παρὰ κυρίου τινὸς ἐν δωρεαῖς λαβόντων, τὰ δὲ
σώματα τῶν πόλεων, ἵνα τὰς καθηκούσας λειτουργίας ἔχωσιν αἱ πόλεις καὶ κατὰ πόλεμον καὶ
κατ' εἰρήνην· ἄτοπον γὰρ τὸ[1] στρατιώτην εἰς
τὸν ὑπὲρ τῆς πατρίδος προϊόντα κίνδυνον, εἰ
τύχοι, πρὸς δάνειον ὑπὸ τοῦ πιστεύσαντος ἀπά-
γεσθαι, καὶ τῆς τῶν ἰδιωτῶν πλεονεξίας ἕνεκα
4 κινδυνεύειν τὴν κοινὴν ἁπάντων σωτηρίαν. δοκεῖ
δὲ καὶ τοῦτον τὸν νόμον ὁ Σόλων εἰς τὰς Ἀθήνας
μετενεγκεῖν, ὃν ὠνόμασε σεισάχθειαν, ἀπολύσας
τοὺς πολίτας ἅπαντας τῶν ἐπὶ τοῖς σώμασι πεπι-
5 στευμένων δανείων. μέμφονται δέ τινες οὐκ
ἀλόγως τοῖς πλείστοις τῶν παρὰ τοῖς Ἕλλησι
νομοθετῶν, οἵτινες ὅπλα μὲν καὶ ἄροτρον καὶ
ἄλλα τῶν ἀναγκαιοτάτων ἐκώλυσαν ἐνέχυρα
λαμβάνεσθαι πρὸς δάνειον, τοὺς δὲ τούτοις χρη-
σομένους συνεχώρησαν ἀγωγίμους εἶναι.

80. Ὑπῆρχε δὲ καὶ περὶ τῶν κλεπτῶν νόμος
παρ' Αἰγυπτίοις ἰδιώτατος. ἐκέλευε γὰρ τοὺς
μὲν[2] βουλομένους ἔχειν ταύτην τὴν ἐργασίαν

---

[1] τὸ Bekker : τόν.
[2] μὲν Dindorf : μὴ D, omitted by all other MSS.

---

[1] The famous *Seisachtheia* ("shaking off of burdens") of
Solon in 594 B.C. declared void existing pledges in land,

with a written bond was forbidden to do more than double the principal from the interest.

In the case of debtors the lawgiver ruled that the repayment of loans could be exacted only from a man's estate, and under no condition did he allow the debtor's person to be subject to seizure, holding that whereas property should belong to those who had amassed it or had received it from some earlier holder by way of a gift, the bodies of citizens should belong to the state, to the end that the state might avail itself of the services which its citizens owed it, in times of both war and peace. For it would be absurd, he felt, that a soldier, at the moment perhaps when he was setting forth to fight for his fatherland, should be haled to prison by his creditor for an unpaid loan, and that the greed of private citizens should in this way endanger the safety of all. And it appears that Solon took this law also to Athens, calling it a " disburdenment," [1] when he absolved all the citizens of the loans, secured by their persons, which they owed. But certain individuals find fault, and not without reason, with the majority of the Greek lawgivers, who forbade the taking of weapons and ploughs and other quite indispensable things as security for loans, but nevertheless allowed the men who would use these implements to be subject to imprisonment.

80. The Egyptian law dealing with thieves was also a very peculiar one. For it bade any who chose to follow this occupation to enter their names with

granted freedom to all men enslaved for debt, and probably cancelled all debts which involved any form of personal servitude, by these measures effecting the complete freedom of all debt slaves or debt serfs in Attica (cp. Adcock in *The Cambridge Ancient History*, 4. p. 37 f.).

ἀπογράφεσθαι πρὸς τὸν ἀρχίφωρα, καὶ τὸ κλαπὲν
ὁμολόγως ἀναφέρειν παραχρῆμα πρὸς ἐκεῖνον,
τοὺς δὲ ἀπολέσαντας παραπλησίως ἀπογράφειν
αὐτῷ καθ᾽ ἕκαστον τῶν ἀπολωλότων, προστι-
θέντας τόν τε τόπον καὶ τὴν ἡμέραν καὶ τὴν
2 ὥραν καθ᾽ ἣν ἀπώλεσεν.[1] τούτῳ δὲ τῷ τρόπῳ
πάντων ἑτοίμως εὑρισκομένων, ἔδει τὸν ἀπολέ-
σαντα τὸ τέταρτον μέρος τῆς ἀξίας δόντα κτή-
σασθαι τὰ ἑαυτοῦ μόνα. ἀδυνάτου γὰρ ὄντος
τοῦ πάντας ἀποστῆσαι τῆς κλοπῆς εὗρε πόρον ὁ
νομοθέτης δι᾽ οὗ πᾶν τὸ ἀπολόμενον σωθήσεται
μικρῶν διδομένων λύτρων.

3 Γαμοῦσι δὲ παρ᾽ Αἰγυπτίοις οἱ μὲν ἱερεῖς
μίαν, τῶν δ᾽ ἄλλων ὅσας ἂν ἕκαστος προαιρῆται·
καὶ τὰ γεννώμενα πάντα τρέφουσιν ἐξ ἀνάγκης
ἕνεκα τῆς πολυανθρωπίας, ὡς ταύτης μέγιστα
συμβαλλομένης πρὸς εὐδαιμονίαν χώρας τε καὶ
πόλεων, νόθον δ᾽ οὐδένα τῶν γεννηθέντων νομίζουσιν, οὐδ᾽ ἂν ἐξ ἀργυρωνήτου μητρὸς γεννηθῇ·
4 καθόλου γὰρ ὑπειλήφασι τὸν πατέρα μόνον
αἴτιον εἶναι τῆς γενέσεως, τὴν δὲ μητέρα τροφὴν
καὶ χώραν παρέχεσθαι τῷ βρέφει, καὶ τῶν δένδρων ἄρρενα μὲν καλοῦσι τὰ καρποφόρα, θήλεα
δὲ τὰ μὴ φέροντα τοὺς καρπούς, ἐναντίως τοῖς
5 Ἕλλησι. τρέφουσι δὲ τὰ παιδία μετά τινος
εὐχερείας ἀδαπάνου καὶ παντελῶς ἀπίστου·
ἑψήματα γὰρ αὐτοῖς χορηγοῦσιν ἔκ τινος μετ᾽

---

[1] ἀπώλεσεν A B D, Vogel: ἀπώλεσαν Bekker, Dindorf,
ἀπέβαλε II.

the Chief of the Thieves and by agreement to bring
to him immediately the stolen articles, while any who
had been robbed filed with him in like manner a list
of all the missing articles, stating the place, the day,
and the hour of the loss. And since by this method
all lost articles were readily found, the owner who
had lost anything had only to pay one-fourth of its
value in order to recover just what belonged to him.
For as it was impossible to keep all mankind from
stealing, the lawgiver devised a scheme whereby
every article lost would be recovered upon payment
of a small ransom.

In accordance with the marriage-customs of the
Egyptians the priests have but one wife, but any other
man takes as many as he may determine;[1] and the
Egyptians are required to raise all their children
in order to increase the population,[2] on the ground
that large numbers are the greatest factor in increasing the prosperity of both country and cities. Nor
do they hold any child a bastard, even though he
was born of a slave mother; for they have taken the
general position that the father is the sole author
of procreation and that the mother only supplies
the fetus with nourishment and a place to live, and
they call the trees which bear fruit " male " and those
which do not " female," exactly opposite to the Greek
usage. They feed their children in a sort of happy-
go-lucky fashion that in its inexpensiveness quite
surpasses belief; for they serve them with stews

[1] According to Herodotus (2. 92) monogamy was the
prevailing custom, but he was certainly in error so far as the
wealthier classes were concerned.
[2] *i.e.* the exposure of children, which was still practised
among some Greeks in Diodorus' day, was forbidden.

εὐτελείας ἑτοίμου[1] γινόμενα, καὶ τῶν ἐκ τῆς
βύβλου πυθμένων τοὺς δυναμένους εἰς τὸ πῦρ
ἐγκρύβεσθαι, καὶ τῶν ῥιζῶν καὶ τῶν καυλῶν τῶν
ἑλείων τὰ μὲν ὠμά, τὰ δ᾽ ἕψοντες, τὰ δ᾽ ὀπτῶντες,
6 διδόασιν. ἀνυποδήτων δὲ καὶ γυμνῶν τῶν πλείστων τρεφομένων διὰ τὴν εὐκρασίαν τῶν τόπων,
τὴν πᾶσαν δαπάνην οἱ γονεῖς, ἄχρι ἂν εἰς ἡλικίαν
ἔλθῃ τὸ τέκνον, οὐ πλείω ποιοῦσι δραχμῶν εἴκοσι.
δι᾽ ἃς αἰτίας μάλιστα τὴν Αἴγυπτον συμβαίνει
πολυανθρωπίᾳ διαφέρειν, καὶ διὰ τοῦτο πλείστας
ἔχειν μεγάλων ἔργων κατασκευάς.

81. Παιδεύουσι δὲ τοὺς υἱοὺς οἱ μὲν ἱερεῖς
γράμματα διττά, τά τε ἱερὰ καλούμενα καὶ τὰ
κοινοτέραν ἔχοντα τὴν μάθησιν. γεωμετρίαν δὲ
2 καὶ τὴν ἀριθμητικὴν ἐπὶ πλέον ἐκπονοῦσιν. ὁ
μὲν γὰρ ποταμὸς κατ᾽ ἐνιαυτὸν ποικίλως μετα-
σχηματίζων τὴν χώραν πολλὰς καὶ παντοίας
ἀμφισβητήσεις ποιεῖ περὶ τῶν ὅρων τοῖς γειτνιῶσι,
ταύτας δ᾽ οὐ ῥᾴδιον ἀκριβῶς ἐξελέγξαι μὴ γεω-
μέτρου τὴν ἀλήθειαν ἐκ τῆς ἐμπειρίας μεθοδεύ-
3 σαντος. ἡ δ᾽ ἀριθμητικὴ πρός τε τὰς κατὰ τὸν
βίον οἰκονομίας αὐτοῖς χρησιμεύει καὶ πρὸς τὰ
γεωμετρίας θεωρήματα, πρὸς δὲ τούτοις οὐκ ὀλίγα
συμβάλλεται καὶ τοῖς τὰ περὶ τὴν ἀστρολογίαν
4 ἐκπονοῦσιν. ἐπιμελοῦς[2] γάρ, εἰ καὶ παρά τισιν

---

[1] μετ᾽ εὐτελείας ἑτοίμου Capps : εὐτελείας ἑτοίμης.
[2] ἐπιμελοῦς Dindorf : ἐπιμελῶς.

---

[1] There were, in fact, three kinds of Egyptian writing, (1)
the hieroglyphic, (2) the hieratic, and (3) the demotic, the last

276

made of any stuff that is ready to hand and cheap, and give them such stalks of the *byblos* plant as can be roasted in the coals, and the roots and stems of marsh plants, either raw or boiled or baked. And since most of the children are reared without shoes or clothing because of the mildness of the climate of the country, the entire expense incurred by the parents of a child until it comes to maturity is not more than twenty drachmas. These are the leading reasons why Egypt has such an extraordinarily large population, and it is because of this fact that she possesses a vast number of great monuments.

81. In the education of their sons the priests teach them two kinds of writing, that which is called " sacred " and that which is used in the more general instruction.[1] Geometry [2] and arithmetic are given special attention. For the river, by changing the face of the country each year in manifold ways, gives rise to many and varied disputes between neighbours over their boundary lines, and these disputes cannot be easily tested out with any exactness unless a geometer works out the truth scientifically by the application of his experience. And arithmetic is serviceable with reference to the business affairs connected with making a living and also in applying the principles of geometry, and likewise is of no small assistance to students of astrology as well. For the positions and arrangements of the stars as

being that in general use in the time of Diodorus. In common with Herodotus (2. 36), Diodorus fails to distinguish between the first and second.

[2] Here " geometry " is used in its original meaning, " measurement of the earth," and " geometer " below means " surveyor."

DIODORUS OF SICILY

ἄλλοις, καὶ παρ' Αἰγυπτίοις παρατηρήσεως
τυγχάνουσιν αἱ τῶν ἄστρων τάξεις τε καὶ κινήσεις·
καὶ τὰς μὲν[1] περὶ ἑκάστων ἀναγραφὰς ἐξ ἐτῶν
ἀπίστων τῷ πλήθει φυλάττουσιν, ἐκ παλαιῶν
χρόνων ἐζηλωμένης παρ' αὐτοῖς τῆς περὶ ταῦτα
σπουδῆς, τὰς δὲ[2] τῶν πλανήτων ἀστέρων κινήσεις
καὶ περιόδους καὶ στηριγμούς, ἔτι δὲ τὰς ἑκάστου
δυνάμεις πρὸς τὰς τῶν ζῴων γενέσεις, τίνων εἰσὶν
ἀγαθῶν ἢ κακῶν ἀπεργαστικαί, φιλοτιμότατα
5 παρατετηρήκασι. καὶ πολλάκις μὲν τοῖς ἀνθρώποις τῶν αὐτοῖς μελλόντων ἀπαντήσεσθαι κατὰ
τὸν βίον προλέγοντες ἐπιτυγχάνουσιν, οὐκ
ὀλιγάκις δὲ καρπῶν φθορὰς ἢ τοὐναντίον πολυ-
καρπίας, ἔτι δὲ νόσους κοινὰς ἀνθρώποις ἢ
βοσκήμασιν ἐσομένας προσημαίνουσι, σεισμούς τε
καὶ κατακλυσμοὺς καὶ κομητῶν ἀστέρων ἐπι-
τολὰς καὶ πάντα τὰ τοῖς πολλοῖς ἀδύνατον ἔχειν
δοκοῦντα τὴν ἐπίγνωσιν, ἐκ πολλοῦ χρόνου[3]
6 παρατηρήσεως γεγενημένης, προγινώσκουσι. φασὶ
δὲ καὶ τοὺς ἐν Βαβυλῶνι Χαλδαίους, ἀποίκους
Αἰγυπτίων ὄντας, τὴν δόξαν ἔχειν τὴν περὶ τῆς
ἀστρολογίας παρὰ τῶν ἱερέων μαθόντας τῶν
Αἰγυπτίων.

7 Τὸ δ' ἄλλο πλῆθος τῶν Αἰγυπτίων ἐκ παίδων
μανθάνει παρὰ τῶν πατέρων ἢ συγγενῶν τὰς
περὶ ἕκαστον βίον ἐπιτηδεύσεις, καθάπερ προει-
ρήκαμεν· γράμματα δ' ἐπ' ὀλίγον διδάσκουσιν[4]
οὐχ ἅπαντες, ἀλλ' οἱ τὰς τέχνας μεταχειριζό-
μενοι μάλιστα. παλαίστραν δὲ καὶ μουσικὴν

---

[1] μὲν omitted by F, Bekker, Dindorf.
[2] δὲ Vogel : τε.
[3] πολλοῦ χρόνου Bekker, Vogel : πολυχροτίου F, Dindorf.

278

well as their motions have always been the subject
of careful observation among the Egyptians, if any-
where in the world; they have preserved to this day
the records concerning each of these stars over an
incredible number of years, this subject of study
having been zealously preserved among them from
ancient times, and they have also observed with the
utmost avidity the motions and orbits and stoppings
of the planets, as well as the influences of each one
on the generation of all living things—the good or
the evil effects, namely, of which they are the cause.
And while they are often successful in predicting to
men the events which are going to befall them in the
course of their lives, not infrequently they foretell
destructions of the crops or, on the other hand,
abundant yields, and pestilences that are to attack
men or beasts, and as a result of their long observations they have prior knowledge of earthquakes and
floods, of the risings of the comets, and of all things
which the ordinary man looks upon as beyond all
finding out. And according to them the Chaldaeans
of Babylon, being colonists from Egypt, enjoy the
fame which they have for their astrology because they
learned that science from the priests of Egypt.

As to the general mass of the Egyptians, they are
instructed from their childhood by their fathers or
kinsmen in the practices proper to each manner of
life as previously described by us; [1] but as for reading
and writing, the Egyptians at large give their
children only a superficial instruction in them, and
not all do this, but for the most part only those who
are engaged in the crafts. In wrestling and music,

[1] Cp. chaps. 43, 70, 74.

---

[4] διδάσκονται Reiske, Bekker, Dindorf.

οὐ νόμιμόν ἐστι παρ' αὐτοῖς μανθάνειν· ὑπολαμβάνουσι γὰρ ἐκ μὲν τῶν καθ' ἡμέραν ἐν
τῇ παλαίστρᾳ γυμνασίων τοὺς νέους οὐχ
ὑγίειαν ἕξειν, ἀλλὰ ῥώμην ὀλιγοχρόνιον καὶ
παντελῶς ἐπικίνδυνον, τὴν δὲ μουσικὴν νομίζουσιν οὐ μόνον ἄχρηστον ὑπάρχειν, ἀλλὰ καὶ
βλαβεράν, ὡς [1] ἐκθηλύνουσαν τὰς τῶν ἀκουόντων
ψυχάς.

82. Τὰς δὲ νόσους προκαταλαμβανόμενοι
θεραπεύουσι τὰ σώματα κλυσμοῖς καὶ νηστείαις
καὶ ἐμέτοις, ἐνίοτε μὲν καθ' ἑκάστην ἡμέραν,
ἐνίοτε δὲ τρεῖς ἢ τέτταρας ἡμέρας διαλείποντες.
2 φασὶ γὰρ πάσης τροφῆς ἀναδοθείσης τὸ πλέον
εἶναι περιττόν, ἀφ' οὗ γεννᾶσθαι τὰς νόσους·
ὥστε τὴν προειρημένην θεραπείαν ἀναιροῦσαν
τὰς ἀρχὰς τῆς νόσου μάλιστ' ἂν παρασκευάσαι
3 τὴν ὑγίειαν. κατὰ δὲ τὰς στρατείας καὶ τὰς
ἐπὶ [2] τῆς χώρας ἐκδημίας θεραπεύονται πάντες
οὐδένα μισθὸν ἰδίᾳ διδόντες· οἱ γὰρ ἰατροὶ τὰς
μὲν τροφὰς ἐκ τοῦ κοινοῦ λαμβάνουσι, τὰς δὲ
θεραπείας προσάγουσι κατὰ νόμον ἔγγραφον,
ὑπὸ [3] πολλῶν καὶ δεδοξασμένων ἰατρῶν ἀρχαίων
συγγεγραμμένον. κἂν τοῖς ἐκ τῆς ἱερᾶς βίβλου
νόμοις ἀναγινωσκομένοις ἀκολουθήσαντες ἀδυ-
νατήσωσι σῶσαι τὸν κάμνοντα, ἀθῷοι παντὸς
ἐγκλήματος ἀπολύονται, ἐὰν δέ τι παρὰ τὰ
γεγραμμένα ποιήσωσι, θανάτου κρίσιν ὑπομένου-
σιν, ἡγουμένου τοῦ νομοθέτου τῆς ἐκ πολλῶν
χρόνων παρατετηρημένης θεραπείας καὶ συντε-

---

[1] ἂν after ὡς deleted by Hertlein.
[2] ἐπὶ omitted by F, Bekker, Dindorf.
[3] ὑπὸ Dindorf : ἀπό.

however, it is not customary among them to receive any instruction at all;[1] for they hold that from the daily exercises in wrestling their young men will gain, not health, but a vigour that is only temporary and in fact quite dangerous, while they consider music to be not only useless but even harmful, since it makes the spirits of the listeners effeminate.

82. In order to prevent sicknesses they look after the health of their bodies by means of drenches, fastings, and emetics,[2] sometimes every day and sometimes at intervals of three or four days. For they say that the larger part of the food taken into the body is superfluous and that it is from this superfluous part that diseases are engendered; consequently the treatment just mentioned, by removing the beginnings of disease, would be most likely to produce health. On their military campaigns and their journeys in the country they all receive treatment without the payment of any private fee; for the physicians draw their support from public funds and administer their treatments in accordance with a written law which was composed in ancient times by many famous physicians. If they follow the rules of this law as they read them in the sacred book and yet are unable to save their patient, they are absolved from any charge and go unpunished; but if they go contrary to the law's prescriptions in any respect, they must submit to a trial with death as the penalty, the lawgiver holding that but few physicians would ever show themselves wiser than the mode of treatment which had been closely followed for a long

[1] Diodorus is contrasting the Egyptian attitude toward these subjects with the emphasis laid upon them in Greek education.

[2] Cp. Herodotus 2. 77.

ταγμένης ὑπὸ τῶν ἀρίστων τεχνιτῶν ὀλίγους ἂν
γενέσθαι συνετωτέρους.

83. Περὶ δὲ τῶν ἀφιερωμένων ζῴων κατ'
Αἴγυπτον εἰκότως φαίνεται πολλοῖς παράδοξον
τὸ γινόμενον καὶ ζητήσεως ἄξιον. σέβονται γὰρ
ἔνια τῶν ζῴων Αἰγύπτιοι καθ' ὑπερβολὴν οὐ
ζῶντα μόνον, ἀλλὰ καὶ τελευτήσαντα, οἷον
αἰλούρους καὶ τοὺς ἰχνεύμονας καὶ κύνας, ἔτι
δ' ἱέρακας καὶ τὰς καλουμένας παρ' αὐτοῖς ἴβεις,
πρὸς δὲ τούτοις τούς τε λύκους καὶ τοὺς κροκοδείλους καὶ ἕτερα τοιαῦτα πλείω, περὶ ὧν τὰς
αἰτίας ἀποδιδόναι πειρασόμεθα, βραχέα πρότερον
ὑπὲρ αὐτῶν διελθόντες.

2   Πρῶτον μὲν γὰρ ἑκάστῳ γένει τῶν σεβασμοῦ
τυγχανόντων ζῴων ἀφιέρωται χώρα φέρουσα
πρόσοδον ἀρκοῦσαν εἰς ἐπιμέλειαν καὶ τροφὴν
αὐτῶν· ποιοῦνται δὲ καὶ θεοῖς τισιν εὐχὰς ὑπὲρ
τῶν παίδων οἱ κατ' Αἴγυπτον τῶν ἐκ τῆς νόσου
σωθέντων· ξυρήσαντες γὰρ τὰς τρίχας καὶ πρὸς
ἀργύριον ἢ χρυσίον στήσαντες διδόασι τὸ νόμισμα τοῖς ἐπιμελομένοις τῶν προειρημένων
3   ζῴων. οἱ δὲ τοῖς μὲν ἱέραξι κρέα κατατέμνοντες
καὶ προσκαλούμενοι μεγάλῃ τῇ φωνῇ πετομένοις
ἀναρρίπτουσι, μέχρι ἂν δέξωνται, τοῖς δ' αἰλού-
ροις καὶ τοῖς ἰχνεύμοσι καταθρύπτοντες τοὺς
ἄρτους εἰς γάλα καὶ ποππύζοντες παρατιθέασιν
ἢ τῶν ἰχθύων τῶν ἐκ τοῦ Νείλου κατατέμνοντες
ὠμῶς σιτίζουσιν· ὡσαύτως δὲ καὶ τῶν ἄλλων
ζῴων ἑκάστῳ γένει τὴν ἁρμόζουσαν τροφὴν χορη-
4   γοῦσι. τὰς δὲ γινομένας περὶ ταῦτα λειτουργίας
οὐχ οἷον ἐκκλίνουσιν ἢ τοῖς ὄχλοις γενέσθαι

period and had been originally prescribed by the ablest practitioners.

83. As regards the consecration of animals in Egypt, the practice naturally appears to many to be extraordinary and worthy of investigation. For the Egyptians venerate certain animals exceedingly, not only during their lifetime but even after their death, such as cats,[1] ichneumons and dogs, and, again, hawks and the birds which they call " ibis," as well as wolves and crocodiles and a number of other animals of that kind, and the reasons for such worship we shall undertake to set forth, after we have first spoken briefly about the animals themselves.

In the first place, for each kind of animal that is accorded this worship there has been consecrated a portion of land which returns a revenue sufficient for their care and sustenance; moreover, the Egyptians make vows to certain gods on behalf of their children who have been delivered from an illness, in which case they shave off their hair and weigh it against silver or gold, and then give the money to the attendants of the animals mentioned. These cut up flesh for the hawks and calling them with a loud cry toss it up to them, as they swoop by, until they catch it, while for the cats and ichneumons they break up bread into milk and calling them with a clucking sound set it before them, or else they cut up fish caught in the Nile and feed the flesh to them raw; and in like manner each of the other kinds of animals is provided with the appropriate food. And as for the various services which these animals require, the Egyptians not only do not try to avoid them or feel

---

[1] The famous discussion of the cats of Egypt is in Herodotus, 2. 66–7.

καταφανεῖς ἐπαισχύνονται, τοὐναντίον δ' ὡς
περὶ¹ τὰς μεγίστας τῶν θεῶν γινόμενοι τιμὰς
σεμνύνονται καὶ μετὰ σημείων ἰδίων περιέρχονται
τὰς πόλεις καὶ τὴν χώραν. πόρρωθεν δ' ὄντες
φανεροὶ τίνων ζῴων ἔχουσι τὴν ἐπιμέλειαν, ὑπὸ
τῶν ἀπαντώντων² προσκυνοῦνται καὶ τιμῶνται.

5 Ὅταν δ' ἀποθάνῃ τι τῶν εἰρημένων, σινδόνι
κατακαλύψαντες καὶ μετ' οἰμωγῆς τὰ στήθη
καταπληξάμενοι φέρουσιν εἰς τὰς ταριχείας·
ἔπειτα θεραπευθέντων αὐτῶν κεδρίᾳ καὶ τοῖς
δυναμένοις εὐωδίαν παρέχεσθαι καὶ πολυχρόνιον
τοῦ σώματος τήρησιν θάπτουσιν ἐν ἱεραῖς θήκαις.

6 ὃς δ' ἂν τούτων τι τῶν ζῴων ἑκὼν διαφθείρῃ,
θανάτῳ περιπίπτει, πλὴν ἐὰν αἴλουρον ἢ τὴν
ἶβιν ἀποκτείνῃ· ταῦτα δὲ ἐάν τε ἑκὼν ἐάν τε
ἄκων ἀποκτείνῃ, πάντως θανάτῳ περιπίπτει,
τῶν ὄχλων συντρεχόντων καὶ τὸν πράξαντα
δεινότατα διατιθέντων, καὶ τοῦτ' ἐνίοτε πρατ-

7 τόντων ἄνευ κρίσεως. διὰ δὲ τὸν ἐπὶ τούτοις
φόβον οἱ θεασάμενοι τεθνηκός τι τούτων τῶν
ζῴων ἀποστάντες μακρὰν βοῶσιν ὀδυρόμενοί τε καὶ
μαρτυρόμενοι κατειλῆφθαι αὐτὸ³ τετελευτηκός.

8 οὕτω δ' ἐν ταῖς τῶν ὄχλων ψυχαῖς ἐντέτηκεν ἡ
πρὸς τὰ ζῷα ταῦτα δεισιδαιμονία καὶ τοῖς
πάθεσιν ἀμεταθέτως ἕκαστος διάκειται πρὸς τὴν
τούτων τιμήν, ὥστε καὶ καθ' ὃν χρόνον Πτολεμαῖος μὲν ὁ βασιλεὺς ὑπὸ Ῥωμαίων οὔπω

---

¹ ὡς περὶ Dindorf : ὥσπερ εἰς.
² ἀπαντώντων Wesseling : ἀπάντων.
³ κατειλῆφθαι τὸ Vulgate ; Vogel deletes τό. Reiske
conjectured αὐτὸ and is followed by Bekker and Dindorf.

ashamed to be seen by the crowds as they perform them, but on the contrary, in the belief that they are engaged in the most serious rites of divine worship, they assume airs of importance, and wearing special insignia make the rounds of the cities and the countryside. And since it can be seen from afar in the service of what animals they are engaged, all who meet them fall down before them and render them honour.

When one of these animals dies they wrap it in fine linen and then, wailing and beating their breasts, carry it off to be embalmed; and after it has been treated with cedar oil and such spices as have the quality of imparting a pleasant odour and of preserving the body for a long time,[1] they lay it away in a consecrated tomb. And whoever intentionally kills one of these animals is put to death, unless it be a cat or an ibis that he kills; but if he kills one of these, whether intentionally or unintentionally, he is certainly put to death, for the common people gather in crowds and deal with the perpetrator most cruelly, sometimes doing this without waiting for a trial. And because of their fear of such a punishment any who have caught sight of one of these animals lying dead withdraw to a great distance and shout with lamentations and protestations that they found the animal already dead. So deeply implanted also in the hearts of the common people is their superstitious regard for these animals and so unalterable are the emotions cherished by every man regarding the honour due to them that once, at the time when Ptolemy their king had not as yet been given by the

---

[1] According to Herodotus (2. 87) this was a less expensive method of embalming.

προσηγόρευτο φίλος, οἱ δ' ὄχλοι πᾶσαν εἰσεφέ-
ροντο σπουδὴν ἐκθεραπεύοντες τοὺς παρεπιδη-
μοῦντας τῶν ἀπὸ τῆς Ἰταλίας καὶ σπεύδοντες
μηδεμίαν ἀφορμὴν ἐγκλήματος ἢ πολέμου δοῦναι
διὰ τὸν φόβον, ἀποκτείναντος Ῥωμαίου τινὸς
αἴλουρον, καὶ τοῦ πλήθους συνδραμόντος ἐπὶ τὴν
οἰκίαν τοῦ πράξαντος, οὔθ' οἱ πεμφθέντες ὑπὸ
τοῦ βασιλέως ἄρχοντες ἐπὶ τὴν παραίτησιν
οὔθ' ὁ κοινὸς ἀπὸ τῆς Ῥώμης φόβος ἴσχυσεν
ἐξελέσθαι τῆς τιμωρίας τὸν ἄνθρωπον, καίπερ
9 ἀκουσίως τοῦτο πεπραχότα. καὶ τοῦτ' οὐκ ἐξ
ἀκοῆς ἡμεῖς ἱστοροῦμεν, ἀλλ' αὐτοὶ κατὰ τὴν
γεγενημένην ἡμῖν ἐπιδημίαν κατ' Αἴγυπτον ἑορα-
κότες.

84. Ἀπίστων δὲ φαινομένων πολλοῖς τῶν
εἰρημένων καὶ μύθοις παραπλησίων πολλῷ
παραδοξότερα φανήσεται τὰ μετὰ ταῦτα ῥηθησό-
μενα. λιμῷ γάρ ποτε πιεζομένων τῶν κατ'
Αἴγυπτόν φασι πολλοὺς ἀλλήλων μὲν ἅψασθαι
διὰ τὴν ἔνδειαν, τῶν δ' ἀφιερωμένων ζῴων τὸ
παράπαν μηδ' αἰτίαν σχεῖν μηδένα προσενη-
2 νέχθαι. ἀλλὰ μήν γε καὶ καθ' ἣν ἂν οἰκίαν
εὑρεθῇ κύων τετελευτηκώς, ξυρῶνται πάντες οἱ
κατ' οἶκον ὄντες ὅλον τὸ σῶμα καὶ ποιοῦνται
πένθος, καὶ τὸ τούτου θαυμασιώτερον, ἐὰν οἶνος
ἢ σῖτος ἤ τι τῶν πρὸς τὸν βίον ἀναγκαίων
τυγχάνῃ κείμενον ἐν τοῖς οἰκήμασιν οὗ τὸ ζῆν
ἐξέλιπέ τι τῶν θηρίων, οὐκ ἂν ἔτι χρήσασθαι
3 πρὸς οὐδὲν αὐτοῖς ὑπομείνειαν. κἂν ἐν ἄλλῃ
χώρᾳ που στρατευόμενοι τύχωσι, λυτρούμενοι
τοὺς αἰλούρους καὶ τοὺς ἱέρακας κατάγουσιν εἰς
Αἴγυπτον· καὶ τοῦτο πράττουσιν ἐνίοτε τῶν

Romans the appellation of "friend"[1] and the
people were exercising all zeal in courting the
favour of the embassy from Italy which was then
visiting Egypt and, in their fear, were intent upon
giving no cause for complaint or war, when one of
the Romans killed a cat and the multitude rushed
in a crowd to his house, neither the officials sent by
the king to beg the man off nor the fear of Rome
which all the people felt were enough to save the man
from punishment, even though his act had been an
accident. And this incident we relate, not from
hearsay, but we saw it with our own eyes on the
occasion of the visit we made to Egypt.

84. But if what has been said seems to many
incredible and like a fanciful tale, what is to follow
will appear far more extraordinary. Once, they
say, when the inhabitants of Egypt were being hard
pressed by a famine, many in their need laid hands
upon their fellows, yet not a single man was even
accused of having partaken of the sacred animals.
Furthermore, whenever a dog is found dead in any
house, every inmate of it shaves his entire body and
goes into mourning, and what is more astonishing
than this, if any wine or grain or any other thing
necessary to life happens to be stored in the building
where one of these animals has expired, they would
never think of using it thereafter for any purpose.
And if they happen to be making a military expedition
in another country, they ransom the captive cats
and hawks and bring them back to Egypt, and this
they do sometimes even when their supply of money

[1] On the date of this incident, cp. the Introduction, p.
viii.

4 ἐφοδίων αὐτοὺς ὑπολιπόντων. τὰ δὲ γινόμενα
περὶ τὸν Ἆπιν τὸν ἐν Μέμφει καὶ τὸν Μνεῦιν
τὸν ἐν Ἡλιουπόλει καὶ τὰ περὶ τὸν τράγον τὸν
ἐν Μένδητι, πρὸς δὲ τούτοις τὸν κροκόδειλον τὸν
κατὰ τὴν Μοίριδος λίμνην καὶ τὸν λέοντα τὸν
τρεφόμενον ἐν τῇ καλουμένῃ Λεόντων πόλει, καὶ
πολλὰ τοιαῦθ᾽ ἕτερα, διηγήσασθαι μὲν εὐχερές,
ἀπαγγείλαντα δὲ πιστευθῆναι παρὰ τοῖς μὴ
5 τεθεαμένοις δύσκολον. ταῦτα γὰρ ἐν ἱεροῖς μὲν
περιβόλοις τρέφεται, θεραπεύουσι δ᾽ αὐτὰ πολλοὶ
τῶν ἀξιολόγων ἀνδρῶν τροφὰς διδόντες τὰς
πολυτελεστάτας· σεμίδαλιν γὰρ ἢ χόνδρον
ἕψοντες ἐν γάλακτι καὶ πέμματα παντοδαπὰ
μέλιτι φυρῶντες, καὶ κρέα χήνεια τὰ μὲν ἕψοντες,
τὰ δ᾽ ὀπτῶντες ἀνεκλείπτως χορηγοῦσι, τοῖς δ᾽
ὠμοφάγοις πολλὰ τῶν ὀρνέων θηρεύοντες παρα-
βάλλουσι, καὶ τὸ καθόλου μεγάλην εἰσφέρονται
6 σπουδὴν εἰς τὴν πολυτέλειαν τῆς τροφῆς. λουτροῖς τε χλιαροῖς χρώμενοι καὶ μύροις τοῖς
κρατίστοις ἀλείφοντες καὶ παντοδαπὰς εὐωδίας
θυμιῶντες οὐ διαλείπουσι, στρωμνάς τε τὰς
πολυτελεστάτας καὶ κόσμον εὐπρεπῆ χορηγοῦσι, καὶ τῶν συνουσιῶν ὅπως τυγχάνῃ κατὰ
φύσιν φροντίδα ποιοῦνται τὴν μεγίστην, πρὸς
δὲ τούτοις ὁμοφύλους θηλείας ἑκάστῳ τῶν ζῴων
τὰς εὐειδεστάτας συντρέφουσιν, ἃς παλλακίδας
προσαγορεύουσι καὶ θεραπεύουσι ταῖς μεγίσταις
7 δαπάναις καὶ λειτουργίαις. ἐὰν δὲ τελευτήσῃ
τι,[1] πενθοῦσι μὲν ἴσα τοῖς ἀγαπητῶν τέκνων
στερομένοις, θάπτουσι δὲ οὐ κατὰ τὴν ἑαυτῶν
δύναμιν, ἀλλὰ πολὺ τὴν ἀξίαν τῆς ἑαυτῶν

---

[1] τι Dindorf: τις.

tor the journey is running short. As for the ceremonies
connected with the Apis of Memphis, the Mnevis of
Heliopolis [1] and the goat of Mendes, as well as with
the crocodile of the Lake of Moeris, the lion kept in
the City of Lions (Leontopolis), as it is called, and
many other ceremonies like them, they could easily
be described, but the writer would scarcely be believed
by any who had not actually witnessed them. For
these animals are kept in sacred enclosures and are
cared for by many men of distinction who offer them
the most expensive fare; for they provide, with
unfailing regularity, the finest wheaten flour or
wheat-groats seethed in milk, every kind of sweet-
meat made with honey, and the meat of ducks,
either boiled or baked, while for the carnivorous
animals birds are caught and thrown to them in
abundance, and, in general, great care is given that
they have an expensive fare. They are continually
bathing the animals in warm water, anointing them
with the most precious ointments, and burning before
them every kind of fragrant incense; they furnish
them with the most expensive coverlets and with
splendid jewellery, and exercise the greatest care
that they shall enjoy sexual intercourse according
to the demands of nature; furthermore, with every
animal they keep the most beautiful females of the
same genus, which they call his concubines and attend
to at the cost of heavy expense and assiduous service.
When any animal dies they mourn for it as deeply as
do those who have lost a beloved child, and bury it
in a manner not in keeping with their ability but

---

[1] The bulls Apis and Mnevis are described in the following
chapter.

8 οὐσίας ὑπερβάλλοντες. μετὰ γὰρ τὴν Ἀλεξάνδρου τελευτήν, Πτολεμαίου τοῦ Λάγου παρειληφότος ἄρτι τὴν Αἴγυπτον, ἔτυχεν ἐν Μέμφει τελευτήσας ὁ Ἆπις γήρᾳ· ὁ δὲ τὴν ἐπιμέλειαν ἔχων αὐτοῦ τήν τε ἡτοιμασμένην χορηγίαν, οὖσαν πάνυ πολλήν, εἰς ταφὴν ἅπασαν ἐδαπάνησε καὶ παρὰ τοῦ Πτολεμαίου πεντήκοντα ἀργυρίου τάλαντα προσεδανείσατο. καὶ καθ᾽ ἡμᾶς δέ τινες τῶν τὰ ζῷα ταῦτα τρεφόντων εἰς τὰς ταφὰς αὐτῶν οὐκ ἔλαττον τῶν ἑκατὸν ταλάντων δεδαπανήκασιν.

85. Προσθετέον δὲ τοῖς εἰρημένοις τὰ λειπόμενα τῶν γινομένων περὶ τὸν ἱερὸν ταῦρον τὸν ὀνομαζόμενον Ἆπιν. ὅταν γὰρ τελευτήσας ταφῇ μεγαλοπρεπῶς, ζητοῦσιν οἱ περὶ ταῦτ᾽ ὄντες ἱερεῖς μόσχον ἔχοντα κατὰ τὸ σῶμα παράσημα

2 τὰ παραπλήσια τῷ προϋπάρξαντι· ὅταν δ᾽ εὑρεθῇ, τὰ μὲν πλήθη τοῦ πένθους ἀπολύεται, τῶν δ᾽ ἱερέων οἷς ἐστιν ἐπιμελὲς ἄγουσι τὸν μόσχον τὸ μὲν πρῶτον εἰς Νείλου πόλιν, ἐν ᾗ τρέφουσιν αὐτὸν ἐφ᾽ ἡμέρας τετταράκοντα, ἔπειτ᾽ εἰς θαλαμηγὸν ναῦν οἴκημα κεχρυσωμένον ἔχουσαν ἐμβιβάσαντες ὡς θεὸν ἀνάγουσιν εἰς

3 Μέμφιν εἰς τὸ τοῦ Ἡφαίστου τέμενος. ἐν δὲ ταῖς προειρημέναις τετταράκονθ᾽ ἡμέραις μόνον ὁρῶσιν αὐτὸν αἱ γυναῖκες κατὰ πρόσωπον ἱστάμεναι καὶ δεικνύουσιν ἀνασυράμεναι τὰ ἑαυτῶν γεννητικὰ μόρια, τὸν δ᾽ ἄλλον χρόνον ἅπαντα κεκωλυμένον ἐστὶν εἰς ὄψιν αὐτὰς ἔρχεσθαι

4 τούτῳ τῷ θεῷ. τῆς δὲ τοῦ βοὸς τούτου τιμῆς αἰτίαν ἔνιοι φέρουσι λέγοντες ὅτι τελευτήσαντος Ὀσίριδος εἰς τοῦτον ἡ ψυχὴ μετέστη, καὶ διὰ

going far beyond the value of their estates. For instance, after the death of Alexander and just subsequently to the taking over of Egypt by Ptolemy the son of Lagus, it happened that the Apis in Memphis died of old age; and the man who was charged with the care of him spent on his burial not only the whole of the very large sum which had been provided for the animal's maintenance, but also borrowed in addition fifty talents[1] of silver from Ptolemy. And even in our own day some of the keepers of these animals have spent on their burial not less than one hundred talents.

85. There should be added to what has been said what still remains to be told concerning the ceremonies connected with the sacred bull called Apis. After he has died and has received a magnificent burial, the priests who are charged with this duty seek out a young bull which has on its body markings similar to those of its predecessor; and when it has been found the people cease their mourning and the priests who have the care of it first take the young bull to Nilopolis, where it is kept forty days, and then, putting it on a state barge fitted out with a gilded cabin, conduct it as a god to the sanctuary of Hephaestus at Memphis. During these forty days only women may look at it; these stand facing it and pulling up their garments show their genitals, but henceforth they are forever prevented from coming into the presence of this god. Some explain the origin of the honour accorded this bull in this way, saying that at the death of Osiris his soul passed into this

---

[1] The intrinsic value of a talent was about one thousand dollars or two hundred and fifty pounds sterling.

ταῦτα διατελεῖ μέχρι τοῦ νῦν ἀεὶ κατὰ τὰς
ἀναδείξεις αὐτοῦ μεθισταμένη πρὸς τοὺς μετα-
5 γενεστέρους· ἔνιοι δὲ λέγουσι τελευτήσαντος
'Οσίριδος ὑπὸ Τυφῶνος τὰ μέλη συναγαγοῦσαν
τὴν 'Ισιν εἰς βοῦν ξυλίνην ἐμβαλεῖν βύσσινα
περιβεβλημένην, καὶ διὰ τοῦτο καὶ τὴν πόλιν
ὀνομασθῆναι Βούσιριν. πολλὰ δὲ καὶ ἄλλα
μυθολογοῦσι περὶ τοῦ Ἄπιδος, ὑπὲρ ὧν μακρὸν
ἡγούμεθα τὰ¹ καθ' ἕκαστον διεξιέναι.

86. Πάντα δὲ θαυμάσια καὶ μείζω πίστεως
ἐπιτελοῦντες οἱ κατ' Αἴγυπτον εἰς τὰ τιμώμενα
ζῷα πολλὴν ἀπορίαν παρέχονται τοῖς τὰς αἰτίας
2 τούτων ζητοῦσιν. οἱ μὲν οὖν ἱερεῖς αὐτῶν ἀπόρ-
ρητόν τι δόγμα περὶ τούτων ἔχουσιν, ὃ προειρή-
καμεν ἐν τοῖς θεολογουμένοις ὑπ' αὐτῶν, οἱ δὲ
πολλοὶ τῶν Αἰγυπτίων τρεῖς αἰτίας ταύτας ἀπο-
διδόασιν, ὧν τὴν μὲν πρώτην μυθώδη παντελῶς
3 καὶ τῆς ἀρχαϊκῆς ἁπλότητος οἰκείαν. φασὶ γὰρ
τοὺς ἐξ ἀρχῆς γενομένους θεούς, ὀλίγους ὄντας
καὶ κατισχυομένους ὑπὸ τοῦ πλήθους καὶ τῆς
ἀνομίας τῶν γηγενῶν ἀνθρώπων, ὁμοιωθῆναί τισι
ζῴοις, καὶ διὰ τοῦ τοιούτου τρόπου διαφυγεῖν τὴν
ὠμότητα καὶ βίαν αὐτῶν· ὕστερον δὲ τῶν κατὰ
τὸν κόσμον πάντων κρατήσαντας, καὶ τοῖς αἰτίοις
τῆς ἐξ ἀρχῆς σωτηρίας χάριν ἀποδιδόντας, ἀφιε-

¹ τὰ Hertlein : τό.

---

[1] The Apis Bull was considered the "living soul of Osiris"
and, according to Plutarch (*On Isis and Osiris*, 43), was
begotten, not by a bull, but by a "generative ray of light,
which streamed from the moon and rested upon a cow when
she was in heat." Apis was a black bull with a white blaze

animal, and therefore up to this day has always passed
into its successors at the times of the manifestation
of Osiris; [1] but some say that when Osiris died at
the hands of Typhon Isis collected the members of
his body and put them in an ox (*bous*), made of wood
covered over with fine linen, and because of this
the city was called Bousiris. Many other stories
are told about the Apis, but we feel that it would
be a long task to recount all the details regarding
them.

86. Since all the practices of the Egyptians in
their worship of animals are astonishing and beyond
belief, they occasion much difficulty for those who
would seek out their origins and causes. Now their
priests have on this subject a teaching which may not
be divulged, as we have already stated in connection
with their accounts of the gods,[2] but the majority of
the Egyptians give the following three causes, the
first of which belongs entirely to the realm of fable
and is in keeping with the simplicity of primitive
times. They say, namely, that the gods who came
into existence in the beginning, being few in number
and overpowered by the multitude and the lawlessness of earth-born men,[3] took on the forms of certain
animals, and in this way saved themselves from the
savagery and violence of mankind; but afterwards,
when they had established their power over all things
in the universe, out of gratitude to the animals which
had been responsible for their salvation at the outset,

upon his forehead; the appearance of a new Apis Bull was
regarded as a new manifestation of Osiris upon earth (cp.
E. A. W. Budge, *Osiris and the Egyptian Resurrection*, 1. pp.
60, 397 ff.).
    [2] In chap. 21.   [3] *i.e.* the Giants.

ρῶσαι τὰς φύσεις αὐτῶν οἷς ἀφωμοιώθησαν, καὶ
καταδεῖξαι τοῖς ἀνθρώποις τὸ τρέφειν μὲν ζῶντα
πολυτελῶς, θάπτειν δὲ τελευτήσαντα.

4 Δευτέραν δὲ λέγουσιν αἰτίαν, ὅτι τὸ παλαιὸν
οἱ κατ᾽ Αἴγυπτον διὰ τὴν ἀταξίαν τὴν ἐν τῷ
στρατοπέδῳ πολλαῖς μάχαις ὑπὸ τῶν πλησιοχώρων ἡττηθέντες ἐπενόησαν σύνθημα φορεῖν
5 ἐπὶ τῶν ταγμάτων. φασὶν οὖν κατασκευάσαντας
εἰκόνας τῶν ζῴων ἃ νῦν τιμῶσι, καὶ πήξαντας
ἐπὶ σαυνίων, φορεῖν τοὺς ἡγεμόνας, καὶ διὰ
τούτου τοῦ τρόπου γνωρίζειν ἕκαστον ἧς εἴη
συντάξεως· μεγάλα δὲ συμβαλλομένης αὐτοῖς
τῆς διὰ τούτων εὐταξίας πρὸς τὴν νίκην, δόξαι
τῆς σωτηρίας αἴτια γεγονέναι τὰ ζῷα· χάριν οὖν
αὐτοῖς τοὺς ἀνθρώπους ἀποδοῦναι βουλομένους
εἰς ἔθος κατατάξαι τῶν εἰκασθέντων τότε μηδὲν
κτείνειν, ἀλλὰ σεβομένους ἀπονέμειν τὴν προειρημένην ἐπιμέλειαν καὶ τιμήν.

87. Τρίτην δ᾽ αἰτίαν φέρουσι τῆς ἀμφισβητή-
σεως τῶν ζῴων τὴν χρείαν, ἣν ἕκαστον αὐτῶν
προσφέρεται πρὸς τὴν ὠφέλειαν τοῦ κοινοῦ βίου
2 καὶ τῶν ἀνθρώπων. τὴν μὲν γὰρ θήλειαν βοῦν
ἐργάτας τίκτειν καὶ τὴν ἐλαφρὰν τῆς γῆς ἀροῦν,
τὰ δὲ πρόβατα δὶς μὲν τίκτειν καὶ τοῖς ἐρίοις
τὴν σκέπην ἅμα καὶ τὴν εὐσχημοσύνην περι-
ποιεῖν, τῷ δὲ γάλακτι καὶ τῷ τυρῷ τροφὰς
παρέχεσθαι προσηνεῖς ἅμα καὶ δαψιλεῖς. τὸν
δὲ κύνα πρός τε τὰς θήρας εἶναι χρήσιμον καὶ
πρὸς τὴν φυλακήν· διόπερ τὸν θεὸν τὸν παρ᾽
αὐτοῖς καλούμενον Ἄνουβιν παρεισάγουσι κυνὸς
ἔχοντα κεφαλήν, ἐμφαίνοντες ὅτι σωματοφύλαξ

they made sacred those kinds whose form they had assumed, and instructed mankind to maintain them in a costly fashion while living and to bury them at death.

The second cause which they give is this—that the early Egyptians, after having been defeated by their neighbours in many battles because of the lack of order in their army, conceived the idea of carrying standards before the several divisions. Consequently, they say, the commanders fashioned figures of the animals which they now worship and carried them fixed on lances, and by this device every man knew where his place was in the array. And since the good order resulting therefrom greatly contributed to victory, they thought that the animals had been responsible for their deliverance; and so the people, wishing to show their gratitude to them, established the custom of not killing any one of the animals whose likeness had been fashioned at that time, but of rendering to them, as objects of worship, the care and honour which we have previously described.

87. The third cause which they adduce in connection with the dispute in question is the service which each one of these animals renders for the benefit of community life and of mankind. The cow, for example, bears workers [1] and ploughs the lighter soil; the sheep lamb twice in the year and provide by their wool both protection for the body and its decorous covering, while by their milk and cheese they furnish food that is both appetizing and abundant. Again, the dog is useful both for the hunt and for man's protection, and this is why they represent the god whom they call Anubis with a dog's head, showing

[1] *i.e.* oxen.

DIODORUS OF SICILY

3 ἦν τῶν περὶ τὸν Ὄσιριν καὶ τὴν Ἶσιν. ἔνιοι δέ
φασι τῆς Ἴσιδος προηγουμένους τοὺς κύνας καθ'
ὃν καιρὸν ἐζήτει τὸν Ὄσιριν, τά τε θηρία καὶ
τοὺς ἀπαντῶντας ἀπείργειν, ἔτι δ' εὐνοϊκῶς
διακειμένους συζητεῖν ὠρυομένους· διὸ καὶ τοῖς
Ἰσείοις προπορεύεσθαι τοὺς κύνας κατὰ τὴν
πομπήν, τῶν καταδειξάντων τοῦτο τὸ νόμιμον
4 σημαινόντων τὴν παλαιὰν τοῦ ζῴου χάριν. καὶ
τὸν μὲν αἴλουρον πρός τε τὰς ἀσπίδας θανάσιμα
δακνούσας εὔθετον ὑπάρχειν καὶ τἄλλα δάκετα
τῶν ἑρπετῶν, τὸν δ' ἰχνεύμονα τῶν κροκοδείλων
παρατηροῦντα τοὺς γόνους τὰ καταληφθέντα τῶν
ᾠῶν συντρίβειν, καὶ ταῦτ' ἐπιμελῶς καὶ φιλο-
5 τίμως ἐνεργεῖν μηδὲν ὠφελούμενον. τοῦτο δ' εἰ
μὴ συνέβαινε γίνεσθαι, διὰ τὸ πλῆθος τῶν γεν-
νωμένων θηρίων ἄβατον ἂν γενέσθαι τὸν ποταμόν.
ἀπόλλυσθαι δὲ καὶ τοὺς κροκοδείλους αὐτοὺς
ὑπὸ τοῦ προειρημένου ζῴου παραδόξως καὶ
παντελῶς ἀπιστουμένῃ μεθόδῳ· τοὺς γὰρ ἰχνεύμονας κυλιομένους ἐν τῷ πηλῷ χασκόντων αὐτῶν
καθ' ὃν ἂν χρόνον ἐπὶ τῆς χέρσου καθεύδωσιν
εἰσπηδᾶν διὰ τοῦ στόματος εἰς μέσον τὸ σῶμα·
ἔπειτα συντόμως τὴν κοιλίαν διαφαγόντας αὐτοὺς
μὲν ἀκινδύνως ἐξιέναι, τοὺς δὲ τοῦτο παθόντας
6 νεκροὺς ποιεῖν παραχρῆμα. τῶν δ' ὀρνέων τὴν
μὲν ἶβιν χρησίμην ὑπάρχειν πρός τε τοὺς ὄφεις
καὶ τὰς ἀκρίδας καὶ τὰς κάμπας, τὸν δ' ἱέρακα
πρὸς τοὺς σκορπίους καὶ κεράστας καὶ τὰ μικρὰ
τῶν δακέτων θηρίων τὰ μάλιστα τοὺς ἀνθρώ-
7 πους ἀναιροῦντα. ἔνιοι δὲ λέγουσι τιμᾶσθαι τὸ
ζῷον τοῦτο διὰ τὸ τοὺς μάντεις οἰωνοῖς τοῖς
ἱέραξι χρωμένους προλέγειν τὰ μέλλοντα τοῖς
296

in this way that he was the bodyguard of Osiris
and Isis. There are some, however, who explain
that dogs guided Isis during her search for Osiris and
protected her from wild beasts and wayfarers, and
that they helped her in her search, because of the
affection they bore for her, by baying; and this is the
reason why at the Festival of Isis the procession is
led by dogs, those who introduced the rite showing
forth in this way the kindly service rendered by this
animal of old. The cat is likewise useful against
asps with their deadly bite and the other reptiles that
sting, while the ichneumon keeps a look-out for the
newly-laid seed of the crocodile and crushes the eggs
left by the female, doing this carefully and zealously
even though it receives no benefit from the act.
Were this not done, the river would have become
impassable because of the multitude of beasts that
would be born. And the crocodiles themselves are
also killed by this animal in an astonishing and quite
incredible manner; for the ichneumons roll themselves over and over in the mud, and when the
crocodiles go to sleep on the land with their mouths
open they jump down their mouths into the centre
of their body; then, rapidly gnawing through the
bowels, they get out unscathed themselves and at
the same time kill their victims instantly.[1] And of
the sacred birds the ibis is useful as a protector against
the snakes, the locusts, and the caterpillars, and
the hawk against the scorpions, horned serpents, and
the small animals of noxious bite which cause the
greatest destruction of men. But some maintain
that the hawk is honoured because it is used as a
bird of omen by the soothsayers in predicting to the

---

[1] Strabo (17. 1. 39) gives much the same account.

8 Αἰγυπτίοις. τινὲς δέ φασιν ἐν τοῖς ἀρχαίοις
χρόνοις ἱέρακα βιβλίον ἐνεγκεῖν εἰς Θήβας τοῖς
ἱερεῦσι φοινικῷ ῥάμματι περιειλημένον, ἔχον
γεγραμμένας τὰς τῶν θεῶν θεραπείας τε καὶ
τιμάς· διὸ [1] καὶ τοὺς ἱερογραμματεῖς φορεῖν
φοινικοῦν ῥάμμα καὶ πτερὸν ἱέρακος ἐπὶ τῆς
9 κεφαλῆς. τὸν δ' ἀετὸν Θηβαῖοι τιμῶσι διὰ τὸ
βασιλικὸν εἶναι δοκεῖν τοῦτο τὸ ζῷον καὶ τοῦ
Διὸς ἄξιον.

88. Τὸν δὲ τράγον ἀπεθέωσαν, καθάπερ καὶ
παρὰ τοῖς Ἕλλησι τετιμῆσθαι λέγουσι τὸν
Πρίαπον, διὰ τὸ γεννητικὸν μόριον· τὸ μὲν
γὰρ ζῷον εἶναι τοῦτο κατωφερέστατον πρὸς τὰς
συνουσίας, τὸ δὲ μόριον τοῦ σώματος τὸ τῆς
γενέσεως αἴτιον τιμᾶσθαι προσηκόντως, ὡς ἂν
ὑπάρχον ἀρχέγονον τῆς τῶν ζῴων φύσεως.
2 καθόλου δὲ τὸ αἰδοῖον οὐκ Αἰγυπτίους μόνον,
ἀλλὰ καὶ τῶν ἄλλων οὐκ ὀλίγους καθιερωκέναι
κατὰ τὰς τελετάς, ὡς αἴτιον τῆς τῶν ζῴων
γενέσεως· τούς τε ἱερεῖς τοὺς παραλαβόντας τὰς
πατρικὰς ἱερωσύνας κατ' Αἴγυπτον τούτῳ τῷ
3 θεῷ πρῶτον μυεῖσθαι. καὶ τοὺς Πᾶνας δὲ καὶ
τοὺς Σατύρους φασὶν ἕνεκα τῆς αὐτῆς αἰτίας
τιμᾶσθαι παρ' ἀνθρώποις· διὸ καὶ τὰς εἰκόνας
αὐτῶν ἀνατιθέναι τοὺς πλείστους ἐν τοῖς ἱεροῖς
ἐντεταμένας καὶ τῇ τοῦ τράγου φύσει παρα-
πλησίας· τὸ γὰρ ζῷον τοῦτο παραδεδόσθαι πρὸς
τὰς συνουσίας ὑπάρχειν ἐνεργέστατον· ἐκείνοις [2]
οὖν διὰ ταύτης τῆς ἐμφάσεως χάριν ἀποδιδόναι
περὶ τῆς πολυτεκνίας τῆς ἑαυτῶν.

[1] διὸ Vogel: διόπερ Vulgate, Bekker, Dindorf.
[2] ἐκείνοις Bekker, Vogel: ἐκείνους Vulgate, Dindorf.

298

Egyptians events which are to come. Others, however, say that in primitive times a hawk brought to the priests in Thebes a book wrapped about with a purple band, which contained written directions concerning the worship of the gods and the honours due to them; and it is for this reason, they add, that the sacred scribes wear on their heads a purple band and the wing of a hawk. The eagle also is honoured by the Thebans because it is believed to be a royal animal and worthy of Zeus.

88. They have deified the goat, just as the Greeks are said to have honoured Priapus,[1] because of the generative member; for this animal has a very great propensity for copulation, and it is fitting that honour be shown to that member of the body which is the cause of generation, being, as it were, the primal author of all animal life. And, in general, not only the Egyptians but not a few other peoples as well have in the rites they observe treated the male member as sacred, on the ground that it is the cause of the generation of all creatures; and the priests in Egypt who have inherited their priestly offices from their fathers are initiated first into the mysteries of this god. And both the Pans and the Satyrs, they say, are worshipped by men for the same reason; and this is why most peoples set up in their sacred places statues of them showing the phallus erect and resembling a goat's in nature, since according to tradition this animal is most efficient in copulation; consequently, by representing these creatures in such fashion, the dedicants are returning thanks to them for their own numerous offspring.

---

[1] Priapus is discussed in Book 4. 6.

4 Τοὺς δὲ ταύρους τοὺς ἱερούς, λέγω δὲ τόν τε
᾿Απιν καὶ τὸν Μνεῦιν, τιμᾶσθαι παραπλησίως
τοῖς θεοῖς, ᾿Οσίριδος καταδείξαντος, ἅμα μὲν διὰ
τὴν τῆς γεωργίας χρείαν, ἅμα δὲ καὶ διὰ τὸ τῶν
εὑρόντων τοὺς καρποὺς τὴν δόξαν ταῖς τούτων
ἐργασίαις παραδόσιμον γεγονέναι τοῖς μετα-
γενεστέροις εἰς ἅπαντα τὸν αἰῶνα. τοὺς δὲ
πυρροὺς βοῦς συγχωρηθῆναι θύειν διὰ τὸ δοκεῖν
τοιοῦτον τῷ χρώματι γεγονέναι Τυφῶνα τὸν
ἐπιβουλεύσαντα μὲν ᾿Οσίριδι, τυχόντα δὲ τιμω-
5 ρίας ὑπὸ τῆς ῎Ισιδος διὰ τὸν τἀνδρὸς φόνον. καὶ
τῶν ἀνθρώπων δὲ τοὺς ὁμοχρωμάτους τῷ Τυφῶνι
τὸ παλαιὸν ὑπὸ τῶν βασιλέων φασὶ θύεσθαι
πρὸς τῷ τάφῳ τῷ[1] ᾿Οσίριδος· τῶν μὲν οὖν
Αἰγυπτίων ὀλίγους τινὰς εὑρίσκεσθαι πυρρούς,
τῶν δὲ ξένων τοὺς πλείους· διὸ καὶ περὶ τῆς
Βουσίριδος ξενοκτονίας παρὰ τοῖς ῞Ελλησιν
ἐνισχῦσαι τὸν μῦθον, οὐ τοῦ βασιλέως ὀνομαζο-
μένου Βουσίριδος, ἀλλὰ τοῦ ᾿Οσίριδος τάφου
ταύτην ἔχοντος τὴν προσηγορίαν κατὰ τὴν τῶν
ἐγχωρίων διάλεκτον.

6 Τοὺς δὲ λύκους τιμᾶσθαι λέγουσι διὰ τὴν
πρὸς τοὺς κύνας τῆς φύσεως ὁμοιότητα· βραχὺ
γὰρ διαλάττοντας αὐτοὺς ταῖς φύσεσι ταῖς ἐπι-
μιξίαις ζωογονεῖν ἐξ ἀλλήλων. φέρουσι δ᾿
Αἰγύπτιοι καὶ ἄλλην αἰτίαν τῆς τοῦ ζῴου
τούτου τιμῆς μυθικωτέραν· τὸ γὰρ παλαιόν φασι
τῆς ῎Ισιδος μετὰ τοῦ παιδὸς ῟Ωρου μελλούσης

---

[1] τῷ Vogel: τοῦ B, Bekker, Dindorf.

The sacred bulls—I refer to the Apis and the
Mnevis—are honoured like the gods, as Osiris commanded, both because of their use in farming and
also because the fame of those who discovered the
fruits of the earth is handed down by the labours of
these animals to succeeding generations for all time.
Red oxen, however, may be sacrificed, because it
is thought that this was the colour of Typhon, who
plotted against Osiris and was then punished by Isis
for the death of her husband. Men also, if they
were of the same colour as Typhon, were sacrificed,
they say, in ancient times by the kings at the tomb
of Osiris; however, only a few Egyptians are now
found red in colour, but the majority of such are
non-Egyptians, and this is why the story spread
among the Greeks of the slaying of foreigners by
Busiris, although Busiris was not the name of the
king but of the tomb of Osiris, which is called that
in the language of the land.[1]

The wolves are honoured, they say, because their
nature is so much like that of dogs, for the natures
of these two animals are little different from each
other and hence offspring is produced by their inter-
breeding. But the Egyptians offer another explanation for the honour accorded this animal, although
it pertains more to the realm of myth; for they
say that in early times when Isis, aided by her son

---

[1] Herodotus (2. 45) denies the existence of human sacrifices
and there was probably none in his day. But the sacrifice of
captives is attested by the monuments of the Eighteenth and
Nineteenth Dynasties, and J. G. Frazer (*The Golden Bough*, 2.
pp. 254 ff.) finds in this account of Diodorus and a similar story
given by Plutarch (*On Isis and Osiris*, 73), on the authority of
Manetho, evidence for the annual sacrifice of a red-haired man
to prevent the failure of the crops.

διαγωνίζεσθαι πρὸς Τυφῶνα παραγενέσθαι βοη-
θὸν ἐξ ᾅδου τὸν Ὄσιριν τῷ τέκνῳ καὶ τῇ γυναικὶ
λύκῳ τὴν ὄψιν ὁμοιωθέντα· ἀναιρεθέντος οὖν
τοῦ Τυφῶνος τοὺς κρατήσαντας καταδεῖξαι τιμᾶν τὸ ζῷον οὗ τῆς ὄψεως ἐπιφανείσης τὸ νικᾶν
7 ἐπηκολούθησεν. ἔνιοι δὲ λέγουσι, τῶν Αἰθιόπων
στρατευσάντων ἐπὶ τὴν Αἴγυπτον, ἀθροισθείσας
παμπληθεῖς ἀγέλας λύκων ἐκδιῶξαι τοὺς ἐπελ-
θόντας ἐκ τῆς χώρας ὑπὲρ πόλιν τὴν ὀνομαζομένην Ἐλεφαντίνην· διὸ καὶ τόν τε νομὸν
ἐκεῖνον Λυκοπολίτην ὀνομασθῆναι καὶ τὰ ζῷα
τὰ προειρημένα τυχεῖν τῆς τιμῆς.

89. Λείπεται δ᾿ ἡμῖν εἰπεῖν περὶ τῆς τῶν κροκοδείλων ἀποθεώσεως, ὑπὲρ ἧς οἱ πλεῖστοι
διαποροῦσι πῶς τῶν θηρίων τούτων σαρκοφα-
γούντων τοὺς ἀνθρώπους ἐνομοθετήθη τιμᾶν ἴσα
2 θεοῖς τοὺς τὰ δεινότατα διατιθέντας. φασὶν οὖν
τῆς χώρας τὴν ὀχυρότητα παρέχεσθαι μὴ μόνον
τὸν ποταμόν, ἀλλὰ καὶ πολὺ μᾶλλον τοὺς ἐν
αὐτῷ κροκοδείλους· διὸ καὶ τοὺς λῃστὰς τούς τε[1]
ἀπὸ τῆς Ἀραβίας καὶ Λιβύης μὴ τολμᾶν
διανήχεσθαι τὸν Νεῖλον, φοβουμένους τὸ πλῆθος
τῶν θηρίων· τοῦτο δ᾿ οὐκ ἄν ποτε γενέσθαι πολε-
μουμένων τῶν ζῴων καὶ διὰ τῶν σαγηνευόντων
3 ἄρδην ἀναιρεθέντων. ἔστι δὲ καὶ ἄλλος λόγος
ἱστορούμενος περὶ τῶν θηρίων τούτων. φασὶ
γάρ τινες τῶν ἀρχαίων τινὰ βασιλέων, τὸν προσαγορευόμενον Μηνᾶν, διωκόμενον ὑπὸ τῶν ἰδίων
κυνῶν καταφυγεῖν εἰς τὴν Μοίριδος καλουμένην
λίμνην, ἔπειθ᾿ ὑπὸ κροκοδείλου παραδόξως ἀνα-

---

[1] τε deleted by Wesseling and all subsequent editors;
retained by Vogel.

Horus, was about to commence her struggle with Typhon, Osiris came from Hades to help his son and his wife, having taken on the guise of a wolf; and so, upon the death of Typhon, his conquerors commanded men to honour the animal upon whose appearance victory followed. But some say that once, when the Ethiopians had marched against Egypt, a great number of bands of wolves (*lykoi*) gathered together and drove the invaders out of the country, pursuing them beyond the city named Elephantine; and therefore that nome was given the name Lycopolite[1] and these animals were granted the honour in question.

89. It remains for us to speak of the deification of crocodiles, a subject regarding which most men are entirely at a loss to explain how, when these beasts eat the flesh of men, it ever became the law to honour like the gods creatures of the most revolting habits. Their reply is, that the security of the country is ensured, not only by the river, but to a much greater degree by the crocodiles in it; that for this reason the robbers that infest both Arabia and Libya do not dare to swim across the Nile, because they fear the beasts, whose number is very great; and that this would never have been the case if war were continually being waged against the animals and they had been utterly destroyed by hunters dragging the river with nets. But still another account is given of these beasts. For some say that once one of the early kings whose name was Menas, being pursued by his own dogs, came in his flight to the Lake of Moeris, as it is called, where, strange as it may seem, a crocodile took him on his

---

[1] *i.e.* "of the City of the Wolves."

ληφθέντα εἰς τὸ πέραν ἀπενεχθῆναι. τῆς δὲ
σωτηρίας χάριν ἀποδιδόναι βουλόμενον τῷ ζῴῳ
πόλιν κτίσαι πλησίον ὀνομάσαντα Κροκοδείλων·
καταδεῖξαι δὲ καὶ τοῖς ἐγχωρίοις ὡς θεοὺς τιμᾶν
ταῦτα τὰ ζῷα καὶ τὴν λίμνην αὐτοῖς εἰς τροφὴν
ἀναθεῖναι· ἐνταῦθα δὲ καὶ τὸν τάφον ἑαυτῷ
κατασκευάσαι πυραμίδα τετράπλευρον ἐπιστή-
σαντα, καὶ τὸν θαυμαζόμενον παρὰ πολλοῖς
λαβύρινθον οἰκοδομῆσαι.

4 Παραπλήσια δὲ καὶ περὶ τῶν ἄλλων λέγουσιν,
ὑπὲρ ὧν τὰ καθ' ἕκαστον μακρὸν ἂν εἴη γράφειν.
ὅτι γὰρ τῆς ὠφελείας ἕνεκα τῆς εἰς τὸν βίον
οὕτως ἑαυτοὺς εἰθίκασι, φανερὸν εἶναι πᾶσιν [1] ἐκ
τοῦ πολλὰ τῶν ἐδωδίμων παρ' αὐτοῖς ἐνίους μὴ
προσφέρεσθαι. τινὰς μὲν γὰρ φακῶν, τινὰς δὲ
κυάμων, ἐνίους δὲ τυρῶν ἢ κρομμύων ἤ τινων
ἄλλων βρωμάτων τὸ παράπαν μὴ γεύεσθαι,
πολλῶν ὑπαρχόντων κατὰ τὴν Αἴγυπτον, δῆλον
ποιοῦντας διότι διδακτέον ἐστὶν ἑαυτοὺς [2] τῶν
χρησίμων ἀπέχεσθαι, καὶ διότι πάντων πάντα
ἐσθιόντων οὐδὲν ἂν ἐξήρκεσε τῶν ἀναλισκο-
5 μένων. καὶ ἑτέρας δ' αἰτίας φέροντές τινές φασιν
ἐπὶ τῶν παλαιῶν βασιλέων πολλάκις ἀφιστα-
μένου τοῦ πλήθους καὶ συμφρονοῦντος κατὰ τῶν
ἡγουμένων, τῶν βασιλέων τινὰ συνέσει διαφέροντα διελέσθαι μὲν τὴν χώραν εἰς πλείω
μέρη, καθ' ἕκαστον δ' αὐτῶν καταδεῖξαι τοῖς
ἐγχωρίοις σέβεσθαί τι ζῷον ἢ τροφῆς τινος μὴ
γεύεσθαι, ὅπως ἑκάστων τὸ μὲν παρ' αὐτοῖς

---

[1] πᾶσιν Vogel : φασὶν Vulgate, Bekker, Dindorf.
[2] ἑαυτοὺς Vogel : αὐτοὺς Vulgate, Bekker, Dindorf.

---

[1] In chap. 61 the builder of the Labyrinth is Mendes.

back and carried him to the other side. Wishing to show his gratitude to the beast for saving him, he founded a city near the place and named it City of the Crocodiles; and he commanded the natives of the region to worship these animals as gods and dedicated the lake to them for their sustenance; and in that place he also constructed his own tomb, erecting a pyramid with four sides, and built the Labyrinth which is admired by many.[1]

A similar diversity of customs exists, according to their accounts, with regard to everything else, but it would be a long task to set forth the details concerning them.[2] That they have adopted these customs for themselves because of the advantage accruing therefrom to their life is clear to all from the fact that there are those among them who will not touch many particular kinds of food. Some, for instance, abstain entirely from lentils, others from beans, and some from cheese or onions or certain other foods, there being many kinds of food in Egypt, showing in this way that men must be taught to deny themselves things that are useful, and that if all ate of everything the supply of no article of consumption would hold out. But some adduce other causes and say that, since under the early kings the multitude were often revolting and conspiring against their rulers, one of the kings who was especially wise divided the land into a number of parts and commanded the inhabitants of each to revere a certain animal or else not to eat a certain food, his thought being that, with each group of

[2] Herodotus (2. 35) sums up this matter by saying that the Egyptians "have made themselves customs and laws contrary to those of all other men."

τιμώμενον σεβομένων, τῶν δὲ παρὰ τοῖς ἄλλοις
ἀφιερωμένων καταφρονούντων, μηδέποτε ὁμονοῆ-
6 σαι δύνωνται πάντες οἱ κατ' Αἴγυπτον. καὶ
τοῦτο ἐκ τῶν ἀποτελεσμάτων φανερὸν εἶναι·
πάντας γὰρ τοὺς πλησιοχώρους πρὸς ἀλλήλους
διαφέρεσθαι, προσκόπτοντας ταῖς εἰς τὰ προειρημένα παρανομίαις.

90. Φέρουσι δὲ καί τινες τοιαύτην αἰτίαν τῆς
τῶν ζῴων ἀφιερώσεως. συναγομένων γὰρ ἐν
ἀρχῇ τῶν ἀνθρώπων ἐκ τοῦ θηριώδους βίου, τὸ
μὲν πρῶτον ἀλλήλους κατεσθίειν καὶ πολεμεῖν,
ἀεὶ τοῦ πλέον δυναμένου τὸν ἀσθενέστερον κατι-
σχύοντος· μετὰ δὲ ταῦτα τοὺς τῇ ῥώμῃ λειπομένους ὑπὸ τοῦ συμφέροντος διδαχθέντας ἀθροί-
ζεσθαι καὶ ποιῆσαι σημεῖον ἑαυτοῖς ἐκ τῶν
ὕστερον καθιερωθέντων ζῴων· πρὸς δὲ τοῦτο τὸ
σημεῖον τῶν ἀεὶ δεδιότων συντρεχόντων, οὐκ
εὐκαταφρόνητον τοῖς ἐπιτιθεμένοις γίνεσθαι τὸ
2 σύστημα· τὸ δ' αὐτὸ καὶ τῶν ἄλλων ποιούντων
διαστῆναι μὲν τὰ πλήθη κατὰ συστήματα, τὸ δὲ
ζῷον τὸ τῆς ἀσφαλείας ἑκάστοις γενόμενον αἴτιον
τιμῶν τυχεῖν ἰσοθέων, ὡς τὰ μέγιστ' εὐηργετηκός·
διόπερ ἄχρι τῶν νῦν χρόνων τὰ τῶν Αἰγυπτίων
ἔθνη διεστηκότα τιμᾶν τὰ παρ' ἑαυτοῖς ἐξ ἀρχῆς
τῶν ζῴων καθιερωθέντα.

Καθόλου δέ φασι τοὺς Αἰγυπτίους ὑπὲρ τοὺς
ἄλλους ἀνθρώπους εὐχαρίστως διακεῖσθαι πρὸς
πᾶν τὸ εὐεργετοῦν, νομίζοντας μεγίστην ἐπι-
κουρίαν εἶναι τῷ βίῳ τὴν ἀμοιβὴν τῆς πρὸς τοὺς
εὐεργέτας χάριτος· δῆλον γὰρ εἶναι διότι πάντες

people revering what was honoured among themselves but despising what was sacred to all the rest, all the inhabitants of Egypt would never be able to be of one mind. And this purpose, they declare, is clear from the results; for every group of people is at odds with its neighbours, being offended at their violations of the customs mentioned above.

90. Some advance some such reason as the following for their deification of the animals. When men, they say, first ceased living like the beasts and gathered into groups, at the outset they kept devouring each other and warring among themselves, the more powerful ever prevailing over the weaker; but later those who were deficient in strength, taught by expediency, grouped together and took for the device upon their standard one of the animals which was later made sacred; then, when those who were from time to time in fear flocked to this symbol, an organized body was formed which was not to be despised by any who attacked it. And when everybody else did the same thing, the whole people came to be divided into organized bodies, and in the case of each the animal which had been responsible for its safety was accorded honours like those belonging to the gods, as having rendered to them the greatest service possible; and this is why to this day the several groups of the Egyptians differ from each other in that each group honours the animals which it originally made sacred.

In general, they say, the Egyptians surpass all other peoples in showing gratitude for every benefaction, since they hold that the return of gratitude to benefactors is a very great resource in life; for it is clear that all men will want to bestow their

πρὸς εὐεργεσίαν ὁρμήσουσι τούτων μάλιστα παρ'
οἷς ἂν ὁρῶσι κάλλιστα θησαυρισθησομένας τὰς
3 χάριτας. διὰ δὲ τὰς αὐτὰς αἰτίας δοκοῦσιν
Αἰγύπτιοι τοὺς ἑαυτῶν βασιλεῖς προσκυνεῖν τε
καὶ τιμᾶν ὡς πρὸς ἀλήθειαν ὄντας θεούς, ἅμα
μὲν οὐκ ἄνευ δαιμονίου τινὸς προνοίας νομίζοντες
αὐτοὺς τετευχέναι τῆς τῶν ὅλων ἐξουσίας, ἅμα
δὲ τοὺς βουλομένους τε καὶ δυναμένους τὰ μέγιστ'
εὐεργετεῖν ἡγούμενοι θείας μετέχειν φύσεως.
4 Περὶ μὲν οὖν τῶν ἀφιερωμένων ζῴων εἰ καὶ
πεπλεονάκαμεν, ἀλλ' οὖν γε τὰ μάλιστα θαυμαζόμενα τῶν παρ' Αἰγυπτίοις νόμιμα διευκρινή-
καμεν.

91. Οὐχ ἥκιστα δ' ἄν τις πυθόμενος τὰ περὶ
τοὺς τετελευτηκότας νόμιμα τῶν Αἰγυπτίων
θαυμάσαι τὴν ἰδιότητα τῶν ἐθῶν. ὅταν γάρ τις
ἀποθάνῃ παρ' αὐτοῖς, οἱ μὲν συγγενεῖς καὶ φίλοι
πάντες καταπλαττόμενοι πηλῷ τὰς κεφαλὰς
περιέρχονται τὴν πόλιν θρηνοῦντες, ἕως ἂν ταφῆς
τύχῃ τὸ σῶμα. οὐ μὴν οὔτε λουτρῶν οὔτε οἴνου
οὔτε τῆς ἄλλης τροφῆς ἀξιολόγου μεταλαμβά-
νουσιν, οὔτε ἐσθῆτας λαμπρὰς περιβάλλονται.
2 τῶν δὲ ταφῶν τρεῖς ὑπάρχουσι τάξεις, ἥ τε πολυ-
τελεστάτη καὶ μέση καὶ ταπεινοτάτη. κατὰ μὲν
οὖν τὴν πρώτην ἀναλίσκεσθαί φασιν ἀργυρίου
τάλαντον, κατὰ δὲ τὴν δευτέραν μνᾶς εἴκοσι,
κατὰ δὲ τὴν ἐσχάτην παντελῶς ὀλίγον τι
3 δαπάνημα γίνεσθαι λέγουσιν. οἱ μὲν οὖν τὰ
σώματα θεραπεύοντές εἰσι τεχνῖται, τὴν ἐπιστήμην ταύτην ἐκ γένους παρειληφότες· οὗτοι δὲ
γραφὴν ἑκάστου τῶν εἰς τὰς ταφὰς δαπανωμένων
τοῖς οἰκείοις τῶν τελευτησάντων προσενέγκαντες

benefactions preferably upon those who they see will most honourably treasure up the favours they bestow. And it is apparently on these grounds that the Egyptians prostrate themselves before their kings and honour them as being in very truth gods, holding, on the one hand, that it was not without the influence of some divine providence that these men have attained to the supreme power, and feeling, also, that such as have the will and the strength to confer the greatest benefactions share in the divine nature.

Now if we have dwelt over-long on the topic of the sacred animals, we have at least thoroughly considered those customs of the Egyptians that men most marvel at.

91. But not least will a man marvel at the peculiarity of the customs of the Egyptians when he learns of their usages with respect to the dead. For whenever anyone dies among them, all his relatives and friends, plastering their heads with mud, roam about the city lamenting, until the body receives burial. Nay more, during that time they indulge in neither baths, nor wine, nor in any other food worth mentioning, nor do they put on bright clothing. There are three classes of burial, the most expensive, the medium, and the most humble. And if the first is used the cost, they say, is a talent of silver, if the second, twenty minae, and if the last, the expense is, they say, very little indeed. Now the men who treat the bodies are skilled artisans who have received this professional knowledge as a family tradition; and these lay before the relatives of the deceased a price-list of every item connected with

ἐπερωτῶσι τινα τρόπον βούλονται τὴν θεραπείαν
4 γενέσθαι τοῦ σώματος. διομολογησάμενοι δὲ
περὶ πάντων καὶ τὸν νεκρὸν παραλαβόντες, τοῖς
τεταγμένοις ἐπὶ τὴν κατειθισμένην ἐπιμέλειαν
τὸ σῶμα παραδιδόασι. καὶ πρῶτος μὲν ὁ γραμ-
ματεὺς λεγόμενος τεθέντος χαμαὶ τοῦ σώματος
ἐπὶ τὴν λαγόνα περιγράφει τὴν εὐώνυμον ὅσον
δεῖ διατεμεῖν· ἔπειτα δ᾿ ὁ λεγόμενος παρασχίστης
λίθον ἔχων Αἰθιοπικὸν καὶ διατεμὼν ὡς ὁ[1] νόμος
κελεύει τὴν σάρκα, παραχρῆμα φεύγει δρόμῳ,
διωκόντων τῶν συμπαρόντων καὶ λίθοις βαλλόν-
των, ἔτι δὲ καταρωμένων καὶ καθαπερεὶ τὸ μύσος
εἰς ἐκεῖνον τρεπόντων· ὑπολαμβάνουσι γὰρ μιση-
τὸν εἶναι πάντα τὸν ὁμοφύλῳ σώματι βίαν προσ-
φέροντα καὶ τραύματα ποιοῦντα καὶ καθόλου τι
κακὸν ἀπεργαζόμενον.

5 Οἱ ταριχευταὶ δὲ καλούμενοι πάσης μὲν τιμῆς
καὶ πολυωρίας ἀξιοῦνται, τοῖς τε ἱερεῦσι συνόντες
καὶ τὰς εἰς ἱερὸν εἰσόδους ἀκωλύτως ὡς καθαροὶ
ποιοῦνται· πρὸς δὲ τὴν θεραπείαν τοῦ παρεσχισ-
μένου σώματος ἀθροισθέντων αὐτῶν εἷς καθίησι
τὴν χεῖρα διὰ τῆς τοῦ νεκροῦ τομῆς εἰς τὸν
θώρακα καὶ πάντα ἐξαιρεῖ[2] χωρὶς νεφρῶν καὶ
καρδίας, ἕτερος δὲ καθαίρει τῶν ἐγκοιλίων ἕκαστον κλύζων οἴνῳ φοινικείῳ καὶ θυμιάμασι.
6 καθόλου δὲ πᾶν τὸ σῶμα τὸ μὲν πρῶτον κεδρίᾳ

---

[1] ὡς ὁ Vogel : ὅσα Vulgate, Bekker, Dindorf.
[2] ἐξαιρεῖ Dindorf : ἐξαίρει.

---

[1] Lit. "one who rips up lengthwise," *i.e.* opens by slitting
[2] The same name is given this knife in Herodotus, 2. 86,
whose description of embalming, although not so detailed as

the burial, and ask them in what manner they wish
the body to be treated. When an agreement has
been reached on every detail and they have taken
the body, they turn it over to men who have been
assigned to the service and have become inured to it.
The first is the scribe, as he is called, who, when the
body has been laid on the ground, circumscribes on
the left flank the extent of the incision; then the one
called the slitter [1] cuts the flesh, as the law commands, with an Ethiopian stone [2] and at once takes
to flight on the run, while those present set out after
him, pelting him with stones, heaping curses on him,
and trying, as it were, to turn the profanation on
his head; for in their eyes everyone is an object
of general hatred who applies violence to the body
of a man of the same tribe or wounds him or, in
general, does him any harm.

The men called embalmers, however, are considered worthy of every honour and consideration,
associating with the priests and even coming and
going in the temples without hindrance, as being
undefiled. When they have gathered to treat the
body after it has been slit open, one of them thrusts
his hand through the opening in the corpse into the
trunk and extracts everything but the kidneys and
heart, and another one cleanses each of the viscera,
washing them in palm wine and spices. And in
general, they carefully dress the whole body for over

that of Diodorus, supplements it in many respects. It was
probably of obsidian or flint, such as are frequently found
in graves with mummies. For the use of such primitive
implements in ancient religious ceremonies, cp. *Joshua*, 5. 3:
"Make thee knives of flint and circumcise again the children
of Israel a second time."

καί τισιν ἄλλοις ἐπιμελείας ἀξιοῦσιν ἐφ᾽ ἡμέρας
πλείους τῶν τριάκοντα, ἔπειτα σμύρνῃ καὶ κινα-
μώμῳ καὶ τοῖς δυναμένοις μὴ μόνον πολυχρόνιον
τήρησιν,[1] ἀλλὰ καὶ τὴν εὐωδίαν παρέχεσθαι·
θεραπεύσαντες δὲ[2] παραδιδόασι τοῖς συγγενέσι
τοῦ τετελευτηκότος οὕτως ἕκαστον τῶν τοῦ
σώματος μελῶν ἀκέραιον τετηρημένον ὥστε καὶ
τὰς ἐπὶ τοῖς βλεφάροις καὶ ταῖς ὀφρύσι
τρίχας διαμένειν καὶ τὴν ὅλην πρόσοψιν τοῦ
σώματος ἀπαράλλακτον εἶναι καὶ τὸν τῆς μορφῆς
7 τύπον γνωρίζεσθαι· διὸ καὶ πολλοὶ τῶν Αἰγυπτίων ἐν οἰκήμασι πολυτελέσι φυλάττοντες τὰ
σώματα τῶν προγόνων, κατ᾽ ὄψιν ὁρῶσι τοὺς
γενεαῖς πολλαῖς τῆς ἑαυτῶν γενέσεως προτετελευ-
τηκότας, ὥστε ἑκάστων τά τε μεγέθη καὶ τὰς
περιοχὰς τῶν σωμάτων, ἔτι δὲ τοὺς τῆς ὄψεως
χαρακτῆρας ὁρωμένους παράδοξον ψυχαγωγίαν
παρέχεσθαι καθάπερ συμβεβιωκότας τοῖς θεωμένοις.[3]

92. Τοῦ δὲ μέλλοντος θάπτεσθαι σώματος
οἱ συγγενεῖς προλέγουσι τὴν ἡμέραν τῆς ταφῆς
τοῖς τε δικασταῖς καὶ τοῖς συγγενέσιν, ἔτι δὲ
φίλοις τοῦ τετελευτηκότος, καὶ διαβεβαιοῦνται
ὅτι διαβαίνειν μέλλει τὴν λίμνην, λέγοντες
2 τοὔνομα τοῦ μετηλλαχότος. ἔπειτα παραγενο-
μένων δικαστῶν δυσὶ πλειόνων[4] τῶν τετταράκοντα, καὶ καθισάντων ἐπί τινος ἡμικυκλίου
κατεσκευασμένου πέραν τῆς λίμνης, ἡ μὲν βᾶρις
καθέλκεται, κατεσκευασμένη πρότερον ὑπὸ τῶν

---

[1] τήρησιν Wesseling : τηρήσειν D, τηρεῖν II.
[2] δὲ Vogel : omitted by Vulgate, Bekker, Dindorf.
[3] θεωμένοις Dindorf : θεωρουμένοις.

thirty days, first with cedar oil and certain other preparations, and then with myrrh, cinnamon, and such spices as have the faculty not only of preserving it for a long time but also of giving it a fragrant odour. And after treating the body they return it to the relatives of the deceased, every member of it having been so preserved intact that even the hair on the eyelids and brows remains, the entire appearance of the body is unchanged, and the cast of its shape is recognizable. This explains why many Egyptians keep the bodies of their ancestors in costly chambers and gaze face to face upon those who died many generations before their own birth, so that, as they look upon the stature and proportions and the features of the countenance of each, they experience a strange enjoyment, as though they had lived with those on whom they gaze.

92. When the body is ready to be buried the family announces the day of interment to the judges and to the relatives and friends of the deceased, and solemnly affirms that he who has just passed away —giving his name—" is about to cross the lake." Then, when the judges, forty-two in number,[1] have assembled and have taken seats in a hemicycle which has been built across the lake, the *baris* [2] is launched, which has been prepared in advance by men espe-

[1] These judges correspond to the forty-two judges or assessors before each of whom the dead man must declare in the next world that he had not committed a certain sin (*Book of the Dead*, Chap. CXXV).

[2] The name given the scows used on the Nile and described in Herodotus 2. 96.

---

[4] πλειόνων Dindorf : πλείω.

ταύτην ἐχόντων τὴν ἐπιμέλειαν, ἐφέστηκε δὲ
ταύτῃ ὁ πορθμεύς, ὃν Αἰγύπτιοι κατὰ τὴν ἰδίαν
3 διάλεκτον ὀνομάζουσι χάρωνα. διὸ καί φασιν
Ὀρφέα τὸ παλαιὸν εἰς Αἴγυπτον παραβαλόντα
καὶ θεασάμενον τοῦτο τὸ νόμιμον, μυθοποιῆσαι
τὰ καθ' ἅδου, τὰ μὲν μιμησάμενον, τὰ δ' αὐτὸν
ἰδίᾳ πλασάμενον· ὑπὲρ[1] οὗ τὰ κατὰ μέρος
4 μικρὸν ὕστερον ἀναγράψομεν. οὐ μὴν ἀλλὰ
τῆς βάρεως εἰς τὴν λίμνην καθελκυσθείσης,
πρὶν ἢ τὴν λάρνακα τὴν τὸν νεκρὸν ἔχουσαν εἰς
αὐτὴν τίθεσθαι, τῷ βουλομένῳ κατηγορεῖν ὁ
νόμος ἐξουσίαν δίδωσιν. ἐὰν μὲν οὖν τις παρελθὼν ἐγκαλέσῃ καὶ δείξῃ βεβιωκότα κακῶς, οἱ
μὲν κριταὶ τὰς γνώμας πᾶσιν[2] ἀποφαίνονται, τὸ
δὲ σῶμα εἴργεται τῆς εἰθισμένης ταφῆς· ἐὰν δ' ὁ
ἐγκαλέσας δόξῃ μὴ δικαίως κατηγορεῖν, μεγάλοις
5 περιπίπτει προστίμοις. ὅταν δὲ μηδεὶς ὑπα-
κούσῃ κατήγορος ἢ παρελθὼν γνωσθῇ συκοφάντης
ὑπάρχειν, οἱ μὲν συγγενεῖς ἀποθέμενοι τὸ πένθος
ἐγκωμιάζουσι τὸν τετελευτηκότα, καὶ περὶ μὲν
τοῦ γένους οὐδὲν λέγουσιν, ὥσπερ παρὰ τοῖς
Ἕλλησιν, ὑπολαμβάνοντες ἅπαντας ὁμοίως εὐ-
γενεῖς εἶναι τοὺς κατ' Αἴγυπτον, τὴν δ' ἐκ παιδὸς
ἀγωγὴν καὶ παιδείαν διελθόντες, πάλιν ἀνδρὸς
γεγονότος τὴν εὐσέβειαν καὶ δικαιοσύνην, ἔτι δὲ
τὴν ἐγκράτειαν καὶ τὰς ἄλλας ἀρετὰς αὐτοῦ
διεξέρχονται, καὶ παρακαλοῦσι τοὺς κάτω θεοὺς
δέξασθαι σύνοικον τοῖς εὐσεβέσι· τὸ δὲ πλῆθος
ἐπευφημεῖ καὶ ἀποσεμνύνει τὴν δόξαν τοῦ τετε-

---

[1] ὑπὲρ Vogel: περὶ C F, Bekker, Dindorf.
[2] πᾶσιν omitted by C F, Bekker, Dindorf.

cially engaged in that service, and which is in the charge of the boatman whom the Egyptians in their language call *charon*.[1] For this reason they insist that Orpheus, having visited Egypt in ancient times and witnessed this custom, merely invented his account of Hades, in part reproducing this practice and in part inventing on his own account; but this point we shall discuss more fully a little later.[2] At any rate, after the *baris* has been launched into the lake but before the coffin containing the body is set in it, the law gives permission to anyone who wishes to arraign the dead person. Now if anyone presents himself and makes a charge, and shows that the dead man had led an evil life, the judges announce the decision to all and the body is denied the customary burial; but if it shall appear that the accuser has made an unjust charge he is severely punished. When no accuser appears or the one who presents himself is discovered to be a slanderer, the relatives put their mourning aside and laud the deceased. And of his ancestry, indeed, they say nothing, as the Greeks do, since they hold that all Egyptians are equally well born, but after recounting his training and education from childhood, they describe his righteousness and justice after he attained to manhood, also his self-control and his other virtues, and call upon the gods of the lower world to receive him into the company of the righteous; and the multitude shouts its assent and extols the glory of the deceased, as of

[1] Professor J. A. Wilson, of the Oriental Institute of the University of Chicago, kindly writes me: "There is no evidence to support the statement of Diodorus that the Egyptians called the underworld ferryman, or any boatman connected with death, *Charon*."

[2] Cp. chap. 96.

λευτηκότος, ὡς τὸν αἰῶνα διατρίβειν μέλλοντος
6 καθ' ᾅδου μετὰ τῶν εὐσεβῶν. τὸ δὲ σῶμα
τιθέασιν οἱ μὲν ἰδίους ἔχοντες τάφους ἐν ταῖς
ἀποδεδειγμέναις θήκαις, οἷς δ' οὐχ ὑπάρχουσι
τάφων κτήσεις, καινὸν οἴκημα ποιοῦσι κατὰ τὴν
ἰδίαν οἰκίαν, καὶ πρὸς τὸν ἀσφαλέστατον τῶν
τοίχων ὀρθὴν ἱστᾶσι τὴν λάρνακα. καὶ τοὺς
κωλυομένους δὲ διὰ τὰς κατηγορίας ἢ πρὸς
δάνειον ὑποθήκας θάπτεσθαι τιθέασι κατὰ τὴν
ἰδίαν οἰκίαν· οὓς ὕστερον ἐνίοτε παίδων παῖδες
εὐπορήσαντες καὶ τῶν τε συμβολαίων καὶ τῶν
ἐγκλημάτων ἀπολύσαντες μεγαλοπρεποῦς ταφῆς
ἀξιοῦσι.

93. Σεμνότατον δὲ διείληπται παρ' Αἰγυπτίοις
τὸ τοὺς γονεῖς ἢ τοὺς προγόνους φανῆναι περιττότερον τετιμηκότας εἰς τὴν αἰώνιον οἴκησιν μετα-
στάντας. νόμιμον δ' ἐστὶ παρ' αὐτοῖς καὶ τὸ
διδόναι τὰ σώματα τῶν τετελευτηκότων γονέων
εἰς ὑποθήκην δανείου· τοῖς δὲ μὴ λυσαμένοις
ὄνειδός τε τὸ μέγιστον ἀκολουθεῖ καὶ μετὰ τὴν
2 τελευτὴν στέρησις ταφῆς. θαυμάσαι δ' ἄν τις
προσηκόντως τοὺς ταῦτα διατάξαντας, ὅτι τὴν
ἐπιείκειαν καὶ τὴν σπουδαιότητα τῶν ἠθῶν οὐκ
ἐκ τῆς τῶν ζώντων ὁμιλίας μόνον, ἀλλὰ καὶ τῆς
τῶν τετελευτηκότων ταφῆς καὶ θεραπείας ἐφ'
ὅσον ἦν ἐνδεχόμενον τοῖς ἀνθρώποις ἐνοικειοῦν
3 ἐφιλοτιμήθησαν. οἱ μὲν γὰρ Ἕλληνες μύθοις
πεπλασμένοις καὶ φήμαις διαβεβλημέναις τὴν
περὶ τούτων πίστιν παρέδωκαν,[1] τήν τε τῶν
εὐσεβῶν τιμὴν καὶ τὴν τῶν πονηρῶν τιμωρίαν·
τοιγαροῦν οὐχ οἷον ἰσχῦσαι δύναται ταῦτα
προτρέψασθαι τοὺς ἀνθρώπους ἐπὶ τὸν ἄριστον

one who is about to spend eternity in Hades among
the righteous. Those who have private sepulchres
lay the body in a vault reserved for it, but those who
possess none construct a new chamber in their own
home, and stand the coffin upright against the
firmest wall. Any also who are forbidden burial
because of the accusations brought against them or
because their bodies have been made security for a
loan they lay away in their own homes; and it sometimes happens that their sons' sons, when they have
become prosperous and paid off the debt or cleared
them of the charges, give them later a magnificent
funeral.

93. It is a most sacred duty, in the eyes of the
Egyptians, that they should be seen to honour their
parents or ancestors all the more after they have
passed to their eternal home. Another custom of
theirs is to put up the bodies of their deceased
parents as security for a loan; and failure to repay
such debts is attended with the deepest disgrace as
well as with deprivation of burial at death. And a
person may well admire the men who established
these customs, because they strove to inculcate in
the inhabitants, so far as was possible, virtuousness
and excellence of character, by means not only of
their converse with the living but also of their burial
and affectionate care of the dead. For the Greeks
have handed down their beliefs in such matters—in
the honour paid to the righteous and the punishment
of the wicked—by means of fanciful tales and dis-
credited legends; consequently these accounts not
only cannot avail to spur their people on to the best

---

¹ παρέδωκαν Vogel : παραδεδώκασι B, Bekker, Dindorf.

βίον, ἀλλὰ τοὐναντίον ὑπὸ τῶν φαύλων χλευα-
ζόμενα πολλῆς καταφρονήσεως τυγχάνουσι·
4 παρὰ δὲ τοῖς Αἰγυπτίοις οὐ μυθώδους, ἀλλ'
ὁρατῆς τοῖς μὲν πονηροῖς τῆς κολάσεως, τοῖς
δ' ἀγαθοῖς τῆς τιμῆς οὔσης, καθ' ἑκάστην ἡμέραν
ἀμφότεροι τῶν ἑαυτοῖς προσηκόντων ὑπομιμνή-
σκονται, καὶ διὰ τούτου τοῦ τρόπου ἡ [1] μεγίστη
καὶ συμφορωτάτη διόρθωσις γίνεται τῶν ἠθῶν.
κρατίστους δ', οἶμαι, τῶν νόμων ἡγητέον οὐκ ἐξ
ὧν εὐπορωτάτους, ἀλλ' ἐξ ὧν ἐπιεικεστάτους τοῖς
ἤθεσι καὶ πολιτικωτάτους συμβήσεται γενέσθαι
τοὺς ἀνθρώπους.

94. Ῥητέον δ' ἡμῖν καὶ περὶ τῶν γενομένων
νομοθετῶν κατ' Αἴγυπτον τῶν οὕτως ἐξηλλαγμένα καὶ παράδοξα νόμιμα καταδειξάντων.
μετὰ γὰρ τὴν παλαιὰν τοῦ κατ' Αἴγυπτον βίου
κατάστασιν, τὴν μυθολογουμένην γεγονέναι ἐπί
τε τῶν θεῶν καὶ τῶν ἡρώων, πεῖσαί φασι
πρῶτον ἐγγράπτοις νόμοις χρήσασθαι τὰ πλήθη
τὸν Μνεύην, ἄνδρα καὶ τῇ ψυχῇ μέγαν καὶ τῷ
βίῳ κοινότατον τῶν μνημονευομένων. προσ-
ποιηθῆναι δ' αὐτῷ τὸν Ἑρμῆν δεδωκέναι τούτους,
ὡς μεγάλων ἀγαθῶν αἰτίους ἐσομένους, καθάπερ
παρ' Ἕλλησι ποιῆσαί φασιν ἐν μὲν τῇ Κρήτῃ
Μίνωα, παρὰ δὲ Λακεδαιμονίοις Λυκοῦργον, τὸν
μὲν παρὰ Διός, τὸν δὲ παρ' Ἀπόλλωνος φήσαντα
2 τούτους παρειληφέναι. καὶ παρ' ἑτέροις δὲ
πλείοσιν ἔθνεσι παραδέδοται τοῦτο τὸ γένος τῆς
ἐπινοίας ὑπάρξαι καὶ πολλῶν ἀγαθῶν αἴτιον

---

[1] ἡ Bekker, Vogel : omitted by Vulgate and Dindorf.

life, but, on the contrary, being scoffed at by worthless men, are received with contempt. But among the Egyptians, since these matters do not belong to the realm of myth but men see with their own eyes that punishment is meted out to the wicked and honour to the good, every day of their lives both the wicked and the good are reminded of their obligations and in this way the greatest and most profitable amendment of men's characters is effected. And the best laws, in my opinion, must be held to be, not those by which men become most prosperous, but those by which they become most virtuous in character and best fitted for citizenship.

94. We must speak also of the lawgivers who have arisen in Egypt and who instituted customs unusual and strange. After the establishment of settled life in Egypt in early times, which took place, according to the mythical account, in the period of the gods and heroes, the first, they say, to persuade the multitudes to use written laws was Mneves,[1] a man not only great of soul but also in his life the most public-spirited of all lawgivers whose names are recorded. According to the tradition he claimed that Hermes had given the laws to him, with the assurance that they would be the cause of great blessings, just as among the Greeks, they say, Minos did in Crete and Lycurgus among the Lacedaemonians, the former saying that he received his laws from Zeus and the latter his from Apollo. Also among several other peoples tradition says that this kind of a device was used and was the cause of much good to such as

---

[1] Apparently Mneves is only a variant of the name Menas of chaps. 43 and 45 (cp. A. Wiedemann, *Ägyptische Geschichte*, p. 163, n. 1).

γενέσθαι τοῖς πεισθεῖσι· παρὰ μὲν γὰρ τοῖς
Ἀριανοῖς Ζαθραύστην ἱστοροῦσι τὸν ἀγαθὸν
δαίμονα προσποιήσασθαι τοὺς νόμους αὐτῷ
διδόναι, παρὰ δὲ τοῖς ὀνομαζομένοις Γέταις τοῖς
ἀπαθανατίζουσι Ζάλμοξιν ὡσαύτως τὴν κοινὴν
Ἑστίαν, παρὰ δὲ τοῖς Ἰουδαίοις Μωυσῆν τὸν
Ἰαὼ ἐπικαλούμενον θεόν, εἴτε θαυμαστὴν καὶ
θείαν ὅλως ἔννοιαν εἶναι κρίναντας τὴν μέλλουσαν
ὠφελήσειν ἀνθρώπων πλῆθος, εἴτε καὶ πρὸς τὴν
ὑπεροχὴν καὶ δύναμιν τῶν εὑρεῖν λεγομένων τοὺς
νόμους ἀποβλέψαντα τὸν ὄχλον μᾶλλον ὑπα-
κούσεσθαι διαλαβόντας.

3 Δεύτερον δὲ νομοθέτην Αἰγύπτιοί φασι γενέσθαι Σάσυχιν, ἄνδρα συνέσει διαφέροντα.
τοῦτον δὲ πρὸς τοῖς ὑπάρχουσι νόμοις ἄλλα τε
προσθεῖναι καὶ τὰ περὶ τὴν τῶν θεῶν τιμὴν
ἐπιμελέστατα διατάξαι, εὑρετὴν δὲ καὶ γεωμετρίας
γενέσθαι καὶ τὴν περὶ τῶν ἄστρων θεωρίαν τε
καὶ παρατήρησιν διδάξαι τοὺς ἐγχωρίους.
4 τρίτον δὲ λέγουσι Σεσόωσιν τὸν βασιλέα μὴ
μόνον τὰς πολεμικὰς πράξεις ἐπιφανεστάτας
κατεργάσασθαι τῶν κατ᾽ Αἴγυπτον, ἀλλὰ καὶ
περὶ τὸ μάχιμον ἔθνος νομοθεσίαν συστήσασθαι,
καὶ τὰ ἀκόλουθα τὰ περὶ τὴν στρατείαν σύμ-
5 παντα διακοσμῆσαι. τέταρτον δὲ νομοθέτην
φασὶ γενέσθαι Βόκχοριν τὸν βασιλέα, σοφὸν

---

[1] This form of the name is much nearer to the old Iranian
form, Zarathustra, than the later corruption Zoroaster.

[2] Herodotus (4. 93 ff.) gives more details about Zalmoxis, or
Gebeleïzis, as he also calls him, and the Getae "who pretend
to be immortal." Strabo (7. 3. 5) calls him Zamolxis and
makes him a former slave of Pythagoras, a story already known
to Herodotus and rejected by him.

believed it. Thus it is recorded that among the
Arians Zathraustes [1] claimed that the Good Spirit
gave him his laws, among the people known as the
Getae who represent themselves to be immortal
Zalmoxis [2] asserted the same of their common goddess Hestia, and among the Jews Moyses referred his
laws to the god who is invoked as Iao.[3] They all did
this either because they believed that a conception
which would help humanity was marvellous and
wholly divine, or because they held that the common
crowd would be more likely to obey the laws if their
gaze were directed towards the majesty and power
of those to whom their laws were ascribed.

A second lawgiver, according to the Egyptians,
was Sasychis,[4] a man of unusual understanding. He
made sundry additions to the existing laws and, in
particular, laid down with the greatest precision the
rites to be used in honouring the gods, and he was
the inventor of geometry and taught his countrymen
both to speculate about the stars and to observe
them. A third one, they tell us, was the king
Sesoösis,[5] who not only performed the most renowned
deeds in war of any king of Egypt but also organized
the rules governing the warrior class [6] and, in conformity with these, set in order all the regulations
that have to do with military campaigns. A fourth
lawgiver, they say, was the king Bocchoris,[7] a wise

[3] This pronunciation seems to reflect a Hebrew form
Yahu; cp. *Psalms* 68. 4 ʒ "His name is Jah."

[4] Sasychis is the Asychis of Herodotus (2. 136), identified
with Shepseskaf of the Fourth Dynasty by H. R. Hall,
Ancient History of the Near East[6], p. 127.

[5] Cp. chaps. 53 ff.

[6] Cp. chap. 73.

[7] Mentioned before in chaps. 45, 65, 79.

τινα καὶ πανουργίᾳ διαφέροντα. τοῦτον οὖν
διατάξαι τὰ περὶ τοὺς βασιλεῖς ἅπαντα καὶ τὰ
περὶ τῶν συμβολαίων ἐξακριβῶσαι· γενέσθαι δ'
αὐτὸν καὶ περὶ τὰς κρίσεις οὕτω συνετὸν ὥστε
πολλὰ τῶν ὑπ' αὐτοῦ διαγνωσθέντων διὰ τὴν
περιττότητα μνημονεύεσθαι μέχρι τῶν καθ'
ἡμᾶς χρόνων. λέγουσι δ' αὐτὸν ὑπάρξαι τῷ
μὲν σώματι παντελῶς ἀσθενῆ, τῷ δὲ τρόπῳ
πάντων φιλοχρηματώτατον.

95. Μετὰ δὲ τοῦτον προσελθεῖν λέγουσι τοῖς
νόμοις Ἄμασιν τὸν βασιλέα, ὃν ἱστοροῦσι τὰ
περὶ τοὺς νομάρχας διατάξαι καὶ τὰ περὶ τὴν
σύμπασαν οἰκονομίαν τῆς Αἰγύπτου. παραδέδοται δὲ συνετός τε γεγονέναι καθ' ὑπερβολὴν
καὶ τὸν τρόπον ἐπιεικὴς καὶ δίκαιος· ὧν ἕνεκα
καὶ τοὺς Αἰγυπτίους αὐτῷ περιτεθεικέναι τὴν
2 ἀρχὴν οὐκ ὄντι γένους βασιλικοῦ. φασὶ δὲ καὶ
τοὺς Ἠλείους, σπουδάζοντας περὶ τὸν Ὀλυμπικὸν [1] ἀγῶνα, πρεσβευτὰς ἀποστεῖλαι πρὸς
αὐτὸν ἐρωτήσοντας πῶς ἂν γένοιτο δικαιότατος·
τὸν δ' εἰπεῖν, ἐὰν μηδεὶς Ἠλεῖος ἀγωνίζηται.
3 Πολυκράτους δὲ τοῦ Σαμίων δυνάστου συντεθει-
μένου πρὸς αὐτὸν φιλίαν, καὶ βιαίως προσφε-
ρομένου τοῖς τε πολίταις καὶ τοῖς εἰς Σάμον
καταπλέουσι ξένοις, τὸ μὲν πρῶτον λέγεται
πρεσβευτὰς ἀποστείλαντα παρακαλεῖν αὐτὸν ἐπὶ
τὴν μετριότητα· οὐ προσέχοντος δ' αὐτοῦ τοῖς
λόγοις ἐπιστολὴν γράψαι τὴν φιλίαν καὶ τὴν
ξενίαν τὴν πρὸς αὐτὸν διαλυόμενον· οὐ γὰρ
βούλεσθαι λυπηθῆναι συντόμως ἑαυτόν, ἀκριβῶς

---

[1] Ὀλυμπικὸν Vogel : Ολυμπιακὸν C, Bekker, Dindorf.

sort of a man and conspicuous for his craftiness. He drew up all the regulations which governed the kings and gave precision to the laws on contracts; and so wise was he in his judicial decisions as well, that many of his judgments are remembered for their excellence even to our day. And they add that he was very weak in body, and that by disposition he was the most avaricious of all their kings.

95. After Bocchoris, they say, their king Amasis [1] 569–526 gave attention to the laws, who, according to their B.C. accounts, drew up the rules governing the nomarchs and the entire administration of Egypt. And tradition describes him as exceedingly wise and in disposition virtuous and just, for which reasons the Egyptians invested him with the kingship, although he was not of the royal line. They say also that the citizens of Elis, when they were giving their attention to the Olympic Games, sent an embassy to him to ask how they could be conducted with the greatest fairness, and that he replied, " Provided no man of Elis participates." And though Polycrates, the ruler of the Samians, had been on terms of friendship with him, when he began oppressing both citizens and such foreigners as put in at Samos, it is said that Amasis at first sent an embassy to him and urged him to moderation; and when no attention was paid to this, he wrote a letter in which he broke up the relations of friendship and hospitality that had existed between them; for he did not wish, as he said, to be plunged into grief in a short while, knowing right

---

[1] Cp. chap. 68. The story of the embassy of Eleans is given more fully in Herodotus (2. 160), where, however, the Egyptian king consulted is called Psammis.

εἰδότα διότι[1] πλησίον ἐστὶν αὐτῷ τὸ κακῶς
παθεῖν οὕτω προεστηκότι τῆς τυραννίδος. θαυ-
μασθῆναι δ' αὐτόν φασι παρὰ τοῖς Ἕλλησι διά
τε τὴν ἐπιείκειαν καὶ διὰ τὸ τῷ Πολυκράτει
ταχέως ἀποβῆναι τὰ ῥηθέντα.

4 Ἕκτον δὲ λέγεται τὸν Ξέρξου πατέρα Δαρεῖον
τοῖς νόμοις ἐπιστῆναι τοῖς τῶν Αἰγυπτίων·
μισήσαντα γὰρ τὴν παρανομίαν τὴν εἰς τὰ κατ'
Αἴγυπτον ἱερὰ γενομένην ὑπὸ Καμβύσου τοῦ
προβασιλεύσαντος ζηλῶσαι βίον ἐπιεικῆ καὶ
5 φιλόθεον. ὁμιλῆσαι μὲν γὰρ αὐτοῖς[2] τοῖς
ἱερεῦσι τοῖς ἐν Αἰγύπτῳ καὶ μεταλαβεῖν αὐτὸν
τῆς τε θεολογίας[3] καὶ τῶν ἐν ταῖς ἱεραῖς
βίβλοις ἀναγεγραμμένων πράξεων· ἐκ δὲ τούτων
ἱστορήσαντα τήν τε μεγαλοψυχίαν τῶν ἀρχαίων
βασιλέων καὶ τὴν εἰς τοὺς ἀρχομένους εὔνοιαν
μιμήσασθαι τὸν[4] ἐκείνων βίον, καὶ διὰ τοῦτο
τηλικαύτης τυχεῖν τιμῆς ὥσθ' ὑπὸ τῶν Αἰγυπτίων
ζῶντα μὲν θεὸν προσαγορεύεσθαι[5] μόνον τῶν
ἁπάντων βασιλέων, τελευτήσαντα δὲ τιμῶν
τυχεῖν ἴσων τοῖς τὸ παλαιὸν νομιμώτατα βασι-
λεύσασι κατ' Αἴγυπτον.

6 Τὴν μὲν οὖν κοινὴν νομοθεσίαν συντελεσθῆναί
φασιν ὑπὸ τῶν εἰρημένων ἀνδρῶν, καὶ δόξης
τυχεῖν τῆς διαδεδομένης παρὰ τοῖς ἄλλοις· ἐν
δὲ τοῖς ὕστερον χρόνοις πολλὰ τῶν καλῶς
ἔχειν δοκούντων νομίμων φασὶ κινηθῆναι, Μακεδόνων ἐπικρατησάντων καὶ καταλυσάντων εἰς
τέλος τὴν βασιλείαν τῶν ἐγχωρίων.

[1] διότι Vogel : ὅτι Vulgate, Bekker, Dindorf.
[2] αὐτοῖς Vogel : αὐτὸν Vulgate, Bekker, Dindorf.
[3] αὐτῶν after θεολογίας added by C, Bekker, Dindorf.

well as he did that misfortune is near at hand for the
ruler who maintains a tyranny in such fashion. And
he was admired, they say, among the Greeks both
because of his virtuous character and because his
words to Polycrates 'were speedily fulfilled.

A sixth man to concern himself with the laws of
the Egyptians, it is said, was Darius the father of
Xerxes; for he was incensed at the lawlessness 521-486 B.C.
which his predecessor, Cambyses, had shown in his
treatment of the sanctuaries of Egypt, and aspired
to live a life of virtue and of piety towards the gods.
Indeed he associated with the priests of Egypt themselves, and took part with them in the study of
theology and of the events recorded in their sacred
books; and when he learned from these books about
the greatness of soul of the ancient kings and about
their goodwill towards their subjects he imitated their
manner of life. For this reason he was the object of
such great honour that he alone of all the kings was
addressed as a god by the Egyptians in his lifetime,
while at his death he was accorded equal honours
with the ancient kings of Egypt who had ruled in
strictest accord with the laws.

The system, then, of law used throughout the land
was the work, they say, of the men just named, and
gained a renown that spread among other peoples
everywhere; but in later times, they say, many
institutions which were regarded as good were
changed, after the Macedonians had conquered and
destroyed once and for all the kingship of the native
line.

---

⁴ τὸν Reiske: τῶν.
⁵ προσαγορεύεσθαι Bekker, Vogel: προσαγορευθῆναι II, Dindorf.

96. Τούτων δ' ἡμῖν διευκρινημένων ῥητέον ὅσοι τῶν παρ' Ἕλλησι δεδοξασμένων ἐπὶ συνέσει καὶ παιδείᾳ παρέβαλον εἰς Αἴγυπτον ἐν τοῖς ἀρχαίοις χρόνοις, ἵνα τῶν ἐνταῦθα νομίμων καὶ 2 τῆς[1] παιδείας μετάσχωσιν. οἱ γὰρ ἱερεῖς τῶν Αἰγυπτίων ἱστοροῦσιν ἐκ τῶν ἀναγραφῶν τῶν ἐν ταῖς ἱεραῖς βίβλοις παραβαλεῖν πρὸς ἑαυτοὺς[2] τὸ παλαιὸν Ὀρφέα τε καὶ Μουσαῖον καὶ Μελάμποδα καὶ Δαίδαλον, πρὸς δὲ τούτοις Ὅμηρόν τε τὸν ποιητὴν καὶ Λυκοῦργον τὸν Σπαρτιάτην, ἔτι δὲ Σόλωνα τὸν Ἀθηναῖον καὶ Πλάτωνα τὸν φιλόσοφον, ἐλθεῖν δὲ καὶ Πυθαγόραν τὸν Σάμιον καὶ τὸν μαθηματικὸν Εὔδοξον, ἔτι δὲ Δημόκριτον τὸν Ἀβδηρίτην καὶ Οἰνοπίδην τὸν 3 Χῖον. πάντων δὲ τούτων σημεῖα δεικνύουσι τῶν μὲν εἰκόνας, τῶν δὲ τόπων ἢ κατασκευασμάτων ὁμωνύμους προσηγορίας, ἔκ τε τῆς ἑκάστῳ ζηλωθείσης παιδείας ἀποδείξεις φέρουσι, συνιστάντες ἐξ Αἰγύπτου μετενηνέχθαι πάντα δι' ὧν παρὰ τοῖς Ἕλλησιν ἐθαυμάσθησαν.

4 Ὀρφέα μὲν γὰρ τῶν μυστικῶν τελετῶν τὰ πλεῖστα καὶ τὰ περὶ τὴν ἑαυτοῦ πλάνην ὀργιαζόμενα καὶ τὴν τῶν ἐν ᾅδου μυθοποιίαν ἀπε-5 νέγκασθαι. τὴν μὲν γὰρ Ὀσίριδος τελετὴν τῇ Διονύσου τὴν αὐτὴν εἶναι, τὴν δὲ τῆς Ἴσιδος τῇ τῆς Δήμητρος ὁμοιοτάτην ὑπάρχειν, τῶν ὀνομάτων μόνων[3] ἐνηλλαγμένων· τὰς δὲ τῶν ἀσεβῶν ἐν ᾅδου τιμωρίας καὶ τοὺς τῶν εὐσεβῶν λειμῶνας καὶ τὰς παρὰ τοῖς πολλοῖς εἰδωλο-

---

[1] τῆς Vogel : omitted Vulgate, Bekker, Dindorf.
[2] ἑαυτοὺς Vogel: αὐτοὺς Vulgate, Bekker, Dindorf.
[3] μόνων Vogel: μόνον Vulgate, Bekker, Dindorf.

96. But now that we have examined these matters, we must enumerate what Greeks, who have won fame for their wisdom and learning, visited Egypt in ancient times, in order to become acquainted with its customs and learning. For the priests of Egypt recount from the records of their sacred books that they were visited in early times by Orpheus, Musaeus, Melampus, and Daedalus, also by the poet Homer and Lycurgus of Sparta, later by Solon of Athens and the philosopher Plato, and that there also came Pythagoras of Samos and the mathematician Eudoxus,[1] as well as Democritus of Abdera and Oenopides[2] of Chios. As evidence for the visits of all these men they point in some cases to their statues and in others to places or buildings[3] which bear their names, and they offer proofs from the branch of learning which each one of these men pursued, arguing that all the things for which they were admired among the Greeks were transferred from Egypt.

Orpheus, for instance, brought from Egypt most of his mystic ceremonies, the orgiastic rites that accompanied his wanderings, and his fabulous account of his experiences in Hades. For the rite of Osiris is the same as that of Dionysus and that of Isis very similar to that of Demeter, the names alone having been interchanged; and the punishments in Hades of the unrighteous, the Fields of the Righteous, and the fantastic conceptions, current among the

[1] The famous astronomer, geographer, and mathematician of Cnidus, pupil of Plato. His stay in Egypt is well attested.
[2] Cp. p. 336, n. 1.
[3] For instance, according to Strabo (17. 1. 29), in Heliopolis were pointed out the houses where Plato and Eudoxus had stopped.

ποίας ἀναπεπλασμένας παρεισαγαγεῖν μιμησάμενον τὰ γινόμενα περὶ τὰς ταφὰς τὰς κατ'
6 Αἴγυπτον. τὸν μὲν γὰρ ψυχοπομπὸν Ἑρμῆν
κατὰ τὸ παλαιὸν νόμιμον παρ' Αἰγυπτίοις ἀνα-
γαγόντα τὸ τοῦ Ἄπιδος σῶμα μέχρι τινὸς παρα-
διδόναι τῷ περικειμένῳ τὴν τοῦ Κερβέρου προτο-
μήν. τοῦ δ' Ὀρφέως τοῦτο καταδείξαντος παρὰ
τοῖς Ἕλλησι τὸν Ὅμηρον ἀκολούθως τούτῳ
θεῖναι κατὰ τὴν ποίησιν

Ἑρμῆς δὲ ψυχὰς Κυλλήνιος ἐξεκαλεῖτο
ἀνδρῶν μνηστήρων, ἔχε δὲ ῥάβδον μετὰ χερσίν.

εἶτα πάλιν ὑποβάντα λέγειν

πὰρ δ' ἴσαν Ὠκεανοῦ τε ῥοὰς καὶ Λευκάδα
πέτρην,
ἠδὲ παρ' Ἠελίοιο πύλας καὶ δῆμον Ὀνείρων
ἤισαν· αἶψα δ' ἵκοντο κατ' ἀσφοδελὸν λειμῶνα,
ἔνθα τε ναίουσι ψυχαί, εἴδωλα καμόντων.

7 Ὠκεανὸν μὲν οὖν καλεῖν τὸν ποταμὸν διὰ τὸ
τοὺς Αἰγυπτίους κατὰ τὴν ἰδίαν διάλεκτον
Ὠκεανὸν λέγειν τὸν Νεῖλον, Ἡλίου δὲ πύλας
τὴν πόλιν τὴν τῶν Ἡλιοπολιτῶν, λειμῶνα δ'
ὀνομάζειν,[1] τὴν μυθολογουμένην οἴκησιν τῶν
μετηλλαχότων, τὸν παρὰ τὴν λίμνην τόπον τὴν
καλουμένην μὲν Ἀχερουσίαν, πλησίον δὲ οὖσαν
τῆς Μέμφεως, ὄντων περὶ αὐτὴν λειμώνων καλλίστων, ἕλους καὶ λωτοῦ καὶ καλάμου. ἀκολούθως δ' εἰρῆσθαι καὶ τὸ κατοικεῖν τοὺς
τελευτήσαντας ἐν τούτοις τοῖς τόποις διὰ τὸ
τὰς τῶν Αἰγυπτίων ταφὰς τὰς πλείστας καὶ
μεγίστας ἐνταῦθα γίνεσθαι, διαπορθμευομένων

---

[1] δ' ὀνομάζειν Eichstädt: δὲ νομίζειν.

many, which are figments of the imagination—all
these were introduced by Orpheus in imitation of the
Egyptian funeral customs. Hermes, for instance,
the Conductor of Souls, according to the ancient
Egyptian custom, brings up the body of the Apis to
a certain point and then gives it over to one who
wears the mask of Cerberus. And after Orpheus
had introduced this notion among the Greeks,
Homer [1] followed it when he wrote :

Cyllenian Hermes then did summon forth
The suitors' souls, holding his wand in hand.

And again a little further [2] on he says:

They passed Oceanus' streams, the Gleaming
    Rock,
The Portals of the Sun, the Land of Dreams ;
And now they reached the Meadow of Asphodel,
Where dwell the Souls, the shades of men
    outworn.

Now he calls the river " Oceanus " [3] because in their
language the Egyptians speak of the Nile as Oceanus ;
the " Portals of the Sun " (Heliopylai) is his name for
the city of Heliopolis ; and " Meadows," the mythical
dwelling of the dead, is his term for the place near
the lake which is called Acherousia, which is near
Memphis, and around it are fairest meadows, of a
marsh-land and lotus and reeds. The same explanation also serves for the statement that the dwelling of
the dead is in these regions, since the most and the
largest tombs of the Egyptians are situated there, the

---

[1] *Odyssey* 24. 1-2.   [2] *Ibid.* 11-14.
[3] As a matter of fact the only name for the Nile in Homer
is *Aigyptos*.

μὲν τῶν νεκρῶν διά τε τοῦ ποταμοῦ καὶ τῆς
Ἀχερουσίας λίμνης, τιθεμένων δὲ τῶν σωμάτων
εἰς τὰς ἐνταῦθα κειμένας θήκας.

8 Συμφωνεῖν δὲ καὶ τἄλλα τὰ παρὰ τοῖς Ἕλλησι καθ᾽ ᾅδου μυθολογούμενα τοῖς ἔτι νῦν
γινομένοις κατ᾽ Αἴγυπτον· τὸ μὲν γὰρ διακομίζον
τὰ σώματα πλοῖον βᾶριν καλεῖσθαι, τὸ δ᾽
ἐπίβαθρον[1] τῷ πορθμεῖ δίδοσθαι, καλουμένῳ
9 κατὰ τὴν ἐγχώριον διάλεκτον χάρωνι. εἶναι
δὲ λέγουσι πλησίον τῶν τόπων τούτων καὶ
σκοτίας Ἑκάτης ἱερὸν καὶ πύλας Κωκυτοῦ καὶ
Λήθης διειλημμένας χαλκοῖς ὀχεῦσιν. ὑπάρχειν
δὲ καὶ ἄλλας πύλας Ἀληθείας, καὶ πλησίον
τούτων εἴδωλον ἀκέφαλον ἑστάναι Δίκης.

97. Πολλὰ δὲ καὶ τῶν ἄλλων τῶν μεμυθο-
ποιημένων διαμένειν παρ᾽ Αἰγυπτίοις, διατη-
ρουμένης ἔτι τῆς προσηγορίας καὶ τῆς ἐν τῷ
2 πράττειν ἐνεργείας. ἐν μὲν γὰρ Ἀκανθῶν πόλει,
πέραν τοῦ Νείλου κατὰ τὴν Λιβύην ἀπὸ σταδίων
ἑκατὸν καὶ εἴκοσι τῆς Μέμφεως, πίθον εἶναι
τετρημένον, εἰς ὃν τῶν ἱερέων ἑξήκοντα καὶ
τριακοσίους καθ᾽ ἑκάστην ἡμέραν ὕδωρ φέρειν
3 εἰς αὐτὸν ἐκ τοῦ Νείλου· τὴν δὲ περὶ τὸν Ὄκνον[2]
μυθοποιίαν δείκνυσθαι πλησίον κατά τινα πανή-
γυριν συντελουμένην, πλέκοντος μὲν ἑνὸς ἀνδρὸς
ἀρχὴν σχοινίου μακράν, πολλῶν δ᾽ ἐκ τῶν

---

[1] νόμισμα τὸν ὀβολὸν after ἐπίβαθρον deleted by Schäfer.
[2] Ὄκνον Stephanus : ὄνον.

---

[1] Cp. chap. 92; baris is also a Greek word for boat.
[2] The bronze bands would resemble the rays of the " Portals
of the Sun,'' in the passage from Homer cited above.

dead being ferried across both the river and Lake Acherousia and their bodies laid in the vaults situated there.

The other myths about Hades, current among the Greeks, also agree with the customs which are practised even now in Egypt. For the boat which receives the bodies is called *baris*,[1] and the passenger's fee is given to the boatman, who in the Egyptian tongue is called *charon*. And near these regions, they say, are also the " Shades," which is a temple of Hecate, and " portals " of Cocytus and Lethe, which are covered at intervals with bands of bronze.[2] There are, moreover, other portals, namely, those of Truth, and near them stands a headless statue [3] of Justice.

97. Many other things as well, of which mythology tells, are still to be found among the Egyptians, the name being still preserved and the customs actually being practised. In the city of Acanthi, for instance, across the Nile in the direction of Libya one hundred and twenty stades from Memphis, there is a perforated jar to which three hundred and sixty priests, one each day, bring water from the Nile;[4] and not far from there the actual performance of the myth of Ocnus [5] is to be seen in one of their festivals, where a single man is weaving at one end of a long

[3] The Greek word may mean " statue " and " shade," the latter meaning occuring in the last line of the passage above from Homer.

[4] This is a reference to the fifty daughters of Danaus, who after death were condemned to the endless labour of pouring water into vessels with holes.

[5] Ocnus was another figure of the Greek underworld who was represented as continually labouring at the weaving of a rope which was devoured by an unseen ass behind him as rapidly as it was woven.

4 ὀπίσω λυόντων τὸ πλεκόμενον. Μελάμποδα δέ
φασι μετενεγκεῖν ἐξ Αἰγύπτου τὰ Διονύσῳ νομι-
ζόμενα τελεῖσθαι παρὰ τοῖς Ἕλλησι καὶ τὰ
περὶ Κρόνου μυθολογούμενα καὶ τὰ περὶ τῆς
Τιτανομαχίας καὶ τὸ σύνολον τὴν περὶ τὰ πάθη
5 τῶν θεῶν ἱστορίαν. τὸν δὲ Δαίδαλον λέγουσιν
ἀπομιμήσασθαι τὴν τοῦ λαβυρίνθου πλοκὴν τοῦ
διαμένοντος μὲν μέχρι τοῦ νῦν καιροῦ, οἰκοδομη-
θέντος δέ, ὡς μέν τινές φασιν, ὑπὸ Μένδητος,
ὡς δ' ἔνιοι λέγουσιν, ὑπὸ Μάρρου τοῦ βασιλέως,
πολλοῖς ἔτεσι πρότερον τῆς Μίνω βασιλείας.
6 τόν τε ῥυθμὸν τῶν ἀρχαίων κατ' Αἴγυπτον
ἀνδριάντων τὸν αὐτὸν εἶναι τοῖς ὑπὸ Δαιδάλου
κατασκευασθεῖσι παρὰ τοῖς Ἕλλησι. τὸ δὲ
κάλλιστον πρόπυλον ἐν Μέμφει τοῦ Ἡφαι-
στείου Δαίδαλον ἀρχιτεκτονῆσαι, καὶ θαυμασθέντα τυχεῖν εἰκόνος ξυλίνης κατὰ τὸ προειρημένον ἱερὸν ταῖς ἰδίαις χερσὶ δεδημιουργημένης,
πέρας δὲ διὰ τὴν εὐφυΐαν ἀξιωθέντα μεγάλης δόξης
καὶ πολλὰ προσεξευρόντα τυχεῖν ἰσοθέων τιμῶν·
κατὰ γὰρ μίαν τῶν πρὸς τῇ Μέμφει νήσων ἔτι
καὶ νῦν ἱερὸν εἶναι Δαιδάλου τιμώμενον ὑπὸ τῶν
ἐγχωρίων.
7 Τῆς δ' Ὁμήρου παρουσίας ἄλλα τε σημεῖα
φέρουσι καὶ μάλιστα τὴν τῆς Ἑλένης γενομένην
παρὰ Μενελάῳ Τηλεμάχου φαρμακείαν καὶ
λήθην τῶν συμβεβηκότων κακῶν. τὸ γὰρ νη-
πενθὲς φάρμακον, ὃ λαβεῖν φησιν ὁ ποιητὴς τὴν
Ἑλένην ἐκ τῶν Αἰγυπτίων Θηβῶν παρὰ Πολυ-

---

1 Cp. chap. 61.
2 i.e. "quieting pain." Cp. Odyssey 4. 220–21: αὐτίκ' ἄρ'
ἐς οἶνον βάλε φάρμακον, ἔνθεν ἔπινον, νηπενθές τ' ἄχολόν τε,

rope and many others beyond him are unravelling
it. Melampus also, they say, brought from Egypt
the rites which the Greeks celebrate in the name of
Dionysus, the myths about Cronus and the War with
the Titans, and, in a word, the account of the things
which happened to the gods. Daedalus, they relate,
copied the maze of the Labyrinth which stands to our
day and was built, according to some, by Mendes,[1]
but according to others, by king Marrus, many years
before the reign of Minos. And the proportions of
the ancient statues of Egypt are the same as in those
made by Daedalus among the Greeks. The very
beautiful propylon of the temple of Hephaestus in
Memphis was also built by Daedalus, who became
an object of admiration and was granted a statue of
himself in wood, which was made by his own hands
and set up in this temple; furthermore, he was
accorded great fame because of his genius and, after
making many discoveries, was granted divine
honours; for on one of the islands off Memphis there
stands even to this day a temple of Daedalus, which
is honoured by the people of that region.

And as proof of the presence of Homer in Egypt
they adduce various pieces of evidence, and especially
the healing drink which brings forgetfulness of all
past evils, which was given by Helen to Telemachus
in the home of Menelaüs. For it is manifest that
the poet had acquired exact knowledge of the
" nepenthic "[2] drug which he says Helen brought
from Egyptian Thebes, given her by Polydamna the

κακῶν ἐπίληθον ἁπάντων. "Straightway she cast into the wine
of which they were drinking a drug to quiet all pain and
strife, and bring forgetfulness of every ill" (tr. Murray in
L.C.L.).

δάμνης τῆς Θῶνος γυναικός, ἀκριβῶς ἐξητακὼς
φαίνεται· ἔτι γὰρ καὶ νῦν τὰς ἐν ταύτῃ γυναῖκας
τῇ προειρημένῃ δυνάμει χρῆσθαι λέγουσι, καὶ
παρὰ μόναις ταῖς Διοσπολίτισιν ἐκ παλαιῶν
χρόνων ὀργῆς καὶ λύπης φάρμακον εὑρῆσθαί
φασι· τὰς δὲ Θήβας καὶ Διὸς πόλιν τὴν αὐτὴν
8 ὑπάρχειν. τήν τε Ἀφροδίτην ὀνομάζεσθαι
παρὰ τοῖς ἐγχωρίοις χρυσῆν ἐκ παλαιᾶς παραδόσεως, καὶ πεδίον εἶναι καλούμενον χρυσῆς
Ἀφροδίτης περὶ τὴν ὀνομαζομένην Μώμεμφιν.
9 τά τε περὶ τὸν Δία καὶ τὴν Ἥραν μυθολογούμενα περὶ τῆς συνουσίας καὶ τὴν εἰς Αἰθιοπίαν
ἐκδημίαν ἐκεῖθεν αὐτὸν μετενεγκεῖν· κατ᾽ ἐνιαυτὸν
γὰρ παρὰ τοῖς Αἰγυπτίοις τὸν νεὼν τοῦ Διὸς
περαιοῦσθαι τὸν ποταμὸν εἰς τὴν Λιβύην, καὶ
μεθ᾽ ἡμέρας τινὰς πάλιν ἐπιστρέφειν, ὡς ἐξ
Αἰθιοπίας τοῦ θεοῦ παρόντος· τήν τε συνουσίαν
τῶν θεῶν τούτων, ἐν ταῖς πανηγύρεσι τῶν ναῶν
ἀνακομιζομένων ἀμφοτέρων εἰς ὄρος ἄνθεσι
παντοίοις ὑπὸ τῶν ἱερέων κατεστρωμένον.

98. Καὶ Λυκοῦργον δὲ καὶ Πλάτωνα καὶ Σόλωνα
πολλὰ τῶν ἐξ Αἰγύπτου νομίμων εἰς τὰς ἑαυτῶν
2 κατατάξαι νομοθεσίας. Πυθαγόραν τε τὰ κατὰ
τὸν ἱερὸν λόγον καὶ τὰ κατὰ γεωμετρίαν θεωρήματα
καὶ τὰ περὶ τοὺς ἀριθμούς, ἔτι δὲ τὴν εἰς πᾶν
ζῷον τῆς ψυχῆς μεταβολὴν μαθεῖν παρ᾽ Αἰγυ-
3 πτίων. ὑπολαμβάνουσι δὲ καὶ Δημόκριτον παρ᾽
αὐτοῖς ἔτη διατρῖψαι πέντε καὶ πολλὰ διδα-
χθῆναι τῶν κατὰ τὴν ἀστρολογίαν. τόν τε
Οἰνοπίδην ὁμοίως συνδιατρίψαντα τοῖς ἱερεῦσι

---

[1] A reference to the epithet constantly used by Homer to
describe Aphrodite.

wife of Thon; for, they allege, even to this day the
women of this city use this powerful remedy, and in
ancient times, they say, a drug to cure anger and
sorrow was discovered exclusively among the women
of Diospolis; but Thebes and Diospolis, they add,
are the same city. Again, Aphrodite is called
" golden " [1] by the natives in accordance with an
old tradition, and near the city which is called
Momemphis there is a plain " of golden Aphrodite."
Likewise, the myths which are related about the
dalliance of Zeus and Hera and of their journey to
Ethiopia he also got from Egypt; for each year
among the Egyptians the shrine of Zeus is carried
across the river into Libya and then brought back
some days later, as if the god were arriving from
Ethiopia; and as for the dalliance of these deities,
in their festal gatherings the priests carry the shrines
of both to an elevation that has been strewn with
flowers of every description.[2]

98. Lycurgus also and Plato and Solon, they say,
incorporated many Egyptian customs into their own
legislation. And Pythagoras learned from Egyptians
his teachings about the gods, his geometrical pro-
positions and theory of numbers, as well as the trans-
migration of the soul into every living thing. Democritus [3] also, as they assert, spent five years among
them and was instructed in many matters relating
to astrology. Oenopides likewise passed some time

[2] The Homeric passage which Diodorus has in mind is in the
14th Book of the *Iliad* (ll. 346 ff.): " The son of Kronos
clasped his consort in his arms. And beneath them the divine
earth sent forth fresh new grass, and dewy lotus, and crocus,
and hyacinth, thick and soft . . ." (tr. Lang, Leaf, Myers).

[3] Democritus of Abdera, the distinguished scientist of the
fifth century B.C., author of the " atomic " theory.

καὶ ἀστρολόγοις μαθεῖν ἄλλα τε καὶ μάλιστα
τὸν ἡλιακὸν κύκλον ὡς λοξὴν μὲν ἔχει τὴν
πορείαν, ἐναντίαν δὲ τοῖς ἄλλοις ἄστροις τὴν
4 φορὰν ποιεῖται.   παραπλησίως δὲ καὶ τὸν
Εὔδοξον ἀστρολογήσαντα παρ' αὐτοῖς καὶ πολλὰ
τῶν χρησίμων εἰς τοὺς Ἕλληνας ἐκδόντα τυχεῖν
ἀξιολόγου δόξης.

5   Τῶν τε ἀγαλματοποιῶν τῶν παλαιῶν τοὺς
μάλιστα διωνομασμένους διατετριφέναι παρ'
αὐτοῖς Τηλεκλέα καὶ Θεόδωρον, τοὺς Ῥοίκου
μὲν υἱούς, κατασκευάσαντας δὲ τοῖς Σαμίοις τὸ
6 τοῦ Ἀπόλλωνος τοῦ Πυθίου ξόανον. τοῦ γὰρ
ἀγάλματος ἐν Σάμῳ μὲν ὑπὸ Τηλεκλέους ἱστο-
ρεῖται τὸ ἥμισυ δημιουργηθῆναι, κατὰ δὲ τὴν
Ἔφεσον ὑπὸ τἀδελφοῦ Θεοδώρου τὸ ἕτερον
μέρος συντελεσθῆναι· συντεθέντα δὲ πρὸς ἄλληλα τὰ μέρη συμφωνεῖν οὕτως ὥστε δοκεῖν
ὑφ' ἑνὸς τὸ πᾶν ἔργον συντετελέσθαι.[1]   τοῦτο

---

[1] ἔργον συντετελέσθαι Vogel: σῶμα κατεσκευάσθαι CF,
Bekker, Dindorf.

---

[1] Oenopides of Chios was a mathematician and astronomer
of the fifth century B.C. According to this statement he
observed the obliquity of the ecliptic, which we now know to
be about 23½°. The fact that the sun's motion on the celestial
sphere is slower than that of the stars causes an apparently
retrograde movement of the sun relative to the stars.

[2] Doubtless the cult statue.

[3] The following sentences are perplexing. The translator is
comforted by the knowledge that they have vexed others who
are more experienced both in Egyptian art and in Greek.
This passage has been discussed last by Heinrich Schäfer
(Von ägyptischer Kunst³, Leipzig, 1930, pp. 350–51), and the
remarks and translation of so distinguished an authority on
Egyptian art deserve to be cited, and in the original.

with the priests and astrologers and learned among
other things about the orbit of the sun, that it has
an oblique course and moves in a direction opposite
to that of the other stars.[1] Like the others, Eudoxus
studied astrology with them and acquired a notable
fame for the great amount of useful knowledge which
he disseminated among the Greeks.

Also of the ancient sculptors the most renowned sojourned among them, namely, Telecles and Theodorus,
the sons of Rhoecus, who executed for the people
of Samos the wooden [2] statue of the Pythian Apollo.
For one half of the statue, as the account is given,
was worked by Telecles in Samos, and the other half
was finished by his brother Theodorus at Ephesus;
and when the two parts were brought together they
fitted so perfectly that the whole work had the
appearance of having been done by one man.   This [3]

" Ich würde die Stelle aus Diodor dem Sizilier (um 50 v.
Chr.), die nicht so einfach ist wie sie scheint, am liebsten nur
griechisch abdrucken, aber damit wäre dem Leser nicht
gedient; ich muss zeigen, wie ich sie auffasse.   W. Schubart
und U.v. Wilamowitz bin ich dafür dankbar, dass sie, denen
der ägyptische Sachverhalt nicht so klar vor Augen steht, mich
an einigen Stellen davor bewahrt haben, ihn in Diodors Worte
hineinzudeuten.   Ein Trost in meiner Verlegenheit ist mir
gewesen, dass v. Wilamowitz mir schrieb, ' Die Übersetzung
der Diodorstelle ist in der Tat knifflich, da er seine Vorlage,
Heraklit [a slip of the pen for " Hecataeus "—Tr.] von Abdera
(um 300 v. Chr.), verschwommen wiedergibt und überhaupt ein
so miserabler Skribent ist.'   Ich wage folgende freie Übersetzung :

" . . . Dieses Werkverfahren (nämlich Statuen aus einzeln
gefertigen Hälften zusammenzusetzen) soll bei den Hellenen
nirgends in Gebrauch sein, dagegen bei den Ägyptern meistens
angewendet werden.   (Nur dort sei es denkbar.)   Bei ihnen
nämlich bestimme man den symmetrischen Bau der Statuen
nicht nach der freien Entscheidung des Auges, wie bei den

δὲ τὸ γένος τῆς ἐργασίας παρὰ μὲν τοῖς Ἕλλησι
μηδαμῶς ἐπιτηδεύεσθαι, παρὰ δὲ τοῖς Αἰγυπτίοις
7 μάλιστα συντελεῖσθαι. παρ' ἐκείνοις γὰρ οὐκ
ἀπὸ τῆς κατὰ τὴν ὅρασιν φαντασίας τὴν συμμετρίαν τῶν ἀγαλμάτων κρίνεσθαι, καθάπερ
παρὰ τοῖς Ἕλλησιν, ἀλλ' ἐπειδὰν τοὺς λίθους
κατακλίνωσι[1] καὶ μερίσαντες κατεργάσωνται,
τὸ τηνικαῦτα τὸ ἀνάλογον ἀπὸ τῶν ἐλαχίστων
8 ἐπὶ τὰ μέγιστα λαμβάνεσθαι· τοῦ γὰρ παντὸς
σώματος τὴν κατασκευὴν εἰς ἓν καὶ εἴκοσι μέρη
καὶ προσέτι τέταρτον διαιρουμένους τὴν ὅλην
ἀποδιδόναι συμμετρίαν τοῦ ζῴου. διόπερ ὅταν
περὶ τοῦ μεγέθους οἱ τεχνῖται πρὸς ἀλλήλους
σύνθωνται, χωρισθέντες ἀπ' ἀλλήλων σύμφωνα
κατασκευάζουσι τὰ μεγέθη τῶν ἔργων οὕτως
ἀκριβῶς ὥστε ἔκπληξιν παρέχειν τὴν ἰδιότητα
9 τῆς πραγματείας αὐτῶν. τὸ δ' ἐν τῇ Σάμῳ
ξόανον συμφώνως τῇ τῶν Αἰγυπτίων φιλοτεχνίᾳ
κατὰ τὴν κορυφὴν[2] διχοτομούμενον διορίζειν

---

[1] κατακλίνωσι Bekker, Vogel: Dindorf conjectured κατα-
ξάνωσι.

[2] κορυφὴν Rhodomann: ὀροφήν.

Hellenen, sondern, nachdem man die Blöcke hingelegt und
gesondert zugerichtet habe, hielten sich die Arbeiter dann,
jeder innerhalb seiner Hälfte, aber auch in bezug auf die
andere, an dieselben Verhältnisse von den kleinsten bis zu den
grössten Teilen. Sie zerlegten nämlich die Höhe des ganzen
Körpers in einundzwanzig und ein Viertel Teile, und erreichten
so den symmetrischen Aufbau der Menschengestalt. Hätten
sich also die (beiden) Bildhauer einmal über die Grösse (der
Statue) geeinigt, so stimmten sie, selbst von einander getrennt,
die Einzelmasse ihrer Werkteile so genau zueinander, dass man
ganz verblüfft sei über dieses ihr eigentümliches Verfahren.
So bestehe das Kultbild in Samos, etc."

[1] No explanation of the "twenty-one and one-fourth"

method of working is practised nowhere among the
Greeks, but is followed generally among the Egyptians. For with them the symmetrical proportions
of the statues are not fixed in accordance with the
appearance they present to the artist's eye, as is
done among the Greeks, but as soon as they lay out
the stones and, after apportioning them, are ready
to work on them, at that stage they take the proportions, from the smallest parts to the largest;
for, dividing the structure of the entire body into
twenty-one parts and one-fourth[1] in addition, they
express in this way the complete figure in its symmetrical proportions. Consequently, so soon as the
artisans agree as to the size of the statue, they
separate and proceed to turn out the various sizes
assigned to them, in such a way that they correspond,
and they do it so accurately that the peculiarity of
their system excites amazement.[2] And the wooden
statue in Samos, in conformity with the ingenious
method of the Egyptians, was cut into two parts
from the top of the head down to the private parts

parts has been found in any modern writer. W. Deonna
(*Dédale ou la Statue de la Grèce Archaïque*, 2 vols., Paris, 1930)
translates this sentence, and then adds (1. p. 229): "Mais
l'étude de l'art égyptien révèle que celui-ci a connu, comme
tout autre art, des proportions très variables, tantôt courtes,
tantôt élancées, suivant les temps, et souvent à même époque,
et qu'il n'est pas possible de fixer un canon précis."

[2] Since the Egyptian artist had no idea of perspective, each
part of a figure, or each member of a group, was portrayed as
if seen from directly in front. Therefore the first training of
an artist consisted in the making of the separate members of
the body, which accounts for the many heads, hands, legs, feet,
which come from the Egyptian schools of art. Schäfer (*l.c.*,
p. 316, cp. p. 389) suggests that this practice may have given
Diodorus the idea that the Egyptians made their statues out
of previously prepared blocks of stone.

τοῦ ζῴου τὸ μέσον μέχρι τῶν αἰδοίων, ἰσάζον
ὁμοίως ἑαυτῷ πάντοθεν· εἶναι δ' αὐτὸ λέγουσι
κατὰ τὸ πλεῖστον παρεμφερὲς τοῖς Αἰγυπτίοις,
ὡς ἂν τὰς μὲν χεῖρας ἔχον παρατεταμένας, τὰ δὲ
σκέλη διαβεβηκότα.

10   Περὶ μὲν οὖν τῶν κατ' Αἴγυπτον ἱστορουμένων
καὶ μνήμης ἀξίων ἀρκεῖ τὰ ῥηθέντα· ἡμεῖς δὲ
κατὰ τὴν ἐν ἀρχῇ τῆς βίβλου πρόθεσιν τὰς
ἑξῆς πράξεις καὶ μυθολογίας ἐν τῇ μετὰ ταύτην
διέξιμεν, ἀρχὴν ποιησάμενοι τὰ κατὰ τὴν Ἀσίαν
τοῖς Ἀσσυρίοις πραχθέντα.

and the statue was divided in the middle, each part exactly matching the other at every point. And they say that this statue is for the most part rather similar to those of Egypt, as having the arms stretched stiffly down the sides and the legs separated in a stride.

Now regarding Egypt, the events which history records and the things that deserve to be mentioned, this account is sufficient; and we shall present in the next Book, in keeping with our profession at the beginning of this Book, the events and legendary accounts next in order, beginning with the part played by the Assyrians in Asia.

BOOK II

Τάδε ἔνεστιν ἐν τῇ δευτέρᾳ τῶν
Διοδώρου βίβλων

Περὶ Νίνου τοῦ πρώτου βασιλεύσαντος κατὰ τὴν Ἀσίαν
καὶ τῶν ὑπ' αὐτοῦ πραχθέντων.

Περὶ τῆς Σεμιράμιδος γενέσεως καὶ τῆς περὶ αὐτὴν
αὐξήσεως.

Ὡς Νίνος ὁ βασιλεὺς ἔγημε τὴν Σεμίραμιν διὰ τὴν
ἀρετὴν αὐτῆς.

Ὡς Σεμίραμις τελευτήσαντος Νίνου διαδεξαμένη τὴν
βασιλείαν πολλὰς καὶ μεγάλας πράξεις ἐπετελέσατο.

Κτίσις Βαβυλῶνος καὶ τῆς κατ' αὐτὴν κατασκευῆς
ἀπαγγελία.[1]

Περὶ τοῦ κρεμαστοῦ λεγομένου κήπου καὶ τῶν ἄλλων
τῶν κατὰ τὴν Βαβυλωνίαν παραδόξων.

Στρατεία Σεμιράμιδος εἰς Αἴγυπτον καὶ Αἰθιοπίαν, ἔτι
δὲ τὴν Ἰνδικήν.

Περὶ τῶν ἀπογόνων ταύτης[2] τῶν βασιλευσάντων κατὰ
τὴν Ἀσίαν καὶ τῆς κατ' αὐτοὺς τρυφῆς τε καὶ ῥαθυμίας.

Ὡς ἔσχατος Σαρδανάπαλλος ὁ βασιλεὺς διὰ τρυφὴν
ἀπέβαλε τὴν ἀρχὴν ὑπὸ Ἀρβάκου τοῦ Μήδου.

Περὶ τῶν Χαλδαίων καὶ τῆς παρατηρήσεως τῶν
ἄστρων.

Περὶ τῶν βασιλέων τῶν κατὰ τὴν Μηδίαν καὶ τῆς περὶ
τούτων διαφωνίας παρὰ τοῖς ἱστοριογράφοις.

Περὶ τοποθεσίας τῆς Ἰνδικῆς καὶ τῶν κατὰ τὴν χώραν
φυομένων καὶ τῶν παρ' Ἰνδοῖς νομίμων.

---

[1] ἀπαγγελία omitted by D, Vogel.
[2] καὶ after ταύτης deleted by Dindorf.

344

CONTENTS OF THE SECOND BOOK
OF DIODORUS

DIODORUS OF SICILY

Περὶ Σκυθῶν καὶ Ἀμαζόνων καὶ Ὑπερβορέων.

Περὶ τῆς Ἀραβίας καὶ τῶν κατ' αὐτὴν φυομένων καὶ μυθολογουμένων.

Περὶ τῶν νήσων τῶν ἐν τῇ μεσημβρίᾳ κατὰ τὸν ὠκεανὸν εὑρεθεισῶν.

CONTENTS OF THE SECOND BOOK

ΒΙΒΛΟΣ ΔΕΥΤΕΡΑ

1. Ἡ μὲν πρὸ ταύτης βίβλος τῆς ὅλης συντάξεως οὖσα πρώτη περιέχει τὰς κατ' Αἴγυπτον
πράξεις· ἐν αἷς ὑπάρχει τά τε περὶ τῶν θεῶν
παρ' Αἰγυπτίοις μυθολογούμενα καὶ περὶ τῆς τοῦ
Νείλου φύσεως καὶ τἄλλα τὰ περὶ τοῦ ποταμοῦ
τούτου παραδοξολογούμενα, πρὸς δὲ τούτοις περί
τε τῆς κατ' Αἴγυπτον χώρας καὶ τῶν ἀρχαίων
βασιλέων τὰ ὑφ' ἑκάστου πραχθέντα. ἑξῆς δὲ
κατετάχθησαν αἱ κατασκευαὶ τῶν πυραμίδων
τῶν ἀναγραφομένων ἐν τοῖς ἑπτὰ θαυμαζομένοις
2 ἔργοις. ἔπειτα[1] διήλθομεν περὶ τῶν νόμων καὶ
τῶν δικαστηρίων, ἔτι δὲ τῶν ἀφιερωμένων ζῴων
παρ' Αἰγυπτίοις τὰ θαυμαζόμενα, πρὸς δὲ τούτοις
τὰ περὶ τῶν τετελευτηκότων νόμιμα, καὶ τῶν
Ἑλλήνων ὅσοι τῶν ἐπὶ παιδείᾳ θαυμαζομένων
παραβαλόντες εἰς Αἴγυπτον καὶ πολλὰ τῶν
χρησίμων μαθόντες μετήνεγκαν εἰς τὴν Ἑλλάδα.
3 ἐν ταύτῃ δ' ἀναγράψομεν τὰς κατὰ τὴν Ἀσίαν
γενομένας πράξεις ἐν τοῖς ἀρχαίοις χρόνοις, τὴν
ἀρχὴν ἀπὸ τῆς τῶν Ἀσσυρίων ἡγεμονίας ποιησάμενοι.
4 Τὸ παλαιὸν τοίνυν κατὰ τὴν Ἀσίαν ὑπῆρχον
ἐγχώριοι βασιλεῖς, ὧν οὔτε πρᾶξις ἐπίσημος οὔτε
ὄνομα μνημονεύεται. πρῶτος δὲ τῶν εἰς ἱστορίαν
καὶ μνήμην παραδεδομένων ἡμῖν Νίνος ὁ βασιλεὺς
τῶν Ἀσσυρίων μεγάλας πράξεις ἐπετελέσατο·

348

BOOK II

THE preceding Book, being the first of the whole work, embraces the facts which concern Egypt, among which are included both the myths related by the Egyptians about their gods and about the nature of the Nile, and the other marvels which are told about this river, as well as a description of the land of Egypt and the acts of each of their ancient kings. Next in order came the structures known as the pyramids, which are listed among the seven wonders of the world. After that we discussed such matters connected with the laws and the courts of law, and also with the animals which are considered sacred among the Egyptians, as excite admiration and wonder, also their customs with respect to the dead, and then named such Greeks as were noted for their learning, who, upon visiting Egypt and being instructed in many useful things, thereupon transferred them to Greece. And in this present Book we shall set forth the events which took place in Asia in the ancient period, beginning with the time when the Assyrians were the dominant power.

In the earliest age, then, the kings of Asia were native-born, and in connection with them no memory is preserved of either a notable deed or a personal name. The first to be handed down by tradition to history and memory for us as one who achieved great deeds is Ninus, king of the Assyrians, and of him

---

¹ ἔπειτα Bekker, Vogel : ἔπειτα δὲ D, Dindorf.

περὶ οὗ τὰ κατὰ μέρος ἀναγράφειν πειρασόμεθα.
γενόμενος γὰρ φύσει πολεμικὸς καὶ ζηλωτὴς τῆς
ἀρετῆς καθώπλισε τῶν νέων τοὺς κρατίστους·
γυμνάσας δ' αὐτοὺς πλείονα χρόνον συνήθεις
ἐποίησε πάσῃ κακοπαθείᾳ καὶ πολεμικοῖς κιν-
5 δύνοις. συστησάμενος οὖν στρατόπεδον ἀξιόλογον συμμαχίαν ἐποιήσατο πρὸς Ἀριαῖον τὸν
βασιλέα τῆς Ἀραβίας, ἣ κατ' ἐκείνους τοὺς
χρόνοις ἐδόκει πλήθειν ἀλκίμων ἀνδρῶν. ἔστι
δὲ καὶ καθόλου τοῦτο τὸ ἔθνος φιλελεύθερον καὶ
κατ' οὐδένα τρόπον προσδεχόμενον ἔπηλυν
ἡγεμόνα· διόπερ οὔθ' οἱ τῶν Περσῶν βασιλεῖς
ὕστερον οὔθ' οἱ τῶν Μακεδόνων, καίπερ πλεῖστον
ἰσχύσαντες, ἠδυνήθησαν τοῦτο τὸ ἔθνος κατα-
6 δουλώσασθαι. καθόλου γὰρ ἡ Ἀραβία δυσπολέ-
μητός ἐστι ξενικαῖς δυνάμεσι διὰ τὸ τὴν μὲν
ἔρημον αὐτῆς εἶναι, τὴν δὲ ἄνυδρον καὶ διειλημ-
μένην φρέασι κεκρυμμένοις καὶ μόνοις τοῖς
7 ἐγχωρίοις γνωριζομένοις. ὁ δ' οὖν τῶν Ἀσσυρίων
βασιλεὺς Νίνος τὸν δυναστεύοντα τῶν Ἀράβων
παραλαβὼν ἐστράτευσε μετὰ πολλῆς δυνάμεως
ἐπὶ Βαβυλωνίους κατοικοῦντας ὅμορον χώραν·
κατ' ἐκείνους δὲ τοὺς χρόνους ἡ μὲν νῦν οὖσα Βαβυ-
λὼν οὐκ ἦν ἐκτισμένη, κατὰ δὲ τὴν Βαβυλωνίαν
ὑπῆρχον ἄλλαι πόλεις ἀξιόλογοι· ῥᾳδίως δὲ
χειρωσάμενος τοὺς ἐγχωρίους διὰ τὸ τῶν ἐν τοῖς
πολέμοις κινδύνων ἀπείρως ἔχειν, τούτοις μὲν
ἔταξε τελεῖν κατ' ἐνιαυτὸν ὡρισμένους φόρους,
τὸν δὲ βασιλέα τῶν καταπολεμηθέντων λαβὼν
8 μετὰ τῶν τέκνων αἰχμάλωτον ἀπέκτεινε. μετὰ
δὲ ταῦτα πολλοῖς πλήθεσιν εἰς τὴν Ἀρμενίαν ἐμ-
βαλὼν καί τινας τῶν πόλεων ἀναστάτους ποιήσας

we shall now endeavour to give a detailed account.
For being by nature a warlike man and emulous of
valour, he supplied the strongest of the young men
with arms, and by training them for a considerable
time he accustomed them to every hardship and all
the dangers of war. And when now he had collected
a notable army, he formed an alliance with Ariaeus,
the king of Arabia, a country which in those times
seems to have abounded in brave men. Now, in
general, this nation is one which loves freedom and
under no circumstances submits to a foreign ruler;
consequently neither the kings of the Persians at a
later time nor those of the Macedonians, though the
most powerful of their day, were ever able to enslave
this nation. For Arabia is, in general, a difficult
country for a foreign army to campaign in, part of it
being desert and part of it waterless and supplied
at intervals with wells which are hidden and known
only to the natives.[1] Ninus, however, the king of the
Assyrians, taking along the ruler of the Arabians as
an ally, made a campaign with a great army against
the Babylonians whose country bordered upon his—in
those times the present city of Babylon had not yet
been founded, but there were other notable cities in
Babylonia—and after easily subduing the inhabitants
of that region because of their inexperience in the
dangers of war, he laid upon them the yearly payment
of fixed tributes, but the king of the conquered,
whom he took captive along with his children, he put
to death. Then, invading Armenia in great force
and laying waste some of its cities, he struck terror

---

[1] Arabia and its peoples are more fully described in chaps.
48 ff.

κατεπλήξατο τοὺς ἐγχωρίους· διόπερ ὁ βασιλεὺς
αὐτῶν Βαρζάνης, ὁρῶν αὐτὸν οὐκ ἀξιόμαχον ὄντα,
μετὰ πολλῶν δώρων ἀπήντησε καὶ πᾶν ἔφησε
9 ποιήσειν τὸ προσταττόμενον. ὁ δὲ Νίνος μεγα-
λοψύχως αὐτῷ χρησάμενος τῆς τε Ἀρμενίας
συνεχώρησεν ἄρχειν καὶ φίλον ὄντα πέμπειν
στρατιὰν καὶ τὴν χορηγίαν τῷ σφετέρῳ στρατοπέδῳ. ἀεὶ δὲ μᾶλλον αὐξόμενος ἐστράτευσεν εἰς
10 τὴν Μηδίαν. ὁ δὲ ταύτης βασιλεὺς Φάρνος
παραταξάμενος ἀξιολόγῳ δυνάμει καὶ λειφθείς,
τῶν τε στρατιωτῶν τοὺς πλείους [1] ἀπέβαλε καὶ
αὐτὸς μετὰ τέκνων ἑπτὰ καὶ γυναικὸς αἰχμάλωτος
ληφθεὶς ἀνεσταυρώθη.

2. Οὕτω δὲ τῶν πραγμάτων τῷ Νίνῳ προχωρούντων δεινὴν ἐπιθυμίαν ἔσχε τοῦ κατα-
στρέψασθαι τὴν Ἀσίαν ἅπασαν τὴν ἐντὸς
Τανάιδος καὶ Νείλου· ὡς ἐπίπαν γὰρ τοῖς εὐτυ-
χοῦσιν ἡ τῶν πραγμάτων εὔροια [2] τὴν τοῦ
πλείονος ἐπιθυμίαν παρίστησι. διόπερ τῆς μὲν
Μηδίας σατράπην ἕνα τῶν περὶ αὐτὸν φίλων
κατέστησεν, αὐτὸς δ' ἐπῄει τὰ κατὰ τὴν Ἀσίαν
ἔθνη καταστρεφόμενος, καὶ χρόνον ἑπτακαιδε-
καετῆ καταναλώσας πλὴν Ἰνδῶν καὶ Βακτριανῶν
2 τῶν ἄλλων ἁπάντων κύριος ἐγένετο. τὰς μὲν
οὖν καθ' ἕκαστα μάχας ἢ τὸν ἀριθμὸν ἁπάντων
τῶν καταπολεμηθέντων οὐδεὶς τῶν συγγραφέων
ἀνέγραψε, τὰ δ' ἐπισημότατα τῶν ἐθνῶν ἀκολούθως Κτησίᾳ τῷ Κνιδίῳ πειρασόμεθα συντόμως
ἐπιδραμεῖν.

3 Κατεστρέψατο μὲν γὰρ τῆς παραθαλαττίου

---

[1] πλείους Vogel: πλείστους Vulgate, Bekker, Dindorf.

into the inhabitants; consequently their king
Barzanes, realizing that he was no match for him in
battle, met him with many presents and announced
that he would obey his every command. But Ninus
treated him with great magnanimity, and agreed that
he should not only continue to rule over Armenia
but should also, as his friend, furnish a contingent
and supplies for the Assyrian army. And as his power
continually increased, he made a campaign against
Media. And the king of this country, Pharnus,
meeting him in battle with a formidable force, was
defeated, and he both lost the larger part of his
soldiers, and himself, being taken captive along with
his seven sons and wife, was crucified.

2. Since the undertakings of Ninus were prospering
in this way, he was seized with a powerful desire to
subdue all of Asia that lies between the Tanaïs [1] and
the Nile; for, as a general thing, when men enjoy
good fortune, the steady current of their success
prompts in them the desire for more. Consequently
he made one of his friends satrap of Media, while he
himself set about the task of subduing the nations of
Asia, and within a period of seventeen years he became
master of them all except the Indians and Bactrians.
Now no historian has recorded the battles with each
nation or the number of all the peoples conquered,
but we shall undertake to run over briefly the most
important nations, as given in the account of Ctesias
of Cnidus.[2]

Of the lands which lie on the sea and of the others

[1] The Don.
[2] On Ctesias see the Introduction, pp. xxvi–xxvii.

---

[2] εὔροια Herwerden : ἐπίρροια.

καὶ τῆς συνεχοῦς χώρας τήν τε Αἴγυπτον καὶ
Φοινίκην, ἔτι δὲ Κοίλην Συρίαν καὶ Κιλικίαν καὶ
Παμφυλίαν καὶ Λυκίαν, πρὸς δὲ ταύταις τήν τε
Καρίαν καὶ Φρυγίαν[1] καὶ Λυδίαν, προσηγάγετο
δὲ τήν τε Τρῳάδα καὶ τὴν ἐφ᾽ Ἑλλησπόντῳ
Φρυγίαν καὶ Προποντίδα καὶ Βιθυνίαν καὶ Καπ-
παδοκίαν καὶ τὰ κατὰ τὸν Πόντον ἔθνη βάρβαρα
κατοικοῦντα μέχρι Τανάϊδος, ἐκυρίευσε δὲ τῆς
τε Καδουσίων χώρας καὶ Ταπύρων, ἔτι δ᾽
Ὑρκανίων καὶ Δραγγῶν, πρὸς δὲ τούτοις
Δερβίκων καὶ Καρμανίων καὶ Χωρομναίων, ἔτι
δὲ Βορκανίων καὶ Παρθυαίων, ἐπῆλθε δὲ καὶ
τὴν Περσίδα καὶ τὴν Σουσιανὴν καὶ τὴν καλουμένην Κασπιανήν, εἰς ἥν εἰσιν εἰσβολαὶ στεναὶ
παντελῶς, διὸ καὶ προσαγορεύονται Κάσπιαι
4 πύλαι. πολλὰ δὲ καὶ ἄλλα τῶν ἐλαττόνων
ἐθνῶν προσηγάγετο, περὶ ὧν μακρὸν ἂν εἴη
λέγειν.   τῆς δὲ Βακτριανῆς οὔσης δυσεισβόλου
καὶ πλήθη μαχίμων ἀνδρῶν ἐχούσης, ἐπειδὴ
πολλὰ πονήσας ἄπρακτος ἐγένετο, τὸν μὲν πρὸς
Βακτριανοὺς πόλεμον εἰς ἕτερον ἀνεβάλετο
καιρόν, τὰς δὲ δυνάμεις ἀναγαγὼν εἰς τὴν
Ἀσσυρίαν ἐξελέξατο τόπον εὔθετον εἰς πόλεως
μεγάλης κτίσιν.

3. Ἐπιφανεστάτας γὰρ πράξεις τῶν πρὸ αὐτοῦ
κατειργασμένος ἔσπευδε τηλικαύτην κτίσαι τὸ
μέγεθος πόλιν ὥστε μὴ μόνον αὐτὴν εἶναι μεγίστην τῶν τότε οὐσῶν κατὰ πᾶσαν τὴν οἰκουμένην,
ἀλλὰ μηδὲ τῶν μεταγενεστέρων ἕτερον ἐπιβαλό-
2 μενον ῥᾳδίως ἂν ὑπερθέσθαι.   τὸν μὲν οὖν τῶν
Ἀράβων βασιλέα τιμήσας δώροις καὶ λαφύροις
μεγαλοπρεπέσιν ἀπέλυσε μετὰ τῆς ἰδίας στρατιᾶς

354

which border on these, Ninus subdued Egypt and
Phoenicia, then Coele-Syria, Cilicia, Pamphylia, and
Lycia, and also Caria, Phrygia, and Lydia; moreover,
he brought under his sway the Troad, Phrygia on
the Hellespont, Propontis, Bithynia, Cappadocia, and
all the barbarian nations who inhabit the shores of
the Pontus as far as the Tanaïs; he also made himself lord of the lands of the Cadusii, Tapyri, Hyrcanii,
Drangi, of the Derbici, Carmanii, Choromnaei, and
of the Borcanii, and Parthyaei; and he invaded both
Persis and Susiana and Caspiana, as it is called, which
is entered by exceedingly narrow passes, known for
that reason as the Caspian Gates. Many other
lesser nations he also brought under his rule, about
whom it would be a long task to speak. But since
Bactriana was difficult to invade and contained
multitudes of warlike men, after much toil and
labour in vain he deferred to a later time the war
against the Bactriani, and leading his forces back
into Assyria selected a place excellently situated for
the founding of a great city.

3. For having accomplished deeds more notable
than those of any king before him, he was eager to
found a city of such magnitude, that not only would
it be the largest of any which then existed in the whole
inhabited world, but also that no other ruler of a later
time should, if he undertook such a task, find it easy
to surpass him. Accordingly, after honouring the
king of the Arabians with gifts and rich spoils from
his wars, he dismissed him and his contingent to

---

¹ καὶ Μυσίαν after Φρυγίαν, omitted by D, is deleted by
Kallenberg, *Textkritik und Sprachgebrauch Diodors*, I. 4.

εἰς τὴν οἰκείαν, αὐτὸς δὲ τὰς πανταχόθεν δυνάμεις καὶ παρασκευὰς πάντων τῶν ἐπιτηδείων ἀθροίσας παρὰ τὸν Εὐφράτην ποταμὸν ἔκτισε πόλιν εὖ τετειχισμένην, ἑτερόμηκες αὐτῆς ὑποστησάμενος τὸ σχῆμα. εἶχε δὲ τῶν μὲν μακροτέρων πλευρῶν ἑκατέραν ἡ πόλις ἑκατὸν καὶ πεντήκοντα σταδίων, 3 τῶν δὲ βραχυτέρων ἐνενήκοντα. διὸ καὶ τοῦ σύμπαντος περιβόλου συσταθέντος ἐκ σταδίων τετρακοσίων καὶ ὀγδοήκοντα τῆς ἐλπίδος οὐ διεψεύσθη· τηλικαύτην γὰρ πόλιν οὐδεὶς ὕστερον ἔκτισε κατά τε τὸ μέγεθος τοῦ περιβόλου καὶ τὴν περὶ τὸ τεῖχος μεγαλοπρέπειαν. τὸ μὲν γὰρ ὕψος εἶχε τὸ τεῖχος ποδῶν ἑκατόν, τὸ δὲ πλάτος τρισὶν ἅρμασιν ἱππάσιμον ἦν· οἱ δὲ σύμπαντες πύργοι τὸν μὲν ἀριθμὸν ἦσαν χίλιοι καὶ πεντα- κόσιοι, τὸ δ' ὕψος εἶχον ποδῶν διακοσίων. 4 κατῴκισε δ' εἰς αὐτὴν τῶν μὲν Ἀσσυρίων τοὺς πλείστους καὶ δυνατωτάτους, ἀπὸ δὲ τῶν ἄλλων ἐθνῶν τοὺς βουλομένους. καὶ τὴν μὲν πόλιν ὠνόμασεν ἀφ' ἑαυτοῦ Νίνον, τοῖς δὲ κατοικισθεῖσι πολλὴν τῆς ὁμόρου χώρας προσώρισεν.

4. Ἐπεὶ δὲ μετὰ τὴν κτίσιν ταύτην ὁ Νίνος ἐστράτευσεν ἐπὶ τὴν Βακτριανήν, ἐν ᾗ Σεμίραμιν ἔγημε τὴν ἐπιφανεστάτην ἁπασῶν τῶν γυναικῶν ὧν παρειλήφαμεν, ἀναγκαῖόν ἐστι περὶ αὐτῆς προειπεῖν πῶς ἐκ ταπεινῆς τύχης εἰς τηλικαύτην προήχθη δόξαν.

---

[1] The city of Nineveh, which lay on the east bank of the Tigris, not on the Euphrates. Strabo (16. 1. 3) says that it was " much greater " than Babylon, whose circuit, as given below (7. 3), was 360 stades.

[2] It is believed with reason that behind the mythical figure of Semiramis, made famous by Greek and Roman legend,

return to their own country and then, gathering his forces from every quarter and all the necessary material, he founded on the Euphrates river a city [1] which was well fortified with walls, giving it the form of a rectangle. The longer sides of the city were each one hundred and fifty stades in length, and the shorter ninety. And so, since the total circuit comprised four hundred and eighty stades, he was not disappointed in his hope, since a city its equal, in respect to either the length of its circuit or the magnificence of its walls, was never founded by any man after his time. For the wall had a height of one hundred feet and its width was sufficient for three chariots abreast to drive upon; and the sum total of its towers was one thousand five hundred, and their height was two hundred feet. He settled in it both Assyrians, who constituted the majority of the population and had the greatest power, and any who wished to come from all other nations. And to the city he gave his own name, Ninus, and he included within the territory of its colonists a large part of the neighbouring country.

4. Since after the founding of this city Ninus made a campaign against Bactriana, where he married Semiramis,[2] the most renowned of all women of whom we have any record, it is necessary first of all to tell how she rose from a lowly fortune to such fame.

" a sort of Assyrian Catherine II, distinguished equally in war and for sensuality " (How and Wells, *A Commentary on Herodotus*, 1. p. 143), lies the historical Sammu-ramat, who was queen-regent in the opening years of the reign of her son Adad-nirari III, 811–782 B.C. About her in the course of the centuries gathered many attributes of the Babylonian goddess Ishtar; her son greatly extended the Assyrian power (see *The Cambridge Ancient History*, 3. pp. 27 f., 183–4).

2 Κατὰ τὴν Συρίαν τοίνυν ἔστι πόλις Ἀσκάλων,
καὶ ταύτης οὐκ ἄπωθεν λίμνη μεγάλη καὶ βαθεῖα
πλήρης ἰχθύων. παρὰ δὲ ταύτην ὑπάρχει τέμενος θεᾶς ἐπιφανοῦς, ἣν ὀνομάζουσιν οἱ Σύροι
Δερκετοῦν· αὕτη δὲ τὸ μὲν πρόσωπον ἔχει
γυναικός, τὸ δ' ἄλλο σῶμα πᾶν ἰχθύος διά τινας
3 τοιαύτας αἰτίας. μυθολογοῦσιν οἱ λογιώτατοι
τῶν ἐγχωρίων τὴν Ἀφροδίτην προσκόψασαν τῇ
προειρημένῃ θεᾷ δεινὸν ἐμβαλεῖν ἔρωτα νεανίσκου
τινὸς τῶν θυόντων οὐκ ἀειδοῦς· τὴν δὲ Δερκετοῦν
μιγεῖσαν τῷ Σύρῳ γεννῆσαι μὲν θυγατέρα, καται-
σχυνθεῖσαν δ' ἐπὶ τοῖς ἡμαρτημένοις τὸν μὲν
νεανίσκον ἀφανίσαι, τὸ δὲ παιδίον εἰς τινας
ἐρήμους καὶ πετρώδεις τόπους ἐκθεῖναι·[1] ἑαυτὴν
δὲ διὰ τὴν αἰσχύνην καὶ λύπην ῥίψασαν εἰς τὴν
λίμνην μετασχηματισθῆναι τὸν τοῦ σώματος
τύπον εἰς ἰχθῦν· διὸ καὶ τοὺς Σύρους μέχρι τοῦ
νῦν ἀπέχεσθαι τούτου τοῦ ζῴου καὶ τιμᾶν τοὺς
4 ἰχθῦς ὡς θεούς. περὶ δὲ τὸν τόπον ὅπου τὸ
βρέφος ἐξετέθη πλήθους περιστερῶν ἐννεοτ-
τεύοντος παραδόξως καὶ δαιμονίως ὑπὸ τούτων
τὸ παιδίον διατρέφεσθαι· τὰς μὲν γὰρ ταῖς
πτέρυξι περιεχούσας τὸ σῶμα τοῦ βρέφους
πανταχόθεν θάλπειν, τὰς δ' ἐκ τῶν σύνεγγυς
ἐπαύλεων, ὁπότε τηρήσειαν τούς τε βουκόλους
καὶ τοὺς ἄλλους νομεῖς ἀπόντας,[2] ἐν τῷ στόματι
φερούσας γάλα διατρέφειν παρασταζούσας ἀνὰ

---

[1] So Rhodomann : ἐκθεῖναι ἐν οἷς πολλοῦ πλήθους περιστερῶν
ἐννοσσεύειν εἰωθότος παραδόξως τροφῆς καὶ σωτηρίας τυχεῖν τὸ
βρέφος ("where a great multitude of doves were wont to
have their nests and where the babe came upon nourishment and safety in an astounding manner"). Almost the
very same words are repeated in the following sentence.

Now there is in Syria a city known as Ascalon, and not far from it a large and deep lake, full of fish. On its shore is a precinct of a famous goddess whom the Syrians call Derceto; [1] and this goddess has the head of a woman but all the rest of her body is that of a fish, the reason being something like this. The story as given by the most learned of the inhabitants of the region is as follows: Aphrodite, being offended with this goddess, inspired in her a violent passion for a certain handsome youth among her votaries; and Derceto gave herself to the Syrian and bore a daughter, but then, filled with shame of her sinful deed, she killed the youth and exposed the child in a rocky desert region, while as for herself, from shame and grief she threw herself into the lake and was changed as to the form of her body into a fish; and it is for this reason that the Syrians to this day abstain from this animal and honour their fish as gods. But about the region where the babe was exposed a great multitude of doves had their nests, and by them the child was nurtured in an astounding and miraculous manner; for some of the doves kept the body of the babe warm on all sides by covering it with their wings, while others, when they observed that the cowherds and the other keepers were absent from the nearby steadings, brought milk therefrom in their beaks and fed the babe by putting it drop

[1] Another name for the Phoenician Astarte. Herodotus (1. 105) calls the goddess of Ascalon the "Heavenly Aphrodite."

---

[2] ἀπόντας Ursinus, Vogel: omitted ACDFG; λιπόντας all other MSS., Bekker, Dindorf.

5 μέσον τῶν χειλῶν. ἐνιαυσίου δὲ τοῦ παιδίου
γενομένου καὶ στερεωτέρας τροφῆς προσδεο-
μένου, τὰς περιστερὰς ἀποκνιζούσας ἀπὸ τῶν
τυρῶν παρέχεσθαι τροφὴν ἀρκοῦσαν. τοὺς δὲ
νομεῖς ἐπανιόντας καὶ θεωροῦντας περιβεβρω-
μένους τοὺς τυροὺς θαυμάσαι τὸ παράδοξον·
παρατηρήσαντας οὖν καὶ μαθόντας τὴν αἰτίαν
6 εὑρεῖν τὸ βρέφος, διαφέρον τῷ κάλλει. εὐθὺς
οὖν αὐτὸ κομίσαντας εἰς τὴν ἔπαυλιν δωρήσασθαι
τῷ προεστηκότι τῶν βασιλικῶν κτηνῶν, ὄνομα
Σίμμᾳ· καὶ τοῦτον ἄτεκνον ὄντα τὸ παιδίον
τρέφειν ὡς θυγάτριον μετὰ πάσης ἐπιμελείας,
ὄνομα θέμενον Σεμίραμιν, ὅπερ ἐστὶ κατὰ τὴν
τῶν Σύρων διάλεκτον παρωνομασμένον ἀπὸ τῶν
περιστερῶν, ἃς ἀπ᾽ ἐκείνων τῶν χρόνων οἱ κατὰ
Συρίαν ἅπαντες διετέλεσαν ὡς θεὰς τιμῶντες.

5. Τὰ μὲν οὖν κατὰ τὴν γένεσιν τῆς Σεμιράμιδος μυθολογούμενα σχεδὸν ταῦτ᾽ ἔστιν. ἤδη
δ᾽ αὐτῆς ἡλικίαν ἐχούσης γάμου καὶ τῷ κάλλει
πολὺ τὰς ἄλλας παρθένους διαφερούσης, ἀπε-
στάλη παρὰ βασιλέως ὕπαρχος ἐπισκεψόμενος
τὰ βασιλικὰ κτήνη· οὗτος δ᾽ ἐκαλεῖτο μὲν
Ὄννης, πρῶτος δ᾽ ἦν τῶν ἐκ τοῦ βασιλικοῦ
συνεδρίου καὶ τῆς Συρίας ἁπάσης ἀποδεδειγμένος
ὕπαρχος. ὃς καταλύσας παρὰ τῷ Σίμμα καὶ
θεωρήσας τὴν Σεμίραμιν ἐθηρεύθη τῷ κάλλει·
διὸ καὶ τοῦ Σίμμα καταδεηθεὶς αὐτῷ δοῦναι τὴν
παρθένον εἰς γάμον ἔννομον, ἀπήγαγεν αὐτὴν εἰς
Νίνον, καὶ γήμας ἐγέννησε δύο παῖδας, Ὑαπάτην
2 καὶ Ὑδάσπην. τῆς δὲ Σεμιράμιδος ἐχούσης καὶ
τἆλλα ἀκόλουθα τῇ περὶ τὴν ὄψιν εὐπρεπείᾳ, συνέβαινε τὸν ἄνδρα τελέως ὑπ᾽ αὐτῆς δεδουλῶσθαι,

by drop between its lips. And when the child was a year old and in need of more solid nourishment, the doves, pecking off bits from the cheeses, supplied it with sufficient nourishment. Now when the keepers returned and saw that the cheeses had been nibbled about the edges, they were astonished at the strange happening; they accordingly kept a look-out, and on discovering the cause found the infant, which was of surpassing beauty. At once, then, bringing it to their steadings they turned it over to the keeper of the royal herds, whose name was Simmas; and Simmas, being childless, gave every care to the rearing of the girl, as his own daughter, and called her Semiramis, a name slightly altered from the word which, in the language of the Syrians, means "doves," birds which since that time all the inhabitants of Syria have continued to honour as goddesses.

5. Such, then, is in substance the story that is told about the birth of Semiramis. And when she had already come to the age of marriage and far surpassed all the other maidens in beauty, an officer was sent from the king's court to inspect the royal herds; his name was Onnes, and he stood first among the members of the king's council and had been appointed governor over all Syria. He stopped with Simmas, and on seeing Semiramis was captivated by her beauty; consequently he earnestly entreated Simmas to give him the maiden in lawful marriage and took her off to Ninus, where he married her and begat two sons, Hyapates and Hydaspes. And since the other qualities of Semiramis were in keeping with the beauty of her countenance, it turned out that her husband became completely enslaved by her,

καὶ μηδὲν ἄνευ τῆς ἐκείνης γνώμης πράττοντα
κατευστοχεῖν ἐν πᾶσι.

3 Καθ' ὃν δὴ χρόνον ὁ βασιλεύς, ἐπειδὴ τὰ περὶ
τὴν κτίσιν τῆς ὁμωνύμου πόλεως συνετέλεσε,
στρατεύειν ἐπὶ Βακτριανοὺς ἐπεχείρησεν. εἰδὼς
δὲ τά τε πλήθη καὶ τὴν ἀλκὴν τῶν ἀνδρῶν,
ἔτι δὲ τὴν χώραν ἔχουσαν πολλοὺς τόπους
ἀπροσίτους διὰ τὴν ὀχυρότητα, κατέλεξεν ἐξ
ἁπάντων τῶν ὑπ' αὐτὸν ἐθνῶν στρατιωτῶν
πλῆθος· ἐπεὶ γὰρ τῆς πρότερον στρατείας ἀπο-
τετευχὼς ἦν, ἔσπευδε πολλαπλασίονι παραγενέ-
4 σθαι δυνάμει πρὸς τὴν Βακτριανήν. συναχθείσης
δὲ τῆς στρατιᾶς πανταχόθεν ἠριθμήθησαν, ὡς
Κτησίας ἐν ταῖς ἱστορίαις ἀναγέγραφε, πεζῶν
μὲν ἑκατὸν ἑβδομήκοντα μυριάδες, ἱππέων δὲ
μιᾷ πλείους τῶν εἴκοσι μυριάδων, ἅρματα δὲ
δρεπανηφόρα μικρὸν ἀπολείποντα τῶν μυρίων
ἑξακοσίων.

5 Ἔστι μὲν οὖν ἄπιστον τοῖς αὐτόθεν ἀκούσασι
τὸ πλῆθος τῆς στρατιᾶς, οὐ μὴν ἀδύνατόν γε
φανήσεται τοῖς ἀναθεωροῦσι τὸ τῆς Ἀσίας
μέγεθος καὶ τὰ πλήθη τῶν κατοικούντων αὐτὴν
ἐθνῶν. εἰ γάρ τις ἀφεὶς τὴν ἐπὶ Σκύθας Δαρείου
στρατείαν μετὰ ὀγδοήκοντα μυριάδων καὶ τὴν
Ξέρξου διάβασιν ἐπὶ τὴν Ἑλλάδα τοῖς ἀνα-
ριθμήτοις πλήθεσι, τὰς ἐχθὲς[1] καὶ πρᾴην συντε-
λεσθείσας πράξεις ἐπὶ τῆς Εὐρώπης σκέψαιτο,
6 τάχιον ἂν πιστὸν ἡγήσαιτο τὸ ῥηθέν. κατὰ μὲν
οὖν τὴν Σικελίαν ὁ Διονύσιος ἐκ μιᾶς τῆς τῶν

---

[1] ἐχθὲς Vogel : χθὲς Vulgate, Bekker, Dindorf.

and since he would do nothing without her advice he prospered in everything.

It was at just this time that the king, now that he had completed the founding of the city which bore his name, undertook his campaign against the Bactrians. And since he was well aware of the great number and the valour of these men, and realized that the country had many places which because of their strength could not be approached by an enemy, he enrolled a great host of soldiers from all the nations under his sway; for as he had come off badly in his earlier campaign, he was resolved on appearing before Bactriana with a force many times as large as theirs. Accordingly, after the army had been assembled from every source, it numbered, as Ctesias has stated in his history, one million seven hundred thousand foot-soldiers, two hundred and ten thousand cavalry, and slightly less than ten thousand six hundred scythe-bearing chariots.

Now at first hearing the great size of the army is incredible, but it will not seem at all impossible to any who consider the great extent of Asia and the vast numbers of the peoples who inhabit it. For if a man, disregarding the campaign of Darius against the Scythians with eight hundred thousand [1] men and the crossing made by Xerxes against Greece with a host beyond number,[2] should consider the events which have taken place in Europe only yesterday or the day before, he would the more quickly come to regard the statement as credible. In Sicily, for instance, Dionysius led forth on his

[1] Herodotus (4. 87) makes the number 700,000, exclusive of the fleet.
[2] Cp. Book 11. 3.

Συρακοσίων πόλεως ἐξήγαγεν ἐπὶ τὰς στρατείας
πεζῶν μὲν δώδεκα μυριάδας, ἱππεῖς δὲ μυρίους
καὶ δισχιλίους, ναῦς δὲ μακρὰς ἐξ ἑνὸς λιμένος
τετρακοσίας, ὧν ἦσαν ἔνιαι τετρήρεις καὶ πεντή-
7 ρεις· Ῥωμαῖοι δὲ μικρὸν πρὸ τῶν Ἀννιβαϊκῶν
καιρῶν, προορώμενοι τὸ μέγεθος τοῦ πολέμου,
κατέγραψαν τοὺς κατὰ τὴν Ἰταλίαν ἐπιτηδείους
εἰς¹ στρατείαν πολίτας τε καὶ συμμάχους, ὧν
ὁ σύμπας ἀριθμὸς μικρὸν ἀπέλιπε τῶν ἑκατὸν
μυριάδων· καίτοι γ' ἕνεκα πλήθους ἀνθρώπων
τὴν Ἰταλίαν ὅλην οὐκ ἄν τις συγκρίνειε πρὸς
ἓν ἔθνος τῶν κατὰ τὴν Ἀσίαν. ταῦτα μὲν οὖν
ἡμῖν εἰρήσθω πρὸς τοὺς ἐκ τῆς νῦν περὶ τὰς
πόλεις οὔσης ἐρημίας τεκμαιρομένους τὴν παλαιὰν
τῶν ἐθνῶν πολυανθρωπίαν.

6. Ὁ δ' οὖν Νίνος μετὰ τοσαύτης δυνάμεως
στρατεύσας εἰς τὴν Βακτριανὴν ἠναγκάζετο,
δυσεισβόλων τῶν τόπων καὶ στενῶν ὄντων, κατὰ
2 μέρος ἄγειν τὴν δύναμιν. ἡ γὰρ Βακτριανὴ
χώρα πολλαῖς καὶ μεγάλαις οἰκουμένη πόλεσι
μίαν μὲν εἶχεν ἐπιφανεστάτην, ἐν ᾗ συνέβαινεν
εἶναι καὶ τὰ βασίλεια· αὕτη δ' ἐκαλεῖτο μὲν
Βάκτρα, μεγέθει δὲ καὶ τῇ κατὰ τὴν ἀκρόπολιν
ὀχυρότητι πολὺ πασῶν διέφερε. βασιλεύων δ'
αὐτῆς Ὀξυάρτης κατέγραψεν ἅπαντας τοὺς ἐν

¹ τὴν after εἰς omitted by CD and deleted by Vogel:
retained by Bekker, Dindorf.

---

[1] Diodorus assumes that his readers are familiar with the
fact that the vessel constituting the body of this fleet was the
trireme, the standard warship of the period of Dionysius (fourth
century B.C.); the quadriremes and quinqueremes were the
next two larger classes. The complement of the trireme was

campaigns from the single city of the Syracusans one hundred and twenty thousand foot-soldiers and twelve thousand cavalry, and from a single harbour four hundred warships, some of which were quadriremes and quinqueremes;[1] and the Romans, a little before the time of Hannibal, foreseeing the magnitude of the war, enrolled all the men in Italy who were fit for military service, both citizens and allies, and the total sum of them fell only a little short of one million; and yet as regards the number of inhabitants a man would not compare all Italy with a single one of the nations of Asia.[2] Let these facts, then, be a sufficient reply on our part to those who try to estimate the populations of the nations of Asia in ancient times on the strength of inferences drawn from the desolation which at the present time prevails in its cities.

6. Now Ninus in his campaign against Bactriana with so large a force was compelled, because access to the country was difficult and the passes were narrow, to advance his army in divisions. For the country of Bactriana, though there were many large cities for the people to dwell in, had one which was the most famous, this being the city containing the royal palace; it was called Bactra, and in size and in the strength of its acropolis was by far the first of them all. The king of the country, Oxyartes, had

at least 200 men, which makes a minimum for the fleet of 80,000 rowers and marines. The larger vessels would, of course, carry larger crews. According to Polybius (1. 26) the quinqueremes of the Romans in the third century B.C. carried 300 rowers and 120 marines.

[2] Polybius (2. 24. 16) estimates the total number of Romans and allies capable of bearing arms at this time (c. 225 B.C.) as 700,000 foot-soldiers and 70,000 cavalry.

ἡλικίᾳ στρατείας ὄντας, οἳ τὸν ἀριθμὸν ἠθροίσ-
3 θησαν εἰς τετταράκοντα μυριάδας. ἀναλαβὼν
οὖν τὴν δύναμιν καὶ τοῖς πολεμίοις ἀπαντήσας
περὶ τὰς εἰσβολάς, εἴασε μέρος τῆς τοῦ Νίνου
στρατιᾶς εἰσβαλεῖν· ἐπεὶ δ' ἔδοξεν ἱκανὸν ἀπο-
βεβηκέναι τῶν πολεμίων πλῆθος εἰς τὸ πεδίον,
ἐξέταξε τὴν ἰδίαν δύναμιν. γενομένης δὲ μάχης
ἰσχυρᾶς οἱ Βακτριανοὶ τοὺς Ἀσσυρίους τρεψά-
μενοι καὶ τὸν διωγμὸν μέχρι τῶν ὑπερκειμένων
ὀρῶν ποιησάμενοι διέφθειραν τῶν πολεμίων εἰς
4 δέκα μυριάδας. μετὰ δὲ ταῦτα πάσης τῆς δυνάμεως εἰσβαλούσης, κρατούμενοι τοῖς πλήθεσι
κατὰ πόλεις ἀπεχώρησαν, ἕκαστοι ταῖς ἰδίαις
πατρίσι βοηθήσοντες. τὰς μὲν οὖν ἄλλας ὁ
Νίνος ἐχειρώσατο ῥᾳδίως, τὰ δὲ Βάκτρα διά τε
τὴν ὀχυρότητα καὶ τὴν ἐν αὐτῇ παρασκευὴν
ἠδυνάτει κατὰ κράτος ἑλεῖν.

5 Πολυχρονίου δὲ τῆς πολιορκίας γινομένης,[1] ὁ
τῆς Σεμιράμιδος ἀνήρ, ἐρωτικῶς ἔχων πρὸς τὴν
γυναῖκα καὶ συστρατευόμενος τῷ βασιλεῖ, μετεπέμψατο τὴν ἄνθρωπον. ἡ δὲ συνέσει καὶ τόλμῃ
καὶ τοῖς ἄλλοις τοῖς πρὸς ἐπιφάνειαν συντείνουσι
κεχορηγημένη καιρὸν ἔλαβεν ἐπιδείξασθαι τὴν
6 ἰδίαν ἀρετήν. πρῶτον μὲν οὖν πολλῶν ἡμερῶν
ὁδὸν μέλλουσα διαπορεύεσθαι στολὴν ἐπραγ-
ματεύσατο δι' ἧς οὐκ ἦν διαγνῶναι τὸν περι-
βεβλημένον πότερον ἀνήρ ἐστιν ἢ γυνή. αὕτη
δ' ἦν εὔχρηστος αὐτῇ πρός τε τὰς ἐν τοῖς
καύμασιν ὁδοιπορίας, εἰς τὸ διατηρῆσαι τὸν τοῦ
σώματος χρῶτα, καὶ πρὸς τὰς ἐν τῷ πράττειν
ὃ βούλοιτο χρείας, εὐκίνητος οὖσα καὶ νεανική,

---

[1] γινομένης Gemistus : γενομένης.

enrolled all the men of military age, and they had been gathered to the number of four hundred thousand. So taking this force with him and meeting the enemy at the passes, he allowed a division of the army of Ninus to enter the country; and when he thought that a sufficient number of the enemy had debouched into the plain he drew out his own forces in battle-order. A fierce struggle then ensued in which the Bactrians put the Assyrians to flight, and pursuing them as far as the mountains which overlooked the field, killed about one hundred thousand of the enemy. But later, when the whole Assyrian force entered their country, the Bactrians, overpowered by the multitude of them, withdrew city by city, each group intending to defend its own homeland. And so Ninus easily subdued all the other cities, but Bactra, because of its strength and the equipment for war which it contained, he was unable to take by storm.

But when the siege was proving a long affair the husband of Semiramis, who was enamoured of his wife and was making the campaign with the king, sent for the woman. And she, endowed as she was with understanding, daring, and all the other qualities which contribute to distinction, seized the opportunity to display her native ability. First of all, then, since she was about to set out upon a journey of many days, she devised a garb which made it impossible to distinguish whether the wearer of it was a man or a woman. This dress was well adapted to her needs, as regards both her travelling in the heat, for protecting the colour of her skin, and her convenience in doing whatever she might wish to do, since it was quite pliable and suitable to a young person, and,

καὶ τὸ σύνολον τοσαύτη τις ἐπῆν αὐτῇ χάρις [1]
ὥσθ' ὕστερον Μήδους ἡγησαμένους τῆς Ἀσίας
φορεῖν τὴν Σεμιράμιδος στολήν, καὶ μετὰ ταῦθ'
7 ὁμοίως Πέρσας. παραγενομένη δ' εἰς τὴν Βακτριανὴν καὶ κατασκεψαμένη τὰ περὶ τὴν πολιορκίαν,
ἑώρα κατὰ μὲν τὰ πεδία καὶ τοὺς εὐεφόδους τῶν
τόπων προσβολὰς γινομένας, πρὸς δὲ τὴν ἀκρόπολιν οὐδένα προσιόντα διὰ τὴν ὀχυρότητα, καὶ
τοὺς ἔνδον ἀπολελοιπότας τὰς ἐνταῦθα φυλακὰς
καὶ παραβοηθοῦντας τοῖς ἐπὶ τῶν κάτω τειχῶν
8 κινδυνεύουσι. διόπερ παραλαβοῦσα τῶν στρατιωτῶν τοὺς πετροβατεῖν εἰωθότας, καὶ μετὰ τούτων
διά τινος χαλεπῆς φάραγγος προσαναβᾶσα, κατ-
ελάβετο μέρος τῆς ἀκροπόλεως καὶ τοῖς πολιορ-
κοῦσι τὸ κατὰ τὸ πεδίον τεῖχος ἐσήμηνεν. οἱ
δ' ἔνδον ἐπὶ τῇ καταλήψει τῆς ἄκρας καταπλα-
γέντες ἐξέλιπον τὰ τείχη καὶ τὴν σωτηρίαν
ἀπέγνωσαν.
9   Τοῦτον δὲ τὸν τρόπον ἁλούσης τῆς πόλεως ὁ
βασιλεὺς θαυμάσας τὴν ἀρετὴν τῆς γυναικὸς
τὸ μὲν πρῶτον μεγάλαις δωρεαῖς αὐτὴν ἐτίμησε,
μετὰ δὲ ταῦτα διὰ τὸ κάλλος τῆς ἀνθρώπου σχὼν
ἐρωτικῶς ἐπεχείρησε τὸν ἄνδρα πείθειν ἑκουσίως
αὐτῷ παραχωρῆσαι, ἐπαγγειλάμενος ἀντὶ ταύτης
τῆς χάριτος αὐτῷ συνοικιεῖν τὴν ἰδίαν θυγατέρα
10 Σωσάνην. δυσχερῶς δ' αὐτοῦ φέροντος, ἠπεί-
λησεν ἐκκόψειν τὰς ὁράσεις μὴ προχείρως ὑπη-
ρετοῦντος τοῖς προστάγμασιν. ὁ δὲ Ὄννης ἅμα

---

[1] χάρις before τις D, Dindorf.

---

[1] The Median dress was distinguished from that of the
Greeks by its covering for the head, a long coat with sleeves

368

in a word, was so attractive that in later times the
Medes, who were then dominant in Asia, always
wore the garb of Semiramis, as did the Persians
after them.[1] Now when Semiramis arrived in
Bactriana and observed the progress of the siege,
she noted that it was on the plains and at positions
which were easily assailed that attacks were being
made, but that no one ever assaulted the acropolis
because of its strong position, and that its defenders
had left their posts there and were coming to the aid
of those who were hard pressed on the walls below.
Consequently, taking with her such soldiers as were
accustomed to clambering up rocky heights, and making
her way with them up through a certain difficult
ravine, she seized a part of the acropolis and gave a
signal to those who were besieging the wall down in
the plain. Thereupon the defenders of the city,
struck with terror at the seizure of the height, left
the walls and abandoned all hope of saving themselves.

When the city had been taken in this way, the king,
marvelling at the ability of the woman, at first
honoured her with great gifts, and later, becoming
infatuated with her because of her beauty, tried to
persuade her husband to yield her to him of his own
accord, offering in return for this favour to give him
his own daughter Sosanê to wife. But when the man
took his offer with ill grace, Ninus threatened to
put out his eyes unless he at once acceded to his
commands. And Onnes, partly out of fear of the

extending to the hands, trousers, and boots. Strabo (11. 13. 9)
expressed the contempt generally felt for it by the Greeks when,
in observing that the Persians adopted this garb, he adds that
" they submitted to wear feminine robes instead of going naked
or lightly clad, and to cover their bodies all over with clothes."

μὲν τὰς τοῦ βασιλέως ἀπειλὰς δείσας, ἅμα δὲ
διὰ τὸν ἔρωτα περιπεσὼν λύττῃ τινὶ καὶ μανίᾳ,
βρόχον ἑαυτῷ περιθεὶς ἀνεκρέμασε. Σεμίραμις
μὲν οὖν διὰ τοιαύτας αἰτίας εἰς βασιλικὸν ἦλθε
πρόσχημα.

7. Ὁ δὲ Νίνος τούς τε ἐν Βάκτροις παρέλαβε
θησαυρούς, ἔχοντας πολὺν ἄργυρόν τε καὶ
χρυσόν, καὶ τὰ κατὰ τὴν Βακτριανὴν κατα-
στήσας ἀπέλυσε τὰς δυνάμεις. μετὰ δὲ ταῦτα
γεννήσας ἐκ Σεμιράμιδος υἱὸν Νιννύαν ἐτελεύτησε,
τὴν γυναῖκα ἀπολιπὼν βασίλισσαν. τὸν δὲ
Νίνον ἡ Σεμίραμις ἔθαψεν ἐν τοῖς βασιλείοις,
καὶ κατεσκεύασεν ἐπ' αὐτῷ χῶμα παμμέγεθες,
οὗ τὸ μὲν ὕψος ἦν ἐννέα σταδίων, τὸ δ' εὖρος, ὥς
2 φησι Κτησίας, δέκα. διὸ καὶ τῆς πόλεως παρὰ
τὸν Εὐφράτην ἐν πεδίῳ κειμένης ἀπὸ πολλῶν
σταδίων ἐφαίνετο τὸ χῶμα καθαπερεί τις ἀκρό-
πολις· ὃ καὶ μέχρι τοῦ νῦν φασι διαμένειν,
καίπερ τῆς Νίνου κατεσκαμμένης ὑπὸ Μήδων,
ὅτε κατέλυσαν τὴν Ἀσσυρίων βασιλείαν.

Ἡ δὲ Σεμίραμις, οὖσα φύσει μεγαλεπίβολος
καὶ φιλοτιμουμένη τῇ δόξῃ τὸν βεβασιλευκότα
πρὸ αὑτῆς ὑπερθέσθαι, πόλιν μὲν ἐπεβάλετο
κτίζειν ἐν τῇ Βαβυλωνίᾳ, ἐπιλεξαμένη δὲ τοὺς
πανταχόθεν ἀρχιτέκτονας καὶ τεχνίτας, ἔτι δὲ
τὴν ἄλλην χορηγίαν παρασκευασαμένη, συνήγαγεν ἐξ ἁπάσης τῆς βασιλείας πρὸς τὴν τῶν
ἔργων συντέλειαν ἀνδρῶν μυριάδας διακοσίας.

---

[1] In 612 B.C.
[2] The following picture of Babylon serves to show the
impression which this great city, whose " circuit was that more

king's threats and partly out of his passion for his wife, fell into a kind of frenzy and madness, put a rope about his neck, and hanged himself. Such, then, were the circumstances whereby Semiramis attained the position of queen.

7. Ninus secured the treasures of Bactra, which contained a great amount of both gold and silver, and after settling the affairs of Bactriana disbanded his forces. After this he begat by Semiramis a son Ninyas, and then died, leaving his wife as queen. Semiramis buried Ninus in the precinct of the palace and erected over his tomb a very large mound, nine stades high and ten wide, as Ctesias says. Consequently, since the city lay on a plain along the Euphrates, the mound was visible for a distance of many stades, like an acropolis; and this mound stands, they say, even to this day, though Ninus was razed to the ground by the Medes when they destroyed the empire of the Assyrians.[1]

Semiramis, whose nature made her eager for great exploits and ambitious to surpass the fame of her predecessor on the throne, set her mind upon founding a city in Babylonia, and after securing the architects of all the world and skilled artisans and making all the other necessary preparations, she gathered together from her entire kingdom two million men to complete the work.[2] Taking the

of a nation than of a city " (Aristotle, *Politics*, 3. 3. 5), made upon the Greeks. The older city was badly damaged by the sack of Sennacherib (*c.* 689 B.C.). The same ruler, however, commenced the work of rebuilding it, a task which was continued by successive kings of Assyria. The Chaldaean Nebuchadrezzar (605–562 B.C.) further embellished it, making it the most magnificent city of Asia, and it is his city which was known to the classical writers.

3 ἀπολαβοῦσα δὲ τὸν Εὐφράτην ποταμὸν εἰς
μέσον περιεβάλετο τεῖχος τῇ πόλει σταδίων
ἑξήκοντα καὶ τριακοσίων, διειλημμένον πύργοις
πυκνοῖς καὶ μεγάλοις,[1] ὥς φησι Κτησίας ὁ
Κνίδιος, ὡς δὲ Κλείταρχος καὶ τῶν ὕστερον
μετ᾽ Ἀλεξάνδρου διαβάντων εἰς τὴν Ἀσίαν τινὲς
ἀνέγραψαν, τριακοσίων ἑξήκοντα πέντε σταδίων·
καὶ προστιθέασιν ὅτι τῶν ἴσων ἡμερῶν εἰς τὸν
ἐνιαυτὸν οὐσῶν ἐφιλοτιμήθη τὸν ἴσον ἀριθμὸν
4 τῶν σταδίων ὑποστήσασθαι. ὀπτὰς δὲ πλίνθους εἰς ἄσφαλτον ἐνδησαμένη τεῖχος κατεσκεύασε τὸ μὲν ὕψος, ὡς μὲν Κτησίας φησί,
πεντήκοντα ὀργυιῶν, ὡς δ᾽ ἔνιοι τῶν νεωτέρων
ἔγραψαν, πηχῶν πεντήκοντα, τὸ δὲ πλάτος
πλέον ἢ δυσὶν ἅρμασιν ἱππάσιμον· πύργους δὲ
τὸν μὲν ἀριθμὸν διακοσίους καὶ πεντήκοντα, τὸ
δ᾽ ὕψος[2] καὶ πλάτος ἐξ ἀναλόγου τῷ βάρει τῶν
5 κατὰ τὸ τεῖχος ἔργων. οὐ χρὴ δὲ θαυμάζειν
εἰ τηλικούτου τὸ μέγεθος τοῦ περιβόλου καθ-
εστῶτος ὀλίγους πύργους κατεσκεύασεν· ἐπὶ
πολὺν γὰρ τόπον τῆς πόλεως ἕλεσι περιεχο-
μένης, κατὰ τοῦτον τὸν τόπον οὐκ ἔδοξεν αὐτῇ
πύργους οἰκοδομεῖν, τῆς φύσεως τῶν ἑλῶν ἱκανὴν
παρεχομένης ὀχυρότητα. ἀνὰ μέσον δὲ τῶν
οἰκιῶν καὶ τῶν τειχῶν ὁδὸς πάντῃ κατελέλειπτο
δίπλεθρος.

---

[1] So Eichstädt, who deletes after μεγάλοις: "And such
was the massiveness of the works that the width of the
walls was sufficient to allow six chariots to drive abreast
upon it, and their height was unbelievable to those who
only hear of it."

[2] Jacoby, *F. Gr. Hist.*, s.v. *Kleitarchos*, frg. 10, adds
ὀργυιῶν after ὕψος and adopts the reading of A B D and

Euphrates river into the centre she threw about the
city a wall with great towers set at frequent intervals,
the wall being three hundred and sixty stades [1]
in circumference, as Ctesias of Cnidus says, but according to the account of Cleitarchus and certain of those
who at a later time crossed into Asia with Alexander,
three hundred and sixty-five stades; [2] and these
latter add that it was her desire to make the number
of stades the same as the days in the year. Making
baked bricks fast in bitumen she built a wall with a
height, as Ctesias says, of fifty fathoms, but, as some
later writers have recorded, of fifty cubits,[3] and
wide enough for more than two chariots abreast to
drive upon; and the towers numbered two hundred
and fifty, their height and width corresponding to
the massive scale of the wall. Now it need occasion
no wonder that, considering the great length of the
circuit wall, Semiramis constructed a small number of
towers; for since over a long distance the city was
surrounded by swamps, she decided not to build
towers along that space, the swamps offering a sufficient
natural defence. And all along between the dwellings and the walls a road was left two plethra wide.

[1] About forty miles.

[2] Herodotus (1. 178) makes the circuit of the walls 480
stades, Strabo (16. 1. 5) 385, although this number has been
generally taken by editors to be an error of the MSS. for 365,
thus bringing him into agreement with Cleitarchus and
Quintus Curtius 5. 4.

[3] *i.e.* either 300 feet high or 75 feet high. Herodotus, *l.c.*,
gives the height as 200 " royal cubits " (*c.* 335 feet).

Tzetzes, *Chil.* 9. 569: τὸ δ' ὕψος ὀργυιῶν ἑξήκοντα, ὡς δ' ἔνιοι
τῶν νεωτέρων φασί, πηχῶν ἑξήκοντα ("their height being sixty
fathoms, but, as some later writers say, sixty cubits").

8. Πρὸς δὲ τὴν ὀξύτητα τῆς τούτων οἰκοδομίας ἑκάστῳ τῶν φίλων στάδιον διεμέτρησε,
δοῦσα τὴν ἱκανὴν εἰς τοῦτο χορηγίαν καὶ διακελευσαμένη τέλος ἐπιθεῖναι τοῖς ἔργοις ἐν
2 ἐνιαυτῷ. ὧν ποιησάντων τὸ προσταχθὲν μετὰ
πολλῆς σπουδῆς, τούτων μὲν ἀπεδέξατο τὴν
φιλοτιμίαν, αὐτὴ δὲ κατὰ τὸ στενώτατον μέρος
τοῦ ποταμοῦ γέφυραν σταδίων πέντε τὸ μῆκος
κατεσκεύασεν, εἰς βυθὸν φιλοτέχνως καθεῖσα
τοὺς κίονας, οἳ διεστήκεσαν ἀπ' ἀλλήλων πόδας
δώδεκα. τοὺς δὲ συνερειδομένους λίθους τόρμοις
σιδηροῖς διελάμβανε, καὶ τὰς τούτων ἁρμονίας
ἐπλήρου μόλιβδον ἐντήκουσα. τοῖς δὲ κίοσι
πρὸ τῶν τὸ ῥεῦμα δεχομένων πλευρῶν γωνίας
προκατεσκεύασεν ἐχούσας τὴν ἀπορροὴν περι-
φερῆ καὶ συνδεδεμένην κατ' ὀλίγον ἕως τοῦ
κατὰ τὸν κίονα πλάτους, ὅπως αἱ μὲν περὶ τὰς
γωνίας ὀξύτητες τέμνωσι τὴν καταφορὰν τοῦ
ῥεύματος, αἱ δὲ περιφέρειαι τῇ τούτου βίᾳ
συνείκουσαι πραΰνωσι τὴν σφοδρότητα τοῦ
3 ποταμοῦ. ἡ μὲν οὖν γέφυρα, κεδρίναις καὶ
κυπαριττίναις δοκοῖς, ἔτι δὲ φοινίκων στελέχεσιν
ὑπερμεγέθεσι κατεστεγασμένη καὶ τριάκοντα
ποδῶν οὖσα τὸ πλάτος, οὐδενὸς ἐδόκει τῶν
Σεμιράμιδος ἔργων τῇ φιλοτεχνίᾳ λείπεσθαι.
ἐξ ἑκατέρου δὲ μέρους τοῦ ποταμοῦ κρηπῖδα

---

[1] Some of the piers of this "most ancient stone bridge of
which we have any record" have been discovered. They are
twenty-one metres long, nine wide, and are placed nine metres

8. In order to expedite the building of these constructions she apportioned a stade to each of her friends, furnishing sufficient material for their task and directing them to complete their work within a year. And when they had finished these assignments with great speed she gratefully accepted their zeal, but she took for herself the construction of a bridge [1] five stades long at the narrowest point of the river, skilfully sinking the piers, which stood twelve feet apart, into its bed. And the stones, which were set firmly together, she bonded with iron cramps, and the joints of the cramps [2] she filled by pouring in lead. Again, before the piers on the side which would receive the current she constructed cutwaters whose sides were rounded to turn off the water and which gradually diminished to the width of the pier, in order that the sharp points of the cutwaters might divide the impetus of the stream, while the rounded sides, yielding to its force, might soften the violence of the river.[3] This bridge, then, floored as it was with beams of cedar and cypress and with palm logs of exceptional size and having a width of thirty feet, is considered to have been inferior in technical skill to none of the works of Semiramis. And on each side of the river she built an expensive

[1] apart. An inscription of Nebuchadrezzar ascribes this bridge to his father Nabopolassar (R. Koldewey, *The Excavations at Babylon* (Eng. transl.), pp. 197–99).

[2] Or " of the stones " (so Liddell-Scott-Jones). But the use of cramps and dowels, sunk into the stones and made fast by pouring in molten lead, was the accepted bonding method in the classic period of Greek architecture, and dove-tailed wooden cramps laid in bitumen have been found in Babylon (Koldewey, *l.c.*, p. 177).

[3] The sides of the piers, as remains show, were convex at the north ends and then sharply receded to a point.

πολυτελῆ κατεσκεύασε παραπλησίαν κατὰ τὸ
πλάτος τοῖς τείχεσιν ἐπὶ σταδίους ἑκατὸν
ἑξήκοντα.

Ὠικοδόμησε δὲ καὶ βασίλεια διπλᾶ παρ' αὐτὸν
τὸν ποταμὸν ἐξ ἑκατέρου μέρους τῆς γεφύρας,
ἐξ ὧν ἅμ'[1] ἔμελλε τήν τε πόλιν ἅπασαν κατοπτεύσειν[2] καὶ καθαπερεὶ τὰς κλεῖς ἕξειν τῶν
4 ἐπικαιροτάτων τῆς πόλεως τόπων. τοῦ δ'
Εὐφράτου διὰ μέσης τῆς Βαβυλῶνος ῥέοντος
καὶ πρὸς μεσημβρίαν καταφερομένου, τῶν
βασιλείων τὰ μὲν πρὸς ἀνατολὴν ἔνευε, τὰ δὲ
πρὸς δύσιν, ἀμφότερα δὲ πολυτελῶς κατεσκεύαστο. τοῦ μὲν γὰρ[3] πρὸς ἑσπέραν κειμένου μέρους ἐποίησε τὸν πρῶτον περίβολον
ἑξήκοντα σταδίων, ὑψηλοῖς καὶ πολυτελέσι
τείχεσιν ὠχυρωμένον, ἐξ ὀπτῆς πλίνθου. ἕτερον δ' ἐντὸς τούτου κυκλοτερῆ κατεσκεύασε, καθ'
ὃν ἐν ὠμαῖς ἔτι ταῖς πλίνθοις διετετύπωτο θηρία
παντοδαπὰ τῇ τῶν χρωμάτων φιλοτεχνίᾳ τὴν
5 ἀλήθειαν ἀπομιμούμενα· οὗτος δ' ὁ περίβολος
ἦν τὸ μὲν μῆκος σταδίων τετταράκοντα, τὸ δὲ
πλάτος ἐπὶ τριακοσίας[4] πλίνθους, τὸ δ' ὕψος,
ὡς Κτησίας φησίν, ὀργυιῶν πεντήκοντα· τῶν δὲ
πύργων ὑπῆρχε τὸ ὕψος ὀργυιῶν ἑβδομήκοντα.
6 κατεσκεύασε δὲ καὶ τρίτον ἐνδοτέρω περίβολον,
ὃς περιεῖχεν ἀκρόπολιν, ἧς ἡ μὲν περίμετρος ἦν
σταδίων εἴκοσι, τὸ δὲ ὕψος[5] καὶ πλάτος τῆς
οἰκοδομίας ὑπεραῖρον τοῦ μέσου τείχους τὴν

---

[1] μὲν after ἅμα deleted by Dindorf.
[2] κατοπτεύσειν Dindorf: κατοπτεύειν.
[3] εἰς τὸ after γὰρ deleted by Dindorf.
[4] τριακοσίας Dindorf: τριακοσίους.　　[5] ὕψος Wurm: μῆκος.

quay [1] of about the same width as the walls and one hundred and sixty stades long.

Semiramis also built two palaces on the very banks of the river, one at each end of the bridge, her intention being that from them she might be able both to look down over the entire city and to hold the keys, as it were, to its most important sections. And since the Euphrates river passed through the centre of Babylon and flowed in a southerly direction, one palace faced the rising and the other the setting sun, and both had been constructed on a lavish scale. For in the case of the one which faced west she made the length of its first or outer circuit wall sixty stades, fortifying it with lofty walls, which had been built at great cost and were of burned brick. And within this she built a second, circular in form,[2] in the bricks of which, before they were baked, wild animals of every kind had been engraved, and by the ingenious use of colours these figures reproduced the actual appearance of the animals themselves; this circuit wall had a length of forty stades, a width of three hundred bricks, and a height, as Ctesias says, of fifty fathoms; the height of the towers, however, was seventy fathoms. And she built within these two yet a third circuit wall, which enclosed an acropolis whose circumference was twenty stades in length, but the height and width of the structure surpassed the dimensions of the middle circuit wall.

[1] Cp. Herodotus 1. 180.
[2] Koldewey (*l.c.*, p. 130) holds that the Greek word may not be translated " circular," preferring " annular, enclosed in itself, not open on one side, like the outer peribolos," his reason being that a " circular peribolos is found nowhere in Babylon."

κατασκευήν. ἐνῆσαν δ' ἔν τε τοῖς πύργοις καὶ
τείχεσι ζῷα παντοδαπὰ φιλοτέχνως τοῖς τε
χρώμασι καὶ τοῖς τῶν τύπων ἀπομιμήμασι
κατεσκευασμένα· τὸ δ' ὅλον ἐπεποίητο κυνήγιον
παντοίων θηρίων ὑπάρχον πλῆρες, ὧν ἦσαν τὰ
μεγέθη πλέον ἢ πηχῶν τεττάρων. κατεσκεύαστο δ' ἐν αὐτοῖς καὶ ἡ Σεμίραμις ἀφ' ἵππου
πάρδαλιν ἀκοντίζουσα, καὶ πλησίον αὐτῆς ὁ
ἀνὴρ Νίνος παίων ἐκ χειρὸς λέοντα λόγχῃ.
7 ἐπέστησε δὲ καὶ πύλας τριττάς,[1] ὧν ὑπῆρχον
διτταὶ[2] χαλκαῖ διὰ μηχανῆς ἀνοιγόμεναι.

Ταῦτα μὲν οὖν τὰ βασίλεια καὶ τῷ μεγέθει
καὶ ταῖς κατασκευαῖς πολὺ προεῖχε τῶν ὄντων
ἐπὶ θάτερα μέρη τοῦ ποταμοῦ. ἐκεῖνα γὰρ εἶχε
τὸν μὲν περίβολον τοῦ τείχους τριάκοντα σταδίων ἐξ ὀπτῆς πλίνθου, ἀντὶ δὲ τῆς περὶ τὰ ζῷα
φιλοτεχνίας χαλκᾶς εἰκόνας Νίνου καὶ Σεμιράμιδος καὶ τῶν ὑπάρχων, ἔτι δὲ Διός, ὃν καλοῦσιν οἱ Βαβυλώνιοι Βῆλον· ἐνῆσαν δὲ καὶ παρατάξεις καὶ κυνήγια παντοδαπά, ποικίλην ψυχαγωγίαν παρεχόμενα τοῖς θεωμένοις.

9. Μετὰ δὲ ταῦτα τῆς Βαβυλωνίας ἐκλεξα-
μένη τὸν ταπεινότατον τόπον ἐποίησε δεξαμενὴν
τετράγωνον, ἧς ἦν ἑκάστη πλευρὰ σταδίων
τριακοσίων, ἐξ ὀπτῆς πλίνθου καὶ ἀσφάλτου
κατεσκευασμένην καὶ τὸ βάθος ἔχουσαν ποδῶν

---

[1] ἐφ' after τριττὰς deleted by Dindorf.
[2] διτταὶ Wurm : δίαιται.

---

[1] Koldewey (l.c., pp. 129–31) identifies this palace with what
he calls the Persian Building, and finds traces of the three
circuit walls (periboloi). It is a striking coincidence that
among the fragments of glazed bricks depicting a chase of

On both the towers and the walls there were again animals of every kind, ingeniously executed by the use of colours as well as by the realistic imitation of the several types; and the whole had been made to represent a hunt, complete in every detail, of all sorts of wild animals, and their size was more than four cubits. Among the animals, moreover, Semiramis had also been portrayed, on horseback and in the act of hurling a javelin at a leopard, and nearby was her husband Ninus, in the act of thrusting his spear into a lion at close quarters.[1] In this wall she also set triple gates, two of which were of bronze and were opened by a mechanical device.

Now this palace far surpassed in both size and details of execution the one on the other bank of the river. For the circuit wall of the latter, made of burned brick, was only thirty stades long, and instead of the ingenious portrayal of animals it had bronze statues of Ninus and Semiramis and their officers, and one also of Zeus, whom the Babylonians call Belus;[2] and on it were also portrayed both battle-scenes and hunts of every kind, which filled those who gazed thereon with varied emotions of pleasure.

9. After this Semiramis picked out the lowest spot in Babylonia and built a square reservoir, which was three hundred stades long on each side; it was constructed of baked brick and bitumen, and had a

wild animals there was found only one human face, that of a woman in white enamel. "We can scarcely doubt, therefore," he says, "that Diodorus was describing the enamels of the Persian building, and that the white face of a woman is the same that Ctesias recognized as a portrait of Semiramis."

[2] "Zeus Belus" was the name by which the Babylonian Bel-Marduk was known among the Greeks.

2 τριάκοντα καὶ πέντε. εἰς ταύτην δ' ἀποστρέ-
ψασα τὸν ποταμὸν κατεσκεύασεν ἐκ τῶν ἐπὶ
τάδε βασιλείων εἰς θάτερα διώρυχα· ἐξ ὀπτῆς
δὲ πλίνθου συνοικοδομήσασα τὰς καμάρας ἐξ
ἑκατέρου μέρους ἀσφάλτῳ κατέχρισεν ἡψημένῃ,
μέχρι οὗ¹ τὸ πάχος τοῦ χρίσματος ἐποίησε πηχῶν
τεττάρων. τῆς δὲ διώρυχος ὑπῆρχον οἱ μὲν τοῖχοι
τὸ πλάτος ἐπὶ πλίνθους εἴκοσι, τὸ δ' ὕψος χωρὶς
τῆς καμφθείσης ψαλίδος ποδῶν δώδεκα, τὸ δὲ
3 πλάτος ποδῶν πεντεκαίδεκα. ἐν ἡμέραις δ' ἑπτὰ
κατασκευασθείσης αὐτῆς ἀποκατέστησε τὸν ποταμὸν ἐπὶ τὴν προϋπάρχουσαν ῥύσιν, ὥστε τοῦ
ῥεύματος ἐπάνω τῆς διώρυχος φερομένου δύνασθαι τὴν Σεμίραμιν ἐκ τῶν πέραν βασιλείων ἐπὶ
θάτερα διαπορεύεσθαι μὴ διαβαίνουσαν τὸν
ποταμόν. ἐπέστησε δὲ καὶ πύλας τῇ διώρυχι
χαλκᾶς ἐφ' ἑκάτερον μέρος, αἳ διέμειναν μέχρι
τῆς² Περσῶν βασιλείας.

4 Μετὰ δὲ ταῦτα ἐν μέσῃ τῇ πόλει κατεσκεύασεν ἱερὸν Διός, ὃν καλοῦσιν οἱ Βαβυλώνιοι, καθάπερ εἰρήκαμεν, Βῆλον. περὶ τούτου
δὲ τῶν συγγραφέων διαφωνούντων, καὶ τοῦ κατασκευάσματος διὰ τὸν χρόνον καταπεπτωκότος,
οὐκ ἔστιν ἀποφήνασθαι τἀκριβές. ὁμολογεῖται
δ' ὑψηλὸν γεγενῆσθαι καθ' ὑπερβολήν, καὶ τοὺς
Χαλδαίους ἐν αὐτῷ τὰς τῶν ἄστρων πεποιῆσθαι
παρατηρήσεις, ἀκριβῶς θεωρουμένων τῶν τ'
ἀνατολῶν καὶ δύσεων διὰ τὸ τοῦ κατασκευά-
5 σματος ὕψος. τῆς δ' ὅλης οἰκοδομίας ἐξ ἀσφάλ-

---

¹ οὗ D, Vogel : ὅτου C, Bekker, Dindorf.
² τῶν after τῆς omitted by C D, Vogel.

depth of thirty-five feet. Then, diverting the river into it, she built an underground passage-way from one palace to the other; and making it of burned brick, she coated the vaulted chambers on both sides with hot bitumen until she had made the thickness of this coating four cubits. The side walls of the passage-way were twenty bricks thick and twelve feet high, exclusive of the barrel-vault, and the width of the passage-way was fifteen feet. And after this construction had been finished in only seven days she let the river back again into its old channel, and so, since the stream flowed above the passage-way, Semiramis was able to go across from one palace to the other without passing over the river. At each end of the passage-way she also set bronze gates which stood until the time of the Persian rule.

After this she built in the centre of the city a temple [1] of Zeus whom, as we have said, the Babylonians call Belus. Now since with regard to this temple the historians are at variance, and since time has caused the structure to fall in ruins, it is impossible to give the exact facts concerning it. But all agree that it was exceedingly high, and that in it the Chaldaeans made their observations of the stars, whose risings and settings could be accurately observed by reason of the height of the structure. Now the entire building was ingeniously constructed at great expense

---

[1] What follows is a description of the great ziggurat, or stage-tower, of E-temen-ana-ki, the "foundation stone of heaven and earth." According to Herodotus (1. 181) it had eight stories, but E. Unger (*Babylon* (1931), pp. 191 ff.) finds evidence for only seven (cp. the Reconstruction, p. 383). The height of this great structure was nearly 300 feet, and in the course of time there gathered about it the Hebrew myth of the Tower of Babel (cp. *The Cambridge Ancient History*, I, pp. 503 ff.).

του καὶ πλίνθου πεφιλοτεχνημένης πολυτελῶς,
ἐπ᾽ ἄκρας τῆς ἀναβάσεως τρία κατεσκεύασεν
ἀγάλματα χρυσᾶ σφυρήλατα, Διός, Ἥρας,
Ῥέας. τούτων δὲ τὸ μὲν τοῦ Διὸς ἑστηκὸς ἦν
καὶ διαβεβηκός, ὑπάρχον δὲ [1] ποδῶν τετταράκοντα τὸ μῆκος σταθμὸν εἶχε χιλίων ταλάντων
Βαβυλωνίων· τὸ δὲ τῆς Ῥέας ἐπὶ δίφρου καθήμενον χρυσοῦ τὸν ἴσον σταθμὸν εἶχε τῷ προει-
ρημένῳ· ἐπὶ δὲ τῶν γονάτων αὐτῆς εἱστήκεσαν
λέοντες δύο, καὶ πλησίον ὄφεις ὑπερμεγέθεις
ἀργυροῖ, τριάκοντα ταλάντων ἕκαστος ἔχων τὸ
6 βάρος. τὸ δὲ τῆς Ἥρας ἑστηκὸς ἦν ἄγαλμα,
σταθμὸν ἔχον ταλάντων ὀκτακοσίων, καὶ τῇ
μὲν δεξιᾷ χειρὶ κατεῖχε τῆς κεφαλῆς ὄφιν, τῇ
7 δ᾽ ἀριστερᾷ σκῆπτρον λιθοκόλλητον. τούτοις
δὲ πᾶσι κοινὴ παρέκειτο τράπεζα χρυσῆ σφυρή-
λατος, τὸ μὲν μῆκος ποδῶν τετταράκοντα, τὸ
δ᾽ εὖρος πεντεκαίδεκα, σταθμὸν ἔχουσα ταλάντων
πεντακοσίων. ἐπὶ δὲ ταύτης ἐπέκειντο δύο
καρχήσια, σταθμὸν ἔχοντα τριάκοντα ταλάντων.
8 ἦσαν δὲ καὶ θυμιατήρια τὸν μὲν ἀριθμὸν ἴσα,
τὸν δὲ σταθμὸν ἑκάτερον ταλάντων τριακοσίων·
ὑπῆρχον δὲ καὶ κρατῆρες χρυσοῖ τρεῖς, ὧν ὁ
μὲν τοῦ Διὸς εἷλκε τάλαντα Βαβυλώνια χίλια
καὶ διακόσια, τῶν δ᾽ ἄλλων ἑκάτερος ἑξακόσια.
9 ἀλλὰ ταῦτα μὲν οἱ τῶν Περσῶν βασιλεῖς ὕστερον
ἐσύλησαν· τῶν δὲ βασιλείων καὶ τῶν ἄλλων
κατασκευασμάτων ὁ χρόνος τὰ μὲν ὁλοσχερῶς
ἠφάνισε, τὰ δ᾽ ἐλυμήνατο· καὶ γὰρ αὐτῆς τῆς
Βαβυλῶνος νῦν βραχύ τι μέρος οἰκεῖται, τὸ δὲ
πλεῖστον ἐντὸς τείχους γεωργεῖται.

10. Ὑπῆρχε δὲ καὶ ὁ κρεμαστὸς καλούμενος

of bitumen and brick, and at the top of the ascent
Semiramis set up three statues of hammered gold, of
Zeus, Hera, and Rhea. Of these statues that of Zeus
represented him erect and striding forward, and,
being forty feet high, weighed a thousand Babylonian
talents; that of Rhea showed her seated on a golden
throne and was of the same weight as that of Zeus;
and at her knees stood two lions, while near by were
huge serpents of silver, each one weighing thirty
talents. The statue of Hera was also standing,
weighing eight hundred talents, and in her right hand
she held a snake by the head and in her left a sceptre
studded with precious stones. A table for all three
statues, made of hammered gold, stood before them,
forty feet long, fifteen wide, and weighing five
hundred talents. Upon it rested two drinking-cups,
weighing thirty talents. And there were censers as
well, also two in number but weighing each three
hundred talents, and also three gold mixing bowls,
of which the one belonging to Zeus weighed twelve
hundred Babylonian talents and the other two six
hundred each. But all these were later carried off as
spoil by the kings of the Persians,[1] while as for the
palaces and the other buildings, time has either
entirely effaced them or left them in ruins; and in
fact of Babylon itself but a small part is inhabited at
this time, and most of the area within its walls is
given over to agriculture.

10. There was also, beside the acropolis, the Hang-

---

[1] Babylon was taken by the Persians in 539 B.C.

---

[1] Vogel follows D in reading δὲ here and deletes it after
σταθμόν.

κῆπος παρὰ τὴν ἀκρόπολιν, οὐ Σεμιράμιδος,
ἀλλά τινος ὕστερον Σύρου βασιλέως κατασκευάσαντος χάριν γυναικὸς παλλακῆς· ταύτην γάρ
φασιν οὖσαν τὸ γένος Περσίδα καὶ τοὺς ἐν τοῖς
ὄρεσι λειμῶνας ἐπιζητοῦσαν ἀξιῶσαι τὸν βασιλέα
μιμήσασθαι διὰ τῆς τοῦ φυτουργείου φιλοτεχνίας
2 τὴν τῆς Περσίδος χώρας ἰδιότητα. ἔστι δ' ὁ
παράδεισος τὴν μὲν πλευρὰν ἑκάστην παρεκ-
τείνων εἰς τέτταρα πλέθρα, τὴν δὲ πρόσβασιν
ὀρεινὴν καὶ τὰς οἰκοδομίας ἄλλας ἐξ ἄλλων ἔχων,
3 ὥστε τὴν πρόσοψιν εἶναι θεατροειδῆ. ὑπὸ δὲ
ταῖς κατεσκευασμέναις ἀναβάσεσιν ᾠκοδόμηντο
σύριγγες, ἅπαν μὲν ὑποδεχόμεναι τὸ τοῦ φυτουργείου βάρος, ἀλλήλων δ' ἐκ τοῦ κατ' ὀλίγον ἀεὶ
μικρὸν ὑπερέχουσαι κατὰ τὴν πρόσβασιν· ἡ δ'
ἀνωτάτω σύριγξ οὖσα πεντήκοντα πηχῶν τὸ
ὕψος εἶχεν ἐπ' αὐτῇ[1] τοῦ παραδείσου τὴν ἀνω-
τάτην ἐπιφάνειαν συνεξισουμένην τῷ περιβόλῳ
4 τῶν ἐπάλξεων. ἔπειθ' οἱ μὲν τοῖχοι πολυτελῶς
κατεσκευασμένοι τὸ πάχος εἶχον ποδῶν εἴκοσι
δύο, τῶν δὲ διεξόδων ἑκάστη τὸ πλάτος δέκα.
τὰς δ' ὀροφὰς κατεστέγαζον λίθιναι δοκοί, τὸ μὲν
μῆκος σὺν ταῖς ἐπιβολαῖς ἔχουσαι ποδῶν ἐκκαί-
5 δεκα, τὸ δὲ πλάτος τεττάρων. τὸ δ' ἐπὶ ταῖς
δοκοῖς ὀρόφωμα πρῶτον μὲν εἶχεν ὑπεστρωμένον
κάλαμον μετὰ πολλῆς ἀσφάλτου, μετὰ δὲ ταῦτα
πλίνθον ὀπτὴν διπλῆν ἐν γύψῳ δεδεμένην, τρίτην
δ' ἐπιβολὴν ἐδέχετο[2] μολιβᾶς στέγας πρὸς τὸ
μὴ διικνεῖσθαι κατὰ βάθος τὴν ἐκ τοῦ χώματος
νοτίδα. ἐπὶ δὲ τούτοις ἐσεσώρευτο γῆς ἱκανὸν

---

[1] ἐφ' αὐτῇ Bekker, Dindorf.
[2] ἐδέχετο Vogel: ἐπεδέχετο C, Bekker, Dindorf.

ing Garden, as it is called, which was built, not by
Semiramis, but by a later Syrian king to please one of
his concubines; for she, they say, being a Persian by
race and longing for the meadows of her mountains,
asked the king to imitate, through the artifice of a
planted garden, the distinctive landscape of Persia.[1]
The park [2] extended four plethra on each side, and
since the approach to the garden sloped like a hillside
and the several parts of the structure rose from one
another tier on tier, the appearance of the whole
resembled that of a theatre. When the ascending
terraces had been built, there had been constructed
beneath them galleries which carried the entire
weight of the planted garden and rose little by little
one above the other along the approach; and the
uppermost gallery, which was fifty cubits high,
bore the highest surface of the park, which
was made level with the circuit wall of the
battlements of the city. Furthermore, the walls,
which had been constructed at great expense, were
twenty-two feet thick, while the passage-way between each two walls was ten feet wide. The roofs
of the galleries were covered over with beams of
stone sixteen feet long, inclusive of the overlap, and
four feet wide. The roof above these beams had
first a layer of reeds laid in great quantities of
bitumen, over this two courses of baked brick bonded
by cement, and as a third layer a covering of lead, to
the end that the moisture from the soil might not
penetrate beneath. On all this again earth had been

[1] The " Hanging Gardens " were built by the Chaldaean
Nebuchadrezzar (605-562 B.C.) for his wife Amyhia, a Median
princess.
[2] *Paradeisos*, " park," a word borrowed from the Persian,
meant no more than a wooded enclosure.

βάθος, ἀρκοῦν¹ ταῖς τῶν μεγίστων δένδρων
ῥίζαις· τὸ δ' ἔδαφος ἐξωμαλισμένον πλῆρες ἦν
παντοδαπῶν δένδρων τῶν δυναμένων κατά τε τὸ
μέγεθος καὶ τὴν ἄλλην χάριν τοὺς θεωμένους
6 ψυχαγωγῆσαι. αἱ δὲ σύριγγες τὰ φῶτα δεχό-
μεναι ταῖς δι' ἀλλήλων ὑπεροχαῖς πολλὰς καὶ
παντοδαπὰς εἶχον διαίτας βασιλικάς· μία δ' ἦν
ἐκ τῆς ἀνωτάτης ἐπιφανείας διατομὰς ἔχουσα
καὶ πρὸς τὰς ἐπαντλήσεις τῶν ὑδάτων ὄργανα,
δι' ὧν ἀνεσπᾶτο πλῆθος ὕδατος ἐκ τοῦ ποταμοῦ,
μηδενὸς τῶν ἔξωθεν τὸ γινόμενον συνιδεῖν δυναμένου. οὗτος μὲν οὖν ὁ παράδεισος, ὡς προεῖπον,
ὕστερον κατεσκευάσθη.

11. Ἡ δὲ Σεμίραμις ἔκτισε καὶ ἄλλας πόλεις
παρὰ τὸν ποταμὸν τόν τε Εὐφράτην καὶ τὸν
Τίγριν, ἐν αἷς ἐμπόρια κατεσκεύασε τοῖς φορτία
διακομίζουσιν ἐκ τῆς Μηδίας καὶ Παραιτακηνῆς καὶ πάσης τῆς σύνεγγυς χώρας. μετὰ
γὰρ τὸν Νεῖλον καὶ Γάγγην ὄντες ἐπισημότατοι
σχεδὸν τῶν κατὰ τὴν Ἀσίαν ποταμῶν Εὐφράτης
καὶ Τίγρις τὰς μὲν πηγὰς ἔχουσιν ἐκ τῶν
Ἀρμενίων ὀρῶν, διεστήκασι δ' ἀπ' ἀλλήλων
2 σταδίους δισχιλίους καὶ πεντακοσίους· ἐνεχθέντες
δὲ διὰ Μηδίας καὶ Παραιτακηνῆς ἐμβάλλουσιν
εἰς τὴν Μεσοποταμίαν, ἣν ἀπολαμβάνοντες εἰς

---

¹ ἀρκοῦν Gemistus: ἀρκούμενον.

¹ Koldewey (l.c., pp. 91–100) would identify a vaulted
building in a corner of Nebuchadrezzar's palace with this
" hanging garden.'' Certain considerations speak strongly
386

piled to a depth sufficient for the roots of the largest
trees; and the ground, when levelled off, was thickly
planted with trees of every kind that, by their great
size or any other charm, could give pleasure to the
beholder. And since the galleries, each projecting
beyond another, all received the light, they contained many royal lodgings of every description;
and there was one gallery which contained openings
leading from the topmost surface and machines for
supplying the garden with water, the machines raising
the water in great abundance from the river, although
no one outside could see it being done. Now this
park, as I have said, was a later construction.[1]

11. Semiramis founded other cities also along the
Euphrates and Tigris rivers, in which she established trading-places for the merchants who brought
goods from Media, Paraetacenê, and all the neighbouring region. For the Euphrates and Tigris, the
most notable, one may say, of all the rivers of Asia
after the Nile and Ganges, have their sources in the
mountains of Armenia and are two thousand five
hundred stades apart at their origin, and after flowing
through Media and Paraetacenê they enter Mesopotamia, which they enclose between them, thus

for this: (1) hewn stone, rarely found elsewhere in Babylon,
was used in its construction; (2) the walls, especially the central
ones, are unusually thick, as if to bear some heavy burden;
(3) the presence of a well, unique among the many found in the
ruins of the city, which consists of three adjoining shafts, the
two outer and oblong ones presumably being used for an endless chain of buckets, and the central and square shaft serving
as an inspection-chamber. L. W. King (*A History of Babylon*,
pp. 46-50) recognizes the force of these arguments, but is
inclined " to hope for a more convincing site for the gardens."
E. Unger (*Babylon*, pp. 216 ff.) accepts the identification of
Koldewey.

μέσον αἴτιοι κατέστησαν τῇ χώρᾳ ταύτης τῆς
προσηγορίας· μετὰ δὲ ταῦτα τὴν Βαβυλωνίαν
διελθόντες[1] εἰς τὴν Ἐρυθρὰν ἐξερεύγονται θάλατ-
3 ταν. μεγάλοι δ' ὄντες καὶ συχνὴν χώραν δια-
πορευόμενοι πολλὰς ἀφορμὰς παρέχονται τοῖς
ἐμπορικῇ χρωμένοις ἐργασίᾳ· διὸ καὶ συμβαίνει
τοὺς παραποταμίους τόπους πλήρεις ὑπάρχειν
ἐμπορίων εὐδαιμόνων καὶ μεγάλα συμβαλλομένων
πρὸς τὴν τῆς Βαβυλωνίας ἐπιφάνειαν.
4   Ἡ δὲ Σεμίραμις ἐκ τῶν Ἀρμενίων ὀρῶν λίθον
ἔτεμε τὸ μὲν μῆκος ποδῶν ἑκατὸν καὶ τριά-
5 κοντα, τὸ δὲ πλάτος καὶ πάχος εἴκοσι καὶ
πέντε· τοῦτον δὲ πολλοῖς πλήθεσι ζευγῶν
ὀρεικῶν τε καὶ βοεικῶν καταγαγοῦσα πρὸς τὸν
ποταμὸν ἐπεβίβασεν ἐπὶ τὴν σχεδίαν· ἐπὶ ταύτης
δὲ παρακομίσασα[2] κατὰ τοῦ ῥεύματος μέχρι τῆς
Βαβυλωνίας ἔστησεν αὐτὸν παρὰ τὴν ἐπισημο-
τάτην ὁδόν, παράδοξον θέαμα τοῖς παριοῦσιν· ὅν
τινες ὀνομάζουσιν ἀπὸ τοῦ σχήματος ὀβελίσκον,
ὃν ἐν τοῖς ἑπτὰ τοῖς κατονομαζομένοις ἔργοις
καταριθμοῦσι.
   12. Πολλῶν δὲ καὶ παραδόξων ὄντων θεαμά-
των κατὰ τὴν Βαβυλωνίαν οὐχ ἥκιστα θαυμά-
ζεται καὶ τὸ πλῆθος τῆς ἐν αὐτῇ γεννωμένης
ἀσφάλτου· τοσοῦτον γάρ ἐστιν ὥστε μὴ μόνον
ταῖς τοσαύταις καὶ τηλικαύταις οἰκοδομίαις
διαρκεῖν, ἀλλὰ καὶ συλλεγόμενον τὸν λαὸν ἐπὶ
τὸν τόπον ἀφειδῶς ἀρύεσθαι καὶ ξηραίνοντα

---

[1] διελθόντες Gemistus : διελόντες.
[2] παρακομίσασα Vogel: κατακομίσασα II, Bekker, Dindorf.

giving this name to the country.[1] After this they
pass through Babylonia and empty into the Red Sea.[2]
Moreover, since they are great streams and traverse
a spacious territory they offer many advantages to
men who follow a merchant trade; and it is due to
this fact that the regions along their banks are filled
with prosperous trading-places which contribute
greatly to the fame of Babylonia.

Semiramis quarried out a stone from the mountains
of Armenia which was one hundred and thirty feet
long and twenty-five feet wide and thick; and this she
hauled by means of many multitudes of yokes of
mules and oxen to the river and there loaded it on a
raft, on which she brought it down the stream to
Babylonia; she then set it up beside the most famous
street, an astonishing sight to all who passed by.
And this stone is called by some an obelisk [3] from its
shape, and they number it among the seven wonders
of the world.

12. Although the sights to be seen in Babylonia
are many and singular, not the least wonderful is the
enormous amount of bitumen which the country
produces; so great is the supply of this that it not
only suffices for their buildings, which are numerous
and large, but the common people also, gathering at
the place,[4] draw it out without any restriction, and

---

[1] Meaning the " region between the rivers." Neither of
the rivers touches either Media or Paraetacenê, which lies
between Media and Persis.

[2] *i.e.* the Persian Gulf. For Diodorus, as for Herodotus (cp.
1. 1), the " Red Sea " was all the water south of Asia. Our
" Red Sea " is the " Arabian Gulf " of Diodorus (cp. 1. 33. 8).

[3] Obelisk is a diminutive of *obelos* (" a spit ").

[4] According to Herodotus (1. 179) the place was eight days'
journey from Babylon at the source of the river Is, which was
a tributary of the Euphrates.

2 κάειν ἀντὶ ξύλων. ἀναριθμήτων δὲ τὸ πλῆθος
ἀνθρώπων ἀρυομένων καθάπερ ἔκ τινος πηγῆς
μεγάλης ἀκέραιον διαμένει τὸ πλήρωμα. ἔστι
δὲ καὶ πλησίον τῆς πηγῆς ταύτης ἀνάδοσις
τῷ μὲν μεγέθει βραχεῖα, δύναμιν δὲ θαυμάσιον
ἔχουσα. προβάλλει[1] γὰρ ἀτμὸν θειώδη καὶ
βαρύν, ᾧ τὸ προσελθὸν ζῷον ἅπαν ἀποθνήσκει,
περιπίπτον ὀξείᾳ καὶ παραδόξῳ τελευτῇ· πνεύματος γὰρ κατοχῇ χρόνον ὑπομεῖναν διαφθείρεται,
καθάπερ κωλυομένης τῆς τοῦ πνεύματος ἐκφορᾶς
ὑπὸ τῆς προσπεσούσης ταῖς ἀναπνοαῖς δυνάμεως·
εὐθὺς δὲ διοιδεῖ καὶ πίμπραται τὸ σῶμα, μάλιστα
3 τοὺς περὶ τὸν πνεύμονα τόπους. ἔστι δὲ καὶ
πέραν τοῦ ποταμοῦ λίμνη στερεὸν ἔχουσα τὸν
περὶ αὐτὴν τύπον,[2] εἰς ἣν ὅταν τις ἐμβῇ τῶν
ἀπείρων, ὀλίγον μὲν νήχεται χρόνον, προϊὼν δ'
εἰς τὸ μέσον καθάπερ ὑπό τινος βίας κατα-
σπᾶται· ἑαυτῷ δὲ βοηθῶν καὶ πάλιν ἀναστρέψαι
προαιρούμενος ἀντέχεται μὲν τῆς ἐκβάσεως, ἀντι-
σπωμένῳ δ' ὑπό τινος ἔοικε· καὶ τὸ μὲν πρῶτον
ἀπονεκροῦται τοὺς πόδας, εἶτα τὰ σκέλη μέχρι
τῆς ὀσφύος, τὸ δὲ τελευταῖον ὅλον τὸ σῶμα νάρκῃ
κρατηθεὶς φέρεται πρὸς βυθόν, καὶ μετ' ὀλίγον
τετελευτηκὼς ἀναβάλλεται.

Περὶ μὲν οὖν τῶν ἐν τῇ Βαβυλωνίᾳ θαυμαζομένων ἀρκείτω τὰ ῥηθέντα.

13. Ἡ δὲ Σεμίραμις ἐπειδὴ τοῖς ἔργοις ἀπέθηκε
πέρας, ἀνέζευξεν ἐπὶ Μηδίας μετὰ πολλῆς δυνά-
μεως· καταντήσασα δὲ πρὸς ὄρος τὸ καλούμενον

[1] προβάλλει Vogel : προσβάλλει Vulgate, Bekker, Dindorf.
[2] τύπον Reiske : τόπον.

drying it burn it in place of wood. And countless as is the multitude of men who draw it out, the amount remains undiminished, as if derived from some immense source. Moreover, near this source there is a vent-hole, of no great size but of remarkable potency. For it emits a heavy sulphurous vapour which brings death to all living creatures that approach it, and they meet with an end swift and strange; for after being subjected for a time to a retention of the breath they are killed, as though the expulsion of the breath were being prevented by the force which has attacked the processes of respiration; and immediately the body swells and blows up, particularly in the region about the lungs. And there is also across the river a lake whose edge offers solid footing, and if any man, unacquainted with it, enters it he swims for a short time, but as he advances towards the centre he is dragged down as though by a certain force; and when he begins to help himself and makes up his mind to turn back to shore again, though he struggles to extricate himself, it appears as if he were being hauled back by something else; and he becomes benumbed, first in his feet, then in his legs as far as the groin, and finally, overcome by numbness in his whole body, he is carried to the bottom, and a little later is cast up dead.

Now concerning the wonders of Babylonia let what has been said suffice.

13. After Semiramis had made an end of her building operations she set forth in the direction of Media with a great force. And when she had arrived at

Βαγίστανον πλησίον αὐτοῦ κατεστρατοπέδευσε,
καὶ κατεσκεύασε παράδεισον, ὃς τὴν μὲν περίμετρον ἦν δώδεκα σταδίων, ἐν πεδίῳ δὲ κείμενος
εἶχε πηγὴν μεγάλην, ἐξ ἧς ἀρδεύεσθαι συνέβαινε
2 τὸ φυτουργεῖον. τὸ δὲ Βαγίστανον ὄρος ἐστὶ
μὲν ἱερὸν Διός, ἐκ δὲ τοῦ παρὰ τὸν παράδεισον
μέρους ἀποτομάδας ἔχει πέτρας εἰς ὕψος ἀνατει-
νούσας ἑπτακαίδεκα σταδίους. οὗ τὸ κατώτατον
μέρος καταξύσασα τὴν ἰδίαν ἐνεχάραξεν εἰκόνα,
δορυφόρους αὐτῇ παραστήσασα ἑκατόν. ἐπέγραψε δὲ καὶ Συρίοις γράμμασιν εἰς τὴν πέτραν
ὅτι Σεμίραμις τοῖς σάγμασι τοῖς τῶν ἀκολου-
θούντων ὑποζυγίων ἀπὸ τοῦ πεδίου χώσασα τὸν
προειρημένον κρημνὸν διὰ τούτων εἰς τὴν ἀκρώ-
ρειαν προσανέβη.

3   Ἐντεῦθεν δ' ἀναζεύξασα καὶ παραγενομένη
πρὸς Χαύονα πόλιν τῆς Μηδίας κατενόησεν ἔν
τινι μετεώρῳ πεδίῳ πέτραν τῷ τε ὕψει καὶ τῷ
μεγέθει καταπληκτικήν. ἐνταῦθ' οὖν ἕτερον
παράδεισον ὑπερμεγέθη κατεσκεύασεν, ἐν μέσῳ
τὴν πέτραν ἀπολαβοῦσα, καθ' ἣν οἰκοδομήματα
πολυτελῆ πρὸς τρυφὴν ἐποίησεν, ἐξ ὧν τά τε
κατὰ τὸν παράδεισον ἀπεθεώρει φυτουργεῖα καὶ
πᾶσαν τὴν στρατιὰν παρεμβεβληκυῖαν ἐν τῷ
4 πεδίῳ. ἐν τούτῳ δὲ τῷ τόπῳ συχνὸν ἐνδιατρί-
ψασα χρόνον καὶ πάντων τῶν εἰς τρυφὴν ἀνηκόντων ἀπολαύσασα, γῆμαι μὲν νομίμως οὐκ ἠθέλη-

---

[1] This is the earliest mention of the modern Behistun, near
the " Gate of Asia " on the old highway between Babylon
and Ecbatana, Diodorus preserving the original form of the
name Bagistana, " place of the Gods " or " of God." The great
inscription, which became the Rosetta Stone of cuneiform, was

the mountain known as Bagistanus,[1] she encamped
near it and laid out a park, which had a circumference of twelve stades and, being situated in the
plain, contained a great spring by means of which
her plantings could be irrigated. The Bagistanus
mountain is sacred to Zeus and on the side facing
the park has sheer cliffs which rise to a height of
seventeen stades. The lowest part of these she
smoothed off and engraved thereon a likeness of
herself with a hundred spearmen at her side. And
she also put this inscription on the cliff in Syrian[2]
letters: " Semiramis, with the pack-saddles of the
beasts of burden in her army, built up a mound from
the plain and thereby climbed this precipice, even to
its very ridge."

Setting forth from that place and arriving at the
city of Chauon in Media, she noticed on a certain
high plateau a rock both of striking height and mass.
Accordingly, she laid out there another park of great
size, putting the rock in the middle of it, and on the
rock she erected, to satisfy her taste for luxury, some
very costly buildings from which she used to look
down both upon her plantings in the park and on the
whole army encamped on the plain. In this place
she passed a long time and enjoyed to the full every
device that contributed to luxury; she was unwilling,
however, to contract a lawful marriage, being afraid

placed there about 516 B.C. to recount the defeat by Darius of
the rebellion which broke out in the reign of Cambyses. It
stands about five hundred feet above the ground and the
magnificent sculptures represent the rebellious satraps, two
attendants of the king, and Darius making the gesture of
adoration before the sacred symbol of Ahuramazda. See
L. W. King and R. C. Thompson, *The Inscription of Darius the
Great at Behistun.*

[2] *i.e.* Assyrian.

σεν, εὐλαβουμένη μήποτε στερηθῇ τῆς ἀρχῆς,
ἐπιλεγομένη δὲ τῶν στρατιωτῶν τοὺς εὐπρεπείᾳ
διαφέροντας τούτοις ἐμίσγετο, καὶ πάντας τοὺς
αὐτῇ πλησιάσαντας ἠφάνιζε.

5   Μετὰ δὲ ταῦτα ἐπ᾽ Ἐκβατάνων τὴν πορείαν
ποιησαμένη παρεγένετο πρὸς ὄρος τὸ Ζαρκαῖον
καλούμενον· τοῦτο δ᾽ ἐπὶ πολλοὺς παρῆκον
σταδίους καὶ πλῆρες ὂν κρημνῶν καὶ φαράγγων
μακρὰν εἶχε τὴν περίοδον. ἐφιλοτιμεῖτο οὖν
ἅμα μὲν μνημεῖον ἀθάνατον ἑαυτῆς ἀπολιπεῖν,
ἅμα δὲ σύντομον ποιήσασθαι τὴν ὁδόν· διόπερ
τούς τε κρημνοὺς κατακόψασα καὶ τοὺς κοίλους
τόπους χώσασα σύντομον καὶ πολυτελῆ κατεσκεύασεν ὁδόν, ἣ μέχρι τοῦ νῦν Σεμιράμιδος
6   καλεῖται. παραγενηθεῖσα δ᾽ εἰς Ἐκβάτανα,
πόλιν ἐν πεδίῳ κειμένην, κατεσκεύασεν ἐν αὐτῇ
πολυτελῆ βασίλεια καὶ τὴν ἄλλην ἐπιμέλειαν
ἐποιήσατο τοῦ τόπου περιττοτέραν. ἀνύδρου
γὰρ οὔσης τῆς πόλεως καὶ μηδαμοῦ σύνεγγυς
ὑπαρχούσης πηγῆς, ἐποίησεν αὐτὴν πᾶσαν
κατάρρυτον, ἐπαγαγοῦσα πλεῖστον καὶ κάλλιστον ὕδωρ μετὰ πολλῆς κακοπαθείας τε καὶ
7   δαπάνης. τῶν γὰρ Ἐκβατάνων ὡς δώδεκα σταδίους ἀπέχον ἔστιν ὄρος ὃ καλεῖται μὲν Ὀρόντης,
τῇ δὲ τραχύτητι καὶ τῷ πρὸς ὕψος ἀνατείνοντι
μεγέθει διάφορον, ὡς ἂν τὴν πρόσβασιν ἔχον
ὄρθιον ἕως τῆς ἀκρωρείας σταδίων εἴκοσι πέντε.
ἐκ θατέρου δὲ μέρους οὔσης λίμνης μεγάλης εἰς
ποταμὸν ἐκβαλλούσης, διέσκαψε τὸ προειρημένον
8   ὄρος κατὰ τὴν ῥίζαν. ἦν δ᾽ ἡ διῶρυξ τὸ μὲν
πλάτος ποδῶν πεντεκαίδεκα, τὸ δ᾽ ὕψος τετταρά-
κοντα· δι᾽ ἧς ἐπαγαγοῦσα τὸν ἐκ τῆς λίμνης

that she might be deprived of her supreme position, but choosing out the most handsome of the soldiers she consorted with them and then made away with all who had lain with her.

After this she advanced in the direction of Ecbatana and arrived at the mountain called Zarcaeus;[1] and since this extended many stades and was full of cliffs and chasms it rendered the journey round a long one. And so she became ambitious both to leave an immortal monument of herself and at the same time to shorten her way; consequently she cut through the cliffs, filled up the low places, and thus at great expense built a short road, which to this day is called the road of Semiramis. Upon arriving at Ecbatana, a city which lies on the plain, she built in it an expensive palace and in every other way gave rather exceptional attention to the region. For since the city had no water supply and there was no spring in its vicinity, she made the whole of it well watered by bringing to it with much hardship and expense an abundance of the purest water. For at a distance from Ecbatana of about twelve stades is a mountain, which is called Orontes and is unusual for its ruggedness and enormous height, since the ascent, straight to its summit, is twenty-five stades. And since a great lake, which emptied into a river, lay on the other side, she made a cutting through the base of this mountain. The tunnel was fifteen feet wide and forty feet high; and through it she brought in the river

[1] The Zagros range.

ποταμὸν ἐπλήρωσε τὴν πόλιν ὕδατος. ταῦτα
μὲν οὖν ἐποίησεν ἐν τῇ Μηδίᾳ.

14. Μετὰ δὲ ταῦτα ἐπῆλθε τήν τε Περσίδα
καὶ τὴν ἄλλην χώραν ἅπασαν ἧς ἐπῆρχε κατὰ
τὴν 'Ασίαν. πανταχοῦ δὲ τὰ μὲν ὄρη καὶ τὰς
ἀπορρῶγας πέτρας διακόπτουσα κατεσκεύασεν
ὁδοὺς πολυτελεῖς, ἐν δὲ τοῖς πεδίοις ἐποίει χώματα,
ποτὲ μὲν τάφους κατασκευάζουσα τοῖς τελευτῶσι
τῶν ἡγεμόνων, ποτὲ δὲ πόλεις ἐν τοῖς ἀναστήμασι
2 κατοικίζουσα. εἰώθει δὲ καὶ κατὰ τὰς στρατοπεδείας μικρὰ χώματα κατασκευάζειν, ἐφ' ὧν
καθιστᾶσα τὴν ἰδίαν σκηνὴν ἅπασαν κατώπτευε
τὴν παρεμβολήν· διὸ καὶ πολλὰ κατὰ τὴν 'Ασίαν
μέχρι τοῦ νῦν διαμένει τῶν ὑπ' ἐκείνης κατασκευασθέντων καὶ καλεῖται Σεμιράμιδος ἔργα.

3 Μετὰ δὲ ταῦτα τήν τε Αἴγυπτον πᾶσαν ἐπῆλθε
καὶ τῆς Λιβύης τὰ πλεῖστα καταστρεψαμένη
παρῆλθεν εἰς Ἄμμωνα, χρησομένη τῷ θεῷ περὶ
τῆς ἰδίας τελευτῆς. λέγεται ' δ' αὐτῇ γενέσθαι
λόγιον ἐξ ἀνθρώπων ἀφανισθήσεσθαι καὶ κατὰ
τὴν 'Ασίαν παρ' ἐνίοις τῶν ἐθνῶν ἀθανάτου
τεύξεσθαι τιμῆς· ὅπερ ἔσεσθαι καθ' ὃν ἂν χρόνον
4 ὁ υἱὸς αὐτῇ Νινύας ἐπιβουλεύσῃ. ἀπὸ δὲ τούτων γενομένη τῆς Αἰθιοπίας ἐπῆλθε τὰ πλεῖστα
καταστρεφομένη καὶ τὰ κατὰ τὴν χώραν θεωμένη
παράδοξα. εἶναι γὰρ ἐν αὐτῇ φασι λίμνην
τετράγωνον, τὴν μὲν περίμετρον ἔχουσαν ποδῶν
ὡς ἑκατὸν ἑξήκοντα, τὸ δ' ὕδωρ τῇ μὲν χρόᾳ
παραπλήσιον κινναβάρει, τὴν δ' ὀσμὴν καθ'
ὑπερβολὴν ἡδεῖαν, οὐκ ἀνόμοιον οἴνῳ παλαιῷ·

---

[1] This is obviously an attempt to explain the many mounds
which dotted the landscape of this region in the time of

which flowed from the lake, and filled the city with water. Now this is what she did in Media.

14. After this she visited Persis and every other country over which she ruled throughout Asia. Everywhere she cut through the mountains and the precipitous cliffs and constructed expensive roads, while on the plains she made mounds, sometimes constructing them as tombs for those of her generals who died, and sometimes founding cities on their tops. And it was also her custom, whenever she made camp, to build little mounds, upon which setting her tent she could look down upon all the encampment. As a consequence many of the works she built throughout Asia remain to this day and are called Works of Semiramis.[1]

After this she visited all Egypt, and after subduing most of Libya she went also to the oracle of Ammon [2] to inquire of the god regarding her own end. And the account runs that the answer was given her that she would disappear from among men and receive undying honour among some of the peoples of Asia, and that this would take place when her son Ninyas should conspire against her. Then upon her return from these regions she visited most of Ethiopia, subduing it as she went and inspecting the wonders of the land. For in that country, they say, there is a lake, square in form, with a perimeter of some hundred and sixty feet, and its water is like cinnabar in colour and the odour of it is exceeding sweet, not unlike that of

Diodorus as well as to-day and are the remains of ancient dwelling sites.

[2] The shrine of Zeus-Ammon in the Oasis of Siwah, which is described in Book 17. 50, in connection with the celebrated visit to it of Alexander.

δύναμιν δ' ἔχειν παράδοξον· τὸν γὰρ πιόντα
φασὶν εἰς μανίαν ἐμπίπτειν καὶ πάνθ' ἃ πρότερον
διέλαθεν ἁμαρτήσας ἑαυτοῦ κατηγορεῖν. τοῖς
μὲν οὖν ταῦτα λέγουσιν οὐκ ἄν τις ῥαδίως
συγκατάθοιτο.

15. Ταφὰς δὲ τῶν τελευτησάντων ἰδίως[1] οἱ
κατὰ τὴν Αἰθιοπίαν ποιοῦνται· ταριχεύσαντες
γὰρ τὰ σώματα καὶ περιχέαντες αὐτοῖς πολλὴν
ὕελον ἱστᾶσιν ἐπὶ στήλης, ὥστε τοῖς παριοῦσι
φαίνεσθαι διὰ τῆς ὑέλου τὸ τοῦ τετελευτηκότος
2 σῶμα, καθάπερ Ἡρόδοτος εἴρηκε. Κτησίας δ' ὁ
Κνίδιος ἀποφαινόμενος τοῦτον σχεδιάζειν, αὐτός
φησι τὸ μὲν σῶμα ταριχεύεσθαι, τὴν μέντοι γε
ὕελον μὴ περιχεῖσθαι γυμνοῖς τοῖς σώμασι· κατα-
καυθήσεσθαι γὰρ ταῦτα καὶ λυμανθέντα τελέως
3 τὴν ὁμοιότητα μὴ δυνήσεσθαι διατηρεῖν. διὸ καὶ
χρυσῆν εἰκόνα κατασκευάζεσθαι κοίλην, εἰς ἣν
ἐντεθέντος τοῦ νεκροῦ περὶ τὴν εἰκόνα χεῖσθαι
τὴν ὕελον· τοῦ δὲ κατασκευάσματος τεθέντος ἐπὶ
τὸν τάφον διὰ τῆς ὑέλου φανῆναι τὸν χρυσὸν
4 ἀφωμοιωμένον τῷ τετελευτηκότι. τοὺς μὲν οὖν
πλουσίους αὐτῶν οὕτω θάπτεσθαί φησι, τοὺς δ'
ἐλάττονας καταλιπόντας οὐσίας ἀργυρᾶς τυγχάνειν εἰκόνος, τοὺς δὲ πένητας κεραμίνης· τὴν δὲ
ὕελον πᾶσιν ἐξαρκεῖν διὰ τὸ πλείστην γεννᾶσθαι

---

[1] ἰδίως Bekker, Vogel : ἰδίας Dindorf.

---

[1] Herodotus (3. 24) says nothing of the sort. According to
him the body is shrunk and covered with gypsum, which is
painted in such a way as to make it resemble a living man;
then "they set it within a hollow pillar of *hyelos*." It is difficult to understand how some translators and commentators
take this word to mean "porcelain," for Herodotus goes on

old wine; moreover, it has a remarkable power; for whoever has drunk of it, they say, falls into a frenzy and accuses himself of every sin which he had formerly committed in secret. However, a man may not readily agree with those who tell such things.

15. In the burial of their dead the inhabitants of Ethiopia follow customs peculiar to themselves; for after they have embalmed the body and have poured a heavy coat of glass over it they stand it on a pillar, so that the body of the dead man is visible through the glass to those who pass by. This is the statement of Herodotus.[1] But Ctesias of Cnidus, declaring that Herodotus is inventing a tale, gives for his part this account. The body is indeed embalmed, but glass is not poured about the naked bodies, for they would be burned and so completely disfigured that they could no longer preserve their likeness. For this reason they fashion a hollow statue of gold and when the corpse has been put into this they pour the glass over the statue, and the figure, prepared in this way, is then placed at the tomb, and the gold, fashioned as it is to resemble the deceased, is seen through the glass. Now the rich among them are buried in this wise, he says, but those who leave a smaller estate receive a silver statue, and the poor one made of earthenware; as for the glass, there is enough of it for everyone,

to say that " it is quarried by them in abundance and is easy to work." In Herodotus' day it probably meant some transparent stone, perhaps alabaster (cp. M. L. Trowbridge, *Philological Studies in Ancient Glass* (University of Illinois Studies in Language and Literature, 1928), pp. 23 ff.); but by the time of Diodorus *hyelos* was the term used for " glass." Strabo (17. 2. 3) agrees with Diodorus in saying that in one manner of burial the Ethiopians " poured glass over " the bodies of the dead.

κατὰ τὴν Αἰθιοπίαν καὶ τελέως παρὰ τοῖς
5 ἐγχωρίοις ἐπιπολάζειν. περὶ δὲ τῶν νομίμων
τῶν παρὰ τοῖς Αἰθίοψι καὶ τῶν ἄλλων τῶν γινομένων ἐν τῇ τούτων χώρᾳ τὰ κυριώτατα καὶ
μνήμης ἄξια μικρὸν ὕστερον ἀναγράψομεν, ὅταν
καὶ τὰς παλαιὰς αὐτῶν πράξεις καὶ μυθολογίας
διεξίωμεν.

16. Ἡ δὲ Σεμίραμις καταστήσασα τά τε κατὰ
τὴν Αἰθιοπίαν καὶ τὴν Αἴγυπτον ἐπανῆλθε μετὰ
τῆς δυνάμεως εἰς Βάκτρα τῆς Ἀσίας. ἔχουσα δὲ
δυνάμεις μεγάλας καὶ πολυχρόνιον εἰρήνην ἄγουσα
φιλοτίμως ἔσχε πρᾶξαί τι λαμπρὸν κατὰ πόλε-
2 μον. πυνθανομένη δὲ τὸ τῶν Ἰνδῶν ἔθνος
μέγιστον εἶναι τῶν κατὰ τὴν οἰκουμένην καὶ
πλείστην τε καὶ καλλίστην χώραν νέμεσθαι,
διενοεῖτο στρατεύειν εἰς τὴν Ἰνδικήν, ἧς ἐβασίλευε μὲν Σταυροβάτης κατ' ἐκείνους τοὺς
χρόνους, στρατιωτῶν δ' εἶχεν ἀναρίθμητον
πλῆθος· ὑπῆρχον δ' αὐτῷ καὶ ἐλέφαντες πολλοὶ
καθ' ὑπερβολὴν λαμπρῶς κεκοσμημένοι τοῖς εἰς
3 τὸν πόλεμον καταπληκτικοῖς. ἡ γὰρ Ἰνδικὴ
χώρα διάφορος οὖσα τῷ κάλλει καὶ πολλοῖς
διειλημμένη ποταμοῖς ἀρδεύεταί τε πολλαχοῦ καὶ
διττοὺς καθ' ἕκαστον ἐνιαυτὸν ἐκφέρει καρπούς·
διὸ καὶ τῶν πρὸς τὸ ζῆν ἐπιτηδείων τοσοῦτον
ἔχει πλῆθος ὥστε διὰ παντὸς ἄφθονον ἀπόλαυσιν
τοῖς ἐγχωρίοις παρέχεσθαι. λέγεται δὲ μηδεποτε
κατ' αὐτὴν γεγονέναι σιτοδείαν ἢ φθορὰν καρπῶν
4 διὰ τὴν εὐκρασίαν τῶν τόπων. ἔχει δὲ καὶ τῶν
ἐλεφάντων ἄπιστον πλῆθος, οἳ ταῖς τε ἀλκαῖς
καὶ ταῖς τοῦ σώματος ῥώμαις πολὺ προέχουσι
τῶν ἐν τῇ Λιβύῃ γινομένων, ὁμοίως δὲ χρυσόν,

since it occurs in great abundance in Ethiopia and is quite current among the inhabitants. With regard to the customs prevailing among the Ethiopians and the other features of their country we shall a little later set forth those that are the most important and deserving of record, at which time we shall also recount their early deeds and their mythology.[1]

16. But after Semiramis had put in order the affairs of Ethiopia and Egypt she returned with her force to Bactra in Asia. And since she had great forces and had been at peace for some time she became eager to achieve some brilliant exploit in war. And when she was informed that the Indian nation was the largest one in the world and likewise possessed both the most extensive and the fairest country, she purposed to make a campaign into India.[2] Stabrobates at that time was king of the country and had a multitude of soldiers without number; and many elephants were also at his disposal, fitted out in an exceedingly splendid fashion with such things as would strike terror in war. For India is a land of unusual beauty, and since it is traversed by many rivers it is supplied with water over its whole area and yields two harvests each year; consequently it has such an abundance of the necessities of life that at all times it favours its inhabitants with a bounteous enjoyment of them. And it is said that because of the favourable climate in those parts the country has never experienced a famine or a destruction of crops. It also has an unbelievable multitude of elephants, which both in courage and in strength of body far surpass those of

[1] This is done in Book 3. 5 ff.
[2] This campaign was doubted already by the ancient writers; cp. Strabo 15. 1. 5 f.

ἄργυρον, σίδηρον, χαλκόν· πρὸς δὲ τούτοις λίθων
παντοίων καὶ πολυτελῶν ἔστιν ἐν αὐτῇ πλῆθος,
ἔτι δὲ τῶν ἄλλων ἁπάντων σχεδὸν τῶν πρὸς
τρυφὴν καὶ πλοῦτον διατεινόντων.

Ὑπὲρ ὧν τὰ κατὰ μέρος ἡ Σεμίραμις ἀκούσασα
προήχθη μηδὲν προαδικηθεῖσα τὸν πρὸς Ἰνδοὺς
5 ἐξενεγκεῖν πόλεμον. ὁρῶσα δ᾽ αὑτὴν μεγάλων
καθ᾽ ὑπερβολὴν προσδεομένην δυνάμεων, ἐξ-
έπεμψεν ἀγγέλους εἰς ἁπάσας τὰς σατραπείας,[1]
διακελευσαμένη τοῖς ἐπάρχοις καταγράφειν τῶν
νέων τοὺς ἀρίστους, δοῦσα τὸν ἀριθμὸν κατὰ τὰ
μεγέθη τῶν ἐθνῶν· προσέταξε δὲ πᾶσι κατασκευάζειν καινὰς πανοπλίας καὶ τοῖς ἄλλοις
ἅπασι λαμπρῶς παραγίνεσθαι κεκοσμημένους
6 μετὰ τρίτον ἔτος εἰς Βάκτρα. μετεπέμψατο δὲ
καὶ ναυπηγοὺς ἔκ τε Φοινίκης καὶ Συρίας καὶ
Κύπρου καὶ τῆς ἄλλης τῆς παραθαλαττίου χώρας,
οἷς ἄφθονον ὕλην μεταγαγοῦσα διεκελεύσατο
7 κατασκευάζειν ποτάμια πλοῖα διαιρετά. ὁ γὰρ
Ἰνδὸς ποταμός, μέγιστος ὢν τῶν περὶ τοὺς τόπους
καὶ τὴν βασιλείαν αὐτῆς ὁρίζων, πολλῶν προσ-
εδεῖτο πλοίων πρός τε τὴν διάβασιν καὶ πρὸς τὸ
τοὺς Ἰνδοὺς ἀπὸ τούτων ἀμύνασθαι· περὶ δὲ τὸν
ποταμὸν οὐκ οὔσης ὕλης ἀναγκαῖον ἦν ἐκ τῆς
Βακτριανῆς πεζῇ παρακομίζεσθαι τὰ πλοῖα.
8 Θεωροῦσα δ᾽ ἡ Σεμίραμις ἑαυτὴν ἐν τῇ τῶν
ἐλεφάντων χρείᾳ πολὺ λειπομένην, ἐπενοήσατο[2]
κατασκευάζειν εἴδωλα[3] τούτων τῶν ζῴων, ἐλπί-
ζουσα καταπλήξεσθαι τοὺς Ἰνδοὺς διὰ τὸ νομίζειν

---

[1] σατραπείας Dindorf : στρατοπεδείας.
[2] τι after ἐπενοήσατο deleted by Hertlein.

Libya, and likewise gold, silver, iron, and copper; furthermore, within its borders are to be found great quantities of precious stones of every kind and of practically all other things which contribute to luxury and wealth.[1]

When Semiramis had received a detailed account of these facts she was led to begin her war against the Indians, although she had been done no injury by them. And realizing that she needed an exceedingly great force in addition to what she had she despatched messengers to all the satrapies, commanding the governors to enrol the bravest of the young men and setting their quota in accordance with the size of each nation; and she further ordered them all to make new suits of armour and to be at hand, brilliantly equipped in every other respect, at Bactra on the third year thereafter. She also summoned shipwrights from Phoenicia, Syria, Cyprus, and the rest of the lands along the sea, and shipping thither an abundance of timber she ordered them to build river boats which could be taken to pieces. For the Indus river, by reason of its being the largest in that region and the boundary of her kingdom, required many boats, some for the passage across and others from which to defend the former from the Indians; and since there was no timber near the river the boats had to be brought from Bactriana by land.

Observing that she was greatly inferior because of her lack of elephants, Semiramis conceived the plan of making dummies like these animals, in the hope that the Indians would be struck with terror because

---

[1] India is more fully described in chaps. 35 ff.

[3] εἴδωλα Vogel: ἰδίωμα.

αὐτοὺς μηδ' εἶναι τὸ σύνολον ἐλέφαντας ἐκτὸς
9 τῶν κατὰ τὴν Ἰνδικήν. ἐπιλέξασα δὲ βοῶν
μελάνων τριάκοντα μυριάδας τὰ μὲν κρέα τοῖς
τεχνίταις καὶ τοῖς πρὸς τὴν τῶν κατασκευασμάτων ὑπηρεσίαν τεταγμένοις διένειμε, τὰς δὲ
βύρσας συρράπτουσα καὶ χόρτου πληροῦσα
κατεσκεύασεν εἴδωλα, κατὰ πᾶν ἀπομιμουμένη
τὴν τῶν ζῴων τούτων φύσιν. ἕκαστον δὲ τούτων εἶχεν ἐντὸς ἄνδρα τὸν ἐπιμελησόμενον καὶ
κάμηλον, ὑφ' οὗ φερόμενον φαντασίαν τοῖς
πόρρωθεν ὁρῶσιν ἀληθινοῦ θηρίου παρείχετο.
10 οἱ δὲ ταῦτα κατασκευάζοντες αὐτῇ τεχνῖται
προσεκαρτέρουν τοῖς ἔργοις ἔν τινι περιβόλῳ
περιῳκοδομημένῳ καὶ πύλας ἔχοντι τηρουμένας
ἐπιμελῶς, ὥστε μηδένα μήτε τῶν ἔσωθεν ἐξιέναι
τεχνιτῶν μήτε τῶν ἔξωθεν εἰσιέναι πρὸς αὐτούς.
τοῦτο δ' ἐποίησεν, ὅπως μηδεὶς τῶν ἔξωθεν ἴδῃ τὸ
γινόμενον μηδὲ διαπέσῃ φήμη πρὸς Ἰνδοὺς περὶ
τούτων.

17. Ἐπεὶ δ' αἵ τε νῆες καὶ τὰ θηρία κατ-
εσκευάσθησαν ἐν τοῖς δυσὶν ἔτεσι, τῷ τρίτῳ
μετεπέμψατο τὰς πανταχόθεν δυνάμεις εἰς τὴν
Βακτριανήν. τὸ δὲ πλῆθος τῆς ἀθροισθείσης
στρατιᾶς ἦν, ὡς Κτησίας ὁ Κνίδιος ἀνέγραψε,
πεζῶν μὲν τριακόσιαι μυριάδες, ἱππέων δὲ εἴκοσι[1]
2 μυριάδες, ἁρμάτων δὲ δέκα μυριάδες. ὑπῆρχον
δὲ καὶ ἄνδρες ἐπὶ καμήλων ὀχούμενοι, μαχαίρας
τετραπήχεις ἔχοντες, τὸν ἀριθμὸν ἴσοι τοῖς
ἅρμασι. ναῦς δὲ ποταμίας κατεσκεύασε διαι-
ρετὰς δισχιλίας, αἷς παρεσκευάσατο καμήλους
τὰς πεζῇ παρακομιζούσας τὰ σκάφη. ἐφόρουν

[1] εἴκοσι Vogel : πεντήκοντα C, Bekker, Dindorf.

of their belief that no elephants ever existed at all apart from those found in India. Accordingly she chose out three hundred thousand black oxen and distributed their meat among her artisans and the men who had been assigned to the task of making the figures, but the hides she sewed together and stuffed with straw, and thus made dummies, copying in every detail the natural appearance of these animals. Each dummy had within it a man to take care of it and a camel and, when it was moved by the latter, to those who saw it from a distance it looked like an actual animal. And the artisans who were engaged in making these dummies for her worked at their task in a certain court which had been surrounded by a wall and had gates which were carefully guarded, so that no worker within could pass out and no one from outside could come in to them. This she did in order that no one from the outside might see what was taking place and that no report about the dummies might escape to the Indians.

17. When the boats and the beasts had been prepared in the two allotted years, on the third she summoned her forces from everywhere to Bactriana. And the multitude of the army which was assembled, as Ctesias of Cnidus has recorded, was three million foot-soldiers, two hundred thousand cavalry, and one hundred thousand chariots. There were also men mounted on camels, carrying swords four cubits long, as many in number as the chariots. And river boats which could be taken apart she built to the number of two thousand, and she had collected camels to carry the vessels overland. Camels also bore the dummies

δὲ καὶ τὰ τῶν ἐλεφάντων εἴδωλα κάμηλοι, καθότι
προείρηται· πρὸς δ' αὐτὰς τοὺς ἵππους οἱ στρα-
τιῶται συνάγοντες συνήθεις ἐποίουν τοῦ μὴ
3 φοβεῖσθαι τὴν ἀγριότητα τῶν θηρίων. τὸ παραπλήσιον δὲ πολλοῖς ἔτεσιν ὕστερον ἔπραξε
Περσεὺς ὁ τῶν Μακεδόνων βασιλεύς, ὅτε πρὸς
Ῥωμαίους ἔμελλε διακινδυνεύειν ἔχοντας ἐκ
Λιβύης ἐλέφαντας. ἀλλ' οὔτ' ἐκείνῳ ῥοπὴν
ἐνεγκεῖν εἰς τὸν πόλεμον συνέβη τὴν περὶ τὰ
τοιαῦτα σπουδὴν καὶ φιλοτεχνίαν οὔτε Σεμιρά-
μιδι· περὶ ὧν ἀκριβέστερον ὁ προϊὼν λόγος
δηλώσει.

4 Ὁ δὲ τῶν Ἰνδῶν βασιλεὺς Σταβροβάτης πυν-
θανόμενος τά τε μεγέθη τῶν ὀνομαζομένων[1] δυνάμεων καὶ τὴν ὑπερβολὴν τῆς εἰς τὸν πόλεμον
παρασκευῆς, ἔσπευδεν ἐν ἅπασιν ὑπερθέσθαι τὴν
5 Σεμίραμιν. καὶ πρῶτον μὲν ἐκ τοῦ καλάμου
κατεσκεύασε πλοῖα ποτάμια τετρακισχίλια· ἡ
γὰρ Ἰνδικὴ παρά τε τοὺς ποταμοὺς καὶ τοὺς
ἑλώδεις τόπους φέρει καλάμου πλῆθος, οὗ τὸ
πάχος οὐκ ἂν ῥᾳδίως ἄνθρωπος περιλάβοι·
λέγεται δὲ καὶ τὰς ἐκ τούτων κατασκευαζομένας
ναῦς διαφόρους κατὰ τὴν χρείαν ὑπάρχειν, οὔσης
6 ἀσήπτου ταύτης τῆς ὕλης. ποιησάμενος δὲ καὶ
τῆς τῶν ὅπλων κατασκευῆς[2] πολλὴν ἐπιμέλειαν
καὶ πᾶσαν ἐπελθὼν τὴν Ἰνδικὴν ἤθροισε δύναμιν
πολὺ μείζονα τῆς Σεμιράμιδι συναχθείσης.

---

[1] ὀνομαζομένων Vogel: ἐτοιμαζομένων F, Bekker, Dindorf.
[2] κατασκευῆς Vogel: παρασκευῆς Π, Bekker, Dindorf.

---

[1] i.e. the elephants.
[2] In the Third Macedonian War, 171–167 B.C., Polyaenus
(4. 20) says that Perseus constructed wooden dummies of

of the elephants, as has been mentioned; and the soldiers, by bringing their horses up to these camels, accustomed them not to fear the savage nature of the beasts.[1] A similar thing was also done many years later by Perseus, the king of the Macedonians, before his decisive conflict with the Romans who had elephants from Libya.[2] But neither in his case did it turn out that the zeal and ingenuity displayed in such matters had any effect on the conflict, nor in that of Semiramis, as will be shown more precisely in our further account.

When Stabrobates, the king of the Indians, heard of the immensity of the forces mentioned and of the exceedingly great preparations which had been made for the war, he was anxious to surpass Semiramis in every respect. First of all, then, he made four thousand river boats out of reeds; for along its rivers and marshy places India produces a great abundance of reeds, so large in diameter that a man cannot easily put his arms about them;[3] and it is said, furthermore, that ships built of these are exceedingly serviceable, since this wood does not rot. Moreover, he gave great care to the preparation of his arms and by visiting all India gathered a far greater force than that which had been collected by Semiramis. Fur-

---

elephants, and that a man within them imitated their trumpeting. The horses of the Macedonians were led up to these and thus accustomed to the appearance and trumpeting of the Roman elephants. Zonaras (9. 22) adds that the dummies were also smeared with an ointment "to give them a dreadful odour."

[3] In Book 17. 90. 5 Diodorus describes trees of India which four men can scarcely get their arms about, and Strabo (15. 1. 56), on the authority of Megasthenes, speaks of reeds some of which are three cubits and others six in diameter.

7 ποιησάμενος δὲ καὶ τῶν ἀγρίων ἐλεφάντων θήραν
καὶ πολλαπλασιάσας τοὺς προϋπάρχοντας, ἐκόσμησεν ἅπαντας τοῖς εἰς τὸν πόλεμον καταπλη-
8 κτικοῖς λαμπρῶς· διὸ καὶ συνέβαινε κατὰ τὴν
ἔφοδον αὐτῶν διά τε τὸ πλῆθος καὶ τὴν ἐπὶ τῶν
θωρακίων κατασκευὴν ἀνυπόστατον ἀνθρωπίνῃ
φύσει φαίνεσθαι τὴν ἐπιφάνειαν.

18. Ἐπεὶ δ' αὐτῷ πάντα τὰ[1] πρὸς τὸν πόλεμον κατεσκεύαστο, πρὸς τὴν Σεμίραμιν καθ' ὁδὸν
οὖσαν ἀπέστειλεν ἀγγέλους, ἐγκαλῶν ὅτι προ-
κατάρχεται τοῦ πολέμου μηδὲν ἀδικηθεῖσα·
πολλὰ δὲ καὶ ἄρρητα κατ' αὐτῆς ὡς ἑταίρας[2]
βλασφημήσας διὰ τῶν γραμμάτων καὶ θεοὺς
ἐπιμαρτυράμενος, ἠπείλει καταπολεμήσας αὐτὴν
2 σταυρῷ προσηλώσειν. ἡ δὲ Σεμίραμις ἀνα-
γνοῦσα τὴν ἐπιστολὴν καὶ καταγελάσασα τῶν
γεγραμμένων, διὰ τῶν ἔργων ἔφησε τὸν Ἰνδὸν
πειράσεσθαι τῆς περὶ αὐτὴν ἀρετῆς. ἐπεὶ δὲ
προάγουσα μετὰ τῆς δυνάμεως ἐπὶ τὸν Ἰνδὸν
ποταμὸν παρεγενήθη, κατέλαβε τὰ τῶν πολεμίων
3 πλοῖα πρὸς μάχην ἕτοιμα. διόπερ καὶ αὐτὴ
καταρτίσασα ταχέως τὰς ναῦς καὶ πληρώσασα
τῶν κρατίστων ἐπιβατῶν συνεστήσατο κατὰ τὸν
ποταμὸν ναυμαχίαν, συμφιλοτιμουμένων καὶ
τῶν παρεμβεβληκότων παρὰ τὸ ῥεῖθρον πεζῶν.
4 ἐπὶ πολὺν δὲ χρόνον τοῦ κινδύνου παρατείνοντος
καὶ προθύμως ἑκατέρων ἀγωνισαμένων, τὸ τελευταῖον ἡ Σεμίραμις ἐνίκησε καὶ διέφθειρε τῶν
πλοίων περὶ χίλια, συνέλαβε δ' αἰχμαλώτους
5 οὐκ ὀλίγους. ἐπαρθεῖσα δὲ τῇ νίκῃ τὰς ἐν τῷ

---

[1] τὰ added by Gemistus.

thermore, holding a hunt of the wild elephants and multiplying many times the number already at his disposal, he fitted them all out splendidly with such things as would strike terror in war; and the consequence was that when they advanced to the attack the multitude of them as well as the towers upon their backs made them appear like a thing beyond the power of human nature to withstand.

18. When he had made all his preparations for the war he despatched messengers to Semiramis, who was already on the road, accusing her of being the aggressor in the war although she had been injured in no respect; then, in the course of his letter, after saying many slanderous things against her as being a strumpet and calling upon the gods as witnesses, he threatened her with crucifixion when he had defeated her. Semiramis, however, on reading his letter dismissed his statements with laughter and remarked, " It will be in deeds [1] that the Indian will make trial of my valour." And when her advance brought her with her force to the Indus river she found the boats of the enemy ready for battle. Consequently she on her side, hastily putting together her boats and manning them with her best marines, joined battle on the river, while the foot-soldiers which were drawn up along the banks also participated eagerly in the contest. The struggle raged for a long time and both sides fought spiritedly, but finally Semiramis was victorious and destroyed about a thousand of the boats, taking also not a few men prisoners. Elated now by her victory, she reduced to

[1] *i.e.* and not in words.

[2] ὡς ἑταίρας Vogel: ὡς ἑταίραν D, εἰς ἑταιρείαν F and accepted by all editors.

ποταμῷ νήσους καὶ πόλεις ἐξηνδραποδίσατο, καὶ
συνήγαγεν αἰχμαλώτων σωμάτων ὑπὲρ τὰς δέκα
μυριάδας.

Μετὰ δὲ ταῦθ' ὁ μὲν τῶν Ἰνδῶν βασιλεὺς
ἀπήγαγε τὴν δύναμιν ἀπὸ τοῦ ποταμοῦ, προσ-
ποιούμενος μὲν ἀναχωρεῖν διὰ φόβον, τῇ δ'
ἀληθείᾳ βουλόμενος τοὺς πολεμίους προτρέ-
6 ψασθαι διαβῆναι τὸν ποταμόν. ἡ δὲ Σεμίραμις,
κατὰ νοῦν αὐτῇ τῶν πραγμάτων προχωρούντων,
ἔζευξε τὸν ποταμὸν κατασκευάσασα πολυτελῆ
καὶ μεγάλην γέφυραν, δι' ἧς ἅπασαν διακο-
μίσασα τὴν δύναμιν ἐπὶ μὲν τοῦ ζεύγματος
φυλακὴν κατέλιπεν ἀνδρῶν ἑξακισμυρίων, τῇ
δ' ἄλλῃ στρατιᾷ προῆγεν ἐπιδιώκουσα τοὺς
Ἰνδούς, προηγουμένων τῶν εἰδώλων, ὅπως οἱ
τῶν πολεμίων κατάσκοποι τῷ βασιλεῖ ἀπαγγεί-
7 λωσι τὸ πλῆθος τῶν παρ' αὐτῇ θηρίων. οὐ
διεψεύσθη δὲ κατά γε τοῦτο τῆς ἐλπίδος, ἀλλὰ
τῶν ἐπὶ κατασκοπὴν ἐκπεμφθέντων τοῖς Ἰνδοῖς
ἀπαγγελλόντων τὸ πλῆθος τῶν παρὰ τοῖς
πολεμίοις ἐλεφάντων, ἅπαντες διηποροῦντο
πόθεν αὐτῇ συνακολουθεῖ τοσοῦτο πλῆθος θη-
8 ρίων. οὐ μὴν ἔμεινέ γε τὸ ψεῦδος πλείω χρόνον
κρυπτόμενον· τῶν γὰρ παρὰ τῇ Σεμιράμιδι
στρατευομένων τινὲς κατελήφθησαν νυκτὸς ἐν τῇ
στρατοπεδείᾳ ῥᾳθυμοῦντες τὰ περὶ τὰς φυλακάς·
φοβηθέντες δὲ τὴν ἐπακολουθοῦσαν τιμωρίαν
ηὐτομόλησαν πρὸς τοὺς πολεμίους καὶ τὴν κατὰ
τοὺς ἐλέφαντας πλάνην ἀπήγγειλαν. ἐφ' οἷς
θαρρήσας ὁ τῶν Ἰνδῶν βασιλεὺς καὶ τῇ δυνάμει
διαγγείλας τὰ περὶ τῶν εἰδώλων, ἐπέστρεψεν ἐπὶ
τοὺς Ἀσσυρίους διατάξας τὴν δύναμιν.

slavery the islands in the river and the cities on them and gathered in more than one hundred thousand captives.

After these events the king of the Indians withdrew his force from the river, giving the appearance of retreating in fear but actually with the intention of enticing the enemy to cross the river. Thereupon Semiramis, now that her undertakings were prospering as she wished, spanned the river with a costly and large bridge, by means of which she got all her forces across; and then she left sixty thousand men to guard the pontoon bridge, while with the rest of her army she advanced in pursuit of the Indians, the dummy elephants leading the way in order that the enemy's spies might report to the king the multitude of these animals in her army. Nor was she deceived in this hope; on the contrary, when those who had been despatched to spy her out reported to the Indians the multitude of elephants among the enemy, they were all at a loss to discover from where such a multitude of beasts as accompanied her could have come. However, the deception did not remain a secret for long; for some of Semiramis' troops were caught neglecting their night watches in the camp, and these, in fear of the consequent punishment, deserted to the enemy and pointed out to them their mistake regarding the nature of the elephants. Encouraged by this information, the king of the Indians, after informing his army about the dummies, set his forces in array and turned about to face the Assyrians.

19. Τὸ δ' αὐτὸ καὶ τῆς Σεμιράμιδος ἐπιτελούσης, ὡς ἤγγισαν ἀλλήλοις τὰ στρατόπεδα, Σταβροβάτης ὁ τῶν Ἰνδῶν βασιλεὺς προαπέστειλε πολὺ πρὸ τῆς φάλαγγος τοὺς ἱππεῖς μετὰ 2 τῶν ἁρμάτων. δεξαμένης δὲ τῆς βασιλίσσης εὐρώστως τὴν ἔφοδον τῶν ἱππέων, καὶ τῶν κατεσκευασμένων ἐλεφάντων πρὸ τῆς φάλαγγος ἐν ἴσοις διαστήμασι τεταγμένων, συνέβαινε 3 πτύρεσθαι τοὺς τῶν Ἰνδῶν ἵππους. τὰ γὰρ εἴδωλα πόρρωθεν μὲν ὁμοίαν εἶχε τὴν πρόσοψιν τοῖς ἀληθινοῖς θηρίοις, οἷς συνήθεις ὄντες οἱ τῶν Ἰνδῶν ἵπποι τεθαρρηκότως προσίππευον· τοῖς δ' ἐγγίσασιν ἥ τε ὀσμὴ προσέβαλλεν ἀσυνήθης καὶ τἄλλα διαφορὰν ἔχοντα πάντα παμμεγέθη τοὺς ἵππους ὁλοσχερῶς συνετάραττε. διὸ καὶ τῶν Ἰνδῶν οἱ μὲν ἐπὶ τὴν γῆν ἔπιπτον, οἱ δὲ τῶν ζῴων ἀπειθούντων τοῖς χαλινοῖς ὡς ἐτύγχανεν[1] εἰς τοὺς πολεμίους ἐξέπιπτον μετὰ τῶν 4 κομιζόντων αὐτοὺς ἵππων. ἡ δὲ Σεμίραμις μετὰ στρατιωτῶν ἐπιλέκτων μαχομένη καὶ τῷ προτερήματι δεξιῶς χρησαμένη τοὺς Ἰνδοὺς ἐτρέψατο. ὧν φυγόντων πρὸς τὴν φάλαγγα Σταβροβάτης ὁ βασιλεὺς οὐ καταπλαγεὶς ἐπήγαγε τὰς τῶν πεζῶν τάξεις, προηγουμένων τῶν ἐλεφάντων, αὐτὸς δ' ἐπὶ τοῦ δεξιοῦ κέρατος τεταγμένος καὶ τὴν μάχην ἐπὶ τοῦ κρατίστου θηρίου ποιούμενος ἐπήγαγε καταπληκτικῶς ἐπὶ τὴν βασίλισσαν κατ' αὐτὸν τυχικῶς τεταγμένην. 5 τὸ δ' αὐτὸ καὶ τῶν ἄλλων ἐλεφάντων ποιησάντων ἡ μετὰ τῆς Σεμιράμιδος δύναμις βραχὺν ὑπέστη χρόνον τὴν τῶν θηρίων ἔφοδον· τὰ γὰρ ζῷα διάφορα ταῖς ἀλκαῖς ὄντα καὶ ταῖς ἰδίαις

19. Semiramis likewise marshalled her forces, and as the two armies neared each other Stabrobates, the king of the Indians, despatched his cavalry and chariots far in advance of the main body. But the queen stoutly withstood the attack of the cavalry, and since the elephants which she had fabricated had been stationed at equal intervals in front of the main body of troops, it came about that the horses of the Indians shied at them. For whereas at a distance the dummies looked like the actual animals with which the horses of the Indians were acquainted and therefore charged upon them boldly enough, yet on nearer contact the odour which reached the horses was unfamiliar, and then the other differences, which taken all together were very great, threw them into utter confusion. Consequently some of the Indians were thrown to the ground, while others, since their horses would not obey the rein, were carried with their mounts pell-mell into the midst of the enemy. Then Semiramis, who was in the battle with a select band of soldiers, made skilful use of her advantage and put the Indians to flight. But although these fled towards the battle-line, King Stabrobates, undismayed, advanced the ranks of his foot-soldiers, keeping the elephants in front, while he himself, taking his position on the right wing and fighting from the most powerful of the beasts, charged in terrifying fashion upon the queen, whom chance had placed opposite him. And since the rest of the elephants followed his example, the army of Semiramis withstood but a short time the attack of the beasts; for the animals, by virtue of their extraordinary courage and the confidence which they felt

---

[1] ἐτύγχανεν Vogel: ἐτύγχανον ABG, Bekker, Dindorf.

ῥώμαις πεποιθότα πάντα τὸν ὑφιστάμενον
6 ῥᾳδίως ἀνῄρει. διόπερ πολὺς καὶ παντοῖος
ἐγίνετο φόνος, τῶν μὲν ὑπὸ τοὺς πόδας ὑποπι-
πτόντων, τῶν δὲ τοῖς ὀδοῦσιν ἀνασχιζομένων,
ἐνίων δὲ ταῖς προβοσκίσιν ἀναρριπτουμένων.
συχνοῦ δὲ πλήθους νεκρῶν σωρευομένου καὶ τοῦ
κινδύνου τοῖς ὁρῶσι δεινὴν ἔκπληξιν καὶ φόβον
παριστάντος, οὐδεὶς ἔτι μένειν ἐπὶ τῆς τάξεως
ἐτόλμα.
7 Τραπέντος οὖν τοῦ πλήθους παντὸς ὁ βασιλεὺς
τῶν Ἰνδῶν ἐπ' αὐτὴν ἐβιάζετο τὴν Σεμίραμιν.
καὶ τὸ μὲν πρῶτον ἐπ' ἐκείνην τοξεύσας ἔτυχε
τοῦ βραχίονος, ἔπειτ' ἀκοντίσας διήλασε διὰ τοῦ
νώτου τῆς βασιλίσσης, πλαγίας ἐνεχθείσης τῆς
πληγῆς· διόπερ οὐδὲν παθοῦσα δεινὸν ἡ Σεμίραμις ταχέως ἀφίππευσε, πολὺ λειπομένου κατὰ
8 τὸ τάχος τοῦ διώκοντος θηρίου. πάντων δὲ
φευγόντων ἐπὶ τὴν σχεδίαν, τοσούτου πλήθους
εἰς ἕνα καὶ στενὸν βιαζομένου τόπον οἱ μὲν τῆς
βασιλίσσης ὑπ' ἀλλήλων ἀπέθνησκον συμ-
πατούμενοι καὶ φυρόμενοι παρὰ φύσιν ἀναμὶξ
ἱππεῖς τε καὶ πεζοί, τῶν δὲ Ἰνδῶν ἐπικειμένων
ὠσμὸς ἐγίνετο βίαιος ἐπὶ τῆς γεφύρας διὰ τὸν
φόβον, ὥστε πολλοὺς ἐξωθουμένους ἐφ' ἑκάτερα
μέρη τῆς γεφύρας ἐμπίπτειν εἰς τὸν ποταμόν.
9 ἡ δὲ Σεμίραμις, ἐπειδὴ τὸ πλεῖστον μέρος τῶν
ἀπὸ τῆς μάχης διασωζομένων διὰ τὸν ποταμὸν
ἔτυχε τῆς ἀσφαλείας, ἀπέκοψε τοὺς συνέχοντας
δεσμοὺς τὴν γέφυραν· ὧν λυθέντων ἡ μὲν σχεδία
κατὰ πολλὰ διαιρεθεῖσα μέρη καὶ συχνοὺς ἐφ'
ἑαυτῆς ἔχουσα τῶν διωκόντων Ἰνδῶν ὑπὸ τῆς
τοῦ ῥεύματος σφοδρότητος ὡς ἔτυχε κατηνέχθη,

in their power, easily destroyed everyone who tried
to withstand them. Consequently there was a great
slaughter, which was effected in various ways, some
being trampled beneath their feet, others ripped up
by their tusks, and a number tossed into the air by
their trunks. And since a great multitude of
corpses lay piled one upon the other and the danger
aroused terrible consternation and fear in those who
witnessed the sight, not a man had the courage to
hold his position any longer.

Now when the entire multitude turned in flight the
king of the Indians pressed his attack upon Semiramis herself. And first he let fly an arrow and struck
her on the arm, and then with his javelin he pierced
the back of the queen, but only with a glancing blow;
and since for this reason Semiramis was not seriously
injured she rode swiftly away, the pursuing beast
being much inferior in speed. But since all were
fleeing to the pontoon bridge and so great a multitude
was forcing its way into a single narrow space, some of
the queen's soldiers perished by being trampled upon
by one another and by cavalry and foot-soldiers being
thrown together in unnatural confusion, and when the
Indians pressed hard upon them a violent crowding
took place on the bridge because of their terror, so
that many were pushed to either side of the bridge
and fell into the river. As for Semiramis, when the
largest part of the survivors of the battle had found
safety by putting the river behind them, she cut the
fastenings which held the bridge together; and when
these were loosened the pontoon bridge, having been
broken apart at many points and bearing great
numbers of the pursuing Indians, was carried down
in haphazard fashion by the violence of the current

καὶ πολλοὺς μὲν τῶν Ἰνδῶν διέφθειρε, τῇ δὲ
Σεμιράμιδι πολλὴν ἀσφάλειαν παρεσκεύασε,
κωλύσασα τὴν τῶν πολεμίων ἐπ' αὐτὴν διάβασιν.
10 μετὰ δὲ ταῦθ' ὁ μὲν τῶν Ἰνδῶν βασιλεύς, διο-
σημιῶν αὐτῷ γενομένων καὶ τῶν μάντεων ἀπο-
φαινομένων σημαίνεσθαι τὸν ποταμὸν μὴ διαβαίνειν, ἡσυχίαν ἔσχεν, ἡ δὲ Σεμίραμις ἀλλαγὴν
ποιησαμένη τῶν αἰχμαλώτων ἐπανῆλθεν εἰς
Βάκτρα, δύο μέρη τῆς δυνάμεως ἀποβεβληκυῖα.
20. Μετὰ δέ τινα χρόνον ὑπὸ Νινύου τοῦ υἱοῦ
δι' εὐνούχου τινὸς ἐπιβουλευθεῖσα, καὶ τὸ παρ'
Ἄμμωνος λόγιον ἀνανεωσαμένη, τὸν ἐπιβουλεύσαντα κακὸν οὐδὲν εἰργάσατο, τοὐναντίον δὲ τὴν
βασιλείαν αὐτῷ παραδοῦσα καὶ τοῖς ὑπάρχοις
ἀκούειν ἐκείνου προστάξασα, ταχέως ἠφάνισεν
ἑαυτήν, ὡς εἰς θεοὺς κατὰ τὸν χρησμὸν μετα-
2 στησομένη. ἔνιοι δὲ μυθολογοῦντές φασιν αὐτὴν
γενέσθαι περιστεράν, καὶ πολλῶν ὀρνέων εἰς
τὴν οἰκίαν καταπετασθέντων μετ' ἐκείνων ἐκπε-
τασθῆναι· διὸ καὶ τοὺς Ἀσσυρίους τὴν περι-
στερὰν τιμᾶν ὡς θεόν, ἀπαθανατίζοντας τὴν
Σεμίραμιν. αὕτη μὲν οὖν βασιλεύσασα τῆς
Ἀσίας ἁπάσης πλὴν Ἰνδῶν ἐτελεύτησε τὸν
προειρημένον τρόπον, βιώσασα μὲν ἔτη ἑξήκοντα
δύο, βασιλεύσασα δὲ δύο πρὸς τοῖς τετταράκοντα.
3 Κτησίας μὲν οὖν ὁ Κνίδιος περὶ Σεμιράμιδος
τοιαῦθ' ἱστόρηκεν· Ἀθήναιος δὲ καί τινες τῶν
ἄλλων συγγραφέων φασὶν αὐτὴν ἑταίραν γεγονέναι εὐπρεπῆ, καὶ διὰ τὸ κάλλος ἐρωτικῶς
4 ἔχειν αὐτῆς τὸν βασιλέα τῶν Ἀσσυρίων. τὸ
μὲν οὖν πρῶτον μετρίας αὐτὴν ἀποδοχῆς τυγχάνειν ἐν τοῖς βασιλείοις, μετὰ δὲ ταῦτα γνησίαν

and caused the death of many of the Indians, but for
Semiramis it was the means of complete safety, the
enemy now being prevented from crossing over
against her. After these events the king of the
Indians remained inactive, since heavenly omens
appeared to him which his seers interpreted to mean
that he must not cross the river, and Semiramis,
after exchanging prisoners, made her way back to
Bactra with the loss of two-thirds of her force.

20. Some time later her son Ninyas conspired
against her through the agency of a certain eunuch;
and remembering the prophecy given her by
Ammon,[1] she did not punish the conspirator, but, on
the contrary, after turning the kingdom over to him
and commanding the governors to obey him, she at
once disappeared, as if she were going to be translated to the gods as the oracle had predicted. Some,
making a myth of it, say that she turned into a dove
and flew off in the company of many birds which
alighted on her dwelling, and this, they say, is the
reason why the Assyrians worship the dove as a god,
thus deifying Semiramis. Be that as it may, this
woman, after having been queen over all Asia with
the exception of India, passed away in the manner
mentioned above, having lived sixty-two years and
having reigned forty-two.

Such, then, is the account that Ctesias of Cnidus has
given about Semiramis; but Athenaeus [2] and certain
other historians say that she was a comely courtesan
and because of her beauty was loved by the king of
the Assyrians. Now at first she was accorded only
a moderate acceptance in the palace, but later, when

[1] Cp. chap. 14.
[2] Nothing is known about this Athenaeus.

ἀναγορευθεῖσαν γυναῖκα πεῖσαι τὸν βασιλέα
πένθ' ἡμέρας αὐτῇ παραχωρῆσαι τῆς βασιλείας.
5 τὴν δὲ Σεμίραμιν ἀναλαβοῦσαν τό τε σκῆπτρον
καὶ τὴν βασίλειον στολὴν κατὰ μὲν τὴν
πρώτην ἡμέραν εὐωχίαν ποιῆσαι καὶ μεγα-
λοπρεπῆ δεῖπνα, ἐν οἷς τοὺς τῶν δυνάμεων
ἡγεμόνας καὶ πάντας τοὺς ἐπιφανεστάτους πεῖσαι
συμπράττειν ἑαυτῇ· τῇ δ' ὑστεραίᾳ τοῦ τε
πλήθους καὶ τῶν ἀξιολογωτάτων ἀνδρῶν ὡς
βασίλισσαν θεραπευόντων τὸν μὲν ἄνδρα καταβαλεῖν εἰς τὴν εἱρκτήν, αὐτὴν δὲ φύσει μεγαλεπίβολον οὖσαν καὶ τολμηρὰν κατασχεῖν τὴν
ἀρχήν, καὶ μέχρι γήρως βασιλεύσασαν πολλὰ
καὶ μεγάλα κατεργάσασθαι. περὶ μὲν οὖν τῶν
κατὰ[1] Σεμίραμιν τοιαύτας ἀντιλογίας εἶναι
συμβαίνει παρὰ τοῖς συγγραφεῦσι.

21. Μετὰ δὲ τὸν ταύτης θάνατον Νινύας ὁ
Νίνου καὶ Σεμιράμιδος υἱὸς παραλαβὼν τὴν
ἀρχὴν ἦρχεν εἰρηνικῶς, τὸ φιλοπόλεμον καὶ
κεκινδυνευμένον τῆς μητρὸς οὐδαμῶς ζηλώσας.
2 πρῶτον μὲν γὰρ ἐν τοῖς βασιλείοις τὸν ἅπαντα
χρόνον διέτριβεν, ὑπ' οὐδενὸς ὁρώμενος πλὴν
τῶν παλλακίδων καὶ τῶν περὶ αὐτὸν εὐνούχων,
ἐζήλου δὲ τρυφὴν καὶ ῥᾳθυμίαν καὶ τὸ μηδέποτε
κακοπαθεῖν μηδὲ μεριμνᾶν, ὑπολαμβάνων βασιλείας εὐδαίμονος εἶναι τέλος τὸ πάσαις χρῆσθαι
3 ταῖς ἡδοναῖς ἀνεπικωλύτως. πρὸς δὲ τὴν ἀσφάλειαν τῆς ἀρχῆς καὶ τὸν κατὰ τῶν ἀρχομένων

---

[1] Vogel follows D in omitting τὴν after κατά.

[1] The following legend contains a reference to the Babylonian
Sacaea, which was almost certainly a New Year's festival. A

she had been proclaimed a lawful wife, she persuaded the king to yield the royal prerogatives to her for a period of five days.[1]   And Semiramis, upon receiving the sceptre and the regal garb, on the first day held high festival and gave a magnificent banquet, at which she persuaded the commanders of the military forces and all the greatest dignitaries to co-operate with her; and on the second day, while the people and the most notable citizens were paying her their respects as queen, she arrested her husband and put him in prison; and since she was by nature a woman of great designs and bold as well, she seized the throne and remaining queen until old age accomplished many great things.   Such, then, are the conflicting accounts which may be found in the historians regarding the career of Semiramis.

21. After her death Ninyas, the son of Ninus and Semiramis, succeeded to the throne and had a peaceful reign, since he in no wise emulated his mother's fondness for war and her adventurous spirit.   For in the first place, he spent all his time in the palace, seen by no one but his concubines and the eunuchs who attended him, and devoted his life to luxury and idleness and the consistent avoidance of any suffering or anxiety, holding the end and aim of a happy reign to be the enjoyment of every kind of pleasure without restraint.   Moreover, having in view the safety of his crown and the fear

prominent feature of this was the killing of a criminal who had been permitted for five days to wear the king's robes, to sit on his throne, to issue decrees, and even to consort with his concubines, and who, after this brief tenure of office, was scourged and executed.   Cp. J. G. Frazer, *The Golden Bough*, Pt. III, *The Dying God*, pp. 113-17.

γινόμενον φόβον κατ' ἐνιαυτὸν μετεπέμπετο
στρατιωτῶν ἀριθμὸν ὡρισμένον καὶ στρατηγὸν
4 ἀπὸ ἔθνους ἑκάστου, καὶ τὸ μὲν ἐκ πάντων
ἀθροισθὲν στράτευμα ἐκτὸς τῆς πόλεως συνεῖχεν,
ἑκάστου τῶν ἐθνῶν τὸν εὐνούστατον τῶν περὶ
αὑτὸν ἀποδεικνύων ἡγεμόνα· τοῦ δ' ἐνιαυτοῦ
διελθόντος μετεπέμπετο πάλιν ἀπὸ τῶν ἐθνῶν
τοὺς ἴσους στρατιώτας, καὶ τοὺς προτέρους ἀπέ-
5 λυεν εἰς τὰς πατρίδας. οὗ συντελουμένου συνέβαινε τοὺς ὑπὸ τὴν βασιλείαν τεταγμένους ἅπαντας[1] καταπεπλῆχθαι, θεωροῦντας ἀεὶ μεγάλας
δυνάμεις ἐν ὑπαίθρῳ στρατοπεδευομένας καὶ τοῖς
ἀφισταμένοις ἢ μὴ πειθαρχοῦσιν ἑτοίμην οὖσαν
6 τιμωρίαν. τὰς δὲ κατ' ἐνιαυτὸν ἀλλαγὰς τῶν
στρατιωτῶν ἐπενόησεν, ἵνα πρὶν ἢ καλῶς γνωσ-
θῆναι τοὺς στρατηγοὺς καὶ τοὺς ἄλλους ἅπαντας
ὑπ' ἀλλήλων, ἕκαστος εἰς τὴν ἰδίαν διαχωρίζηται
πατρίδα· ὁ γὰρ πολὺς χρόνος τῆς στρατείας
ἐμπειρίαν τε τῶν κατὰ τὸν πόλεμον καὶ φρόνημα
τοῖς ἡγεμόσι περιτίθησι, καὶ τὸ πλεῖστον ἀφορμὰς
παρέχεται μεγάλας πρὸς ἀπόστασιν καὶ συνω-
7 μοσίαν κατὰ τῶν ἡγουμένων. τὸ δὲ μηδ' ὑφ'
ἑνὸς τῶν ἔξωθεν θεωρεῖσθαι τῆς μὲν περὶ αὑτὸν
τρυφῆς ἄγνοιαν παρείχετο πᾶσι, καθάπερ δὲ
θεὸν ἀόρατον διὰ τὸν φόβον ἕκαστος οὐδὲ λόγῳ
βλασφημεῖν ἐτόλμα. στρατηγοὺς δὲ καὶ σατράπας καὶ διοικητάς, ἔτι δὲ δικαστὰς καθ' ἕκαστον
ἔθνος ἀποδείξας καὶ τἆλλα πάντα διατάξας ὡς
ποτ' ἔδοξεν αὑτῷ συμφέρειν, τὸν τοῦ ζῆν χρόνον
κατέμεινεν ἐν τῇ Νίνῳ.
8   Παραπλησίως δὲ τούτῳ καὶ οἱ λοιποὶ βασιλεῖς,

---

[1] ἅπαντας Vogel : πάντας Vulgate, Bekker, Dindorf.

he felt with reference to his subjects, he used to summon each year a fixed number of soldiers and a general from each nation and to keep the army, which had been gathered in this way from all his subject peoples, outside his capital, appointing as commander of each nation one of the most trustworthy men in his service; and at the end of the year he would summon from his peoples a second equal number of soldiers and dismiss the former to their countries. The result of this device was that all those subject to his rule were filled with awe, seeing at all times a great host encamped in the open and punishment ready to fall on any who rebelled or would not yield obedience. This annual change of the soldiers was devised by him in order that, before the generals and all the other commanders of the army should become well acquainted with each other, every man of them would have been separated from the rest and have gone back to his own country; for long service in the field both gives the commanders experience in the arts of war and fills them with arrogance, and, above all, it offers great opportunities for rebellion and for plotting against their rulers. And the fact that he was seen by no one outside the palace made everyone ignorant of the luxury of his manner of life, and through their fear of him, as of an unseen god, each man dared not show disrespect of him even in word. So by appointing generals, satraps, financial officers, and judges for each nation and arranging all other matters as he felt at any time to be to his advantage, he remained for his lifetime in the city of Ninus.

The rest of the kings also followed his example, son

παῖς παρὰ πατρὸς διαδεχόμενος τὴν ἀρχήν, ἐπὶ
γενεὰς τριάκοντα ἐβασίλευσαν μέχρι Σαρδανα-
πάλλου· ἐπὶ τούτου γὰρ ἡ τῶν Ἀσσυρίων ἡγεμονία μετέπεσεν εἰς Μήδους, ἔτη διαμείνασα
πλείω τῶν χιλίων καὶ τριακοσίων,[1] καθάπερ
φησὶ Κτησίας ὁ Κνίδιος ἐν τῇ δευτέρᾳ βίβλῳ.

22. Τὰ δ' ὀνόματα πάντα[2] τῶν βασιλέων καὶ
τὸ πλῆθος τῶν ἐτῶν ὧν ἕκαστος ἐβασίλευσεν
οὐ κατεπείγει γράφειν διὰ τὸ μηδὲν ὑπ' αὐτῶν
πεπρᾶχθαι μνήμης ἄξιον. μόνη γὰρ τέτευχεν
ἀναγραφῆς ἡ πεμφθεῖσα συμμαχία τοῖς Τρωσὶν
ὑπ' Ἀσσυρίων, ἧς ἐστρατήγει Μέμνων ὁ Τιθωνοῦ.
2 Τευτάμου γὰρ βασιλεύοντος τῆς Ἀσίας, ὃς ἦν
εἰκοστὸς ἀπὸ Νίννου τοῦ Σεμιράμιδος, φασὶ τοὺς
μετ' Ἀγαμέμνονος Ἕλληνας ἐπὶ Τροίαν στρατεῦ-
σαι, τὴν ἡγεμονίαν ἐχόντων τῆς Ἀσίας τῶν
Ἀσσυρίων ἔτη πλείω τῶν χιλίων. καὶ τὸν μὲν
Πρίαμον βαρυνόμενον τῷ πολέμῳ καὶ βασιλεύοντα τῆς Τρῳάδος, ὑπήκοον δ' ὄντα τῷ βασιλεῖ
τῶν Ἀσσυρίων, πέμψαι πρὸς αὐτὸν πρεσβευτὰς
περὶ βοηθείας· τὸν δὲ Τεύταμον μυρίους μὲν
Αἰθίοπας, ἄλλους δὲ τοσούτους Σουσιανοὺς σὺν
ἅρμασι διακοσίοις ἐξαποστεῖλαι, στρατηγὸν ἐπι-
3 καταστήσαντα Μέμνονα τὸν Τιθωνοῦ. καὶ τὸν

[1] ἔτι δ' ἑξήκοντα after τριακοσίων deleted by Dindorf ; cp.
ch. 28. 8.
[2] πάντα Vogel : πάντων F, Bekker, Dindorf.

---

[1] Names of kings of Assyria are now known from as early as
ca. 2500 B.C.
[2] The earliest Greek tradition knew the Ethiopians as " the
farthest of men,'' who dwelt on the stream Oceanus. Hero-

succeeding father upon the throne, and reigned for
thirty generations down to Sardanapallus; for it was
under this ruler that the Empire of the Assyrians
fell to the Medes, after it had lasted more than 612 B.C.
thirteen hundred years,[1] as Ctesias of Cnidus says in
his Second Book.

22. There is no special need of giving all the names
of the kings and the number of years which each of
them reigned because nothing was done by them which
merits mentioning. For the only event which has
been recorded is the despatch by the Assyrians to
the Trojans of an allied force, which was under the
command of Memnon the son of Tithonus. For
when Teutamus, they say, was ruler of Asia, being
the twentieth in succession from Ninyas the son of
Semiramis, the Greeks made an expedition against *ca.* 1190
Troy with Agamemnon, at a time when the Assyrians B.C.
had controlled Asia for more than a thousand years.
And Priam, who was king of the Troad and a vassal
of the king of the Assyrians, being hard pressed by
the war, sent an embassy to the king requesting aid;
and Teutamus despatched ten thousand Ethiopians
and a like number of the men of Susiana along with
two hundred chariots, having appointed as general
Memnon the son of Tithonus.[2] Now Tithonus, who

dotus (7. 70) speaks of " the Ethiopians of the East," probably
meaning the Assyrians. Plato (*Laws* 685 c) also mentions
help sent to Priam by the Assyrians. The account here has
more of the appearance of genuine history than that in Book
4. 75, where Diodorus reverts to mythology in presenting
Tithonus as the son of Laomedon and brother of Priam, and
having him travel to the east " as far as Ethiopia," where he
begot Memnon by Dawn. When tradition began to place the
Homeric Ethiopians in Libya, Memnon came to be associated
with Thebes in Egypt.

μὲν Τιθωνόν, κατ' ἐκείνους τοὺς χρόνους τῆς
Περσίδος ὄντα στρατηγόν, εὐδοκιμεῖν παρὰ τῷ
βασιλεῖ μάλιστα τῶν καθεσταμένων ἐπάρχων,
τὸν δὲ Μέμνονα τὴν ἡλικίαν ἀκμάζοντα διαφέρειν
ἀνδρείᾳ τε καὶ ψυχῆς λαμπρότητι. οἰκοδομῆσαι
δ' αὐτὸν ἐπὶ τῆς ἄκρας τὰ ἐν Σούσοις βασίλεια
τὰ διαμείναντα μέχρι τῆς Περσῶν ἡγεμονίας,
κληθέντα δ' ἀπ' ἐκείνου Μεμνόνεια· κατασκευάσαι
δὲ καὶ διὰ τῆς χώρας λεωφόρον ὁδὸν τὴν μέχρι
4 τῶν νῦν χρόνων ὀνομαζομένην Μεμνόνειαν. ἀμφισβητοῦσι δὲ καὶ οἱ περὶ τὴν Αἴγυπτον Αἰθίοπες,
λέγοντες ἐν ἐκείνοις τοῖς τόποις γεγονέναι τὸν
ἄνδρα τοῦτον, καὶ βασίλεια παλαιὰ δεικνύουσιν,
ἃ μέχρι τοῦ νῦν ὀνομάζεσθαί φασι Μεμνόνεια.
5 οὐ μὴν ἀλλὰ τοῖς Τρωσὶ λέγεται βοηθῆσαι τὸν
Μέμνονα μετὰ δισμυρίων μὲν πεζῶν, ἁρμάτων δὲ
διακοσίων· ὃν θαυμασθῆναί τε δι' ἀνδρείαν καὶ
πολλοὺς ἀνελεῖν ἐν ταῖς μάχαις τῶν Ἑλλήνων,
τὸ δὲ τελευταῖον ὑπὸ Θετταλῶν ἐνεδρευθέντα
κατασφαγῆναι· τοῦ δὲ σώματος τοὺς Αἰθίοπας
ἐγκρατεῖς γενομένους κατακαῦσαί τε τὸν νεκρὸν
καὶ τὰ ὀστᾶ πρὸς Τιθωνὸν ἀποκομίσαι. περὶ
μὲν οὖν Μέμνονος τοιαῦτ' ἐν ταῖς βασιλικαῖς
ἀναγραφαῖς ἱστορεῖσθαί φασιν οἱ βάρβαροι.
23. Σαρδανάπαλλος δέ, τριακοστὸς μὲν ὢν
ἀπὸ Νίνου τοῦ συστησαμένου τὴν ἡγεμονίαν,
ἔσχατος δὲ γενόμενος Ἀσσυρίων βασιλεύς, ὑπερῆ-
ρεν ἅπαντας τοὺς πρὸ αὐτοῦ τρυφῇ καὶ ῥαθυμίᾳ.
χωρὶς γὰρ τοῦ μηδ' ὑφ' ἑνὸς τῶν ἔξωθεν ὁρᾶσθαι
βίον ἔζησε γυναικός, καὶ διαιτώμενος μὲν μετὰ

---

[1] The following account of the dissolute Sardanapallus is not
borne out by the documents, nor indeed by Diodorus himself

was at that time general of Persis, was the most
highly esteemed of the governors at the king's court,
and Memnon, who was in the bloom of manhood,
was distinguished both for his bravery and for his
nobility of spirit. He also built the palace in the
upper city of Susa which stood until the time of the
Persian Empire and was called after him Memnonian;
moreover, he constructed through the country a
public highway which bears the name Memnonian
to this time. But the Ethiopians who border upon
Egypt dispute this, maintaining that this man was
a native of their country, and they point out an
ancient palace which to this day, they say, bears the
name Memnonian. At any rate, the account runs that
Memnon went to the aid of the Trojans with twenty
thousand foot-soldiers and two hundred chariots;
and he was admired for his bravery and slew many
Greeks in the fighting, but was finally ambushed
by the Thessalians and slain; whereupon the
Ethiopians recovered his body, burned the corpse,
and took the bones back to Tithonus. Such is the
account concerning Memnon that is given in the
royal records, according to what the barbarians
say.

23. Sardanapallus, the thirtieth in succession from
Ninus, who founded the empire, and the last king of
the Assyrians, outdid all his predecessors in luxury and
sluggishness.[1] For not to mention the fact that he
was not seen by any man residing outside the palace,
he lived the life of a woman, and spending his days

(cp. chaps. 25 ff.). Sin-shar-ishkun, the last king of Assyria,
was a worthy descendant of his vigorous predecessors on the
Assyrian throne, and defended a dying empire with energy.
Cp. *The Cambridge Ancient History*, 3. pp. 128 ff., 296 f.

τῶν παλλακίδων, πορφύραν δὲ καὶ τὰ μαλακώ-
τατα τῶν ἐρίων ταλασιουργῶν, στολὴν μὲν
γυναικείαν ἐνεδεδύκει, τὸ δὲ πρόσωπον καὶ πᾶν
τὸ σῶμα ψιμυθίοις καὶ τοῖς ἄλλοις τοῖς τῶν
ἑταιρῶν ἐπιτηδεύμασιν ἁπαλώτερον πάσης γυ-
2 ναικὸς τρυφερᾶς κατεσκεύαστο. ἐπετήδευσε δὲ
καὶ τὴν φωνὴν ἔχειν γυναικώδη καὶ κατὰ τοὺς
πότους οὐ μόνον ποτῶν καὶ βρωτῶν τῶν δυναμένων μάλιστα τὰς ἡδονὰς παρέχεσθαι συνεχῶς
ἀπολαύειν, ἀλλὰ καὶ τὰς ἀφροδισιακὰς τέρψεις
μεταδιώκειν ἀνδρὸς ἅμα καὶ γυναικός· ἐχρῆτο
γὰρ ταῖς ἐπ᾽ ἀμφότερα συνουσίαις ἀνέδην, τῆς
ἐκ τῆς πράξεως αἰσχύνης οὐδὲν ὅλως φροντίζων.
3 ἐπὶ τοσοῦτο δὲ προήχθη τρυφῆς καὶ τῆς αἰσχίστης
ἡδονῆς καὶ ἀκρασίας ὥστ᾽ ἐπικήδειον εἰς αὑτὸν
ποιῆσαι καὶ παραγγεῖλαι τοῖς διαδόχοις τῆς
ἀρχῆς μετὰ τὴν ἑαυτοῦ τελευτὴν ἐπὶ τὸν τάφον
ἐπιγράψαι τὸ συγγραφὲν μὲν ὑπ᾽ ἐκείνου βαρβαρι-
κῶς, μεθερμηνευθὲν δὲ ὕστερον ὑπό τινος Ἕλληνος,

εὖ εἰδὼς ὅτι θνητὸς ἔφυς, σὸν θυμὸν ἄεξε[1]
τερπόμενος θαλίῃσι· θανόντι σοι οὔτις ὄνησις.
καὶ γὰρ ἐγὼ σποδός εἰμι, Νίνου μεγάλης
βασιλεύσας.
ταῦτ᾽ ἔχω ὅσσ᾽ ἔφαγον καὶ ἐφύβρισα καὶ μετ᾽
ἔρωτος
τέρπν᾽ ἔπαθον, τὰ δὲ πολλὰ καὶ ὄλβια κεῖνα
λέλειπται.[2]

4 τοιοῦτος δ᾽ ὢν τὸν τρόπον οὐ μόνον αὐτὸς
αἰσχρῶς κατέστρεψε τὸν βίον, ἀλλὰ καὶ τὴν

---

[1] ἄεξε Tzetzes, *Chiliades*, III. 453, who preserves the first
three lines of the poetry : δέξαι A D, δείξαι B.

in the company of his concubines and spinning
purple garments and working the softest of wool, he
had assumed the feminine garb and so covered his face
and indeed his entire body with whitening cosmetics
and the other unguents used by courtesans, that he
rendered it more delicate than that of any luxury-
loving woman. He also took care to make even his
voice to be like a woman's, and at his carousals not only
to indulge regularly in those drinks and viands which
could offer the greatest pleasure, but also to pursue
the delights of love with men as well as with women;
for he practised sexual indulgence of both kinds
without restraint, showing not the least concern for
the disgrace attending such conduct. To such an
excess did he go of luxury and of the most shameless
sensual pleasure and intemperance, that he composed
a funeral dirge for himself and commanded his successors upon the throne to inscribe it upon his tomb
after his death; it was composed by him in a foreign
language but was afterwards translated by a Greek
as follows:

> Knowing full well that thou wert mortal born,
> Thy heart lift up, take thy delight in feasts;
> When dead no pleasure more is thine. Thus I,
> Who once o'er mighty Ninus ruled, am naught
> But dust. Yet these are mine which gave me joy
> In life—the food I ate, my wantonness,
> And love's delights. But all those other things
> Men deem felicities are left behind.

Because he was a man of this character, not only did
he end his own life in a disgraceful manner, but he

---

² λέλυνται in Athenaeus 336a.

Ἀσσυρίων ἡγεμονίαν ἄρδην ἀνέτρεψε, πολυ-
χρονιωτάτην γενομένην τῶν μνημονευομένων.

24. Ἀρβάκης γάρ τις, Μῆδος μὲν τὸ γένος,
ἀνδρείᾳ δὲ καὶ ψυχῆς λαμπρότητι διαφέρων,
ἐστρατήγει Μήδων τῶν κατ᾽ ἐνιαυτὸν ἐκπεμπο-
μένων εἰς τὴν Νίνον. κατὰ δὲ τὴν στρατείαν
γενόμενος συνήθης τῷ στρατηγῷ τῶν Βαβυλωνίων, ὑπ᾽ ἐκείνου παρεκλήθη καταλῦσαι τὴν
2 τῶν Ἀσσυρίων ἡγεμονίαν. ἦν δ᾽ οὗτος ὄνομα
μὲν Βέλεσυς, τῶν δ᾽ ἱερέων ἐπισημότατος, οὓς
Βαβυλώνιοι καλοῦσι Χαλδαίους. ἐμπειρίαν οὖν
ἔχων μεγίστην ἀστρολογίας τε καὶ μαντικῆς
προέλεγε τοῖς πολλοῖς τὸ ἀποβησόμενον ἀδια-
πτώτως· διὸ καὶ θαυμαζόμενος ἐπὶ τούτοις τῷ
στρατηγῷ τῶν Μήδων ὄντι φίλῳ προεῖπεν ὅτι
πάντως αὐτὸν δεῖ βασιλεῦσαι πάσης τῆς χώρας
3 ἧς ἄρχει Σαρδανάπαλλος. ὁ δ᾽ Ἀρβάκης ἐπαι-
νέσας τὸν ἄνδρα, τούτῳ μὲν ἐπηγγείλατο δώσειν
σατραπείαν τῆς Βαβυλωνίας, τῆς πράξεως ἐπὶ
τέλος ἐλθούσης, αὐτὸς δὲ καθαπερεί τινος θεοῦ
φωνῇ μετεωρισθεὶς τοῖς τε ἡγεμόσι τῶν ἄλλων
ἐθνῶν συνίστατο καὶ πρὸς τὰς ἑστιάσεις καὶ
κοινὰς ὁμιλίας ἐκτενῶς ἅπαντας παρελάμβανε,
4 φιλίαν κατασκευάζων[1] πρὸς ἕκαστον. ἐφιλοτιμήθη δὲ καὶ τὸν βασιλέα κατ᾽ ὄψιν ἰδεῖν καὶ
τὸν τούτου βίον ὅλον κατασκέψασθαι. διόπερ
δούς τινι τῶν εὐνούχων χρυσῆν φιάλην εἰσήχθη

---

[1] κατασκευάζων Gemistus : ἐγκατασκευάζων.

caused the total destruction of the Assyrian Empire, which had endured longer than any other known to history.

24. The facts are these:[1] A certain Arbaces, a Mede by race, and conspicuous for his bravery and nobility of spirit, was the general of the contingent of Medes which was sent each year to Ninus. And having made the acquaintance during this service of the general of the Babylonians, he was urged by him to overthrow the empire of the Assyrians. Now this man's name was Belesys, and he was the most distinguished of those priests whom the Babylonians call Chaldaeans. And since as a consequence he had the fullest experience of astrology and divination, he was wont to foretell the future unerringly to the people in general; therefore, being greatly admired for this gift, he also predicted to the general of the Medes, who was his friend, that it was certainly fated for him to be king over all the territory which was then held by Sardanapallus. Arbaces, commending the man, promised to give him the satrapy of Babylonia when the affair should be consummated, and for his part, like a man elated by a message from some god, both entered into a league with the commanders of the other nations and assiduously invited them all to banquets and social gatherings, establishing thereby a friendship with each of them. He was resolved also to see the king face to face and to observe his whole manner of life. Consequently he gave one of the eunuchs a golden

---

[1] The kernel of truth in the account which follows lies in the fact that Nineveh fell before the combined attacks of the Median Cyaxares and the Chaldaean Nabopolassar.

πρὸς τὸν Σαρδανάπαλλον, καὶ τήν τε τρυφὴν
αὐτοῦ καὶ τὸν γυναικώδη τῶν ἐπιτηδευμάτων
ζῆλον ἀκριβῶς κατανοήσας κατεφρόνησε μὲν τοῦ
βασιλέως ὡς οὐδενὸς ἀξίου, προήχθη δὲ πολὺ
μᾶλλον ἀντέχεσθαι τῶν δοθεισῶν ἐλπίδων ὑπὸ
5 τοῦ Χαλδαίου. τέλος δὲ συνωμοσίαν ἐποιήσατο
πρὸς τὸν Βέλεσυν, ὥστε αὐτὸν μὲν Μήδους
ἀποστῆσαι καὶ Πέρσας, ἐκεῖνον δὲ πεῖσαι Βαβυλωνίους κοινωνῆσαι τῆς πράξεως καὶ τὸν τῶν
Ἀράβων ἡγεμόνα φίλον ὄντα προσλαβέσθαι
πρὸς τὴν τῶν ὅλων ἐπίθεσιν.

6   Ὡς δ' ὁ ἐνιαύσιος τῆς στρατείας διεληλύθει
χρόνος, διαδοχῆς δ' ἑτέρας ἐλθούσης ἀπελύθησαν
οἱ πρότεροι κατὰ τὸ ἔθος εἰς τὰς πατρίδας,
ἐνταῦθα ὁ Ἀρβάκης ἔπεισε τοὺς μὲν Μήδους
ἐπιθέσθαι τῇ βασιλείᾳ, Πέρσας δ' ἐπ' ἐλευθερίᾳ
κοινωνῆσαι τῆς συνωμοσίας.[1] παραπλησίως δὲ
καὶ ὁ Βέλεσυς τούς τε Βαβυλωνίους ἔπεισεν
ἀντέχεσθαι τῆς ἐλευθερίας, καὶ πρεσβεύσας εἰς
Ἀραβίαν παρεστήσατο τὸν ἡγούμενον τῶν
ἐγχωρίων, ὄντα φίλον αὐτοῦ καὶ ξένον, μετασχεῖν
7 τῆς ἐπιθέσεως. τοῦ δ' ἐνιαυσίου χρόνου διελθόντος πάντες οὗτοι πλῆθος στρατιωτῶν συν-
αγαγόντες ἧκον πανδημεὶ πρὸς τὴν Νίνον, τῷ
μὲν λόγῳ διαδοχὴν ἄγοντες, ὡς ἦν σύνηθες, τῇ
δ' ἀληθείᾳ καταλύσοντες τὴν τῶν Ἀσσυρίων
8 ἡγεμονίαν. ἀθροισθέντων οὖν τῶν προειρημένων
τεττάρων ἐθνῶν εἰς ἕνα τόπον, ὁ μὲν σύμπας
αὐτῶν ἀριθμὸς ὑπῆρχεν εἰς τετταράκοντα μυ-

---

[1] συνωμοσίας Dindorf : ἡγεμονίας.

[1] Cp. chap. 21.

bowl as a present and gained admittance to Sardanapallus; and when he had observed at close hand both
his luxuriousness and his love of effeminate pursuits
and practices, he despised the king as worthy of no
consideration and was led all the more to cling to the
hopes which had been held out to him by the Chaldaean. And the conclusion of the matter was that he
formed a conspiracy with Belesys, whereby he should
himself move the Medes and Persians to revolt while
the latter should persuade the Babylonians to join the
undertaking and should secure the help of the commander of the Arabs, who was his friend, for the
attempt to secure the supreme control.

When the year's time of their service in the king's
army [1] had passed and, another force having arrived
to replace them, the relieved men had been dismissed as usual to their homes, thereupon Arbaces
persuaded the Medes to attack the Assyrian kingdom
and the Persians to join in the conspiracy, on the
condition of receiving their freedom.[2] Belesys too
in similar fashion both persuaded the Babylonians
to strike for their freedom, and sending an embassy
to Arabia, won over the commander of the people
of that country, a friend of his who exchanged
hospitality with him, to join in the attack. And
after a year's time all these leaders gathered a multitude of soldiers and came with all their forces to
Ninus, ostensibly bringing up replacements, as was
the custom, but in fact with the intention of destroy-
ing the empire of the Assyrians. Now when these
four nations had gathered into one place the whole
number of them amounted to four hundred thousand

[2] *i.e.* from the Assyrians.

ριάδας, εἰς μίαν δὲ παρεμβολὴν συνελθόντες
ἐβουλεύοντο κοινῇ περὶ τοῦ συμφέροντος.

25. Σαρδανάπαλλος δὲ γνοὺς τὴν ἀπόστασιν
εὐθὺς ἐξήγαγεν ἐπ᾿ αὐτοὺς τὰς ἀπὸ τῶν ἄλλων
ἐθνῶν δυνάμεις. καὶ τὸ μὲν πρῶτον γενομένης ἐν
τῷ πεδίῳ παρατάξεως ἐλείφθησαν οἱ τὴν ἀπόστασιν ποιησάμενοι, καὶ πολλοὺς ἀποβαλόντες
συνεδιώχθησαν εἰς ὄρος ἀπέχον τῆς Νίνου
2 σταδίους ἑβδομήκοντα· μετὰ δὲ ταῦτα πάλιν
καταβάντων αὐτῶν εἰς τὸ πεδίον καὶ πρὸς
μάχην παρασκευαζομένων, ὁ μὲν Σαρδανάπαλλος
ἀντιτάξας τὴν ἰδίαν στρατιὰν προαπέστειλε
πρὸς τὸ τῶν πολεμίων στρατόπεδον τοὺς κηρύ-
ξοντας διότι Σαρδανάπαλλος τοῖς μὲν ἀνελοῦσιν
Ἀρβάκην τὸν Μῆδον δώσει χρυσίου διακόσια
τάλαντα, τοῖς δὲ ζῶντα παραδοῦσι χρήματα
μὲν δωρήσεται δὶς τοσαῦτα, τῆς δὲ Μηδίας
3 ὕπαρχον [1] καταστήσει. παραπλησίως [2] δ᾿ ἐπηγγείλατο δώσειν δωρεὰς τοῖς Βέλεσυν τὸν Βαβυ-
λώνιον ἀνελοῦσιν ἢ ζωγρήσασιν. οὐδενὸς δὲ
προσέχοντος τοῖς κηρύγμασι, συνῆψε μάχην,
καὶ πολλοὺς μὲν ἐφόνευσε τῶν ἀποστατῶν, τὸ
δ᾿ ἄλλο πλῆθος συνεδίωξεν εἰς τὴν ἐν τοῖς ὄρεσι
παρεμβολήν.

4 Οἱ δὲ περὶ τὸν Ἀρβάκην διὰ τὰς ἥττας
ἀθυμοῦντες συνήγαγον τῶν φίλων συνέδριον καὶ
5 προέθηκαν βουλὴν τί δέοι πράττειν. οἱ πλεῖστοι μὲν οὖν ἔφασαν δεῖν εἰς τὰς πατρίδας
ἀπιέναι καὶ τόπους ὀχυροὺς καταλαμβάνεσθαι
καὶ τῶν ἄλλων τῶν εἰς τὸν πόλεμον χρησίμων

---

[1] ὕπαρχον Vogel : ἔπαρχον Vulgate, Bekker, Dindorf.

men, and when they had assembled into one camp
they took counsel together concerning the best plan
to pursue.

25. As for Sardanapallus, so soon as he became
aware of the revolt, he led forth against the rebels
the contingents which had come from the rest of
the nations. And at first, when battle was joined
on the plain, those who were making the revolt were
defeated, and after heavy losses were pursued to a
mountain which was seventy stades distant from
Ninus; but afterwards, when they came down again
into the plain and were preparing for battle, Sardanapallus marshalled his army against them and despatched heralds to the camp of the enemy to make
this proclamation: " Sardanapallus will give two
hundred talents of gold to anyone who slays Arbaces
the Mede, and will make a present of twice that
amount to anyone who delivers him up alive and will
also appoint him governor over Media." Likewise he
promised to reward any who would either slay
Belesys the Babylonian or take him alive. But
since no man paid any attention to the proclamation,
he joined battle, slew many of the rebels, and
pursued the remainder of the multitude into their
encampment in the mountains.

Arbaces, having lost heart because of these defeats,
now convened a meeting of his friends and called
upon them to consider what should be done. Now
the majority said that they should retire to their
respective countries, seize strong positions, and so far
as possible prepare there whatever else would be

---

² For παραπλησίως Gemistus, followed by Bekker and
Dindorf, conjectured παραπλησίας.

τὴν ἐνδεχομένην παρασκευὴν ποιεῖσθαι· Βέλεσυς
δ' ὁ Βαβυλώνιος, φήσας τοὺς θεοὺς αὐτοῖς
σημαίνειν μετὰ πόνων καὶ κακοπαθείας ἐπὶ
τέλος ἄξειν τὴν προαίρεσιν, καὶ τἆλλα παρακα-
λέσας ἐνδεχομένως, ἔπεισεν ἅπαντας ὑπομένειν
6 τοὺς κινδύνους. γενομένης οὖν τρίτης παρατάξεως πάλιν ὁ βασιλεὺς ἐνίκησε, καὶ τῆς τε
παρεμβολῆς τῶν ἀποστατῶν ἐκυρίευσε καὶ τοὺς
ἡττηθέντας ἐδίωξε μέχρι τῶν ὅρων τῆς Βαβυλω-
νίας· συνέβη δὲ καὶ τὸν Ἀρβάκην αὐτὸν λαμ-
πρότατα κινδυνεύσαντα καὶ πολλοὺς ἀνελόντα
7 τῶν Ἀσσυρίων γενέσθαι τραυματίαν. τηλικούτων δ' ἐλαττωμάτων κατὰ τὸ συνεχὲς γινομένων τοῖς ἀφεστηκόσιν, οἱ τὰς ἡγεμονίας
ἔχοντες ἀπελπίσαντες περὶ τῆς νίκης παρ-
εσκευάζοντο διαχωρίζεσθαι πρὸς τοὺς οἰκείους
8 ἕκαστοι τόπους. ὁ δὲ Βέλεσυς ἐν ὑπαίθρῳ τὴν
νύκτα διηγρυπνηκὼς καὶ περὶ τὴν τῶν ἄστρων
παρατήρησιν φιλοτιμηθείς, ἔφησε τοῖς ἀπηλπι-
κόσι τὰ πράγματα, ἂν πένθ' ἡμέρας ἀναμείνωσιν,
αὐτομάτην ἥξειν βοήθειαν καὶ μεταβολὴν ἔσεσθαι
τῶν ὅλων παμμεγέθη εἰς τοὐναντίον· ταῦτα γὰρ
ὁρᾶν διὰ τῆς τῶν ἄστρων ἐμπειρίας προσημαί-
νοντας αὐτοῖς τοὺς θεούς. καὶ παρεκάλει ταύτας
τὰς ἡμέρας μείναντας πεῖραν λαβεῖν τῆς ἰδίας
τέχνης καὶ τῆς τῶν θεῶν εὐεργεσίας.

26. Μετακληθέντων οὖν πάντων πάλιν καὶ
τὸν ὡρισμένον χρόνον ἀναμεινάντων, ἧκέ τις
ἀπαγγέλλων διότι δύναμις ἐκ τῆς Βακτριανῆς
ἀπεσταλμένη τῷ βασιλεῖ πλησίον ἐστὶ πορευο-
2 μένη κατὰ σπουδήν. ἔδοξεν οὖν τοῖς περὶ τὸν
Ἀρβάκην ἀπαντῆσαι τοῖς στρατηγοῖς τὴν

useful for the war; but Belesys the Babylonian, by
maintaining that the gods were promising them by
signs that with labours and hardship they would bring
their enterprise to a successful end, and encouraging
them in every other way as much as he could, persuaded them all to remain to face further perils. So
there was a third battle, and again the king was
victorious, captured the camp of the rebels, and
pursued the defeated foe as far as the boundaries of
Babylonia; and it also happened that Arbaces
himself, who had fought most brilliantly and had
slain many Assyrians, was wounded. And now that
the rebels had suffered defeats so decisive following
one upon the other, their commanders, abandoning
all hope of victory, were preparing to disperse each
to his own country. But Belesys, who had passed a
sleepless night in the open and had devoted himself
to the observation of the stars, said to those who had
lost hope in their cause, " If you will wait five days
help will come of its own accord, and there will be a
mighty change to the opposite in the whole situation;
for from my long study of the stars I see the gods
foretelling this to us." And he appealed to them to
wait that many days and test his own skill and the
good will of the gods.

26. So after they had all been called back and had
waited the stipulated time, there came a messenger
with the news that a force which had been despatched
from Bactriana to the king was near at hand, advancing with all speed. Arbaces, accordingly, decided to
go to meet their generals by the shortest route,

ταχίστην ἀναλαβόντας τῶν στρατιωτῶν τοὺς
κρατίστους καὶ μάλιστ' εὐζώνους, ὅπως, ἂν μὴ
διὰ τῶν λόγων τοὺς Βακτριανοὺς δύνωνται πεῖσαι
συναποστῆναι, τοῖς ὅπλοις βιάσωνται μετα-
3 σχεῖν τῶν αὐτῶν ἐλπίδων. τέλος δὲ[1] πρὸς τὴν
ἐλευθερίαν ἀσμένως ὑπακουσάντων τὸ μὲν πρῶτον τῶν ἡγεμόνων, ἔπειτα καὶ τῆς ὅλης δυνάμεως,
πάντες ἐν ταὐτῷ κατεστρατοπέδευσαν.
4 Ὅτε δὴ συνέβη τὸν βασιλέα τῶν Ἀσσυρίων
τὴν μὲν ἀπόστασιν τῶν Βακτριανῶν ἀγνοοῦντα,
ταῖς δὲ προγεγενημέναις εὐημερίαις μετεωρισ-
θέντα, τραπῆναι πρὸς ἄνεσιν, καὶ τοῖς στρατιώ-
ταις διαδοῦναι πρὸς εὐωχίαν ἱερεῖα καὶ πλῆθος
οἴνου τε καὶ τῶν ἄλλων ἐπιτηδείων. διόπερ τῆς
δυνάμεως ἁπάσης ἑστιωμένης, οἱ περὶ τὸν
Ἀρβάκην παρά τινων αὐτομόλων πυθόμενοι τὴν
ἐν τῇ παρεμβολῇ τῶν πολεμίων ῥαθυμίαν καὶ
μέθην, νυκτὸς ἀπροσδοκήτως τὴν ἐπίθεσιν ἐποιή-
5 σαντο. προσπεσόντες δὲ συντεταγμένοι μὲν
ἀσυντάκτοις, ἕτοιμοι δ' ἀπαρασκεύοις, τῆς τε
παρεμβολῆς ἐκράτησαν καὶ τῶν στρατιωτῶν
πολλοὺς ἀνελόντες τοὺς ἄλλους μέχρι τῆς πό-
6 λεως κατεδίωξαν. μετὰ δὲ ταῦτα ὁ μὲν βασιλεὺς
Γαλαιμένην τὸν ἀδελφὸν τῆς γυναικὸς ἀποδείξας
στρατηγόν, αὐτὸς τῶν κατὰ τὴν πόλιν ἐπιμέλειαν ἐποιεῖτο· οἱ δ' ἀποστάται κατὰ τὸ πεδίον
τὸ πρὸ τῆς πόλεως παραταξάμενοι δυσὶ μάχαις
ἐνίκησαν τοὺς Ἀσσυρίους, καὶ τόν τε Γαλαιμένην ἀνεῖλον καὶ τῶν ἀντιταξαμένων τοὺς μὲν
ἐν τῇ φυγῇ κατέσφαξαν, τοὺς δ' ἀποκλεισθέντας
τῆς εἰς τὴν πόλιν ἐπανόδου καὶ συναναγκα-
σθέντας ἑαυτοὺς ῥιπτεῖν εἰς τὸν Εὐφράτην

taking along the best and most agile of his troops, so that, in case they should be unable to persuade the Bactrians by arguments to join in the revolt, they might resort to arms to force them to share with them in the same hopes. But the outcome¹ was that the new-comers gladly listened to the call to freedom, first the commanders and then the entire force, and they all encamped in the same place.

It happened at this very time that the king of the Assyrians, who was unaware of the defection of the Bactrians and had become elated over his past successes, turned to indulgence and divided among his soldiers for a feast animals and great quantities of both wine and all other provisions. Consequently, since the whole army was carousing, Arbaces, learning from some deserters of the relaxation and drunkenness in the camp of the enemy, made his attack upon it unexpectedly in the night. And as it was an assault of organized men upon disorganized and of ready men upon unprepared, they won possession of the camp, and after slaying many of the soldiers pursued the rest of them as far as the city. After this the king named for the chief command Galaemenes, his wife's brother, and gave his own attention to the affairs within the city. But the rebels, drawing up their forces in the plain before the city, overcame the Assyrians in two battles, and they not only slew Galaemenes, but of the opposing forces they cut down some in their flight, while others, who had been shut out from entering the city and forced to leap into

---

¹ For τέλος δὲ Vogel proposes τούτων δὲ or ὧν, unless, as he suggests, there is a large lacuna.

7 ποταμὸν πλὴν ὀλίγων ἅπαντας ἀνεῖλον. τοσοῦτο
δὲ πλῆθος ἦν τῶν φονευθέντων ὥστε τὸ φερόμενον ῥεῦμα κραθὲν αἵματι τὴν χρόαν ἐφ᾽ ἱκανὸν
τόπον μεταβαλεῖν. ἔπειτα τοῦ βασιλέως συγ-
κλεισθέντος εἰς πολιορκίαν πολλὰ τῶν ἐθνῶν
ἀφίστατο, ἑκάστου πρὸς τὴν ἐλευθερίαν αὐτομο-
λοῦντος.

8 Ὁ δὲ Σαρδανάπαλλος ὁρῶν τὴν ὅλην βασιλείαν ἐν τοῖς μεγίστοις οὖσαν κινδύνοις, τοὺς
μὲν υἱοὺς τρεῖς ὄντας καὶ θυγατέρας δύο μετὰ
πολλῶν χρημάτων εἰς Παφλαγονίαν ἀπέστειλε
πρὸς Κότταν τὸν ἔπαρχον, ὄντα τῶν ἀρχομένων
εὐνούστατον, αὐτὸς δὲ βιβλιαφόρους ἀποστείλας
πρὸς ἅπαντας τοὺς ὑπ᾽ αὐτὸν τεταγμένους μετεπέμπετο δυνάμεις καὶ τὰ πρὸς τὴν πολιορκίαν
9 παρεσκευάζετο. ἦν δ᾽ αὐτῷ λόγιον παραδεδο-
μένον ἐκ προγόνων ὅτι τὴν Νίνον οὐδεὶς ἑλεῖ
κατὰ κράτος, ἐὰν μὴ πρότερον ὁ ποταμὸς τῇ
πόλει γένηται πολέμιος. ὑπολαμβάνων οὖν τοῦτο μηδέποτε ἔσεσθαι, ταῖς ἐλπίσιν ἀντεῖχε,
διανοούμενος ὑπομένειν τὴν πολιορκίαν καὶ τὰ
παρὰ τῶν ὑποτεταγμένων[1] ἀποσταλησόμενα
στρατόπεδα προσδέχεσθαι.[2]

27. Οἱ δ᾽ ἀποστάται τοῖς προτερήμασιν ἐπαρ-
θέντες προσέκειντο μὲν τῇ πολιορκίᾳ, διὰ δὲ τὴν
ὀχυρότητα τῶν τειχῶν οὐδὲν ἠδύναντο βλάψαι
τοὺς ἐν τῇ πόλει· πετροβόλοι γὰρ ἢ χελῶναι
χωστρίδες ἢ κριοὶ πρὸς ἀνατροπὴν μεμηχανη-
μένοι τειχῶν οὔπω κατ᾽ ἐκείνους τοὺς καιροὺς

[1] ὑποτεταγμένων Vogel : ἐπάρχων A B D, Bekker, Dindorf.
[2] προσδέχεσθαι Vogel : προσεδέχετο Vulgate, Bekker, Dindorf.

the Euphrates river, they destroyed almost to a man. So great was the multitude of the slain that the water of the stream, mingled with the blood, was changed in colour over a considerable distance. Furthermore, now that the king was shut up in the city and besieged there, many of the nations revolted, going over in each case to the side of liberty.

Sardanapallus, realizing that his entire kingdom was in the greatest danger, sent his three sons and two daughters together with much of his treasure to Paphlagonia to the governor Cotta, who was the most loyal of his subjects, while he himself, despatching letter-carriers to all his subjects, summoned forces and made preparations for the siege. Now there was a prophecy which had come down to him from his ancestors: " No enemy will ever take Ninus by storm unless the river shall first become the city's enemy." Assuming, therefore, that this would never be, he held out in hope, his thought being to endure the siege and await the troops which would be sent from his subjects.

27. The rebels, elated at their successes, pressed the siege, but because of the strength of the walls they were unable to do any harm to the men in the city; for neither engines for throwing stones, nor shelters for sappers,[1] nor battering-rams devised to overthrow walls had as yet been invented at that time. More-

---

[1] The χελῶναι ("tortoises"; cp. the Roman *testudo*) χωστρίδες were strong moveable sheds or roofs, under whose protection sappers and miners could work. In Book 20. 91. 8 they are contrasted with sheds which carried battering-rams (χελῶναι κριοφόροι).

εὕρηντο. τῶν δ' ἐπιτηδείων ἁπάντων οἱ κατὰ
τὴν πόλιν πολλὴν εἶχον δαψίλειαν, προνενοη-
μένου τοῦ βασιλέως τούτου τοῦ μέρους. διὸ καὶ
χρονιζούσης τῆς πολιορκίας ἐπ' ἔτη μὲν δύο
προσέκειντο προσβολὰς ποιούμενοι τοῖς τείχεσι
καὶ τῆς ἐπὶ τὴν χώραν ἐξόδου τοὺς ἐκ τῆς πόλεως
εἴργοντες· τῷ τρίτῳ δ' ἔτει συνεχῶς ὄμβρων
μεγάλων καταρραγέντων συνέβη τὸν Εὐφράτην
μέγαν γενόμενον κατακλύσαι τε μέρος τῆς πόλεως καὶ καταβαλεῖν τὸ τεῖχος ἐπὶ σταδίους
2 εἴκοσιν. ἐνταῦθα ὁ βασιλεὺς νομίσας τετε-
λέσθαι τὸν χρησμὸν καὶ τῇ πόλει τὸν ποταμὸν
γεγονέναι φανερῶς πολέμιον, ἀπέγνω τὴν σωτηρίαν. ἵνα δὲ μὴ τοῖς πολεμίοις ὑποχείριος
γένηται, πυρὰν ἐν τοῖς βασιλείοις κατεσκεύασεν
ὑπερμεγέθη, καὶ τόν τε χρυσὸν καὶ τὸν ἄργυρον
ἅπαντα, πρὸς δὲ τούτοις τὴν βασιλικὴν ἐσθῆτα
πᾶσαν ἐπὶ ταύτην ἐσώρευσε, τὰς δὲ παλλακίδας
καὶ τοὺς εὐνούχους συγκλείσας εἰς τὸν ἐν μέσῃ
τῇ πυρᾷ κατεσκευασμένον οἶκον ἅμα τούτοις
ἅπασιν ἑαυτόν τε καὶ τὰ βασίλεια κατέκαυσεν.
3 οἱ δ' ἀποστάται πυθόμενοι τὴν ἀπώλειαν τὴν
Σαρδαναπάλλου, τῆς μὲν πόλεως ἐκράτησαν
εἰσπεσόντες κατὰ τὸ πεπτωκὸς μέρος τοῦ τείχους,
τὸν δ' Ἀρβάκην ἐνδύσαντες τὴν βασιλικὴν
στολὴν προσηγόρευσαν βασιλέα, καὶ τὴν τῶν
ὅλων ἐξουσίαν ἐπέτρεψαν.

28. Ἔνθα δὴ τοῦ βασιλέως τοῖς συναγωνισα-
μένοις στρατηγοῖς δωρεάς τε διαδόντος κατὰ τὴν
ἀξίαν καὶ σατράπας ἐθνῶν καθιστάντος, προσελ-
θὼν αὐτῷ Βέλεσυς ὁ Βαβυλώνιος, ὁ προειπὼν
ὅτι βασιλεὺς ἔσται τῆς Ἀσίας, τῆς τε εὐεργεσίας

over, the inhabitants of the city had a great abundance of all provisions, since the king had taken thought on that score. Consequently the siege dragged on, and for two years they pressed their attack, making assaults on the walls and preventing the inhabitants of the city from going out into the country; but in the third year, after there had been heavy and continuous rains, it came to pass that the Euphrates, running very full, both inundated a portion of the city and broke down the walls for a distance of twenty stades. At this the king, believing that the oracle had been fulfilled and that the river had plainly become the city's enemy, abandoned hope of saving himself. And in order that he might not fall into the hands of the enemy, he built an enormous pyre [1] in his palace, heaped upon it all his gold and silver as well as every article of the royal wardrobe, and then, shutting his concubines and eunuchs in the room which had been built in the middle of the pyre, he consigned both them and himself and his palace to the flames. The rebels, on learning of the death of Sardanapallus, took the city by forcing an entrance where the wall had fallen, and clothing Arbaces in the royal garb saluted him as king and put in his hands the supreme authority.

28. Thereupon, after the new king had distributed among the generals who had aided him in the struggle gifts corresponding to their several deserts, and as he was appointing satraps over the nations, Belesys the Babylonian, who had foretold to Arbaces that he would be king of Asia, coming to him, reminded him

---

[1] Diodorus greatly abridged the description of this pyre by Ctesias, since Athenaeus (12. 38), who derived his account of it also from Ctesias, gives many more details concerning it.

ὑπέμνησε καὶ τὴν Βαβυλῶνος ἀρχὴν ἠξίου
2 δοῦναι, καθάπερ ἐξ ἀρχῆς ὑπέσχετο. ἀπεφαί-
νετο δὲ καὶ κατὰ τοὺς κινδύνους ἑαυτὸν εὐχὴν
πεποιῆσθαι τῷ Βήλῳ Σαρδαναπάλλου κρατη-
θέντος καὶ τῶν¹ βασιλείων ἐμπυρισθέντων ἀπο-
κομιεῖν τὴν σποδὸν τὴν ἐκ τούτων εἰς Βαβυλῶνα, καὶ πλησίον τοῦ τεμένους τοῦ θεοῦ καὶ
τοῦ ποταμοῦ καταθέμενον χῶμα κατασκευάσειν
τὸ παρεξόμενον τοῖς κατὰ τὸν Εὐφράτην πλέου-
σιν ἀθάνατον ὑπόμνημα τοῦ καταλύσαντος τὴν
3 Ἀσσυρίων ἀρχήν. τοῦτο δ' ᾐτεῖτο πυθόμενός
τινος εὐνούχου τὰ περὶ τὸν ἄργυρον καὶ χρυσόν,
ὃν διαδράντα καὶ πρὸς αὐτὸν αὐτομολήσαντα
4 κατέκρυψεν. ὁ δ' Ἀρβάκης τούτων οὐδὲν εἰδὼς
διὰ τὸ πάντας τοὺς ἐν τοῖς βασιλείοις συγκατα-
καῆναι τῷ βασιλεῖ, τήν τε σποδὸν ἀποκομίσαι
καὶ τὴν Βαβυλῶνα ἔχειν ἀτελῆ συνεχώρησεν.
εἶθ' ὁ μὲν Βέλεσυς πλοῖα παραστησάμενος μετὰ
τῆς σποδοῦ τὸ πλεῖστον τοῦ τε ἀργύρου καὶ τοῦ
χρυσοῦ συντόμως ἀπέστειλεν εἰς Βαβυλῶνα· ὁ
δὲ βασιλεύς, μηνυθείσης αὐτῷ τῆς πράξεως
αὐτοφώρου,² δικαστὰς ἀπέδειξε τοὺς συναγωνι-
5 σαμένους στρατηγούς. τοῦ πράξαντος δ' ὁμολο-
γοῦντος ἀδικεῖν, τὸ μὲν δικαστήριον αὐτοῦ θάνατον κατέγνω, ὁ δὲ βασιλεύς, μεγαλόψυχος ὢν
καὶ τὴν ἀρχὴν τῆς ἡγεμονίας βουλόμενος ἐπιεικῆ
παρέχεσθαι, τῶν τε κινδύνων ἀπέλυσε τὸν
Βέλεσυν καὶ τὸν ἀποκεκομισμένον ἄργυρον καὶ
χρυσὸν ἔχειν συνεχώρησεν· ὁμοίως δὲ καὶ τὴν
ἐξ ἀρχῆς δοθεῖσαν ἐξουσίαν τῆς Βαβυλῶνος

---

¹ ἄλλων after τῶν added by Vulgate, Bekker, Dindorf.

of his good services, and asked that he be given the governorship of Babylon, as had been promised at the outset. He also explained that when their cause was endangered he had made a vow to Belus that, if Sardanapallus were defeated and his palace went up in flames, he would bring its ashes to Babylon, and depositing them near the river and the sacred precinct of the god he would construct a mound which, for all who sailed down the Euphrates, would stand as an eternal memorial of the man who had overthrown the rule of the Assyrians. This request he made because he had learned from a certain eunuch, who had made his escape and come to Belesys and was kept hidden by him, of the facts regarding the silver and gold. Now since Arbaces knew nothing of this, by reason of the fact that all the inmates of the palace had been burned along with the king, he allowed him both to carry the ashes away and to hold Babylon without the payment of tribute. Thereupon Belesys procured boats and at once sent off to Babylon along with the ashes practically all the silver and gold; and the king, having been informed of the act which Belesys had been caught perpetrating, appointed as judges the generals who had served with him in the war. And when the accused acknowledged his guilt, the court sentenced him to death, but the king, being a magnanimous man and wishing to make his rule at the outset known for clemency, both freed Belesys from the danger threatening him and allowed him to keep the silver and gold which he had carried off; likewise, he did not even take from him the governorship over Babylon which had originally

---

² αὐτοφώρου Rhodomann: αὐτοφόρου.

οὐκ ἀφείλετο, φήσας μείζονας εἶναι τὰς ἐξ αὐτοῦ
προγεγενημένας εὐεργεσίας τῶν ὕστερον ἀδικη-
6 μάτων. διαβοηθείσης δὲ τῆς ἐπιεικείας οὐ τὴν
τυχοῦσαν εὔνοιαν ἅμα[1] καὶ δόξαν παρὰ τῶν
ἐθνῶν ἀπηνέγκατο, πάντων κρινόντων ἄξιον εἶναι
τῆς βασιλείας τὸν οὕτω προσενεχθέντα τοῖς
7 ἀδικήσασιν. ὁ δ' οὖν Ἀρβάκης τοῖς κατὰ τὴν
πόλιν ἐπιεικῶς προσενεχθεὶς αὐτοὺς μὲν κατὰ
κώμας διῴκισε, τὰς ἰδίας κτήσεις ἑκάστοις
ἀποδούς, τὴν δὲ πόλιν εἰς ἔδαφος κατέσκαψεν.
ἔπειτα τόν τε ἄργυρον καὶ χρυσὸν τὸν ἐκ τῆς
πυρᾶς ὑπολειφθέντα πολλῶν ὄντα ταλάντων
ἀπεκόμισε τῆς Μηδίας εἰς Ἐκβάτανα.
8   Ἡ μὲν οὖν ἡγεμονία τῶν Ἀσσυρίων ἀπὸ Νίνου
διαμείνασα τριάκοντα μὲν γενεάς, ἔτη δὲ πλείω
τῶν χιλίων καὶ τριακοσίων, ὑπὸ Μήδων κατελύθη
τὸν προειρημένον τρόπον.
    29. Ἡμῖν δ' οὐκ ἀνάρμοστον εἶναι δοκεῖ περὶ
τῶν ἐν Βαβυλῶνι Χαλδαίων καὶ τῆς ἀρχαιότητος
αὐτῶν βραχέα διελθεῖν, ἵνα μηδὲν παραλείπωμεν
2 τῶν ἀξίων μνήμης. Χαλδαῖοι τοίνυν τῶν ἀρχαιοτάτων ὄντες Βαβυλωνίων τῇ μὲν διαιρέσει τῆς
πολιτείας παραπλησίαν ἔχουσι τάξιν τοῖς κατ'
Αἴγυπτον ἱερεῦσι· πρὸς γὰρ τῇ θεραπείᾳ τῶν
θεῶν τεταγμένοι πάντα τὸν τοῦ ζῆν χρόνον
φιλοσοφοῦσι, μεγίστην δόξαν ἔχοντες ἐν ἀστρολογίᾳ. ἀντέχονται δ' ἐπὶ πολὺ καὶ μαντικῆς,
ποιούμενοι προρρήσεις περὶ τῶν μελλόντων, καὶ
τῶν μὲν καθαρμοῖς, τῶν δὲ θυσίαις, τῶν δ'
ἄλλαις τισὶν ἐπῳδαῖς ἀποτροπὰς κακῶν καὶ
3 τελειώσεις ἀγαθῶν πειρῶνται πορίζειν. ἐμπειρίαν

[1] ἅμα Dindorf: ἀλλά.

been given to him, saying that his former services were greater than his subsequent misdeeds. When this act of clemency was noised about, he won no ordinary loyalty on the part of his subjects as well as renown among the nations, all judging that a man who had conducted himself in this wise towards wrongdoers was worthy of the kingship. Arbaces, however, showing clemency towards the inhabitants of the city, settled them in villages and returned to each man his personal possessions, but the city he levelled to the ground. Then the silver and gold, amounting to many talents, which had been left in the pyre, he collected and took off to Ecbatana in Media.

So the empire of the Assyrians, which had endured from the time of Ninus through thirty generations, for more than one thousand three hundred years, was destroyed by the Medes in the manner described above.

29. But to us it seems not inappropriate to speak briefly of the Chaldaeans of Babylon and of their antiquity, that we may omit nothing which is worthy of record. Now the Chaldaeans, belonging as they do to the most ancient inhabitants of Babylonia, have about the same position among the divisions of the state as that occupied by the priests of Egypt; for being assigned to the service of the gods they spend their entire life in study, their greatest renown being in the field of astrology. But they occupy themselves largely with soothsaying as well, making predictions about future events, and in some cases by purifications, in others by sacrifices, and in others by some other charms they attempt to effect the averting of evil things and the fulfilment of the good. They are

445

δ' ἔχουσι καὶ τῆς διὰ τῶν οἰωνῶν μαντικῆς, ἐνυπνίων τε καὶ τεράτων ἐξηγήσεις ἀποφαίνονται. οὐκ ἀσόφως δὲ ποιοῦνται καὶ τὰ περὶ τὴν ἱεροσκοπίαν ἄκρως ἐπιτυγχάνειν νομίζοντες.[1]

4 Τὴν δὲ τούτων μάθησιν ἁπάντων οὐχ ὁμοίαν ποιοῦνται τοῖς τὰ τοιαῦτ' ἐπιτηδεύουσι τῶν Ἑλλήνων. παρὰ μὲν γὰρ τοῖς Χαλδαίοις ἐκ γένους ἡ τούτων φιλοσοφία παραδέδοται, καὶ παῖς παρὰ πατρὸς διαδέχεται, τῶν ἄλλων λειτουργιῶν πασῶν ἀπολελυμένος. διὸ καὶ γονεῖς ἔχοντες διδασκάλους ἅμα μὲν ἀφθόνως ἅπαντα μανθάνουσιν, ἅμα δὲ τοῖς παραγγελλομένοις προσέχουσι πιστεύοντες βεβαιότερον. ἔπειτ' εὐθὺς ἐκ παίδων συντρεφόμενοι τοῖς μαθήμασι μεγάλην ἕξιν περιποιοῦνται διά τε τὸ τῆς ἡλικίας εὐδίδακτον καὶ διὰ τὸ πλῆθος τοῦ προσκαρτερουμένου χρόνου.

5 Παρὰ δὲ τοῖς Ἕλλησιν ὁ πολλοῖς ἀπαρασκεύως[2] προσιὼν ὀψέ ποτε τῆς φιλοσοφίας ἅπτεται, καὶ μέχρι τινὸς φιλοπονήσας ἀπῆλθε περισπασθεὶς ὑπὸ βιωτικῆς χρείας· ὀλίγοι δέ τινες ἐπὶ φιλοσοφίαν ἀποδύντες ἐργολαβίας ἕνεκεν παραμένουσιν ἐν τῷ μαθήματι, καινοτομοῦντες ἀεὶ περὶ τῶν μεγίστων δογμάτων καὶ

6 τοῖς πρὸ αὐτῶν οὐκ ἀκολουθοῦντες. τοιγαροῦν οἱ μὲν βάρβαροι διαμένοντες ἐπὶ τῶν αὐτῶν ἀεὶ βεβαίως ἕκαστα λαμβάνουσιν, οἱ δ' Ἕλληνες τοῦ

---

[1] νομίζοντες D, Vogel: Bekker and Dindorf follow the Vulgate in reading νομίζονται, and think that some words have been lost after ἀσόφως δέ.

[2] πολλοῖς ἀπαρασκεύως Vogel: πολὺς ἀπαράσκευος.

also skilled in soothsaying by the flight of birds, and they give out interpretations of both dreams and portents. They also show marked ability in making divinations from the observation of the entrails of animals, deeming that in this branch they are eminently successful.

The training which they receive in all these matters is not the same as that of the Greeks who follow such practices. For among the Chaldaeans the scientific study of these subjects is passed down in the family, and son takes it over from father, being relieved of all other services in the state. Since, therefore, they have their parents for teachers, they not only are taught everything ungrudgingly but also at the same time they give heed to the precepts of their teachers with a more unwavering trust. Furthermore, since they are bred in these teachings from childhood up, they attain a great skill in them, both because of the ease with which youth is taught and because of the great amount of time which is devoted to this study.

Among the Greeks, on the contrary, the student who takes up a large number of subjects without preparation turns to the higher studies only quite late, and then, after labouring upon them to some extent, gives them up, being distracted by the necessity of earning a livelihood; and but a few here and there really strip for the higher studies and continue in the pursuit of them as a profit-making business, and these are always trying to make innovations in connection with the most important doctrines instead of following in the path of their predecessors. The result of this is that the barbarians, by sticking to the same things always, keep a firm hold on every detail, while the Greeks, on

κατὰ τὴν ἐργολαβίαν κέρδους στοχαζόμενοι καινὰς
αἱρέσεις κτίζουσι, καὶ περὶ τῶν μεγίστων θεωρη-
μάτων ἀλλήλοις ἀντιδοξοῦντες διχονοεῖν ποιοῦσι
τοὺς μανθάνοντας καὶ τὰς ψυχὰς αὐτῶν πλανᾶ-
σθαι, τὸν πάντα βίον ἐν αἰώρᾳ γινομένας[1] καὶ
μηδὲν ὅλως πιστεῦσαι δυναμένας βεβαίως· τὰς
γοῦν ἐπιφανεστάτας αἱρέσεις τῶν φιλοσόφων εἴ τις
ἀκριβῶς ἐξετάζοι, πλεῖστον ὅσον εὑρήσει διαφε-
ρούσας ἀλλήλων καὶ περὶ τῶν μεγίστων δοξῶν
ἐναντία δοξαζούσας.

30. Οἱ δ' οὖν Χαλδαῖοι τὴν μὲν τοῦ κόσμου
φύσιν ἀίδιόν φασιν εἶναι καὶ μήτε ἐξ ἀρχῆς
γένεσιν ἐσχηκέναι μήθ' ὕστερον φθορὰν ἐπι-
δέξεσθαι, τὴν δὲ τῶν ὅλων τάξιν τε καὶ διακόσμησιν θείᾳ τινὶ προνοίᾳ γεγονέναι, καὶ νῦν ἕκαστα
τῶν ἐν οὐρανῷ γινομένων οὐχ ὡς ἔτυχεν οὐδ'
αὐτομάτως ἀλλ' ὡρισμένῃ τινὶ καὶ βεβαίως
2 κεκυρωμένῃ θεῶν κρίσει συντελεῖσθαι. τῶν δ'
ἄστρων πολυχρονίους παρατηρήσεις πεποιημένοι,
καὶ τὰς ἑκάστου κινήσεις τε καὶ δυνάμεις ἀκριβέστατα πάντων ἀνθρώπων ἐπεγνωκότες, πολλὰ
τῶν μελλόντων συμβαίνειν προλέγουσι τοῖς
3 ἀνθρώποις. μεγίστην δέ[2] φασιν εἶναι θεωρίαν
καὶ δύναμιν περὶ τοὺς πέντε ἀστέρας τοὺς πλάνητας καλουμένους, οὓς ἐκεῖνοι κοινῇ μὲν ἑρμηνεῖς
ὀνομάζουσιν, ἰδίᾳ δὲ τὸν ὑπὸ τῶν Ἑλλήνων Κρόνον
ὀνομαζόμενον, ἐπιφανέστατον δὲ καὶ πλεῖστα καὶ

---

[1] γινουένας Coraës : γενομένας.   [2] δὲ Dindorf : τε.

---

[1] i.e. to mankind of the will of the gods, as explained
below.
[2] Saturn.

the other hand, aiming at the profit to be made out of the business, keep founding new schools and, wrangling with each other over the most important matters of speculation, bring it about that their pupils hold conflicting views, and that their minds, vacillating throughout their lives and unable to believe anything at all with firm conviction, simply wander in confusion. It is at any rate true that, if a man were to examine carefully the most famous schools of the philosophers, he would find them differing from one another to the uttermost degree and maintaining opposite opinions regarding the most fundamental tenets.

30. Now, as the Chaldaeans say, the world is by its nature eternal, and neither had a first beginning nor will at a later time suffer destruction; furthermore, both the disposition and the orderly arrangement of the universe have come about by virtue of a divine providence, and to-day whatever takes place in the heavens is in every instance brought to pass, not at haphazard nor by virtue of any spontaneous action, but by some fixed and firmly determined divine decision. And since they have observed the stars over a long period of time and have noted both the movements and the influences of each of them with greater precision than any other men, they foretell to mankind many things that will take place in the future. But above all in importance, they say, is the study of the influence of the five stars known as planets, which they call " Interpreters "[1] when speaking of them as a group, but if referring to them singly, the one named Cronus[2] by the Greeks, which is the most conspicuous and presages more events and such as are of greater importance than the others,

449

μέγιστα προσημαίνοντα, καλοῦσιν Ἡλίου· τοὺς
δ' ἄλλους τέτταρας ὁμοίως τοῖς παρ' ἡμῖν ἀστρολόγοις ὀνομάζουσιν, Ἄρεος, Ἀφροδίτης, Ἑρμοῦ,
4 Διός. διὰ τοῦτο δ' αὐτοὺς ἑρμηνεῖς καλοῦσιν,
ὅτι τῶν ἄλλων ἀστέρων ἀπλανῶν ὄντων καὶ
τεταγμένῃ πορείᾳ μίαν περιφορὰν ἐχόντων οὗτοι
μόνοι πορείαν ἰδίαν ποιούμενοι τὰ μέλλοντα
γίνεσθαι δεικνύουσιν, ἑρμηνεύοντες τοῖς ἀνθρώποις τὴν τῶν θεῶν ἔννοιαν.[1] τὰ μὲν γὰρ διὰ τῆς
ἀνατολῆς, τὰ δὲ διὰ τῆς δύσεως, τινὰ δὲ διὰ τῆς
χρόας προσημαίνειν φασὶν αὐτοὺς τοῖς προσέχειν
5 ἀκριβῶς βουληθεῖσι· ποτὲ μὲν γὰρ πνευμάτων
μεγέθη δηλοῦν αὐτούς, ποτὲ δὲ ὄμβρων ἢ καυμάτων ὑπερβολάς, ἔστι δὲ ὅτε κομητῶν ἀστέρων
ἐπιτολάς, ἔτι δὲ ἡλίου τε καὶ σελήνης ἐκλείψεις,
καὶ σεισμούς, καὶ τὸ σύνολον πάσας τὰς ἐκ τοῦ
περιέχοντος γεννωμένας περιστάσεις ὠφελίμους
τε καὶ βλαβερὰς οὐ μόνον ἔθνεσιν ἢ[2] τόποις,
ἀλλὰ καὶ βασιλεῦσι καὶ τοῖς τυχοῦσιν ἰδιώταις.
6   Ὑπὸ δὲ τὴν τούτων φορὰν λέγουσι τετάχθαι
τριάκοντα ἀστέρας, οὓς προσαγορεύουσι βου-
λαίους θεούς· τούτων δὲ τοὺς μὲν ἡμίσεις τοὺς
ὑπὲρ γῆν τόπους ἐφορᾶν, τοὺς δ' ἡμίσεις τοὺς[3]
ὑπὸ τὴν γῆν, τὰ κατ' ἀνθρώπους ἐπισκοποῦντας
ἅμα καὶ τὰ κατὰ τὸν οὐρανὸν συμβαίνοντα· διὰ
δ' ἡμερῶν δέκα πέμπεσθαι τῶν μὲν ἄνω πρὸς
τοὺς κάτω καθάπερ ἄγγελον ἕνα τῶν ἀστέρων,

---

[1] ἔννοιαν Dindorf : εὔνοιαν.
[2] ἢ Vogel, following C D F; καὶ Bekker and Dindorf,
following the other MSS.
[3] τοὺς added by Reiske.

---

[1] Mars, Venus, Mercury, Jupiter.

they call the star of Helius, whereas the other four they designate as the stars of Ares, Aphrodite, Hermes, and Zeus,[1] as do our astrologers. The reason why they call them "Interpreters" is that whereas all the other stars are fixed and follow a single circuit in a regular course, these alone, by virtue of following each its own course, point out future events, thus interpreting to mankind the design of the gods. For sometimes by their risings, sometimes by their settings, and again by their colour, the Chaldaeans say, they give signs of coming events to such as are willing to observe them closely; for at one time they show forth mighty storms of winds, at another excessive rains or heat, at times the appearance of comets, also eclipses of both sun and moon, and earthquakes, and in a word all the conditions which owe their origin to the atmosphere and work both benefits and harm, not only to whole peoples or regions, but also to kings and to persons of private station.

Under the course in which these planets move are situated, according to them, thirty stars,[2] which they designate as "counselling gods"; of these one half oversee the regions above the earth and the other half those beneath the earth, having under their purview the affairs of mankind and likewise those of the heavens; and every ten days one of the stars above is sent as a messenger, so to speak, to the stars

[2] According to Bouché-Leclercq, L'Astrologie Grecque, p. 43, n. 4, Diodorus has confused here two distinct systems, that of the thirty-six stars known as decans, which Babylonian astrology designated as rulers of ten degrees in each zodiac, and that of the thirty stars which the Egyptians believed to be gods, each of whom presided over one of the thirty days of the month.

τῶν δ' ὑπὸ γῆν πρὸς τοὺς ἄνω πάλιν ὁμοίως ἕνα, καὶ ταύτην ἔχειν αὐτοὺς φορὰν ὡρισμένην καὶ
7 περιόδῳ κεκυρωμένην αἰωνίῳ. τῶν θεῶν δὲ τούτων κυρίους εἶναί φασι δώδεκα τὸν ἀριθμόν, ὧν ἑκάστῳ μῆνα καὶ τῶν δώδεκα λεγομένων ζῳδίων ἐν προσνέμουσι. διὰ δὲ τούτων φασὶ ποιεῖσθαι τὴν πορείαν τόν τε ἥλιον καὶ τὴν σελήνην καὶ πέντε τοὺς πλάνητας ἀστέρας, τοῦ μὲν ἡλίου τὸν ἴδιον κύκλον ἐν ἐνιαυτῷ τελοῦντος, τῆς δὲ σελήνης ἐν μηνὶ τὴν ἰδίαν περίοδον διαπορευομένης.

31. Τῶν δὲ πλανήτων ἴδιον ἕκαστον[1] ἔχειν δρόμον καὶ διηλλαγμένως καὶ ποικίλως χρῆσθαι τοῖς τάχεσι καὶ τῇ τῶν χρόνων διαιρέσει. πλεῖστα δὲ πρὸς τὰς γενέσεις τῶν ἀνθρώπων συμβάλλεσθαι τούτους τοὺς ἀστέρας ἀγαθά τε καὶ κακά· διὰ δὲ τῆς τούτων φύσεώς τε καὶ θεωρίας μάλιστα γινώσκειν τὰ συμβαίνοντα τοῖς ἀνθρώ-
2 ποις. πεποιῆσθαι δέ φασι προρρήσεις ἄλλοις τε βασιλεῦσιν οὐκ ὀλίγοις καὶ τῷ καταπολεμή- σαντι Δαρεῖον Ἀλεξάνδρῳ καὶ τοῖς μετὰ ταῦτα βασιλεύσασιν Ἀντιγόνῳ τε καὶ Σελεύκῳ τῷ Νικάτορι, ἐν ἅπασι δὲ τοῖς ῥηθεῖσιν εὐστοχη- κέναι δοκοῦσιν· ὑπὲρ ὧν ἡμεῖς[2] τὰ κατὰ μέρος
3 ἐν οἰκειοτέροις ἀναγράψομεν καιροῖς. προλέ- γουσι δὲ καὶ τοῖς ἰδιώταις τὰ μέλλοντα συμβαί- νειν οὕτως εὐστόχως ὥστε τοὺς πειραθέντας θαυμάζειν τὸ γινόμενον καὶ μεῖζον ἢ κατ' ἄνθρω- πον ἡγεῖσθαι.
4 Μετὰ δὲ τὸν ζῳδιακὸν κύκλον εἴκοσι καὶ

---

[1] ἴδιον ἕκαστον Vogel: ἕκαστον ἴδιον Vulgate, Bekker, Dindorf.

below, and again in like manner one of the stars
below the earth to those above, and this movement of
theirs is fixed and determined by means of an orbit
which is unchanging for ever. Twelve of these gods,
they say, hold chief authority, and to each of these
the Chaldaeans assign a month and one of the signs
of the zodiac, as they are called. And through the
midst of these signs, they say, both the sun and
moon and the five planets make their course, the
sun completing his cycle in a year and the moon
traversing her circuit in a month.

31. Each of the planets, according to them, has its
own particular course, and its velocities and periods
of time are subject to change and variation. These
stars it is which exert the greatest influence for both
good and evil upon the nativity of men; and it is
chiefly from the nature of these planets and the
study of them that they know what is in store for
mankind. And they have made predictions, they
say, not only to numerous other kings, but also to
Alexander, who defeated Darius, and to Antigonus
and Seleucus Nicator who afterwards became kings,
and in all their prophecies they are thought to have
hit the truth. But of these things we shall write in
detail on a more appropriate occasion.[1] Moreover,
they also foretell to men in private station what will
befall them, and with such accuracy that those who
have made trial of them marvel at the feat and believe
that it transcends the power of man.

Beyond the circle of the zodiac they designate

[1] For prophecies to Alexander cp. Book 17. 112, and to
Antigonus, Book 19. 55.

---

[2] ἡμεῖς Vogel: omitted by Vulgate, Bekker, Dindorf.

τέτταρας ἀφορίζουσιν ἀστέρας, ὧν τοὺς μὲν
ἡμίσεις ἐν τοῖς βορείοις μέρεσι, τοὺς δ' ἡμίσεις
ἐν τοῖς νοτίοις τετάχθαι φασί, καὶ τούτων τοὺς
μὲν ὁρωμένους τῶν ζώντων εἶναι καταριθμοῦσι,
τοὺς δ' ἀφανεῖς τοῖς τετελευτηκόσι προσωρίσθαι
νομίζουσιν, οὓς δικαστὰς τῶν ὅλων προσαγο-
5 ρεύουσιν. ὑπὸ πάντα δὲ τὰ προειρημένα τὴν
σελήνην φέρεσθαι λέγουσιν, ἔγγιστα μὲν τῆς γῆς
οὖσαν διὰ τὴν βαρύτητα, διαπορευομένην δ' ἐν
ἐλαχίστῳ χρόνῳ τὸν ἑαυτῆς δρόμον, οὐ διὰ τὴν
ὀξύτητα τῆς φορᾶς, ἀλλὰ διὰ τὴν βραχύτητα
6 τοῦ κύκλου. ὅτι δὲ τὸ φῶς ἀλλότριον ἔχει καὶ
διότι τὰς ἐκλείψεις ποιεῖται διὰ τὸ σκίασμα τῆς
γῆς παραπλήσια λέγουσι τοῖς Ἕλλησι. περὶ δὲ
τῆς κατὰ τὸν ἥλιον ἐκλείψεως ἀσθενεστάτας
ἀποδείξεις φέροντες οὐ τολμῶσι προλέγειν οὐδ'
ἀκριβῶς ὑπὲρ ταύτης περιγράφειν[1] τοὺς χρόνους.
7 περὶ δὲ τῆς γῆς ἰδιωτάτας ἀποφάσεις ποιοῦνται,
λέγοντες ὑπάρχειν αὐτὴν σκαφοειδῆ καὶ κοίλην,
καὶ πολλὰς καὶ πιθανὰς ἀποδείξεις εὐποροῦσι
περί τε ταύτης καὶ περὶ τῶν ἄλλων τῶν κατὰ
τὸν κόσμον· ὑπὲρ ὧν τὰ κατὰ μέρος διεξιέναι
τῆς ὑποκειμένης ἱστορίας ἀλλότριον εἶναι νομί-
8 ζομεν. τοῦτο μέντοι γε διαβεβαιώσαιτ' ἄν τις
προσηκόντως ὅτι Χαλδαῖοι μεγίστην ἕξιν ἐν
ἀστρολογίᾳ τῶν ἁπάντων ἀνθρώπων ἔχουσι καὶ
διότι πλείστην ἐπιμέλειαν ἐποιήσαντο ταύτης
9 τῆς θεωρίας. περὶ δὲ τοῦ πλήθους τῶν ἐτῶν, ἐν
οἷς φασι τὴν θεωρίαν τῶν κατὰ τὸν κόσμον πεποιῆσθαι τὸ σύστημα τῶν Χαλδαίων, οὐκ ἄν τις
ῥᾳδίως πιστεύσειεν· ἐτῶν γὰρ ἑπτὰ καὶ τεσσαρά-
κοντα μυριάδας καὶ τρεῖς ἐπὶ ταύταις χιλιάδας

twenty-four other stars, of which one half, they
say, are situated in the northern parts and one half
in the southern, and of these those which are
visible they assign to the world of the living, while
those which are invisible they regard as being
adjacent to the dead, and so they call them
" Judges of the Universe." And under all the
stars hitherto mentioned the moon, according to
them, takes her way, being nearest the earth because
of her weight and completing her course in a very
brief period of time, not by reason of her great
velocity, but because her orbit is so short. They also
agree with the Greeks in saying that her light is
reflected and that her eclipses are due to the shadow
of the earth. Regarding the eclipse of the sun,
however, they offer the weakest kind of explanation,
and do not presume to predict it or to define the times
of its occurrence with any precision. Again, in
connection with the earth they make assertions
entirely peculiar to themselves, saying that it is
shaped like a boat and hollow, and they offer many
plausible arguments about both the earth and all
other bodies in the firmament, a full discussion of
which we feel would be alien to our history. This
point, however, a man may fittingly maintain, that
the Chaldaeans have of all men the greatest grasp of
astrology, and that they have bestowed the greatest
diligence upon the study of it. But as to the number
of years which, according to their statements, the
order of the Chaldaeans has spent on the study of
the bodies of the universe, a man can scarcely
believe them; for they reckon that, down to

---

¹ περιγράφειν Wesseling : παραγράφειν.

εἰς τὴν Ἀλεξάνδρου διάβασιν γεγονέναι κατ-
αριθμοῦσιν, ἀφ' ὅτου τὸ παλαιὸν ἤρξαντο τῶν
ἄστρων τὰς παρατηρήσεις ποιεῖσθαι.

10 Καὶ περὶ μὲν Χαλδαίων ἀρκεσθησόμεθα τοῖς
ῥηθεῖσιν, ἵνα μὴ μακρότερον ἀποπλανώμεθα τῆς
οἰκείας ἱστορίας· περὶ δὲ τῆς Ἀσσυρίων βασιλείας ὡς ὑπὸ Μήδων κατελύθη προειρηκότες
ἐπάνιμεν ὅθεν ἐξέβημεν.

32. Ἐπεὶ δὲ διαφωνοῦσιν οἱ παλαιότατοι τῶν
συγγραφέων περὶ τῆς μεγίστης τῶν Μήδων
ἡγεμονίας, οἰκεῖον εἶναι διαλαμβάνομεν τοῖς
φιλαλήθως τὰς πράξεις ἱστορεῖν βουλομένοις τὴν
διαφορὰν τῶν ἱστοριογράφων παρ' ἄλληλα
2 θεῖναι. Ἡρόδοτος μὲν οὖν κατὰ Ξέρξην γεγονὼς
τοῖς χρόνοις φησὶν Ἀσσυρίους ἔτη πεντακόσια
πρότερον τῆς Ἀσίας ἄρξαντας ὑπὸ Μήδων κατα-
λυθῆναι, ἔπειτα βασιλέα μὲν μηδένα γενέσθαι
τὸν ἀμφισβητήσοντα τῶν ὅλων ἐπὶ πολλὰς
γενεάς, τὰς δὲ πόλεις καθ' ἑαυτὰς ταττομένας
διοικεῖσθαι δημοκρατικῶς· τὸ δὲ τελευταῖον
πολλῶν ἐτῶν διελθόντων αἱρεθῆναι βασιλέα
παρὰ τοῖς Μήδοις ἄνδρα δικαιοσύνῃ διάφορον,
3 ὄνομα Κυαξάρην. τοῦτον δὲ πρῶτον ἐπιχειρῆσαι
προσάγεσθαι τοὺς πλησιοχώρους, καὶ τοῖς Μήδοις
ἀρχηγὸν γενέσθαι τῆς τῶν ὅλων ἡγεμονίας·
ἔπειτα τοὺς ἐκγόνους ἀεὶ προσκατακτωμένους
πολλὴν τῆς ὁμόρου χώρας αὐξῆσαι τὴν βασιλείαν μέχρι Ἀστυάγους τοῦ καταπολεμηθέντος

----

[1] King of Persia, 486–464 B.C.; Herodotus was born in the
decade 490–80 B.C. The passage is Herodotus 1. 95 ff., where,
however, the years are given as five hundred and twenty.

Alexander's crossing over into Asia, it has been four hundred and seventy-three thousand years, since they began in early times to make their observations of the stars. 334 B.C.

So far as the Chaldaeans are concerned we shall be satisfied with what has been said, that we may not wander too far from the matter proper to our history; and now that we have given an account of the destruction of the kingdom of the Assyrians by the Medes we shall return to the point at which we digressed.

32. Since the earliest writers of history are at variance concerning the mighty empire of the Medes, we feel that it is incumbent upon those who would write the history of events with a love for truth to set forth side by side the different accounts of the historians. Now Herodotus, who lived in the time of Xerxes,[1] gives this account: After the Assyrians had ruled Asia for five hundred years they were conquered by the Medes, and thereafter no king arose for many generations to lay claim to supreme power, but the city-states, enjoying a regimen of their own, were administered in a democratic fashion; finally, however, after many years a man distinguished for his justice, named Cyaxares,[2] was chosen king among the Medes. He was the first to try to attach to himself the neighbouring peoples and became for the Medes the founder of their universal empire; and after him his descendants extended the kingdom by continually adding a great deal of the adjoining country, until the reign of Astyages who was conquered by Cyrus and 612 B.C.

[2] Herodotus mentions three kings, Deioces, Phraortes, and Cyaxares, before Astyages. The Cyaxares mentioned here by Diodorus is really the Deioces of Herodotus 1. 96 ff., but Diodorus, in Book 8. 16, mentions a Deioces, " the king of the Medes."

ὑπὸ Κύρου καὶ Περσῶν. περὶ ὧν νῦν ἡμεῖς τὰ
κεφάλαια προειρηκότες τὰ κατὰ μέρος ὕστερον
ἀκριβῶς ἀναγράψομεν, ἐπειδὰν ἐπὶ τοὺς οἰκείους
χρόνους ἐπιβάλωμεν· κατὰ γὰρ τὸ δεύτερον ἔτος
τῆς ἑπτακαιδεκάτης Ὀλυμπιάδος ᾑρέθη βασιλεὺς
ὑπὸ Μήδων Κυαξάρης καθ' Ἡρόδοτον.

4 Κτησίας δὲ ὁ Κνίδιος τοῖς μὲν χρόνοις ὑπῆρξε
κατὰ τὴν Κύρου στρατείαν ἐπὶ Ἀρταξέρξην τὸν
ἀδελφόν, γενόμενος δ' αἰχμάλωτος, καὶ διὰ τὴν
ἰατρικὴν ἐπιστήμην ἀναληφθεὶς ὑπὸ τοῦ βασιλέως, ἑπτακαίδεκα ἔτη διετέλεσε τιμώμενος ὑπ'
αὐτοῦ. οὗτος οὖν φησιν ἐκ τῶν βασιλικῶν
διφθερῶν, ἐν αἷς οἱ Πέρσαι τὰς παλαιὰς πράξεις
κατά τινα νόμον εἶχον συντεταγμένας, πολυπραγ-
μονῆσαι τὰ καθ' ἕκαστον καὶ συνταξάμενος[1] τὴν
5 ἱστορίαν εἰς τοὺς Ἕλληνας ἐξενεγκεῖν. φησὶν
οὖν μετὰ τὴν κατάλυσιν τῆς Ἀσσυρίων ἡγεμονίας
Μήδους προστῆναι τῆς Ἀσίας Ἀρβάκου βασιλεύοντος τοῦ Σαρδαναπάλλον καταπολεμήσαντος,
6 καθότι προείρηται. τούτου δ' ἄρξαντος ἔτη δυσὶ
λείποντα τῶν τριάκοντα διαδέξασθαι τὴν βασιλείαν τὸν υἱὸν Μαυδάκην, ὃν ἄρξαι τῆς Ἀσίας
ἔτη πεντήκοντα. μετὰ δὲ τοῦτον τριάκοντα μὲν
ἔτη βασιλεῦσαι Σώσαρμον, πεντήκοντα δὲ
Ἀρτύκαν, δύο δὲ πρὸς τοῖς εἴκοσι τὸν προσαγορευόμενον Ἀρβιάνην, τετταράκοντα δὲ Ἀρ-
ταῖον.

33. Ἐπὶ δὲ τούτου συστῆναι μέγαν πόλεμον

---

[1] συνταξάμενος Gemistus : συνταξάμενον.

---

[1] Herodotus puts the accession of Deioces (the Cyaxares of
Diodorus) in 699 B.C. (cp. How and Wells, *A Commentary on
Herodotus,* 1. pp. 383 ff.), if the defeat of Astyages by Cyrus

the Persians. We have for the present given only the 549 B.C.
most important of these events in summary and shall
later give a detailed account of them one by one
when we come to the periods in which they fall; for
it was in the second year of the Seventeenth Olympiad,
according to Herodotus, that Cyaxares was chosen 711–10
king by the Medes.[1] B.C.

Ctesias of Cnidus, on the other hand, lived during
the time when Cyrus [2] made his expedition against 401 B.C.
Artaxerxes his brother, and having been made
prisoner and then retained by Artaxerxes because of
his medical knowledge, he enjoyed a position of
honour with him for seventeen years.[3] Now Ctesias
says that from the royal records, in which the Persians in accordance with a certain law of theirs kept
an account of their ancient affairs, he carefully investigated the facts about each king, and when he
had composed his history he published it to the
Greeks. This, then, is his account : After the destruction of the Assyrian Empire the Medes were the
chief power in Asia under their king Arbaces, who
conquered Sardanapallus, as has been told before.[4]
And when he had reigned twenty-eight years his
son Maudaces succeeded to the throne and reigned
over Asia fifty years. After him Sosarmus ruled for
thirty years, Artycas for fifty, the king known as
Arbianes for twenty-two, and Artaeus for forty years.

33. During the reign of Artaeus a great war broke

occurred in 549 B.C. (cp. *The Cambridge Ancient History*, 4.
p. 7) and not, as formerly held, in 550.

[2] Cyrus the Younger, the story of whose struggle with his
brother for the throne is told in the *Anabasis* of Xenophon.

[3] According to Plutarch (*Artaxerxes*, 11 ff.), Ctesias was
already in the king's retinue at the time.

[4] Cp. chaps. 23 ff.

τοῖς Μήδοις πρὸς Καδουσίους διὰ τοιαύτας
αἰτίας. Παρσώνδην τὸν Πέρσην, θαυμαζόμενον ἐπ'
ἀνδρείᾳ καὶ συνέσει καὶ ταῖς ἄλλαις ἀρεταῖς, φίλον
τε ὑπάρξαι τῷ βασιλεῖ καὶ μέγιστον ἰσχῦσαι τῶν
2 μετεχόντων τοῦ βασιλικοῦ συνεδρίου. τοῦτον δ'
ὑπὸ τοῦ βασιλέως ἔν τινι κρίσει λυπηθέντα φυγεῖν
μετὰ πεζῶν μὲν τρισχιλίων, ἱππέων δὲ χιλίων εἰς
Καδουσίους, παρ' οἷς ἦν ἐκδεδομένος τὴν ἰδίαν
ἀδελφὴν τῷ μάλιστα δυναστεύοντι κατὰ τούτους
3 τοὺς τόπους. γενόμενον δ' ἀποστάτην καὶ πεί-
σαντα τὸ σύμπαν ἔθνος ἀντέχεσθαι τῆς ἐλευθερίας, αἱρεθῆναι στρατηγὸν διὰ τὴν ἀνδρείαν.
ἔπειτα πυνθανόμενον ἀθροιζομένην ἐπ' αὐτὸν
μεγάλην δύναμιν, καθοπλίσαι τοὺς Καδουσίους
πανδημεί, καὶ καταστρατοπεδεῦσαι πρὸς ταῖς εἰς
τὴν χώραν εἰσβολαῖς ἔχοντα τοὺς σύμπαντας
4 οὐκ ἐλάττους εἴκοσι μυριάδων. τοῦ δὲ βασιλέως
Ἀρταίου στρατεύσαντος ἐπ' αὐτὸν μυριάσιν
ὀγδοήκοντα μάχῃ κρατῆσαι καὶ πλείους μὲν τῶν
πεντακισμυρίων ἀνελεῖν, τὴν δ' ἄλλην δύναμιν
ἐκβαλεῖν ἐκ τῆς Καδουσίων χώρας. διὸ καὶ
παρὰ τοῖς ἐγχωρίοις θαυμαζόμενον αἱρεθῆναί τε
βασιλέα καὶ τὴν Μηδίαν συνεχῶς λεηλατεῖν καὶ
5 πάντα τόπον καταφθείρειν. μεγάλης δὲ δόξης
τυχόντα, καὶ γήρᾳ μέλλοντα καταστρέφειν τὸν
βίον, ἀρὰν θέσθαι παραστησάμενον τὸν διαδεχό-
μενον τὴν ἀρχήν, ὅπως μηδέποτε διαλύσωνται
τὴν ἔχθραν Καδούσιοι πρὸς Μήδους· εἰ δὲ σύν-
θοιντο ὁμολογίας, ἐξώλεις γενέσθαι τούς τε ἀπὸ
6 τοῦ γένους αὐτοῦ καὶ Καδουσίους ἅπαντας. διὰ
δὴ ταύτας τὰς αἰτίας ἀεὶ πολεμικῶς ἐσχηκέναι
Καδουσίους πρὸς Μήδους, καὶ μηδέποτε τοῖς

out between the Medes and the Cadusii, for the following reasons. Parsondes, a Persian, a man renowned for his valour and intelligence and every other virtue, was both a friend of the king's and the most influential of the members of the royal council. Feeling himself aggrieved by the king in a certain decision, he fled with three thousand foot-soldiers and a thousand horsemen to the Cadusii, to one of whom, the most influential man in those parts, he had given his sister in marriage. And now that he had become a rebel, he persuaded the entire people to vindicate their freedom and was chosen general because of his valour. Then, learning that a great force was being gathered against him, he armed the whole nation of the Cadusii and pitched his camp before the passes leading into the country, having a force of no less than two hundred thousand men all told. And although the king Artaeus advanced against him with eight hundred thousand soldiers, Parsondes defeated him in battle and slew more than fifty thousand of his followers, and drove the rest of the army out of the country of the Cadusii. And for this exploit he was so admired by the people of the land that he was chosen king, and he plundered Media without ceasing and laid waste every district of the country. And after he had attained great fame and was about to die of old age, he called to his side his successor to the throne and required of him an oath that the Cadusii should never put an end to their enmity towards the Medes, adding that, if peace were ever made with them, it meant the destruction of his line and of the whole race of the Cadusii. These, then, were the reasons why the Cadusii were always inveterate enemies of the Medes, and had never been

τούτων βασιλεῦσιν ὑπηκόους γεγονέναι, μέχρι
οὗ Κῦρος εἰς Πέρσας μετέστησε τὴν ἡγεμονίαν.

34. Τῶν δὲ Μήδων βασιλεῦσαι μετὰ τὴν
Ἀρταίου τελευτὴν Ἀρτύνην μὲν ἔτη δύο πρὸς
τοῖς εἴκοσι, Ἀστιβάραν δὲ τετταράκοντα. ἐπὶ
δὲ τούτου Πάρθους ἀποστάντας Μήδων Σάκαις
2 τήν τε χώραν καὶ τὴν πόλιν ἐγχειρίσαι· διόπερ
συστάντος πολέμου τοῖς Σάκαις πρὸς Μήδους
ἐπ' ἔτη πλείω γενέσθαι τε μάχας οὐκ ὀλίγας
καὶ συχνῶν παρ' ἀμφοτέροις ἀναιρεθέντων τὸ
τελευταῖον εἰρήνην αὐτοὺς ἐπὶ τοῖσδε συνθέσθαι,
Πάρθους μὲν ὑπὸ Μήδους τετάχθαι, τῶν δὲ
προϋπαρχόντων ἑκατέρους κυριεύσαντας φίλους
εἶναι καὶ συμμάχους ἀλλήλοις εἰς τὸν ἅπαντα
χρόνον.

3 Βασιλεῦσαι δὲ τότε τῶν Σακῶν γυναῖκα τὰ
κατὰ πόλεμον ἐζηλωκυῖαν καὶ τόλμῃ τε καὶ
πράξει πολὺ διαφέρουσαν τῶν ἐν Σάκαις γυναικῶν, ὄνομα Ζαρίναν. καθόλου μὲν οὖν τὸ ἔθνος
τοῦτο γυναῖκας ἀλκίμους ἔχειν καὶ κοινωνούσας
τοῖς ἀνδράσι τῶν ἐν τοῖς πολέμοις κινδύνων,
ταύτην δὲ λέγεται τῷ τε κάλλει γενέσθαι πασῶν
ἐκπρεπεστάτην[1] καὶ ταῖς ἐπιβολαῖς καὶ τοῖς
4 κατὰ μέρος ἐγχειρήμασι θαυμαστήν. τῶν μὲν
γὰρ πλησιοχώρων βαρβάρων τοὺς ἐπηρμένους
τῷ θράσει καὶ καταδουλουμένους τὸ ἔθνος τῶν
Σακῶν καταπολεμῆσαι, τῆς δὲ χώρας πολλὴν
ἐξημερῶσαι, καὶ πόλεις οὐκ ὀλίγας κτίσαι, καὶ
τὸ σύνολον εὐδαιμονέστερον τὸν βίον τῶν ὁμο-
5 εθνῶν ποιῆσαι. διὸ καὶ τοὺς ἐγχωρίους μετὰ

---

[1] ἐκπρεπεστάτην D, Vogel : εὐπρεπεστάτην Vulgate, Bekker, Dindorf.

subjected to the Median kings up to the time when
Cyrus transferred the Empire of the Medes to the
Persians.

34. After the death of Artaeus, Ctesias continues,
Artynes ruled over the Medes for twenty-two years,
and Astibaras for forty. During the reign of the
latter the Parthians revolted from the Medes and
entrusted both their country and their city to the
hands of the Sacae. This led to a war between the
Sacae and the Medes, which lasted many years, and
after no small number of battles and the loss of many
lives on both sides, they finally agreed to peace on
the following terms, that the Parthians should be
subject to the Medes, but that both peoples should
retain their former possessions and be friends and
allies for ever.

At that time the Sacae were ruled by a woman
named Zarina, who was devoted to warfare and was in
daring and efficiency by far the foremost of the women
of the Sacae. Now this people, in general, have
courageous women who share with their husbands
the dangers of war, but she, it is said, was the most
conspicuous of them all for her beauty and remarkable as well in respect to both her designs and whatever she undertook. For she subdued such of the
neighbouring barbarian peoples as had become proud
because of their boldness and were trying to enslave
the people of the Sacae, and into much of her own
realm she introduced civilized life, founded not a few
cities, and, in a word, made the life of her people
happier. Consequently her countrymen after her

DIODORUS OF SICILY

τὴν τελευτὴν αὐτῆς χάριν ἀποδιδόντας τῶν
εὐεργεσιῶν καὶ τῆς ἀρετῆς μνημονεύοντας τάφον
οἰκοδομῆσαι πολὺ τῶν ὄντων παρ' αὐτοῖς ὑπερ-
έχοντα· ὑποστησαμένους γὰρ πυραμίδα τρίγωνον
τριῶν μὲν σταδίων ἑκάστην πλευρὰν αὐτῆς κατασκευάσαι τὸ μῆκος, τὸ δ' ὕψος σταδιαῖον, εἰς ὀξὺ
συνηγμένης τῆς κορυφῆς· ἐπιστῆσαι δὲ τῷ τάφῳ
καὶ χρυσῆν εἰκόνα κολοττικήν, καὶ τιμὰς ἡρωικὰς
ἀπονεῖμαι, καὶ τἆλλα πάντα μεγαλοπρεπέστερα
ποιεῖν τῶν τοῖς προγόνοις αὐτῆς συγχωρηθέντων.
6 Ἀστιβάρα δὲ τοῦ βασιλέως τῶν Μήδων ἐν
Ἐκβατάνοις γήρᾳ τελευτήσαντος τὴν ἀρχὴν
Ἀσπάνδαν τὸν υἱὸν διαδέξασθαι, τὸν ὑπὸ τῶν
Ἑλλήνων Ἀστυάγην καλούμενον. τούτου δ'
ὑπὸ Κύρου τοῦ Πέρσου καταπολεμηθέντος μετα-
πεσεῖν τὴν βασιλείαν εἰς Πέρσας, περὶ ὧν ἡμεῖς
τὰ κατὰ μέρος ἐν τοῖς ἰδίοις χρόνοις ἀκριβῶς
ἀναγράψομεν.
7 Περὶ μὲν οὖν τῆς Ἀσσυρίων καὶ Μήδων βασιλείας καὶ τῆς τῶν συγγραφέων διαφωνίας ἱκανῶς
εἰρῆσθαι νομίζομεν· περὶ δὲ τῆς Ἰνδικῆς καὶ τῶν
ἐν αὐτῇ μυθολογουμένων ἐν μέρει διέξιμεν.

death, in gratitude for her benefactions and in remembrance of her virtues, built her a tomb which was far the largest of any in their land; for they erected a triangular pyramid, making the length of each side three stades and the height one stade, and bringing it to a point at the top; and on the tomb they also placed a colossal gilded statue of her and accorded her the honours belonging to heroes, and all the other honours they bestowed upon her were more magnificent than those which had fallen to the lot of her ancestors.

When, Ctesias continues, Astibaras, the king of the Medes, died of old age in Ecbatana, his son Aspandas, whom the Greeks call Astyages, succeeded to the throne. And when he had been defeated by Cyrus the Persian, the kingdom passed to the Persians. Of them we shall give a detailed and exact account at the proper time.[1]

Concerning the kingdoms of the Assyrians and of the Medes, and concerning the disagreement in the accounts of the historians, we consider that enough has been said; now we shall discuss India and then, in turn, recount the legends of that land.

---

[1] This was in the Ninth Book.

A PARTIAL INDEX OF PROPER NAMES [1]

[1] A complete Index will appear in the last volume.

INDEX

INDEX

INDEX

MAPS

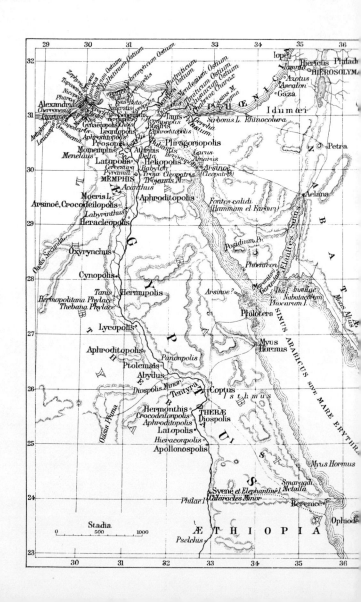

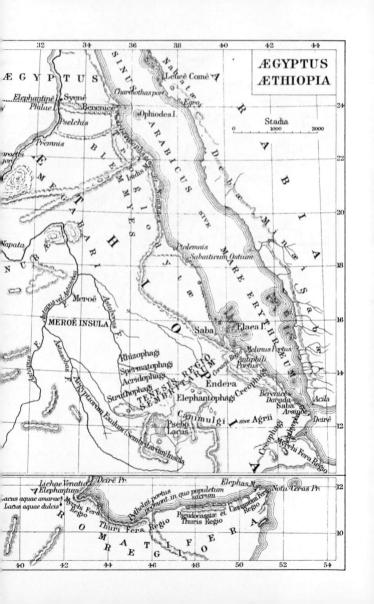

ÆGYPTUS
ÆTHIOPIA

Stadia
0   1000   2000

ÆGYPTUS

SINUS

Leucê Comê

Charmothas port.

Elephantinê Syenê
Philae
Berenicê
Pselchis   Ophiodes I.

Premnis

ARABICUS

AEGABARI

BLEMMYES

Napata

F. Meroê

MEROË INSULA

Astaboras F.

Astasobas F.

Astapus vel Astusapes

Astusabas F.

NUB

Rhizophagi
Spermatophagi
Acridophagi
Struthophagi

Saba   Elaea I.

MARE ERYTHRAEUM

Ptolemais
Sabaticum Ostium

sive

REGIO

Coracii Bello

Melinus Portus
Antiphili
Portius

Endera   Creophagi

Berenicê
Darada   Saba
Arsinoe

Acila

Deirê

Elephantophagi

TENESIS
SEMBRITARUM

Psebo
Lacus

Colimulgi sive Agrii

Sembritarum Insula

Creophagi

Myrrha Fera Regio

A

Lichae Venatio
Elephantum
Lacus aquae amarae
Lacus aquae dulcis

Deirê Pr.

Myrrha Fera
Regio

Thuri Fera Regio

Psetholai portus
promont. in quo populetum
sacrum

Pseudocassiae et
Thuris Regio

Elephas M.

Tanganum Fera
Regio

Notu Ceras Pr.

F

AROMATIFERA

ASIA

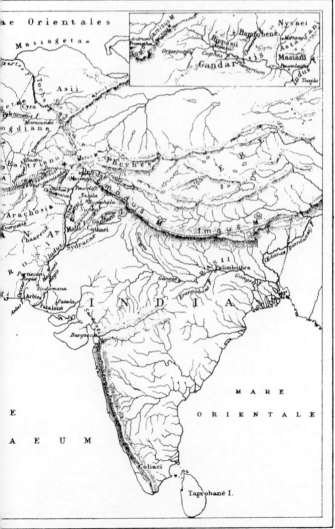

THE LOEB CLASSICAL LIBRARY

Latin Authors

AMMIANUS MARCELLINUS. J. C. Rolfe. 3 Vols.

APULEIUS: THE GOLDEN ASS (METAMORPHOSES). W. Adlington (1566). Revised by S. Gaselee.

ST. AUGUSTINE: CITY OF GOD. 7 Vols. Vol. I. G. E. McCracken. Vols. II and VII. W. M. Green. Vol. III. D. Wiesen. Vol. IV. P. Levine. Vol. V. E. M. Sanford and W. M. Green. Vol. VI. W. C. Greene.

ST. AUGUSTINE, CONFESSIONS. W. Watts (1631). 2 Vols.

ST. AUGUSTINE, SELECT LETTERS. J. H. Baxter.

AUSONIUS. H. G. Evelyn White. 2 Vols.

BEDE. J. E. King. 2 Vols.

BOETHIUS: TRACTS and DE CONSOLATIONE PHILOSOPHIAE. Rev. H. F. Stewart and E. K. Rand. Revised by S. J. Tester.

CAESAR: ALEXANDRIAN, AFRICAN and SPANISH WARS. A. G. Way.

CAESAR: CIVIL WARS. A. G. Peskett.

CAESAR: GALLIC WAR. H. J. Edwards.

CATO: DE RE RUSTICA. VARRO: DE RE RUSTICA. H. B. Ash and W. D. Hooper.

CATULLUS. F. W. Cornish. TIBULLUS. J. B. Postgate. PERVIGILIUM VENERIS. J. W. Mackail. Revised by G. P. Goold.

CELSUS: DE MEDICINA. W. G. Spencer. 3 Vols.

CICERO: BRUTUS and ORATOR. G. L. Hendrickson and H. M. Hubbell.

[CICERO]: AD HERENNIUM. H. Caplan.

CICERO: DE ORATORE, etc. 2 Vols. Vol. I. DE ORATORE, Books I and II. E. W. Sutton and H. Rackham. Vol. II. DE ORATORE, Book III. DE FATO; PARADOXA STOICORUM; DE PARTITIONE ORATORIA. H. Rackham.

CICERO: DE FINIBUS. H. Rackham.

CICERO: DE INVENTIONE, etc. H. M. Hubbell.

CICERO: DE NATURA DEORUM and ACADEMICA. H. Rackham.

CICERO: DE OFFICIIS. Walter Miller.

CICERO: DE RE PUBLICA and DE LEGIBUS. Clinton W. Keyes.

NEPOS, CORNELIUS. J. C. Rolfe.

OVID: THE ART OF LOVE and OTHER POEMS. J. H. Mozley. Revised by G. P. Goold.

OVID: FASTI. Sir James G. Frazer. Revised by G. P. Goold.

OVID: HEROIDES and AMORES. Grant Showerman. Revised by G. P. Goold.

OVID: METAMORPHOSES. F. J. Miller. 2 Vols. Revised by G. P. Goold.

OVID: TRISTIA and EX PONTO. A. L. Wheeler. Revised by G. P. Goold.

PERSIUS. Cf. JUVENAL.

PERVIGILIUM VENERIS. Cf. CATULLUS.

PETRONIUS. M. Heseltine. SENECA: APOCOLOCYNTOSIS. W. H. D. Rouse. Revised by E. H. Warmington.

PHAEDRUS and BABRIUS (Greek). B. E. Perry.

PLAUTUS. Paul Nixon. 5 Vols.

PLINY: LETTERS, PANEGYRICUS. Betty Radice. 2 Vols.

PLINY: NATURAL HISTORY. 10 Vols. Vols. I.–V. and IX. H. Rackham. VI.–VIII. W. H. S. Jones. X. D. E. Eichholz.

PROPERTIUS. H. E. Butler.

PRUDENTIUS. H. J. Thomson. 2 Vols.

QUINTILIAN. H. E. Butler. 4 Vols.

REMAINS OF OLD LATIN. E. H. Warmington. 4 Vols. Vol. I. (ENNIUS AND CAECILIUS) Vol. II. (LIVIUS, NAEVIUS PACUVIUS, ACCIUS) Vol. III. (LUCILIUS and LAWS OF XII TABLES) Vol. IV. (ARCHAIC INSCRIPTIONS).

RES GESTAE DIVI AUGUSTI. Cf. VELLEIUS PATERCULUS.

SALLUST. J. C. Rolfe.

SCRIPTORES HISTORIAE AUGUSTAE. D. Magie. 3 Vols.

SENECA, THE ELDER: CONTROVERSIAE, SUASORIAE. M. Winterbottom. 2 Vols.

SENECA: APOCOLOCYNTOSIS. Cf. PETRONIUS.

SENECA: EPISTULAE MORALES. R. M. Gummere. 3 Vols.

SENECA: MORAL ESSAYS. J. W. Basore. 3 Vols.

SENECA: TRAGEDIES. F. J. Miller. 2 Vols.

SENECA: NATURALES QUAESTIONES. T. H. Corcoran. 2 VOLS.

SIDONIUS: POEMS and LETTERS. W. B. Anderson. 2 Vols.

SILIUS ITALICUS. J. D. Duff. 2 Vols.

STATIUS. J. H. Mozley. 2 Vols.

SUETONIUS. J. C. Rolfe. 2 Vols.

TACITUS: DIALOGUS. Sir Wm. Peterson. AGRICOLA and GERMANIA. Maurice Hutton. Revised by M. Winterbottom, R. M. Ogilvie, E. H. Warmington.

TACITUS: HISTORIES and ANNALS. C. H. Moore and J. Jackson. 4 Vols.

TERENCE. John Sargeaunt. 2 Vols.

TERTULLIAN: APOLOGIA and DE SPECTACULIS. T. R. Glover. MINUCIUS FELIX. G. H. Rendall.

TIBULLUS. Cf. CATULLUS.
VALERIUS FLACCUS. J. H. Mozley.
VARRO: DE LINGUA LATINA. R. G. Kent. 2 Vols.
VELLEIUS PATERCULUS and RES GESTAE DIVI AUGUSTI. F. W. SHIPLEY.
VIRGIL. H. R. Fairclough. 2 Vols.
VITRUVIUS: DE ARCHITECTURA. F. Granger. 2 Vols.

Greek Authors

ACHILLES TATIUS. S. Gaselee.
AELIAN: ON THE NATURE OF ANIMALS. A. F. Scholfield. 3 Vols.
AENEAS TACTICUS. ASCLEPIODOTUS and ONASANDER. The Illinois Greek
    Club.
AESCHINES. C. D. Adams.
AESCHYLUS. H. Weir Smyth. 2 Vols.
ALCIPHRON, AELIAN, PHILOSTRATUS: LETTERS. A. R. Benner and F. H.
    Fobes.
ANDOCIDES, ANTIPHON. Cf. MINOR ATTIC ORATORS Vol. I.
APOLLODORUS. Sir James G. Frazer. 2 Vols.
APOLLONIUS RHODIUS. R. C. Seaton.
APOSTOLIC FATHERS. Kirsopp Lake. 2 Vols.
APPIAN: ROMAN HISTORY. Horace White. 4 Vols.
ARATUS. Cf. CALLIMACHUS.
ARISTIDES: ORATIONS. C. A. Behr.
ARISTOPHANES. Benjamin Bickley Rogers. 3 Vols. Verse trans.
ARISTOTLE: ART OF RHETORIC. J. H. Freese.
ARISTOTLE: ATHENIAN CONSTITUTION, EUDEMIAN ETHICS, VICES AND
    VIRTUES. H. Rackham.
ARISTOTLE: GENERATION OF ANIMALS. A. L. Peck.
ARISTOTLE: HISTORIA ANIMALIUM. A. L. Peck. Vols. I.–II.
ARISTOTLE: METAPHYSICS. H. Tredennick. 2 Vols.
ARISTOTLE: METEOROLOGICA. H. D. P. Lee.
ARISTOTLE: MINOR WORKS. W. S. Hett. On Colours, On Things
    Heard, On Physiognomies, On Plants, On Marvellous Things
    Heard, Mechanical Problems, On Indivisible Lines, On Situations
    and Names of Winds, On Melissus, Xenophanes, and Gorgias.
ARISTOTLE: NICOMACHEAN ETHICS. H. Rackham.
ARISTOTLE: OECONOMICA and MAGNA MORALIA. G. C. Armstrong (with
    METAPHYSICS, Vol. II).
ARISTOTLE: ON THE HEAVENS. W. K. C. Guthrie.
ARISTOTLE: ON THE SOUL, PARVA NATURALIA, ON BREATH. W. S. Hett.
ARISTOTLE: CATEGORIES, ON INTERPRETATION, PRIOR ANALYTICS. H. P.
    Cooke and H. Tredennick.

ARISTOTLE: POSTERIOR ANALYTICS, TOPICS. H. Tredennick and E. S. Forster.

ARISTOTLE: ON SOPHISTICAL REFUTATIONS.
On Coming-to-be and Passing-Away, On the Cosmos. E. S. Forster and D. J. Furley.

ARISTOTLE: PARTS OF ANIMALS. A. L. Peck; MOTION AND PROGRESSION OF ANIMALS. E. S. Forster.

ARISTOTLE: PHYSICS. Rev. P. Wicksteed and F. M. Cornford. 2 Vols.

ARISTOTLE: POETICS and LONGINUS. W. Hamilton Fyfe; DEMETRIUS ON STYLE. W. Rhys Roberts.

ARISTOTLE: POLITICS. H. Rackham.

ARISTOTLE: PROBLEMS. W. S. Hett. 2 Vols.

ARISTOTLE: RHETORICA AD ALEXANDRUM (with PROBLEMS. Vol. II). H. Rackham.

ARRIAN: HISTORY OF ALEXANDER and INDICA. Rev. E. Iliffe Robson. 2 Vols. New version P. Brunt.

ATHENAEUS: DEIPNOSOPHISTAE. C. B. Gulick. 7 Vols.

BABRIUS and PHAEDRUS (Latin). B. E. Perry.

ST. BASIL: LETTERS. R. J. Deferrari. 4 Vols.

CALLIMACHUS: FRAGMENTS. C. A. Trypanis. MUSAEUS: HERO AND LEANDER. T. Gelzer and C. Whitman.

CALLIMACHUS, Hymns and Epigrams and LYCOPHRON. A. W. Mair; ARATUS. G. R. Mair.

CLEMENT OF ALEXANDRIA. Rev. G. W. Butterworth.

COLLUTHUS. Cf. OPPIAN.

DAPHNIS AND CHLOE. Thornley's translation revised by J. M. Edmonds: and PARTHENIUS. S. Gaselee.

DEMOSTHENES I.: OLYNTHIACS, PHILIPPICS and MINOR ORATIONS I.–XVII. and XX. J. H. Vince.

DEMOSTHENES II.: DE CORONA and DE FALSA LEGATIONE. C. A. Vince and J. H. Vince.

DEMOSTHENES III.: MEIDIAS, ANDROTION, ARISTOCRATES, TIMOCRATES and ARISTOGEITON I. and II. J. H. Vince.

DEMOSTHENES IV.–VI.: PRIVATE ORATIONS and IN NEAERAM. A. T. Murray.

DEMOSTHENES VII.: FUNERAL SPEECH, EROTIC ESSAY, EXORDIA and LETTERS. N. W. and N. J. DeWitt.

DIO CASSIUS: ROMAN HISTORY. E. Cary. 9 Vols.

DIO CHRYSOSTOM. J. W. Cohoon and H. Lamar Crosby. 5 Vols.

DIODORUS SICULUS. 12 Vols. Vols. I.–VI. C. H. Oldfather. Vol. VII. C. L. Sherman. Vol. VIII. C. B. Welles. Vols. IX. and X. R. M. Geer. Vol. XI. F. Walton. Vol. XII. F. Walton. General Index. R. M. Geer.

DIOGENES LAERTIUS. R. D. Hicks. 2 Vols. New Introduction by H. S. Long.

DIONYSIUS OF HALICARNASSUS: ROMAN ANTIQUITIES. Spelman's translation revised by E. Cary. 7 Vols.

DIONYSIUS OF HALICARNASSUS: CRITICAL ESSAYS. S. Usher. 2 Vols.
EPICTETUS. W. A. Oldfather. 2 Vols.
EURIPIDES. A. S. Way. 4 Vols. Verse trans.
EUSEBIUS: ECCLESIASTICAL HISTORY. Kirsopp Lake and J. E. L. Oulton. 2 Vols.
GALEN: ON THE NATURAL FACULTIES. A. J. Brock.
GREEK ANTHOLOGY. W. R. Paton. 5 Vols.
GREEK BUCOLIC POETS (THEOCRITUS, BION, MOSCHUS). J. M. Edmonds.
GREEK ELEGY AND IAMBUS with the ANACREONTEA. J. M. Edmonds. 2 Vols.
GREEK LYRIC. D. A. Campbell. 4 Vols. Vols. I. and II.
GREEK MATHEMATICAL WORKS. Ivor Thomas. 2 Vols.
HERODAS. Cf. THEOPHRASTUS: CHARACTERS.
HERODIAN. C. R. Whittaker. 2 Vols.
HERODOTUS. A. D. Godley. 4 Vols.
HESIOD AND THE HOMERIC HYMNS. H. G. Evelyn White.
HIPPOCRATES and the FRAGMENTS OF HERACLEITUS. W. H. S. Jones and E. T. Withington. 7 Vols. Vols. I.–VI.
HOMER: ILIAD. A. T. Murray. 2 Vols.
HOMER: ODYSSEY. A. T. Murray. 2 Vols.
ISAEUS. E. W. Forster.
ISOCRATES. George Norlin and LaRue Van Hook. 3 Vols.
[ST. JOHN DAMASCENE]: BARLAAM AND IOASAPH. Rev. G. R. Woodward, Harold Mattingly and D. M. Lang.
JOSEPHUS. 10 Vols. Vols. I.–IV. H. Thackeray. Vol. V. H. Thackeray and R. Marcus. Vols. VI.–VII. R. Marcus. Vol. VIII. R. Marcus and Allen Wikgren. Vols. IX.–X. L. H. Feldman.
JULIAN. Wilmer Cave Wright. 3 Vols.
LIBANIUS. A. F. Norman. 2 Vols..
LUCIAN. 8 Vols. Vols. I.–V. A. M. Harmon. Vol. VI. K. Kilburn. Vols. VII.–VIII. M. D. Macleod.
LYCOPHRON. Cf. CALLIMACHUS.
LYRA GRAECA, III. J. M. Edmonds. (Vols. I.and II. have been replaced by GREEK LYRIC I. and II.)
LYSIAS. W. R. M. Lamb.
MANETHO. W. G. Waddell.
MARCUS AURELIUS. C. R. Haines.
MENANDER. W. G. Arnott. 3 Vols. Vol. I.
MINOR ATTIC ORATORS (ANTIPHON, ANDOCIDES, LYCURGUS, DEMADES, DINARCHUS, HYPERIDES). K. J. Maidment and J. O. Burtt. 2 Vols.
MUSAEUS: HERO AND LEANDER. Cf. CALLIMACHUS.
NONNOS: DIONYSIACA. W. H. D. Rouse. 3 Vols.
OPPIAN, COLLUTHUS, TRYPHIODORUS. A. W. Mair.
PAPYRI. NON-LITERARY SELECTIONS. A. S. Hunt and C. C. Edgar. 2 Vols. LITERARY SELECTIONS (Poetry). D. L. Page.

PARTHENIUS. Cf. DAPHNIS AND CHLOE.

PAUSANIAS: DESCRIPTION OF GREECE. W. H. S. Jones. 4 Vols. and Companion Vol. arranged by R. E. Wycherley.

PHILO. 10 Vols. Vols. I.–V. F. H. Colson and Rev. G. H. Whitaker. Vols. VI.–IX. F. H. Colson. Vol. X. F. H. Colson and the Rev. J. W. Earp.

PHILO: two supplementary Vols. (*Translation only*.) Ralph Marcus.

PHILOSTRATUS: THE LIFE OF APOLLONIUS OF TYANA. F. C. Conybeare. 2 Vols.

PHILOSTRATUS: IMAGINES; CALLISTRATUS: DESCRIPTIONS. A. Fairbanks.

PHILOSTRATUS and EUNAPIUS: LIVES OF THE SOPHISTS. Wilmer Cave Wright.

PINDAR. Sir J. E. Sandys.

PLATO: CHARMIDES, ALCIBIADES, HIPPARCHUS, THE LOVERS, THEAGES, MINOS and EPINOMIS. W. R. M. Lamb.

PLATO: CRATYLUS, PARMENIDES, GREATER HIPPIAS, LESSER HIPPIAS. H. N. Fowler.

PLATO: EUTHYPHRO, APOLOGY, CRITO, PHAEDO, PHAEDRUS. H. N. Fowler.

PLATO: LACHES, PROTAGORAS, MENO, EUTHYDEMUS. W. R. M. Lamb.

PLATO: LAWS. Rev. R. G. Bury. 2 Vols.

PLATO: LYSIS, SYMPOSIUM, GORGIAS. W. R. M. Lamb.

PLATO: REPUBLIC. Paul Shorey. 2 Vols.

PLATO: STATESMAN, PHILEBUS. H. N. Fowler; ION. W. R. M. Lamb.

PLATO: THEAETETUS and SOPHIST. H. N. Fowler.

PLATO: TIMAEUS, CRITIAS, CLEITOPHON, MENEXENUS, EPISTULAE. Rev. R. G. Bury.

PLOTINUS: A. H. Armstrong. 7 Vols.

PLUTARCH: MORALIA. 16 Vols. Vols. I.–V. F. C. Babbitt. Vol. VI. W. C. Helmbold. Vols. VII. and XIV. P. H. De Lacy and B. Einarson. Vol. VIII. P. A. Clement and H. B. Hoffleit. Vol. IX. E. L. Minar, Jr., F. H. Sandbach, W. C. Helmbold. Vol. X. H. N. Fowler. Vol. XI. L. Pearson and F. H. Sandbach. Vol. XII. H. Cherniss and W. C. Helmbold. Vol. XIII. 1–2. H. Cherniss. Vol. XV. F. H. Sandbach.

PLUTARCH: THE PARALLEL LIVES. B. Perrin. 11 Vols.

POLYBIUS. W. R. Paton. 6 Vols.

PROCOPIUS. H. B. Dewing. 7 Vols.

PTOLEMY: TETRABIBLOS. F. E. Robbins.

QUINTUS SMYRNAEUS. A. S. Way. Verse trans.

SEXTUS EMPIRICUS. Rev. R. G. Bury. 4 Vols.

SOPHOCLES. F. Storr. 2 Vols. Verse trans.

STRABO: GEOGRAPHY. Horace L. Jones. 8 Vols.

THEOCRITUS. Cf. GREEK BUCOLIC POETS.

THEOPHRASTUS: CHARACTERS. J. M. Edmonds. HERODAS, etc. A. D. Knox.